5. **Program Operations and Facilities Management**

Knowledge and application of policies and procedures that meet state/local regulations and professional standards pertaining to the health and safety of young children. Knowledge of nutritional and health requirements for food service. The ability to design and plan the effective use of space based on principles of environmental psychology and child development. Knowledge of playground safety design and practice.

6. **Family Support**

Knowledge and application of family systems and different parenting styles. Knowledge of community resources to support family wellness. The ability to implement program practices that support families of diverse cultural, ethnic, linguistic, and socio-economic backgrounds. The ability to support families as valued partners in the educational process.

7. **Marketing and Public Relations**

Knowledge of the fundamentals of effective marketing, public relations, and community outreach. The ability to evaluate the cost benefit of different marketing and promotional strategies. The ability to communicate the program's philosophy and promote a positive public image to families, business leaders, public officials, and prospective funders. The ability to promote linkages with local schools. Skill in developing a business plan and effective promotional literature, handbooks, newsletters, and press releases.

8. **Leadership and Advocacy**

Knowledge of organizational theory and leadership styles as they relate to early childhood work environments. Knowledge of the legislative process, social issues, and public policy affecting young children and their families. The ability to articulate a vision, clarify and affirm values, and create a culture built on norms of continuous improvement and ethical conduct. The ability to evaluate program effectiveness. The ability to define organizational problems, gather data to generate alternative solutions, and effectively apply analytical skills in its solution. The ability to advocate on behalf of young children, their families and the profession.

9. **Oral and Written Communication**

Knowledge of the mechanics of writing including organizing ideas, grammar, punctuation, and spelling. The ability to use written communication to effectively express one's thoughts. Knowledge of oral communication techniques including establishing rapport, preparing the environment, active listening, and voice control. The ability to communicate ideas effectively in a formal presentation.

10. **Technology**

Knowledge of basic computer hardware and software applications. The ability to use the computer for program administrative functions.

Early Childhood Knowledge and Skills

Administrators need a strong foundation in the fundamentals of child development and early childhood education in order to guide the instructional practices of teachers and support staff.

1. **Historical and Philosophical Foundations**

Knowledge of the historical roots and philosophical foundations of early childhood care and education. Knowledge of different types of early childhood programs, roles, funding, and regulatory structures. Knowledge of current trends and important influences impacting program quality. Knowledge of research methodologies.

2. **Child Growth and Development**

Knowledge of different theoretical positions in child development. Knowledge of the biological, environmental, cultural, and social influences impacting children's growth and development from prenatal through early adolescence. Knowledge of developmental milestones in children's physical, cognitive, language, aesthetic, social, and emotional development. Knowledge of current research in neuroscience and its application to the field of early childhood.

3. **Child Observation and Assessment**

Knowledge and application of developmentally appropriate child observation and assessment methods. Knowledge of the purposes, characteristics, and limitations of different assessment tools and techniques. Ability to use different observation techniques including formal and informal observation, behavior sampling, and developmental checklists. Knowledge of ethical practice as it relates to the use of assessment information. The ability to apply child observation and assessment data to planning and structuring developmentally appropriate instructional strategies.

4. **Curriculum and Instructional Methods**

Knowledge of different curriculum models; appropriate curriculum goals; and different instructional strategies for infants, toddlers, preschoolers, and kindergarten children. Ability to plan and implement a curriculum based on knowledge of individual children's developmental patterns, family and community goals, institutional and cultural context, and state standards. Ability to design integrated and meaningful curricular experiences in the content areas of language and literacy, mathematics, science, social studies, art, music, drama, movement, and technology. Ability to implement anti-bias instructional strategies that take into account culturally valued content and children's home experiences. Ability to evaluate outcomes of different curricular approaches.

5. Children with Special Needs

Knowledge of atypical development including mild and severe disabilities in physical, health, cognitive, social/emotional, communication, and sensory functioning. Knowledge of licensing standards, state and federal laws (e.g., ADA, IDEA) as they relate to services and accommodations for children with special needs. Knowledge of the characteristics of giftedness and how educational environments can support children with exceptional capabilities. The ability to work collaboratively as part of family-professional team in planning and implementing appropriate services for children with special needs. Knowledge of special education resources and services.

6. Family and Community Relationships

Knowledge of the diversity of family systems; traditional, non-traditional and alternative family structures, family life styles; and the dynamics of family life on the development of young children. Knowledge of socio-cultural factors influencing contemporary families including the impact of language, religion, poverty, race, technology, and the media. Knowledge of different community resources, assistance, and support available to children and families. Knowledge of different strategies to promote reciprocal partnerships between home and center. Ability to communicate effectively with parents through written and oral communication. Ability to demonstrate awareness and appreciation of different cultural and familial practices and customs. Knowledge of child rearing patterns in other countries.

7. Health, Safety, and Nutrition

Knowledge and application of practices that promote good nutrition, dental health, physical health, mental health, and safety of infants/toddlers, preschool, and kindergarten children. Ability to implement practices indoors and outdoors that help prevent, prepare for, and respond to emergencies. Ability to model healthful lifestyle choices.

8. Individual and Group Guidance

Knowledge of the rationale for and research supporting different models of child guidance and classroom management. Ability to apply different techniques that promote positive and supportive relationships with children and among children. Ability to reflect on teaching behavior and modify guidance techniques based on the developmental and special needs of children.

9. Learning Environments

Knowledge of the impact of the physical environment on children's learning and development. The ability to use space, color, sound, texture, light, and other design elements to create indoor and outdoor learning environments that are aesthetically pleasing, intellectually stimulating, psychologically safe, and nurturing. The ability to select age-appropriate equipment and materials that achieve curricular goals and encourage positive social interaction.

10. Professionalism

Knowledge of laws, regulations, and policies that impact professional conduct with children and families. Knowledge of different professional organizations, resources, and issues impacting the welfare of early childhood practitioners. Knowledge of center accreditation criteria. Ability to make professional judgments based on the NAEYC *Code of Ethical Conduct and Statement of Commitment*. Ability to reflect on one's professional growth and development and make goals for personal improvement. Ability to work as part of a professional team and supervise support staff or volunteers.

Source: From the National Association for the Education of Young Children. 2005. *NAEYC Early Childhood Program Standards and Accreditation Criteria: The Mark of Quality in Early Childhood Education.* Washington, DC: Author. Reprinted with permission from the National Association for the Education of Young Children.

NAEYC ACCREDITATION STANDAI PROGRAMS

Fresno City College
Social Science Division
1101 E University Ave
Fresno, CA 93741
(559) 442-4600

STANDARD 1: RELATIONSHIPS

Topic Areas

1.A.: Building Positive Relationships among Teachers and Families

1.B.: Building Positive Relationships between Teachers and Children

1.C.: Helping Children Make Friends

1.D.: Creating a Predictable, Consistent, and Harmonious Classroom

1.E.: Addressing Challenging Behaviors

1.F.: Promoting Self-Regulation

STANDARD 2: CURRICULUM

Topic Areas

2.A.: Curriculum: Essential Characteristics

2.B.: Areas of Development: Social-Emotional Development

2.C.: Areas of Development: Physical Development

2.D.: Areas of Development: Language Development

2.E.: Curriculum Content Area for Cognitive Development: Early Literacy

2.F.: Curriculum Content Area for Cognitive Development: Early Mathematics

2.G.: Curriculum Content Area for Cognitive Development: Science

2.H.: Curriculum Content Area for Cognitive Development: Technology

To avoid confusion in the numbering system, there are no criteria labeled 2.I.

2.J.: Curriculum Area for Cognitive Development: Creative Expression and Appreciation for the Arts

2.K: Curriculum Content Area for Cognitive Development: Health and Safety

2.L.: Curriculum Content Area for Cognitive Development: Social

STANDARD 3: TEACHING

Topic Areas

3.A.: Designing Enriched Learning Environments

3.B.: Creating Caring Communities for Learning

3.C.: Supervising Children

3.D.: Using Time, Grouping, and Routines to Achieve Learning Goals

3.E.: Responding to Children's Interests and Needs

3.F.: Making Learning Meaningful for All Children

3.G.: Using Instruction to Deepen Children's Understanding and Build Their Skills and Knowledge

STANDARD 4: ASSESSMENT OF CHILD PROGRESS

Topic Areas

4.A.: Creating an Assessment Plan

4.B.: Using Appropriate Assessment Methods

4.C.: Identifying Children's Interests and Needs and Describing Children's Progress

4.D.: Adapting Curriculum, Individualizing Teaching, and Informing Program Development

4.E.: Communicating with Families and Involving Families in the Assessment Process

STANDARD 5: HEALTH

Topic Areas

5.A.: Promoting and Protecting Children's Health and Controlling Infectious Disease

5.B.: Ensuring Children's Nutritional Well-being

5.C.: Maintaining a Healthful Environment

STANDARD 6: TEACHERS

Topic Areas

6.A.: Preparation, Knowledge, and Skills of Teaching Staff

6.B.: Teachers' Dispositions and Professional Commitment

STANDARD 7: FAMILIES

Topic Areas

7.A.: Knowing and Understanding the Program's Families

7.B.: Sharing Information Between Staff and Families

7.C.: Nurturing Families as Advocates for Their Children

STANDARD 8: COMMUNITY RELATIONSHIPS

Topic Areas

8.A.: Linking with the Community

8.B.: Accessing Community Resources

8.C.: Acting as a Citizen in the Neighborhood and the Early Childhood Community

STANDARD 9: PHYSICAL ENVIRONMENT

Topic Areas

9.A.: Indoor and Outdoor Equipment, Materials, and Furnishings

9.B.: Outdoor Environmental Design

9.C.: Building and Physical Design

9.D.: Environmental Health

STANDARD 10: LEADERSHIP AND MANAGEMENT

Topic Areas

10.A.: Leadership

10.B.: Management Policies and Procedures

10.C.: Fiscal Accountability Policies and Procedures

10.D.: Health, Nutrition, and Safety Policies and Procedures

10.E.: Personnel Policies

10.F.: Program Evaluation, Accountability, and Continuous Improvement

Source: From the National Association for the Education of Young Children. 2005. *NAEYC Early Childhood Program Standards and Accreditation Criteria: The Mark of Quality in Early Childhood Education.* Washington, DC: Author. Reprinted with permission from the National Association for the Education of Young Children.

PLANNING AND ADMINISTERING EARLY CHILDHOOD PROGRAMS

Ninth Edition

Celia A. Decker
Northwestern State University

John R. Decker
Sabine Parish, Louisiana, School System

Nancy K. Freeman
University of South Carolina, Columbia

Herman T. Knopf
University of South Carolina, Columbia

Merrill
is an imprint of

Upper Saddle River, New Jersey
Columbus, Ohio

Library of Congress Cataloging-in-Publication Data

Planning and administering early childhood programs / Celia A. Decker … [et al.]. — 9th ed.
  p. cm.
  Rev. ed. of: Planning and administering early childhood programs / Celia A. Decker,
John R. Decker. 8th ed. c2005.
  Includes bibliographical references and index.
  ISBN-13: 978-0-13-513549-5
  ISBN-10: 0-13-513549-4
1. Early childhood education—United States. 2. Educational planning—United States.
3. Day care centers—United States—Administration. 4. Instructional systems—United
States. I. Decker, Celia Anita. II. Decker, Celia Anita. Planning and administering early
childhood programs.
  LB1139.25.D43 2009
  372.210973—dc22

                                                                        2008029394

Vice President and Executive Publisher: Jeffery W. Johnston
Acquisitions Editor: Julie Peters
Editorial Assistant: Tiffany Bitzel
Senior Managing Editor: Pamela D. Bennett
Senior Project Manager: Linda Hillis Bayma
Production Coordinator: Bruce Hobart, Pine Tree Composition, Inc.
Design Coordinator: Diane C. Lorenzo
Cover Designer: Candace Rowley
Cover image: PhotoDisc
Operations Specialist: Laura Messerly
Director of Marketing: Quinn Perkson
Marketing Manager: Erica DeLuca
Marketing Coordinator: Brian Mounts

This book was set in Garamond by Laserwords Pvt. Ltd., Chennai. It was printed and bound by Edwards Brothers. The cover was printed by Phoenix Color Corp.

Photo Credits: Mac H. Brown/Merrill.

Pearson Education Ltd., London
Pearson Education Singapore, Pte. Ltd.
Pearson Education Canada, Inc.
Pearson Education–Japan
Pearson Education Australia PTY, Limited

Pearson Education North Asia, Ltd., Hong Kong
Pearson Educación de Mexico, S.A. de C.V.
Pearson Education Malaysia, Pte. Ltd.
Pearson Education Upper Saddle River, New Jersey

Merrill
is an imprint of

PEARSON

www.pearsonhighered.com

10 9 8 7 6 5 4 3 2
ISBN-13: 978-0-13-513549-5
ISBN-10:   0-13-513549-4

C and J. D.: *To Kelcey and Keith, our twin sons, and Kristiana, our daughter.*

N.K.F.: *To my husband John, my grandchildren Beatrice, Julia, and Connor, and their parents.*

H.T.K.: *To Kristin, Donna, and Jim for their continued support, and to my children Tyler and Elise.*

About the Authors

Celia A. Decker retired after 38 years of service in early childhood education. At the time of her retirement, she held the position of professor of early childhood education at Northwestern State University and served as the program coordinator of graduate studies in early childhood education. In addition to coauthoring this text, she is the author of *Children: The Early Years* and its supplements and coauthor of *Parents and Their Children,* both published by Goodheart-Willcox Company. She has presented papers at national, regional, and state annual meetings of many professional early childhood associations. She has served as a consultant for Head Start, Even Start, and local school systems.

During her years of teaching as a kindergarten teacher in an inner-city school system and as a college professor, she has received many honors. In 1994, she was selected as the Outstanding Professor at Northwestern State University.

John R. Decker retired after an elementary teaching and administrative career of 37 years. Before entering the field of education, he served as a district scout executive for Kaw Council, Boy Scouts of America, Kansas City, Kansas. His educational career included elementary teaching positions in inner-city schools, in an open education program, and in rural public schools. He also served as assistant professor of education and taught college courses in education and supervised preservice teachers in a federally supported college-based program. He has frequently given speeches and workshops for professional organizations. He has been recognized for his 30-year membership in Phi Delta Kappa.

Nancy K. Freeman is an associate professor of early childhood education and director of the Child Development and Research Center at the University of South Carolina. A former child care director and teacher, she currently consults for the campus child care center. Nancy has authored scholarly publications and given conference presentations on topics such as professional ethics, service learning, and the preparation of the child care workforce. She is chair of the Governor's Advisory Committee on the Regulation of Child Day Care Facilities, has served on the governing board of the National Association of Early Childhood Teacher Educators (NAECTE), and will assume its presidency in 2009.

Herman T. Knopf is an assistant professor of early childhood education at the Child Development and Research Center at the University of South Carolina. A former child care director, teacher, and professional development coordinator, he is currently a consultant for the university-based child care center and is engaged in research exploring the use of computer technology to enhance assessment practices and family communication among early care and education providers. He has published scholarly articles focused on family involvement, enhancing literacy practices, and professionalism in the field of early childhood education. He is currently on the board of directors for the Southern Early Childhood Association and the South Carolina Early Childhood Association.

Preface

Planning and Administering Early Childhood Programs, ninth edition, continues the tradition begun by Celia and John Decker. Its purpose is to contribute to the professional preparation of prospective and in-service program administrators by providing specific guidance on how to plan for, implement, market, and evaluate programs serving children from birth through school age.

NEW CONTENT

The ninth edition represents a significant revision of the text. It has been made more practical and readable with the contributions of two new co-authors, Dr. Nancy Freeman and Dr. Herman Knopf. Each chapter is aligned with NAEYC's 2007 Program Administrator Competencies, and the text includes expanded discussions of:

- Leadership and the roles of effective administrators
- Program marketing
- Professional ethics
- Quality rating systems
- Guidelines for developing a board of directors, among other topics of interest to new and experienced program administrators

This edition's basic premise is that by providing high-quality early childhood programs we help all children and families reach their fullest potential. All aspects of early childhood programs are linked. For that reason it is important to appreciate that administrators hold the key to quality. The extensive references and resources listed in this edition can provide readers with in-depth understandings of many topics. Readers who access the identified Internet resources can stay even more up-to-date in this quickly changing field.

PEDAGOGICAL FEATURES

Readers will find the three subdivisions of the book helpful because they parallel the administrator's planning processes: developing the program's goals and vision, creating a framework for the program's successful operation, and implementing a quality program that supports children's learning, growth, and development.

- New "Application Activities" provide practical, relevant assignments to practice what directors actually do.

- Photographs, tables, and figures are used throughout the text to (a) summarize research or show conflicting points of view, (b) visually present the organization of a concept, and (c) give practical examples.
- The Trends and Issues and Summary sections will also help readers focus on the main themes of the book.

We have raised issues to stimulate early childhood leaders to reexamine their beliefs and then take another look at their programs' rationales and practices. The text provides information needed by all early childhood programs. Although early childhood programs are operated under a wide variety of auspices, there remains a great deal of overlap among the types of competencies needed in various programs. We have attempted to provide a balance among research and supported statements, applied ideas for implementation, and resources for further thought and consideration.

Like the eight editions that have come before, this edition will aid in the initial planning of early childhood programs and be a source of helpful information after programs are under way. The purpose of this book will be fulfilled when the reader makes wiser judgments about planning and administering early childhood programs.

TEXT ORGANIZATION

Chapter 1 emphasizes the importance of quality programming and summarizes recent developments to enhance the quality available to young children and their families.

Part One, Constructing the Early Childhood Program's Framework, includes three chapters. Chapter 2 explains that planning begins with a vision and mission development and then proceeds to a needs assessment to help planners choose program features in response to local needs and values. The chapter includes a description of the processes that program directors might consider in order to reach concensus regarding the program vision and mission. The chapter closes with general guidelines for implementing and evaluating the program. Chapter 3 examines regulations related to many aspects of the program's operation. Chapter 4 guides administrators developing program policies and procedures as well as handbooks for staff, families, and administrators.

Part Two, Operationalizing the Early Childhood Program, includes four chapters addressing important administrative topics. Chapter 5 provides an overview of staffing trends and the roles and qualifications of various staff members. A discussion of needs assessment and staff recruitment follows. The chapter also addresses how effective directors develop and use knowledge of the local community and explains in depth the director's leadership, collaborative, and management roles. Chapter 6 identifies issues to consider when planning a program's physical facility, addressing issues ranging from site selection and classroom floor plans, to equipping classrooms to support children's learning, growth, and development. Chapter 7 explains how funding impacts the quality of programs and discusses innovative funding ideas, sources of funds, the process of developing a budget, and proposals for financing a system. Chapter 8 presents an introduction to marketing a child care and education program. Through this chapter the reader learns that marketing is much more than an advertising campaign; instead it is the actual fulfillment of the program vision and mission and how the program services are percieved by the children and families who are served. The chapter concludes with a description of specific strategies that can be used to effectively market your program to potential clients and families.

Part Three, Implementing the Children's Program, discusses the administrator's role in planning and overseeing the program's services. Chapter 9 addresses the director's role in deciding curricular content and organization, implementing the program, and providing needed program supports. Chapter 10 concerns the administrator's role in meeting nutritional requirements, controlling infectious diseases, and ensuring a safe environment while instilling lifelong nutrition, health, and safety habits. Chapter 11 examines the issues and gives practical suggestions concerning assessing, recording, and reporting children's development and learning. Chapter 12 describes effective strategies for creating respectful collaborative relationships with diverse families and working with stakeholders in the community. Chapter 13 identifies the characteristics that set professionals apart from other workers, examines the ethical dimensions of early childhood program administration, and identifies strategies for becoming an effective advocate for children and families.

ACKNOWLEDGMENTS

We thank Rita Paul, director of South Carolina's Child Care Licensing and Regulatory Services; Sherry King, director of the Children's Center at the University of South Carolina; Judy Reddekopp, administrative assistant, and Nur Tanyel, Mallary McManus, and Erika Livingston, research assistants, all of the University of South Carolina; Danny Stevens and Andy Sherrard, founding partners of O2B Kids, Inc., Gainesville, Florida; and Denise DaRos-Voseles for their contributions to the development of this text.

We thank the following reviewers of this edition for their helpful comments: LaDonna Atkins, University of Central Oklahoma; Karen Bennett, Santa Fe Community College; Colleen Fawcett, Palm Beach Community College; Ann Gadzikowski, Oakton Community College; Barbara Haschke, Baylor University; Hengameh Kermani, University of North Carolina, Wilmington; Donna Rafanello, Long Beach City College; and Janice Sean, Sarasota County Technical Institute Sarasota, Florida.

Brief Contents

1 Overview of Early Care and Education and Program Administration   1

PART I   CONSTRUCTING THE EARLY CHILDHOOD PROGRAM'S FRAMEWORK

2 Developing a Vision, Mission, and Program Evaluation   14
3 Understanding Regulations, Accreditation Criteria, and Other Standards of Practice   36
4 Establishing Policies and Procedures   60

PART II   OPERATIONALIZING THE EARLY CHILDHOOD PROGRAM

5 Leading and Managing Personnel   84
6 Creating Quality Learning Environments   122
7 Financing and Budgeting   173
8 Marketing Your Child Care and Education Program   196

PART III   IMPLEMENTING THE CHILDREN'S PROGRAM

9 Planning the Children's Program   210
10 Providing Nutrition, Health, and Safety Services   245
11 Assessment: An Essential Component of Effective Early Childhood Programming   278
12 Working with Families and Communities   307
13 Contributing to the Profession   339

APPENDICES

1 Suppliers of Materials and Equipment for Early Childhood Programs 352

2 NAEYC Code of Ethical Conduct and Statement of Commitment 355

3 NAEYC Code of Ethical Conduct Supplement for Early Childhood Program Administrators 363

4 Suggested Furniture and Furnishings 370

5 Poisonous Plants 380

6 Governing Board Profile Worksheets 382

7 Governing Board Job Description and Agreement 385

8 Professional Organizations of Interest to Early Childhood Educators 386

References 388

Author Index 414

Subject Index 420

Contents

1   Overview of Early Care and Education and Program Administration   1

    Why are the Early Years Important?   3
      Influences of Early Care and Education Programs   *3*
    Types of Early Childhood Programs   4
      Most Common Types of Child Care   *5*   •   *Special Services in Child Care*   *7*
    Quality: The Overriding Concern   8
      Characteristics of Quality   *9*
      Parent Choice and Quality   *9*
    How Can Directors Move Their Programs Toward Excellence?   10
      The Roles of a Director   *10*   •   *Leadership Styles*   *11*   •   *The Journey Begins*   *12*
    Summary   12
    Useful Web Sites   13
    To Reflect   13

PART I   CONSTRUCTING THE EARLY CHILDHOOD PROGRAM'S FRAMEWORK

2   Developing a Vision, Mission, and Program Evaluation   14

    Program Influences   15
      Considering the Values of the Community   *15*   •   *Developing the Program Philosophy*   *16*   •   *Brief Review of Early Childhood Theory and Philosophy*   *16*
    Program Components   19
      Curriculum: The Program for Children and Families   *20*   •   *Deciding on Curriculum*   *20*   •   *Services Offered*   *21*   •   *Daily Operations Management*   *22*   •   *Financial Management*   *26*
    Developing a Vision: The Foundation for All Other Program Components   27
    Developing the Program's Mission Statement   28
    Implementing the Program   29
    Program Evaluation and Goal Development   30
    Evaluating the Program   31
      Intuitive Evaluation   *31*   •   *Formal Evaluation*   *32*   •   *An Important Consideration*   *33*
    Summary   34
    Useful Web Sites   34
    To Reflect   35

3 Understanding Regulations, Accreditation Criteria, and Other Standards of Practice   36

Considering Regulations   37
Specific Types of Regulations   37 • Regulations to Address When Establishing a New Program   38 • Regulations That Guide Program Development and Implementation   39 • Child Care Center Regulations   39 • Family Child Care Regulations   42 • Concerns About Regulatory Policies   43 • Certification of Teachers in Public School Early Childhood Programs   46 • Specialized Teacher Qualifications   47 • Accreditation   47
Quality Rating Systems   49
Meeting Legal Requirements   50 • Legal Existence of Private Programs   50 • Fiscal Regulations   55 • Laws That Protect the Staff and the Program   56 • Laws in Addition to Licensing That Protect Children   57
Summary   58
Useful Web Sites   58
To Reflect   59

4 Establishing Policies and Procedures   60

Considering Policies and Procedures   61
Policies and Procedures Guide for Employees and Families   61
Regulations and Standards Often Specify Required Policies and Procedures   63
Licensing Requirements   63 • Requirements Addressed by Voluntary Standards   64 • Why Are Policies and Procedures Important?   65 • Who Is Responsible for Developing Policies and Procedures?   65 • Developing or Revising the Family Handbook and Staff Manual for an Existing Program   66 • Developing the Family Handbook and Staff Manual for a New Program   67 • Using Established Policies and Procedures   68 • Characteristics of Viable Policies and Procedures   68
Policy and Procedure Categories   69
What Topics Need to Be Addressed in a Staff Manual?   71
What Topics Need to Be Addressed in the Family Handbook?   76
What Information Should Be in the Administrator's Manual?   81
Summary   82
Useful Web Sites   82
To Reflect   83

PART II OPERATIONALIZING THE EARLY CHILDHOOD PROGRAM

5 Leading and Managing Personnel   84

Trends in Staffing   85
Staff Shortage: A Deep-Rooted Problem   85
Staffing an Early Childhood Program   87
Roles and Qualifications of Personnel   87 • Assessing Needs and Recruiting Staff Members   94
Laying the Foundation for a Community   99
Building a Positive and Productive Work Climate for Staff   100
Creating and Communicating a Culturally Relevant Vision   101 • Collaborating   102 • Managing   105

Enriching the Professional Life of the Staff   105
Assessing Staff Professional Development Needs   105   •   Providing
Professional Development   106
Personnel Services and Records   116
Contract and Terms of Employment   116   •   Job
Description   117   •   Insurance and Retirement
Plans   117   •   Personnel Records   119
Summary   120
Useful Web Sites   121
To Reflect   121

6   Creating Quality Learning Environments   122

Planning a New or Renovated Facility   123
Entry/Exit Area   125
Indoor Space   126
Colors, Lighting, and Sound   126   •   Floors, Ceilings, and
Walls   128   •   Storage and Display   129   •   Arranging and Furnishing
Classrooms   130   •   General Criteria for Learning/Activity
Centers   135   •   Activity Centers for Infants and
Toddlers   136   •   Learning/Activity Centers for
Preschoolers   138   •   Additional Areas in Classrooms   150   •   Food
Preparation, Feeding and Dining Areas   152   •   Developing Classroom
Floor Plans   153   •   Adult Areas   154   •   Environmental Control   155
Outdoor Space   155
General Criteria and Specifications for Child Care
Playgrounds   155   •   Outdoor Space Arrangement   157
The Early Childhood Facility   163
Other Considerations   163
Safety   163   •   Planning Facilities for Accommodating Special
Needs   166   •   Purchasing Equipment and Materials   166   •   Caring
for Equipment and Materials   170   •   Purchasing Insurance   171
Trends and Issues   171
Summary   171
Useful Web Sites   172
To Reflect   172

7   Financing and Budgeting   173

Costs of Early Childhood Programs   174
Estimates of Program Costs   175   •   Costs to Families   176   •
Costs of Local Programs   178
Financing Early Childhood Programs   178
Government and Foundation Financing   178   •   Securing Federal
Funds   182   •   Proposal Planning   183   •   Writing the
Proposal   183   •   Employer Assistance   185   •   Fees, Tuition, and
Miscellaneous Sources of Funds   185
Budgeting   187
Regulations Governing Budget Making and Adoption   187   •   Developing
a Budget   187   •   Reporting the Budget   190
Trends and Issues   190
Providing Adequate Subsidies   191   •   Compensating a Skilled and Stable
Workforce   193   •   Financing a System of Early Childhood Education   193

Summary   194
Useful Web Sites   194
To Reflect   195

8   Marketing Your Child Care and Education Program   196

Marketing Is Important   197
What Is Marketing?   198
*Facility Design   200   •   Service Delivery   201   •   Marketing
Plan   203   •   Strategies to Publicize Your Program: Internal and External
Marketing   205   •   Guidelines for Print Media   206   •   Web Site
Design   207   •   Strategies for the Initial Point of Contact   207
•   The Power of the Purple Cow   208*
Summary   209
Useful Web Sites   209
To Reflect   209

PART III   IMPLEMENTING THE CHILDREN'S PROGRAM

9   Planning the Children's Program   210

Program Planning   211
*Starting with the Program Vision and Mission   212   •   Developmentally
Appropriate Practices: The Foundation of Excellence   212   •   Stating
Goals   217   •   Translating Goals into Child Outcomes   217
•   Organizing the Curriculum   218   •   Themes Versus Projects: Authentic
Learning Opportunities   222*
Implementing the Curriculum   224
*Designing Teaching Strategies   225   •   Using Computers and Other
Technologies   226   •   Facilitating Effective Classroom
Transitions   228   •   Providing for Physical Care
Routines   228   •   Planning for Special Times   228   •   Developing
Supportive Relationships   231   •   Considering Other Aspects of
Implementing the Curriculum   234*
Creating Appropriate Program Supports   234
*Grouping   234   •   Scheduling   237   •   Determining the Responsibilities
of Staff   238*
Trends and Issues   240
*Defining Quality Curriculum: The Standards Movement   240   •   Issuing
Standards on Standards   241   •   Balancing Teaching
Strategies   241   •   Considering Inclusion   242*
Summary   243
Useful Web Sites   243
To Reflect   244

10   Providing Nutrition, Health, and Safety Services   245

Promoting Good Nutrition   246
*Providing and Serving Nutritious Meals and Snacks   248   •
Guidelines for Feeding Infants   251   •   Guidelines for Providing Enjoyable
Meals and Snacks   251   •   Hiring Staff and Meeting Requirements for the
Food Service Program   256   •   Planning Nutrition Education   257*

Promoting Good Health 259
  *Assessing Health Status 260 • Advocating for Preventive Health
  Care 262 • Providing Health Care 266 • Caring for Children with
  Noninfectious Chronic Illnesses and Disabilities 266*
Being Safe 271
  *Addressing Environmental Safety 271 • Vehicular
  Safety 272 • Preparing for Emergencies 273*
Summary 276
Useful Web Sites 276
To Reflect 277

11 Assessment: An Essential Component of Effective Early Childhood
Programming   278
Call for "Responsible Assessment" 279
Purposes of Assessment and Documentation 280
  *Promoting Children's Development and Learning 280 • Naturalistic
  Observations 282 • Structured Observations 285 • Tools for
  Structuring Authentic Assessments 288 • Identifying Children Needing
  Additional Intervention Services 289 • Determining Program
  Effectiveness and Making Policy Decisions 289*
Recording *292*
  *Types of Records 293 • Record Collections 298 • Family
  Educational Rights and Privacy Act* (FERPA) *300*
Reporting 301
  *Determining the Purposes of Reporting 301 • Facilitating Reporting
  Through Assessment Data 301 • Selecting the Methods of
  Reporting 302 • Rethinking Reporting Practices 304*
Trends and Issues 304
Summary 305
Useful Web Sites 306
To Reflect 306

12 Working with Families and Communities   307
Early Childhood Educators Have a Long History of Partnering with
Families 308
  Collaboration: A Crucial Element of Quality Programming 308
Benefits and Challenges of Working with Families 309
  *Threefold Benefits of Family–School Collaboration 309 • Challenges to
  Family Involvement 312 • Meeting the Challenges of Collaboration 316*
Collaboration with Families 318
  *Family–Staff Communication 318 • Family
  Participation 331 • Parent Education and Family Resource and Support
  Programs 333*
Early Childhood Educators Have a Long History of Partnering with Their
Communities 334
  *Tapping into Family and Community Support Through Advisory Committees
  and Boards of Directors 335*
Trends and Issues 337

Summary   338
Useful Web Sites   338
To Reflect   338

13   Contributing to the Profession   339

Promoting Professionalization   340
   *Moving Toward Professionalism: Professional Preparation and Reliance on
   the NAEYC Code of Ethical Conduct   341*
Engaging in Informed Advocacy   343
   Becoming an Effective Advocate   345   •   An Advocate's Toolbox   346
Helping Others Find a Place in the Profession   348
Becoming Involved in Research   349
   Teachers as Researchers   349
Trends and Issues   349
Summary   350
Useful Web Sites   351
To Reflect   351

APPENDIXES

APPENDIX 1   Suppliers of Materials and Equipment for Early Childhood Programs   352
APPENDIX 2   NAEYC Code of Ethical Conduct and Statement of Commitment   355
APPENDIX 3   NAEYC Code of Ethical Conduct Supplement for Early Childhood
             Program Administrators   363
APPENDIX 4   Suggested Furniture and Furnishings   370
APPENDIX 5   Poisonous Plants   380
APPENDIX 6   Governing Board Profile Worksheets   382
APPENDIX 7   Governing Board Job Description and Agreement   385
APPENDIX 8   Professional Organizations of Interest to Early Childhood Educators   386

References   388

Author Index   414

Subject Index   420

NOTE: Every effort has been made to provide accurate and current Internet information in this book. However, the Internet and information posted on it are constantly changing, so it is inevitable that some of the Internet addresses listed in this textbook will change.

1

OVERVIEW OF EARLY CARE AND EDUCATION AND PROGRAM ADMINISTRATION

NAEYC Director Competencies addressed in this chapter:

Early Childhood Knowledge and Skills

1. Historical and Philosophical Foundations
   Knowledge of current trends and important influences impacting program quality. Knowledge of research methodologies.
8. Leadership and Advocacy
   Knowledge of organizational theory and leadership styles as they relate to early childhood work environments.

Child care is a way of life for many of America's young children. It is estimated that 71.5% of mothers with children under 6 are in the labor force (U.S. Census Bureau, 2006), and nearly three out of four children with working mothers are cared for by persons who are not their parents (Urban Institute, 2004). This represents a major change in the American family during the past 30 years. In 1976, when the women's movement had just begun, 31% of mothers of young children were in the labor force (Lerman & Schmidt, 1999). Today's figures indicate there has been more than a twofold increase in maternal employment and child care participation in just one generation.

Just as the demand for child care has changed over the years, so has our country's interest in, and support for, programs of early care and education. Consider the differences between:

- Family-focused programs of the 1940s that provided child care and other services for "Rosie the Riveter" who was building ships and other materials needed by the war effort.
- Comprehensive Head Start programs that were the centerpiece of the 1960's War on Poverty. Head Start was designed to provide care and education, medical screenings, and needed social services to bootstrap children and families out of poverty.
- Child care that was designed to meet the needs of "liberated women" who entered the workforce in record numbers in the 1970s.
- Programs since the turn of the century that focus on meeting the first benchmark of the Goals 2000 panel that challenged America to ensure all children the opportunities they need to come to school "ready to learn."

The field's knowledge base has expanded as it has responded to current needs, interests, and the existing level of political support. Today early childhood programs are likely to advocate for increased public support by relying on recently popularized brain research and longitudinal studies that provide evidence that young children reap lifelong benefits from high-quality early childhood programming, particularly when coupled with intensive parent involvement and education (Center on the Developing Child, 2007; Schweinhart et al., 2005; Shonkoff & Phillips, 2000).

Programs of early care and education have the opportunity to realize the promise of these strands of research while meeting the current needs of America's children and families.

1. We need available and affordable child care for working families (Olson, 2002).
2. We have a responsibility to minimize the effects of identified risk-producing conditions such as poverty, low birth weight, maternal depression, family violence, parents with low educational attainment and low levels of literacy, and chronic health conditions and disabilities. Each of these factors increases the likelihood that children will struggle in school. The chances for success are greatly reduced when children face multiple risk factors in their early years (Center on the Developing Child, 2007).
3. We need a workforce that can compete in the worldwide knowledge economy (Carnegie Task Force on Meeting the Needs of Young Children, 1994; Committee for Economic Development, Research, and Policy, 1987, 1991, 1993; Rolnick & Grunewald, 2003).

Although America does not yet have a robust infrastructure that provides all families affordable, accessible high-quality programming for their young children, early childhood initiatives have attracted unprecedented attention in recent years. One example illustrating the current interest in early childhood is the fact that federal No Child Left Behind legislation requires states to develop *Good Start Grow Smart* standards describing what preschool children should know and be able to do. Some locales have also recently adopted, or are in the process of developing, infant and toddler early learning guidelines that provide a common language to describe the developmental trajectory of typically developing infants and toddlers (California Department of Education, 2006).

Application Activity

Visit the Web site at the end of this chapter to find information about your state's requirements to serve as a program administrator. Are you qualified now? What would you need to do to be eligible to serve as a director? Are the qualifications the same or different in neighboring states? What are these differences?

Another example of increased support for early chidhood programs is the number of states that have recently instituted programs for preschoolers, particularly 4-year-olds (4K). In 2005–2006 38 states had state-funded preKindergarten programs serving 20 percent of all 4-year-olds, up from 17% in 2004–2005 and just 14% in 2001–2002 (Barnett, Hustedt, Hawkinson, & Robin, 2006). Even in this period of rapid expansion, however, preschool programs are consistently less well funded than are programs for primary-age children, and there is great variation in teacher qualifications and other characteristics of quality (Barnett et al.).

Many efforts to improve quality have focused on teachers' qualifications. Head Start (Administration for Children and Families, 2007), National Association for the Education of Young Children (NAEYC, 2005) Accreditation Standards and some state-supported 4K programs have raised the educational bar to require an associate degree and, for some positions, a baccalaureate degree for teachers and administrators. States' requirements for program administrators are found by following links from the Web site listed at the end of this chapter.

Challenges remain as the field strives to increase quality, affordability, and accessibility to meet the needs of increasingly diverse communities. It is our hope that this book equips current and future administrators to provide high-quality programming in their own centers. We also hope that it prepares you to advocate for the societal and governmental support needed to provide all young children the opportunities they need to enhance their chances for success in school and beyond.

WHY ARE THE EARLY YEARS IMPORTANT?

Many young children attend child care more than 2,000 hours per year. That is about twice the amount of time older children spend annually in public school classrooms. In fact, the cumulative total time youngsters spend in child care may equal the total time they spend in school from the beginning of kindergarten until they graduate from high school (Children's Defense Fund, 2006).

These figures describing children's extensive experiences in child care make it easy to appreciate why child care has a lasting impact on young children's learning, growth, and development. Potential benefits of high-quality care have been documented to include enhanced social, emotional, learning, language, and cognitive development that increase a child's chances for success in school and beyond (Barnett, 1995; Burchinal, Roberts, Nabors, & Bryant, 1996; Howes, 2000; NICHD Early Child Care Research Network, 1998; Ramey & Ramey, 1998). As a program administrator, you will have an opportunity to ensure program quality so that these potential benefits are realized.

Influences of Early Care and Education Programs

Effective program administration begins with an understanding of the history and traditions of early care and education. This overview will provide a starting point as you learn about program planning and implementation, effective management, and leadership.

The caregiver is facilitating a group game with her children.

Today's early childhood programs continue the field's rich traditions. They are an indication of society's commitment to its youngest and most vulnerable members. The current level of investment in programs for young children points to growing acceptance of the fact that a child's earliest experiences have lifelong implications and, to a large extent, set the stage for success (Shonkoff & Phillips, 2000). This conviction is based, in large measure, on an appreciation for the vulnerability of very young children's developing brains, and the windows of opportunity that are uniquely open during the first three years (Center on the Developing Child, 2007; Cranley Gallagher, 2005).

Although science has provided mounting evidence of the importance of the early years, too many children begin school with disadvantages that are very hard, and sometimes impossible, to overcome. As many as 18.5% of America's young children live in poverty (Center for Law and Social Policy/Children's Defense Fund, 2006). Minorities shoulder the biggest burden of poverty: Thirty-five percent of African American, 35% of American Indian, and 28% of Hispanic or Latino children live in households of three with less than $15,577 in income per year (Annie E. Casey Foundation, 2006: Center on the Developing Child, 2007).

The effects of poverty during infancy and early childhood can have lifelong effects. Low-income families are less likely to seek prenatal care; are less able to provide pregnant women and young children adequate nutrition; may not fully immunize their children against childhood illnesses; and are more likely to live in unsafe, stress-producing neighborhoods (Center for the Developing Child, 2007; Children's Defense Fund, 2006). Advocates who appreciate the potential benefits of experiences in quality programs need to focus, in particular, on those children most at risk for school failure as they map the course of early childhood in the years to come.

TYPES OF EARLY CHILDHOOD PROGRAMS

One of the first challenges encountered when studying programs of early care and education is the confusion about the meaning of *early childhood*. Professional organizations, state departments of education, researchers, and other stakeholders sometimes use vague synonyms or different chronological ages or developmental milestones when they refer to "young children."

The National Association for the Education of Young Children (NAEYC) has defined *early childhood* as the period from birth through age 8 (NAEYC, 1991, p. 1). That is the definition we will use throughout this book, with a particular emphasis on young children served in community child care settings.

One way to classify early childhood programs is by considering the program's sponsor. Early childhood programs are operated by:

- State agencies (e.g., 4K or public school kindergarten)
- Federal agencies (e.g., Head Start and Early Head Start)
- Colleges and universities that use them as clinical settings and as research laboratories
- Private for-profit or nonprofit organizations (e.g., community preschools or parent cooperatives; employer-sponsored child care; faith-based programs; programs operated by service or philanthropic organizations)

Early childhood programs may also be described by referring to their historical roots which include health care, social services, home economics or family and consumer science, and education (Meisels & Shonkoff, 2000). Today, as in the past, early childhood programs reflect the social interests, political trends, and community priorities of the day (Garbarino & Ganzel, 2000; Sameroff & Fiese, 2000).

Most Common Types of Child Care

State-operated public schools and federally funded Head Start programs serve particular populations of young children from birth through 4 years of age. These programs have specific operating procedures and are governed by mandated standards. You will want to learn more about these programs if you anticipate a career in a government-operated program of early care and education.

Figure 1.1 depicts the primary child care arrangements for children under 5. It illustrates that the two most commonly encountered types of child care are the primary focus of this book: child care centers and family child care. A **child care center** is a nonresidential facility serving 13 or more children that operates fewer than 24 hours a day (NARA/NCCIC, 2006). Many programs serve children from birth through school age for 10 to 12 hours a day, adjusting their schedule to meet the needs of working families. Most serve the same children and families on a regular basis, but others accept children on an occasional drop-in basis. Child care centers are regulated by states' licensing agencies.

While many for-profit centers are owned and operated by individuals or family corporations, some are operated as large chains or are franchises. Not-for-profit centers are typically sponsored by state and local governments, religious groups, service or philanthropic organizations, or parent cooperatives. About 57% of America's 3- to 5-year-olds participate in child care on a full-time or part-time basis (Annie E. Casey Foundation, 2007).

Family child care is nonresidential care provided in a private home other than the child's own. About 27% of America's children under 6 attend family-based child care at least once a week (Kids Count, 2007). In small family child care homes, the group of children is small—approximately 6 children, including the caregiver's own children. Many states differentiate between small home programs and those serving 7 to 12 children in **large family child care homes** or

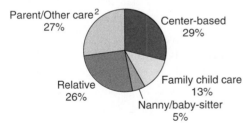

Primary Child Care Arrangements for Children Under Age 5 with Employed Mothers[1]

Parent/Other care[2]
27%

Center-based
29%

Relative
26%

Family child care
13%

Nanny/baby-sitter
5%

Figure 1.1
Nearly 3 Out of 4 Young Children with Employed Mothers Are Regularly in Child Care

[1]Data on child care arrangements were obtained by conducting interviews with the adult most knowledgeable about the child. Since this person was most often the mother (71.5 percent), the term "mother" is used here to refer to this respondent.

[2]The survey did not ask questions about parental care, which can include care provided by the other parent or care by the mother while she worked. Children whose mothers did not report them to be in a regular child care arrangement are assumed to be in parent/other care.

Source: 2002 National Survey of America's Families. Used by permission of the Urban League.

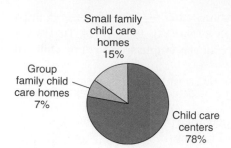

Figure 1.2
The 2005 Licensed Capacity Report

Source: National Association for Regulatory Administration (NARA) & Technical Assistance Center (NCCIC) (2006). *The 2005 child care licensing study.* Conyers, GA: Author.

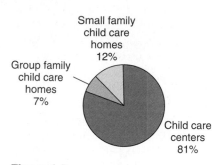

Figure 1.3
The 2007 Licensed Capacity Report

Source: National Association for Regulatory Administration (NARA) & Technical Assistance Center (NCCIC) (2006). *The 2005 child care licensing study.* Conyers, GA: Author.

group child care homes. Family child care homes are most frequently operated as independent businesses, but they are occasionally part of a **system** (i.e., have a sponsoring organization that has been authorized by the state to approve and monitor its services), as is the case for home providers operating on military bases.

There is wide variation among states' regulatory requirements for small and large family child care programs. In some states, operators must simply submit evidence that providers have undergone criminal background checks and have taken other essential steps to ensure children's safety and well-being. In others, home-based programs are held to standards similar to those applied to child care centers. You will want to become familiar with your state's requirements if you are considering opening a program for young children in your home.

Informal care includes a large network of unregulated "kith-and-kin" providers caring for children in their homes. They are usually relatives, friends, or neighbors of the children they serve. Some researchers estimate that nearly one-half of all young children, particularly infants, in nonparental care use informal, unregulated child care arrangements at least some of the time (Brown-Lyons, Robertson, & Layzer, 2001; Paulsell, Mekos, Del Grosso, Rowand, & Banghart, 2006).

As you study Figures 1.2, 1.3, and 1.4, note that the supply of spaces in center-based child care centers and group family and small family child care homes remained relatively stable between the years 2005 and 2007. The notable variation was a small shift from small homes to center-based care. This shift indicates, perhaps, that operating a small day care home is the most difficult, and least financially sustainable, form of child care. This is possibly because providers are isolated as they shoulder the important responsibilities of caring for other families' young children and the fees families are able to afford hardly cover the expenses involved in operating a quality program.

The changes in enrollment may also be an indication that efforts to increase the oversight of home providers have resulted in increased numbers of registered or licensed providers leaving the system of regulated care to enter the informal, unregulated "kith-and-kin" network.

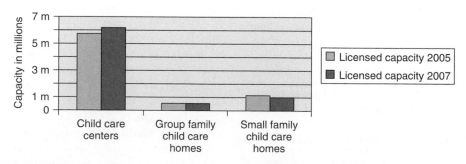

Figure 1.4
The Licensed Program Capacity Report for 2005 and 2007

Source: National Association for Regulatory Administration (NARA) & Technical Assistance Center (NCCIC) (2006). *The 2005 child care licensing study.* Conyers, GA: Author.

Special Services in Child Care

Infant and toddler child care serves children from birth to age 3. There is great demand for services for very young children: In 2005, 42% of 1-year-olds and 53% of children 12 to 24 months old experienced nonparental care at least once a week (Zero to Three, 2007). But, in spite of this high demand, there is an inadequate supply of infant/toddler care, in large measure because of the high cost of maintaining the low ratios (one caregiver to three or four children) that are the hallmark of quality. It is also difficult to provide consistently high-quality care for very young children. The now-classic Cost, Quality, and Outcomes study reported that 40% of infant/toddler programs were of poor quality, and only 8% were determined to provide quality care (Cost, Quality and Child Outcomes Study Team, 1995).

Federal initiatives, including the targeted Child Care and Development Fund (CCDF) infant-toddler set-aside, are designed to funnel increased funds to programs for young children to provide specialized training and technical assistance for caregivers of very young children (Zero to Three, 2007). Some of these efforts designed to increase the availability of quality infant/toddler care are still in the early stages of implementation. Their effectiveness will be evidenced in the years to come.

Another trend affecting child care providers is an increase in the demand for, and number of programs offering, **school-age child care (SACC).** SACC is nonparental care for children from kindergarten through 15 years of age. It includes services provided by child care centers; large and small family child care homes; parks and recreational departments; and youth groups such as YM/YWCAs, scouts, and Boys' and Girls' Clubs.

SACC operates when school is not in session—before and after school, on school holidays, and during the summer. Many states exempt programs for school-age children from child care regulations (NARA/NCCIC, 2006). As of 2005, 13 states had adopted separate school-age licensing standards addressing, most frequently, the physical environment, child-staff ratios, maximum group size, staff qualifications and background, health and hygiene, and program activities (U.S. DHHS, 2006).

Children with **identified special needs** are another population served, in increased numbers, by community child care programs. According to the U.S. Department of Education, Office of Special Education and Rehabilitative Services, Office of Special Education Programs (2005), 34% of all young children with disabilities are being served primarily in early childhood programs and an additional 16.4% of children with disabilities are enrolled in early childhood programs part time. While the Americans with Disabilities Act (ADA) requires early childhood programs to make reasonable accommodations to serve young children with disabilities, the inclusion of children with disabilities among their same-age peers is just as much a moral obligation.

Research has shown that inclusive early childhood programming benefits all children, not just children with disabilities. When used in this manner the term **inclusion** refers to the complete integration of children with disabilities into the community they live in. This complete integration is not simply a matter of placement (the child physically in the proximity of typically developing peers), but rather all children (regardless of disability) becoming part of the community of children that is established within a classroom or program. In this way, effective inclusion results in meaningful engagement of typically developing children with children who have disabilities and the establishment of durable social relationships.

Effective inclusion, however, is not easily accomplished and requires collaboration among child care administrators, general education teachers, special education service providers, and local education agencies to ensure that the children and staff get the needed services and professional development necessary to be effective.

A final trend is the growing need for care for children who are **mildly ill** or who are recovering from surgery. Programs for these children provide a valuable service to working families who would otherwise have to miss work when their child is unable to participate in child care because of a minor noncontagious condition. There are five popular types of care for children who are mildly ill:

1. Centers that care only for sick children
2. Programs within hospitals
3. "Sick rooms" at regular child care centers
4. Specialized family day care homes
5. In-home care or visiting nurse services

Programs vary on what illness or conditions they will admit or exclude; for example, many programs are not able to serve children with infectious diarrhea or those with a very high fever (Beierlein & Van Horn, n.d.). Some states have separate regulations for programs serving children who are ill.

Application Activity

Review your state's child care regulations (see the Web site at the end of this chapter) to identify the kinds of programs they address and to identify any programs that are exempt from regulation, such as those serving school-age children.

QUALITY: THE OVERRIDING CONCERN

The growing appreciation for the potential benefits of quality programs of early care and education has strengthened funding agencies' and policy makers' commitment to ensuring all families have access to programming that can support and enhance young children's development, growth, and learning. These benefits can be realized, however, only in high-quality programs with characteristics linked to positive outcomes for children.

Children comfortably engaged in independent reading is a signal that the environment is safe and secure for the children.

Characteristics of Quality

Researchers and policy makers assess a child care program's quality by evaluating its structural and process characteristics. Measures of **structural quality** include group size, child-adult ratio, and the extent of teachers' and administrators' specialized education and training. Many of these features are readily observable and are addressed in states' licensing regulations.

Dimensions of **process quality** include some assessments that are straightforward and easy to evaluate, and others that are more nuanced and difficult to quantify. An example of an easy-to-observe dimension of process quality is an evaluation of the center's health and safety practices. Dimensions more difficult to assess include measures of caregivers' sensitivity and responsiveness; measures of cognitive and language stimulation; and characterizations of peer interactions as positive or negative. While an observer might develop an opinion about a program's quality by observing these kinds of teacher-child interactions, assessments of these dimensions of quality require trained assessors using standardized instruments that are generally not available to program administrators.

Parent Choice and Quality

Families may not consider quality differences in choosing programs. In fact, discrepancies often exist between parent and expert ratings (Helburn & Culkin, 1995a, 1995b). The following reasons may explain the discrepancies:

1. Parents may not have good consumer information on choosing child care. Some parents choose programs without expert advice or knowledge of quality characteristics they should look for. Other parents may have information, but they may not read or understand it. Many parents have never seen good programs for comparison purposes. Child Care Resource and Referral Agencies (CCR&Rs) are moving toward providing parents with more specific information, such as the staff's education or training given as percentages, the director's qualifications, the adult–child ratio, and regulatory compliance. Some states are rating centers, which is the easiest way to make parents good consumers.

2. Parents may have few choices in some geographical locations. Due to limited consumer demand and a host of other factors common in rural and/or economically depressed areas, there may be few child care options from which parents can choose. The child care options that are available in these areas might also offer substandard programming as a result of the high costs associated with providing high quality care, a lack of competition, and a need to keep the price of care affordable to the families living in these economically depressed areas.

3. The values parents place on a specific aspect of a program may overshadow quality aspects. Parents may be considering costs, hours of services, and convenience of location. Research findings suggest that parents also seem to look for a shared value system with providers. Several studies indicate that experts need to reevaluate the "fit" between program goals and what families perceive as their needs. For example, Zinzeleta and Little (1997) found that parents were seeking programs with a heavy academic emphasis and shared religious values. Mitchell, Cooperstein, and Larner (1992) found that parents often choose child care in an attempt to protect their children *from* certain values. Thus, family members must be involved in designing and implementing high-quality services for children.

A strategy many states have adopted to help families become more informed consumers of child care is the adoption of a quality rating system (QRS). These systems use easy-to-understand symbols, like stars, to represent differing levels of quality. Like the diamonds the American Automobile Association (AAA) uses to rank restaurants and hotels, the symbols summarize a comprehensive evaluation of the program's structural and process characteristics, indicating a range of quality from adequate to exemplary (AAA, n.d.). Quality rating systems can be either voluntary or mandatory. Either way, they are an effective way to help families make informed decisions when they select care for their young children.

HOW CAN DIRECTORS MOVE THEIR PROGRAMS TOWARD EXCELLENCE?

We now turn to the description of the roles, responsibilities, and professional attributes of early childhood program administrators. As the "person in charge" the director of any center-based early childhood program will engage in different types of activities that ultimately influence the level of quality and significantly impact a center's ability to be successful. (See inside front cover for NAEYC's definition of administrator and competencies for program administration.)

The Roles of a Director

An effective early childhood program administrator must be able to assume different roles within the organization and attend to different aspects of the program to ensure that the services provided are indeed the services that are valued and/or warranted. It is likely that the effective director will assume each of the following roles within the organization.

Leader: In this role, a director must maintain a future orientation, focusing on the continuous improvement of the services provided to children and their families. As the leader of the program, the director's role is to ensure that there is a vision for what the program aspires to become. This vision is created by considering the values and needs of relevant stakeholders, the professional knowledge borne from current theories and research, and the professional wisdom gained from experiences in the field of early childhood education. Once the vision is developed and agreed upon by staff and other stakeholders, the director must develop a plan to facilitate continuous improvement efforts that will result in achievement (or an approximation) of the vision.

Manager: In this role, a director is primarily focused on the daily operations of the program. The effective program administrator works to ensure that children and families are receiving the services they need. To accomplish this, in the role of the manager, the director observes staff to ensure they are fulfilling their responsibilities, while at the same time interacting with children and families to gauge their level of satisfaction. The effective administrator actively monitors the financial health of the organization—the organization's income and expenditures. Using the skills of an effective marketer, the director works to ensure that the center has sufficient enrollment by effectively publicizing the program to the community.

Coach: In the role of the coach, the director focuses on providing professional development and technical assistance to all staff members as a means to increase their level of performance. While the knowledge and skills of the staff will be enhanced through a variety of strategies, the coach is keenly aware that to be effective he or she must first acknowledge the strengths of individual staff members, identify areas of needed improvement, and develop a plan to increase these skills and competencies. By focusing on continuous improvement, the coach acts as a bridge between the roles of manager and leader. The coach, aware of the vision for excellence, is continually monitoring daily performance, looking for opportunities to propel the entire team forward, closer to achieving to ultimate goal—highest quality child care and education services.

Leadership Styles

The studies of effective leadership styles from the past were focused on identifying the characteristics and behaviors of effective leaders in the hope of being able to describe very specifically what one might learn and then do to become an effective leader (Dulewicz & Higgs, 2005). More recent investigation in this area has resulted in the identification of areas of competence and personal characteristics exhibited by effective leaders (Dulewicz & Higgs, 2005, p. 107).

An effective leader must be able to:

- **Envision:** Identify a clear picture for the future and clearly articulate the vision in a way that inspires others toward action.
- **Engage:** Communicate effectively with each individual so they understand how they will contribute to the achievement of the vision.
- **Enable:** Act on a belief in the talent and potential of individuals and create the environment in which these can be released.
- **Inquire:** Be open to real dialogue with those involved in the organization and encourage free and frank debate of all issues.
- **Develop:** Work with people to build their capability and help them to make the envisioned contribution.

Personal characteristics of an effective leader include the following:

- **Authenticity:** Being genuine and not attempting to "play a role," or acting in a manipulative way
- **Integrity:** Being consistent in what one says and does
- **Will:** Possesing a drive to lead and persistence in working toward a goal
- **Self-belief:** Evaluating one's capabilities realistically and belief in achieving required goals
- **Self-awareness:** Understanding oneself—who you are, how you feel, and how others see you

While an awareness of these competencies and traits is important, it is even more important that effective leaders employ strategies and select from a repertoire of behaviors that are uniquely suited to the context they are currently working in. Recent researchers have identified three distinct classifications of leadership styles (goal oriented, involving, engaging) and the organizational context (low change, moderate change, and high change) for which they are best suited. Table 1.1 illustrates how different leadership behaviors match different organizational contexts.

As you can see from the table, an effective leader will at times take charge of a situation and at other times act more as a facilitator. In instances when an organization is mainly in a low-change mode of operating, it is often more efficient for the leader to make decisions critical to continued operation and provide specific guidance to staff to ensure that the organization continues providing high-quality services. In instances where there is a high degree of change (e.g., beginning a new program or service), it is most often desirable for the leader to facilitate high levels of collaboration among many relevant stakeholders to capitalize on the collective wisdom of the group and to ensure that all engaged parties agree that the change is necessary.

One of the most important tasks facing a program director in the context of significant change is encouraging stakeholder ownership of the process and the end result. An effective director facilitates this high level of buy-in through a collaborative process where all key stakeholders believe they have a voice.

Table 1.1
Match Between Leadership Styles and Organizational Context

Leadership Styles	Change Context		
	Low Change	Moderate Change	High Change
Goal Oriented: Leader sets direction and plays a significant role in specifically directing others to achieve key goals. Leader-centric.	Yes	Maybe	No
Involving: Less leader-centric than goal oriented. Focus is on providing strong sense of direction but encourages collaboration in identifying specific tasks and how goals will be achieved.	Maybe	Yes	Maybe
Engaging: Focus is on facilitating others in identifying the direction and the means for achieving necessary goals. The leader is more concerned with the development of others than on maintaining a specific direction of change.	No	Maybe	Yes

The Journey Begins

You will not become an effective early care and education administrator by simply reading this book or any other book on early childhood programs. It takes years of experience in concert with a process of continual program evaluation and reflection. It is our hope that this text will help you on your journey to becoming an effective program administrator by providing a description of characteristics of quality program development and management.

Throughout the text you will find authentic examples from successful early care and education programs. In addition, we have developed worksheets and forms that might also be useful to you as you work to either develop or improve a program for young children. While we do not attempt to provide solutions to all situations you might encounter, we have endeavored to identify the essential knowledge and skills that will set you on the path toward success.

SUMMARY

Early childhood programs have experienced growth unlike any other U.S. enterprise except technology. The increased demand for child care and education in a society whose workforce involves and will continue to involve more women and greater ethnic and racial diversity has fostered this growth. There is also a strong desire to help children in poverty get a better start in life. This has been underscored by the expanding body of research demonstrating the benefits of high-quality programs.

Early childhood programs, taken collectively, constitute a diverse, rather uncoordinated system supported by various individuals and by public and private organizations with differing historical roots. The quality of early childhood programs has become an overriding concern following the release of data from national studies of child care. Besides the concern over quality, other trends and issues include:

1. Very diverse program practices
2. More emphasis on the child within the family setting and meeting the family's needs
3. A belief in the need to build community partnerships that consider local needs and cultural values
4. An emphasis on collaboration and linkages across various auspices funding early childhood programs
5. A comprehensive view (i.e., care and education) of high-quality programs for *all* children

USEFUL WEB SITES

Individual states' child care regulations can be found by following links from

>   nrc.uchsc.edu/STATES/states.htm

Individual states' licensing requirements for program administrators can be found by following links from

>   nccic.acf.hhs.gov/pubs/cclicensingreq/cclr-directors.html

TO REFLECT

1. As you embark on the process of becoming an effective program administrator of a high-quality early care and education program, think about the reasons or life circumstances that have led you to this point in your career. Why do you want to be an early childhood program administrator? What personal characteristics or skills do you possess that will help you?

2. As the director of a respected child care program, you have been asked to address an upcoming local school board meeting about the importance of early care and education. The board is planning to implement a new systemwide preschool program. What arguments for care would be effective when addressing this group that is more likely to be concerned about educational benefits such as school readiness and academic skills?

2

DEVELOPING A VISION, MISSION, AND PROGRAM EVALUATION

NAEYC Director Competencies addressed in this chapter:

Management Knowledge and Skills

1. Personal and Professional Self-Awareness
Knowledge of one's own beliefs, values, and philosophical stance.

8. Leadership and Advocacy
The ability to articulate a vision, clarify and affirm values, and create a culture built on norms of continuous improvement and ethical conduct. The ability to evaluate program effectiveness. The ability to define organizational problems, gather data to generate alternative solutions, and effectively apply analytical skills in its solution. The ability to advocate on behalf of young children, their families and the profession.

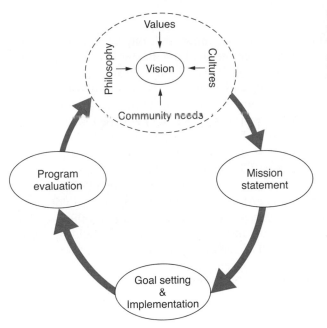

Figure 2.1
Process for Program Planning and Evaluation

An effective early childhood administrator or director must be aware of all the influences and components that contribute to the development of a high-quality program for young children. With this awareness, the director begins planning for success by developing a **vision** for a high-quality program designed to support children's development and learning. The program's vision must be aligned with the sponsor's **purpose**, based on an articulated **philosophy** of care and education, reflect the **cultures** and **values** of the children and families served, and meet the **community's needs**.

Next steps include sharing the vision with all stakeholders (revising when necessary) and working collaboratively to develop a program **mission statement**, creating an implementation and **program assessment plan** and time line, and, finally, implementing the program using these tools as a roadmap to success. As Figure 2.1 illustrates, program planning is a continuous cycle for the successful administrator.

The director will use information from the program assessment activities as a starting point for future planning. Of utmost importance are the congruence and alignment among all these program components. Misalignment of any program component is likely to impact the overall effectiveness of the program and will inhibit the ability to meet the needs of the children and families being served. The service Delivery Planning sheet will help you use information from your needs assessment to identify services to offer.

PROGRAM INFLUENCES

Whether you are planning for an early childhood program currently operating or managing one that is under development, values of the stakeholders and the local community and the program philosophy must be taken into account to ensure that the program meets the needs of the intended clientele. These influences are likely to impact all aspects of the program.

Considering the Values of the Community

The values of all people who might have a stake in the outcomes of the child care and education program (director, staff, parents, children, public school professionals, and the local community) should be carefully identified and thoughtfully incorporated into the vision for the center. Each stakeholder group expects that certain things will result from early care and education services, and the values actually have a direct impact on the ultimate outcomes. In order to identify the key values of the stakeholders you will be serving, consider asking the following questions:

1. What do you expect your child to know or be able to do to be a successful adult? Why are these knowledge and skills important?
2. From your perspective, what value might an early childhood program add to your community?
3. What do you expect of teachers and caregivers who interact with your child?
4. What are the most important services that our program might provide to the community?

While early childhood professionals might be interested in different outcomes than other stakeholder groups, it is the responsibility of the program administrator to mediate conflicting interests when they arise.

Developing the Program Philosophy

When thinking of the program philosophy, the first things that often come to mind are **epistemological** (the nature of learning) and **pedagogical** (the nature of teaching) beliefs. Although these are important considerations for all early care and education programs, they are not the only aspects of the program that should inform the program philosophy.

Here again it is important to mention the importance of alignment between program philosophy and the program's vision and mission. The program philosophy is not only the beliefs that guide the selection of curriculum; it should also be the guide for all interactions within the organization including interactions between administration and staff, staff and clients (children and families), and all those affiliated with the organization and the community. For example, if an administrator values the work of John Dewey (1897), then the importance of democratic values should pervade all interactions among staff, children, and families, resulting in the cultivation of a truly democratic culture throughout the program.

The philosophy of an early childhood care and education program should be heavily influenced by the knowledge base of the field of early childhood education. Although the field of early childhood education is not in total agreement regarding the research and theories that most accurately describe the nature of development and learning, the field is unified in the understanding that practice should be informed and guided by a combination of child development theory (that is, based on direct observation of children) and philosophical beliefs regarding the purpose and function of educational programs.

Brief Review of Early Childhood Theory and Philosophy

The two most prevalent sources for determining program foundations are theoretical and philosophical positions. The theoretical positions come from (a) psychological theories that help answer questions regarding what and how children can learn and (b) the ecological perspective of the child (the sociocultural context) that examines the impact of socialization processes on the child's development. The philosophical position comes from values for children individually and collectively, both now and in the future and is thus concerned with what children ought to know.

In addition to these commonly used guides for curriculum development and selection, there is an emerging position that education programs should base curricular and instructional decisions on scientific evidence. While basing curricular decisions on "scientific" research is a relatively new trend in the field of education, it is important that, as professionals, we don't limit our instructional selection decisions by what has historically been done (Odom & Wolery, 2000). Instead, we should base our decisions on evidence, in the form of research, professional wisdom, and family and professional values (Buysse & Wesley, 2006).

Psychological Theories.   Three major views of children's development and learning have influenced early childhood education. The first school of thought, which permeated the literature from the 1930s through the 1950s, is the **maturational view.** In this view, development is seen as the result of the maturation of structures within the individual (Gesell, 1931). The dominant aspect of development is a genetic construction.

Genetic influences are substantial (Plomin, 1997). The maturational view holds that teachers should provide educative experiences when the child shows interest. Today's maturationists believe that the genes guide the process of maturation, and teaching or nurturing determines the specific content of what an individual learns (e.g., naming colors) and influences to some degree the rate and extent of learning. Through the use of norms, the maturationists have developed "expectations" for children at different ages that prevent a child from being hurried by poorly timed experiences. In the 1950s, the integration of assumptions from the psychoanalytic theories with the maturational theory brought about the child development approach (Jersild, 1946).

The second school of thought is the **behavioral-environmental view** (Skinner, 1938). In this view, the environment, rather than genetic construction, has the dominant role in learning. Learning is viewed as environmental inputs and behavioral outputs. The focus is not on mental processes, but on eliciting and reinforcing verbal, perceptual, and motor behaviors. Behaviorism provides a theoretical rationale for the traditional view of teaching as direct instruction with sequenced goals and objectives and corresponding materials. The teacher verbally communicates the desired behavior or physically models the behavior and reinforces the child for making the appropriate response through effective praise.

Some psychologists see this approach as having two serious limitations

1. Learning is limited to the acquisition of specific items of information.
2. The child's motivation for learning may be different from what the teacher intended (e.g., the child was motivated by individual attention from the teacher rather than by his or her own success).

The third school of thought is the **constructivist view.** Constructivism, as formulated by Jean Piaget in the 1920s, saw children as interacting with their environment and constructing their own intellect. Constructivists, who directly challenge the behaviorists, see genetic makeup and environment (nature and nurture) as more or less equal in shaping development. Unlike the behaviorists, both the maturationists and the constructivists describe the child as moving from one stage to another. Unlike the maturationists, who see the progression of development at more or less predictable ages, constructivists see development as the result of experience with objects and consultation with people coupled with the way in which the individual interprets, recognizes, or modifies experience.

Vygotsky was a contemporary of Piaget. His theory (Vygotsky, 1978) complements Piaget's by emphasizing socially constructed knowledge. Although Vygotsky agreed with Piaget concerning the role of personal experiences, he also felt that knowledge was constructed as a result of social experiences with peers and adults.

For Vygotsky, initial learning begins on the social plane—that is, learners are guided by the instruction of others. Cognitive strategies are eventually transferred to the psychological plane (i.e., humans learn of their own volition), but these learnings are permanently imbued with their social origins. Because Vygotsky theorized that cognitive development occurs in a social–cultural context, his theory can be classified as **social constructivism.** Along with the ideas of Vygotsky, post-Piagetian theorists speak of more than one type of intelligence (Gardner, 1983).

Ecological Perspectives.   Ecological perspectives are concerned with how learning and development are influenced by the uniqueness of a person's environments. Bronfenbrenner (1979, 1989) advocated applying an ecological perspective to all behaviors. Bronfenbrenner (1986) suggested that people live in multiple environments simultaneously. He described the ecological context that a child experiences and that affects development as four different, but overlapping, systems.

- The microsystem, the immediate and powerful socializer of children, comprises the family, child care or school, peers, media, and community.
- The mesosystem consists of overlapping microsystems, such as parent–teacher interaction or employer-supported child care.
- The exosystem consists of parents' jobs, city government, the school board, community services, and the federal government. A child may be influenced indirectly

by the exosystem. For example, parents whose employment requires conformity are likely to adopt an autocratic or authoritarian parenting style.

- The macrosystem or culture consists of socioeconomic, racial or ethnic, geographic and American ideological, religious, and political cultures. Because culture has a profound effect, Cole (1998) embedded environments within a cultural context.

Two theories with ecological perspectives are of interest to early childhood educators. Erikson's (1950) *psychosocial theory* describes how children develop the foundation for personality and mental health. Erikson noted that the environment shapes personality through both limitations and freedoms. That is, it provides the range of behaviors and learning circumscribed by society as directed through significant relations, such as parents, and provides freedom of choice for the individual throughout life. He stated that his eight developmental crises (e.g., sense of trust versus mistrust) are universal, but that the central problem (e.g., weaning) faced in a given crisis period is culturally determined.

Vygotsky's theory, which he aptly described as "mind in society" (Vygotsky, 1978), has a decided ecological perspective. According to Vygotsky, the learner engages in problem-solving activities in which an adult or more capable peer guides and models ways to solve the task that are between each child's independent problem-solving capability and what he or she can do with assistance. (This was called *scaffolding* by Wood, Bruner, and Ross, 1976.) Vygotsky called it the **zone of proximal development (ZPD).**

Through participation in authentic cultural activities with social interactions, children learn cultural "tools of the mind" (i.e., symbol systems, such as language) and eventually use these tools to engage in internal cognitive activity. Thus, the child's social environment provides the needed support system that allows the child to develop new competencies; that is, learning in a social context leads to development.

Philosophical Positions.   Schools are designed to meet social purposes. This fact has been recognized since the time of Plato, who described education in *The Republic* as preparation of children to do the state's bidding. Like Plato, Dewey believed that education is the fundamental lever of social progress (Dewey, 1897). Conversely, during the 1960s the emphasis on psychological theories almost overshadowed philosophical positions. Some early childhood professionals expressed the opinion that psychological theory alone cannot be the sole basis for determining program design (Egan, 1983; Hunt, 1961).

Several program designers suggested that a blend of the psychological and philosophical views was needed. Kohlberg and Mayer (1972) stated that philosophically desirable ends must be rooted in the "facts of development." "Philosophical principles cannot be stated as ends of education until they can be stated psychologically" (p. 485). They also saw psychological theories as having either implicit or explicit values and stated that when theories are used as the basis for program design they become ideologies.

The need for a philosophical position as a foundation for program design seems clear. Whether the lack of a philosophical basis is the result of a vague ideology, dominance of psychological theories, or other causes, the dilemma posed by this gap in value base was pinpointed by Sommerville (1982). He stated, "Children are going to school for an ever-longer period, but we seem less and less sure about what they should be getting from it" (p. 16). Thus, the critical question is, What kind of U.S. citizen do we need to meet the challenges and opportunities of the 21st century? Like Dewey (1916), we must emphasize the importance of communicating with each other the values we will share in our programs and schools.

Several ideas for values have been suggested, including the Golden Rule, which is seen as a common value taught in most major religions. Other values often suggested are "honesty, caring, fairness, respect, and perseverance" (Smith, 1997, p. 233). The NAEYC and the National Association of Early Childhood Specialists in State Departments of Education (1991) have suggested that a free society "should reflect the ideals of a participatory democracy, such as personal autonomy, decision making, equality, and social justice" (p. 28).

Synthesis of Theories and Philosophies.   When the NAEYC first issued its position statements on developmentally appropriate practice (DAP; Bredekamp, 1987), the statements seemed to lean heavily on psychological theories for age-appropriate and individually appropriate curricula. Some asserted that DAP did not address (or obscured) other aspects of program planning (Kostelnik, 1992; Spodek, 1991; Swadener & Kessler, 1991). In an attempt to address these concerns, the NAEYC (1997a) issued a revised statement acknowledging that curricular decisions must be based on a knowledge of child development and learning, individual children's characteristics and strengths, and the social and cultural contexts in which children live.

Spodek's (1991) dimensions for program planning and evaluation seem to be a synthesis of psychological theories, ecological perspectives, and philosophical positions. Spodek called for the use of three dimensions for judging educational programs:

1. Developmental (considers what children can learn and the methodology employed in teaching)
2. Cultural (acknowledges society's values, that is, what we want children to be and become)
3. Knowledge (addresses what children need to know today and in the future to function successfully)

Katz (1991a) said that three interrelated a priori questions must be asked to identify appropriate program development: (a) What should be learned? (this deals with goals), (b) When should it be learned? (this deals with child development), and (c) How is it best learned? (this considers program implementation of goals).

PROGRAM COMPONENTS

There are countless interactions between early childhood professionals and the clientele (children and families) they serve each day. It is the sum of these interactions that establishes the ultimate level of quality that is attained. Program planning and attending to the essential components of high-quality care and education will increase the effectiveness and consistency of the interactions throughout the child care and education setting.

For instructional purposes, we have identified three aspects of programs for young children that must be planned, implemented, and evaluated:

- Curriculum (programming and services directly designed to meet the care and education needs of the children and their families)
- Daily operations management (staff management, systems development, and daily problem solving)
- Financial management

Decisions made about each of these program components have an effect on all other programmatic components. For example, if Sara, the new director of a proprietary child care center, was interested in establishing a child care program that included children with significant special needs with typically developing children, the curriculum must consider the wide variety of abilities that the children in each classroom are likely to have. Likewise, she would also have to ensure that the staff working in these classrooms have the requisite training, experience, and professional support to ensure that each child receives the instruction and services that he or she is entitled to so they develop to their maximum potential. Financial considerations might involve collaboration with the local agency that oversees IDEA Part C programming to procure necessary equipment and support services.

Curriculum: The Program for Children and Families

Early childhood curriculum includes much more than the daily activities and learning centers that are planned by the teacher. Curriculum includes all aspects of the program that influence what and how the children might learn. Such components include the daily planned engagements and the learning centers. They also include the incidental conversations between caregivers and the children, the physical layout of the facility, the provision of materials and supplies that the children have access to, the expectations for children's behavior, procedures for transitioning between activities, eating, sleeping, toileting, and the age grouping of the children.

While the specific process for designing the curriculum is described in chapter 9, at this stage in the planning process it is important to begin investigating and identifying how to go about curriculum design and implementation. In the next section we will provide information for you to consider as you embark on the decision to use an established curriculum model or a design of your own.

Deciding on Curriculum

Curriculum models have had a major impact on program goals, administrative and pedagogical decisions, and program outcomes. However, the very nature of models raises many issues and research uncertainties.

Theory as Program Informant.   A question often raised is whether one approach should be selected to promote consistency or whether a curriculum model should be one of several program informants. Some programs are based on several developmental theories, and some professionals call for other disciplines, such as philosophy, sociology, and anthropology, to be used as informants.

Many professionals believe that the cultural context of children's development should be considered; that is, one size does not fit all. The universality of development has been challenged (Gardner, 1999); that is, children develop many valued skills and knowledge in many types of environments (Goncu, 1999). Except during the 1960s and 1970s, the cultural context has been considered important in understanding development. During the 1980s the work of Vygotsky and Bronfenbrenner, which stressed the importance of culture, again aroused interest in the cultural nature of development (Rogoff & Chavajay, 1995).

Many researchers are now calling for culturally sensitive approaches that take familial and community cultural values into account in assessing needs for a program service, in planning and delivering services, and in measuring program outcomes. This approach is in sharp contrast to the idea of "cultural deprivation" that was prominent in the 1960s.

Another problem of using developmental theory as an informant is that theory is continually changing. Stott and Bowman (1996) discussed how programs informed by developmental or learning theory thus promote practices based on concepts no longer supported in theory.

Finally, some professionals believe that curriculum models should not be standardized. They see children, teachers, and even families as designers of an emergent curriculum. Conversely, the demand for accountability has led to interest in curriculum models developed by experts and then transported to various sites for implementation.

Within-model variation has led to questions as to whether "typical" programs can have the same effects as exemplary programs using the same model (Barnett, 1986; Haskins, 1989). Kagan (1991a) believed that transporting models will not work and that program developers should launch site-specific models. Furthermore, even if a model has been adopted at another site, it is not known how far the program can deviate from its model (e.g., in expenditures per child) before the positive effects disappear. Weikart (1981, 1983) emphasized that the success of a program for young children was based on the quality of the program implementation rather than the model.

Program Quality and Effectiveness of Models. Some professionals believe that the best way to promote program quality is through the adoption of models (Pogrow, 1996). Frede (1998) found the following commonalities in models with long-term effectiveness:

1. Coherent programs with curriculum content based on needed school-related knowledge and skills
2. Qualified teachers who use reflective teaching practices aided by qualified supervisors
3. Low teacher-child ratios and small group sizes
4. Collaborative relationships with parents

Search for the "Best" Model. Even among high-quality programs, effectiveness must be interpreted with caution. Programs differ in their target populations, duration, and administrative and pedagogical components. Furthermore, the effects of high-quality programs also depend on their reception by children, teachers, and families. Thus, researchers need to determine which aspects of a program (curriculum, other aspects, or both) are beneficial and for whom (Barnett, Frede, Mobasher, & Mohr, 1987; Hauser-Cram, 1990; Horowitz & O'Brien, 1989; Jacobs, 1988; Powell, 1987a, 1987b; Sigel, 1990).

This problem is confounded by the association between the curriculum goals selected and the teaching techniques employed (Miller, Bugbee, & Hyberton, 1985). Thus, the question that needs to be answered is, Under what conditions does the model work? (Guralnick, 1988; Meisels, 1985). Other questions still not answered are as follows:

1. Can exposure to a high-quality program serve as a barrier to environmental risks, or are other efforts needed (e.g., housing) to maximize benefits (Horowitz & O'Brien, 1989)?
2. Can benefits of quality programs accrue to *all* children? (Target populations who receive interventions have been rather limited.)

The search for the "best" model is still an issue. Recently, researchers noted the consistency between program goals and program outcomes. This finding brings us back to philosophical questions. In choosing a model, what outcomes are most important?

Services Offered

While the services offered by an early childhood program are likely to be focused primarily on the care and education of the children, how a single program defines appropriate care and education will be determined by the program vision, sponsorship, and the values of the families and community served by the program.

Some centers provide comprehensive care and education services that might include access to on-site health care professionals (medical, dental, counseling); transportation to and from the center; extended hours of care; after-school programming for elementary aged children; family (adult) education programming; child care staff professional development training; academic tutoring; or developmental screening for children with special needs.

Once a center administrator has evaluated the needs of the stakeholders who are served by the program and decided on the services that will be offered, a significant amount of planning will be required to ensure that the center has the resources and professional knowledge and skill to effectively deliver needed services. (See Table 2.1 for a *service delivery planning sheet*.)

Table 2.1
Service Delivery Planning Sheet

Family/Community Need	Service to Meet the Need	Necessary Resources (Human or Material)	Anticipated Cost	Will Service Be Provided? Yes/No and Rationale for Decision
List the results of your family/community needs assessment in this column. Reserve each block for individual needs.	Describe or list service(s) that is/are likely to address this need for families.	List any and all resources that will be necessary to deliver this service.	Identify the real cost of providing this service by identifying labor costs, facility costs, and any equipment and supplies that are necessary to provide the service.	Based on the impact this service might have on the perceived quality of the program, and the determination that the costs associated with the service are reasonable and affordable regardless of the decision. Include a rationale for the service for later reference.

Daily Operations Management

Operations management includes the active facilitation by the program administrator to ensure that both process and structural program characteristics are consistently being maintained. Part of the planning process is establishing **systems** that are needed to ensure a minimum level of service is provided consistently to your clientele.

Systems are simply a structured plan for service delivery that include explicit description of desired results, articulation of the complete process for delivering the service, and a process for continually monitoring to ensure that the desired results are actually being achieved. For example, in an attempt to ensure that the facility is clean, organized, and well maintained, a child care administrator might design a facility checklist (Figure 2.2) that identifies all aspects of the center that should be clean, organized, and maintained. Embedded in the checklist is the expected frequency that the outcomes are achieved and monitored.

In addition to checklists, program directors also create staff manuals that articulate program goals and staff performance expectations. These manuals, if done well, include all necessary procedures that help establish the minimum level of performance for all job responsibilities and duties. An example of such a procedure detailing how staff are expected to handle situations when children are injured while at the center can be seen in Figure 2.3.

For further description of the purpose and process of developing employee handbooks and training manuals, see Chapter 4.

The Facility Maintenance Checklist identifies the areas of the classroom that are to be monitored for cleanliness, organization, and maintenance. Each staff member is expected to complete this checklist at the conclusion of his or her shift. If an item on the checklist is not clean or organized, take the appropriate action to ensure that it is as it should be prior to leaving the facility. If an item is in need of repair, please take the appropriate action to ensure the children's safety. This may require that the item be removed from the children's access. If an item is broken and is not repairable, discard the item and make a note indicating that a replacement is needed. Use the notes section of the checklist to document anything you are not able to address immediately and might need the attention of the building administrator.

CLASSROOM	4-year-olds					SHIFT: AM / MIDDAY / PM (Please Circle)
TEACHER						

M	T	W	TH	F	AREA	Notes
					Entryway to the classroom: Free of litter, cubby area is organized, all children's names are clearly legible.	
					Block center: Blocks and other toys are appropriately stored, clean, and in good repair.	
					Dramatic Play: All materials are in appropriate bins, and clothes are hanging.	
					Table Manipulatives: All materials are in labeled bins and all labels are facing out.	
					Book Nook: All books are organized on the book shelf. All books are right side up, with front cover facing out.	
					Circle Time Rug: Whiteboard is clean, rug is free of litter, materials for the next group time are prepared and in the green tub.	
					Snack/Lunch Area: All tables are clean, chairs are tucked under the table, and trash cans are empty.	
					Rest Mats: Stacked neatly in storage closet.	
				WEEKLY TASKS		
					Sanitize blocks	
					Dramatic play	
					Materials laundered	
					Table manipulatives sanitized	
					Rest mats sanitized	

Figure 2.2
Facility Checklist

First Aid

First Aid Kit

All of our classrooms have a small first-aid kit consisting of Band-Aids, plastic gloves, antibiotic ointment, cotton swabs, and a thermometer. These items are in the classrooms so that the teachers can treat level 1 injuries. A complete first aid kit is kept at the preschool receptionist station. This kit is to be used for more severe injuries (level 2) and contains the following items:

- Alcohol
- Syrup of ipecac
- Bandages
- Scissors
- Tweezers
- Adhesive tape
- Cotton balls
- Latex gloves
- Anti-bacterial salve
- First aid handbook
- Thermometer
- Tylenol/Motrin

In the event of illness or injury, we cannot apply or administer any medication without parental consent. This includes but is not limited to antibiotic ointment, Tylenol/ Motrin, bug spray, sunscreen, etc. In the event that parental consent is given, we must document any administration of medicine in the child's file.

What should I do when a child is injured?

Cuts, Scrapes, or Punctures

- Wash your hands
- Put on gloves
- Wash wound with soap and water
- Apply Neosporin ointment to wound (if parental consent is given)
- Cover wound with Band-Aid or gauze if too big for a Band-Aid
- Wash your hands
- Fill out accident report
- Notify parents (if severe)

Bumps

- Apply cold pack or ice for 15 minutes or less
- If there is no cold pack available in the room, get an ice bag from the employee lounge refrigerator or Odabee's Café.
- Fill out accident report
- Notify parents

Bleeding

- Wash your hands
- Put on gloves

Figure 2.3
Example from Employee Manual
Source: From the initial training manual of O2B Kids College, Gainesville, FL. Adapted with permission.

- Gently apply pressure to site with gauze to stop the bleeding
- After bleeding has stopped follow procedure for "cuts, scrapes and punctures."
- Fill out accident report
- Notify parents

When to take the child to the front desk

- Rash
- Vomiting situation that requires the retrieval of the child by the parent
- Illness requires isolation
- Suspected fever

When to call 911

- Severe bleeding
- Unnatural loss of teeth
- Loss of consciousness
- Seizures
- Vomiting or passing blood
- Possible broken bones

What should I do after I have attended to the child's needs?

We have categorized typical child injuries into three levels. The levels are grouped according to the severity of the injury. The following describes the procedures that must be followed in the event of an injury. If you are faced with an injury that does not fall into one of the following categories, seek the help of a supervisor immediately after you have attended to the needs of the child.

LEVEL 1: Fill out an incident report

The following types of injuries require that you attend to the child's needs and document the situation leading to the injury by completing an accident report. After you have completed the accident report turn it in to the receptionist at the front desk.

Level 1 injuries:
Minor bumps and bruises
Bug bites
Skinned knee or elbow
Any injury below the neck that can be covered with a Band-Aid

LEVEL 2: Follow the above procedures and contact the parent and the director

The following types of injuries are considered more severe than level 1 injuries. After the level 1 procedures have been completed, contact the child's parents and make the director aware of the incident.

Level 2 injuries:
Any injury above the shoulders (minor head injuries)
    Scratch on the face
    Cut head
    Knot on the head

Child bites
Fever
Unexplained rash
Vomiting
Illness requiring that the child go home

Figure 2.3 (Continued)

LEVEL 3: Contact the director immediately. The director will contact the parents. If necessary call 911.

The following are severe injuries. Due to the severity and sensitivity of such injuries, the director will inform the parents of the incident. Make sure to contact the director immediately. If the situation warrants, call 911. **Do not wait until you get in touch with the director**. Although you cannot make regular phone calls from the classroom phones, **you CAN call 911**.

Level 3 injuries:
Any injury that requires the immediate care of a physician:

> Broken bone
> Stitches
> Seizure

The following incidents are not severe in the sense that the child is in immediate danger, but these types of situations are very serious and require immediate parental notification.

> Bloody nose
> Cut hair

The above mentioned injuries are only examples. This is not an all-inclusive list. If you are not sure how to categorize an accident, consult another teacher or supervisor.

Figure 2.3 (Continued)

Financial Management

To ensure that the early care and education program is able to operate, the financial health of the organization must be planned for and actively monitored. This includes monitoring the flow of funding (income and expenses) and reporting the financial health of the organization to sponsoring organizations.

While the actual process of financial management will be discussed in Chapter 7, it is important, from the planning vantage point, that the child care administrator identify how he or she intends to monitor the financial standing of the program. For example, will you use a financial software program to help with billing and payroll? Or will you use a comprehensive child care management tool such as *Child Care Manager,* or *ProCare?*

Program planning should be a collaborative process.

You will also need to determine if the program will be proprietary or nonprofit and identify any local agencies or programs that might be able to subsidize the costs of providing high-quality care and education services.

DEVELOPING A VISION: THE FOUNDATION FOR ALL OTHER PROGRAM COMPONENTS

All high-quality early childhood programs have some characteristics in common. All adhere to appropriate licensing regulations. All are situated in facilities designed or adapted for use by young children; provide appropriate equipment and supplies to support caregiving routines and active and quiet play. All plan carefully for the curriculum they offer the children in their care.

Beyond these basic features, high-quality programs vary enormously. There is little consensus as to what goals are the best for children. There are no universally accepted strategies to reach these goals, and there are many approaches to program evaluation. A successful program administrator knows what he or she wants to accomplish, the niche he or she hopes the center will fill, and has a vision for the program.

This vision is not a roadmap to program implementation. Instead, it is a broad and ambitious view of what you hope the program can accomplish and, more specifically, what the program will look like in operation. For example, you may want to serve the children of low-income mothers pursuing higher education in hopes that reliable child care will increase their chances to break the cycle of poverty. Or you may, instead, envision a small faith-based program to provide socialization experiences for the children of working mothers in an upper-middle-class neighborhood.

No matter what the purpose of the program, the chances of realizing its potential will depend, in large measure, on how clearly you understand what you want to accomplish. In small, privately owned programs, the director (who is often the owner as well) usually identifies this vision by taking into account his or her professional and financial goals.

In nonprofit programs and large proprietary programs, this strategic planning might be carried out collaboratively. The director may present the vision of what contribution he or she hopes the program will make to the community and the children and families it serves to the board of directors for discussion and approval. Or the director may work with a board of advisors (a group constituted by families, staff, and community members) to develop the program's vision collaboratively. A program's vision should be future oriented. It is an opportunity to "dream big" and should describe what the program hopes to accomplish for children, families, and the community.

In developing the vision for your center, it might be wise to consult potential stakeholders to conduct a needs assessment for the community where the center is located or will be located in the future. The needs assessment should include a survey of what child care and education services are offered, stakeholder satisfaction with these services, and an assessment of the demographic information for the population of the area.

In addition, the vision for your program should be influenced by professional knowledge of what constitutes high-quality programming. Such programming draws upon theoretical, philosophical, and empirical understandings of the aims of education and best practices that support both academic and social development of young children.

The vision for the program should include absolutely every aspect of the program as each has an impact on all others. This includes the curriculum for the children, the nature of services offered, management of staff and daily operations, and financial management.

When visualizing the ultimate goal of the program, the director could contemplate the sights, sounds, emotions, and outcomes of all stakeholders. Imagine walking into this ideal

Developing Your Vision

Step 1:   Reflect on your personal values, hopes, and dreams. Close your eyes and visualize the ideal child care and education program on a typical day of operation. In this visualization, take a tour of the facility and answer the following questions:

- What do you see on the walls, floor, and ceiling?
- What sounds do you hear?
- What are the children, families, and teachers doing?
- If you were to interview child, parent, and teacher, how would they describe their experience at the center?
- What services are provided?
- What are the ultimate outcomes you hope to achieve through provision of these services?

Step 2:   Articulate a complete narrative description of this visualization. Be sure to include every perceptible characteristic of this visualization (sights, sounds, smells, touch). As you are putting this visualization into words, think of not only the physical characteristics, but also the feelings that you experienced while touring this ideal setting.

Step 3:   Share this narrative with a group of stakeholders. Elicit feedback by asking the following questions:

- What aspects of this visualization do you find appealing?
- Are there aspects of typical child care programs that are absent from this description?
- Are there characteristics of the visualization that are troubling?
- What suggestions do you have to strengthen this vision?
- If the center is in operation, what are the shortcomings of our present functioning?

Step 4:   Taking the feedback from the stakeholder group meeting, revise the vision statement, print it out, frame it, and hang it in a location where you will see it frequently.

Figure 2.4
Vision Development Worksheet

center: How are you greeted? What do you hear? What do you see? What people are in this setting and how are they interacting with each other? As you observe and walk around the facility, what color are the walls? What types of materials are present?

Once you have engaged in this visualization, you must then articulate this vision in a way that other people can understand. This is important because the next step in drafting your vision is sharing it with others. If your center is currently in operation, you will need to share this vision with your staff, the families being served, and other community members who might have a stake in the ultimate outcome (e.g. public or private schools that typically accept the children once they graduate from your program), of the service you provide.

If, on the other hand, the center is not yet operating, you will need to get input from potential stakeholders, or, if appropriate, a board of directors/advisors. To help you with the process, use the worksheet presented in Figure 2.4.

DEVELOPING THE PROGRAM'S MISSION STATEMENT

Once the program's vision has been identified and agreed upon, the next step is to create the organization's mission statement. This is a clear expression of the program's purpose. A program's mission statement should be a simple, short, easy to remember statement

Creating a vision and mission involves actually visualizing the types of experiences you hope the children will engage in.

that all employees will be able to understand, memorize, and use as a guide in their day-to-day practice (Meshanko, 1996). The mission statement should be applicable to all decisions made throughout the program, including major programmatic decisions, classroom-level curriculum decisions, and decisions that impact individual children and families. Because of the broad-reaching nature and importance of the mission statement, it is highly recommended that all stakeholders be included in the development or refinement of your organization's mission.

A clear and well-understood mission statement should be the foundation for everything that happens in the center. It can be used by the director when coaching a teacher in appropriate guidance strategies, answering a father's questions about his toddler's day, and helping the cook plan healthy, but affordable, meals.

Application Activity

For the next week, look for the mission statements of community businesses and agencies in your area. As you read these mission statements, ask the following questions:

1. Is the mission statement short enough to be memorized by all employees?
2. Is the mission statement specific enough that it applies only to this type of business or agency (or could it be applied to any organization?)?
3. Based on your experience in this setting, is it likely that the mission statement *actually* guides the employees' decision making?

IMPLEMENTING THE PROGRAM

After carefully considering all the factors that influence the program and after the vision and mission of the program have been articulated, the director or board must **operationalize the program**. The "ideal" program seems to be the one that best suits the needs of the children and families served. Personal beliefs, whether articulated or maintained as a preconscious set of values, influence decision making.

To operationalize the program, the director needs to develop and write the pedagogical and operational components of the program. Using the program mission statement, think through questions pertaining to the pedagogical components of your program. To begin this process, ask yourself the following questions.

1. What are the goals and objectives of my early childhood program?   To provide an environment conducive to the development of the whole child? To teach young children academic skills? To provide intensive instruction in areas of academic deficits and thinking skills? To develop creativity? To build a healthy self-concept? To spur self-direction in learning?

2. What provisions for children's individual differences are consistent with my program's goals?   Should I expect the same level or varying levels of achievement? Are individual differences acceptable in some or all academic areas? in some or all developmental areas (psychomotor, affective, cognitive)? Are activities chosen by the child appropriate to the child's own interest and developmental level, or are they staff tailored to meet individual differences? Are activities presented for one or several learning styles?

3. What schedule format is needed to facilitate my program's objectives?   A full- or half-day schedule? The same session length for all children, or length of session tailored to each child's and parents' needs? a predetermined or flexible daily schedule based on children's interests?

Administrators must also consider questions pertaining to the operational components of the program, such as the following.

1. What staff roles are necessary to implement the learning environment as set forth in my program philosophy?   Persons who dispense knowledge, resource persons, or persons who prepare the environment? Persons who use positive or negative reinforcement? Group leaders or individual counselors? Academic content specialists or social engineers? Persons who work almost exclusively with young children or those who provide parent education?

2. What staff positions (director, teachers, volunteers) are needed to execute my program?   What academic or experiential qualifications are required or desired? What type of orientation or in-service training is needed? What child–staff ratio is required?

3. What equipment and materials are required?   Equipment and materials that are self-correcting or that encourage creativeness? that are designed to stress one concept (e.g., color paddles) or many concepts (e.g., blocks)? that require substantial or minimal adult guidance? that are designed for group or individual use? that provide for concrete experiences or abstract thinking?

4. What physical arrangement is compatible with the goals of my program?   Differentiated or nondifferentiated areas for specific activities? fixed or flexible areas? outside area used primarily for learning or for recess? equipment and materials arranged for self-service by the child or for teacher distribution?

And then the crucial question must be answered: Do the answers have a supportable rationale? Make sure you carefully consider your answers. Try to weed out irrelevant beliefs, inappropriate values, and outdated information. Is what you have written culturally relevant, supported by research, developmentally appropriate, and timely? Bowman (1986) stated that the tremendous increase of knowledge from interdisciplinary sources provides us with a rich base to plan for children, but it also encourages us to "tolerate faddism, quackism, and just plain foolishness" (p. 6).

PROGRAM EVALUATION AND GOAL DEVELOPMENT

Once the program vision and mission statements have been developed and agreed upon and an implementation plan has been adopted by all appropriate stakeholders, the next step in the process of program development and enhancement is to conduct a program evaluation to identify areas of necessary improvement. This program evaluation is an assessment of the program that examines the extent to which program operations or implementation align with or have the potential to fulfill the program mission and vision.

The program evaluation should be comprehensive, covering all aspects of the program. It should include administration effectiveness, staff effectiveness, curriculum implementation, child and family satisfaction, and employee satisfaction. Early childhood administrators need to target their efforts in response to local needs and values. Being

Table 2.2
Assessing Local Needs Through Culturally Sensitive Questions

- What are the needs of local families? What services are valid for the group to be served?
- What are the local values (e.g., tradition versus change; competition versus cooperation; perceived value of early child-hood programs)? How diverse is the local population, and how does this diversity affect generalizations concerning local values?
- What communication skills are needed?
- What services are now available? Are there children or families who do not get needed, but locally available, services? Are there any cultural barriers preventing these children or families from being served?
- What human resources are available in the local community? How can the community be involved in the planning and delivery of these services? How should you organize to get these services? What type of leadership style is preferred in the local community?
- What material resources (e.g., parks, health care, social agencies) are available in the community? How are these resources perceived by the local population? Is there a single institution serving as the center of a service network?

able to address local conditions effectively is often referred to as being **culturally competent** or **sensitive** (see Table 2.2).

EVALUATING THE PROGRAM

Administrators are held accountable for the programs under their leadership and direction. With a constant demand for excellence, evaluation has become one of the administrator's most significant responsibilities. Why? One reason is that funding and legal sources require evaluation reports. Accreditation is based on standards set by the accrediting agencies, such as professional groups. Furthermore, the staff objectively and subjectively make judgments as they work in the program. In addition, parents question program quality, and public interest in program value is heightened, especially on the part of taxpayers. Administrators must answer to each of these groups.

A discussion of evaluation leads to classification of the types of evaluation. Dopyera and Lay-Dopyera (1990) identified two types of evaluation: intuitive and formal.

Intuitive Evaluation

Intuitive evaluation might be called a personal construct or practical knowledge. Intuitive evaluation is a notion about what constitutes the right way to achieve something. Unlike planned formal evaluation, intuitive evaluation concerns how people perform on a minute-by-minute basis.

Early childhood teachers and administrators have notions about their professional practice. Although these notions guide their day-to-day practice, they are difficult to articulate. These notions come to light when a clash occurs between one's own ideas or actions and those of another who is respected or when the outcomes of what one expects and what ensues differ.

Through studies of intuitive evaluation (Clark & Peterson, 1986; Katz, 1984; Spodek, 1987), two points seem to be established:

1. Early childhood educators take their book-learned knowledge and guided observations and integrate them with their values and practical knowledge. This knowledge

is integrated by each individual teacher from his or her theory-based knowledge, accumulated experience, and understanding of milieu and self.

2. Intuitive evaluation is important because educators must often make judgment calls so quickly that they do not have time to reflect on theory and empirical findings; thus, intuitive evaluation guides practice.

Formal Evaluation

Planned (or formal) evaluation has its roots in concern over accountability to the funding agencies. With an increasing number of mandates for evaluation, the evaluation profession has grown, and activities involving formal evaluation have increased. Many educational endeavors require formal evaluation, such as needs assessment, program analysis, cost effectiveness (the effectiveness of a program as it relates to cost per child), and program impact (positive changes in the child or family that affect society).

Administrators must determine the appropriate type of evaluation to serve their needs (objectives-based evaluation, standards-based evaluation, and evaluation research). Objectives-based and standards-based evaluation are both concerned with accountability. Evaluation research is concerned with the interplay of various aspects of a given program related to outcomes.

Objectives-Based Evaluation.   **Objectives-based evaluation** focuses on what children achieve as a result of participation in a specific program. Objectives-based evaluation is the most common form of formal evaluation. Thus, the criteria used for evaluation are program specific (developed by examining the program's goals and objectives). The analyses of evaluation data provide information on the degree to which program goals and objectives are met.

Evaluation may be conducted at two points in the program. **Formative evaluation** is used to determine the effectiveness of various aspects of the program (e.g., grouping practices) while program changes are still being made. **Summative evaluation** determines the effectiveness of the overall program at some ending point.

Standards-Based Evaluation.   **Standards-based evaluation** is an appraisal of a program based on a set of standards (criteria) developed outside any specific program. These standards may be deemed worthwhile by a professional association (e.g., the National Academy of Early Childhood Programs' Accreditation), the funding or monitoring agency (e.g., Head Start Performance Objectives), or a researcher (e.g., The Early Childhood Environment Rating Scale).

There are several standards-based evaluations that focus on the overall environment of the classroom or program and are designed to measure the quality of the learning environment.

1. **High/Scope Program Quality Assessment (PQA).**   The PQA was developed by the High/Scope Educational Research Foundation (1998). The PQA has 72 items that cover the following attributes of quality: learning environment, daily routine, adult–child interaction, curriculum planning and assessment, parent involvement and family services, staff qualifications and staff development, and program management. Each item is scored on a 5-point rating scale.

2. **Early Childhood Environment Rating Scale: Revised Edition (ECERS).**   The ECERS was developed by Harms and Clifford in 1980 and revised by Harms, Clifford, and Cryer (1998). They see an early childhood program as an ecological system with more parts than just the individual within the program. The ECERS is used to examine 43 attributes that cover the following areas of quality: space and furnishings, personal care routines, language

and reasoning, activities, interactions, program structure, and parents and staff. Ratings are given for each area, and a total rating can be calculated for each group. Scores on all the groups within a center may be compiled to get a quality score for a center.

3. Family Day Care Rating Scale (FDCRS).   The FDCRS was developed by Harms and Clifford (1989) and follows the same pattern as their ECERS. The FDCRS is used to examine 32 attributes that cover the following areas of quality: space and furnishings for care and learning, basic care, language and reasoning, learning activities, social development, and adult needs. Each item is described in four levels of quality: inadequate, minimal, good, and excellent. Eight "supplementary items" are provided for centers enrolling children with special needs.

4. Infant/Toddler Environment Rating Scale. Revised Edition (ITERS).   The ITERS was developed by Harms, Cryer, and Clifford (2003) and follows the same pattern as their ECERS and FDCRS. The ITERS consists of 39 items for the assessment of the quality of center-based child care for children up to 30 months of age. Items are organized under the following categories: space and furnishings, personal care routines, listening and talking, activities, interaction, program structure, and parents and staff. Each item is presented on a 7-point scale, with descriptors for 1 (inadequate), 3 (minimal), 5 (good), and 7 (excellent).

5. School-Age Care Environment Rating Scale (SACERS).   The SACERS was developed by Harms, Jacobs, and White (1995) and follows the same pattern as the ECERS, FDCRS, and ITERS. The SACERS consists of 49 items for the assessment of the quality of child care programs offered by schools and other organizations. Items are organized under the following attributes: space and furnishings, health and safety, activities, interactions, program structure, staff development, and supplementary items (for children with special needs).

6. Assessment of Practices in Early Elementary Classrooms (APEEC).   The APEEC was developed by Hemmeter, Maxwell, Ault, and Schuster (2001) and follows the same pattern as the ECERS, EDCRS, ITERS, and SACERS. The APEEC, designed for kindergarten through Grade 3 classrooms, consists of 16 items in the following domains of classroom practice: physical environment, instructional context, and social context.

Specific aspects of programs can be checked, too. Some examples include (a) Child's Adjustment to the Program (Nilsen, 2000, p. 265); (b) Early Childhood Work Environment Survey (Professional Development Project of National-Louis University); (c) Parent Evaluation of Child Care Program (*Child Care Information Exchange,* June 1989, pp. 25–26); and (d) Safety Checklist (Frost, 1992a, pp. 346–350).

Researchers are working on instruments for empirical studies of DAP. Different types of instruments have been developed to fit the researchers' investigations. For example, Hitz and Wright (1988) developed an instrument to note the degree of change in academic emphasis of early childhood programs (from Developmentally Inappropriate Practices to DAP). Bryant, Clifford, and Peisner (1991) developed an instrument to determine teachers' knowledge and attitudes about DAP. Similarly, Oakes and Caruso (1990) measured teachers' attitudes about authority in the classroom and developed observation instruments to confirm the "self-reports." Charlesworth and colleagues (1993) thought of DIP and DAP on a continuum. They developed the Teachers Belief Statements, the Instructional Activities Scale, and the Checklist for Rating Developmentally Appropriate Practice in Kindergarten Classrooms. (Other standards-based assessments are discussed in chapter 11.)

An Important Consideration

Evaluation generates information that should be used for program enhancement. The most meaningful evaluations are most often those stimulated by internal factors rather than those resulting from external mandates. Evaluations mandated by external sources are perceived as useful only when data are also used for local program purposes. Program quality needs to go beyond structural variables that researchers have associated with high-quality child and family outcomes (Katz, 1999) and also include process characteristics such as teacher-child interaction.

To overcome the negative effects of evaluation, staff must acknowledge the interdependent effects of all program components, and evaluation must include all components, be ongoing, and include all those involved in a program. Pressures for answers from within and without the program will not seem so unbearable, or the difficulties involved in overcoming content and methodological problems so insurmountable, if one keeps in mind the major purpose of program evaluation: to identify opportunities for improvement. If evaluation is seen as a means for program improvement, it becomes a continuous process, and its results become starting points for future planning.

SUMMARY

The administrator's main task is providing leadership in program planning, implementation, and evaluation. The administrator, as an early step, will identify and articulate the vision he or she has for the program. The factors that should influence the program vision are a synthesis of community and stakeholder values, empirical evidence, psychological theories, ecological perspectives, and philosophical positions. Once the program vision has been developed, a succinct mission statement should be created and communicated to stakeholders and staff members to guide them in all interactions with children and families.

The administrator must then understand and choose a curriculum approach and implementation plan that address the needs of all stakeholders and, as supported by evidence, will likely result in desired outcomes for children and families. A curriculum model consists of the program philosophy, the administrative and pedagogical components, and the program evaluation. The choice of the program base is critical because programmatic research points to a consistent relationship between program focus and program outcomes. Every aspect of implementation of the program's administrative and pedagogical components should be in keeping with the vision, mission, and philosophy of the program.

The administrator's final step is planning for program evaluation. Evaluation may be of two types: intuitive and formal. Unplanned, intuitive evaluation is constantly functioning; thus, attempts should be made to understand the criteria being used by all involved in the local program. Formal or planned evaluation may be objectives based, standards based, or outcomes based. The administrator and the staff should jointly determine the reasons for evaluation (e.g., needs assessment, program effectiveness), the appropriate type of evaluation, the specific instrument to be used, and the timing of the implementation for both formative and summative evaluations. Evaluation results should provide feedback for future program planning.

USEFUL WEB SITES

Free Management Library

This site features links to a wide range of management topics that are helpful for both profit and nonprofit programs.

www.managementhelp.org

Early Childhood Assessment Consortium

The Early Childhood Education Assessment (ECEA) Consortium provides resources to inform program evaluation and

assessment systems to lead higher levels of quality programming.

http://www.ccsso.org/projects/SCASS/Projects/Early_Childhood_Education_Assessment_Consortium/

TO REFLECT

1. A local corporation is interested in providing child care for its employees. The personnel manager has been asked to ascertain whether the corporation should plan for an on-site program or make a community investment in child care (by encouraging family satellite programs or using corporate reserve slots). What type of data should the personnel manager collect and analyze before making a decision?

2. A potential proprietor is considering child care as a small business. As the first step, a needs assessment instrument should be devised and implemented. What types of items should be included in the needs assessment instrument?

3. In a final seminar session connected with student teaching, a student teacher asks, "What should a new teacher do if his or her philosophical notions come into conflict with those of an administrator?" Rusher, McGrevin, and Lambiotte (1992) say there are four options: (a) disregard the direction of the administrator, (b) teach in ways that are inconsistent with one's beliefs, (c) leave the profession, and (d) teach using "best practices" and make a concerted effort to change the beliefs of the administrator. What are the pros and cons of each option?

3

UNDERSTANDING REGULATIONS, ACCREDITATION CRITERIA, AND OTHER STANDARDS OF PRACTICE

NAEYC Director Competencies addressed in this chapter:

Management Knowledge and Skills

2. Legal and Fiscal Management
   Knowledge and application of the advantages and disadvantages of different legal structures. Knowledge of different codes and regulations as they relate to the delivery of early childhood program services. Knowledge of child custody, child abuse, special education, confidentiality, anti-discrimination, insurance liability, contract, and labor laws pertaining to program management.
5. Program Operations and Facilities Management
   Knowledge and application of policies and procedures that meet state/local regulations and professional standards pertaining to the health and safety of young children.

Early Childhood Knowledge and Skills

5. Children with Special Needs
   Knowledge of licensing standards, state and federal laws (e.g., ADA, IDEA) as they relate to services and accommodations for children with special needs.
10. Professionalism
    Knowledge of laws, regulations, and policies that impact professional conduct with children and families. Knowledge of center accreditation criteria.

Large numbers of families rely on out-of-home care for their infants, toddlers, preschoolers, and school-age children during the work day. In 2005 there were 335,520 licensed child care facilities in the United States with a capacity to serve over 9 million children. Interestingly, while two thirds of the licensed facilities are child care homes, more then 70% of the children served are enrolled in child care centers (NARA/NCCIC, 2006).

Regulations and standards guide the life of an early childhood care and education program—its children and their families, its staff, director, and board. They are designed to give families that rely on child care peace of mind that the health and welfare of their children are safeguarded while their youngsters are away from home. Although regulations and standards may be defined in various ways, we use the following definitions in this book:

1. A **regulation** is a binding rule that has been created by a governing body outside of the early childhood program.
2. A **standard** is a statement of expectations for program characteristics and performance (CCSSO, 2006).

Regulations and standards are closely linked. Together they create benchmarks related to a program's facility, programming, staffing, and other dimensions of quality. Child care programs must comply, for example, with licensing regulations related to the staff-child ratio, that is, the number of children one adult may legally be responsible for.

While state child care regulations set a minimum accepted standard of care, accreditation standards identify criteria that improve the quality of children's experiences. Returning to the example of staff-child ratios, you might see that your state's regulations allow one caregiver to care for up to five infants, but the higher NAEYC Accreditation Standards allow one caregiver to be responsible for only four infants at a time (NAEYC, 2005).

In this chapter we discuss regulations and standards, and in chapter 4 we will explore policies and procedures, that is, how specific programs operate within applicable regulations and standards.

CONSIDERING REGULATIONS

Regulations are the rules, directives, statutes, and standards that prescribe, direct, limit, and govern early childhood programs. They set mininum standards to (1) protect young children's health and safety, (2) ensure equal access to care for eligible children and families, and (3) ensure compliance with zoning and other business-related aspects of the center's operation. These regulations are standards of practice no program is expected to fall below.

Some of the specific regulations that apply to a particular program depend on the auspices under which it operates. Is it a nonprofit organization that is part of a public elementary school or operated by a faith-based organization? Is the center a federally funded Head Start or a corporate-sponsored work-site program? Is it part of a for-profit chain, or operated by an individual entrepreneur? Is it located in an urban, suburban, or rural setting? The next section identifies the kinds of regulations, rules, and statutes you must be aware of and, when applicable, abide by when you are a center director.

Specific Types of Regulations

If you are creating a new center, you are likely to be particularly attentive to certain regulations, such as those related to zoning and the required square footage of classrooms. These are two of many issues that must be addressed before you receive a Certificate of

Occupancy, a statement from the appropriate local governmental agency indicating that a building is suitable for use. A new center must have a Certificate of Occupancy before applying for initial licensure and permission to legally operate as a child care program.

Other regulations, such as those governing staff-child ratio and group size, affect the center's day-to-day operations and require you to be constantly vigilant to be certain you are in compliance. Our discussion will begin with issues related to facilities and the business of child care. Most of these regulations apply to all programs (e.g., zoning, fire regulations, and laws governing services for children with special needs). Other regulations apply only to specific kinds of programs (e.g., public schools or Head Start).

Regulations to Address When Establishing a New Program

Zoning Regulations.   Zoning regulations define how land may be used. Each city and town is enabled by state zoning laws to divide its land into districts. Within those districts, the municipality can enact zoning codes that regulate the use of land and can include specifications related to buildings' structure and their use. Generally, zoning regulations become more stringent as population density increases; that is, there are likely to be more rules about land use in the center city than there are in the suburbs, and suburbs are likely to have more regulations than do rural areas.

Interestingly, child care is frequently treated as a "problem use." Child care centers are often prohibited from residential neighborhoods because of concerns about the noise and traffic they are likely to generate. They are also often not permitted in commercial areas because business districts are not considered good places for children. Some states are working to prevent localities from enacting restrictive policies related to the construction and operation of child care facilities.

Building Codes and Requirements Related to Fire Safety and Sanitation.   Building codes and regulations related to fire safety and sanitation are parts of laws addressing public safety and health. A child care center in a particular locale may be covered under municipal ordinances or locally enforced state regulations. Building codes address the structure's wiring, plumbing, and building materials. Fire regulations describe allowable types of building construction and set standards related to alarm systems, sprinkler systems, and fire extinguishers. They specify how combustible materials are to be stored and require that building evacuation plans be posted. The Life Safety Code Handbook of the National Fire Protection Association (NFPA) provides guidelines for appropriate fire codes for centers, group homes, and family child care. The handbook is available online (its Web site is included in the list at the end of this chapter).

Sanitation codes are mainly concerned with food service operations; diaper changing and bathroom facilities; and procedures for washing toys, equipment, and furniture. Sanitation standards specify, for example, where sinks are to be located (i.e. in the same area as the toilet and in the central diapering area) and require that washable toys are to be sanitized daily. These issues are often addressed in licensing standards established and enforced by state departments of social services but are sometimes the responsibility of local health departments. The American Academy Of Pediatrics (AAP), American Public Health Association (APHA), and the National Resource Center for Health and Safety in Child Care and Early Education (NRCHSCCEE) have joined together to produce *Caring for Our Children: National Health and Safety Performance Standards: Guidelines for Out-of-Home Child Care,* 2nd ed. This book provides an overview of issues to consider when planning and operating a child care program. The standards are available online in English and Spanish. The Web site for this comprehensive resource is included in the list at the end of this chapter.

Regulations That Guide Program Development and Implementation

Licensing: Minimal Quality Regulations.   **Licensing** is the procedure by which a person, association, or corporation obtains from its state licensing agency a permit to operate or continue operating a child care facility. The District of Columbia, the Department of Defense, and 49 states (all except Idaho) license child care facilites (NARA/NCCIC, 2006). The licensing agency (typically the state's department of health and human services or department of social services) is a regulatory body with both quasi-legislative and quasi-judicial authority (Class, 1968). Quasi-legislative powers include responsibility for establishing standards; quasi-judicial powers include responsibility for making decisions to issue or deny a license application and for conducting hearings in grievance cases.

Child care licenses are valid for varied periods of time. Twelve states offer nonexpiring licenses, in 31 states a license is good for 1 or 2 years; and licenses are good for varied periods of time in the other 8 states (NACCRRA, 2007; NARA/NCCIC, 2006).

Features of Child Care Licensing Laws.   A **child care center** is generally defined as a nonresidential facility providing child care services for less than 24 hours a day (NAEYC, 1997). Many states have specific standards for small family child care homes (usually up to 6 children), large family or group child care homes (typically 7 to 12 children cared for by the provider and a full-time assistant), and child care centers serving 13 or more children on a regular basis, usually more than 30 days per year (AAP/APHA/NRCHSCCEE, 2002b). In addition, some states have separate regulations for programs that serve school-age children, infants and toddlers, mildly ill children, or provide drop-in services (NARA/NCCIC, 2006). Each state defines these terms and explains the rules that govern their operations in their regulations.

States' child care regulations are generally reviewed on a regular 4- or 5-year cycle by an appointed child care advisory board (Morgan, 1996). States are encouraged to take care that this advisory board reflects the state's cultural and ethnic diversity and includes representatives from all stakeholder groups: for-profit and not-for-profit operators and caregivers, parents of children enrolled in child care, agency personnel, child development and health care professionals, citizens, and politicians (AAP/APHA/NRCHSCCEE, 2002a). This board typically proposes changes to licensing regulations based on current beliefs about how to safeguard children's physical and emotional well-being. Proposed changes are, eventually, submitted to the state legislature for adoption.

Regulations must balance the state's responsibility to protect children in out-of-home care with the pressures of the marketplace, that is, the ability of providers to meet the established minimum standards. The advisory board usually presents proposed regulations in a series of public hearings, giving concerned citizens the opportunity to express their concerns and/or support for recommended changes to existing regulations. Changes to the proposed regulations may be necessary before revised regulations are enacted into law. Some states provide a gradual phase-in of new rules, particularly when the changes have economic ramifications as do changes to group size or staff-child ratios.

Child Care Center Regulations

Regulatory laws governing child care centers differ widely from state to state.[1] Their purpose is to set minimum standards of care; that is, they are designed to prevent harm to children rather than to ensure the provision of exemplary care. In 2007 the National Association

[1]In this discussion of child care regulations, the District of Columbia is considered to be a state.

It is important that all personnel attend training sessions to help them become thoroughly familiar with applicable licensing regulations.

of Child Care Resource and Referral Agencies (NACCRRA) compared the regulations of all states and the Department of Defense (DOD). They considered how the standards measured up to accepted levels of quality in three specific areas: preventing the spread of infectious diseases, ensuring the safety of the facility, and requiring appropriate training for providers. Rating states' regulations on a 150-point scale, this report indicates that, excluding scores of the DOD and the top two states (Illinois and New York), the average score was only 70.2. The authors conclude "We can do better." They recommend that the U.S. Congress raise the standards for programs eligible for federal child care block grant subsidies, a strategy they propose will motivate states to revise regulations to mandate higher levels of quality.

All states' regulations are now online. You may want to compare your state's regulations with those of another nearby state to identify how they are alike and how they are different. To review regulations of a specific state, follow the links from the Web site of the National Resource Center for Health and Safety in Child Care and Early Education listed at the end of this chapter.

Areas addressed in most licensing codes include the following (AAP et al., 2002b):

1. Introduction to licensing laws and procedures.   For purposes of licensing, states permit individuals to care for other people's children if they apply for and are given permission (a license) by the authorized agency of the government. The introductory section of the licensing regulations defines terms such as "child care center" and "director"; identifies the programs that must be licensed and, when appropriate, those that are exempt; describes how applicants obtain and submit an application for a license; identifies required inspections and approvals; indicates the duration of the license and describes the renewal process; identifies situations that would result in license denial, revocation, or nonrenewal; stipulates how the license is to be posted on the premises; and provides other state-specific general information. (An overview of licensing procedures is provided in Figure 3.1.)

2. Organization and administration.   State licensing laws require an applicant to identify the program's purposes and its sponsoring organization, to indicate whether the program is for-profit or not-for-profit, and to describe its administrative structure (e.g., director, board of directors). They often require programs to have policies describing the services

> 1. Become familiar with state licensing regulations, paying particular attention to
>   • Background checks required of staff
>   • Age, education, and experience requirements for director and other staff
>   • Requirement that staff trained in First Aid and CPR be on-site during operating hours
> 2. Obtain zoning approval
> 3. Submit building plans to the Fire Marshal for approval
> 4. Schedule Fire, Sanitation, and Child Care Licensing Inspections (to occur in that order)
> 5. Post license and open for business

Figure 3.1
An Overview of the Process of Opening a Licensed Child Care Center

they provide children (e.g., eligibility and admission criteria, termination policies, nondiscrimination provision, and fees) and may also require plans to ensure the center's financial solvency.

3. Staffing. This section of the regulations describes required staff-child ratios, educational prerequisites, mandated criminal background and abuse and neglect registry checks, and the minimum age requirements for center employees. Regulations might, for example, permit a 16-year-old with a high school diploma or GED (certificate given for completing tests of General Educational Development considered to be equivalent to a high school diploma) to serve as a director in one state but might require the director to be at least 21 and hold a bachelor's degree in another. Likewise, there are states where an employee enrolled in high school or a GED program is qualified to be a lead teacher, and in other states lead teachers must hold, at a minimum, a CDA (Child Development Associate) credential (NARA/NCCIC, 2006). We will address issues related to staff requirements in more detail later in this chapter.

4. Facilities, supplies, equipment, and transportation. Licensing codes typically require applicants to satisfy health department and fire marshal requirements before applying for a license to operate a child care center. All states that regulate child care specify the amount of indoor space (square footage) available per child. Most states regulate the amount of outdoor space, require that indoor and outdoor equipment be safe and in good repair, and require outdoor fencing. The majority of states require centers to ensure children's security by keeping daily attendance records and establishing policies for accepting children in the morning and releasing them at the end of the day. Many require programs to create emergency preparedness plans and to conduct regular fire drills. Almost all states have regulations related to transporting children in vehicles. Most require the driver to have a valid driver's license, address the driver's minimum age, and require the vehicle be kept in good repair. Many require children to be secured in safety restraints (NARA/NCCIC, 2006).

5. Health and safety. All states that regulate child care require participating children to have specified immunizations before they are allowed to participate, or documentation indicating why they are exempt from this requirement. All also describe procedures for administering medications to children while they are in care. In addition, most require children and staff to have a physical exam. Other health and safety issues often addressed in regulations include descriptions of required health forms for children and staff, requirements for reporting injuries and infectious illnesses, handwashing requirements for children and staff, diapering procedures, rules related to smoking and firearms, and guidelines for keeping animals (NARA/NCCIC, 2006). An area receiving particularly serious attention in most states' regulations is the prevention of the spread of infectious disease, especially in programs serving infants (Morgan, 1986).

6. Activities and equipment.   Almost all states (49 of 51) have some regulations specifiying the types of activities centers must make part of children's daily schedule. Regulations typically require active and quiet play indoors and out, nap or rest time, individual and group activities, and regular meals and snacks. Many states also require programs to explicitly address social, emotional, physical, cognitive, and language and literacy development. Specific regulations are likely to require, at a minimum, fine motor toys and manipulatives, books and materials to support literacy, props to support dramatic play and make believe, and art supplies (NARA/NCCIC, 2006).

Application Activity

Working in small groups, refer to your state's online child care regulations to become familiar with requirements related to required activities and equipment (follow links from the Web site of the National Resource Center for Health and Safety in Child Care and Early Education at the end of this chapter). Assume you have the basic tables, chairs, resting cots, and book shelves you need to equip a classroom for infants, toddlers, and 3- or 4-year-olds. What would you purchase if you had $1,000 to spend to enhance the collection of fine-motor toys, books and literacy materials, dramatic play, or art center? Use a catalog or the Web site of a school-supply company (see appendix 1) to identify specifically what you would select.

---

7. Discipline.   Most states (49 of 51) have regulations related to behavior management, guidance, and discipline. Many states stipulate that programs use "no harsh discipline" and give suggestions for appropriately guiding children's behavior. In some locales certain religious groups have worked to exempt their child care programs from licensing because local regulations prohibit corporal punishment (NARA/NCCIC, 2006).

8. Parent involvement and communication.   Most states require that parents be involved in, and informed about, the program their child attends. Strategies for involving families include providing them written copies of the program's policies and procedures, logging children's daily activities, regularly scheduling parent/teacher conferences, and permitting families to visit the facility during hours of operation with and without prior notice (NARA/NCCIC, 2006).

9. Nutrition and food services.   All states that regulate child care specify the required nutritional content of the meals and snacks served to children while in care. Most have specific rules related to feeding infants, indicate the number of snacks and meals for older children and the time intervals between them, and require the center to post a menu of the meals and snacks they serve (NARA/NCCIC, 2006).

Family Child Care Regulations

Regulation of small and large family child care remains inconsistent and largely voluntary. Forty-five states (88%) regulate small family child care homes and 39 states (76%) regulate large group homes, but this oversight remains largely voluntary. Many states continue to stuggle with the fact that the majority of child care homes remain outside the state's regulatory system (NARA/NCCIC, 2006).

Regulations that apply to family child care homes are typically very similar to those for child care centers. The main differences in the family child care regulations concern

1. How the number of children will be counted (all children on the premises for supervision, including the caregiver's own children, are counted in the home's approved capacity)
2. How keeping infants and toddlers affects the count (most family child care homes have mixed-age groups)
3. How the inside and outside areas of the home, and the family's personal possessions, must be child-proofed to ensure children's health and safety.

These accident-prevention regulations are likely to address how children are to be kept from dangerous constructions, such as stairs, and dangerous items, such as weapons, which are found in some homes. Some professionals question whether center-based regulations should apply to family child care programs. Others are concerned, however, that regulations for home-based centers remain largely voluntary.

Registration is a process by which providers certify that they have complied with a state's licensing regulations. Eligible programs that complete registration are often qualified to participate in assistance programs such as the U.S. Department of Agriculture food program or are able to accept children who receive a child care subsidy.

States differ in their definitions of what child care facilities must be licensed and which may be simply registered (NARA/NCCIC, 2006). Registered (nonlicensed) facilities may include programs operated under public auspices (e.g., public school programs), day camps, programs sponsored by religious organizations, programs operated by private schools or agencies (e.g., the YMCA), and those that care for children for a limited amount of time each day or a limited number of days (fewer than 30) per year.

Registered providers are usually required to certify that they have met identified health and fire standards. Some states also require registered child care homes to conduct criminal background checks on individuals who work with, or are around, children. In many instances, however, registration is simply a sign-up procedure.

Concerns About Regulatory Policies

In spite of advocates' efforts to enact child care licensing regulations that set high expectations, concerns about the quality of current licensing standards remain.

1. Some states' child care regulations exempt a large number of programs. The most frequent exemptions apply to part-day programs, those operated by faith-based organizations, public schools, and programs that serve just a few children (Children's Foundation, 2001, 2002; NAEYC, 1998b). Services before and after school have generally also been outside of the regulatory system. This gap is closing, however. To date 13 states have adopted abbreviated licensing standards for services for school-age children. These less comprehensive regulations most often create standards related to the physical environment, child-staff ratios and maximum group size, staff qualifications and background, health and hygiene, and program activities (U.S. Department of Health and Human Services, 2006).

2. Licensing codes often fall below standards recommended by the American Academy of Pediatrics or NAEYC (AAP et al., 2002a; NAEYC, 1998a) in critical indicators of quality, such as child-staff ratios, group size, and the education and training of staff members (Children's Foundation, 2001, 2002; NAEYC, 1998b; NACCRRA, 2007; Snow, Teleki, & Reguero-de-Atiles, 1996).

3. Many states' licensing agencies face challenges providing training to licensing staff, keeping caseloads at recommended levels, and having adequate resources to provide regular on-site monitoring to ensure effective enforcement and meaningful technical assistance (Gormley, 1997; NAEYC, 1998b; NARA/NCCIC, 2006; U.S. General Accounting Office, 2000).

Advocates calling for higher licensing standards recommend that states eliminate exemptions and create incentives for all programs caring for children to be licensed. They also recommend reduced licensing staff caseloads so that inspectors will be able to visit programs regularly and will be able to provide technical support as needed.

Additional issues that advocates in some states are working to change relate to staff qualifications, group size, and staff-child ratios. They call for licensing standards that reflect current research identifying characteristics of quality related to positive child outcomes and for streamlined licensure processes (Cost, Quality, Outcomes Study Team, 1995; NAEYC, 1998; NARA/NCCIC, 2006).

Public Agency Regulations.   Publicly funded early childhood programs are typically not subject to state child care licensing regulations. Instead, programs operated by the public school system fall within the jurisdiction of the state's educational agency (SEA), and Head Start programs are regulated by federal guidelines.

Many states have an office of early childhood education within its department of education. That state office works with

- Districts, principals, and teachers providing oversight and technical assistance
- The public sharing information about standards, regulations, and trends and issues in early childhood education
- Legislators and other policy makers who shape and influence legislation that affects early childhood programs

The National Association of Early Childhood Specialists in State Departments of Education (NAECS/SDE) is a national organization, founded in 1972, that provides resources and networking opportunities for state-level early childhood leaders. It also helps unify members' efforts to advocate for policies that support quality programming for young children.

Application Activity

Compare Head Start Performance Standards with your states' licensing standards (Internet addresses to both can be found at the end of this chapter). Identify the ways this federal program for low-income families sets a higher standard of care than is required for many programs operated under different auspices.

Staff Credentials.   Recognition of an administrator's and teacher's expertise is called *credentialing, certification,* or *licensure.* High demand for early childhood program personnel, inadequate compensation, high staff turnover, and the lack of professional consensus regarding relevant qualifications have contributed to, in many instances, programs with minimally qualified teachers and caregivers.

Regulations Concerning Administrator Qualifications.   Advocates for quality urge policy makers to require directors to satisfy the same requirements regardless of who is sponsoring the early childhood program they lead (Morgan, 2000b). The fact remains, however, that states' child care regulations continue to set minimal educational, age, and experience requirements for directors working in licensed facilities. The implementation of a required administrator's credential is in its infancy in most locales (NARA/NCCIC, 2006).

Most directors are former classroom teachers. Their training and experience are likely to have made them familiar with young children and the fundamentals of developmentally appropriate instruction. These experiences, however, have not equipped them with the expertise in organization theory and leadership, management, staff development, legal issues, fiscal management, and marketing they need as a program administrator (Bloom, 1989; Mitchell, 2000; Morgan, 1997, 2000a).

The most frequently required qualification needed to be a center director is the Child Development Associate (CDA) credential. Only three states, Florida, Oklahoma, Texas, require directors to hold a state credential in administration (NARA/NCCIC, 2006). A number of states offer a director's credential, most often in their community college or technical college system. Most states also offer a number of alternative routes for preservice qualifications that specify varying combinations of education and experience (NARA/NCCIC, 2006). Unfortunately most directors are not well prepared for their administrative responsibilities—they simply learn on the job or by turning to their licensing or funding agency for assistance.

Administrators' qualifications are another area where early childhood programs operated by state and federal governments are bound by different regulations than child care programs operated by nongovernmental entities. Administrators of public schools offering early childhood programs including prekindergarten (or child development) classes, kindergarten, and primary grades must hold a state administrator's certificate. This means they are required to hold a valid teaching certificate, have had teaching experience, and have taken specified graduate courses in administration. Although public school administrators are well educated and experienced in "school matters," few states require specialized knowledge in early childood education serving children from birth to age 8 and are ill-equipped to provide supervision and instructional leadership to early childhood teachers.

Head Start does not require any specific training for directors. Just as in other child care settings, most directors come from the ranks of classroom teachers. Those who come from outside Head Start usually have extensive experience in programs serving low-income children. Head Start offers new directors' workshops, week-long regional training sessions, tailored administrative consultation, and the Head Start Management Fellows program to prepare new directors to meet Performance Standards and other regulations.

There is evidence that neither principals (Charlesworth, Hart, Burts, & DeWolf, 1993) nor child care directors (Caruso, 1991) have had thorough training in developmentally appropriate instructional strategies that create curriculum from children's choices reflecting individuals' needs, interests, and strengths (Bredekamp & Copple, 1997). While those who have had training in early childhood care and education tended to see the importance of this developmental appropriate approach to instruction (Charlesworth et al.), teachers continue to struggle with administrators who lack these understandings (Goldstein, 1997; West, 2001).

NAEYC's Accreditation Standards (2005) identify directors' core competencies (see inside front cover). These competencies as well as the management and the leadership functions listed next are a helpful place to begin a consideration of what effective directors must need to know and be able to do. Program administrators have responsibilities related to:

- **Pedagogy.**   Creating a learning community of children and adults that promotes optimal child development and healthy families.
- **The Center's Organization and Systems.**   Establishing systems for smooth program functioning and managing staff to carry out the program's mission; planning and budgeting the program's fiscal resources; managing organizational change; and establishing systems to monitor and evaluate organizational performance.
- **Human Resources.**   Recruiting, selecting, and orienting personnel. Overseeing systems for the supervision, retention, and professional development of staff that affirm program values and promote a shared vision.
- **Collaboration.**   Establishing partnerships with program staff, family members, board members, community representatives, civic leaders, and other stakeholders to provide quality services for children and their families.

- **Advocacy.**   Taking action and encouraging others to work on behalf of high quality services that meet the needs of children and their families (NAEYC, 2005).

The director's knowledge and skill are increasingly recognized as essential components of quality. Bachelor's or master's degree programs in early childhood administration are being offered by a number of colleges and universities (e.g., Carnegie Mellon University's H. John Heinz III School of Public Policy and Management; National Louis University's Center for Early Childhood Leadership; Nova University; University of Missouri at Kansas City's Forum for Early Childhood Organization and Leadership Development). These degree programs represent important steps toward increasing directors' knowledge, skill, and professionalism and should lead the way in efforts to document how the director's level of skill and expertise contribute to quality.

Regulations Concerning Teacher Qualifications.   Teachers' qualifications, including the extent and duration of their preservice field experiences and the characteristics of their ongoing professional development, have a signficant impact on the program's quality. They are an important factor in determining the likelihood that the program will contribute to children's growth and development and their success in school and beyond (Darling-Hammond, 1998; Darling-Hammond, Wise, & Klein, 1999; Early et al., 2006; Epstein, 1999; Fischer & Eheart, 1991; Howes, 1997; Kontos & File, 1992; Kontos, Howes, & Galinsky, 1997; Mitchell, 1988; Snider & Fu, 1990).

Certification of Teachers in Public School Early Childhood Programs

Even though all states require teachers working with young children in public schools to be certified, states' requirements vary greatly. All require teachers working with young children to hold at least a bachelor's degree, some require a master's degree for initial certification, and many require candidates to pass standardized tests such as PRAXIS exams. All but two states (Montana and Nevada) have some form of specialized early childhood teacher certification. Some states' early childhood credential qualifies teachers to work with children from birth to age 8 or third grade; in others they are qualified only for preschool to second or third grade.

States also use different terms to describe the same kind of programming. It is not clear, for example, if *pre-K, nursery,* and *3-year-olds* are the same kinds of programs (Fields & Mitchell, 2007). In addition, certification requirements vary from requiring an in-depth preparation in growth and development, instruction in appropriate strategies for teaching young children, and supervised student teaching to add-on and alternative certification programs that require just a few courses and little or no supervised practical experience.

Students graduating in good standing from a state-approved early childhood program can expect to be recommended for certification in the state where their college or university is located. They would also be eligible for certificiation in states that have developed reciprocal certification agreements with the state of the institution granting their degree.

The National Board of Professional Teaching Standards (NBPTS) has been offering early childhood certification since 1987. The rigorous NBPTS certification process requires candidates to submit a portfolio documenting their teaching skills and to pass a comprehensive writen exam. Many states supplement the salaries of NBPTS certified teachers. NBPTS certification is a nationally recognized credential so teachers can maintain their certification if they move from one state to another.

In recent years the importance of placing appropriately certified teachers in public school early childhood classrooms has become more important than ever. Federal No Child Left Behind (NCLB) legislation enacted in 2001 requires classroom teachers in public schools receiving federal funds to be "highly qualified," that is, working with the age group for which they are fully certified by the 2005–2006 academic year. This is one criterion included in mandated school report cards that evaluate public schools' ability to reach expected levels of excellence.

Specialized Teacher Qualifications

The instructional staff of Montessori schools that belong to the American Montessori Society (AMS) must, in addition to satisfying state licensing or certification requirements, meet AMS certification requirements for working with infants and toddlers and in early childhood (ages 2 1/2 to 6 years), elementary, or secondary programs.

The High/Scope Foundation also offers specialized training in the High/Scope curriculum that qualifies teachers for High/Scope certification. In addition the High/Scope Educational Research Foundation awards accreditation to qualified programs that demonstrate their ability to implement the High/Scope curriculum accurately.

Teacher Qualifications in Head Start and Child Care Programs.   Although child care is still seen by some as an unskilled occupation, there is a rising tide of commitment to increasing the professionalism of the child care workforce. Head Start's 2007 reauthorization mandates that by 2013 at least 50 percent of all Head Start teachers in center-based programs have at least an associate degree (ACF, 2007).

States' child care regulations also address teachers' qualifications. A number of states require lead teachers to hold at least a Child Development Associate (CDA) credential. That means they must have a high school diploma or GED and have 120 clock hours of education distributed over eight subject areas as shown in Figure 3.2. The CDA credential is considered to be equivalent to 9 to 12 credit hours of professional education. The popularity and usefulness of this credential has recently declined, however, because of the Head Start reauthorization and other initiatives to raise the bar of professionalism in child care (Freeman & Feeney, 2006).

Accreditation

Accreditation is a voluntary system of evaluation that measures a program's success meeting the accrediting organization's established standards of practice. Review Table 3.1 for a comparison of licensure and program accreditation programs.

Accreditation represents a recognized standard of excellence. As publically funded 4K (or pre-K) programs have grown in popularity, some states have enacted regulations requiring programs receiving state monies to be accredited or to be actively working toward accreditation (ECS, 2002).

1. Planning a safe, healthy learning environment
2. Advancing children's physical and intellectual development
3. Supporting children's social and emotional development
4. Establishing productive relationships with families
5. Managing effective program operation
6. Maintaining a commitment to professionalism
7. Observing and recording children's behavior
8. Knowing and adhering to principles of child development and learning

Figure 3.2
Education Subject Areas Required to Receive CDA Credential

Table 3.1

A Comparison of Licensure and Program Accreditation

Licensure	Accreditation
Mandatory	Voluntary
Developed by governmental agencies and funding agencies.	Developed by professional organizations.
Minimal level of quality.	Higher-than-minimal standard of quality.
Requires full compliance.	Requires substantial compliance.
Enforced at state and local levels.	Nationally validated and enforced.
Failure to comply can result in revocation of the center's license. It cannot operate legally.	Failure to comply may mean the center loses accreditation, but it can continue to operate legally.

A study of directors' perceptions of the benefits of accreditation found that 55% of directors of accredited programs thought their programs were more visible, and 38% reported that accreditation made marketing easier. More than 90% of directors reported that they believed the quality of their programs increased because they pursued accreditation. They identified improvements in areas of curriculum, administration, health and safety, and the physical environment. The directors also stated that children benefited from better staff morale, improved knowledge and understanding of DAP, and parent understanding of the components and standards necessary for high-quality care (Herr, Johnson, & Zimmerman, 1993).

Accredited and nonaccredited early childhood programs have been shown to differ in the following areas: innovations and acceptance of change; goal consensus; opportunities for staff development; and clarity about policies, procedures, and communication (Jorde-Bloom, 1996).

The NAEYC Academy for Early Childhood Program Accreditation was established in 1985 and is generally accepted as the "gold standard" stamp of quality programming. It is the most well known and most widely respected accreditation in the field. There were just a few hundred accredited centers in 1988, but by 2007 there were more than 10,000 accredited programs serving nearly 1 million children. The number of accredited centers has grown as the public has become more informed about the importance of quality early care and education (NAEYC, n.d.).

In 1999 the NAEYC Governing Board embarked on the process of reinventing the Academy's accreditation system. Revised Early Childhood Program Standards and Accreditation Criteria were approved in 2005 and took effect in September 2006. Revisions were designed to increase the reliability of program evaluation, improve the system's responsiveness and the timeliness of on-site validation visits, and to raise the bar of quality. Specifics about NAEYC accreditation can be found by following links to *Accreditation of Programs for Young Children* from the NAEYC Web site (see p. iii for the NAEYC Accreditation Standards).

There are four steps to acquiring NAEYC Accreditation. Centers must:

1. Enroll in a **self-study** that helps the program identify the strengths they bring to the accreditation process, identify areas where they need to concentrate improvement efforts, and make and implement specific program improvement plans to address all accreditation standards. Programs can take as long as they need to complete this self study.
2. Submit an **application for accreditation** in which the program indicates it will complete the formal self-assessment, document how it has met each standard, and make progress toward meeting identified accreditation criteria within one year.

3. Become a **candidate** for accreditation by submitting the required Self-Assessment Report and other documentation describing the program's structure and qualifications of administrators and staff.
4. Host an **on-site visit** scheduled for within 6 months of the submission of their candidacy materials.

Once they have earned accreditation, centers must submit four annual reports over the 5-year term of accreditation. Fees are assessed at each step of the process. The initial cost of accreditation for small centers (10 to 60 children) totals $1,275, with an annual report fee of $300. Centers enrolling between 241 to 360 children pay $2,375 to become accredited as well as an annual renewal fee of $450. Larger centers are assessed $275 during the application process for every additional 120 children, and an additional $100 per year for every additional 120 children. Accredited programs must reapply and successfully complete the entire process before the end of their 5-year accreditation term.

Many programs begin accreditation but stall during self-study either in the initial process or during reaccreditation. Talley (1997) found several reasons for abandoning the process. Almost two fifths of the directors reported a lack of time, and almost one third reported problems with staff turnover or program instability as the major reasons for failure to complete the accreditation process. Three other frequently mentioned barriers to success were new directors who felt ill-equipped to successfully achieve accreditation, saw the application process as overwhelming, and viewed other program concerns as higher priorities. Although a few programs with strong, stable staffs and healthy environments believed accreditation was not important, most programs failed to complete the required self-study because they were unsure about the quality of their program and their chances for success.

In addition to NAEYC, the following professional associations have developed accreditation criteria and procedures for early childhood programs: the Association of Christian Schools International (ACSI), the Council on Accreditation (COA), the National Accreditation Commission for Early Care and Education Programs (NAC), the National After School Association (NAA), the National Early Childhood Program Accreditation (NECPA), the National Lutheran School Accreditation (NLSA), and the National Association for Family Child Care (NAFCC).

Public schools are accredited by their state education agency and may be accredited by the Southern Association of Colleges and Schools. Among the six regional accrediting associations, only the Southern Association of Colleges and Schools has an arrangement for accrediting elementary schools. Accreditation from some of the organizations identified above is also to available to programs operated by public schools.

QUALITY RATING SYSTEMS

Quality rating systems (QRS) are "a method to assess, improve and communicate the level of quality in early care and education settings" (NCCIC, 2006). Quality rating systems are designed to inform parents and other interested citizens about the quality of participating child care programs and to increase the quality of programming available in their community.

A quality rating system provides a systematic and gradual stair-step process for bridging the gap between the minimum standards set by each state's child care licensing standards and the high standards that reflect research-based best practices. The number of steps between basic licensure and the highest level of quality varies from two steps, in Montana, to five in Vermont. The majority of existing QRS identify four steps above licensing, and in most cases the highest level of quality includes national accreditation by an accepted national accreditation system (Mitchell, 2005).

All quality rating systems include components of the following elements (NCCIC, 2006):

1. Standards identify two or more levels of quality above the floor created by mandatory licensing regulations.
2. Valid and reliable assessments of quality are used to assign ratings and monitor compliance with standards. Twelve of 14 statewide systems use an environmental rating scale, for example, the Early Childhood Environment Rating Scale (Harms, Clifford, & Cryer, 2005) as one measure of quality (NCCIC, 2007).
3. Outreach and support efforts promote participation in voluntary rating systems and provide technical assistance to programs striving to attain a higher-than-minimal rating.
4. Financial incentives are specifically linked to compliance with higher-than-minimal quality standards.
5. Parent and community education is designed to help the public understand the system and how it benefits children, families, and the community's early care and education system. QRS use easily understood symbols, most frequently an increasing number of stars, to identify each level of quality (Mitchell, 2005).

States' approaches to creating a QRS vary. In some systems all centers are required to participate, and in others participation is voluntary. Many quality rating systems are linked to tiered systems of reimbursement, that is, they create incentives for centers to increase the quality of their program by linking higher quality ratings with higher levels of reimbursement. By identifying documented levels of quality, the system provides participating centers an incentive to reach higher levels of excellence.

Since the implementation of the first quality rating system in Oklahoma in 1998, quality rating systems have attracted the attention of communities from coast to coast. By 2007, 14 states had a QRS in place and more than 25 were in the process of exploring or designing a tiered quality rating system (NCCIC, 2007). Some communities make their QRS a statewide venture; others limit their implementation to particular counties or metropolitan areas, particularily during their pilot phase. Follow links from the Web site at the end of the chapter for a listing of Web sites for existing quality rating systems.

Meeting Legal Requirements

Some standards do not directly involve the protection of children and their families. They concern the business aspects of early childhood programs, such as the legal existence of private programs, fiscal regulations, and regulations applying to hiring and terminating personnel. It is critically important that owners and operators of child care programs think carefully about the risks they assume when they and their employees are responsible for the safety and well-being of other people's children. They need to be well aware of the financial liabilities they may face, for example, if a child were to be seriously injured while under the supervision of their employees, or their responsibility if an employee were to injure a child in care. For these reasons potential owners and operators of child care programs need to be informed as they make decisions about a number of legal aspects related to child care program operation.

Legal Existence of Private Programs

Proprietorship, partnership, limited liability company (sometimes called an "LLC"), and *corporation* are legal categories for four types of private ownership. Legal requirements for operating an early childhood program under any of these categories vary from state to state. This discussion focuses on common features of the laws. If you are planning to establish a private early childhood program, you should seek legal advice about laws and regulations that may apply. Various forms for business entities are summarized in Table 3.2.

Table 3.2
Comparisons Between Entities

Entities	Sole Proprietorship	General Partnership	Limited Partnership	Limited Liability Corporation	S Corporation	C Corporation
Liability protection	No	No	General partnership has unlimited liability; limited partners are like corporation shareholders.	Yes	Yes	Yes
Reduced entity taxation	Yes	Yes	Yes	Yes	Yes	No
Business debts separate from owners?	No	No	No for general partnership; yes for limited partnership.	Yes, unless guaranteed.	Yes, unless guaranteed.	No
Easy to form?	Yes	Yes	No	No	No	No
Filing requirements other than business license	None	None	Yes	Yes	Yes	Yes
Management	Owner controls	Partners	General partner controls.	Either member managed, like a general partnership or manager managed, like a corporation.	Both these entities are usually managed by board of directors, though special management agreements may be permitted; directors typically delegate to officers and other agents.	
Permanence	No	No	Harder to dissolve.	Harder to dissolve.	Normally	Normally
Transferability of interests	Can assign	Same as GP	Freely transferable; subject to agreement.	Freely transferable; subject to agreement.	Freely transferable subject to share transfer agreement,	

Note: The most two important entity choice factors are liability protection and reduced tax liability. As the chart reflects, the most favored entities in these regards are the LLC and the S Corporation. Each entity offers different benefits and features different drawbacks. State laws vary. You should consult with your tax advisor before deciding which form of entity is best for you.

Proprietorship.   Under a **proprietorship,** a program is owned by one person. Another name for this type of business entity is **sole proprietorship**. The owner has no partners or other co-owners, and there is no separate legal entity, that is, there is no LLC or incorporation. Sole proprietorships may consist purely of a single owner-operator or may have more than one person doing the work for the single owner. The legal requirements are simple. To create a proprietorship, the owner simply must start a business and comply with any business license, fictitious name, or other requirements imposed on small businesses by state or local law. Thus, if the owner is not going to name the center after himself, a fictitious name registration, such as "Jack and Jill Center" may need to be filed.

In a sole proprietorship, the owner has full decision-making authority as long as decisions are consistent with governmental regulations (e.g., the owner must report business revenue and expenses on his or her personal tax return). The owner may sell, give away, or go out of the business with no restrictions except the payment of outstanding debts and the completion of contractual obligations.

A major drawback relates to the potential for full personal liability on the part of the owner for the liabilities of the business. Because of the risks inherent in ownership of a child care program, the proprietorship form of doing business is not recommended, even assuming the owner carries liability insurance to protect against legal risks. The owner may be held personally liable for contractual or other liabilities beyond the owner's ability to control, and the liability may exceed the owner's personal funds, leading to personal bankruptcy.

Partnership.   In a **partnership,** two or more people join together for the purpose of running an enterprise as co-owners. A partnership may involve several individuals or entities as co-partners. For example, other partnerships or corporations may serve as partners in a child care center's operation.

A partnership is a distinct legal entity, meaning it exists apart from the owners. Unless there is an agreement to the contrary, a partner may sell or give away his or her interest in the partnership only if all other partners consent. If one partner dies, the partnership is dissolved.

The law recognizes two types of partnerships:

1. General partnership.   In this partnership, each partner is a legal coequal. Subject to agreements to the contrary, each partner has a right to an equal share of the profits and losses from the business, and an equal right to control the company. Each partner faces personal liability to creditors or tort claimants (a tort is a civil wrong). Operating a child care program as a general partnership can be risky because the partnership can be held responsible for wrongs committed by the center's employees, and each partner operating on behalf of the business has full authority to make binding decisions independently of other partners. As with a proprietorship, the partnership may have to obtain a business license and may have to file a true name certificate. As with the sole proprietorship, the general partnership is not taxed as a separate entity. It must, however, file an information return, reporting its revenues and expenses to federal and state taxing authorities. As with the limited partnership discussed next, many partnerships have written partnership agreements spelling out how the business is to be run and the partners' rights in relation to each other.

2. Limited partnership.   This partnership requires a filing with the state government, typically with the Secretary of State, in order to become legally formed. It consists of one or more general partners and one or more limited partners. Each general partner faces risks identical to those of a general partnership. Limited partners are different. They do not face unlimited personal liability for the losses of the company. Each limited partner is responsible for, and may be held liable to the extent of his or her capital contribution to the partnership. In other words, if the business suffers a catastrophic loss, the general partners may be personally wiped out financially; the limited partners stand to lose only whatever financial investment they made in the limited partnership; their other personal assets are not at risk. Tax and business filing requirements for the limited partnership mirror those for the general partnership once the business begins operating. In exchange for limited liability, limited partners are not allowed to participate in the day-to-day control of the partnership.

Limited Liability Company.   An LLC, like a limited partnership and a corporation, is a separate legal entity in the eyes of the law. Thus, owners of an LLC must file with the state government, typically with the Secretary of State, to establish their business. In many states an LLC may consist of as few as one member. In other words, if state law permits, a single owner can establish the business as an LLC.

There are typically two key benefits to doing business as an LLC. The first is shared with sole proprietorships and partnerships; the second is a benefit those entity forms do not have. The shared benefit is flow-through taxation. An LLC owner has the ability to declare that the business will be taxed as if it were a partnership, meaning that there is no separate tax levied on the business entity itself. Alternatively, the owner may declare that the LLC will be taxed as if it were a corporation.

The second major benefit of LLC status separates the LLC from sole proprietorships and general partnerships and is very valuable. That benefit is "limited liability." With limited liability, the owner is freed from personal liability for wrongs committed by others that lead to claims against the entity. Like the limited partner in the limited partnership, the owner of an LLC risks his or her personal investment in the business but does not face unlimited personal liability for the business' debts or actions of employees or co-owners.

The LLC is a very flexible entity when it comes to management structure. If there are multiple owners, the LLC can be operated with corporate formalities (through a board of directors, for example) or like a partnership, with the members each playing a role in decision making. This latter type of management style, called "member-managed," is the standard way LLCs are run, but a more formal "board of directors" system can be agreed to by the members.

LLCs are typically more difficult to dissolve than partnerships. For example, depending on state law, an LLC may not dissolve when one of the members dies. As with partnerships, LLC members typically agree on a contract, called an "operating agreement," spelling out rules on how the business is to be operated and the members' rights.

Corporation.   A **corporation** is a legal entity, just like the limited partnership and the LLC. It may be established on a for-profit or not-for-profit basis. Corporations typically exist forever unless dissolved by the board of directors or through court proceedings. Like LLCs, corporations offer the benefit of limited liability to its members.

Many private early childhood programs are legally organized as LLCs or corporations due to the protection from personal liability for the owners. Work-site child care programs may be organized as divisions of the parent company, subsidiary entities, or as independent not-for-profit corporations.

The corporation protects individuals from certain liabilities by creating a decision-making and accountable board of directors. Although the board may delegate decision-making power to a manager or to a single director, it may still be ultimately responsible if a lawsuit were to be brought against the center. Board members are typically protected, however, for their good faith business decisions under the "business judgment rule," even where the decisions turn out poorly.

Individual board members can be held personally liable in certain circumstances, however, such as for their own personal wrongdoing (for example, fraud) or for the failure of the corporation to pay withholding taxes on employees' salaries. However, personal financial liability is greatly diminished in a corporation, as compared with the proprietorship or partnership.

In addition to diminished personal financial liability, regulations governing taxation may provide incentives for a child care center to operate as a corporation. It is possible to limit corporate taxes on the entity by qualifying for "Subchapter S" status. Any program owner should seek professional tax advice before deciding on a proposed entity's form and final structure.

Because the corporation is a legal entity, several documents must be filed with appropriate state offices. The forms are usually somewhat different for for-profit and not-for-profit corporations. Three documents are required to complete the incorporation process:

1. Articles of incorporation or certificate of incorporation. The organization's legal creators, or incorporators, use this form to provide information about the corporation, such as the name and address of the agency; its purposes; whether it is a for-profit or not-for-profit corporation; its powers, for example, to purchase property and make loans; membership, if the state requires members; names and addresses of the initial board of directors; initial officers; and the date of the annual meeting.

2. Bylaws. The IRS requires bylaws if the corporation is seeking tax-exempt status. Bylaws operate as internal rules of order. They explain how the corporation will conduct its business, what tasks are to be performed by the various officers and the board, and describe voting and meeting requirements.

3. Minutes of the incorporators' meeting. After the incorporators prepare the documents identified above, an incorporators' meeting is held. The name of the corporation is approved, and the articles of incorporation and bylaws are signed. The incorporators elect officers and the board of directors, who will serve until the first meeting of the members. In for-profit corporations, the incorporators vote to authorize the issuance of stock. Formal minutes of the incorporators' meeting, including votes taken, are written and signed by each incorporator.

Once the state accepts the articles of incorporation for filing, the corporation's life begins. The incorporators no longer have power. Board members carry out the purposes of the organization, and the members own the organization.

When corporations dissolve, they must follow state law if they are for-profit corporations and must follow federal regulations if they are not-for-profit corporations. Early childhood programs may operate either as **for-profit** or **not-for-profit** corporations. For-profit corporations are organized for the purpose of making a profit. Early childhood programs in this category, as well as proprietorships and partnerships, are businesses.

A for-profit corporation may be a closed corporation, in which members of a family or perhaps a few friends own stock, or a public corporation, in which stock is traded on exchanges.

If the corporation makes a profit, it pays taxes on the profits; individual stockholders file personal income tax forms listing such items as salaries and dividends received from the corporation. A closed corporation with a Subchapter S status functions like a partnership for the most part.

Earnings are typically not subjected to corporate tax. The corporation reports its income, and taxes on the owners' shares of the profits are paid by each individual owner on his or her personal tax return.

The main purpose of not-for-profit corporations is other than to make a profit, but such corporations are permitted to make a profit. Any surplus, or profit, however, must be used to promote the purposes of the organization as set forth in the articles of incorporation. In other words, the profit may be used for the center's purposes.

Child care has two types of not-for-profit corporations: (a) those organized for charitable, educational, literary, religious, or scientific purposes under Section 501(c) (3) of the Internal Revenue Code and (b) those organized for social welfare purposes under

Section 501(c) (4) of the Internal Revenue Code. Tax-exempt status is not automatic. The not-for-profit corporation must file for and be granted tax-exempt status at both the federal and state levels.

When it comes to operational formalities for early childhood programs, there are some standard procedures. Separate bank accounts should be obtained for any early childhood program. The failure of an LLC or corporation to maintain financial records separate from those of its owners will jeopardize limited liability protection. Creditors or tort claimants may seek to "pierce the corporate veil," stripping away limited liability protection and holding the owners personally liability for the company's obligations.

Careful record keeping for financial and management purposes is a basic standard requirement. Not-for-profit corporations with a certain income level, and other programs receiving monies from certain funding sources, are required to have an audit. In most states, not-for-profit corporations are required to file an annual financial report following the audit.

Franchises and chains may fall under any of the foregoing legal categories of private organizations but are most often corporations or LLCs. Franchises and chains are differentiated as follows:

1. A **franchise** is an organization that allows an individual or an entity to use its name, follow its standardized program and administrative procedures, and receive assistance (e.g., in selecting a site, building and equipping a facility, and training staff) for an agreed-upon sum of money, royalty, or both. Two popular child care franchises are Kiddie Academy and The Learning Experience.
2. A **chain** is ownership of several facilities by the same proprietorship, partnership, or corporation. These facilities are administered by a central organization. Kinder Care Learning Centers is an example of a chain.

Fiscal Regulations

Many fiscal regulations are specific to given programs. Contractual undertakings and Internal Revenue Service regulations, however, must be complied with by all early childhood programs. Fraud or failure to comply with fiscal regulations may result in serious consequences, including the risk of civil or criminal liability.

Contracts. **Contracts** are legally enforceable agreements that may be oral or written (e.g., insurance policies; employment contracts; contracts with parents for fees; contracts for food, supplies, and services; contracts with funding sources; and leases). A contract has three elements:

1. The **offer**—the buyer's proposal to the seller or the seller's invitation to the buyer to purchase a given object or service at a stated price (money or service)
2. **Acceptance**—the buyer's acceptance of an offer or the seller's acknowledgment of the buyer's willingness to accept an offer
3. **Consideration**—the legal term for the price or value of what each party exchanges (e.g., a subscription to a professional journal for $40 per year)

Breaking a contract is called a **breach,** and the potential penalty is referred to as **damages.**

IRS Regulations. Many Internal Revenue Service (IRS) regulations apply to all early childhood programs:

1. **Employer identification number.** Each organization employing people on a regular salaried basis is required to obtain a federal employer identification number. A

program cannot file for a tax-exempt status without first having obtained this number using IRS Form SS-4.

2. Tax returns.   Employers file quarterly tax returns, IRS Form 941. This form is filed with the regional IRS service center. A penalty is assessed for late filing. Salaried employers of public early childhood programs file the appropriate schedule on IRS Form 1040. All private programs must file tax returns. Sole proprietors and partnerships with other income file the appropriate schedule on Form 1040, partnerships without other income file IRS Form 1065, for-profit corporations file Form 1120, and not-for-profit corporations file Form 990.

3. Withholding Exemption Certificates and IRS Form 1099.   A Withholding Exemption Certificate, IRS Form W-4, is required for each employee. The certificates are used for determining the amount to withhold for federal, state, and city income taxes. The form indicates marital status and the number of dependents and must be completed before the first paycheck is issued. Employees must sign new forms if their marital status or the number of dependents changes or if they want more of their wages to be withheld. An annual statement of taxes withheld from an employee's earnings (Form W-2) is sent to each employee no later than January 31 of the year following the year in which the employee was paid. Occasionally, early childhood programs hire someone to do a temporary job, such as plumbing or electrical work. Because withholding taxes would not have been deducted from the wages, all centers paying $600 or more to any individual who is not a regular employee must file IRS Form 1099 reporting the transaction.

Laws That Protect the Staff and the Program

Certain regulations are designed to protect the employee and the program. Laws that protect the staff include those that prevent discrimination, relate to minimum wages, ensure adherence to regulations created by the owner/operator or the board, determine eligibility of staff who meet identified qualifications to serve in particular positions, staff members' potential vulnerability to legal actions, and the civil rights of employees with disabilities.

Title VII of the Civil Rights Acts of 1964 and as Amended by the Equal Opportunity Act of 1972.   Fair employment practices are mandatory for organizations, companies, and people having contracts with the federal government. The practices are also mandatory for any company employing or composed of 15 or more people. Employees subject to this act and its amendment must not discriminate against any individual on the grounds of race, creed, color, gender, national origin, or age. Employment practices must be based on relevant measures of merit and competence. The employer must also base job qualifications on bona fide occupational qualifications (BFOQ); thus, job descriptions must clearly specify the tasks to be performed.

Americans with Disabilities Act.   The Americans with Disabilities Act (ADA), P.L. 101–336, was signed into law on July 26, 1990. The ADA established civil rights for people with disabilities. The part of the law concerning employment states that employers with 15 or more employees must avoid job-related discrimination based on the employee's disability. To be protected under the law, the employee must satisfy BFOQ that are job related and be able to perform those tasks that are essential to the job with reasonable accommodations (e.g., making the facility accessible, modifying equipment, modifying work schedules, providing readers or interpreters), if necessary. Furthermore, the employer is legally liable if other employees discriminate or do not make adjustments to accommodate employees with disabilities (Surr, 1992).

Fair Labor Standards Act.   The Fair Labor Standards Act of 1938 as amended applies equally to men and women. Employers subject to this act and its amendments must pay employees the current minimum wage; overtime (hours worked over the 40-hour week) at the rate of 1 1/2 times the employee's regular rate of pay; regular wages and overtime pay for attendance at training sessions, whether the sessions are conducted at the place of work or at another site; and equal wages for equal work. The act does not apply to members of one's immediate family.

Family and Medical Leave Act.   The Family and Medical Leave Act (FMLA) of 1993 requires companies and organizations with 50 or more employees to grant those who have worked for them for at least 12 months up to a total of 12 workweeks of unpaid leave during any 12-month period for one or more of the following reasons:

- for the birth or adoption of a child
- to care for an immediate family member (spouse, child, or parent) with a serious health condition; or
- to take medical leave when unable to work because of a serious health condition

Potential Vulnerability to Legal Actions.   Three legal principles often apply in legal actions involving any business.

1. An employee is hired to perform certain types of duties, with certain expectations as to how these duties will be performed. When an employee's actions are consistent with those expectations, an employee is said to be "acting within the scope of authority." An employee is not liable when acting within the scope of authority but is liable when acting beyond it.
2. Except for negligence on the part of employees, employers are responsible for all torts (civil wrongs) committed by employees. The legal phrase used for this principle is *respondent superior* ("the boss is responsible"). This principle does not apply to independent contractors, who are responsible for their own torts.
3. Principals (e.g., boards of directors) are responsible for torts committed by their agents (e.g., directors) acting on the business of the principal and within the scope of employment.

Laws in Addition to Licensing That Protect Children

In every state child care providers are **mandated reporters**. Mandated reporters are professionals who have a legal responsibility to report suspected neglect or physical or sexual abuse to appropriate child protective service authorities. Failure to report suspected abuse or neglect can result in criminal or civil penalties. That means that a mandated reporter who does not comply with this law can face fines and/or imprisonment and can lose her job or her license for not reporting. For these reasons, early childhood professionals must be familiar with the indications of child maltreatment and state laws regarding reporting suspected cases.

In most cases individuals are responsible for reporting suspected abuse or neglect. A director, principal, or other supervisor cannot prevent an employee who has reason to suspect that a child has been mistreated from making a report. Programs should include information about requirements related to abuse and neglect in handbooks distributed to families and staff. Suggested guidelines are included in the discussion of policies and procedures in the next chapter.

Legal Responsibilities and Vulnerabilities.   Individuals' legal and financial vulnerability vary, as described earlier, depending on the program's ownership and the agreements that have been formalized between and among owners. Programs that are fully liable for compliance with laws and in the case of personal injury are sole proprietorships, partnerships, and for-profit corporations.

Liability is limited in some states by the charitable immunity doctrine for programs operated as not-for-profit corporations. Public agency programs, such as public school early childhood programs and Head Start, have generally been immune from full liability as provided by Section 1983 of the Civil Rights Act (Mancke, 1972). Under the Civil Rights Act, immunity was not extended to the following three types of suits:

1. Intentional injury (e.g., corporal punishment resulting in lasting injury to body or health; restraint of a person, such as physically enforcing time-out; and defamation, such as implying a student's lack of ability in nonprofessional communication)
2. Negligence (e.g., failure to give adequate instruction, failure to take into account a child's abilities, improper supervision, inadequate inspection of equipment)
3. Educational negligence (careless or incompetent teaching practices) (Scott, 1983)

Several implications can be drawn concerning the potential vulnerability to legal action. First, all employees should have job descriptions spelling out their scope of authority. Second, adequate staffing, safe housing and equipment, administrative diligence, staff awareness and training in care of children, and documentation will do much to reduce the risk of torts (acts that may result in legal suits brought against the center and/or its employees). Finally, everyone involved in programs should realize that situations leading to liability are ever-present concerns and that all employees are vulnerable to legal actions.

SUMMARY

Regulations are the rules, directives, statutes, and laws that prescribe, direct, limit, and govern early childhood programs. They are designed to create a safety net for young children and to identify a level of quality no program should fall below. Standards describe expectations for programs. Like regulations, they can apply to program facilities, teachers' qualifications, curriculum construction, and many other aspects of early care and education programming.

Some standards are optional, such as the high standards of NAEYC Program Accreditation, and others pertain to certain kinds of programs, such as the Head Start Performance Standards. Regulations and standards go hand-in-hand. They create a context for early childhood programs provided under a wide range of auspices and are an important part of your study of early childhood program planning and administration.

USEFUL WEB SITES

Model licensing standards and other information about quality care are available at *Caring for Our Children: National Health and Safety Performance Standards,* 2nd ed. It is available in English and Spanish by following links from

www.healthykids.us

Information about existing quality rating systems can be found by following links from

nccic.acf.hhs.gov/pubs/qrs-defsystems.html

Head Start Standards can be following links from this Head Start 101 Toolkit found at

www.headstartinfo.org/infocenter/hs101.htm

The National Fire Protection Handbook is available at

www.nfpa.org/

National Resource Center for Health and Safety in Child Care and Early Education has links to all states' child care regulations from

nrc.uchsc.edu/STATES/states.htm

The 2005 Child Care Licensing Study includes in-depth information about all states' regulations. The executive summary and full report can be located by following links from

www.nara.affiniscape.com/displaycommon.cfm?an=1&subarticlenbr=104

The National Association of Child Care Resource and Referral Agency's NACCRRA's Ranking of State Child Care Center Standards and Oversight is at

www.naccrra.org/policy/scorecard.php

TO REFLECT

1. Serving as the director of a program caring for children is a tremendous responsibility. The existing system of laws, regulations, and voluntary standards provides guidance and protection to newcomers as well as experienced veterans. Which of these guides do you find most beneficial? Can you point to particular sections that you find most helpful? Why?

2. Review the process to become an NAEYC Accredited Center. How would you lead a program through that process? What skills do you now have and which would you need to develop to pursue NAEYC Program Accreditation?

4

ESTABLISHING POLICIES AND PROCEDURES

NAEYC Director Competencies addressed in this chapter:

Management Knowledge and Skills

4. Educational Programming
   The ability to develop and implement a program to meet the needs of young children at different ages and developmental levels (infant/toddler, preschool, kindergarten). Knowledge of administrative practices that promote the inclusion of children with special needs.

5. Program Operations and Facilities Management
   Knowledge and application of policies and procedures that meet state/local regulations and professional standards pertaining to the health and safety of young children.

6. Family Support
   Knowledge and application of policies and procedures that meet state/local regulations and professional standards pertaining to the health and safety of young children.

9. Oral and Written Communication
   Knowledge of the mechanics of writing including organizing ideas, grammar, punctuation, and spelling. The ability to use written communication to effectively express one's thoughts.

Αs discussed in chapter 3, regulations, policies, and procedures are closely linked. In this chapter we discuss how policies and procedures guide a program's operations. They ensure compliance with applicable federal, state, and local laws, regulations, and standards while helping the program achieve its particular mission and reach its goals.

CONSIDERING POLICIES AND PROCEDURES

Policies address issues that are critical to the center's operations and include rules employees must follow. *Procedures* are step by step instructions for following established policies.

Policies describe the program's specific plans for achieving particular goals. They can apply to employees as well as participating families. Policies often answer the question, "What is to be done and by whom?" For example, a policy might state that the director is responsible for recruiting and retaining qualified staff. Other policies clarify expectations of employment. An example of this kind of policy is one that establishes how much vacation each employee is allowed. A third group of policies describes rules participating families are expected to follow. An example of this kind of policy might state that children's birthday celebrations are not to include sugar-filled treats such as cupcakes and candy.

Policies should be written as comprehensive statements describing previously made decisions, identified guiding principles, or already agreed-upon courses of action that will help the program achieve its goals. Many policies will be included in a program's family handbook and/or staff manual, but other written policies might serve as a resource for program administrators to ensure consistency and fair treatment for employees and families alike.

Procedures describe specific strategies for complying with established policies. They may identify, step-by-step, how to reach agreed-upon goals and may include forms developed to accomplish these tasks. Like policies, most, but not all procedures, will be included in appropriate staff manuals and family handbooks; others apply only to administrators and are less widely circulated.

An example of procedures that apply to all employees are those that describe applying for vacation time. These procedures should indicate where the form for requesting a vacation can be found, how far in advance and to whom requests are to be submitted, and when employees can expect a response to their vacation request.

Procedures that apply to families which should be included in the handbook include information about how they are to notify the center if their child is sick and will not be attending for several days, or how they are to identify nonfamily members authorized to pick their child up at the end of the day.

Some procedures apply only to administrators. For example, when filling a staff vacancy, the director may be required to (1) post a notice in the staff break room, (2) advertise in the local paper, and (3) list the job opening in an online job bank. It would not be appropriate to include this procedure in the widely circulated staff manual, but it would be important that the director follow it consistently.

Policies and Procedures Guide for Employees and Families

Policies and procedures describe each stakeholder's responsibilities and guide their interactions with each other. In addition to addressing laws, regulations, and standards, policies and procedures should reflect the profession's *Code of Ethical Conduct* designed to "offer guidelines for responsible behavior" (NAEYC, 2005). These ethical guidelines contribute an additional layer of guidance by describing how "good early childhood professionals" are expected to behave and what they aspire to be like as they work with young children and their families, colleagues, employers, and the community.

The **Staff Manual** is an internal document that describes qualifications for employment, includes job descriptions, and spells out employees' rights and responsibilities. It also includes policies and procedures describing how employees are expected to comply with laws, regulations, and standards designed to safeguard the health, safety, and well-being of children, families, employees, employers, and the community. The staff manual should additionally create clear expectations related to employees' professionalism and reliance on ethical standards. It should serve as an absolutely critical tool that helps to create the center's culture of caring, contributes to a center's smooth operation, and helps it stay on course for accomplishing its goals. The lack of a comprehensive staff manual leaves policies and procedures open to interpretation by staff. This can create discrepancies and misunderstandings on the part of staff, which can be problematic for the director.

Families, like employees, play a critical role in ensuring that the program's operations comply with applicable laws, regulations, and standards, and that it is on-track for accomplishing its mission and reaching its goals. A program's **Family Handbook** is distributed to the parents and/or guardians of all participating children and may also be posted on the program's Web site. It should include information about the program's operations, policies, and procedures. Examples of regulations-based policies families are responsible for following include those that require children to submit proof of specific immunizations and those that require children with identified contagious conditions to be isolated or excluded until they are no longer contagious.

The family handbook also includes specifics about the program's day-to-day operations. It is likely to provide guidance about how children should dress, describe nap-time routines, as well as drop-off and pickup procedures. Many programs also have policies addressing holiday observances and create guidelines about bringing toys from home.

In addition, the family handbook should make it clear that this program's operations and interactions are guided by the *NAEYC Code of Ethical Conduct*. In fact, the Code requires that programs "shall inform families of program philosophy, policies, curriculum, assessment system, and personnel qualifications, and explain why we teach as we do" (Code of Ethics, Principle 2.2). The family handbook is an essential tool for systemically communicating this information to all families.

Finally, the **administrative manual** is a tool for program administrators describing policies and procedures that guide the administrator's decision-making process. It is likely to address employee salaries; waiting list policies; or benefits, like reduced tuition for an employee's child, that are at the director's discretion when trying to attract particularly desirable personnel.

Like the program's staff manual and family handbook, the administrative manual should be developed in such a way that the program's operations reflect the core values, principles, and ideals identified in the *NAEYC Code of Ethical Conduct*. It should also reflect knowledge of, and reliance on, the supplements to the NAEYC Code of Ethics that address the particular responsibilities shouldered by administrators. See the *NAEYC Code of Ethical Conduct* in Appendix 2 and the *Supplement for Program Administrators* in Appendix 3.

Unlike the staff manual and the family handbook, the administrative policies and procedures manual is not distributed. Only the program's director and the governing and/or advisory boards have access to this sensitive information. It is important, nonetheless, even in small proprietary programs, to write down administrative policies and procedures. This ensures fair and equitable treatment and simplifies the director's day-to-day decision making by addressing in advance the commonly occurring issues he is likely to face on a regular basis.

When the development of the staff manual, family handbook, and administrative manual are guided by the *NAEYC Code of Ethical Conduct* (2005) as well as its Supplements for Program Administrators (2006) and Adult Educators (2004) (a role the director plays within her own center), many problems can be avoided or addressed proactively. For example, policies related to conferences with families should be guided by Principle 1.4: "We shall involve all those with relevant knowledge (including families and staff) in decisions concerning a child, as appropriate, ensuring confidentiality of sensitive information." Principle 2.9 identifies issues about which families need to be informed: "We shall inform the family of injuries and incidents involving their child, of risks such as exposures to communicable diseases that might result in infection, and of occurrences that might result in emotional stress."

The Code also guides employees' relationships with one another. Ideals 3A.1, 3A.2 and 3A.3 urge teachers to establish and maintain relationships of respect, trust, confidentiality, collaboration, and cooperation; share resources; and support co-workers in meeting their professional needs and in their professional development. It also provides guidance when problems emerge. Principle 3A.2 states: "When we have concerns about the professional behavior of a co-worker, we shall first let that person know of our concern in a way that shows respect for personal dignity and for the diversity to be found among staff members, and then attempt to resolve the matter collegially and in a confidential manner."

All employees need to be very familiar with, and to be held accountable for, consistently and reliably following, both the family handbook and the staff manual. The family handbook guides their interactions with participating children and families. The staff manual guides employees' relationships with their co-workers, administrator, clients, and employer. Together they create shared understandings about the program's operations. When the director follows the administrator's manual, the program is assured that established administrative policies and procedures will be followed, even when there are changes in administrative personnel.

REGULATIONS AND STANDARDS OFTEN SPECIFY REQUIRED POLICIES AND PROCEDURES

Licensing Requirements

Many states' child care regulations require that licensed programs have written policies and procedures for staff and families covering particular aspects of their operation. Manuals for center personnel may be required to address issues such as:

- Job qualifications
- Essential job functions
- Staff performance evaluation procedures
- Termination procedures

Licensing regulations in many states require that topics such as the following be addressed in handbooks for families:

- Ages of children served
- Hours and days of operation
- Procedures for releasing children at the end of the day
- Procedures for handling illness and injuries
- Procedures for notifying families of field trips
- Notification that child care providers are mandated reporters of suspected child abuse and neglect
- Accepted forms of discipline (NARA/NCCIC, 2006)

The state board of education may also require school-based programs for young children, such as prekindergarten and after-school programs, to create policies and procedures addressing specific aspects of their operation.

Requirements Addressed by Voluntary Standards

The family handbook, employee manual, and written administrative policies (the administrative manual) of programs participating in voluntary accreditation or the quality rating systems, which are in place in some states, are required to meet additional standards, above and beyond those imposed by licensing regulations. NAEYC Accreditation Standards, for example, require programs to provide families information, including policies and procedures, *in a language the family can understand* (NAEYC, 2005). This is a good example that shows how accreditation standards that exceed minimal state licensing requirements shape a program's operations.

NAEYC Accreditation Standards also address teachers' preparation, knowledge, and skills. While state regulations may allow lead teachers to be enrolled in high school or a GED program, NAEYC requires that lead teachers in accredited programs have at least an associate's degree or the equivalent. In addition, NAEYC requires that at least 75% of the lead teachers in an accredited program hold a bachelor's degree in early childhood or a related field (2005). That means the staff manual in an accredited center must describe minimal requirements for lead teachers and the administrative manual should specify that the director is responsible for ensuring that at least 75% of the program's lead teachers have at least a bachelor's degree. These policies will guide the director when making hiring and promotion decisions and will ensure compliance with applicable accreditation standards.

NAEYC requires other written personnel policies that go substantially beyond requirements of licensing. For example, they must describe:

- Roles and responsibilities, qualifications, and specialized training required of staff *and volunteers*
- Nondiscriminatory hiring procedures, that is, hiring personnel based on the applicant's ability, qualifications, and experience, and not on gender, race, ethnicity, or other characteristics not related to the applicant's ability to perform the duties of the position
- Salary scales and descriptions of benefits for full-time employees including health insurance, leave, education, and retirement plans

While accreditation standards require that written policies and procedures address all these issues, it is possible that not all this information, such as detailed salary scales, will be included in the widely circulated staff manual but will, instead, be part of the administrative manual.

Centers that are part of a franchise or chain may also be required to satisfy specific non-licensure-related requirements. For example, the operator may require all employees to wear shirts with the center's logo, or all classrooms might be required to include specific information in an "introducing the staff" flyer posted outside each classroom. Dress codes and other organization-specific rules would be included in the center's staff manual.

Application Activity

Working in small groups, review the *NAEYC Code of Ethical Conduct* in appendix 2. Develop an item you think would make a good addition to a program's staff manual that is suggested by one of the Code's Core Values, Ideals, or Principles.

Why Are Policies and Procedures Important?

When programs thoughtfully and carefully create comprehensive policies and procedures and include them as appropriate in family handbooks and staff and administration manuals, they eliminate any number of potential problems that would otherwise require a great deal of the director's time and energy. Well-developed policies and procedures can, for example, help determine how you should prioritize families on your waiting list.

Suppose two families paid the registration fee and put their children's names on the waiting list for a space in your 3-year-old classroom just days apart. Now, after several months, you have a long-awaited opening. Do you offer the slot to the first child on the list whose stay-at-home mother wants him to have a wider circle of friends? Or do you offer it to the family that came to you a few days later and now needs full-time child care so the mother, who has been job hunting for months and needs the money because the family has faced unexpected medical expenses, can accept the position she was recently offered?

A clear-cut policy aligned with your program's mission, goals, and core values would help you reach a fair, equitable, and defensible decision. If your family handbook and program policies indicate you will *always* fill vacancies on a first-come, first-served basis, you would be bound to offer enrollment to the first family to pay the application fee. If, on the other hand, your mission prioritizes supporting families' economic self-sufficiency, and your policies state that you are *guided by* the established waiting list, you may elect to offer the spot to the second family that needs reliable child care to support the mother's employment.

Policies and procedures provide guidelines for achieving the program's goals. They can help the director act decisively and confidently because he is able to follow written procedures that address commonly faced situations in ways that are aligned with laws, regulations, and applicable standards, as well as the program's mission and goals.

Well-conceived policies and procedures also make program administrators more efficient. Instead of ricocheting from one emergency to the next, the director can turn to established policies and procedures to guide day-to-day decision making.

And finally, carefully crafted policies and procedures ensure consistency. Instead of relying on memory about how sensitive situations have been handled in the past, a director can turn to established policies and procedures, confident that the course of action will be fair to children, families, employees, and the community. Time invested in writing a complete administrator's manual can save time and reduce stress in the long run.

Who Is Responsible for Developing Policies and Procedures?

In small family-operated centers, owners or operators often serve as hands-on directors working directly with children, families, and employees. The director in these centers is likely to develop, interpret, and implement policies and procedures and probably has the autonomy to make decisions as the need arises.

Medium-sized centers operated by a local sponsor such as a church, community organization, college, or university may have a board of directors and/or an advisory committee that works with the director in policy and procedure development and implementation. The director and the board may have an informal give-and-take relationship rather than one involving a formal chain of command. In these programs, the board is responsible for representing the sponsor's interests in areas such as the maintenance and use of space and utilities, the program's fiscal health, days and hours of operation, and the program's success meeting the sponsor's goals and its purpose in operating the early childhood program.

While the board focuses on creating a context for the center's operations, the director should be relied upon as the expert on matters related to young children and early care and education. He is expected to be aware of employees' strengths and needs, to have developed positive relationships with the children and families served, and to have a good reputation in the community which reflects well on the sponsoring agency.

Large chains and franchises, Head Start, and public school programs usually have a formal organizational structure with established lines of authority. In these programs, policy formulation, interpretation, and implementation are likely to be formally structured, with the responsibilities of the director and board clearly identified. In these large organizations, the director is likely to serve as an expert and spokesperson for the early childhood program, working within this formal structure to advocate for the children and staff.

For example, a superintendent in a public school works with the school board on policies and procedures and sees that the adopted policies and procedures are implemented, but this work is carried out by assistant superintendents, principals, early childhood coordinators, and classroom teachers who directly implement programs for young children at the local level.

Application Activity

Develop a *policy* (a rule about a critical issue) and *procedures* (step-by-step instructions for following that policy) for a staff manual or family handbook. Make sure that it addresses a complex topic likely to require the director to make a difficult decision. Topics to consider are responding to a family's request for a particular teacher or classroom; working with a teacher who is going through a difficult divorce and whose attendance has not met the program's expectations; a family who has been regularly bringing their child to the center during his class's nap time.

Developing or Revising the Family Handbook and Staff Manual for an Existing Program

If you become a director in a small center, you might single-handedly create its family handbook and staff manual. If you work in a medium-size or large center, you may have the opportunity to lead in their development or refinement. Assuming the program has a record of regulatory compliance and success, your job when developing these materials for a program already in operation is to begin by making "the way we do things here" explicit. That is, you would work to describe how the center's "business as usual" approach has helped it (to date) comply with laws, regulations, and standards, and achieve its goals in the service of young children and their families.

A director embarking on a substantial revision of the center's staff manual and/or family handbook, or creating these materials for an existing program, will want to work with the center's governing or advisory board and a small group of staff to be certain drafts of newly developed materials accurately reflect current policies and procedures.

It would also be wise to ask a few families to review a proposed family handbook to be certain it is clear from their unique perspective. This would also be a good time to ask a lawyer to review the materials to be certain the policies and procedures they describe keep the center in compliance with applicable laws related to hiring, termination, including children who have special needs, handling confidential information, and other issues that may have legal components. You may be able to ask a parent of a child enrolled in the program to provide this review, or a member of your governing or advisory board may be able to provide this service or know someone who can.

Once a preliminary draft of a new family handbook or staff manual is ready for staff review, administrators should give employees an opportunity to provide feedback so they will have ownership of the materials and will agree that their descriptions of existing policies and procedures are accurate, reasonable, and fair.

Feedback on draft materials should be carefully considered when developing the final version of these documents. Although it is unlikely administrators and boards will incorporate every suggestion, it is essential that staff can see evidence that their feedback has been thoughtfully considered. It is important to remember that they are the face of the center, both within the program and out in the community. They must know and agree with program policies and procedures because their compliance with both the spirit and the letter of the center's policies and procedures will contribute to employees' morale, the program's reputation, and its overall success.

Once the staff manual and family handbook have been adopted, staff should be required to "sign off" on them annually to signify that they know and are committed to following the policies and procedures they describe.

Because professionals are continually engaged in reflective practice, the director should embark on a thorough review to be certain all policies and procedures reflect not only where the center *is* on its journey toward excellence, but also *where it can make progress* achieving its goals. This reflective review should consider whether the families and staff have become comfortable relying on these documents to guide their day-to-day interactions.

These documents are the center's official vehicles for communicating the center's current understanding of where it is and where it plans to go in the future. The family handbook and staff manual should be updated at least annually, but, while revised manuals and handbooks can be expected to be published annually, the process of their revision should be an ongoing one that culminates at the start of the new year, which may be the calendar year (January), the center's fiscal year, or the academic year (August or September).

Whether creating new policies and procedures, or updating handbooks and manuals already in place, child care administrators, advisory boards, and boards of directors should view policies and procedures and the manuals and handbooks that describe them as tools to help the center fulfill its mission by operationalizing its vision, core values, and goals.

Developing the Family Handbook and Staff Manual for a New Program

The difference between creating the staff manual and family handbook for a new center and working to formalize operations at an existing one is that when launching a new program, instead of describing "business as usual," you will be developing policies and procedures to set the course of the program for the foreseeable future. It is important for these documents to create a culture that respects children, families, and colleagues; one that encourages and nurtures relationships based on trust and respect; and that they put into place policies and procedures that anticipate as many frequently asked questions and ordinarily occurring situations as possible so the program operates smoothly and efficiently.

The place to begin the process of developing these materials is with appropriate licensing and accreditation standards. You want to be certain you address all topics required by these standards. The next step is to consider how the program will contribute to the mission and achieve the goals of the founders of the business, the education committee of the sponsoring church, the board of a publicly funded agency, or whoever is preparing to begin serving young children and families.

Since the director of a new program will probably have neither a staff nor families to review preliminary drafts, it will be particularly important for him to rely on the program's board or founder, professional resources such as this book, and, if possible, experienced colleagues to give feedback as he finalizes these foundational documents. Once the center begins operations, it will also be particularly important to keep systematic notes indicating policies and procedures that are working well and those that will need attention when the time comes for their revision.

Using Established Policies and Procedures

Whether implementing existing or newly established policies and procedures, it is the program administrator's responsibility, either alone or with the center's corporate office or board of directors, to interpret and ensure consistent compliance with these programmatic guidelines. That means not only that he follows them without fail, but also that he holds each employee and all participating families accountable for abiding by them consistently. Together they must accept their responsibility to ensure the program's smooth operation in compliance with appropriate laws and regulations and in keeping with the particular program's mission, goals, and objectives.

Characteristics of Viable Policies and Procedures

Administrators and boards developing policies and procedures need to consider if proposed items are (1) aligned with laws, regulations, and standards; (2) reasonable and needed; (3) have the potential to contribute to the program's efforts to fulfill its mission and achieve its goals; and (4) help the program take a proactive stance rather than a reactive approach to operations and decision making.

Directors and boards responsible for developing the program's staff manual and family handbook need to be committed to devoting the time and effort required for creating and evaluating policies and procedures during their development and when refinements are needed. They must concentrate on keeping policies and procedures aligned with changing laws, regulations, and standards; understandings of best practice; and must be ready to correct identified gaps, oversights, or duplications. Some characteristics of viable policies and procedures follow:

1. They conform to state laws and regulations, accreditation standards (when applicable), and to the policies of the funding agency.
2. They address as many situations as possible that can be expected to occur frequently.
3. The staff manual and family handbook must be internally consistent throughout and must be aligned with each other. The likelihood of consistency among policies and procedures is greater when they are developed with an eye on the program's mission, goals, and core values.
4. They should be relatively constant. Policies should not change every time there are new members on the board. Procedures should be changed only when better strategies for accomplishing particular goals have been identified. They can change without resulting in a change of policy.
5. They should be readily available so they can be interpreted with consistency by those concerned.
6. Generally speaking, policies and procedures should be followed consistently. When there are situations which frequently require the director to make an exception to an existing policy or procedure, the fact that a stated policy or procedure is not always followed should be clearly indicated. For example, consider the scenario described earlier when the director had to decide to whom she would offer an opening in the 3-year-old classroom. The policy on filling openings from the waiting list might say, "Spaces will be offered to families on the waiting list on a

first-come, first-served basis unless there are compelling extraordinary circumstances." If exceptions to a policy or procedure are frequently made, that is likely to be an indication that the policy or procedure needs to be revised.

7. They should be reviewed regularly and modified as needed. Their relevance and usefulness depend on their alignment with current state laws and the regulations of other agencies and their success guiding the program toward fulfilling its mission. Policies may include a stipulation that they be reviewed by the director or the board on a regular basis, for example, one year from the date they go into effect.

POLICY AND PROCEDURE CATEGORIES

Policies and procedures should cover as many aspects of the early care and education program's operation as possible. There are, of course, wide variations across programs, but most programs of early care and education have policies and procedures in the following categories:

1. **Program overview.**   Any discussion of policies and procedures should begin by providing an overview of the program, its purpose, vision, goals, and objectives.

2. **Program services.**   These policies and procedures state the primary program services to be provided (e.g., care, education), along with other services (e.g., food, transportation, social services, parent education) offered by the program.

3. **Administration.**   Some specific areas included in administrative policies and procedures are the makeup of, and procedures for, selecting or electing members to the board of directors, board committees (e.g., executive, personnel, finance, building, program, nominating), advisory group, parent council, or other councils or committees; policies related to the appointment and functions of the director and supervisory personnel; and the administrative operations, such as the organizational chart and membership and functions of various administrative bodies.

4. **Personnel policies.**   All programs need to have the following in place:
- Job descriptions and qualifications
- Recruitment, selection and appointment procedures
- Staff training and development requirements
- Performance review procedures
- Salary schedules and fringe benefits
- Payroll dates
- Policies related to excused and unexcused absences
- Personal leave and vacation policies
- Termination policies

Personnel policies of publicly funded programs must include nondiscrimination, equal opportunity clauses and must be in compliance with the Americans with Disabilities Act. Employees may also be covered by the Pregnancy Discrimination Act of 1978 and the Family Leave Act of 1993. The Web sites of the U.S. Equal Employment Opportunity Commission and the U.S. Department of Justice, Americans with Disabilities Act (ADA) home page listed at the end of this chapter include advice about how to avoid discriminatory practices and indicate information related to these issues that should be included in staff manuals. (e.g., causes of termination, procedures for termination, appeal process for termination). You may want to review the Web site of the U.S. Equal Employment Opportunity Commission (see the address for this Web site at the end of this chapter) for additional specifics.

5. **Services to children.**   These policies and procedures describe who is eligible for the program's services. Sometimes eligibility is determined by governmental or agency

mandates; sometimes families must document financial need; and in other instances programs may give priority to particular populations, for example, the members of the sponsoring church, or employees of a particular business. These policies also describe:

- Maximum group (class) size
- Child-staff ratio
- Enrollment options (e.g. full time, part time, drop-in)
- Program services and provisions for child welfare (e.g., accident procedures, insurance coverage)
- Types of assessments used to document children's progress and procedures for sharing assessment information with families
- Termination of program services

6. Health and safety.   This category of policies and procedures may cover:
- Physical exams required before employment or admission
- Daily health screenings
- Care or exclusion of ill children
- Procedures for medication administration
- Health services offered by the program (e.g., screening, immunizations)
- Management of injuries and emergencies
- Nutrition and food handling guidelines
- Provision for rest or sleep
- Health and safety education
- Staff training in health and safety
- Surveillance of environmental problems

Rely on appropriate professional resources such as NAEYC's *Healthy Young Children* (Aronson & Spahr, 2002) for specific guidelines created by health care professionals.

7. Business and financial issues.   Some areas included in policies related to the program's finances include:
- The identification of person(s) responsible for the program's financial management, including the creation and monitoring of the budget
- The system of accounting
- Requirements for fiscal record keeping
- Audit requirements

Financial policies should also describe the sources of funding (e.g., fees, grants, contracts) and guidelines and procedures for purchasing goods and services. Financial policies should additionally describe how the program will create and manage the contingency fund which should be established to pay for significant unplanned expenses, such as a new roof or furnace; or how to pay employees in case the program should have to close for a week, a month, or even longer because of illness or a facility problem.

8. Record keeping.   Policies and procedures should also indicate:
- What kinds of records are kept on each employee and each child
- Where records are kept, including provisions for their security
- Identify who, under what circumstances, has access to these records

They should identify procedures for ensuring compliance with the Family Educational Rights and Privacy Act (FERPA) as it relates to children's and families' rights to privacy in educational settings. Refer to the Web site listed at the end of this chapter for a description of applicable provisions of FERPA.

9. Families.   These policies and procedures describe ways the program interacts with families and meets families' needs. Particular issues to address in this category include:
- Description of the program philosophy

- Procedures and policies related to enrolling and withdrawing children
- Days and hours of operation
- The calendar for the coming year including scheduled holidays
- Policies related to families visiting their child's classroom (i.e., Is there an "open door" policy? Can family members visit at any time of the day? Is an appointment necessary before entering the classroom?)
- Descriptions of how program personnel will communicate with families including daily or weekly logs, newsletters, email, teacher conferences

Policies related to families should also include information about opportunities for them to be involved in the program by accompanying children on field trips and contributing as a classroom volunteer. And finally, it should include information about the structure and purpose of the parent/teacher organization including information about planned family events and fundraising.

10. Public relations and marketing.   These policies guide outreach into the community including community representation on advisory committees or governing boards, relationships with allied agencies and associations, and the use of facilities by outside groups. There will also be expectations about how the administrator creates a "presence" in the community and how the program creates its unique identity. These policies may also indicate if the center advertises when applications are being accepted or when registration opens to the public. These issues will be discussed in depth in chapter 8.

WHAT TOPICS NEED TO BE ADDRESSED IN A STAFF MANUAL?

Your program's staff manual is the vehicle that communicates and formalizes many of the program's policies and procedures. It serves as a reference and roadmap for administrators and employees alike. The staff manual builds on and expands state regulations. In addition to including a statement that all employees are required to know and adhere to applicable licensing regulations, major topics that you may want to address and elaborate on in the staff manual include

1. **Program Overview**
   - States the program's purpose, philosophy, mission, vision, goals, and objectives.
   - Includes the program's address, phone and fax numbers, email address, Web site and Federal Employer Identification Number (FEIN) number.
   - Affirms that the program is committed to the field's core values, ideals, and principles as stated in the *NAEYC Code of Ethical Conduct*.
2. **Program Services**
   - Identifies ages served and hours of operation.
   - Identifies curriculum models (e.g. Creative Curriculum, High/Scope) or approaches to early care and education (e.g., Program for Infant/Toddler Care) teachers and caregivers are expected to implement.
   - Summarizes age-appropriate expectations including suggestions for creating an appropriate learning environment as well as strategies for appropriately challenging, communicating with, guiding, and nurturing young children.
   - Identifies learning standards addressed at each age level (e.g., *Good Start Grow Smart* Standards for 3- and 4-year-olds, state Learning Standards if appropriate for 4- and 5-year-olds).
   - Describes required documentation of curriculum planning. Are teachers required to submit lesson plans in advance? What should they include?

- Provides parents information about their child's growth, development, and learning using agreed-upon assessment strategies at regularly scheduled parent conferences.

3. **Administration**
   - Includes an organizational chart with a description of the makeup of advisory and/or governing boards
   - Identifies who is responsible if the director is not on-site. Indicates who has leadership duties if that person is not there. Establishes a chain of command and indicates who will be contacted for help in the case of an emergency.

4. **Personnel Policies**
   - Gives notice that the program adheres to applicable nondiscriminatory, equal opportunity, American with Disabilities, and Family Leave laws.
   - Indicates, if applicable, that employment is "at will" and briefly describes this policy.
   - Summarizes job descriptions and qualifications for all positions.
   - Identifies all information and forms required for employment (i.e., background checks, physical exams, educational records, references, Federal Employment Eligibility Verification [I-9] and Internal Revenue Employee's Withholding Allowance Certificate [W-4] forms).
   - Summarizes required fringe benefits (e.g., worker's compensation, and Social Security) and other benefits available to employees (e.g., health insurance, retirement) who wish to participate.
   - Describes indicators of possible abuse or neglect, puts teachers and caregivers on notice that they are mandated reporters of suspected child abuse or neglect, and identifies where they can find additional information about their community's child protective services.
   - Describes staffing patterns (e.g., lead teacher, assistant teacher, floater) and how teaching teams are expected to share instructional, caregiving, and housekeeping responsibilities.
   - Identifies daily work hours, break and lunch time scheduling, and how work hours are to be recorded.
   - Identifies schedule and frequency of pay days (e.g., every other Friday, the 1st and 15th of each month, etc.).
   - Describes when the program will conduct an orientation for new employees and includes a general description of its content.
   - Describes the probationary period, if any, for new employees. Indicates its length and how it effects terms of employement (e.g., eligibility for benefits, earned leave).
   - Describes policies and procedures related to sick leave, personal leave, family leave (e.g., maternity, paternity, or family illness or death), jury duty, time off for medical/dental appointments, and vacation. Identifies forms used to request leave or vacation, where those forms can be found, and to whom they are to be submitted. Indicates how far in advance they should be submitted and when employees will know if leave/vacation has been granted.
   - Identifies whom to call when sick and unable to work.
   - Describes when substitutes are used and how they are contacted and scheduled.
   - Identifies staff meetings employees are required to attend. Indicates how often required meetings are usually scheduled (e.g., monthly at lunch time) and indicates if employees are paid for this time.
   - Stipulates the number of hours of in-service training required annually. Is in-service training offered on-site? Are employees paid during training? Are

employees supported if they attend local, regional, or national conferences? Is support available for courses at local colleges or universities? Does the program participate in the Education and Compensation Helps (T.E.A.C.H.©) scholarship program offered by many states? (See the Web site listed at the end of this chapter for more information about the T.E.A.C.H.© program).

- Describes procedures used to evaluate staff performance and either includes copies of observation and performance evaluation forms or indicates how they can be attained.
- Describes policies related to raises and bonuses. Can employees expect annual cost-of-living raises? Are raises based on merit? Are bonuses regularly awarded? Do raises and bonuses depend on the program's financial status?
- Describes displinary/corrective action procedures including procedures for filing an appeal.
- Describes where staff can locate supplies and how they can request needed materials and equipment.
- Describes the program's policies related to the use of personal cell phones, the center's phones, computers and office equipment, and the Internet.
- Describes dress code for all staff.
- Identifies where staff are to park.
- Indicates that the center is a nonsmoking facility or identifies where smoking is permitted.
- Indicates if employees are allowed to bring their preschool or school-age children with them to work and if they are, under what circumstances.
- Describes resignation and termination procedures and indicates if exit interviews are offered, and if so, with whom.

5. Services to Children
- Describes admission criteria and identifies any populations (i.e., siblings of currently enrolled children, members of the sponsoring church) who are eligible for preferential admissions.
- Indicates if the program is inclusive, that is, if children with identified special needs are welcome to enroll and describes development and use of Individual family service plan (IFSP) and Individual Educational Program (IEP), if appropriate.
- Includes annual calendar indicating dates the program is closed and dates of required staff work days.

- Identifies staff-child ratios for each age group served.
- Identifies group size for each age group served.
- Describes how transitions from one room to the next are planned (are they based on children's age or on their developmental level?) and how they are implemented.
- Stipulates that teachers and caregivers are responsible for supervising the children in their care at all times, both indoors and out, when they are awake and asleep.
- Describes policies related to child guidance and discipline and summarizes recommended practices.
- Describes the program's assessment practices, identifies assessment instruments used (i.e., Ages and Stages Questionnaire, Work Sampling System) and includes a general description of expected documentation of learning and development, including the content of children's portfolios, anecdotal records, and so on.
- Describes morning drop-off and afternoon pickup routines including expectations about how teachers and caregivers are expected to help children adjust to the program.

- Indicates expectations about lesson and unit plans. Are they to be turned in regularly? To whom? What are they to include?
- Describes the program's policies about classroom pets and animal visitors. Are they allowed or encouraged? Are they allowed to be out of a cage? What hand-washing practices are required?
- Describes expections about outdoor play. Where are outdoor play areas? Do infants spend time outdoors? Do children regularly visit near-by parks? Are children expected to play outside every day except during extreme weather? When would they stay indoors?
- ⊙ Describes appropriate activities for days when children must remain indoors.
- Describes the program's policy about field trips. How are field trips approved, scheduled, and supervised? How are children transported?

Harvest Feast

- ⊙ Describes the program's policies related to holiday and birthday celebrations, being sensitive that some families' beliefs mean that they prohibit their children from participating in any celebrations.
- Descibes any extra optional activities offered on a fee-for-services basis.
- Describes procedures to follow if a child has not been picked up at the end of the day.
- Describes how staff and families are notified in the event of severe weather.

6. Health and Safety

- Summarizes universal precautions that reduce the likelihood that infectious and contagious diseases, including blood-borne pathogens, will be spread.
- Describes handwashing practices for children and adults.
- Describes practices specific to infant rooms:

  - Details diaper changing practices designed to protect children's health and safety.
  - Indicates that adults must remove their shoes upon entry.
  - Requires infants be placed on their backs to sleep to prevent sudden infant death syndrome (SIDS).
  - Indicates if families provide formula and baby food and where they are stored if provided by the center.
  - Indicates how bottles of formula or breast milk are heated (Microwaves are NEVER used to heat breast milk or formula).
  - Describes how food and bottles brought from home are stored and labeled and when they must be discarded.
  - Describes provisions in place for nursing mothers who want to visit the classroom to nurse their babies.
  - Indicates if families provide diapers, wipes, creams and ointments where they are stored if provided by the center.
  - Describes how infants are fed (e.g. Are bottle-fed babies always held? Are older infants placed in high chairs or do they sit in child-sized chairs?)

- Describes appropriate labeling and storage of children's cribs and rest cots.
- Details sanitizing and washing procedures for toys, cots and cribs, sheets, bibs, and so on. (Sanitizing solution is made by mixing 1 tbl of bleach to 1 qt of water or ¼ cup bleach to 1 gal water. This solution must be made daily.)
- Describes procedures for storing and giving children prescription and over-the-counter medications.
- Explains fire and emergency evacuation procedures, including where children would be taken if they could not return to their classrooms and how families would be notified in case of an emergency.

- Details sick child exclusion policies, identifying when children should not come to school and when they are ready to return.
- Describes plans to provide children needed first aid, including how minor injuries will be handled (e.g., What incident reports are to be filed?) and how parents will be notified if emergency medical care, including transport by ambulance, is needed.
- Describes procedures if a teacher becomes ill or is injured, how children's safety will be safeguarded and how supervision will be assured.
- Describes how children will be released at the end of the day. Indicates how families notify the program if someone other than the usual parent or caregiver will take their child home, including what form of identification is required before a child will be released to someone other than the usual parent or caregiver.
- Sets expectations for toilet training and describes toileting routines. Indicates if children of particular ages are required to be potty trained. Describes how the program supports potty training. Indicates if children are always accompanied in the bathroom and if bathroom time is part of the daily routine.
- Indicates if the program provides breakfast, lunch, and/or snacks. Does the center follow U.S. Department of Agriculture (USDA) or other published dietary guidelines? If children bring food from home does the program provide any guidelines about what should or should not be brought to school (e.g., Is it a peanut-free program)? May children and staff bring fast food (e.g., McDonald's)?
- Describes steps to be taken when certain allergies or other dietary restrictions are observed.
- Describes mealtime routines. Are meals served family style? Are teachers and caregivers expected to eat with the children? Is conversation encouraged?
- Indicates teachers' housekeeping responsibilities (e.g., Do they take out the trash, sweep their floors, clean sinks and bathrooms at the end of the day?).
- Details, by whom, and how often the facility and playground are checked to note their condition and identify repairs that may be needed.

7. **Business and Financial Issues**
- Details established fees and tuition.
- Describes how fees and tuition are collected and teachers' responsibilities (if any) related to fee collection.
- Indicates how payments are handled if enrichment activities are provided on a fee-for-services basis (e.g., dance, gymnastics, art).

8. **Records**
- Describes content of employees' personnel files and identifies individuals who have access to these records.
- Describes content of children's files and identifies individuals who have access to these records.
- Summarizes teachers' and caregivers' responsibilities to comply with the Family Educational Rights and Privacy Act (FERPA).

9. **Families**
- Describes how teachers and caregivers are expected to communicate with families (e.g., daily logs, communication notebooks, regular emails, monthly newsletters).
- Indicates if the center has an open-door policy that welcomes parents at any time. Are there any restrictions about when they can visit (e.g., not at nap time)? Are siblings welcome?
- Describes how teachers and caregivers are expected to communicate concerns about a child's behavior. Indicates how confidentiality of all children and families is maintained.

The director should review the staff manual with all employees when they are hired and regularly thereafter.

- Indicates how families notify the center if an individual unknown to the center staff will be picking up their child at the end of the day.
- Describes frequency and content of parent/teacher conferences.
- Indicates if the program offers parenting classes. If so, when are they held? Who is eligible to participate?
- Indicates if the program has a Parent/Teacher Organization or PTA. Describes its purpose and major activities. Indicates how teachers can become involved.

10. **Public Relations and Marketing**
   - Some teachers may be willing to speak to civic groups, or they might reach out to other child care programs or neighborhood religious communities in need of training or parent education classes. When it is seen as a community resource, the program reflects well on itself and the field of early care and education.
   - Employees should be reminded that they are the face and voice of the program in the community. Even when they are not working their behavior reflects on the center.

Remember that employees are expected to know and consistently abide by all policies and procedures included in the employee manual as well as the family handbook. Some topics, such as job descriptions, are most appropriately addressed in the employee manual while others, such as guidelines for birthday celebrations, are described in the family handbook.

What Topics Need to Be Addressed in the Family Handbook?

It is important that the family manual have a warm and friendly tone and that it be polished and professional. That means it is easy to read and understand, carefully avoids professional jargon, and incudes no errors in spelling or grammar. Illustrations should be respectful of children and families (avoid "cute") and should reflect the cultural and ethnic diversity of the families you serve. In addition, you should make every effort to have the manual translated into the home language of every family enrolled in your program. It does not communicate with your children's parents if they cannot read and understand its contents.

Consider addressing the topics listed next as you prepare a family handbook. Some information, such as the program's overview and description of services, belongs in both the staff manual and the family handbook. Other information, such as specifics about when and how to pay fees, is appropriately covered in more depth in the family handbook than in the staff manual. Additional topics, such as staff qualifications, are addressed more briefly in the family handbook than in the staff manual. The emphasis you put on each topic in these program-specific materials, will reflect the audience you are addressing, the program's purpose, and the population it serves.

1. **Program Overview**
   - States the program's purpose, philosophy, mission, vision, goals, and objectives and its general approach to instruction (e.g., Is this a play-based program?)
   - Indicates the program's licensure and, when applicable, accreditation or quality rating.
   - Affirms that the program is committed to the field's core values, ideals, and principles as stated in the *NAEYC Code of Ethical Conduct*.

2. **Program Services**
   - Identifies ages served and hours of operation.
   - Gives notice that the program adheres to applicable nondiscriminatory, equal opportunity, and Americans with Disabilities laws.
   - Identifies curriculum models (e.g., Creative Curricum, High/Scope) or approaches to early care and education (e.g., Program for Infant/Toddler Care) implemented by the program and briefly describes their essential characteristics.
   - Describes services provided and routines for before and/or after school for school-age children (e.g., homework time, activity options).
   - Indicates where parents are to park at drop-off and pickup times.
   - Describes policies related to termination of services, including notice families are expected to give if they plan to withdraw their child from the center.

3. **Administration**
   - Includes organizational chart including a description and makeup of advisory and/or governing boards.
   - Lists current staff and their assignments.

4. **Services to Children**
   - Describes admission requirements, including birth-date cutoffs and identifies any populations (e.g., siblings of currently enrolled children, members of the sponsoring church) who are eligible for preferential admissions.
   - Includes the annual calendar indicating dates the program is closed.
   - Indicates staff-child ratios and group size for each age group served.
   - Describes how transitions from one room to the next are planned (are they based on children's age or on their developmental level?)and how they are implemented.
   - Describes the amount of interaction between children of different ages, particularly if the program serves school-age children.
   - Describes how children should dress (e.g., playclothes that may get dirty or wet, shoes that are safe for running and climbing) and reminds families children will play outdoors in all but extreme weather.
   - Indicates the program's ability and willingness to meet the needs of children with identified special needs and any requirements (e.g., an extra employee in the classroom under certain circumstances) that may apply.
   - Describes the program's policies related to child guidance and discipline.
   - Describes morning drop-off and afternoon pickup routines including advice on helping children transition into the program and adjust to its day-to-day routines.
   - Describes the program's policy about classroom pets and animal visitors.

- Describes expectations about outdoor play. Where are outdoor play areas? Do children regularly visit near-by parks? Are children expected to play outside every day except during extreme weather?
- Describes the program's policy about field trips, including a description of how families will be notified of an upcoming trip, what kind of permission form will be required for children to participate, how children will be transported and, if appropriate, invites families to help with supervision.
- Describes the program's policies related to holiday and birthday celebrations.
- Lists supplies children are expected to bring from home (e.g., rest mats, tooth-brush, blanket for nap time, change of clothes).
- Describes procedures that will be followed if a child has not been picked up at the end of the day.
- Describes any extra optional activities offered on a fee-for-services basis and the related responsibilities of regular center staff.
- Describes how families are notified if the program will be closed, will open late, or close early because of severe weather.

5. **Health and Safety**
   - Identifies required immunizations and health exams required for enrollment.
   - Describes handwashing practices followed by children and adults.
   - Describes plans to provide children needed first aid, including how minor injuries will be handled and how parents will be notified if emergency medical care, including transport by ambulance, is needed.
   - Describes procedures for giving children prescription and over-the-counter medications. Indicates if a form must be completed to give the program permission to administer medications and where that form can be found.
   - Explains emergency evacuation procedures, including where children would be taken if they could not return to their classrooms and how families would be notified in case of an emergency.
   - Describes practices specific to infant rooms:
     - Indicates that adults must remove their shoes upon entry.
     - Notifies families infants will be placed on their backs to sleep to prevent sudden infant death syndrome (SIDS).
     - Indicates if formula and baby food are provided by the center or if they are brought by children's families.
     - Stipulates that bottles of formula or breast milk are heated (Microwaves are NEVER used to heat breast milk or formula.)
     - Describes how food and bottles brought from home are stored and labeled and when they must be discarded.
     - Describes provisions in place for nursing mothers who want to visit the classroom to nurse their babies.
     - Indicates if the center provides diapers, wipes, creams, and ointments or if they are brought by children's families.
     - Describes how infants are fed (e.g. Are bottle-fed babies always held? Are older infants placed in high chairs or do they sit in child-sized chairs?)
   - Sets expectations for toilet training and describes toileting routines. Indicates if children of particular ages are required to be potty trained. Describes how the program supports potty training. Indicates if children are always accompanied in the bathroom and if bathroom time is part of the daily routine.
   - Details sick child exclusion policies, identifying when children should not come to school and when they will be permitted to return.

See Figure 4.1 for an example of how your family handbook might describe when a child should stay home from school.

When Should Your Child Stay Home?

We hope your child will be able to come to the center regularly, but there are times when children should stay home for their own safety and well-being or to prevent the spread of a contagious condition.

Children should stay home when they are ill.

These are symptoms that mean your child should not come to school:

Blood in stools
Diarrhea (negative stool cultures required for some illnesses)
Difficult breathing
Fever accompanied by behavior changes or symptoms of an illness until the child receives a professional evaluation
Inexplicable irritability or persistent crying
Lethargy (more than usual tiredness)
Mouth sores with drooling
Persistent abdominal pain
Rash with fever or behavior change
Uncontrolled coughing
Unspecified respiratory tract illness
Vomiting (two or more times in 24 hours)
Wheezing

Your child should not come to school if he or she has:

Chicken pox (until lesions have dried)
Haemophilus influenza, type b (HIb) infection
Head lice (until after first treatment)
Hepatitis A (until one week after onset)
Herpes simplex (sores and drooling)
Impetigo (until 24 hours after treatment begins)
Measles (until 6 days after rash appears)
Meningitis
Mumps (until 9 days after swelling)
Pertussis (until 14 days after laboratory confirmed onset)
Purulent conjunctivitis (until 24 hours after treatment begins)
Rubella (until 6 days after rash appears)
Scabies (until treatment is completed)
Shingles (if sores have not crusted)
Streptococcal pharyngitis (until 24 hours after treatment begins) or other streptococcal infections
Tuberculosis

Family Emergency

Your child probably needs to be with you or other familiar family members in the case of the death or serious illness of a loved one. You know your child best, however, and we want to help if the familiar school routine would be a comfort. Please be in touch in these kinds of circumstances so that we can know how to help you and your child.

During Extreme Weather

The center will be closed when local schools close because of extreme weather. Listen to local radio and TV stations or check the Internet. We follow the decision made by the Richland School District in case of school closings. You will NOT hear an announcement specifically from our school.

Figure 4.1
Sample of a family handbook's description of when children should stay home from school and when they may return.

- Requests that children bring a complete change of clothes (including socks) to be left at the center in case of accidents.
- Describes how children will be released at the end of the day. Indicates how families notify the program if someone other than the usual parent or caregiver will take their child home, including what form of identification is required before a child will be released to someone other than the usual parent or caregiver.
- Indicates if the program provides breakfast, lunch, and snacks and follows U.S. Department of Agriculture (USDA) or other published dietary guidelines.
- Provides guidelines about what should or should not be brought to school if children bring food from home (e.g., Is it a peanut free program? Will food from home be refrigerated? Can it be heated? May children bring fast food, such as McDonald's).
- Details what steps are taken to be certain food allergies and other dietary restrictions are respected (e.g., those based on religious practices or preferences for only organic foods).
- Describes mealtime routines. Are meals served family style? Do teachers and caregivers eat with the children? Is conversation encouraged?

6. **Business and Financial Issues**
   - Details established fees and tuition for each age group, including registration fees, materials fees, late fees, and returned check policy.
   - Describes when fees and tuition are due and how they are collected (e.g., Are they mailed, dropped into a box on the director's desk?).
   - Describes when late fees and returned check fees are assessed and how they are to be handled.

7. **Records**
   - Identifies birth, immunization, physical examination, residency, or other documentation requirement for admission.
   - Identifies materials families must submit before their child can participate in the program, such as emergency contact information, acknowledgement of having received the family handbook, and so on.

8. **Families**
   - Puts parents on notice that teachers and caregivers are mandated by law to report suspected child abuse or neglect to the local child protective service agency.
   - Identifies how families can expect teachers and caregivers to communicate with them (e.g., daily logs, communication notebooks, regular emails, monthly newsletters).
   - Indicates if the center has an open-door policy that welcomes parents at any time. Are there any restrictions about when they can visit (e.g., not at nap time)? Are siblings welcome?
   - Describes how teachers teachers and caregivers are expected to communicate concerns about a child's behavior. Indicates how confidentiality of all children and families is maintained.
   - Describes frequency and content of parent/teacher conferences.
   - Indicates if the program offers parenting classes. If so, when are they held? Who is eligible to participate?
   - Indicates if the program has a Parent/Teacher Organization or PTA. Describes its purpose and major activities. Indicates how can families become involved.

See Figure 4.2 for an example of a Family Member's Checklist to briefly communicate beginning-of-school routines.

Family Member's Checklist

We are looking forward to a productive and fun school year. We want to be certain your child gets off to the very best start possible. Please read this handbook carefully and complete this checklist to be sure you and your child have everything ready for school to begin.

Have you read this handbook? _____

Have you completed and signed the emergency information form?_____

Have you asked your emergency contacts if they are willing to be "on call" if your child needs them? _____

Have you completed and signed the health history form? _____

Has your physician completed and signed the physical examination form? _____

Has your physician completed and signed the immunization record form? _____

Has your dentist signed the dental report form? _____

Does your child have comfortable play clothes and sturdy shoes to wear to school? _____

Do you have the needed supplies? (book bag, blanket for rest time, etc.) _____

Are all sweaters, jackets, hats, and mittens labeled? _____

Have you put an extra set of clothes (head to toe) in a labeled zip-lock bag? _____

Are you helping your child anticipate your family's school day routine? _____

Do you have any questions you'd like to discuss with center personnel?

Figure 4.2
This checklist helps ensure a smooth start to a new school year.

9. **Public Relations and Marketing**
   - Indicates that the director and selected teachers may be willing to speak to civic groups or may be available to work with other childcare programs or neighborhood religious communities in need of training or parent education classes. When seen as a community resource, the program reflects well on itself and the field of early care and education.

WHAT INFORMATION SHOULD BE IN THE ADMINISTRATOR'S MANUAL?

This material will, in all likelihood, be available only to the director and, in the case of mid-size and large programs, the supervisor(s), which may be an advisory or governing board or the corporation's regional and/or national coordinator.

The issues addressed in an administrator's manual are likely to be more idiosyncratic than those addressed in either the family handbook or the staff manual. Examples of items that may be addressed in the administrative manual include

- Details related to salary scales, raises, and bonuses (if applicable).
- Details of hiring procedures. Are potential employees approved by a board or its representatives?
- Details of termination procedures.

- Conditions for the availability of employee tuition discounts. Is this benefit available to all employees? Is it a discretionary benefit that may be offered to employees with specific credentials?
- Describes how the yearly calendar is developed. Does the director consult with local schools? Professional organizations whose conferences the staff attends?
- The director's responsibilities related to recruitment of both staff and families.
- The time lines related to licensure and accreditation. When is the program up for renewal? What reports are required to licensure and accrediting bodies?

If you become a program director, you will want to find out about existing guidelines you will be expected to follow. During your tenure you will want to continue to develop this resource. It will make your life, and that of your successor, much easier if all this information can be found in a central, organized location.

SUMMARY

While regulations, statues, and standards as well as the program's mission statement, goals, and objectives create a framework for a program's operations, it is the program-specific materials—its family handbook, staff manual, and administrative manual—that apply these rules and regulations to a program's day-to-day operations. The formulation, implementation, and evaluation of these materials are the responsibilities of the board of directors and the program administrator.

When a program has thoughtfully developed policies and procedures that are clearly and consistantly communicated to staff and families, many potential problems can be elimiated. Well-conceived policies and procedures also save the program director a great deal of time and energy. They give him or her the opportunity to focus on the important work of caring for and educating the young children entrusted to the program and its staff. You will find that time devoted to the creation of these materials is time well spent. They put your program on track for smooth operation. Where morale of staff is high, parents are the program's biggest boosters, and children's days are spent in an environment that enhances their learning, growth, and development.

USEFUL WEB SITES

Information about the T.E.A.C.H. Early Childhood© Project is available from

www.childcareservices.org/ps/teach.html

Information about the U.S. Department of Education Family Educational Rights and Privacy Act (FERPA)is available from

www.ed.gov/policy/gen/guid/fpco/ferpa/index.html

Information about the Americans with Disabilities Act is available from

www.usdoj.gov/crt/ada/adahom1.htm.

Answers to questions commonly asked about child care centers is available from

www.ada.gov/childq&a.htm

Information from the U.S. Equal Employment Opportunity Commission is available from

www.eeoc.gov/

Information about the Family and Medical Leave Act (FMLA) is available from

www.dol.gov/esa/whd/fmla/

TO REFLECT

1. What might be some consequences if a director did not consistently apply policies and procedures described in the family handbook or staff manual? How would the program's operations be affected? What effect would this behavior have on morale? Who would be responsible for bringing these issues to her attention? Would the *NAEYC Code of Ethical Conduct* or the *Supplement for Program Administrators* guide your decisions?

2. We recommend that you ask a few trusted families to review your program's family handbook as it is being developed and finalized. What are the benefits and the risks of asking for feedback before the document has been finalized?

5

LEADING AND MANAGING PERSONNEL

NAEYC Administrator Competencies addressed in this chapter:

Management Knowledge and Skills

Staff Management and Human Relations

Knowledge and application of group dynamics, communication styles, and techniques for conflict resolution. Knowledge of different supervisory and group facilitation styles. The ability to relate to staff and board members of diverse racial, cultural, and ethnic backgrounds. The ability to hire, supervise, and motivate staff to high levels of performance. Skill in consensus building, team development, and staff performance appraisal.

Leadership and Advocacy

Knowledge of organizational theory and leadership styles as they relate to early childhood work environments. Knowledge of the legislative process, social issues, and public policy affecting young children and their families. The ability to articulate a vision, clarify and affirm values, and create a culture built on norms of continuous improvement and ethical conduct. The ability to evaluate program effectiveness. The ability to define organizational problems, gather data to generate alternative solutions, and effectively apply analytical skills in its solution. The ability to advocate on behalf of young children, their families and the profession.

The staff is the single most important influence on the quality of early childhood programs. The best programs tend to have highly qualified staff and low teacher turnover. A disparity exists between the professional preparation, access to many roles in the field, adequate compensation of staff, and the growing expectations for optimal care and education of young children. Furthermore, if working conditions are not good for staff members, children do not do well in programs.

To ensure job satisfaction for staff as well as program quality, three criteria must be met in staffing:

1. The staff must meet at least minimal qualifications for their specific duties, although an employer hopes to select employees who have the most potential.
2. Those selected must understand and agree with the program vision and mission.
3. The staff must accept personal ownership and responsibility for the program.

It is the responsibility of the program director to ensure that these criteria are met. Through careful selection of applicants and effective hiring practices you help set the stage for a high-quality program. Once the stage is set, however, you must actively work to retain staff by establishing and maintaining a positive organizational culture, providing appropriate training and professional development, ensuring that staff are adequately compensated for their work, and that staff have an overall sense of satisfaction as a result of their work in your program.

TRENDS IN STAFFING

Advocacy efforts have resulted in an increased recognition of the importance of early childhood education. In addition to the acceptance of kindergartens and primary programs as an integral part of public education, the growing consensus is that enough high-quality infant, toddler, and preschool programs should exist to meet the developmental needs of these children and the needs of their families, all at a cost that families and society can afford.

All the characteristics of high-quality programs depend on adequate numbers of well-trained staff members. Early childhood programs need increasingly larger staffs for several reasons. First, more early childhood programs are becoming comprehensive in nature, which necessitates additional staff. Second, an adequate adult–child ratio based on the ages and needs of children served and a small group size are major factors in program quality. Third, with the inclusion of children with special needs, support staff are needed for screening and identifying these children and for helping to engage children with special needs into general education classrooms (Hebbeler, 1995).

The demographic data on early childhood program staff are not encouraging. Regrettably, as a result of today's economic problems, the tendency is toward fewer staff and larger groups for preschool children (Snow, Teleki, & Reguero-de-Atiles, 1996). As discussed previously, several national studies have confirmed the mediocre quality of most early childhood programs. Thus, more and more families are struggling to find adequate child care at an affordable cost.

Staff Shortage: A Deep-Rooted Problem

The biggest quality issue facing early childhood care and education programs is the difficulty to recruit and retain staff members. Retention of staff especially affects program quality in several ways. As reported by Hale-Jinks, Knopf, and Kemple (2006), staff turnover impacts the emotional security of children enrolled in the program, increases stress among teachers and caregivers who remain employed at the center, and increases operating costs for the center. All these impacts can make fulfilling your program vision and mission increasingly difficult.

The **turnover rate,** the number of teachers who leave a program during the year, has been extremely high. A recent estimate reports an annual turnover rate as high as 40% among early care and education personnel in the United States (Center for the Child Care Workforce, 2004). Recent reviews of professional literature have reported that low compensation, high job stress, inadequate training, and a lack of administrative support contribute to high levels of staff turnover (Hale-Jinks et al., 2006).

Low Compensation.   The Worthy Wage Campaign, initiated by the Center for the Child Care Workforce, sought to expose the association of low pay with the difficulty in recruiting qualified staff and the association of high turnover rates among child care workers with low-quality programs. As a group, child care teachers earn less than half as much as kindergarten teachers. When compared to other occupations, child care workers earn less than janitors, cooks, and chauffeurs (Barnett, 2003). Predictably, the highest turnover rates tend to occur in programs that pay the lowest salaries; conversely, the lowest turnover rates were in programs that paid the highest salaries (Quality, Compensation, and Affordability, 1998; Whitebook, Sakai, Gerber, & Howes, 2001).

Staff compensation and turnover rate are also associated with measured program quality, such as accreditation. For example, the NAEYC-accredited programs had the lowest center turnover rate, but the centers that did not maintain their accreditation did not differ in turnover rate from programs that had never sought accreditation ("Quality, Compensation, and Affordability," 1998).

Compensation, however, should not be limited to hourly wages or annual salary. It is also common for child care professionals to not have health insurance, sick leave, paid vacation, reimbursement for professional development, and performance bonuses as part of standard compensation packages (Hale-Jinks et al., 2006). A report that investigated changes in child care staffing from 1994 to 2000 found that the key factors that led to lower turnover among teachers and directors were higher than average salary and compensation packages (Whitebook et al., 2001).

With this in mind, it is wise for the program director and/or governing board to contact an appropriate professional (insurance provider/accountant) to explore the provision of a compensation package that exceeds the market standard. While inadequate compensation is likely to have a significant impact on job satisfaction and staff turnover, there are other factors that you, as the child care director, should be mindful of when endeavoring to reduce staff turnover.

High Job Stress.   Job stress experienced by individuals working in early care and education settings has been linked by researchers to lower job satisfaction, teacher burnout, and ultimately job turnover (Deery-Schmitt & Todd, 1995; McClelland, 1986; Manlove, 1993; 1994; Whitebook, Howes, Phillips, & Pemberton, 1991). Factors identified by early childhood caregivers that contribute to high levels of stress include long hours, the physical demands of the job, and being constantly overwhelmed by unpredictable stress-inducing situations (conflict among children, malfunctioning toilet facilities, angry parents, etc.). In addition, increased focus on children's academic performance and preparation for school has led to pressure to achieve and a collective sense of failure (Curbow, Spratt, Ungaretti, McDonnell, & Breckler, 2001).

Inadequate Training.   The work of early care and education professionals is difficult and complex. Entering this profession ill-prepared is likely to lead to increased stress as described in the previous section. Teachers with limited specific preparation to work in early childhood settings are less likely to view their work as professional and thus are less likely to feel a personal commitment to their work with children.

While the research describing the need for a specific level of education hasn't clearly identified a link between specific educational qualifications of teaching staff and early childhood outcomes (Childhood Education Study; Early, Maxwell, Burchinal, Bender, Bryant et al., 2007), there is consensus within the field regarding the need for increased professional development in order to raise the level of quality experiences by young children in center-based care and education program (Marshall et al., 2001; Phillips, Mekos, Scarr, McCartney, & Abbott-Shim, 2000; Whitebook, 2001; Whitebook, Howes, & Phillips, 1990). Early care and education teachers hold a complex and difficult job, which entails the provision of quality care, nurturing, and providing educational experiences for a diverse population of young children. In order to deliver high-quality care, teachers must achieve a standard of professionalism, in which they willingly accept the awesome responsibility of teaching and caring for a very vulnerable population. To ensure high-quality services and experiences are provided, these professionals must reflect and learn from their daily teaching experiences. In order to achieve and further such professionalism, caregivers should be knowledgeable of evidence-based best practices and the process of assessment and self-evaluation. This knowledge and skill are likely to result only from systemized teacher preparation programs and professional development.

A staffing crisis is detrimental to all involved. Children are affected by the change in rituals and by the loss of people associated with the rituals. Insecure children spend less time involved with peers and more time in "aimless wandering" and show drops in cognitive activities (Whitebook et al., 1990). Changes in staff are especially detrimental to infants and toddlers. Those who experience more staff turnover do not score as well on cognitive tests (Clarke-Stewart & Gruber, 1984) and develop less secure attachments (Carnegie Task Force on Meeting the Needs of Young Children, 1994; Howes & Hamilton, 1992), as compared with infants and toddlers experiencing no turnover in care. Families find that it takes time to feel comfortable with new staff. Of course, staff are affected, too. An unstable work environment caused, by high levels of turnover tends to decrease predictability for children and staff which has the effect of raising stress levels. This unstable work environment leads to even more turnover which over time leads to lower quality care and education services (Whitebook & Sakai, 2003). There is hope, however, that program administrators, through their role as leaders and managers, have influence over the organizational climate, and many of the factors that tend to influence staff turnover. Through this chapter we present strategies that will help program administrators set the stage for success in attracting and retaining staff, the cornerstone of a high-quality program.

STAFFING AN EARLY CHILDHOOD PROGRAM

After developing a program vision and mission, an administrator is faced with the task of determining the staff needed and of matching job requirements with existing staff members. This task is a continual one; staffing patterns change as a program expands or as vacancies occur.

Roles and Qualifications of Personnel

Although all staff members must be in good physical and psychological health and have the personal qualities necessary to work with young children, a person's needed qualifications depend on his or her specific role. And even roles with the same title may vary from program to program.

Personnel may be classified as either primary program personnel or support program personnel. **Primary program personnel** have direct, continuous contact with children. **Support program personnel** provide services that support or facilitate caregiving and the instructional program. Although a staff member is classified by the major role, he or she may occasionally function in another capacity. For example, a teacher may occasionally clean the room or serve food, or a dietitian might discuss good eating habits with children or console a child who drops a carton of milk.

Director.   A **director** is someone who is typically in charge of the total program. Directors of early childhood education programs in public schools are often supervisors or resource personnel. In Montessori programs, teachers are traditionally given this title. The title of *director* is frequently given to the person legally responsible for the total program and services. Caruso and Fawcett (1999) used the following terms to define the roles of directors:

Executive director: One who administers a large child care agency that may comprise several social services programs

Program director: One who runs the day-to-day operations of a program

Educational coordinator: One who is responsible for the educational component, including staff development and curriculum development, of an agency or a single program

Head teacher: One who oversees one or more classrooms

Supervisor: One who oversees teachers and support personnel

Although this book's focus is primarily on the role of the program director, organizations differ; as programs differ, so do the roles of their directors.

Director's Role.   Regardless of the type of early childhood program or the title of the director, many responsibilities are similar. Professionals have categorized the responsibilities in different ways. For example, Hayden (1996) described the following five administrative roles:

- Technical responsibilities (e.g., regulations and policies, budgets)
- Staff relations
- Educational planning
- Public relations (e.g., advocacy, networking, fund-raising, marketing)
- Symbolic (i.e., director as a symbol for the identity of the group)

Carter and Curtis (1998) used the equilateral triangle to conceptualize the role of a director. The roles, which are of equal importance, are managing and overseeing, coaching and mentoring, and building and supporting community. Morgan (2000) listed eight roles of directors and competencies for each role. Bloom (2000b) interviewed directors regarding their perceptions of their roles and used linguistic metaphorical analysis of the data. Almost 29% of all directors talked about "leading and guiding"; 28% referred to their role as balancing multiple tasks; and 25% saw their role as "caring and nurturing" of the entire community.

For this text, directors' responsibilities include both a **leadership component** (i.e., the people-oriented or human resources role) and a **management component** or the technical (i.e., organizational, program, business), nonperson aspects of administration. (For more specific examples of leadership and management roles, see Figure 5.1.)

Bloom (1997a) suggested that clear distinctions cannot be made between leadership and management functions in most early childhood programs; most directors have both responsibilities, and the functions themselves overlap. For example, the director may write the program's goals and then articulate the goals to others. The administrative role becomes more complex with the size of the program and the location (i.e., a program located at multiple sites is usually more complex than a program located at one site).

Director's Responsibilities

Leadership

Articulates program vision, mission, and philosophy.

Works with staff to plan entire program component based on goals.

Communicates policies and procedures, needs, program objectives, and problems with all interested parties—board, staff, parents, and their agencies; motivates others to take their responsibilities; resolves conflicts.

Affirms values of program and serves in advocacy roles in concert with various community agencies through community-wide endeavors and through professional organizations.

Serves as a model in terms of the code of ethics (see Chapter 13).

Delegates leadership roles and certain responsibilities to others when appropriate and takes on responsibilities when appropriate to delegate responsibilities.

Continues his or her own professional development.

Management

Writes or adopts and implements all regulations, policies, and procedures.

Abides by all contracts.

Serves as personnel manager by doing the following:

- Conducting a needs assessment
- Recruiting and selecting
- Hiring
- Planning placement
- Filling staff roles with substitutes when needed
- Developing a communications system (e.g., meetings)
- Supervising staff and planning professional development
- Evaluating staff
- Maintaining personnel records

Enrolls and places children and family members.

Plans and maintains records on children and family members.

Develops program calendar and overall daily scheduling (e.g., eating times).

Follows procedures and manages property by doing the following:

- Planning or locating adequate housing and maintaining building and grounds
- Ordering and maintaining equipment, materials, and supplies
- Maintaining all property records (e.g., mortgage or lease payments, insurance, inventories)

Plans finances by doing the following:

- Mobilizing resources
- Developing the budget
- Planning marketing strategies
- Working with funding and regulatory agencies
- Writing proposals for grants and governmental assistance programs

Develops an efficient internal and external (public relations) communications system.

Plans program evaluation if needed.

Figure 5.1
Program Director's Responsibilities: Leadership and Management

The need to balance the leadership and management roles for program success has been studied on a historical basis by Hewes (2000). In stressing the need for a balance among tasks, Neugebauer (2000) likened a successful program director to an orchestra director; that is, he or she must "be able to blend all the talents of the individual performers" (p. 98). In sum, the director has the leadership role in managing quality in the program.

Professional Qualifications of Directors. The professional qualifications of directors vary, depending on the program's organizational pattern. Several initiatives have examined the director's role and debated the possibilities for credentials as part of the licensing and/or accreditation requirements for center-based sites. While some states have begun to require a specific director credential, this is not a universal requirement. Be sure to review the rules and regulations for your location and take appropriate action.

Essential knowledge and competencies have been identified by the NAEYC through their program accreditation standards and continue to be refined (see inside front cover for NAEYC Program Administrator Competencies). The general consensus is that administrators should have early childhood professional knowledge and administrative competence. More specifically, Brown and Manning (2000) identified four areas of knowledge needed by directors, and Neugebauer (2000) and Morgan (2000) developed comprehensive lists of needed competencies.

Many competencies have been described in depth. Some of these competencies include visionary skills (Carter & Curtis, 1998); communication skills and team building (Jorde-Bloom, 1997a); human resource management (Stonehouse & Woodrow, 1992); financial management (Morgan, 1999); supervision (Caruso & Fawcett, 1999); and culturally relevant leadership and community partnership skills ("Taking the Lead Initiative," 1999).

In reality, however, many administrators step into their roles without the needed competencies. Less than 20% of all directors have planned a career in administration. Most said they reached their current position because others saw their leadership potential. About 90% come from the ranks of teachers (Bloom, 1997a), often in Katz's (1995) "renewal stage" when teachers are looking for new challenges or in Vander Ven's (1988) "direct care: advanced" stage in which teachers make logical decisions. Thus, competencies are learned through work experience, and work experience becomes a critical factor in program quality (Cost, Quality, and Child Outcomes Study Team, 1995). As new directors learn the needed competencies, they go through stages as shown in Figure 5.2.

Along with work experience, directors use other tools for developing competencies. Many engage in self-study. (Some resources are listed at the end of the chapter.) Besides professional reading materials, other frequently used means of self-study include professional conferences, workshops, and interest groups. Often community business groups conduct forums and other programs of benefit to early childhood program directors. Other directors learn through director mentors ("Taking the Lead Initiative," 2000). Directors also use assessment tools (Freeman & Brown, 2000; Schiller & Dyke, 2001; Sciarra & Dorsey, 1998) for professional development.

Personal Qualifications of Directors. Regardless of the program, personal characteristics of effective directors are similar. Because of the numbers and complexities of their responsibilities, successful directors are usually focused and organized. Effective directors must be able to see the program holistically and recognize interconnections. Other characteristics include:

- Physical and mental stamina
- Openness to new ideas
- Communication skills
- Flexibility of expression and thought
- Acceptance of capabilities and fallibilities

Stages Given by Anthony (1998)

Stage 1: Organizing and Surviving (first year)

Learn by trial and error

Learn much new information

Manage stress

Stage 2: Managing and Focusing (second year)

Develop expertise in specific program areas

Extend knowledge and support beyond local program

Develop time management skills

Stage 3: Leading and Balancing (third or fourth year)

Develop a vision for the program

Include others in achieving goals

Stage 4: Advocating and Mentoring (fifth or sixth year)

Share professional expertise

Expand current program

Avoid burnout

Stages Given by Bloom (1997b)

Beginning directors (first year)

Eager to make a contribution and to be liked

Face reality shocks (e.g., needed stamina, amount of paperwork, needs of others, lack of support)

Major problems are lack of management skills, seeing single solutions to complex problems, and seeing events from personal perspective

Competent directors (between first and fourth years)

Have problems with time management

Know their strengths and weaknesses

Often overcome problems of beginning directors

Master directors

See themselves as change agents, mentors, role models, and advocates

Engage in reflective practice

Make role expectations clear to others and use flexible style to meet needs of staff members

Seek consistency between espoused theory and reality

Stages Given by Caruso and Fawcett (1999)

Beginning

Try to conceptualize roles

Imitate models from past experiences

Figure 5.2
Stages of Directors' Development

Use different approaches (trial and error)

Avoid responsibilities by pretending not to have enough time

Gradually work out authority relationships

Extending

Somewhat ambivalent about role

Discuss problems and conflicts objectively

See differences in staff members

Understand program better

Maturing

Make conscious decisions

Are accountable for their actions

Are more sensitive to others

Assess themselves accurately

Not as burdened by problems

Figure 5.2 (Continued)

- Ability to learn from mistakes
- Willingness to share credit with others
- Cheerfulness, warmth, and sensitivity to both children and adults
- Personal sense of security
- Desire to succeed
- Honesty

Primary Program Personnel.   Just as distinctions between care and education should not be made, distinctions between child care workers and teachers are no longer useful. The following definitions for teaching staff are currently being used by the NAEYC as part of the program accreditation criteria (NAEYC, 2005):

> **Teachers** are defined as the adult with *primary* responsibility for a group of children. For the purposes of NAEYC Accreditation a *group or classroom of children* is defined by the criteria for maximum group size for children of different ages/developmental levels. The teacher must spend the vast majority of time with one group of children who attend at the same time, rather than dividing time between classrooms or floating between groups. Primary responsibility for multiple groups of children, who attend at the same time, cannot be assigned to any one or single teacher.

> **Assistant Teachers** (or **Teacher Aides**) are defined as adults who work under the direct supervision of a teacher. Assistant teachers/teacher aides can work independently in a teacher's absence, but for the vast majority of the time, the assistant teacher/teacher aide works directly with the teacher in the same space with the same group of children.

Role of Primary Personnel.   Except for tasks specific to the age group served, very little distinction can be made among the roles performed by teachers in the various early childhood programs. Roles may include the following responsibilities:

- Serve in a leadership capacity with other staff members.
- Implement the program vision, mission, and philosophy by observing and determining children's needs in relation to program goals and by planning activities.

- Communicate verbally and sympathetically with children.
- Respond effectively to children's behavior.
- Model and articulate to families and other staff members practices in keeping with the program's rationale.

Professional Qualifications of Primary Personnel.   Because the tasks performed by teachers are essentially the same, entry-level qualifications are similar in all programs. Isenberg (1999) stated that a strong liberal arts background seems essential as the base of professional qualifications. Regardless of whether professional development occurs as preservice or inservice or whether it is primarily in the form of formal education or a workshop type of training, it should be knowledge based as opposed to conventional wisdom (Griffin, 1999). A good source for determining the core content of early childhood professionals' knowledge base is the NAEYC's (2005) standards for early childhood professional preparation, which can be revisited at greater depth and breadth at higher levels of preparation.

Personal Qualifications of Primary Personnel.   Personal characteristics associated with an effective teacher are difficult to define. Opinion varies as to what constitutes a good teacher of young children. In addition, teaching styles (personality traits, attitudes) are interwoven with teaching techniques (methodology). Characteristics of effective teachers may be specific to the age of the children and vary with the cultural group served. Because teaching is so complex and multifaceted, more research needs to be conducted on personal characteristics and teaching effectiveness (Spodek, 1996).

Characteristics and skills often associated with effective early childhood teachers include warmth, flexibility, integrity, sense of humor, physical and mental stamina, vitality, emotional stability and confidence, naturalness, and an ability to support development without being overprotective (Elicker & Fortner-Wood, 1995). Feeney and Christensen (1979) wrote that the most important characteristic of a good teacher is the ability to be with young children rather than do for young children. Balaban (1992) described 12 ways in which teachers are with young children; among these ways are as anticipators and planners, listeners and watchers, protectors, providers of interesting environments, elicitors of language, and smoothers of jangled feelings. In addition to having these characteristics, teachers who work with infants should be able to develop very close bonds with infants, "read" behavioral cues (e.g., distinguish among cries), and make long-term commitments to programs so that infants are provided continuity (Balaban, 1992; Honig, 1993).

Support Program Personnel.   The major role of support program personnel is to furnish services that support or facilitate the program. Support program personnel include dietitians and food service personnel, medical staff, psychologists, caseworkers, maintenance staff, general office staff, transportation staff, and volunteers. A new category of support program personnel is the **case manager,** a position created through the Individualized Family Service Plan (IFSP) requirements of Part C of P.L. 105–17. Similar to caseworkers, case managers are child and family advocates who serve as a linking agent between families and needed service agencies. Unlike caseworkers, who are traditionally from the social work profession, IFSP case managers are chosen because of expertise in relation to a given child's primary problem and thus may be, for example, nutritionists, physical therapists, or speech pathologists.

Some categories of support personnel are found mainly in public school and government-funded early childhood programs. For example, **early intervention specialists** are teachers or consultants who specialize in the development and learning of children with special needs. Other special education consultants include occupational therapists, physical therapists, and speech-language pathologists (Wesley, 2002). In very small proprietorships, food service, maintenance, and office work are often done by the director, teachers, and volunteers.

Prepare children for the possibility of a substitute; for example, have potential substitutes visit the room.

Write the following procedures in detail:

- Greeting of children as they arrive
- Meals, snacks, and toileting routines
- Basic activities for each block of time in the schedule and frequently used transitions
- Routines for moving children outdoors and to other places in the building (e.g., library)
- Routines for emergencies
- Administrative duties (e.g., attendance count, meal count, snack money, sending notes home)
- Routines for departure, including a listing of those who ride buses, travel in private cars, and so on.

Write plans for 2 to 3 days that do not overburden the substitute; place materials needed for plans in a given drawer or on a given shelf noted in written plans.

Have an up-to-date list of children and note any children with special needs and how those needs are handled (children's name tags can be helpful).

Leave note on desk with semiregular activities such as "duty" responsibilities.

Keep a notebook with all of the above on the desk.

If the substitute did a good job, call and express appreciation. Inform the director or the building principal of the quality of the substitute's work so that a decision can be made about possible rehiring of the substitute. (Also remember that many teachers begin their teaching careers by doing substitute work.)

Figure 5.3
Plans for Substitute Teachers

Support program personnel must have the qualifications of their respective professions. They must also be knowledgeable about age-level expectations of young children. Personal qualifications include the ability to communicate with children and to work with all adults involved in the program.

Substitute personnel should have the same professional qualifications and personal characteristics as the regularly employed personnel. To ensure program continuity, careful plans should be made for substitute teachers (see Figure 5.3). Such plans are most essential when substitute personnel will be working alone (e.g., in a self-contained classroom), especially in kindergartens and primary grades.

Assessing Needs and Recruiting Staff Members

The director with a board determines the specific characteristics of the personnel wanted and the minimum accepted. The director may seek a diverse staff through an informal needs assessment or a rigorous affirmative action plan. Because the budget is usually limited, the director must also determine priorities. Other considerations may include the potential staff available and the amount of training and supervision to be conducted. The necessary positions must then be translated into job descriptions.

The director, the personnel administrator, or a committee from the board is responsible for advertising the positions. Programs must follow affirmative action guidelines in recruiting and hiring. **Affirmative action** entails identifying and changing discriminatory employment practices and taking positive steps to recruit and provide an accepting working environment for minorities and women. Manuals on affirmative action programs are available. The ADA outlaws employment discrimination based on disability. The Economic

Employment Opportunity Commission will consider the job description and whether reasonable accommodations can be made.

The NAEYC adopted a general (comprehensive) antidiscriminatory policy in 1988 stating that employment decisions must be based solely on the competence and qualifications of persons to perform "designated duties" ("NAEYC Business," 1988). Possible steps in recruiting staff include developing and gathering recruitment materials, advertising, having applicants complete job applications, obtaining documentation of credentials, interviewing, and hiring for a probationary period.

Developing and Gathering Recruitment Materials.   Recruitment materials must include job descriptions that list duties in terms of "essential functions" and how frequently each function must be performed, responsibilities, and authority and must list the qualifications and skills required. Public relations brochures and policy manuals are also good recruitment materials.

The director should first notify persons already involved in the program of an opening and then make the advertisement public. The advertisement should be in keeping with the job description and state all nonnegotiable items, such as required education and experience, so that unqualified applicants can quickly be eliminated. The advertisement should also include the method of applying and the deadline for application. Figure 5.4 is an example of a newspaper advertisement.

The method of applying and the acceptance of applications will depend on the abilities and experiences of applicants and the director's time. Thus, the method of application may vary from a telephone call or completion of a simple application form to a lengthy application form, a résumé, and a letter requesting transcripts and credentials. For example, if written communication abilities are not part of the job description, applicants could apply in person or over the telephone. A simple application form is given in Figure 5.5 as an example.

After the application deadline, the director or other staff member in charge of hiring will screen applications to eliminate unqualified applicants. Eliminated applications should be retained for affirmative action requirements. Finally, the administrator is required by affirmative action guidelines to list the reasons for rejection and to notify applicants.

Obtaining Documentation of Credentials.   The director or person(s) interviewing should obtain the following documents:

1. **References.**   The director can legally contact all references given on the application and all former employers concerning work history and character. These references are aids in seeing how the applicant performed in the eyes of others. A sample introductory letter and accompanying reference form are shown in Figure 5.6.

Early childhood teachers wanted for a college-sponsored child development center. Responsibilities include planning and implementing developmentally appropriate activities for a group of twelve 3-year-old children. A.A./A.S. degree in child development/early childhood education or a CDA certificate required; teaching experience preferred. Essential functions include constantly maintaining visual supervision of children to ensure safety and occasionally lifting, carrying, and holding children. Write for an application to Mrs. A. Jones, Director, Johnson County Community College Child Development Center, (*address*) or call (*telephone/fax*) Monday through Thursday between 2:00 and 4:00 P.M. Deadline for applications, August 1. We are an Equal Opportunity Employer.

Figure 5.4
Job Advertisement

Application For Teacher Position

JOHNSON COUNTY COMMUNITY COLLEGE CHILD DEVELOPMENT CENTER

Name of application _____   _____   _____
                          Last   First   Middle or maiden

Address _____   Zip _____

Telephone number ( ) _____

RECORD OF EDUCATION

High school(s) attended

Name of school   School address   Years attended   Years completed (check)

1. _____   _____   From _____   Fr. _____ Soph. _____ Jr. _____
                        _____   to _____   Sr. _____ Graduated _____

2. _____   _____   From _____   Fr. _____ Soph. _____ Jr. _____
                        _____   to _____   Sr. _____ Graduated _____

College(s) attended

Name of college   Address   Years attended   Level completed (check)

1. _____   _____   From _____   No degree: _____
                        _____   to _____   Degree received: _____
                                                                         Major: _____

2. _____   _____   From _____   No degree: _____
                        _____   to _____   Degree received: _____
                                                                         Major: _____

Teaching certificates _____

_____ (Name of certificate)

RECORD OF WORK EXPERIENCE

Name and address of employer(s)	Date(s) of employment	Nature of work (Describe)
1. _____	From _____ to _____	_____
2. _____	From _____ to _____	_____
3. _____	From _____ to _____	_____

List names and addresses of three references who are familiar with your educational progress and/or work experiences.

1. _____
2. _____
3. _____

I understand that my signature on this application legally permits authorized administrators of the Johnson County Community College Child Development Center to contact all former employers concerning my work history and character as it pertains to the position for which I have applied.

_____ (Signature)

_____ (Date)

Figure 5.5
Application for Teacher Position

Johnson County Community College Child Development Center

TO: _____

FROM: _____

RE: _____
(Name of applicant)

The applicant has given your name as a person who can provide a reference on his or her qualifications. We want to select teachers whose professional preparation, experience, and personality can be expected to produce the best results at our Child Development Center. Please give your full and frank evaluation. Your reply will be kept in strict confidence. Please assist both us and the applicant by replying promptly.

Teaching Position Reference

How would you describe the applicant's ability in each of the following areas?

1. Knowledge of young children's development:

2. Ability to plan developmentally appropriate activities to enrich and extend children's development:

3. Ability to implement planned activities to enrich and extend children's development:

4. Ability to use positive guidance including disciplining techniques with children:

5. Ability to assess children's progress:

6. Ability to organize a physical setting:

7. Ability to work with family members:

8. Ability to work with other staff members as a team:

9. Capacity for professional and personal growth:

On the basis of your present knowledge, would you employ this applicant in a program for which you were responsible? _____

Please explain: _____

What opportunity have you had to form your judgment of this applicant? _____
_____

Additional remarks: _____

_____   _____   _____
        (Date)   (Signature)   (Title)

Figure 5.6
Sample Introductory Letter and Reference Form

2. **Employment Eligibility Verification.**   The U.S. Department of Justice, Bureau of Citizenship and Immigration Services has a form with instructions for obtaining employment eligibility verification that is used to establish identity and employment eligibility.

3. **Criminal History Records Checks.**   Since 1985, many states have passed laws requiring national criminal history records checks for child care center employees. These laws were implemented to comply with federal legislation. Criminal history record checks are the only way to defend against a claim of *negligent hire,* in which an employer is held responsible for injuries to a third party if the injury was foreseeable or if the employer did not investigate before hiring.

Interviewing.   Following the screening of applicants and obtaining documentation, all promising applicants should be interviewed. The following steps should be used in the interview process:

1. The director must follow established board policies concerning the nature, setting, and person(s) conducting the interview (e.g., board's personnel committee in large programs or the board member, director, or staff member(s) responsible to the new employee), along with determining who will make the final decision regarding selection.

2. The director must be careful to follow Title VII of the 1964 Civil Rights Act prohibiting discriminatory hiring practices. The rule of thumb is that all questions asked of the applicant must have a "business necessity." Some questions to avoid are date of birth or age, marital status, spouse's occupation; pregnancy issues and number of children; child care arrangements; religious affiliation (although inquiry may be made whether the scheduled workdays are suitable); membership in organizations (except those pertaining to the position); race or national origin (except for affirmative action information); arrest record; type of discharge from the military; union memberships; and disabilities (ask only whether the person can perform job specific functions).

3. For teaching positions, the beliefs and values of teachers need to be consonant with those of the program vision, mission, and philosophy. The interview should reveal the applicant's ideas and attitudes toward children. To understand what values and beliefs might support an interviewee's teaching practices, the interviewer should ask questions about how the applicant sees his or her role in working with young children. Interviewers who prefer a written discussion guide can use Bloom, Sheerer, and Britz's (1991) assessment tool "Beliefs and Values" (pp. 232–233), which is designed to get adults to reflect on their attitudes and beliefs about children, families, and the teacher's role. Some teachers bring professional teaching portfolios that can be used to document interview answers (Hurst, Wilson, & Cramer, 1998). Interview questions should also match the type of candidate (e.g., with older candidates, focus on experiences rather than on career paths; Newman et al., 1992).

4. After ascertaining the applicant's ideas and attitudes toward children, the interviewer should discuss and answer questions about the program, such as the program vision, mission, nad philosophy; the ages of enrolled children; the guidance and discipline practices; how children are assessed; the degree of family involvement; a complete description of the job; salary; the length of school day and year; opportunities for promotion; fringe benefits; sick leave and retirement plans; consulting and supervisory services; and the nature and use of assessment to determine job performance and advancement. (For future reference, a staff policy handbook containing such information should be made available to those hired.)

Hiring.   The applicants are informed about the selection at a given date and in a specified manner. The person who is hired must usually sign a contract and other required personnel papers. If no applicant is hired, the recruitment process is repeated.

Many programs give the hired applicant a trial work period in which the director or hiring committee tries to see how compatible the person is with program practices. The conditions of the probationary period must be clearly communicated to the new employee before hiring. The trial period should last 6 months or less, and pay should be slightly less than full salary.

LAYING THE FOUNDATION FOR A COMMUNITY

An early childhood program is an organization that operates within the cultural and community contexts in which it is located. Programs are affected by the local community—its human and financial resources. On the human side, directors interact with other community leaders (i.e., leaders serving various agencies and social interest groups and directors of other early childhood programs), select and hire staff members and recruit volunteers from within the community, and serve community clients (i.e., children and their families). On the financial side, the program is affected by the community economic base and resources devoted to children and families.

Because each community has a culture that affects the early childhood program, directors must understand the local community. In building a knowledge base of the community culture, the director lays the foundation for a quality program (Brown & Manning, 2000) by doing the following:

1. Using the type of organizational structure (e.g., democratic) and the definition of leadership (e.g., collaborative) and characteristics (e.g., open communication style) that are most effective
2. Developing program services based on a vision of community needs and values
3. Being sensitive to the needs of staff members and volunteers
4. Providing a welcoming physical environment
5. Promoting a sense of belonging and a sense of community through the involvement of families and members of the broader community
6. Exploring other values, explaining why certain policies are needed, and resolving conflicts between professional and personal values
7. Gaining the insight needed for resource development, marketing, and advocacy and networking within the local community for in-service training of staff members, connecting families to other community resources, and promoting community projects.

BUILDING A POSITIVE AND PRODUCTIVE WORK CLIMATE FOR STAFF

As previously discussed, administrators' responsibilities include both leadership and management components. Leadership is the ability to balance the organization's need for productivity and quality with the needs of the staff. For example, task performance cannot be at the expense of work relationships. Leadership involves the process of making decisions that mold ever-changing goals and of securing the needed commitment to achieve the program's goals. Because leadership directly affects program quality, the term **leadership** seems to be replacing the term *administration*.

Even with great visions and commitment, all programs must function smoothly on a day-to-day basis. Thus, administrators are also responsible for the management component, which focuses on the specific tactics of getting and keeping the program running and provides continuity for program functioning.

Leadership in early childhood care and education is different from leadership in other organizations. Ideas about leadership in early childhood programs have not been based on traditional constructs. Kagan and Bowman (1997) suggested that traditional theories may not have been appropriate because these constructs represent a hierarchical model with a top-down view (i.e., vested right to use unilateral decision making) and a male-oriented (i.e., power-oriented) stance. This hierarchical model emphasizes results, not relations.

For over 2 decades, researchers have noted that the leadership styles in fields in which women predominate are more collaborative in nature (Hennig & Jardin, 1976; Lawler, Mohrman, & Ledford, 1992; Morrison, 1992). Collaborative models see leadership as authoritative rather than authoritarian (Rodd, 1998). Leaders in these models are committed to the growth of those under their leadership and thus to closing the status gap. These leaders use their authority mainly in implementing ideas coming out of the group process and in handling emergencies. Followers of collaborative leaders are committed to the ideas of the leader because they feel involved and valued (Kelley, 1991). Thus, collaborative leadership emphasizes both results and relations.

The early childhood field has had a long history of "shared leadership" (Kagan, 1994) or "participatory management" (Jorde-Bloom, 1995). Parents and professionals shared leadership in parent cooperatives and Head Start. Today, the emerging effort is toward networking and collaboration, but the team approach is not always carried out in the real world.

People in an early childhood program are not only individuals, but also part of a group—called the **faculty** or **staff.** Along with the personalities of these individuals, their roles and positions within the group shape their collective behavior or form the group's personality (Barker, Wahlers, Watson, & Kibler, 1987). In all organizations, including early childhood programs, responsibilities are carried out as a result of interpersonal relations more than of formal roles. Interpersonal relations include the way planning is conducted, decisions are made, and conflicts are resolved (Hoy & Miskel, 1987).

Staff members develop perceptions about their program. The collective perceptions are called the **climate** (Bloom, 1997a). The climate can be described in terms of the degree to which (a) the group understands and supports the leader's visions for the program, (b) the staff is involved in the collaborative effort and maintains collegiality during the process, and (c) the staff believes the administrator can provide both the expertise and time to manage the program.

Creating and Communicating a Culturally Relevant Vision

Leaders can shape their organizational environment and can transform the lives of those in their program and even the wider community. Carter and Curtis (1998) called for directors to have big dreams about the roles their programs can play in reshaping their communities. Many professionals admire the schools of Reggio Emilia because they were created from a culturally relevant vision.

To have a culturally relevant vision, program directors must constantly reexamine their programs in terms of the changing needs of clients and trends in the field. Rapid social changes have occurred in the lives of young children and their families. Drucker (1990) speaks of leaders seeing the connection between the missions of organizations and marketing (Who are your clients? What do they need and value? Do you offer what they need and value?).

In response to these changes, a new transdisciplinary knowledge base is forming in early childhood care and education (Stott & Bowman, 1996), and a growing need for family-centered services and collaboration with other community agencies is occurring (Kagan, Rivera, Brigham, & Rosenblum, 1992). Effective leaders have adapted their programs to meet the needs of clients and to make use of "best practices" knowledge.

The constant adaptation of services has required leaders who can create and communicate a culturally relevant vision. Carter and Curtis (1998) provided these practical suggestions for creating such a vision:

- Recall the vision that brought you to this field.
- Share memories of positive childhood experiences.
- Discuss positive experiences portrayed in children's books and how those could be implemented in your program.
- Ask family members to share their hopes for their children who are entering your program.

The vision provides the direction for innovative decisions to bridge the gap between present services and projected needs. Without a vision, the leader will be caught too frequently in *crisis change* (i.e., response to an unexpected occurrence) or *transformational change* (i.e., radical alteration of the organization in order to survive; Rodd, 1998). Visions always involve changes. Unlike reacting to crisis and transformational changes, initiating innovative changes allows leaders to move their programs in the desirable direction for the following reasons:

1. Leaders can ponder the best- and worst-case scenarios and take only carefully calculated risks. Once they have foresight into the needed changes, they are willing to accept change and convince others to accept it; in short, they are mission driven (Collins & Porras, 1994).

2. Leaders can study the entire picture of change from a systems perspective. A systems perspective, according to Bloom and colleagues (1991), involves (a) changing people's knowledge, skills, or attitudes; (b) changing the process (e.g., goal setting, decision making); and (c) changing the structure (e.g., goals, policies, housing, budget). If all three are not changed, dysfunction occurs in the system. Looking at changes from a systems perspective allows the leader to look at costs (time, money, disruption) versus positive results (services wanted or needed by clients, effectiveness, efficiency).

3. Leaders can evaluate results. For example, results may be considered positive when they bring status to a program, are cost effective, or produce efficiency. Because change takes time and occurs in stages, Likert (1967) suggested that leaders need to wait a minimum of 2 years to see real change. As noted in longitudinal programmatic research, output can be delayed. Even when the change in programs seems simple, often intervening variables cause delay (e.g., How long would it take to change staff attitudes concerning the inclusion of children with developmental delay in general education classrooms?).

Leaders must communicate—literally sell—their visions to their staff. If innovative change is to be effective, the leader must begin with the vision, identify why the change is needed, set goals and objectives, delegate responsibilities, set standards of performance, and establish time frames. Change through collaborative endeavors takes longer than top-down change. Although some changes may be mandated by a leader, lack of trust in the vision or even in the leader often occurs in authoritarian situations. Many changes require collaboration to be effective because they are often implemented by the staff (e.g., curriculum changes).

Collaborating

Program effectiveness is most efficiently achieved through collaboration. Often, directors view their early childhood programs as having more effective collaboration than do staff members (Bloom, 1995). It is important, in establishing a collaborative culture, for the staff to perceive the center administration as collaborative. Staff perceptions can be checked through individual interviews or conversations and through other formal means (Bloom et al., 1991, pp. 192–196; Smylie, 1992). Early childhood programs must go beyond a verbal commitment to collaboration to actually using the process.

The following are four levels of decision making that, when used appropriately can foster the development of a collaborative work environment:

a. **Unilateral**—The director makes the call.
b. **Consultative**—The director seeks input from others before making the call.
c. **Collaborative**—The director and others analyze the problem, generate and evaluate possible solutions, and then decide on the action.
d. Delegative—The director provides information, and others make the decision. (Bloom, 2000a).

In business, names for shared decision making include *total quality management, site-based management, quality circles, management by consensus,* and *participatory management.* Leaders must determine whether a decision should be determined through

For collaboration to truly be effective, the program director must engage in meaningful, nonthreatening communication.

collaboration. Collaborative decision making is more appropriate for novel situations that call for problem solving than for routine decisions. Bloom also stated that directors should consider the personal interests or stakes of others in the issue and others' degree of input-competence. Directors must be forthright about how input from others will be used.

Steps in Collaborating.   The steps in decision making through collaborative means are much like the steps involved in any process of decision making. The first step is pinpointing the problem. Assessing needs makes others understand that improvement is a shared responsibility. To pinpoint a problem, one has to realize that the symptoms are not necessarily the problem itself. Thus, one has to collect accurate data on the problem. Data can be collected through anonymous questionnaires or interviews (see Bloom et al., 1991) or through documents or records on staff, children, and family members. It is important, however, that multiple stakeholders be engaged in the process of identifying the problem. This way the process is collaborative right from the start.

The second step involves considering different potential solutions and assessing each one. The main question is, What do we need to do to achieve our goal? Decisions should be based more on evidence than on personal opinion or tradition. The code of ethics (see chapter 13) should also guide the process when dealing with ethical dilemmas.

Finally, the group must select the best alternative, develop a plan of action, and implement it. Other decisions must be made, such as who will do each aspect of the plan, what is needed to accomplish the plan (time and monetary resources), and how and when improvements will be measured.

Roles of the Leader During Collaboration.   Collaborative teamwork occurs when individual needs are subordinated to achieve program goals. The director serves as the leader of the team. During the process of collaborating, the leader keeps the task structure clear (i.e., helps the group determine the problem or issue, the goal to be achieved, and the process of attaining the goal or desired results) and ensures constructive relationships. To be successful, a leader must assume several responsibilities.

Motivating Collaborative Efforts.   The leader must encourage the participation of the entire group involved in the proposed change. Rodd (1998) stated that individuals have "the right to be cautious about anything new but not the right to not grow and develop" (p. 132). Several suggestions for motivating are as follows:

1. The leader must convince others that the job itself is important. Because early childhood care and education are inherently important work, leaders find it relatively easy to convince others that their jobs are important. Still, leaders must build a sense of community and foster the "we" feeling of meeting the dynamic needs of children and their families.

2. The leader must know staff attitudes. Several instruments are available to help with this (see Bloom et al., 1991, pp. 42, 170–176, 255–255). Shoemaker (2000) developed an "Analysis of Staff Motivation" questionnaire (pp. 158–160).

3. Leaders need to build self-esteem in employees. Bandura (1982) theorized that people must be convinced that they will be successful before they attempt goals. Thus, leaders need to (a) have a democratic organizational climate that provides appropriate autonomy, (b) coach for collaborative work, (c) provide staff needed training and time to learn new skills, and (d) reward individuals with recognition and greater responsibility along with external rewards (e.g., salary increases, job security).

Communicating with Others.   The success of leadership rests almost totally on the ability to communicate because it is the method of attaining shared meanings. During collaboration, leaders must communicate with others their commitment to have an impact on the lives of young children and their families and to implement the visions for their programs. Understanding differences in values and using culturally sensitive communication are important.

To be successful, leaders must recognize barriers to communication (e.g., differences in cultures, staff members working in separate rooms and/or with different age groups of children, interruptions and noise level). To move the collaborative process forward, they must listen, reflect, provide support and objective feedback, and consider the effects their words have on others. See Figure 5.7.

Overseeing Conflicts.   Collaborative decision making leads to fewer conflicts. Conflicts are higher both under authoritarian leadership in which people feel left out of decision making and under permissive leadership in which people want guidance but do not have it. In collaborative decision making, conflicts most often arise because many beliefs are subjective (Clyde & Rodd, 1989) and because collaboration is not majority rule, but consensus building.

Reflective Listening Skills

- Understanding content
- Comprehending body language and paralinguistics (tone of voice)

Response Skills

- Setting decision-making parameters
- Stating one's reflections of another's comments as part of the response
- Being sensitive to others' values and feelings
- Using appropriate self-assertion when needed

Figure 5.7
Needed Communication Skills

Leaders can manage conflicts in a constructive way by describing the conflict situation, communicating understandings of the various perspectives, brainstorming for alternatives, and trying and evaluating alternatives to find the best solution. Sustaining issue-based conflict—not hurting individuals—is desirable because it can lead to "collective wisdom" (Jones & Nimmo, 1999).

Delegating Responsibilities.   Leaders must distinguish between the tasks the leader must do and those others can do. When delegating responsibilities, the leader must match the tasks to staff members' skills and interests. People can also volunteer for tasks, but it is still important for the leader to ensure a match between individual competence and the desired result.

As part of the delegating process, leaders must be clear about what needs to be done, the deadlines for completion, and the levels of authority and accountability. Leaders must explain that they will not be supervising the tasks but are available to help gather needed tools and information and for support.

Managing

Management skills are necessary for program survival. Managing is the technical aspect of administration. The director is the technical expert who is responsible for the execution of the program. The specific tasks vary from program to program.

Excellent managers are good at time management (getting things done quickly without undue stress). Interruptions and not keeping contacts with others to the point are the main enemies of time management in early childhood programs. Effective time management requires organizing the office; setting goals and matching smaller tasks to goals; establishing priorities among activities and investing maximum time in productive activities; doing the necessary but undesirable tasks, and analyzing impediments to completing tasks.

ENRICHING THE PROFESSIONAL LIFE OF THE STAFF

The most important role of the director is to enable conditions that lead to an enriching professional life for the staff. To enrich the professional life of the staff, directors must assess both collective and individual needs and then plan ways to meet both.

Assessing Staff Professional Development Needs

Defining competence in terms of the exact background needed is difficult. Certain core knowledge and skills are needed and must be acquired through experience by all early childhood professionals because these are correlated with classroom quality and positive teacher behaviors. All personnel need to refresh current skills and learn new ones that will help with the changes that are occurring in teaching and enable them to discard inappropriate practices and rebuild appropriate practices.

Because early childhood personnel differ widely in their educational backgrounds and are at different stages in their careers, they experience unique individual needs. Early childhood professionals serve in different roles, too. For example, family child care providers have different needs from personnel in child care centers (Trawick-Smith & Lambert, 1995). Thus, to be effective, leaders must assess both the collective and the individual needs of staff members if they hope to improve the quality of the program and provide opportunities for professional growth accordingly.

Professional development should continue throughout a staff member's tenure, as each staff member continually works to improve knowledge and skills in their work with young children. To be effective, professional development must be seen as an active process of growing and learning, and not a product (e.g., a workshop presented by someone else). Thus, professional development plans should be based on a systematic review of staff knowledge and performance and include self-reflection as part of the process in determining specific topics for professional development. Abbott-Shim (1990) recommended the use of data from individual job performance assessments, needs assessment surveys, and program evaluations. Data can be collected in the following ways:

1. **Staff job performance assessments** show the strengths and weaknesses of individual staff members. A summary of strengths and weaknesses of staff members can be used to determine potential training areas.
2. **Needs assessment surveys** are surveys in which staff check topics of perceived needs. The director summarizes the responses and identifies training needs. A simple needs assessment survey is given in Figure 5.8.
3. **Program evaluation measures** provide comprehensive evaluation, including sections measuring staff competencies, family perceptions of program strengths and weaknesses, and child outcomes.

Application Activity

Think about the current staff evaluation system that you have in place. When was the most recent formal evaluation of staff performance and knowledge? What was the outcome of such an evaluation? Based on the information presented up to this point, what ways could you strengthen the staff evaluation process at your center, and how could you better use the results to inform professional development?

Identifying Individual Needs.   Staff training has to be individualized because staff members are unique individuals at different stages of development, with different abilities and teaching styles and different roles. For example, Katz (1995) identified four stages of development and the training needs of in-service teachers at each stage:

1. Survival.   The first year of teaching is filled with self-doubt. Teachers need on-site support and technical assistance.
2. Consolidation.   During the second and perhaps third year, teachers consolidate the gains they have made and focus on specific skills. They need on-site assistance, access to specialists, and advice from colleagues.
3. Renewal.   During the third and fourth years, job stress is alleviated through assistance in the analysis of teaching and participation in professional associations.
4. Maturity.   After the fifth year, teachers benefit from additional formal education, professional conferences, and contributions to the profession (e.g., journal writing).

Providing Professional Development

As previously noted, early childhood care and education is a two-tiered system of teacher regulation. Unlike public school teachers, who have a preservice credential, many other teachers are hired without credential (Mitchell, 1996). This trend has important implications for professional development in traditional child care centers. We are much more reliant on in-service training to ensure that all staff members are able to meet the care and education needs of the children in their charge. Thus, the director is often responsible for planning and implementing **staff development activities** (all activities that aid staff in providing quality for the early childhood program).

Needs Assessment Survey of
Johnson County Community College Child Development Center

We need some information regarding your specific needs for training. After reading the entire list below, check 6 topics (from the 48 listed) that you would like to have covered in in-service training. After checking, rank the topics in order of importance, with "1" being the most important to you.

Child care

_____ Regulations/legal issues
_____ Evaluation of children
_____ Mainstreaming exceptional children
_____ Health and safety

Child development

_____ Physical development (general)
_____ Social development
_____ Cognitive development
_____ Emotional development
_____ Morals/values development
_____ Language development
_____ Motor skill development

Curriculum (preschool through primary)

_____ Art
_____ Oral language
_____ Writing
_____ Literature
_____ Prereading skills
_____ Mathematics
_____ Social studies
_____ Science
_____ Music
_____ Gross-motor play
_____ Fine-motor play
_____ Incorporating computers
_____ Incorporating multicultural/multilingual learnings
_____ Cooking experiences

_____ Sand/water/mud play
_____ Woodworking experiences
_____ Block-building experiences
_____ Dramatic play experiences

Organization and management

_____ Arranging physical environments
_____ Use of indoor equipment/materials
_____ Use of outdoor equipment/materials
_____ Scheduling problems
_____ Transitions
_____ Grouping
_____ Encouraging effective child–child interactions
_____ Encouraging effective child–adult interactions
_____ Encouraging effective child–material interactions
_____ Guiding children's behavior (discipline)

Staff needs

_____ Credentials/training requirements
_____ Communication skills
_____ Team teaching
_____ Evaluation
_____ Policy development

Families

_____ Family education
_____ Family involvement
_____ Family support
_____ Meeting needs of special families
   (e.g., single parents)

Figure 5.8
Staff Training Needs Assessment Survey

Staff development is designed to ensure that all staff members receive/construct needed knowledge, skills, and attitudes that will facilitate the provision of high-quality services to children and families. Most professionals see staff development as a major catalyst to the development of high-quality programs for young children.

Regrettably, planning and implementing staff development have not been easy tasks for directors. The Cost, Quality, and Child Outcomes Study Team (1995) found that centers scored low on opportunities for professional growth. Regardless of the difficulties involved, directors play critical roles in the quality of their programs through leadership in professional growth opportunities (Bredekamp, 1990; Jorde-Bloom, Sheerer, & Britz 1991). Improving the quality of personnel has been accomplished by encouraging and supporting more formal education; mentoring and coaching for professional development; providing various group professional development activities; urging professional affiliations; and assessing job performance.

All staff development activities need to involve the following:

1. Active learning.   Active learning involves activities such as collaborating on a project, debating issues, and participating in community activities. Active learning is a way to balance practical and theoretical knowledge, allow adults to learn in the same ways we want children to learn, and stimulate creativity (Cuffaro, 1995; Jones, 1986; Piscitelli, 2000).

2. Reflective practice.   Reflective practice requires teachers to think about their experiences and interactions and adjust activities based on their reflections. Many resources are available to help teachers become more reflective (Rand, 2000; Tertell, Klein, & Jewett, 1998).

3. Individualized activities.   Staff training must move away from the cookie-cutter approach to an individualized one. Content is determined by assessing collective (i.e., local program) and individual needs. Staff members need to have input into the planning.

Encouraging Formal Education.   From its beginning, the kindergarten movement required a course of study for prospective teachers. As kindergartens and other early childhood programs became part of the public schools, teachers were required to obtain degrees from postsecondary institutions and state-granted teaching certificates. Local boards of education also required refresher courses or work toward an advanced degree for renewal of a contract and pay raises. Katz (1995) indicated that teachers in the stages of renewal and maturity (after 3 to 5 years of experience) are in need of college work.

Unlike public school teachers, preschool teachers, especially those working in child care centers, more often pursue formal education after being employed. To encourage staff members to pursue formal education as an in-service activity, directors must

  a. Coordinate training offered by institutions and staff members' needs and availability for training
  b. Work out other problems associated with training (e.g., classroom coverage during work hours and babysitting and transportation services for after-hours training)
  c. Supervise field experiences
  d. Provide salary increments or career advancement as recognition for completed work

To encourage staff members to acquire more formal education, a growing number of states have launched initiatives. The best known initiative is the TEACH (Teacher Education and Compensation Helps) Early Childhood Project, which began in North Carolina in 1990 and has spread to 17 other states. Teachers receive scholarships to attend school and bonus pay when they complete their study; in turn, teachers commit to working in their sponsoring program for at least one more year (Olson, 2002).

Mentoring for Professional Development.   **Mentoring** is the supporting and coaching of a *protégé* (novice staff member) by a *mentor* (educated, experienced, and dedicated staff member). In some cases, mentoring may involve peer coaching (i.e., between two inexperienced teachers), but this model is seldom used. The overall purpose of mentoring is to serve as a bridge between preservice training and early practice or as a way to learn new skills anytime.

Performance supervision is an idea that dates to the 1920s. School supervisors provided help to novice teachers and also evaluated them. Today's mentoring models, which evolved from the industrial concept called **quality circles,** seldom use directors as mentors.

Values of Mentoring.   As a result of problems faced by beginning teachers and high rates of teacher turnover and attrition, mentoring is gaining support. Mentoring enhances the work of the mentor and the knowledge and skills of the protégé. More specifically, research on mentoring shows that mentoring builds leadership (Whitebook, Hnatiuk, & Bellm, 1994), helps counter high turnover rates (Kremer-Hazon & Ben-Peretz, 1996), increases feelings of professional growth (Rosenholtz, Bassler, & Hoover-Dempsey, 1986), and instills a sense of community (Newman, Rutter, & Smith, 1989).

Mentoring seems especially appropriate in predominantly female careers because women appear to benefit from more mentor-initiated contact, more feedback, and more modeling than men (Schneider, 1991). Because of its success, mentoring is now seen in public schools and in many states' early childhood care and education career lattices.

Mentoring Models and Processes.   Mentoring models may work in various ways. For example, some mentors work with one type of program (e.g., family child care), whereas others work with more than one type of program. Some serve as mentors in specific areas (e.g., in the use of assistive technologies or developing literacy skills in children), whereas others work with their protégés on all aspects of their tasks (e.g., in the process of obtaining a CDA credential). Variations in the setting (e.g., the protégé's classroom) and approaches (e.g., one-on-one mentoring, one mentor to several protégés) are also common (Bellm, Whitebook, & Hnatiuk, 1997; Center for Career Development in Early Care and Education at Wheelock College, 2000; "Taking the Lead Initiative," 2000).

The mentoring process usually works this way:

1. The mentor gets to know the responsibilities and program settings of the protégé.
2. With the protégé, the mentor helps establish expectations for the process.
3. The protégé discusses perceived needs. (For example, the protégé might want to use Bellm and colleagues' [1997] "Self-Evaluation Checklist" [pp. 91–93].)
4. The protégé and mentor agree on specific goals.
5. The mentor and protégé develop a plan of action (i.e., meeting times and how the mentoring will work).
6. The mentor and protégé prepare a plan of action; the protégé tries out the plan; the mentor observes and gathers data; the mentor and protégé both take some time to reflect on outcomes before discussing the results; the protégé reflects on his or her teaching with the mentor's help (e.g., What do you think happened? How did _____ affect the outcome?). The protégé draws inferences.
7. Together the protégé and mentor decide whether goals and strategies should be incorporated into the teaching repertoire or whether they need to be refined or alternative ideas selected.

Requirements for Effective Mentoring.   Some requirements of effective mentoring follow:

1. Select the best mentors possible. Although some qualities of mentors may vary by culture, generally mentors should
    a. Have training and experience in child development and early childhood education, adult learning, reflective practice, and leadership
    b. Have the ability to be supportive of protégés and build a collaborative approach (see "Taking the Pulse of Your Relationship: A Checklist for Mentors" in Bellm et al., 1997, p. 74)

    c. Use different mentoring methods to match protégés' abilities and learning styles and the goals to be achieved, and be creative problem solvers

    d. Have good communication skills and be able to observe and record protégés' performances

    e. Be able to clarify differences in opinions, knowledge-based "best practices," and mandates

    f. Be good role models

2. Match the mentor with the protégé based on the protégé's needs, abilities, and learning style.

3. Find release time for the mentor, the protégé, or both.

4. Provide necessary coverage of the mentor's and protégé's responsibilities during the process.

5. Collect resources on mentoring (see end of chapter).

6. Budget stipends and wage increases for both mentors and protégés.

Providing Group Professional Development Activities. Group techniques for staff development are also used. Like mentoring, group techniques should fit staff members' abilities, skills, and interests as well as possess appropriate training content. For example, Latimer (1994) gave some pointers on training older adults. The method of presentation should be varied to hold interest. And, most important, staff members must be involved and able to see the direct application of the training to their professional responsibilities.

Finding time for group activities is difficult. Staff development cannot occur during nap time. Staff development needs to occur on a regular basis, with staff receiving release time or appropriate compensation. The following are several ways of handling staff development:

1. The center or school may be closed on certain days for staff development. (Parents should have them on their calendar at the time of enrollment.)

2. The center may close for a week during periods of low enrollment. These are also excellent times for hiring substitute help or getting volunteers.

3. Evening sessions can work. (Serving dinner and having child care for staff are nice touches.)

Discussions. Staff meetings can be used for discussions (see Figure 5.9 for general tips). Staff should *share* ideas rather than have the director do all the presenting. Staff can learn through discussing and solving problems. Teachers can gain much from reflection on their own work. After sharing ideas, each staff member should try one or more ideas during work.

Staff can also gain from the sharing of personal narratives. Change in teaching occurs through the process of listening and responding (Cinnamond & Zimpher, 1990). Narratives are not new in early childhood education (Ashton-Warner, 1963; Pratt, 1948). Recently published narratives (listed at the end of the chapter) are good for staff development.

Discussions can occur on any aspect of the program. Because of staff diversity, beliefs and values about program goals and policies should be explored through discussions (Carter, 1992). Exchanges of ideas and feelings about issues and role clarification (see Bloom et al., 1991, pp. 233–252) are most helpful.

Workshops and Consultation. Workshops are the most common form of training (Kisker, Hofferth, Phillips, & Farquhar, 1991). They may be provided through outside sources (e.g., professional organizations) or developed by staff members themselves. The term *workshop* implies an activity-oriented, as opposed to a presentation-only, session and often centers on one topic. Teachers need to have options on topics. (See Abbott-Shim, 1990; Bloom, 2000c; and Carter, 1993 for some ideas.)

- Divide discussion content into categories (e.g., children's program, parents, administration). Decide which category is covered at a given time (e.g., children's program—first Tuesday of each month; parents—second Tuesday of every other month). Routine announcements may be distributed at the end of each meeting or handled in other ways.
- Make meetings relevant to those in attendance. Thus, in some cases, assistant teachers may not need to meet with lead teachers.
- Prepare an agenda a few days before a scheduled meeting. Make any needed materials available at this time. The agenda should indicate the amount of time for presentation and for discussion.
- Start and stop the meeting on time.
- Distribute minutes of the meeting to staff.

Figure 5.9
Tips on Staff Meeting Discussions

If consultation is to yield lasting results, consultants must be viewed as resource people and not as "experts" hired to solve problems. They need to be aware of the real-life concerns of staff (Trawick-Smith & Lambert, 1995) and facilitate staff members in resolving their own problems. If consultant work is to be secured, the administrator must identify potential resource people, describe (in writing) training needs, and provide a format to be completed by potential resource people. Figure 5.10 is an example of a workshop proposal format. Both proposals and presentations should be evaluated as shown in Figure 5.11.

Self-Study in Accreditation and Program Evaluation.   The accreditation process is a major avenue for staff development because it involves self-study. Certain items from other program evaluations are appropriate for staff development, too.

Workshop Proposal

The following information must be submitted for consideration as a resource person for the Johnson County Community College Child Development Center.

Name, address, day and evening phone numbers of individuals submitting request.

Main presenter résumé (title, academic and professional background).

Names and addresses and résumés of other presenters.

Objectives of presentation.

Outline of presentation.

   Concept:

   Delivery strategy:

   Time required:

Method to be used to evaluate workshop effectiveness.

Resource materials provided by consultant.

Special requests (e.g., observation in center before presentation, audiovisual equipment).

Figure 5.10
Example of a Workshop Proposal Format

Evaluation of_____
Johnson County Community College Child Development Center

Rank each item on a 3-point scale: 1 (Excellent), 2 (Satisfactory), and 3 (Poor).

	Proposal	*Presentation*
Objectives related to training needs	_____	_____
Content related to training needs	_____	_____
Content applicable to work with children	_____	_____
Content organized	_____	_____
Content clearly presented	_____	_____
Delivery strategies held interests of participants	_____	_____
Delivery strategies encouraged give-and-take among staff members and between staff and resource person(s)	_____	_____
Evaluation seemed effective	_____	_____
Resource materials seemed practical	_____	_____

Comments: _____

_____

_____

_____

Figure 5.11
Example of an Evaluation Format for Workshops and Consultation

Use of Professional Development Resources.   All programs can benefit from the use of professional journals, books, and audiovisual materials. Professional organizations publish many useful materials in many formats.

Urging Professional Affiliations.   Membership in professional organizations offers various opportunities for personnel to improve their qualifications. Regrettably, many staff members do not belong to any professional group (Galinsky, Howes, Kontos, & Shinn, 1994; Whitebook et al., 1990).

Professional organizations publish literature such as journals, position papers, and other materials to aid members in professional growth and competence. Almost all professional organizations have regular national, regional, and state meetings that provide a means for hearing and seeing the "latest" and for sharing ideas with others. Professional organizations serve as public representation—advocacy—of members' views to local, state, and national governing bodies. Some organizations offer opportunities for travel and study, research assistance, and consultation. Others provide personal services to members, such as insurance policies and loans. Finally, membership in a professional organization says to families and the community in general, "I am joining with others in an effort to provide the best for our children." See appendix 8 for a list of many professional organizations concerned with the development of young children.

Assessing Job Performance.   Directors have the overall responsibility for staff assessment. Sometimes a board member is also involved. Large corporate systems use regional staff administrators to do the assessment. In public schools, principals and central office supervisors assess staff.

Purposes.   Assessing job performance provides a mirror for what is happening in the program; that is, assessing job performance can aid in determining the effectiveness of the program in attaining its vision and diagnosing some of its problems. Caruso and Fawcett (1999) stated that "probably no other supervisory process has the *potential* to affect the quality of learning experiences for children as what staff members learn about themselves" (p. 151). The process of assessing job performance aids staff members in realizing that they are professionals (Duff, Brown, & Van Scoy, 1995).

Assessment may be formative or summative. **Formative assessment** is focused on the diagnostic (reflects the strengths and weaknesses of a staff member) and is thus used to promote growth. Formative assessment is usually focused on one problem or a group of related problems at one time (e.g., planning or arranging the physical facility). Teachers want the assessment process to imply that there are always areas in which one can learn and improve. Teachers should also use self-assessment as formative assessment.

Summative assessment lets persons know how they perform against certain predetermined criteria. Summative assessment "sums up" performance in that it looks at overall performance. Thus, summative assessment is used for such decisions as continuing employment, offering tenure, and advancing merit pay. For the present purposes, only formative assessment is considered because all other purposes of assessment, such as tenure and merit pay, should be based on performance.

Criteria for Assessment.   Criteria for assessment should reflect the specific responsibilities of a staff member and be appropriate for the professional level of that person. Generally, personnel who provide similar services should be assessed according to the same criteria, but personnel serving in dissimilar roles should be assessed according to different criteria, although some assessment items might be the same.

Assessments should be based on observations of performance and the observer's perceptions of the staff member's intentions. Several assessment tools are available and can be adapted to fit local needs. Some sources of criteria include the following:

1. The common elements that "define what all early childhood professionals must know and be able to do" (p. 13) based on a position statement of the NAEYC (Willer, 1994)
2. The CDA competency standards (Council for Early Childhood Professional Recognition, 1996)
3. "Criteria for High-Quality Early Childhood Programs" given in the guide to accreditation by the National Academy of Early Childhood Programs (NAEYC, 2005)

Besides having the director observe their performance, staff members need to be reflective of their own performance through self-assessment. Although few self-assessment scales are available, the University of South Carolina Children's Center has developed a scale that requires the teacher to reflect on his or her satisfaction with career choice, professional performances, collaborative relations, and long-term career goals (Duff et al., 1995).

Methods of Observing and Recording.   After criteria for assessing personnel performance have been determined, they must be incorporated into an appraisal instrument. Locally devised assessment procedures may include the following:

1. **Narratives** are based on observations. These observations may be open ended or may focus on specific areas, such as guidance of children or planning. During observations, the director observes the staff member and notes specific strengths and weaknesses of the performance on the basis of the criteria selected for that particular job category. Sometimes

a staff member is asked to make a self-assessment based on personal recollections. Video-tapes are also becoming a popular means of affirming the director's observations, the staff member's self-assessment, or both. Videotapes do not seem as judgmental as verbal or written critiques.

2. Portfolios are also being used in some programs. A portfolio is a collection of materials (e.g., written work, tapes, photographs) that teachers collect and assemble to represent their performance. Thus, portfolios are an extension of narratives.

3. Interview procedures may be developed as assessment instruments. On the one hand, an interview may take the form of an open-ended discussion concerning strengths, performance areas needing improvement, and discussions on how to make needed improvements. On the other hand, some interview forms may, in actuality, be verbal rating scales.

4. Checklists and **rating scales** usually list assessment criteria in categories. Many check sheets and rating scales also include an overall assessment for each category of characteristics, for total performance, or for both. Although check sheets and rating scales are written assessment instruments, each instrument has a distinctive style. The check sheet can be used to indicate those behaviors satisfactorily completed by a staff member. The administrator may check "yes," "no," or "not applicable" (see Figure 5.12). A rating scale, a qualitative assessment of performance, represents successive levels of quality along an inferior–superior continuum. The levels of quality may be described in different ways. (See Figures 5.13, 5.14, 5.15, and 5.16 .)

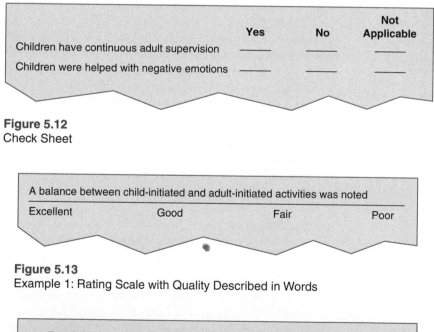

Figure 5.12
Check Sheet

Figure 5.13
Example 1: Rating Scale with Quality Described in Words

Figure 5.14
Example 2: Rating Scale with Quality Described in Words

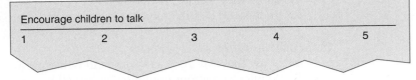

Figure 5.15
Rating Scale with Quality Described in Numerals

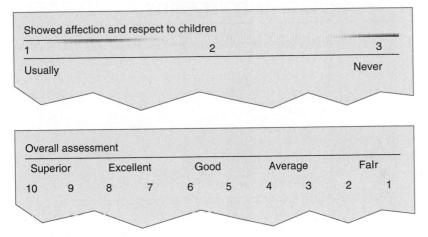

Figure 5.16
Rating Scale with Quality Described in Words and Numerals

Steps in Assessing. Directors should observe staff members many times before doing a formal observation. Caruso and Fawcett (1999) suggested these steps:

1. Do a pre-observation conference to review the purposes of the observation, discuss concerns, and plan procedures.
2. Conduct the formal observation.
3. Conduct the supervisory conference by setting the agenda, reviewing goals, discussing strengths and weaknesses, and making future plans.
4. Do a postconference analysis.

Frequency of Assessment. Informal assessment, especially self-assessment, should be conducted continually; however, the policy-making body should plan, determine the frequency of, and schedule formal assessment. Formative assessment should be conducted several times per year. Inexperienced teachers often need more assessments than do experienced teachers. Summative assessments are most often conducted annually.

Concerns. Directors need training and experience in assessing job performance. They must realize that observations are not totally objective but are affected by beliefs and values, stress, and program constraints beyond their control. Directors can also avoid some bias by getting a second opinion (i.e., asking another administrator to observe and look over the completed forms) before conferencing. Directors should ask themselves, Can I prove this statement? In talking about either strengths or weaknesses, directors should be careful about using superlatives, which can be misleading.

Regardless of the criteria chosen and the instruments selected, several basic principles need to be followed out of respect for each teacher and because appraisal records are legal documents. Staff must:

1. Know they will be assessed
2. Understand that their assessment is based on program goals and their job description
3. Be informed of the process
4. Know they will receive verbal and written results
5. Be informed about how the results will be used
6. Be assured that their assessment results are confidential and accessible only to those entitled to the information

PERSONNEL SERVICES AND RECORDS

State boards of education and licensing agencies require that certain personnel services be provided and records kept by early childhood programs under their respective jurisdictions. In addition to providing those mandated personnel services and records, local boards of education or boards of directors may provide additional services and require other records permitted by state law.

Contract and Terms of Employment

A **contract** is an agreement between two or more parties. In early childhood programs, a contract is an agreement between each staff member and the director or board specifying the services the staff member must provide and the specific sum of money to be paid for services rendered. Contracts may differ, depending on the job description (e.g., teacher and assistant teacher). All contracts should conform to the following guidelines:

A written agreement as opposed to an oral one

A specific designation of the parties to the contract

A statement of the legal capacity of the parties represented

A provision for signatures by the authorized agent(s) of and by the teacher

A clear stipulation of the salary to be paid

A designation of the date and duration of the contract and the date when service is to begin

A definition of the assignment

In signing a contract, an employee indirectly consents to obey all rules and regulations in force at the time of employment or adopted during the period of employment. Policies that most directly affect employees may include hours per day and days per week; vacation; specific requirements, such as a uniform or driver's license; sick, emergency, and maternity leaves; substitutes; insurance; salary increases and fringe benefits; and retirement plans. Each employee should have a written copy of all current policies.

The employee may receive a contract for some specified period of time, perhaps an annual or a continuing contract. Contracts for a specified period of time must be renewed at the end of such time period. The two types of continuing contracts are **notification** and **tenure.**

An individual having a notification continuing contract must be notified on or before a given date if the contract is not to be renewed. A tenure contract guarantees that an employee cannot be dismissed except for certain specific conditions, such as lack of funds to pay salaries, neglect of duty, incompetency, failure to observe regulations, and immorality. Furthermore, a dismissed tenured employee has the right to a hearing in which the board must prove just cause for the dismissal. Programs offering tenure require that an employee serve a probationary period of a given number of years (usually 3 or 5) before receiving a tenure contract.

Special service contracts must also be written when a limited service is to be performed by a temporary employee (e.g., consultant). This type of contract must clearly specify the services to be rendered; the date(s) services are to be performed, including any follow-up services; any special arrangements, such as materials to be supplied by a temporary employee (or by the employer); and the fee. The signatures of the temporary employee and the requester should be affixed to the contract, and the transaction should be dated.

Job Description

A job description for each personnel category should be written and kept current and should include the following:

1. Job title
2. Minimum qualifications
3. Primary duties and responsibilities
4. Working conditions
5. Additional duties
6. Reporting relationships and limits of authority
7. Benefits.

The Economic Employment Opportunity Commission (EEOC) will examine job descriptions for a section called *essential functions* (a part of the primary duties and responsibilities). If someone is not employed because of a disability, the director or board must be prepared to show that the function is essential to the job and cannot reasonably be performed by another staff member. (Essential functions must be in each job description prior to advertising.) Job descriptions should be specific to the particular early childhood program and position rather than adopted from another program. A potential employee should review the job description before signing a contract; all employees should keep their job descriptions in their files.

Application Activity

Do you have a job description for each hired position at your center? If not, create one that addresses all seven of the job description previously items identified. If you currently have a job description for each hired position at your center, review them to make sure they contain all the recommended information and the job description is up to date. A sample job description is shown in Figure 5.17.

Insurance and Retirement Plans

Various kinds of insurance and retirement plans protect employees and organizations. Adequate coverage is expensive, but essential. Some types of insurance and retirement plans may be mandated by state or federal laws, whereas other types may be voluntary.

Federal Insurance Contributions Act (FICA).   Most centers are required to pay FICA, or Social Security, tax. FICA tax is generally used for retirement purposes. Tax rates are set at a percentage of the employee's salary. The employer deposits quarterly the amount of the employee's contributions collected as payroll deductions plus an equal amount from the employer. (This money is deposited in a separate account because commingling of federal funds is prohibited by law.) A quarterly report on FICA taxes is also required. All organizations, including tax-exempt programs, are responsible for keeping up with current tax laws.

Johnson County Community College Child Development Center

Title: Teacher

Qualifications: A teacher shall have at least an A.A. degree in child development/early childhood education or hold a child development associate certificate. A teacher must also meet licensing regulations concerning minimum age and health status. The essential functions include constantly maintaining visual supervision of children to ensure safety and occasionally lifting, carrying, and holding children.

Primary duties and responsibilities: A teacher shall (1) plan and execute developmentally appropriate activities, (2) observe and evaluate children's progress, (3) provide a written report (on the forms provided) to the director and parents at least two times per year, (4) be available for informal parent-teacher contacts at the beginning and end of each session, and (5) perform other duties particular to the program.

Working conditions: A teacher is paid for an 8-hour working day. Reporting time is 7:15 a.m. Monday through Friday. A teacher should be prepared to receive children at 7:30 a.m. A teacher will eat at the noon meal with the children and will have two 15-minute breaks during the 6-hour day. The teacher's planning period is from 1:30 until 3:15 p.m. daily.

The director must be notified in the event of illness or emergencies. Paid vacation periods must be planned 3 months in advance and approved by the director. Other optional benefits include a group health insurance plan, employee retirement fund, and others particular to the program.

Additional duties: A teacher is expected to attend staff development activities on the first Tuesday of each month from 3:30 until 5:30 p.m. and a monthly parent function usually held in the evenings from 7:00 until 9:00 p.m. on the third Thursday of each month.

Reporting relationships and limits of authority: A teacher reports directly to the director of the program. *Prior commitment from the director must be obtained* for purchasing any item, approving additional or terminating any services for children, and releasing information on center activities to the media. A teacher *may take action but must inform* when releasing a child to an authorized adult during normal attendance hours, administering authorized medications, and informing a parent about a child's nonsevere illness. A teacher *may take action without informing* when developing new activities in keeping with the program's philosophy, changing sequence of daily activities except for snack and mealtimes, and talking with parents about children's development.

Benefits: Sick and emergency leave without loss of pay is 12 days for a 12-month period of employment. A 2-week paid vacation plus Thanksgiving and other national holidays are observed.

Figure 5.17
Sample Job Description

Workers' Compensation Insurance.   Workers' compensation is liability insurance compensating an employee injured by an accident in the course of and arising out of employment. (Independent contractors are not covered. Directors should insist that any contractors doing work for a program certify that they are adequately insured so that they cannot later claim to have been acting as an employee.) Workers' compensation is required in most states, but many states have exceptions for certain classes of employers, such as organizations with few employees or organizations wishing to self-insure. The insurance company pays 100% of all workers' compensation benefits required by state law. Injured employees and, in the case of death, their dependents are eligible for one half to two thirds of their weekly wages, plus hospital and medical benefits. In most states, employees, in turn, give up their right to sue employers for damages covered by the law.

State Unemployment Insurance.   State unemployment insurance is required in most states and varies considerably from state to state. A questionnaire must be completed about the employees' activities and the tax status of the early childhood program. The insurance rates are figured as a percentage of total wages and are different for for-profit and not-for-profit corporations.

Liability Insurance.   Liability insurance protects the organization or employee from loss when persons have been injured or property has been damaged as a result of negligence (rather than accident) on the part of the institution or its employees. However, almost any "accident" that occurs is usually considered the result of negligence. The extent to which an institution or its employees can be held liable varies from state to state, and a liability policy should cover everything for which an institution is liable. In most states, programs providing transportation services are required to have vehicle insurance, including liability insurance.

Health Insurance and Hospital-Medical Insurance.   Health insurance, whether fully or partially paid for by the employer or taken on a voluntary basis and paid for by the employee, may assume any of three forms: (a) medical reimbursement insurance, (b) medical service or prepaid medical care, and (c) disability income benefits. Hospital medical plans fall into three groups: (a) basic hospitalization and medical coverage, (b) major medical insurance, and (c) closed-panel operation (service available from a limited number of physicians, clinics, or hospitals).

Crime Coverages.   Protection against loss resulting from dishonesty of employees or others is available under four forms of coverage: (a) fidelity bonds, (b) board-form money and securities policy, (c) "3-D policy" (dishonesty, disappearance, and destruction), and (d) all-risk insurance.

Retirement Programs.   Federal Social Security coverage, FICA tax, is usually mandatory. Generally, the tax is used as a federal "retirement program." Most public school program personnel are also under state retirement programs, paid on a matching fund basis by employer and employee. Other programs may also have retirement plans in addition to Social Security coverage.

Personnel Records

Personnel administration involves keeping records and making reports in accordance with state laws, the program's governing body requirements, and federal legislation concerning privacy of personal information. Public and private schools must keep personnel records on each regulation pertaining to employees—both program and support personnel. In most cases, personnel records are kept by the local programs, and reports are submitted to their respective state governing boards (licensing agency or state board of education). However, the governing board may inspect locally kept records.

Personnel records is a collective term for all records containing information about employees. Although these records vary from program to program, they usually embody the following details:

1. *Personal information records* are kept by all early childhood programs. Most of the personal information is given by a potential employee on the application form, and the information is kept current. Personal information includes name, age, gender, address, telephone number, citizenship, Social Security number, and names and addresses of those who will give references.

2. *Personal health records* signed by an appropriate medical professional are required by all early childhood programs. These records may be detailed, requiring specific medical results of a physical examination or specified laboratory tests, or may be a general statement that the employee is free from any mental or physical illness that might adversely affect the health of children or other adults.

3. *Emergency information* is required by many programs. This information includes the names, addresses, and telephone numbers of one or more persons to be contacted in an emergency; the name of a physician and hospital; and any medical information, such as allergies to drugs or other conditions, deemed necessary in an emergency.

4. *Records of education and other qualifications* are required by all programs. They must include the names of schools attended, diplomas or degrees obtained, transcripts of academic work, and the registration number and type of teacher's or administrator's certificate or any other credential needed by an employee (e.g., a chauffeur's license).

5. *Professional or occupational information records,* including the places and dates of employment, names of employers, and job descriptions, are kept by all programs.

6. *Professional or occupational skill and character references* are included in the personnel records. In most cases, these references are for confidential use by the employer.

7. *Service records* are kept by some programs. These records contain information concerning the date of current employment; level or age of children cared for or taught or program directed; absences incurred or leaves taken; in-service education received and conferences attended; committees served on; salary received; and date and reason for termination of service.

8. *Insurance records* are kept by all programs involved in any group insurance.

9. *Job performance assessment records* are placed on file in many programs. Certain forms must be treated as legal documents, but observers' informal notes should be shredded after they have fulfilled their purposes.

Personnel of many early childhood programs, especially Head Start and others receiving federal funding, are covered under the Privacy Act of 1974 (P.L. 93–579). Because a person's legal right to privacy must be guarded, administrators must keep abreast of the laws pertaining to record keeping and record security. For example, the Privacy Act of 1974 requires federal agencies to take certain steps to safeguard the accuracy, currentness, and security of records concerning individuals and to limit record keeping to necessary and lawful purposes. Individuals also have a right to examine federal records containing such information and to challenge the accuracy of data with which they disagree (Title V. Section 522a, 1977).

SUMMARY

The factors that influence the effectiveness of early childhood programs are incredibly multifaceted and hence complex. All research studies support the contention that the behavior of adults in early childhood programs has an important impact on children.

The qualities of effective staff members have been studied. Although no simple, definitive source answers the question concerning what professional qualifications (knowledge and skills) and personal characteristics (personality traits and values) people need to work effectively with young children, a great deal of consensus does exist. Directors have the responsibilities of laying the foundation for a community, building a positive and productive work climate for staff, enriching the professional life of staff members, and providing personnel services and keeping records. Better job conditions support job satisfaction and act to reduce staff turnover, which, in turn, leads to quality of services.

USEFUL WEB SITES

Human Resources About.com

http://humanresources.about.com/od/interviewing/a/one_stop.htm

This site presents important information regarding the interviewing and hiring of potential employees.

NAEYC Public Policy

http://www.naeyc.org/policy/

This section of the NAEYC website provides links to information and strategies regarding the public policy process and recent developments and initiatives that have potential to impact the compensation, hiring, training, and management of staff in early childhood programs.

TO REFLECT

1. Preschool and kindergarten teachers in public school settings are often at the bottom of a pecking order. Sometimes the discrimination is subtle (e.g., their opinions on schoolwide matters are not acknowledged), and sometimes the discrimination is very open (e.g., they are teased about "playing all day" or majoring in "Sandbox 101"). How can early childhood teachers in public schools gain the respect of their colleagues and administrators?

2. Director X is frustrated because she knows her staff does not particularly respect her as their administrator. She was picked for her position from the ranks of a teacher, although she knew she wasn't the best teacher. She had not actively sought the position and was surprised but pleased when it was offered to her. She has tried three approaches to leadership, and all have failed. First, she tried praise (and very sparse criticism) as a way to please everyone. Next, she tried putting less emphasis on her position (and the authority that goes with it) by taking the smallest office and answering her own phone, and so forth. Finally, she tried to show her staff that she "earned her salary" by becoming a workaholic and working as much as she could—early, late, and on weekends. Why did each approach fail? What should Director X do to gain respect?

3. Director X has four candidates for a teaching position with preschool children. From her interviews, she notes the following: Candidate 1 sees herself in a mothering role. Candidate 2 sees herself aiding children's development, especially their academic development. Candidate 3 wants to build a "little democratic community" in which children's decision making is most important. Candidate 4, who has read some of Montessori's writings, believes in order and organization. What would the classroom be like under each of these four candidates? What criteria should the director use in selecting one of the four candidates?

4. Before taking her position as director of a large corporate early childhood program, Director X has been sent to a weeklong seminar for directors. She is disappointed because she feels that many of the skills she is learning are not applicable to early childhood program leadership. How is leadership in early childhood programs different from leadership in other organizations? What are the implications?

6

CREATING QUALITY LEARNING ENVIRONMENTS

NAEYC Director Competencies addressed in this chapter:

Management Knowledge and Skills

5. Program Operations and Facilities Management
   Knowledge and application of policies and procedures that meet state/local regulations and professional standards pertaining to:
   - the health and safety of young children.
   - the ability to design and plan the effective use of space based on principles of environmental psychology and child development.
   - knowledge of playground safety design and practice.

Early Childhood Knowledge and Skills

1. Historical and Philosophical Foundations
   Knowledge of current trends and important influences impacting program quality.
9. Learning Environments
   Knowledge of the impact of the physical environment on children's learning and development.
   - The ability to use space, color, sound, texture, light, and other design elements to create indoor and outdoor learning environments that are aesthetically pleasing, intellectually stimulating, psychologically safe, and nurturing.
   - The ability to select age-appropriate equipment and materials that achieve curricular goals and encourage positive social interaction.

Learning environments speak to both children and adults in powerful ways. Our use of space tells children how to behave and how to feel. Wide open spaces invite them to "run like the wind," whereas small intimate areas suggest quiet play and can provide a private moment in the midst of a busy classroom. Materials also suggest ways to behave and feel. Some say, "Play with me, I'm sturdy. I'm here for you to manipulate and explore; you can figure me out and be successful when you work with me." Others say "Touch carefully because I'm fragile. I might break" or "I'm hard to figure out. I'm not meant for you."

The learning environment also communicates the program's values and goals to adults. Visitors to the Reggio Emilia schools in Italy are, for example, invariably impressed by the attention invested in aesthetics. classrooms are inviting and light filled, areas for active play are separate from spaces for quiet concentration; there are safe places to keep works in progress; and the lunch room has furniture and furnishings that create a relaxed and homey atmostphere.

An intentionally created environment reflects an understanding of how children develop and learn while providing opportunities for child–child, child–material, and child–adult interactions. It supports adults in their work, giving them ready access to the resources they need and a place to relax for a while in the middle of a busy day.

In this chapter we discuss how the center's environment can be either inviting, relaxed, and comfortable, letting children know they are free to explore; or intimidating, formal, and stiff, making them feel reluctant to enter, stressed, and on guard. We also provide guidelines for making indoor and outdoor spaces engaging, attractive, and safe places that bring out the best in young children and the adults who work with them each day.

PLANNING A NEW OR RENOVATED FACILITY

Some early childhood programs have brand-new buildings designed and built to their specifications; others are housed in existing structures renovated for their use; and still others are located in newly constructed additions to older buildings. Each of these arrangements can be successful. Whatever the setting, the facility should be designed to meet the particular needs of the children for whom it is planned.

If you have the opportunity to design a new center or modify an existing one, your first task is to consider the following issues:

1. The structure must adhere to all applicable building and zoning regulations. Refer to chapter 3 for a discussion of what these regulations are likely to addresss.

2. The safety of the children and staff is your primary concern. Consider outside hazards, such as near-by water or busy streets, when selecting a potential property. Keep these potential hazards in mind when selecting the location of doorways, driveways, and parking areas and design safeguards to protect children and adults from danger.

3. Zoning laws in many areas, and federal laws applying to programs to receive direct or indirect federal assistance, require that buildings accommodate students and employees with physical, vision, hearing, and other disabilities. Their needs should be taken into account in all stages of facility planning.

4. Most of the building's occupants will be young children who are likely to be there as many as 2,000 hours per year. The facility should be child-oriented and also comfortable for adults.

5. Flexibility is essential. Both indoor and outdoor spaces should be planned to accommodate children's changing interests.

6. If you are establishing a new center, you will need to select furniture, equipment, and materials. These are complex decisions that will take a significant amount of time and effort.

7. Cost is always a consideration. Building the facility and equipping its classrooms will require a large initial investment. The program's sponsor will recoup these costs over many years if high-quality materials are purchased from the very beginning.

8. The arrangements of space and materials should be varied and intentional. Some furniture and equipment should be placed near the ceiling, some at children's eye level, and other items should be low enough for children to reach. Consider the item's function, who will use it, where it will be most convenient. There should be areas of different sizes. Large areas invite children to run and climb, small spaces encourage them to fit themselves into hardly big-enough nooks and crannies. There should be also places for boisterous play and for being quiet. The need for children to be together and also to be alone should be considered. There should be interesting architectual features such as inviting alcoves, skylights, or porches, as well as furnishings such as nonpoisonous plants and flowers, artwork, and curtains, wall hangings, and tablecloths made of beautiful fabrics that soften the environment. All these features add to the center's livability and to its aesthetics (Olds, 2001).

The program's vision, goals, and values (described in chapter 2) reflect the needs of the community of children, families, and staff. Their creation is the first step when planning the program's facility. The process of facility planning will, then, take different forms depending on the size and scope of the project.

Planning for a large center or a multisite program often begins with the appointment of a committee charged with developing preliminary or conceptual plans which are then turned over to a draftsman or architect who will develop a specific proposal. In small programs, the director is likely to single-handedly plan facility construction or renovation. Corporate chains and franchises usually have employees who manage the construction and renovation of their centers based on a prototypical design. Facilities for public school prekindergartens and kindergartens are planned by the local board with input from the principal and sometimes classroom teachers.

Regardless of whether the structure is old or new, whether the program is operated by a public, private, or nonprofit entity, facility planners should take the following steps to progress from facility planning, to building and equipping the center, to finally opening the doors to children and families:

1. Program planners should identify the program's specific needs. Consider its maximum enrollment, the ages of children served, anticipated special needs of children served, expected group sizes, and the hours of operation.
2. Planners should familiarize themselves with construction issues they need to address by reading about facility planning in this book and other professional resources, meeting with experts in the field, and visiting programs similar to the one they are planning.
3. Planners need to work closely with all appropriate agencies to be certain their plans are in compliance with building, fire prevention, licensing, and, when appropriate, accreditation regulations. Refer to the discussion about facilities in chapter 3 for an in-depth discussion of building issues addressed in licensing and other relevant regulations.
4. Programs operated by a board of directors will probably be required to submit their plans to the board for approval before construction begins. They will be expected to meet identified benchmarks along the way to document progress toward project completion.

5. The director or the board's designee needs to work with the architect and contractor, accountant, and attorney to be certain planning and construction go smoothly.

Sometimes early childhood programs share facilities with other groups. In some communities, weekday preschool and Sunday school programs use the same classrooms, activity rooms, and kitchens on different days of the week. In other locales, programs for early care and education are housed in community centers where classes and meetings are held in the evenings and weekends when the children are not there. Programs that successfully share space create clear expectations about:

- Cleaning (i.e., Who will clean the rooms and buildings and how often will they be cleaned?)
- Equipment storage (i.e., Where will materials be stored and who will have access to them?)
- Classroom setup (i.e., May the weekday program use the bulletin boards? Can they label children's cubbies? Can decorations and materials for religious holidays used by Sunday school be left up during the week?)

Clear channels of communication are needed for these arrangements to be successful, but it is worth the effort when well-designed community resources are used to benefit many children and families.

In other instances early childhood programs lease their facilities. Program personnel should seek long-term leases and should determine in advance if the lease is renewable, clarify who is responsible for repairs, and determine how the building and the grounds can be altered (i.e., Can the center build ramps, paint walls, erect fences and playgrounds?).

Each of these arrangements can work very well, but it takes time and effort to ensure a well-planned environment that will support the program's goals and objectives and help it realize its mission to serve young children and their families.

Program planners need to address many issues related to the building's exterior and interior design. Even small details can communicate the program's values, goals, and purpose. They create a first and often lasting impression on the community, families, and children.

ENTRY/EXIT AREA

Children and families see the entry/exit area when they arrive every morning and when they leave every afternoon. It is their first and last image of the facility every day. It has the potential to be warm and inviting or to be intimidating, cold, and institutional, creating barriers for children and their families. The entry/exit area is also the view most often seen by the public, and the public's opinion of a program may be based, in large measure, on what can be seen from the street.

The area should be a comfortable scale rather than large, imposing, and institutional. It should use landscaping, lighting, ramps, and natural materials that invite children and parents to enter (Read, 2007). Windows are an important feature because they help children and parents feel comfortable as they prepare to transition into child care in the morning. Some entryways provide views of indoor and outdoor activity areas from a foyer, porch, or courtyard. Displays of children's work; photos of families, children, and staff members; and information about upcoming events are all welcome additions that can create a sense of belonging for children and families. They also communicate the center's purpose and goals to visitors (Curtis & Carter, 2003).

There should be convenient parking near the center's front door so parents will feel able to linger at drop-off and pickup times (Greenman, 1988). It is important to incorporate a curb cut and ramp near the parking lot to accommodate individuals with disabilities. The ramp should be at least 36 in. wide; the slope should be gradual, at least 12 ft long for each 1 ft of incline, and should include handrails. In addition, thresholds to entrances should be no more than 3 in. high and doors should open easily and have at least 32-in. clearings.

For safety purposes, the entry/exit area should be designed to control access to the center. A receptionist should be stationed near the entrance area when family members are arriving in the morning and leaving in the afternoon. Many programs now require parents to ring a doorbell or enter a personal code to unlock the front door, and some have installed observation cameras near all entry/exit areas and in the parking lot to add an extra measure of security.

INDOOR SPACE

Each group of children has its own classroom with space for active, quiet, and messy play; cubbies for children to store personal belongings; and areas for caregiving routines such as diapering and toileting, snack preparation, and storage. The facility must also have adult restrooms, administrative and storage areas, and a custodial closet with access to water and safe storage of cleaning supplies. Many programs also have a kitchen, lunch room, an activities area, a reception area, and a staff break room.

Colors, Lighting, and Sound

Colors.   Much of the color in a room comes from its walls. Color choice depends on several criteria: Bright colors and busy patterns are apt to be overstimulating, while neutral colors are relaxing and help children focus their attention on classroom materials and events (Lally & Stewart, 1990).

When selecting colors for classrooms and other areas in the center take these factors into consideration:

1. **The amount of light in the room.**   Soft pastels may be best for a southern or western exposure, but a northern exposure may need a strong, light-reflecting color such as yellow. Sussman (1998) likes using lightly pigmented pastels with a few intense highlight colors.

2. **The size and shape of the room.**   Mirrors and light wall colors make rooms look larger. If slightly different shades of the same color are used on opposite walls, narrow rooms appear wider. Bright colors make walls look closer and for that reason are more appropriate in large rooms (Olds, 2001). Bright colors should be used with extreme caution, however. Brightly colored rooms often become cluttered and may make it difficult for children and adults to be at their best.

3. **The perception of clutter.**   The environment of many early childhood programs is full of bright colors, commercial classroom materials, and too many decorations (Tarr, 2004). These can create stress and make it difficult for children and adults to focus on materials that showcase what children are interested in and what they can do. Bright colors, permanent murals, and decorative classroom materials may look fine in empty rooms. Once these rooms are occupied, however, they often become overstimulating because materials, furniture, children's work, and the children and adults who fill the room add to the room's brightness.

4. **The influence of color on academic achievement.**   A limited amount of research has been reported on this topic. Findings indicate, however, that red is a good choice for

areas planned for gross motor activities and concept development activities; yellow is good for music and art activities; and green, blue, and purple are effective in reading areas. The use of various colors may be most important in infant and toddler programs because children perceive color over form (shape) until 4 years of age. In rooms with young infants, yellow may be a good choice because it is the first color babies can perceive (Olds, 2001).

5. The psychological impact of colors. Bright reds create excitement. Yellows, deep purples, and greens are restful. "Ethnic" color pallets may help create a sense of belongingness (Caples, 1996).

Lighting. It is important to maximize your use of natural light because it is inviting and homelike. Natural light from large windows, balconies, and porches improves children's and adults' moods, reduces fatigue and eyestrain, helps the body maintain circadian rhythms, destroys bacteria and mold, and is a source of vitamin D (Edwards & Torcellini, 2002; Olds, 2001). Furthermore, children learn many things by looking out the window (they can see best from windowsills 18 to 24 in. high). Children learn about the weather by observing frost, fog, rain, and snow; they learn about the passage of time by noticing patterns of light and shade; and they learn about the natural and man-made world when they can see it from their classroom.

How you use natural light will depend to a great extent on your climate and other site-specific considerations. Determine how much sun is ideal as you plan each classroom's directional orientation. Is your weather cold and snowy, where warming sun would be welcome? Do you have many months that are hot and steamy, making it important that you avoid direct sun as much as possible? The answers to those questions will help you decide if it is better for classrooms to face east toward the morning sun, west so they are bathed in afternoon light, or if a southern or northern exposure, without direct sun is best. Do not forget to take into account the impact of large buildings or nearby trees that block the light.

After you have planned to maximize natural light in such a way that you have avoided excessive heat or glare, you will need to plan how you will supplement sunlight with artificial lighting. Optimum lighting plans use light purposefully, making decisions based on how each space will be used. That means some lighting will be direct and some will be indirect, fixtures will be mounted at various heights, and task lighting will illuminate workspaces where children and adults need to see details well, such as when they are reading and writing. Regulatory agencies often specify the minimum amount of light required in different areas of the center, for example 30-ft candles may be required in play areas, 20-ft candles in restrooms, 10-ft candles in hallways, and less than 5-ft candles in sleeping areas. Because lighting should be tailored to meet children's specific needs, dimmers are good additions to the lighting plan.

Your plan for artificial light should strive to provide light that is as much like natural light as possible. That means that you will install full-spectrum fluorescent or incandescent bulbs, rather than traditional fluorescent bulbs which produce light that is harsh and apt to leave children and adults tired at the end of the day (Edwards & Torcellini, 2002; Olds, 2001; Schreiber, 1996).

Of course, each classroom in most buildings will have a different directional orientation and a different exposure to natural light, so it will be important to plan window coverings, appropriate color schemes, and artificial lighting techniques based on each classroom's particular needs.

Sound. We are bombarded all day long with noises from highways, airplanes, telephones, vacuum cleaners and dishwashers, and lawn mowers and leaf blowers. When working in child care, the sounds surrounding us are likely to also include crying children, noises from play such as those created by hammering toys and falling towers of blocks, and the voices of children and adults. As adults we have learned to tune out many of the sounds in our environment, but children are acutely aware of them. Overexposure to high noise levels can create chronic stress including persistent startle or "fight-or-flight" reactions. Other physical responses can include headaches, hyperactivity, tense muscles, indigestion, the inability to concentrate, irritability, and poor sleep habits (Olds, 2001). In short, high noise levels are harmful to children and adults alike.

The first strategy to keep sound at a healthy level is to keep group sizes small and to have rooms large enough that you can separate areas for noisy active play from those for quiet pursuits. You can take additional steps to make sure that the sounds children hear most are human voices directed personally to them, noises that characterize the productive hum of children at play, live and recorded music, and the sounds of nature.

The first step is to provide plenty of materials that absorb sound such as carpets, stuffed furniture, curtains, and acoustical ceiling tiles. The next is to cushion the sounds of noisy play; for example, consider an area rug in the block center. And, finally, be certain doors to noisy areas can close tightly to help keep noise out (Gonzalez-Mena & Eyer, 2007).

Floors, Ceilings, and Walls

Floors, ceilings, and walls must be both functional and durable. The materials used on their surfaces should be coordinated so they are aesthetically pleasing and comfortable.

Floors.   Young children need flooring that is comfortable to play on, will tolerate getting wet during messy play activities, will not stain if there are spills at mealtimes, and can be cleaned when they have bathroom accidents. Flooring materials should be able to withstand hard wear, be easy to clean, should not become slippery when wet, and should not give off toxic fumes.

Carpet and resilient flooring such as vinyl and linoleum are the most frequently used flooring materials in child care settings. Resilient floorings with a matte finish that are not slippery when wet are best for areas designed for water play, painting, sand play, and for toileting areas. Vinyl and linoleum generally come as 10-in. or 12-in. squares or as sheet goods. They are both good choices.

Carpet is softer, more comfortable, and better at absorbing noise than resilient flooring. It can also help minimize injuries. All child care settings are enhanced by carpeted areas, but it is particularly important to include carpet in infant rooms because very young children spend so much time on the floor. When choosing carpet, consider the fiber (nylon and natural fibers such as wool are the most durable); the pile (cut pile or cut and loop pile are more desirable than loop pile because they are softer and feel more like home); and construction (woven and tufted carpets usually wear better). It is very important to consider the carpet's backing, padding, and glue. Even though they are not visible, they have the potential to add allergens and toxins into the environment. When possible, select backings, padding, and glues that are natural and free of pesticide residues and latex-based products that are not apt to emit toxic fumes (Olds, 2001).

Most programs create zones for active and quiet play by combining resilient flooring with wall-to-wall carpet or area and throw rugs. The area with resilient flooring accommodates activities like eating and messy play. Carpet or rugs add visual interest, define activity areas, and add softness. Be sure to secure area rugs with double-sided tape to prevent trip-and-fall accidents and be alert to repair them if they begin to ravel or fray.

A final issue to consider is how you will keep floors warm and free from drafts. Radiant heating is one solution to consider, particularly in cold climates, but this kind of heat does not solve draft problems. Baseboard heating provides floor warmth and freedom from drafts if they are a problem.

Ceilings.   When possible, ceiling heights and finishes should be varied to create intimate spaces, visual interest, and to accommodate furnishings of various heights. These variations can reduce noise and are aesthetically pleasing. Even when ceilings are all the same height, mobiles, banners, canopies, and hanging fabrics can create intimate spaces and can expand play opportunities. One way to create ceiling interest is to mount a beam across the room from which you can hang basket chairs, plants, toys, or fabric. It is essential to be certain nothing hung from the ceiling creates a fire hazard and that everything satisfies regulations of the fire marshal (Olds, 2001).

Walls.   Walls play important roles in every child care facility. They define spaces, provide acoustical separation, and are used for storage, display and as communication centers. When possible walls should have varied surfaces such as carpet, fabric, mirrors, brick, wood, tile, stone, or stucco in addition to traditional drywall (Olds, 2001).

Paint and vinyl coverings are the most popular wall finishes for spaces with children. Paint is an economical choice, comes in a virtually endless variety of colors, and semigloss and gloss finishes are able to withstand frequent washing. It is easy to repaint and freshen up painted surfaces. Vinyl wall coverings come in a variety of grades and price ranges and are very stain-resistant and durable. They can be difficult to apply, however, and can be difficult and expensive to remove. Hard plastic surfacing can be practical in areas like bathrooms that receive very heavy use. This material is not appropriate for general use, however. It creates a sterile and institutional feel rather than one that is warm and inviting (Olds, 2001).

Corner moldings and wall bumpers may be needed in high-traffic areas. When possible, choose natural materials to retain a homelike rather than institutional feel.

Consider adding visual interest by using mirrors, fabric, display areas, and murals on walls, particularly in hallways and common areas. They can create a sense of place, define areas for a variety of purposes, and can be attractive and welcoming.

Storage and Display

Storage and display areas are essential elements of a well-designed child care program. They are too important to be left to chance and should be addressed in the very earliest stages of facility planning.

Storage.   Child care programs never seem to have enough storage! Planners should anticipate the need to store consumables used by children:

- Rest mats or cots
- Childrens' belongings
- Indoor large motor equipment
- Bulk supplies like paint and paper
- Administrative materials, supplies, and archived records
- Shared curriculum and audiovisual materials including those used on a rotating basis
- Seasonal materials such as holiday decorations
- Extra furniture and equipment
- Food and kitchen supplies
- Outdoor toys and equipment
- Custodial and maintenance equipment
- Cleaning supplies (Olds, 2001)

Adequate storage contributes to a rich curriculum because teachers are able to accumulate and use a variety of resources to respond to children's interests (Prescott, 1984). Well-designed storage in classrooms and adult areas also enhances efficiency, creates predictability, reduces clutter, extends children's play, enhances children's developing classification and sorting skills, and contributes to the creation of a community of learners where children share responsibility for the learning environment.

A general rule-of-thumb is that 10% of the center's square footage should be devoted to storage areas that are not accessible to children (Olds, 2001). Isbell and Exelby (2001) classify storage as (a) open and closed and (b) fixed, movable, and portable. Some materials for children should be in open storage that gives them opportunities to make choices. Other materials should be in closed storage to allow staff to regulate their availability.

Generally speaking, constructivist programs and those serving older children have a significant amount of open storage. Programs for infants and toddlers and those that emphasize teacher-directed activites provide fewer choices. Some items, such as cleaning supplies, medicines, teachers' professional libraries, personal records of children and staff, business records, and personal items of staff, always need to be in closed, secured (locked) storage.

Storage units that are built-in (fixed) cannot be altered. Freestanding units (movable) allow for flexible arrangement and can serve as room dividers. Care must be taken, however, that all freestanding units are tip-proof (Isbell & Exelby, 2001). Baskets, tote bags, and boxes are useful for portable storage and for organizing loose parts.

For infant and toddler programs, 2-ft-high shelves are appropriate for open storage, but they must be very sturdy because babies will use them to pull themselves up. For preschool and primary programs, shelf height should be approximately 3 ft. Shelves or racks should be placed near the area where they will be used.

The design and materials from which storage units are made should be compatible with their purpose. Large, low open shelves provide room to store blocks in an orderly fashion. Resting-cot closets with louvered doors allow air circulation. Waterproof containers are needed in water play centers.

Well-designed storage helps children and staff find what they need, keep materials and equipment in good condition, and can be aesthetically pleasing. Bins are inappropriate storage except for moving heavy materials (e.g., hollow blocks) because they do not allow easy access and children are likely to "dump" toys in at cleanup time rather than arranging them so they can easily be found later.

Display.   Display areas create opportunities to communicate the program's activities, history, and values while shaping its identity on a day-to-day basis. Displays can also be useful in creating connections between the center and children's home life. They contribute to the creation of a sense of belonging for all who enter the doors (Curtis & Carter, 2003).

Displays can also enhance and document children's learning by making learning visible to themselves, their families, and visitors (Katz & Chard, 2000). Materials documenting curriculum should be accessible to children (Cost, Quality, and Child Outcomes Study Team, 1995). That means they are mounted on the wall at children's eye level or on low shelves where children can study them in depth. Infant/toddler caregivers can mount documentation on the floor or on walls near the floor.

When displays become documentation of children's learning, as they do in programs based on the Reggio Emilia approach, they move beyond describing what children did to include the teacher's interpretation and explanation. They provide insights into what children were thinking and coming to understand.

Arranging and Furnishing Classrooms

Classrooms are the most important areas of the building because they are where children spend most of their time.

Room Size.   Room size is one of the most important things to consider when planning a center. Classrooms should be small enough to be intimate. Children are happier, interact more, and dramatize fantasy themes more in smaller rooms than they do in larger ones

(Howes, 1983). They are also likely to be more talkative and to be less reluctant to come to school (Howes & Rubenstein, 1985 as cited in Trawick-Smith, 1992) when they are coming to a smaller classroom.

Many states' licensing regulations require at least 35 sq ft per child. For young infants, 35 sq ft per child in the primary activity area is adequate (Lally, Provence, Szanton, & Weissbourd, 1986), but an additional 30 sq ft per child is needed for each crib and the 2- to 3-foot clearance required between adjacent cribs (Olds, 2001).

It is easy to appreciate that older children need more room for active play. Their classrooms also need zones for different kinds of activities. Experts recommend 50 to 75 sq ft per child (Bergen, Reid, & Torelli, 2001; Lally et al., 1995; Olds, 2001). Rooms of this size provide children space to become actively involved with each other and materials, make it possible to provide spaces for one or two children to work quietly together, create opportunities for adults to work with individual children or small groups, and are likely to be more accommmodating for children who are physically disabled.

Regardless of the number of children or the length of the session, the children's classrooms should have at least 900 sq ft of clear floor space, exclusive of rest rooms, eating, and separate napping areas. Designs for many new classrooms call for 1,200 to 1,500 sq ft (Hohmann & Buchleitner, 1992).

When floor space is limited and ceilings are high, space can often be stretched vertically with lofts and climbing structures. To protect children from injury if they should fall, indoor climbing structures should be surrounded by the same kinds of safe surfaces they would have if they were outdoors. Options include the kinds of mats or surfacing used outdoors or secured 4-in. mats (Thompson & Hudson, 2003).

In many climates, centers with minimal indoor space can compensate by using sheltered outdoor play spaces, like a covered porch or patio, for much of the year.

Room Shape.   Long, narrow classrooms encourage running and sliding. Square rooms often have dead space in the center because activity areas are apt to be placed along walls instead of toward the center of the room. A classroom that is slightly longer than it is wide is the easiest to arrange and is likely to be inviting to children and their families.

Room Arrangement.   The arrangement of each classroom affects the quality of children's and adults' daily experiences. Every classroom should provide safety and security; should be predictable and promote autonomy; should meet the learning needs of children with varied abilities, temperaments, and learning styles; and should be convenient for children and adults.

The *Infant/Toddler Environment Rating Scale* (Harms, Cryer, & Clifford, 2003), the *Early Childhood Environment Rating Scale* (Harms, Clifford, & Cryer 2005), and the *School-Age Care Environment Rating Scale* (Harms, Jacobs, & White, 1996) are widely used and readily available environment assessment tools that we believe can be very valuable in helping programs arrange rooms; select, store, and use materials; and develop daily schedules that are associated with positive outcomes for children.

These rating scales have a strong research base and are used by many states as a part of their licensing and/or quality rating systems. For those reasons they are excellent tools to guide you as you furnish and equip classrooms for children from birth through school age.

1. The room arrangement should help the program meet its goals.   Programs that embrace a constructivist approach to early education need an environment that gives children opportunities to move freely and to choose which activites they want to actively pursue. These classrooms are divided into learning centers with low partitions. The size of each center depends on the space required for the use and storage of needed equipment and materials as well as the number of children likely to work in that area at one time.

Learning centers should communicate their purpose clearly to children. The block center looks different from the area for dramatic play, and areas to work with puzzles and other small manipulatives are set apart from the cozy area to enjoy books. Open areas and small tables allow adults to work with children individually or in small groups. An open floor plan also makes it possible for adults to supervise children from many locations throughout the room. See Figures 6.1 through 6.10 in later sections of this chapter for model floor plans designed for active learning.

2. The room should feel open and inviting while providing children opportunities to concentrate and become engaged in their activities. The size, scale, and arrangment of toys, shelves, and partitions contribute to whether children find the classroom inviting or intimidating. Open rooms with clearly defined zones welcome children, let them clearly see the available play options, promote active learning and collaboration, provide children with needed privacy, can prevent negative behaviors such as aggression or withdrawal, and reduce children's tendency to wander about the room (Neill & Denham, 1982; Trawick-Smith, 1992). Classrooms with high partitions, with learning centers that are almost completely surrounded by room dividers, and where toys are not clearly in sight are uninviting and intimidating. They do not invite young children to enter or to become actively involved.

3. The room arrangement should provide children spaces that feel private. Chaotic and frantic behaviors are associated with classrooms that do not have private spaces for chidren to escape the busyness of classroom activities. Children benefit from areas that offer them privacy to construct a sense of self (Laufer & Wolfe, 1977), to "cocoon" when the noise and other stimuli overwhelm them (Greenman, 1988; Hyson, 1994; NAEYC, 1998), to be cuddled (Hyson, 1994), and to focus on their special endeavors (Meltz, 1990) before gradually moving into the group (Olds, 2001).

Window seats, cozy corners, small closets with the doors removed, and a few learning centers or workstations for one child all help meet indoor privacy needs (Greenman, 1988; Johnson, 1987; Kennedy, 1991; Olds, 2001). Private places can also be created with rocking, gliding, or beanbag chairs; pillows; and by using dividers and storage cabinets that are high enough to give children a sense of privacy, but low enough for adults to see over.

4. The needs of children with disabilities should be considered when a room is being arranged. Room arrangements must permit *all* children **accessibility,** the ability to enter all parts of the environment including bathrooms and to access equipment and materials (Winter, Bell, & Dempsey, 1994; Cryer, Harms, & Riley, 2003), and **availability,** the ability to participate in all experiences (Cavallaro, Haney, & Cabello, 1993). A child who uses an assistive device is likely to require more space for movement. Wheelchairs require an aisle of 36 in. and corners of at least 42 in. Lofts, play pits, and other popular features included in many classrooms can limit access to children who use assistive devices.

Furniture and Other Essentials. Once the scene has been set for quality care by selecting the building's color scheme, planning for natural and artificial light, installing floor coverings that support active and quiet play, and other details related to the center's structure and design have been addressed, it is time to select furniture and furnishings that will make the program come alive. All furniture selected for programs of early care and education should be **comfortable.** That means much of the furniture is **child sized.** The tables and chairs in the toddler room are smaller than those in spaces used by 3-year-olds. Children can easily reach toys on open shelves, and lofts and other equipment are appropriately scaled. There should also be furniture that is comfortable for adults. Ideas to consider are cozy rocking chairs or gliders (which are safer for little fingers), hammocks, and appropriately sized cubes or storage bins designed for adults to sit on.

Furniture and equipment should also be **flexible** and **open-ended.** It should be easy to rearrange the room to respond to children's needs and interests. Movable platforms,

Risers are versatile because they provide storage while creating play spaces and play surfaces.

risers, large hollow blocks, movable tables, boxes, large pieces of fabric, clothespins, and other open-ended materials give children opportunities to arrange spaces to suit their needs. They enhance children's imaginative play, provide opportunities for problem solving, cooperation, and collaboration (Curtis & Carter, 2003).

Teachers and caregivers also benefit from flexible arrangements. At rest time it should be easy to arrange cots so children can rest comfortably and undisturbed. On rainy days it should be possible to push the tables aside and lay down tumbling mats. On the spur of the moment you should be able to create a cozy corner to read a book or just talk with a child needing special one-on-one attention.

Furnishings should be **practical** and **attractive.** All furnishings should be easy to keep clean. That means tables and shelves are finished to withstand frequent washing and disinfecting. Upholstered platforms, couches, and chairs are covered with durable washable coverings. And finally, all classrooms should be designed with an eye toward aesthetics.

Furniture should be the appropriate size and proportions for the children it serves, should be durable and lightweight, and have rounded corners. If space is at a premium, stacking chairs and storage systems are attractive options.

We recommend rectangular tables that can accommodate four to six children. They are very flexible because they can be inviting and intimate during snacks and meals, are large enough for many arts and crafts projects, and can easily be combined to make larger workspaces when needed. Children's chairs should be sturdy and should allow children's feet to rest comfortably on the floor without bending their legs more than 90°.

Refer to Table 6.1 for a chart indicating the size of tables and chairs that are typically appropriate for children of different ages. Note that the distance between the seat of the chair and the table surface should be approximately 8 in., so tables must be sized to fit with the chairs. Vendors of school supplies such as Community Playthings and Environments provide guidelines to help you fit tables and chairs for each age group you serve. (See appendix 1 for the Web sites of these vendors and other suppliers of furniture, equipment, and supplies.)

It is important to remember that children can grow very quickly. You need to have extra chairs and tables on hand so that all children can always be accommodated for meals, snacks, and other table activities.

You will also want to provide open and closed storage units including cubbies for children and storage for adults' personal belongings; furniture such as light, sand and water, and carpentry tables for activity centers; book racks; computer stations; lofts and risers; and soft furniture for relaxation.

While the furniture and furnishings needed by infants and toddlers are, in most respects, no different from those of older children, caregiving routines do create the need for some special equipment. While toddlers and preschoolers usually use cots for naptime, infants need cribs to sleep safely. In addition, classrooms for both infants and toddlers need an area dedicated to preparing bottles and food as well as a diaper changing area apart from all food preparation.

We advise against high chairs and other restraining equipment such as baby swings or standing toys. In their place we recommend comfortable rockers so caregivers can hold children while feeding bottles and beginning them on solid food; and small, low chairs that

Table 6.1
Recommended Table and Chair Heights for Young Children

Recommended Table Heights (inches)	12″	14″	16″	18″	20″	22″	24″	26″	28″–30″
Recommended Seat Heights (inches)	5″	6.5″	8″	10″	12″	14″	16″	Adult	
1-year-olds	50%	50%							
2-year-olds			60%	40%					
3-year-olds				100%					
4-year-olds				40%	60%				
5-year-olds					100%				
6-year-olds					50%	50%			
7-year-olds					20%	80%			
8-year-olds						80%	20%		
9-year-olds						40%	60%		
10-year-olds							100%		
11-year-olds							80%	20%	
12-year-olds							20%	80%	
13-year-olds and up								20%	80%

Based on international averages. Young children grow rapidly. If at all possible, have chairs of various heights on hand so you can provide each child a comfortable table and chair.

Source: Adapted from Community Playthings, (2008). Used by permission.

Comfortable tables and chairs invite children to become engaged with interesting table-top activities.

children can sit in when they are ready to begin to feed themselves. If you decide to use high chairs, be certain they have restraining straps that go around children's waists and between their legs. They should be folded and put out of the way when not in use because children are apt to climb on them if they are stored in the room.

It is also important that your program be inviting to breast-feeding mothers who want to visit their babies during the workday. This means you will arrange a comfortable place where mothers and their babies can concentrate on nursing and being together. This can be in the classroom or in another comfortable and cozy place nearby.

Refer to part 1 of appendix 4 for a list of suggested basic furniture and furnishings.

Other furnishings to consider are clocks, wastebaskets, storage bins and baskets, and non-poisonous plants. Remember to plan for window treatments including curtains that can add softness, color, and texture, and blinds that can help control light and heat. Plan for securing the cords from blinds well out of children's reach. They can be a strangulation hazard.

General Criteria for Learning/Activity Centers

Each classroom needs to be equipped with age-appropriate activity and learning centers. Plan for both active and quiet zones that offer these five kinds of experiences every day:

1. *Quiet activities* such as listening to books, reading, and cuddling
2. *Stuctured activities* such as puzzles, construction toys, and manipulatives
3. *Craft and discovery activities* such as paint, play dough, water, sand, and wood-working
4. *Dramatic play activities* such as puppets, dress-up, and dramatic play
5. *Large motor actities* such as slides, climbing equipment, balls, and large blocks (Olds, 2001)

The *Environment Rating Scales* identified earlier can be very helpful as you identify activity centers that are appropriate for infants and toddlers, preschoolers, and school-age children. These resources also describe how each center should be equipped.

Learning/activity centers are "carefully designed areas that contain planned learning activites and materials" (Kostelnik, Soderman & Whiren, 2007, p. 112). They support hands-on learning; contribute to children's learning as they work on particular projects or themes; and accommodate children of various developmental levels, interests, and abilities. Classrooms with learning centers also provide teachers opportunities to evaluate children's progress across developmental domains by observing their purposeful interactions with peers and carefully selected materials.

Each learning center should be arranged so that children can see what it has to offer and can understand how it is used. Learning centers should be:

1. Located in a specific place well suited for the activity
2. Have clearly marked boundaries
3. Provide areas for play and for observing
4. Provide for storage and display of materials related to the specific center
5. Create a mood that sets it apart from other areas in the classroom (Olds, 2001)

Defining Space.   Boundaries between learning centers should be clearly defined, but they should be flexible so they can be expanded or made smaller to respond to children's interest. Consider the classroom traffic patterns and make certain there are clear paths between centers.

Space can be defined by the placement of shelves, partitions, low walls, or other furniture such as sofas and chairs. Boundaries can be created by varying the floor level through the use of platforms or lofts. Space can also be defined by differences in colors or shades of wall paint or carpet and by the use of targeted task lighting. It is important to be certain teachers can visually supervise every area of the classroom. Spaces can be made to feel safe and secure for children by creating partitions children are not able to see over, but adults can (Olds, 2001).

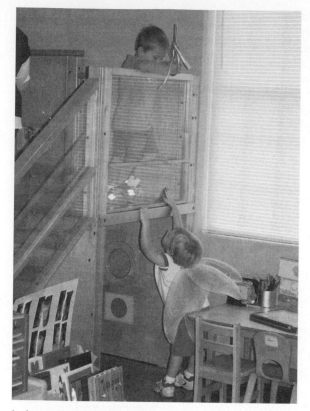

Lofts create variety and can accommodate many different learning centers.

Before deciding how to define space for a learning/activity center, you will want to decide whether the space will be permanently used in this way. The colors of walls and carpet and the levels of floors are somewhat permanent, but movable partitions and storage units are not. Being able to add, eliminate, or change centers makes the room more flexible and responsive to children's interests and needs.

Allowing Sufficient Space.   Each center needs to be large enough to accommodate the kinds of activities for which it is intended. More space is needed in centers designed for several children to play together as they do during dramatic play, and those where children need room to spread out as they do when they use unit blocks. Centers should be planned to provide both room to play and room for storage of related materials.

Providing Acoustic Isolation.   Noise can easily become a problem, particularly in a small classroom. Sounds from one learning center should not interfere with activities in another. That means the block center that typically involves several children and materials that can be noisy should not adjoin the reading center where children come to quietly enjoy books. Noise-absorbing floor and wall coverings and acoustical ceiling tiles can help reduce the classroom's noise level. Other strategies to reduce noise include providing ear phones in the listening center, low-pile carpet in the block center, and by locating particularly noisy activities such as woodworking outdoors.

Arranging Equipment and Materials.   Equipment and materials should be arranged and displayed in the center where they will be used. Open shelves encourage children to select materials independently and to return them when they are finished. It is helpful to label shelves, bins, and baskets with a picture or silhouette of items stored there to help children return them correctly.

Children's safety should be your guide when arranging the classroom and organizing its storage. Heavy but portable items like large trucks should be placed on the lower shelves of cabinets. The CD player should be near an electric outlet so you don't need to use a long extension cord. Equipment that is not used every day should be stored to prevent damage but should be readily available. Everything in storage should be clearly labeled. If there are loose parts, they should be kept in a box with a lid or a bag to keep them together. Store food, paper, paint, and other consumables so that you use the oldest materials first.

Activity Centers for Infants and Toddlers

As mentioned earlier, classroom environments for infants and toddlers share many characteristics with classrooms serving older children. Protecting children's health and keeping them safe is always the first concern. Spaces for infants and toddlers should be comfortable, convenient, and child-sized. They need areas where children can be active, places to enjoy the company of their peers, and opportunities for one-on-one time with their primary caregiver. Their classrooms also need to be designed so that caregiving routines such as feeding, diaper changing, and sleeping are comfortable and convenient for caregivers. Caregivers must be alert, ready to adapt classrooms to match infants' and toddlers' rapidly changing developmental levels, interests, and abilities (Lally & Stewart, 1990).

It is particularly important that areas for infants and toddlers be interesting places full of beautiful sights, sounds, and textures that capture these babies' attention and lead them to explore and problem solve in their sensory and motor world.

Infant and Toddler Rooms. Quality infant and toddler care is not simply a scaled-down version of quality preschool. "A well designed environment . . . supports infants' and toddlers' emotional well-being, stimulates their senses, and challenges their motor skills" (Torelli cited in Gonzalez-Mena & Eyer, 2007, p. 262). The following principles should guide your creation of infant/toddler environments:

1. **Infants and toddlers need an environment that will keep them safe and healthy.** Very young children explore toys with their mouths as well as their fingers. They pull up and climb on furniture and can be counted on to explore the environment in ways you never expected. Their health and safety must always be your number one concern. Frequent and proper hand washing is the single most important thing you can do to keep children and caretakers healthy. Classrooms should have convenient sinks so that children and adults can wash their hands after every diaper change or trip to the bathroom, before every meal and snack, whenever their hands have been used to cover a cough or wipe a nose, and after being outside or touching pets.

It is also important to keep all dangerous materials locked and out of reach. Window blinds can be stangulation hazards; they need to be secured well out of the way of curious fingers. There should also be a routine for washing sheets, blankets, pillows, dress-up clothes, and other soft furnishings and for sanitizing toys that have gone in children's mouths.

2. **Infants and toddlers need an aesthetically pleasing environment with beautiful colors, sounds, forms, and textures.** This means that you need to consider the color scheme, room arrangement, and furnishings of infant/toddler facilities to create a welcoming, home-like setting for your youngest children. They need to hear the sounds of live human voices, to enjoy natural sunlight and the outdoors, and to be fascinated by the beautiful colors and interesting textures that surround them.

3. **Infant and toddler rooms should be designed to be "baby scale" and also "adult scale."** An infant's perspective is very different from that of adults. We recommend that you get down on the floor to consider how the world looks from a baby's perspective. Take care to avoid harsh lights that shine in their eyes. Offer interesting things to look at, to feel, and to hear. It is important that the adults who care for babies have comfortable adult-size furniture such as gliders, hammocks, sofas, and easy chairs that let them nurture and care for infants and toddlers in a relaxed, comfortable, and convenient environment.

4. **Activity centers should have open-ended materials and duplicates of popular toys.** Simple toys are best for infants and toddlers. They enjoy household items like pots and pans; simple art materials like crayons and papers of different colors; balls of different sizes and textures, tray puzzles with three or four pieces; board books; soft dolls; and simple props for make-believe, particularly blankets and bottles so they can care for their "babies."

Infants and toddlers are egocentric. They are able to see the world from only their own perspective. They do not yet realize, for example, that their classmate wants a turn with the ball they find fascinating. They like to play side-by-side, but it is not appropriate to expect them to be able to share or to wait their turn. That is why it is important to have duplicates of the same toy—several identical red trucks, blue balls, and baby dolls in pink dresses. That gives each child the opportunity to play with attractive and appropriate toys without having to wait their turn or give up popular selections before they are ready.

5. Infants and toddlers need opportunities to be alone.   Young infants are exploring their own bodies. They are fascinated by their fingers, are amazed when they find their toes, and are busy making sense of the sights and sounds that surround them. They need protected spaces where they can concentrate on learning about themselves and the world around them.

Mobile infants and toddlers need private areas for a different reason. They are active explorers, crawling into, climbing over, and running around everything in sight. It sometimes seems as if they never slow down. Quiet places to be alone or to spend time with a special caretaker help them relax and can prevent their becoming overstimulated.

6. Small activity centers for one or two children are more appropriate than the larger centers typical of programs for older children.   A center for a young infant can be as small as a throw rug, mat, or window (Greenman & Stonehouse, 1996). For mobile infants and toddlers, an activity center might accommodate two children playing side-by-side. The important thing is to provide young children interesting vantage points, a variety of materials to examine, and freedom to explore their environments with their entire bodies.

7. Infants and toddlers need predictablity and familiarity as well as novelty.   Predictable routines and familiar environments comfort infants and toddlers. They are able to relax when caregiving routines and surroundings stay the same day after day, week after week. That is not to say they don't enjoy novelty, but it does mean that classrooms for infants and toddlers should not be rearranged overnight, nor should all familiar toys be suddenly exchanged for new ones. Thoughtful caregivers add new materials to familiar centers; for example, they add scarves to the dress-up corner to provide children the chance to experiment with their shimmering colors and silky feel, but the dress-up corner hasn't moved and favorite items are still there. Another example of how you can add novelty while maintaining familiarity is by adding new books to the book corner, but keeping the book center where it is and keeping some favorite books along with the new ones.

Classroom areas for infants and toddlers can be described as being for large-motor, dramatic, messy, and quiet play (Lowman & Ruhmann, 1998). Consider these centers for infants and toddlers:

- Blocks and vehicles
- Manipulative toys like puzzles
- Quiet area
- Art center
- Listening center
- Dramatic play/housekeeping center
- Area for seeing and touching
- Water and sand area
- Area for gross-motor play
- Music-making area (Adams and Taylor, 1985; Cataldo, 1982; Stewart, 1982)

See Figure 6.1 for an example of a floor plan of an infant room and Figure 6.2 for a floor plan of a toddler room. They illustrate some of the principles discussed above. Napping, feeding, and changing and toileting areas are discussed later in this chapter.

Learning/Activity Centers for Preschoolers

Preschoolers have interests, needs, and abilities that set them apart from younger children. These activity centers are recommended for preschool and kindergarten children.

Block Center.   The **block center** is devoted to building with unit blocks and props such as people, animals, cars, and trucks. The block center might also have paper, pencils, Post-it®

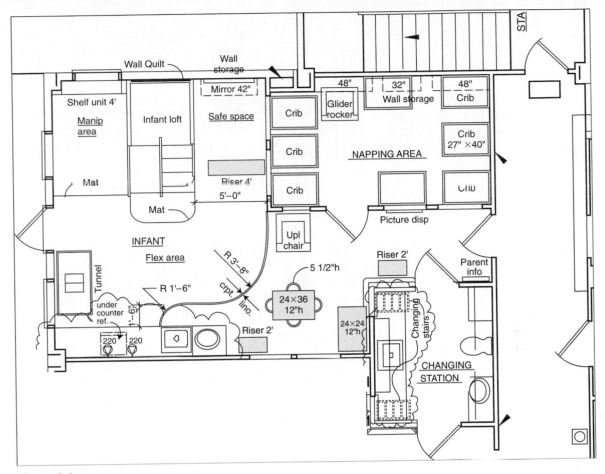

Figure 6.1
Infant Floor Plan

Source: Floor plan developed by Louis Torelli for the Children's Center at the University of South Carolina, Columbia, South Carolina. Used by permission of the University of South Carolina.

notes, and other writing materials for labeling structures or to support block play in other ways. Block centers are noisy and are best located on dense carpet, out of the flow of traffic. Various group sizes may be accommodated in the block center:

1. A small block center, about 75 sq ft, is appropriate for one or two children. Small block centers, if protected by storage units or if defined by a pit or low platform, may be placed near the room entrance. Experienced teachers have noticed that playing with blocks can smooth some children's transition to school in the morning. Usually, about 100 to 150 blocks and a few accessories are shelved in a small block center.

2. A large block center, about 260 sq ft, can accommodate up to seven children. From 700 to 1,000 unit blocks or 80 or more hollow blocks are recommended for a large block area. A large block area should be located out of the flow of traffic where structures can be left up for more than one day.

3. A small set of hollow blocks (e.g., 10 long, 10 square, 10 boards), used in conjunction with dramatic play, are often stored in or near dramatic play centers, especially those that change themes throughout the year (e.g., store, post office, veterinarian's office, beauty shop, or farm).

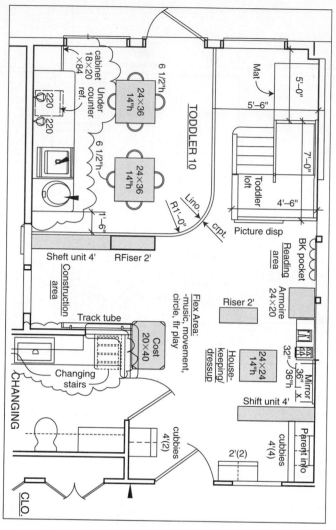

Figure 6.2
Toddler Floor Plan

Source: Floor plan developed by Louis Torelli for the Children's Center at the University of South Carolina, Columbia, South Carolina. Used by permission of the University of South Carolina.

4. Large outside block areas, for building with a full set of hollow blocks or unit blocks, are usually temporary arrangements. Because wooden blocks must stay dry, they will have to be transported in block carts or wagons to and from the outdoor block building area.

Storage units found in the catalogs and on the Web sites of popular vendors are well suited for unit blocks. Blocks and accessories should be carefully stored so that block builders can find what they want. We recommend that you:

a. Store blocks lengthwise for quick identification (blocks cannot be identified by their ends)

b. Label each section of the shelves with tracings of the blocks so they can be returned after use

c. Draw children's attention to the size of various blocks by shelving them seriated by length, with larger blocks on the bottom shelf

d. Do not pack shelves too tightly

e. Vary accessories from time to time to reflect children's current interests and units of study

Consider displaying pictures of buildings, bridges, and other structures near the block center. They can be photographs of neighborhood structures, pictures taken during class trips or can be cut from magazines. Figure 6.3 is an example of a floor plan for an indoor block center.

Dramatic Play Center.   Dramatic play centers are like a stage. They invite children to play make-believe as they reenact family life; role play various occupations such as teacher, doctor, or barber; and act out familiar stories (Beaty, 1996). Props are usually displayed in the area that is designed specifically for children's spontaneous pretend play, but the truth is that dramatic play can occur almost anywhere in the room.

The most common theme for dramatic play, particularly for children 3 and under, is housekeeping. Older preschoolers and primary-age children often continue to play "house" but can enjoy a variety of play themes, particularly when their play is based on a field trip or other shared experience. Prop boxes are a good way to organize and store materials to support a particular theme such as grocery store, beauty shop, veterinary hospital, or flower shop (Boutte, Van Scoy, & Hendley, 1996; Myhre, 1993;). Families often enjoy getting involved in dramatic play by sharing appropriate artifacts and expertise.

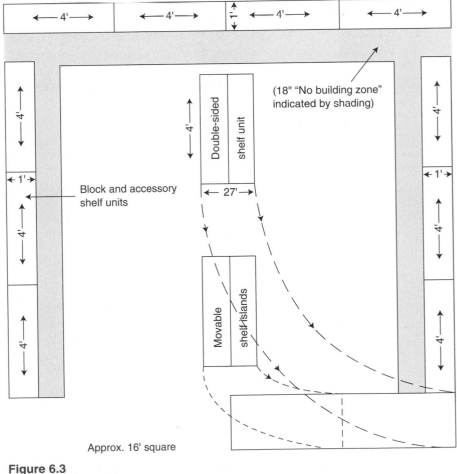

Figure 6.3
Large Indoor Block Center/Area

Many early childhood programs also have a puppet theater near the dramatic play or language arts center. Usually storage and display shelves and a freestanding puppet theater are all children need to use puppets as part of their make-believe play.

Art Center.   This section of the room is devoted to the creation and display of children's artistic representations. These activities are important because they help young children develop their sensory and perceptual concepts of color, form, size, texture, and light and dark. They use artists' tools to awaken their aesthetic sensitivities, represent their thoughts in artistic products rather than in words, display their creativity, express their emotions, and refine their small-motor skills.

The art center can be considered to be a small studio. It should offer a comfortable place to work without unrealistic constraints (e.g., "Don't drip paint on the floor because it will stain the carpet!"). It should provide shelves, racks, and cupboards for children to store supplies and works in progress and to display completed projects for others to admire.

Reggio Emilia schools provide a model for honoring the arts. The Reggio preschools have a separate art studio called an *atelier*. Their *atelieristas,* art teachers with a specialized background in visual art, music, dance, theater, or design, scaffold children's explorations of a wide variety of artisitic media.

Whether you have just a corner of the classroom or a separate room devoted to children's artistic expresssions, the goal is to provide children multiple opportunities, over time, to use art materials in satisfying ways. Consider these guidelines for creating a well-designed art center:

1. It should look like a joy-filled studio. Ideally, it will be bathed in natural glare-free light, but you may need to rely on artificial light to give children plenty of illumination for their work. An art center near the playground allows art activities to expand to outdoor areas. A sense of productive activity is enhanced when children's work is displayed in or near the art center.

2. The art center should have places for individual and group work. Work surfaces include the wall (porcelain boards and murals), tilted surfaces (easels), and flat surfaces (tables). Movable stand-up tables should be approximately 20 in. high, and sit-down/stand-up tables should be about 18 in. high. Built-in work surfaces should be 20 in. high and between 2 and 3 ft deep. The art center needs many storage shelves for supplies. Storage shelves for paper should have doors, although other storage shelves may be open. Drying art products will require lines or racks for paintings and mobiles, and shelves for three-dimensional products.

3. Tables, wall coverings, and floors of the art center should be durable and easy to clean. Pretest surfaces to be certain they will not be stained by red paint. Floors should not be slippery when wet, and all surfaces should be made of quick-drying materials.

4. A sink in the art center or in an adjacent rest room with plenty of counter space on both sides is essential for mixing paints, plaster of paris, modeling compounds, and the like, as well as for cleanup. The sink should have appropriate strainers to catch clay, paste, and other materials, and should have an accessible U-trap. The sink counter and the wall behind the sink should be covered with a durable, easy-to-clean wall covering.

5. The art center must be roomy enough to accommodate tables, easels, and children moving about with wet paintings. It needs to be approximately 190 sq ft. (See Figure 6.4 for a sample layout of an art center.)

Music Center.   The music center is devoted to children's explorations of melody, pitch, rhythm, and harmony. It also exposes them to a wide range of musical genres such as jazz,

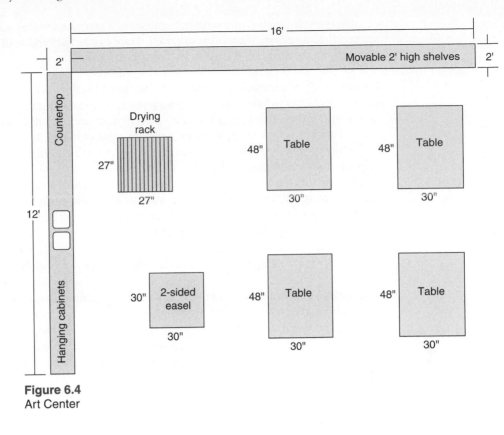

Figure 6.4
Art Center

folk, classical, reggae, and other musical traditions. Some musical activities such as listening to music, watching videos of music or dance performances, and looking at books and pictures associated with music and dance are receptive. Others are active, involving children in singing, playing instruments, and creating dances. Music is often part of circle time or other whole group activities, so it may be convenient to locate the music center near the area used for whole-group meetings.

The music center may need only about 80 sq ft, especially if its activities can easily expand into the whole-group area. Because singing, playing instruments, and dancing are noisy, the center should be located where the music will not disturb others. Sound-absorbing materials should, if possible, be used on the floor.

The music center should be arranged with listening stations; displays of CDs and books related to music, dance, and the performing arts (stored so children can see the front of the book or CD); counters for xylophones, autoharps, tape players, and other "sound makers;" and shelving or baskets for other rhythm and percussion instruments as well as scarves, capes, and other dress-up clothes for dancing or marching.

Water and Sand Center.   This is where children explore two of nature's most intriguing raw materials—water and sand. Because of concerns about allergies, sand is sometimes replaced with flax seed or other nonallergenic material, but the lessons remain the same. Sand and and water tables help children learn many basic math and science concepts such as empty and full, heavy and light, more and less, shallow and deep, and measurement. Sand and water tables can be also used for other sensory explorations and messy activities (West & Cox, 2001).

The sand and water area is relatively small; approximately 60 sq ft is sufficient. Sand and water tables need to be located near a sink and drain. They should be placed on a waterproof floor that does not get slippery when wet.

Shelving for water and sand toys must be waterproof. Many sand and water play toys are small so tote boxes usually work well. They can be labeled with pictures or words (e.g., *floating, measuring*) so they can be rotated as desired.

Carpentry or Woodworking Center.   Older preschoolers and primary-age children enjoy carpentry and woodworking. Handling natural materials and real tools, hearing the sounds of cutting and hammering, and smelling sawdust are valuable sensory experiences. The woodworking center also provides children opportunities to refine fine motor skills and eye-hand coordination; helps develop logico-mathematical understandings; and gives them opportunitites to represent the real world through play.

Woodworking is a noisy center that requires about 60 sq ft. It must be located out of the flow of traffic in an easy-to-supervise area. Children need plenty of light and should be able to concentrate without distraction. The area must be equipped with a sturdy work-bench and high-quality tools (Sosna, 2000). A storage rack with tracings of tools simplifies storage. The workbench and tools should be portable so they can be stored when not in use. Keep wood scraps nearby in boxes, baskets, and wooden bins.

Science and Mathematics Center.   This area invites children to wonder, reflect, and problem solve about the scientific and mathematical world. Here they can see how science and mathematics are part of their everyday lives, learn to respect and appreciate the world of nature, and develop physical and logico-mathematical concepts related to math and science. All too often the science and mathematics center consists simply of a window ledge with a plant and a small "discovery table." This approach misses many opportunities—science and math are fascinating to children and should be central to the curriculum.

That is why plants, an aquarium, and a cage for a small animal should be welcome in any corner of the room. Science and mathematical concepts are also taught outdoors and in the cooking, block, water and sand, and manipulative centers.

Generally speaking, science and mathematics centers should be at least 60 sq ft. That is large enough for the center to be the home base for caring for animals and plants and for other messy activities. The center should be near a sink; electrical outlets are needed for aquariums and incubators; and it should have flooring that is easily cleaned. Be careful to comply with state licensing regulations concerning food preparation areas and their proximity to animals in cages.

Some science and mathematics materials are left out throughout the year, but others are changed regularly. Consider the following criteria when planning a science and math center:

1.   There should be plenty of display and work space. A counter at children's sitting or standing height can hold an aquarium, terrarium, plants, or animal cages. Tables or counter space can also hold materials that are not out all the time—magnets, prisms, seeds, rocks, sound makers, models of spaceships, dinosaurs, mathematics manipulatives, and so on. A centrally located table draws children's attention to the current activity (e.g., getting seeds from a pumpkin). A book display rack with a small area rug or floor cushions makes a nice reading area. Plenty of display area is needed to document children's work and to display science pictures and posters.

2.   Closed storage space such as a built-in closet can have open shelves at the top and built-in drawers to store science and mathematics items at the bottom. Units with tote bins are also ideal for storage of math and science materials.

Cooking Center.   Cooking is a real activity. It is not pretend! Cooking activities are not designed to teach children how to cook. They are designed to promote good nutrition and healthy habits; to teach safety concepts; to enhance language, mathematics, science

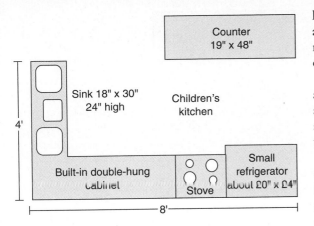

Figure 6.5
Cooking Center

learning; and to provide multicultural experiences. Cooking also promotes social interactions, fine motor skills, decision making, and problem solving through enjoyable firsthand experiences.

Many early childhood programs do not have space for a separate cooking center so it is often combined with the art and/or science/math center. An ideal cooking center, whether a separate or shared area, requires approximately 30 sq ft and would look like a small kitchen (see Figure 6-5).

The center needs a stove with a see-through glass oven door, a refrigerator, a sink, and storage cabinets. Storage cabinets that hold dangerous items such as knives, electrical appliances, and cleaning supplies, need to be locked. Pantry items need to be stored carefully to keep them fresh and pest-free.

Manipulatives and Small Construction Toy Center. This area gives children opportunities to work with small objects that help them develop fine motor skills and eye–hand coordination, solve problems, and develop spatial concepts.

The center is usually located in a quiet part of the room with resilient flooring or low-pile carpet. It does not need to be very large, approximately 100 sq ft should suffice. Children generally sit or stand at tables while using Legos and other interlocking blocks, parquetry blocks, beads, sewing cards, or working on puzzles with just a few pieces. They need some open floor space for building with Tinkertoys or Junior Erector sets; for playing with a marble chute; and for working on floor puzzles. Storage cabinets with open shelves and clear plastic totes, baskets, or trays or boxes labeled with pictures and words keep materials in view and give children opportunities to independently choose what they want to work with. See Figure 6.6 for a sample floorplan for a manipulative and small construction toy center.

Language, Literacy, Writing and Book Center. While you will want to have books and writing materials throughout the room, this is the area designed specifically to give children opportunities for looking and listening activities. It also offers children hands-on experiences with the written and spoken word. The ideal center would be large (approximately 150 sq ft) but subdivided into cozy sections for reading, writing, and listening. The center should be located in a quiet section of the room. Figure 6-7 provides a sample plan for a language, literacy, writing and book center.

Consider the following criteria when planning a language and literacy center:

1. A loft can provide space for two book nooks. The loft itself could be equipped with a small book rack or book pockets that show the front covers of books (not their spines), a small puppet theater, and puppets. Beneath the loft, cozy floor pillows and task lighting could serve as a book nook for one or two children.
2. Adjacent to the loft can be an area equipped as a communications center, with computers and listening stations, as well as a writing center with a variety of pencils, pens, and markers, and several kinds of lined and unlined paper, envelopes, shopping lists, and so on.
3. The third area could be equipped as a reading and storytelling area with book storage and display; flannel and magnetic boards; a wall pocket chart. It needs places to sit at a table, on a couch, or on the floor. The back of the reading center can serve as a language game area, with storage cabinets, a low table with floor cushions, a chalkboard room divider, and a magnetic board.

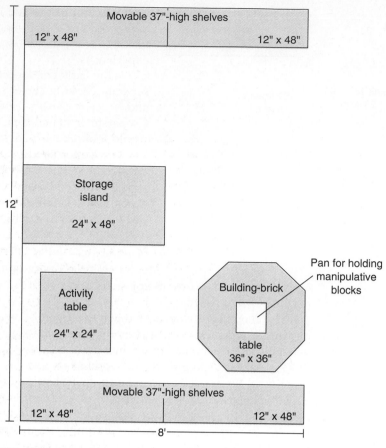

Figure 6.6
Manipulative and Small Constructive Toy Center

Other Areas.   Many centers overlook the importance of providing private cozy spaces in all classrooms. This is important, particularly for children who spend long days in child care (Cost, Quality, and Child Outcomes Study Team, 1995). Private areas serve as places to tune out, to enjoy being by oneself for a few minutes, or to reduce excitement (Isbell & Exelby, 2001). A small block center, a rocking horse or riding toy, a window seat, or a playhouse also give children places to watch from before entering play. These areas may be particularly critical to the development of children with disabilities (Prescott, 1987).

Children also enjoy special-interest areas, such as an aquarium or terrarium; a rock, insect, or shell collection; a garden or bird feeder to observe from a window; a flowering hanging basket; and displays related to specific curriculum themes. Special-interest areas can also be used to display "treasures" from home, with the understanding that preschool is not the best place for very valuable or very fragile items that cannot be replaced.

Learning Centers for Primary-Level Children.   Learning centers for primary-grade children (ages 6 through 8) do not have to be as clearly defined as do centers for younger children. Related activities and content areas can also be combined for older children. For example, a primary program might have these learning centers: cooking/science/art, dramatic play/music, reading, and mathematics/block construction. This is another way to cluster centers: art/cooking, construction, mathematics/computer, and language/reading and writing. Similar to preschool/kindergarten room design, messy and noisy areas are separated

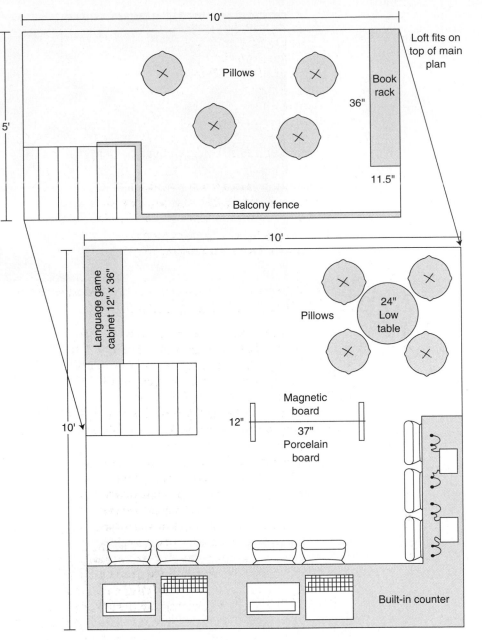

Figure 6.7
Emerging Literacy and Book Center

from less messy and quieter areas. The space, furniture, and furnishings requirements for each center are the same as those for centers previously described.

School-Age Child Care Activity Centers.   Activity centers for children who come to child care after school are unique for three reasons. First, school-age programs must accommodate a wide age range, often 5 through 10 or 12 years. Second, programs operate just 2 to 3 hours a day during the school year and typically all day during school holidays and summer vacation periods. Third, school-age programs often share their space with a school, preschool child care, or faith-based program.

School-age children enjoy cooking and other activities they would do if they went directly home after school.

Since school-age programs seldom have a space that is solely theirs, activity centers are often created by arranging mobile storage units or room dividers to fit their needs. It is also very helpful to have access to a large storage closet or storage workroom to supplement the classroom storage units. The activities offered to school-age children are similar to what school-age children would do if they went home after school. School-age care centers should include:

a. Cooking or snack areas
b. Quiet areas for reading, doing homework, listening to music with headphones, creative writing, or just resting
c. Workspaces for arts and crafts, including woodworking if possible
d. Table games and manipulative areas
e. A computer center with Internet access (with appropriate parental controls in place) and a printer

Other areas children enjoy are science centers, and games such as Ping-Pong or Foosball.

See suggested floor plans for classrooms for 3-year-olds, (Figure 6-8), 4-year-olds, (Figure 6-9), and school-age children who come after school and during school holidays and vacations (Figure 6-10).

Application Activity

Assume you are working with a class of 3- to 5-year-olds. Select a learning center as the focus of this project. Propose a layout for this learning center. Begin by selecting furniture, equipment, and toys by consulting appendix 4 for suggested materials as well as recommendations on vendors' Web sites (see appendix 1 for suppliers) and other professional resources. Once you have selected the furniture, toys, and equipment, arrange that equipment in the classroom. Give the director an estimate for how much your recommendation will cost.

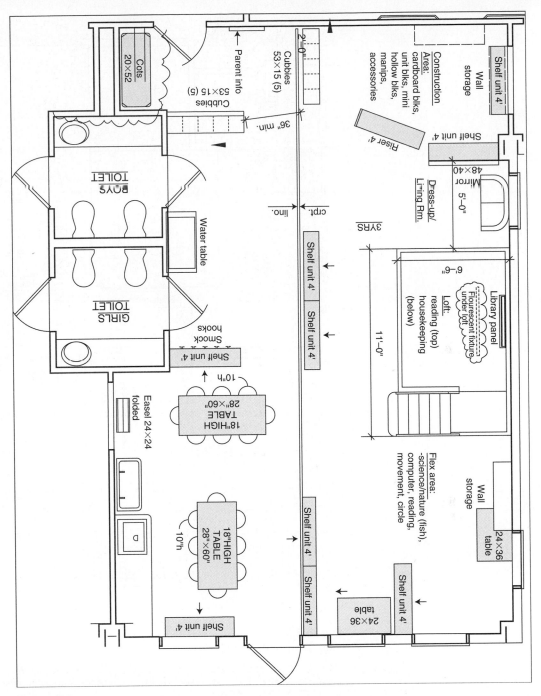

Figure 6.8
Floor Plan for 3-year-olds

Source: Floor plan developed by Louis Torelli for the Children's Center at the University of South Carolina, Columbia, South Carolina. Used by permission of the University of South Carolina.

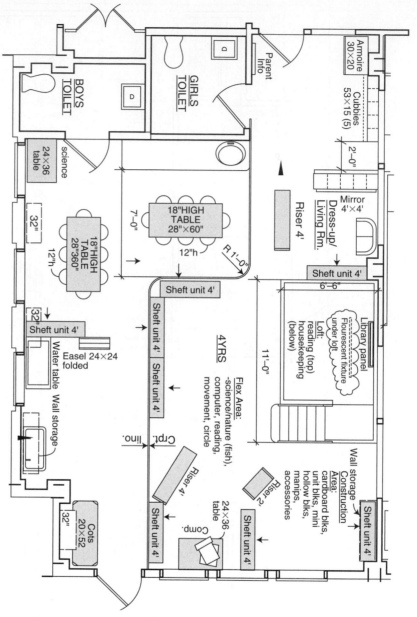

Figure 6.9
Floor Plan for 4-year-olds

Source: Floor plan developed by Louis Torelli for the Children's Center at the University of South Carolina, Columbia, South Carolina. Used by permission of the University of South Carolina.

Additional Areas in Classrooms

Young children are learning all the time—in learning centers and while being cared for and learning to care for themselves. Facility planners need to consider areas for personal belongings and for caregiving routines, in addition to the activity areas described above, as they plan a child care facility.

Children's Cubbies.   Children should have their own individual cubbies for storing book bags, lunch boxes, coats, hats, special toys, and other items from home. They create a

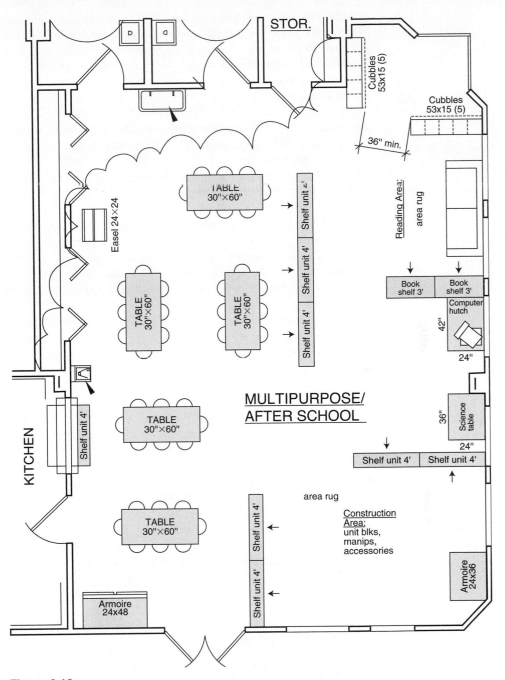

Figure 6.10
Floor plan for School-Age Care

Source: Floor plan developed by Louis Torelli for the Children's Center at the University of South Carolina, Columbia, South Carolina. Used by permission of the University of South Carolina.

personal space for each child, help children learn to care for their possessions and respect those of others, and reduce the spread of contagious diseases. The area for cubbies should be close to the door and should have enough room for parents and teachers to help children settle in for the day. The floor covering in this area should be easily cleaned because it will get quite dirty during inclement weather.

Infants' Diapering and Toileting Areas. Diapering and toileting areas should be spacious enough for children and the adults who are supervising and helping them. They should be easy to clean and disinfect. They should be attractive and cheerful, decorated with mirrors and interesting pictures, communicating to children that this is an important and comfortable place. Ideally, diapering and toileting areas have windows for sunlight and ventilation.

Diapering Area. The diapering area should be carefully arranged so that the caregiver can easily reach all needed supplies: diapers, wipes, creams or lotions, latex gloves, a foot-operated wastebasket with a plastic liner for sanitary disposal of soiled diapers, and disinfecting solution for cleaning the diapering surface. Often changing tables for older children are designed with steps so they can climb up, saving the caregiver's back from the strain of frequent lifting. If paper is used on the changing table, place the roll at the end of the table so it can easily be replaced after each diaper change (Lally & Stewart, 1990). The diapering area must have a sink with warm running water, liquid soap, and paper towels. This sink cannot be used for food preparation or for washing dishes (Gonzalez-Mena & Eyer, 2007). The diapering area should be situated so the caregiver can keep an eye on other children while meeting individual children's caregiving needs.

Children's Toileting Areas. Children's toileting areas should be conveniently located in or very near classrooms. Plan one toilet for 10 to 20 children over 2 years of age. Toilets should be small enough for children to use independently or sturdy step stools should be available to make children comfortable when using them by themselves. The height of the toilet seat must be appropriate for wheelchair users, and toilet tissue should be not more than 6 in. from the front of the toilet bowl. Handrails should be mounted on the wall for additional safety. Low partitions between, and in front of, toilets provide privacy while permitting easy supervision. Because young children are apt to surprise you with what they flush down the toilet, you will want to install multiple clean-outs, easily accessible U-traps, and separate shutoff valves for each toilet.

Lavatory sinks should be adjacent to, but outside, the toilet areas. Children should be able to reach sinks independently. Provide sturdy step stools if needed. Water faucets with levers or blades are easier to use than ones with knobs. They help children become independent. Water heaters should be set to 100° to 120°F to prevent scalding. Dishwashing requires hotter water, so you will need a separate water heater for the kitchen. Children need access to liquid soap, paper towels, and a trash receptacle for towel disposal.

If you plan to install a drinking fountain it should be located near the rest rooms, out of the flow of traffic, and should be low enough for children to use independently or a sturdy step stool should be provided. Select a fountain that will accommodate children with disabilities. You will want to have paper cups available for children not yet able to get enough water to quench their thirst from a fountain.

Food Preparation, Feeding and Dining Areas

Infants' bottles and food are usually prepared in their classrooms. Classrooms need to be equipped with a sink specifically for food preparation, a small refrigerator, and a bottle warmer. Infants' milk and food should never be heated in a microwave oven. Microwaves create hot spots that can be dangerous. Infants should be held when they are bottle fed and as they start solid foods. When they are able to sit on their own, they are ready to sit at a small table and to enjoy family style meals with their classmates.

Older children are likely to eat snacks in their classrooms and lunch either in their classrooms or in a central dining room. Mealtimes should be opportunities for relaxed conversation. Tables and chairs should be child-size and comfortable. Dishes and cutlery should be sized for small hands. All surfaces should be able to withstand frequent sanitizing.

Conveniently located child-size sinks contribute to children's autonomy and help develop healthy habits.

All-day programs that serve breakfast and lunch usually have a commercial kitchen, bring in catered food, or children bring their meals from home. Programs that serve only snacks do not need a separate kitchen—snacks, serving utensils, and disposable cups, plates, and napkins can be kept in classrooms.

Napping Areas.   Napping areas should be cozy and relaxing. Each infant needs to follow his or her individual napping schedule and must have an individual crib that is in the same location every day. Licensing regulations are likely to specify spacing between cribs and may have other rules addressing the location of sleeping rooms for infants. It is important that infants always be placed on their backs to sleep to reduce the risk of sudden infant death syndrome (SIDS).

Toddlers and preschoolers usually nap after lunch and can be expected to adjust to a regular napping schedule. Most programs plan for toddlers and preschoolers to rest in their classrooms. That means you will need room darkening shades and an individual cot for each child. Children's cots should be placed in the same location every day. A calm atmosphere, books to look at, soft music, a favorite blanket or "lovey" from home, and a back rub often help children sleep restfully (Gonzalez-Mena & Eyer, 2007).

Developing Classroom Floor Plans

You need to systematically develop floor plans to create an environment that will help you meet the program's goals. We recommend that you take the following steps as you design classroom layouts:

1. The first step is to determine how each classroom will be used. You need to identify the specific caregiving, educational and developmental activities it is meant to support.

2. Next, you will want to consider which activities create a lot of traffic or are likely to be messy and wet (like entryways, painting, and eating), and which activities require quiet, cozy environments. When designing infant rooms, you also need to plan an area for cribs. They should be placed in a location that can be made dark and comfortable for sleeping. Select areas in each classroom for these wet and active functions, as well as spaces for quiet and cozy ones.

3. Now it is time to identify the centers that best fit the program's goals. Each classroom should include at least five different interest areas (Harms et al., 2005). Calculate the number of places needed for center play by multiplying the number of children by 1.5; for example, 20 children require 30 activity places. Having more choices than children lessens waiting time and offers a reasonable number of options.

List the centers you plan to incorporate and note the maximum number of children you expect to be in each center at one time, as shown in Table 6.2.

This process will create a framework for the center you are creating and will generate priorities to guide your work.

Isolation Area.   An isolation area is needed to care for ill or hurt children until a family member arrives to take them home. It is good for the isolation area to have a bed or cot and to have a few toys and books nearby. A small bathroom adjacent to the isolation area can be very helpful.

Table 6.2
Determining the Anticipated Capacity of Each Learning Center

Center	Maximum Activity Places
Cooking	3
Dramatic play	4
And so on	And so on
	Total of 30 places

Adult Areas

Working in an early childhood program is physically and emotionally demanding. The quality of the work environment directly affects an adult's abilities to perform well.

Family Reception Area.   The family reception area should be comfortable and well defined. It should invite adults to gather and can provide a place for family members and staff to work together (Olds, 2001). It should provide information about the program, can be used to announce parent organization activities such as social events and fund-raisers, and can be a clearinghouse for information about the community. The reception area is an ideal place for displays that put the spotlight on children's learning. This area might also include materials designed to answer families' questions about child development, parenting, or other particular needs.

Adult Lounge/Rest Room.   A comfortable lounge should be provided for all staff so they have a place to relax during breaks. The lounge should have a sink, refrigerator, microwave, and a coffee machine so staff can prepare and eat snacks. This is also an appropriate place to display professional magazines and journals. If possible, provide a computer with Internet access so that teachers can email parents or search for professional information. For greater privacy, adult rest rooms should not be part of the lounge but should be located nearby.

Staff Workroom.   Sometimes the adult lounge and workroom are combined, but ideally they are separate. The workroom is likely to be shared by teachers in several classrooms, and perhaps by all teachers in the facility. It needs desks or tables and chairs, shelves and cabinets for professional materials and supplies, office machines (e.g., paper cutter, laminator, photocopier, computer and printer), and a sink. This is a good place for staff members' personal belongings. If it is used this way, each individual needs a spacious locker with a lock.

Professional Library.   An early childhood program should have a professional library to keep staff informed and to help them in planning. The library is usually a storage and display area located in, or adjacent to, the director's office or the workroom. The library should include professional books; curriculum materials; journals and other publications of professional associations; advocacy materials; catalogs from suppliers of equipment and materials; and professional development software, tapes, or DVDs.

Office.   The program director needs a place for private conversations with parents and staff and a secure place to store confidential financial, personnel, and child records. The director needs a secure computer, a printer, telephone with answering machine, and a comfortable and convenient workspace. This office is sometimes near or part of the reception area located by the front door and is sometimes a separate room.

Environmental Control

Controlling noise and light and installing and maintaining effective heating, cooling, and ventilation systems are important considerations when planning for a comfortable early childhood environment. Acoustics and lighting were discussed earlier in this chapter.

Heating, Cooling, and Ventilating.   Child care regulations typically specify that rooms should be kept between 68°F and 80°F at floor level. In most states, regulations also stipulate that all indoor areas must have good ventilation designed to minimize drafts, odors, extreme temperatures, and humidity, which can be achieved either by opening the windows or by using air conditioning or safely installed fans.

OUTDOOR SPACE

Outdoor play is very important to young children. Theorists such as Piaget and Vygotsky recognized the important contributions play can make to all developmental domains, and we recognize that outdoor play gives children opportunities to pursue vigorous, boisterous, self-directed pursuits. In fact, researchers have shown that outdoor play uniquely enhances motor development (Poest, Williams, Witt, & Atwood, 1990); provides sensory stimulation (Olds, 2001; Tilbury, 1994); presents opportunities to use language and solve problems (Rivkin, 1995); contributes to cognitive development (Bodrova & Leong, 2003; Perry, 2003; Sallis et al., 1999); and provides children opportunities to practice and develop social skills (Klein, Wirth, & Linas, 2003; Frost, Wortham, & Reifel, 2001).

For these reasons, facility planners should devote at least as much time, care, and creativity designing outdoor areas as they do planning classrooms. A playground is not a frill—it is an absolutely essential part of a quality program of early care and education. In fact, when adults were asked about their favorite kinds of play as children, over 70% described outdoor play experiences (Henniger, 1994). We are making memories for the children in our care!

General Criteria and Specifications for Child Care Playgrounds

Playgrounds have the potential to enhance every developmental domain, foster children's sense of wonder, appeal to all the senses, create a sense of place, preserve and enhance the site's natural features, and to be aesthetically pleasing (Koralek, 2002; Olds, 2001; Talbot & Frost, 1989; Wilson, Kilmer, & Knauerhase, 1996). They can contribute to the program's success in meeting its goals while meeting every child's needs for active play.

Planners should consider the playground's location, size, terrain, and surface. They must be certain the playground meets all safety standards and is accessible, or has the potential to be made accessible, to children with disabilities. These issues are discussed later in this chapter.

Location.   If your facility has one playground, it should not surround the building because that arrangement would make supervision almost impossible. If each age group has its own playground, they can ring the facility, giving each group access to the play area designed especially for them.

If the facility will have just one playground, the south side of the building, which will have sun throughout the day, is generally the most desirable. To minimize the chance of accidents as children go in and out, a facility should have:

- A door threshold flush with the indoor/outdoor surfaces, or a ramp if an abrupt change in surface levels is unavoidable

Well-designed outdoor environments enhance children's quality of life.

- Floor treatments that provide maximum traction as children transition from the playground to the classroom
- A sliding door or a door prop
- A door with windows to prevent collisions

To ensure constant supervision for all children, the bathroom should be directly accessible from the playground or just inside the door. A drinking fountain should also be easily accessible to children during outdoor play.

Size.   Most states' licensing regulations require outdoor activity areas to have at least 75 sq ft per child. The amount of space required sometimes varies according to the age of the children, with infants and toddlers requiring less space than older children. NAEYC accreditation criteria (2005) require at least 75 sq ft per child "for each child playing outside at any one time. The total amount of required play space is based on a maximum of one-third of the total center enrollment being outside at one time" (NAEYC, 2005). Other experts recommend 100 to 200 sq ft per child and advise, when possible, that the playground be large enough to accommodate all children at the same time so that every child will be able to spend a significant amount of time outdoors every day (Olds, 2001).

The Fence.   Most states and NAEYC Accreditation Standards (2005) require that playgrounds be surrounded by a fence or a natural barrier and gates that children cannot open. We recommend nonclimbable barriers 4 to 6 ft high, with a gap at the bottom of no more than 3 1/2 in. A fence is essential when the playground is bordered by a dangerous area such as a parking lot, street, swimming pool, or a natural body of water (Frost, 1992). Many states also require fences as boundaries between areas for infant/toddlers and older children (Olds, 2001). These interior fences do not have to be as tall as those around the playground's perimeter.

When selecting fencing material, consider what children will hear and see on the other side of the fence. If the view is interesting, select chain link, lattice, or other materials that permit visibility. When the view is not desirable, the site is very noisy, or there are concerns about vandalism, fences made of wood or concrete are better choices. Solid fences can incorporate different textures and colors or plantings to soften the view and create visual interest. Remember to consider how the fence looks from the inside of the playground and also how it fits into the neighborhood and whether it makes the center inviting or intimidating from the street (Olds, 2001).

In addition to having an entry from the building, the outdoor area should have a locking 12-ft gate large enough for large lawn maintenance equipment and trucks delivering sand. Be careful not to install permanent structures in such a way that they block sand delivery trucks from the sand play area.

Terrain.   Outdoor play spaces with varied terrain are more interesting and more challenging than flat ones. When possible, retain the natural vegetation and incorporate existing slopes, trees, rock outcroppings, and other interesting features. If the play space is flat and barren, however, it is not difficult to create small hills which give children opportunities to climb, roll, and slide. It is also possible to add vegetation by planting a mix of shrubs, trees, and flowers. These features create private areas that invite exploration and make-believe (Olds, 2001).

Hills do not have to be large to be challenging. A hill that rises just 3 ft and has a gentle slope of no more than $10°$ is perfect for preschoolers. These hills and mounds easily become part of the playscape; for example, a slide can be mounted on the slope of a small mound. Interesting paths for wheeled toys can also be created in rolling terrain.

Surface.   Surfaces for infants and toddlers should be mainly grass, wood, sand, and dirt. Outdoor activity areas for older children should also have a variety of surfaces. All playgrounds need to be well drained, with the fastest drying areas nearest the building. Approximately one-half to two-thirds of the total square footage of the outdoor playground should be covered with grass, and about 1,000 sq ft should be covered in hard surfaces for activities such as wheeled-toy riding and block building. Some areas should be left as dirt for gardening and for realizing "a satisfaction common to every child—digging a big hole!" (Baker, 1968, p. 61). Areas underneath equipment need special resilient materials that are described below in the "Safety" and other "Other Considerations" discussions.

Shade and Shelter.   Every playground should provide shelter and shade to protect children from wind and exposure to the sun. The amount of shelter you need to add will depend, in part, on your climate and the shade and shelter provided by trees, terrain, and nearby buildings. No matter what your climate, a covered play area, such as a verandah that gets plenty of air circulation, can serve as an extension of children's classrooms. It will be an inviting place for quiet play during warm weather and for active play when it is cold or inclement.

Storage.   Storage is needed for loose parts such as wheeled toys, sand and water play accessories, balls, trucks, big blocks, and gardening tools. Since these toys are more likely to be used if they are stored near where they will be used, their storage area should either be attached to the main building in an area adjoining the playground, in an area children pass on their way to the playground, or in a free-standing outdoor shed located on the playground. If detached from the building, the outdoor shed should fit in and not detract from the main building and should, if possible, be positioned to break the wind. A single storage unit 12 ft long, 10 ft wide, and 7 to 8 ft high is sufficient for most early childhood programs.

Create a place for everything by equipping the storage area with hooks and shelves mounted within children's reach and bins children can manage on their own. This way children are able to get the equipment out and to help put it away. A high shelf to store seasonal items or materials for staff use is also useful.

Smaller lockable storage cabinets located near particular centers, such as sand, block building, and dramatic play, are ideal for some materials. These cabinets, like storage sheds, must be made of durable materials that can withstand moisture.

All outdoor storage areas should have slightly raised flooring to prevent flooding after a heavy rain. A ramp makes it easier to move equipment into and out of the storage shed and minimizes tripping.

Outdoor Space Arrangement

The indoor space should be extended outdoors, and the outdoor space should be extended indoors. Together they enhance children's growth and development, and support the program's goals.

Before planning an outdoor space, talk with staff, family members, and older children and see what they would like to do outside. Visit other playgrounds and analyze the current site. In planning or redesigning outside play areas, evaluation tools can help identify what is missing and point you toward elements you would most like to include (DeBord, Hestenes, Moore, Cosco, & McGinnis, 2002; Frost, Wortham, & Reifel, 2007).

Outdoor Areas for Infants and Toddlers.   Many people think of playgrounds as spaces designed for vigorous rough-and-tumble play. They often assume there is no reason to create outdoor areas for very young children. But infants and toddlers are no different from older children. They too need fresh air and sunlight, delight in exploring nature, and benefit from time outdoors. But it is true that infants' and toddlers' outside environment is different from spaces for older children.

Four specific criteria are extremely important to consider when planning an outdoor area for infants and toddlers. First, it must be safe, that is, it should provide a gentle terrain for crawling, walking, running, and stepping up and down; be free of materials that would be harmful if eaten such as gravel, mushrooms, and plants with potentially dangerous leaves, flowers, or stems; and it must not have sand areas that could be used as a litterbox by neighborhood cats. See appendix 5 for a list of poisonious and nonpoisonious plants that might be in your environment.

Second, the area must be scaled to be comfortable and accessible for the very young. Young infants enjoy blankets put on soft grass in shady, protected areas. Lawns also encourge early crawlers to explore and toddlers to roll, tumble, and relax. Cruisers enjoy low benches or logs to support their explorations and for them to crawl over or around. Crawlers and beginning walkers also enjoy paths with interesting textures such as patterned rocks, colored bricks, and half logs buried along the way. Raised (15-in. maximum) walkways with railings also create appropriate challenges. Beginning walkers also need smooth surfaces to enjoy push and pull and ride-on toys (Gonzalez-Mena & Eyer, 2007; Lally & Stewart, 1990).

Third, outdoor areas should invite the sensory motor explorations of the very young. Differences in hardness, texture, color, temperature, and areas in the sun and shade are interesting places to crawl and walk and to use pull, push, or riding toys.

Fourth, infants and toddlers need loose materials for play. Many of the rattles, stacking toys, soft blocks, board books, and other materials they enjoy indoors can come outside with them. If teachers are going to be able to manage getting children and toys outdoors, the playground must be very close and very convenient to the classroom.

Spaces Specifically for Young Infants.   Nonmobile infants enjoy an enclosed area with a surface that encourages reaching, grasping, and kicking. The area should stimulate visual and auditory senses with colorful streamers, soft wind chimes, prisms and mirrors, and natural sounds such as breezes rustling in the trees and birdsongs. A stroller path adds an additional opportunity for exploration and might make it possible for babies to visit older siblings playing in other areas of the playground.

Spaces Specifically for Mobile Infants and Toddlers.   Four design principles can guide your efforts to create an appropriate play environment for mobile infants and toddlers:

1. Allow for a wide range of child-initiated movements via pathways, hills, ramps, and tunnels.
2. Stimulate their senses.
3. Provide for novelty, variety, and challenge.
4. Make the area safe and comfortable. (Frost, 1992).

The safe, natural environment—trees, shrubs, flowers, pine cones, and tree stumps—should be left undisturbed. As much as possible, play areas for mobile infants and toddlers need to integrate sensory, exploratory, and action-oriented devices. For example, a structure can have panels to look at and feel; objects like pulleys, drums, and steering wheels to manipulate; and climbers and slides that promote large muscle play.

Figure 6.11 is a plan for an infant and toddler outdoor play space. It illustrates some of the principles described above.

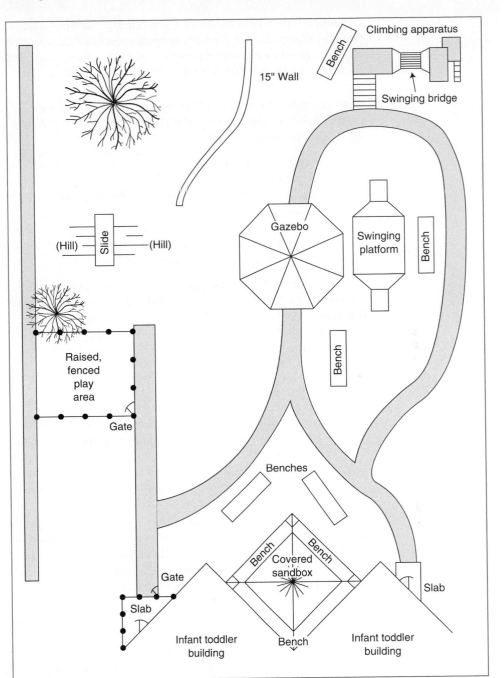

Figure 6.11
Infant and Toddler Outdoor Activity Area

Outdoor Areas for Older Children. Older children need playgrounds that enhance their developing motor skills, their advancing cognitive skills, and their growing peer interactions. Playgrounds for preschoolers should build on and extend the experiences they had in infancy and toddlerhood. For example, preschoolers still need structures that integrate sensory, exploratory, and action-oriented activities, but the structures should be more complex than those seen on toddler playgrounds. Like toddlers, preschoolers need dramatic play materials, but their props need to encourage more advanced symbolism and more cooperative play than do props for toddlers. Likewise, a smooth transition in playground design must occur in programs serving preschool and primary-age children. Primary-age children need more open grassy areas, more gymnastic types of apparatuses, and more pretend toys than do preschool children (Frost, 1992).

Play Experiences and Zones.   Like play indoors, outdoor play needs to meet the developmental needs of the whole child. Four types of play enhance preschoolers' and primary-age children's development:

1. Functional or exercise play that involves practice and repetition of gross-motor activities
2. Constructive play during which children use materials such as paint or sand to create
3. Dramatic or pretend play that often occurs in small, private spaces
4. Cooperative social play such as games with rules and sustained dramatic play (Johnson, Christie, & Yawkey, 1987)

Like indoor classrooms, playgrounds have activity centers or zones (Perry, 2003). Some experts suggest that outdoor centers should duplicate the play experiences found indoors (Henniger, 1993), but others believe outdoor centers should be unique and different (Jensen & Bullard, 2002). Playgrounds with the following five play zones bridge these contrasting views:

1. A nature zone with plants, animals, and rocks that can be located in either an active or quiet area.
2. An adventure zone for construction and digging.
3. An active zone for play on play structures, sand/water play, and for chase and ball games. Preschoolers need open grassy areas; primary-level children can handle chase and ball games on grassy or hard-surface areas.
4. A quiet area with easels, water/sand tables, a book nook, and a snack area.
5. A quiet play zone for dramatic play. (Guddemi & Eriksen, 1992)

General Criteria for Arranging Zones.   Outdoor play is different from indoor play in several important ways. First, there are fewer restrictions. Children can be boisterous, rambunctious, and energetic, and there are less likely to be rules governing how materials are to be used and how many children can play in each center. That means children usually have more freedom to do as they please when they are outdoors (Perry, 2003). This is why you are more likely to see children combine several kinds of activities into one theme outdoors than inside. For example, playing "car wash" is likely to involve children combining water play, dramatic play, and vigorous physical activity as they push, pull, and ride on wheeled toys. There are also more likely to be multiple opportunities for particular kinds of play outdoors; for example, the playhouse under the play structure, tents under the trees, or the garden may all support cooperative dramatic play.

Outdoor playscapes should be designed to provide opportunities for quiet play as well as the vigorous activities we often think of as being typical on the playground. Children playing quietly need protection from their peers' rambunctious play as well as from wind or heat. Boulders, logs, park benches, and picnic tables can provide attractive seating for those engaged in quiet play. Smooth surfaces that are good for jumping rope, playing jacks, and for board or card games can also be good for quiet play. Quiet play areas can be situated near shrubbery or large stones, in nooks created by changes in terrain, or in a veranda or other playground shelter.

Both active and quiet players need pathways to guide their transitions from one part of the playground to another. Clear paths can minimize conflict and prevent accidents (e.g., getting too close to swings). Pathways should lead to places of interest, like a garden, should connect equipment within a zone, and connect play zones with each other. They can be made interesting by using curves and intersections; by including bridges; by having gates to open and close; by varying the path's texture and composition by using materials such as stepping stones, mosaics made of pavers or pretty rocks, or timber rounds; and by including special attractions like flowers, a butterfly or ladybug house, a wind chime, or a weather station along the path; and by including places to sit.

Specific Zones and Equipment.   Plan for your playground to have five play spaces per child. That way every child will have several play options from which to choose. Consider the following guidelines when planning for playground zones:

1. **Open area.**   The open area needs to be large for playing with balls, Frisbees, and hula hoops, as well as for just running.

2. **Road for wheeled toys.**   A hard-surfaced area can form a tricycle, wagon, or doll stroller road extending through the outdoor space and returning to its starting point. The road should be wide enough to permit passing. A curving road is more interesting than a straight one. Avoid right-angle turns because they cause accidents. Like pathways, the road should have some challenges (e.g., a slight rise). Roads are more interesting if there are attractions like store fronts or gas stations along the way or archways to ride through. They should be made aesthetically pleasing by including flowers and shrubs.

3. **Sandpit or sandbox.**   Sand play is preschool children's most popular outside activity (Berry, 1993). Sand play can be provided by creating a sandpit or a sandbox. A sandpit can be a large mound or a narrow, winding river of sand. Children should have flat working surfaces, such as wooden boards or flat boulders, beside or in the sand. An outdoor sandpit should have a boundary element that "provides a 'sense' of enclosure for the playing children, keeps out unwanted traffic, protects the area against water draining from adjacent areas, and helps keep the sand within the sand play areas" (Osmon, 1971, p. 77). Boundaries can be built or created by the landscape.

A sandbox provides many of the same play opportunities as a sand pit but is smaller and is more clearly defined. Whether you provide sand play in a sandpit or a sand box, the work area should sometimes be exposed to the sanitizing and drying rays of the sun but should also have shade available to protect children from the sun. Water should be available to enhance sand play.

All sand areas must be covered when not in use to prevent neighborhood cats from using them as a litterbox. Sandbox covers are available from playground equipment vendors or can be made by securing shade cloth with heavy objects.

4. **Water areas.**   Water play is likely to be more energetic outdoors than it is inside. Playgrounds can feature birdbaths, fountains, elevated streams, water tables, sprinklers, and splash and wading pools. Water temperature should be between $60°F$ and $80°F$ ($16°C$ and $27°C$). Water play equipment need not be expensive. Children enjoy an inflatable or plastic pool and a spray nozzle or sprinkler on a garden hose as much as more expensive water play equipment. Be certain to follow licensing regulations, particularly as to required ratios, and health department regulations whenever children are near water.

5. **Gardens.**   Children enjoy gardens with any kind of plant life—flowers, vegetables, herbs, vines, shrubs, trees, and even weeds! An outdoor garden should be fenced to protect it from animals or from being accidentally trampled. Raised garden beds allow children in wheelchairs to participate.

6. Play structures.   Complex play structures are very popular additions to many playgrounds. They are likely to include ladders, chains, ropes, and/or tire nets, making it possible for children with varied skill levels and abilities to get up to, and down from, any number of play platforms. Preschoolers usually find climbing up easier than climbing down. That is one reason there should be multiple ways to navigate these structures. Additional features of many complex play structures include tunnels, swings, spiral and tube slides, horizontal ladders, and climbing walls. They accommodate vigorous play, often as part of cooperative social play that is so popular with this age group.

Figure 6.12, is a plan for a playground for preschool children. It illustrates some of the principles discussed above.

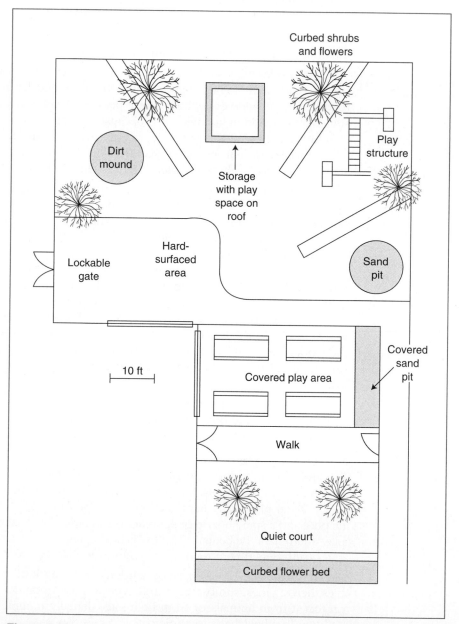

Figure 6.12
Preschool, Kindergarten, and Primary-Level Outdoor Activity Area

THE EARLY CHILDHOOD FACILITY

An essential part of planning an early childhood facility is determining how much space you will need to accomplish your goals. You must accommodate the building, the outdoor play space, paths and parking spaces, and will want to include landscaping so that the facility fits into the neighborhood. Experts recommend that the site provide 325 sq ft to 574 sq ft per child (Olds, 2001). Regrettably, many facilities are situated on sites that are too small to meet program goals, to comfortably accommodate children and adults for long hours each day, or to have opportunities for future growth.

For centers serving more than 150 children, the facility can seem formidable to young children and can be tiring for adults. Large centers would be wise to create a campus with linked buildings, multiple entrances and exits, and convenient parking.

Figures 6.1 through 6.2 illustrate possible arrangements for classrooms, selected classroom activiity areas, and outdoor activity areas for infants/toddlers and older children. The figures are not intended as models but are designed to graphically depict some of the ideas discussed in this chapter.

OTHER CONSIDERATIONS

Designing the indoor and outdoor spaces and selecting furniture, equipment, and supplies are just two aspects of facility planning. Early childhood administrators must always be mindful of safety standards and be certain their center accommodates the needs of children and adults with disabilities. Purchasing furniture, equipment, and supplies; maintaining the inside and outside of the facility; and securing insurance coverage for the facility and its contents are also important responsibilities of effective program administrators.

Safety

The safety of children, staff, parents, and others is of utmost importance. A safe environment gives children opportunities to work and play without undue restrictions that wear on both children and adults. The playground is the most hazardous area in most facilities. Playground safety needs to be a priority.

Regulations.   There are few, if any, regulations ensuring the safety of outdoor play areas (Runyan, Gray, Kotch, & Kreuter, 1991; Wallach & Afthinos, 1990). In fact, many states' child care regulations say little or nothing about playground safety, and even public school outdoor play areas are largely unregulated (Wallach & Edelstein, 1991). But even though mandatory regulations are scarce, there is a growing body of research that has documented the hazards commonly found on playgrounds and widely accepted guidelines are now available to help ensure the safety of your center's outdoor play areas.

The U.S. Consumer Product Safety Commission's *Handbook for Public Playground Safety* is the definitive resource addressing safety issues that those responsible for playgrounds in parks, schools, child care facilities, and other public places should be aware of. The Handbook is frequently updated and is available online, (see the Web address at the end of the chapter). It is a must-have reference that describes the characteristics of safe play spaces, identifies common risks, and describes how to avoid them.

Supervision.   The single most important thing you can do to ensure children's safety on the playground is to provide consistent supervision. Teachers must be aware of where every child is and must know what every child is doing. Even though it may be tempting to view outside play time as a break from classroom responsibilities, teachers need to be particularly vigilant to protect children from harm when they are outdoors. It may help teachers realize how important supervision is when they hear that almost 206,000 preschool- and elementary-age children receive emergency care from injuries that occurred on playground equipment every year. About 10% of those accidents occurred in child care settings. About three fourths of all injuries on public playgrounds resulted from falls, primarily onto the surface under the equipment. For children under age 5, 60% of all serious injuries involved the head and face. Children 5 and older most frequently suffered fractures to their wrists, lower arms, and elbows (Tinsworth & McDonald, 2001).

Ropes, shoestrings, cords, leashes, strings on clothing, and items tied to equipment can entrap children. More than half of all playground fatalities are caused by stangulation. *No ropes of any kind should ever be attached to playground equipment.* Teachers should also be particularly watchful around climbing equipment, particulary monkey bars and horizontal ladders, where more than half of all injuries that resulted in hospital visits occurred. Other injuries were caused by swings, colliding with stationary equipment, and injuries caused by protruding nails and screws, pinch points, sharp edges, hot surfaces and playground debris (CPSC, 2008).

Adequate supervision requires the following:

1. Teachers need training in playground safety. Materials have been developed in recent years that help teachers become better at ensuring their children's safety on the playground. See the addresses for Web-based resources from the National Program for Playground Safety and others at the end of this chapter.

2. Adequate supervision also requires that teachers be able to see the entire play area. Playgrounds should be designed with the importance of adequate supervision in mind, and teachers need to learn how to station themselves in different areas of the play yard so that, together, they can cover all areas used by children.

3. Teachers should be actively involved with children while they are on the playground. Young children are learning all the time, indoors and out, so that means the effective teacher is alert for opportunities to teach children new skills, to challenge them to reach their goals, to support their social and emotional development, to ask questions that prompt cognitive development, and to help them have fun.

Separating Play Areas.   The *Handbook for Public Playground Safety* identifies "use zones" (formally called "fall zones"), which are the surfaces under and around specific pieces of playground equipment into which a child exiting or falling from that equipment is likely to land. These use zones must have protective surfacing and are to be kept clear. Toys must not be left in use zones, and children's paths from one part of the playground to another must not pass through them.

Equipment Hazards.   Safe playgrounds are designed to meet the needs of a particular age group. Playgrounds for preschoolers include appropriate equipment, are scaled to fit typical 2- to 5-year-olds, and are laid out to create appropriate challenges for this age group. Playgrounds for preschoolers should be different in significant ways from areas planned for infants and toddlers and should also be distinct from playgrounds designed for 5- through 12-year-olds.

Safe playgrounds are also constructed from high-grade nontoxic materials that are appropriate for climate conditions, are correctly installed, and are well maintained.

A complete discussion of playground safety is beyond the scope of this book, but Table 6.3 summarizes safety specifications for some of the most popular equipment most likely to be on your playground. We recommend that you consult the CPSC handbook for specific guidelines related to climbing structures, see-saws, spring rockers, and other equipment you are considering for your program.

Table 6.3
Safety Specifications for Selected Playground Equipment

Swings: Single Axis Swings That Go Back and Forth

- Surround swings with a low barrier such as a fence or a hedge to prevent children from running into the use zone.
- No more than two swings should be hung from one support.
- Swing seats should be lightweight. Rubber and plastic are recommended.
- Provide at least 24" between swings; 30" between swings and support posts.
- Provide full bucket seats for children under 4 years.
- Animal figure swings are *not* recommended.
- S-hooks holding swing seats and those connected to the supporting structure must be completely closed (the gap should not admit a dime).
- Cushioning material must cover 6' on either side of the swing and 2 times the height of the supporting structure in the front and back.

Slides: Straight Chute Slide

- The platform at the top of the slide should be at least 22" long and should be at least as wide as the slide.
- Guardrails or protective barriers should surround the slide platform.
- There should be *no gaps* between the platform and the start of the chute.
- The slide's average incline should be no more than 30°.
- Sides should be at least 4" along the entire length of the slide.
- Metal slides should be placed out of the sun to prevent burning.
- The exit area should include at least 11" of horizontal surface and should be a designated distance from protective surfacing (this distance depends on the height of the slide).

Source: U.S. Consumer Product Safety Commission (2008). *Handbook for Public Playground Safety* available at http://www.cpsc.gov/cpscpub/pubs/325.pdf.

Surfacing Under Playground Equipment.   Hard-packed surfaces are to blame for many playground injuries. Dirt and grass are not enough to protect children from injury. Protective surfacing is needed under any equipment from which a child might fall because when a child falls, either the surface gives to absorb the impact or the child gives with a resulting bruise, broken bone, spinal injury, head injury, or even death.

The following are three types of commonly used surfaces. We consulted the *Handbook for Public Playground Safety* to describe some pros and cons for each. You will want to consult with a playground safety expert when making decisions about which surface is best for your climate, your budget, and the playground equipment you plan to install.

1. **Organic loose material.**   (wood chips, bark mulch, engineered wood fibers, etc.). These are the least expensive options. They are readily available, easy to install, drain well, are less abrasive, and less likely to attract animals than sand. It is difficult to maintain the recommended depth of 6 to 12 in. of organic material, however. These materials' cushioning potential is reduced when they are wet or frozen, they decompose and become compacted over time, are subject to microbacterial growth when wet, and must be frequently refurbished.

2. **Inorganic loose material.**   (sand, gravel, pea gravel, shredded tires). These are also low-cost options. They are readily available, easy to install, and do not encourge the growth of undesirable microbes. Maintaining a depth of 6 to 12 in. can be a challenge, however, because children's activities tend to scatter them all. The cushioning potential of sand, gravel and pea gravel are reduced when they are wet, frozen, and when there is high humidity, but shredded tires retain their resiliency and are less likely to compact than other

loose-fill materials. Each of these options has drawbacks, however. Sand blows away, gets on children's clothes and in their pockets and cuffs, is abrasive and damages interior floors and surfaces, and attracts cats who use it as a litter box. Pea gravel is unsuitable for children under 5 and dangerous for children under 3 years of age because it can get into small children's eyes, ears, and noses. Gravel is hard to walk on. Shredded tires can stain clothing, may contain steel wires from steel belted tires, and may be swallowed.

   3. Unitary materials.   (rubber mats poured into place on-site). These materials require virtually no maintenance, are easy to clean, have consistent shock absorbency, and are accessible to the handicapped. They require professional installation, however, are appropriate only for level surfaces, and their initial cost is relatively high. Some types are susceptible to frost damage.

Application Activity

Evaluate a particular piece of playground equipment at your facility's playground or a playground at a park nearby. Is it appropriate for the age group that uses it? Is it safely constructed? Does it have appropriate cushioning material? Report your findings to the class. If possible, use photos to illustrate your conclusions about the appropriateness and safety of this piece of equipment.

Planning Facilities for Accommodating Special Needs

The American with Disabilities Act (ADA) requires early childhood programs to accommodate children and adults with special needs in the "least restrictive environment." It provides a foundation for efforts to provide inclusive programs that benefit all participants—individuals who have disabilities and their able-bodied peers.

ADA mandates that indoor and outdoor facilities be accessible for all children and adults so that those with and without disabilities can safely take part in activities and can choose from the range of activities it offers. Accessibility is a priority because it is the first step toward welcoming children with disabilities into an inclusive setting. Accessibility is often achieved by simplifying the activity, by creating more open space, or by modifying the environment by installing doors and paths that accommodate wheelchairs, ramps with appropriate slopes, grab bars, and handrails (Sandall, 2003). Accessiblity is increased when raised tables with wheelchair indentations are available, when needed materials are on lower shelves that can be reached from a wheelchair; and when the facility is equipped with accessible water fountains and doorknobs.

Descriptions of specific features of integrated settings are beyond the scope of this book. Review the Web sites listed at the end of this chapter for recommendations for detailed information to guide your efforts to create a fully inclusive setting.

Purchasing Equipment and Materials

Some of the most important decisions a director makes when planning a facility are those related to the purchase of furniture, furnishings, equipment, and materials. They will impact the center's operations from its first day in operation forward. It takes forethought and planning to have the needed furniture, furnishings, equipment, and materials on hand to support the program's basic operations and children's day-to-day activities. If purchasing decisions are not thoughtfully made, caregivers will not have what they need to keep children safe; will not be able to create smooth routines for arrivals, departures, mealtimes, and naptimes; will not have materials to engage children in meaningful activities; and will be stressed by a classroom that seems to be always chaotic and disorganized.

Furthermore, if the wear and tear of daily use is not taken into account when purchasing tables, chairs, toys, and furnishings, there will undoubtedly be disappointments when they break and they will soon have to be replaced, creating unanticipated expense.

Systematic planning for purchases of furniture, furnishings, equipment, and supplies makes it possible to compare similar products' materials, construction, and cost. Comparison shopping is quite painless now that suppliers' catalogs are posted online. Careful shopping will make it more likely you will get what you need, the items you select will meet your expectations, and you will be able to avoid disappointments and costly mistakes and restocking fees that are often charged for returns.

Fortunately, even in new centers, many purchases can be made over time. You will want to make major purchases with start-up monies and at the beginning of each budget year. Consumables such as arts and crafts materials, seasonal supplies, and toys and books can be refreshed as needed throughout the year. It is always wise to set monies aside to purchase big-ticket items that may need to be replaced unexpectedly; to be able to offer teachers discretionary funds to refresh books, toys, and other materials that get hard wear; and to be able to purchase innovative products that you think are a good fit to help the program achieve its goals.

Purchasing Guidelines.   You will consider many factors when making purchasing decisions. These suggestions may help you think systematically about purchases:

1.   Select only safe, durable, relatively maintenance free, and aesthetically pleasing funiture, furnishings, equipment, materials, and supplies. To do otherwise is to risk being penny wise and pound foolish.

2.   Be certain to purchase equipment and materials that are aligned with the program's theoretical foundation and will help achieve its goals. Materials that encourage creativity, experimentation, and peer social interaction are appropriate for constructivist programs that value hands-on active learning. These materials can be used in child-directed ways and can accommodate children with varying degrees of competence and differing interests. Programs that implement different approaches to curriculum, such as Montessori or direct instruction, will use materials that are task-directed, autotelic (self-rewarding), and self-correcting.

Regardless of the program's theoretical foundation, all materials must meet the needs of children with disabilities and must convey multicultural, inclusive, and nonsexist values. Look for multiethnic dolls and hand puppets as well as dolls with disabilities that come with assistive devices such as wheelchairs, walkers, braces, glasses, and hearing aids. Similarly books, puzzles, and pictures selected for classroom use should depict various ethnic and racial groups and nontraditional sex-role behaviors. Consider equipment and materials that can be used in a variety of situations and that embrace individual differences. As much as possible teachers' input should guide the selection of classroom materials and supplies.

3.   The director or business manager should keep an ongoing **inventory,** a record of the quantity of materials already purchased and the location of these items, as well as a "wish list" identifying items the center plans to purchase in the future. The inventory is an essential tool when planning purchases. It helps avoid duplication, determines what equipment and materials need to be replaced, determines insurance needs, can help calculate losses from theft, and contributes to the annual budget planning process. The inventory should be kept electronically in a spreadsheet (such as Excel) or database (such as FileMaker Pro) format. It should be backed up regularly to a secure location.

The inventory should list and identify all equipment and materials that have been purchased and delivered with the date of acquisition. For nonconsumable items, the inventory record should indicate any maintenance performed and provide the current cost of replacement (often more than the initial cost). Inventoried equipment should be marked with the name of the program, the classroom (when appropriate), and an inventory number.

4. The diretor or business manager should save by negotiating prices whenever possible. When comparing costs, be sure taxes (when appropriate), shipping, and handling charges are included.

5. Be alert for sales and specials on consumable items, but take care not to overbuy.

6. Purchase only from reputable companies. There are many well-established vendors of furniture, supplies, and equipment. (See appendix 1.)

Purchasing Instructional Materials.   A wide variety of instructional materials are available for caregivers and teachers of infants, toddlers, preschoolers and primary-age children. Some, like kits and sets, require a significant investment to purchase a package designed to deliver specific content, like literacy skills or themed monthly activities. Most emphasize teacher-directed activities designed to be used in particular ways.

Other materials, like books and computer software, are less substantial investments and offer teachers and caregivers opportunities to pick and choose the ones they think best suited for the particular children with whom they work.

Purchasing Kits and Sets.   We advise you to carefully evaluate any kits or sets before investing in them by answering the following questions:

1. Do *all* the materials align with the program's theoretical foundation? Are their content and format developmentally appropriate?
2. How does having the kit benefit teachers? Does it save them time collecting or making materials? Do teachers need the kit or set as a guide in presenting concepts or skills?
3. How does the kit benefit children? Does it reflect the children in this community? Does it convey respect for diversity and inclusion? Are its activities authentic and is it likely they will be meaningful for these children?
4. What is the total cost of this package including shipping and taxes? Can several teachers use the same kit or set with their groups of children? Are special services such as training, installation, and maintenance needed? Are these extras included in the cost? What is the cost of replacement or consumable parts? Is other equipment, such as audiovisual equipment, needed for using the kit or set?
5. Are the materials and storage case durable, easily maintained, and safe?
6. How much space is needed to use and store these materials?

Purchasing Children's Books.   Children's books should be a cornerstone in every early childhood program. It is important that children have access every day to quality children's literature. Children should have access to books representing various genres, including fiction, nonfiction, poetry, wordless picture books, books for emerging readers, and, for older children, chapter books to be read aloud or independently. Classrooms are enriched by board books that infants and toddlers can handle themselves, big books that entire classes can enjoy together, and quality hardcover and paperback books children can enjoy alone or with peers.

It is important to give children free access to a wide selection of quality books. They should not be kept nice and clean on the shelf but should be in children's hands where they can be enjoyed time and again, even if that means they sometimes get torn, stepped on, even written on in the process. Use the following criteria when selecting books for the classroom:

1. Does the book "promote the development of knowledge and understanding, processes and skills, as well as dispositions to use and apply skills and to go on learning?" (Bredekamp & Copple, 1997, p. 20). For example,

    a. Is the book's theme likely to be interesting to most young children (e.g., nature, machines, pets, babies)?

    b. Does the book have the potential to meet children's social and emotional needs? Does it explore issues such as welcoming a new baby, making friends, overcoming fears, resolving conflicts peacefully, or other issues faced at home or at school?

    c. Does the book contribute to a project or thematic study? Books to extend and enrich almost every concept are available.

    d. Does the book have a predictable outcome, rhyming words, alliteration? It could be a good opportunity to teach related skills to early readers.

    e. Would it be possible to "stretch" the book with follow-up activities like dramatic play, a cooking activity, artwork, or story writing?

  2. Is the book considered high-quality literature (i.e., received an award such as the Caldecott)? Are the author and illustrator known for their quality work? Early childhood educators can use several sources such as those listed in appendix 1 to identify quality literature that would make a valuable contribution to their classroom.

When thinking about books for the classroom, do not forget the local library. You have a limited book-buying budget, but a large collection of quality children's literature is as close as your neighborhood library or bookmobile. This is a resource that is too valuable to overlook.

Purchasing Computers, Cameras, and Related Hardware and Software. Center directors need to consider two different issues when purchasing computers, cameras, printers, data storage, peripherals, and related software. Administrators and teachers need to use technology in their work, and children over 3 benefit when they have access to developmentally appropriate computer programs, cameras, and printers in their classrooms.

Both hardware and software change so rapidly that it is impossible to make specific recommendations here, but suffice it to say that you should stay abreast of technological advances and bring them into the center to benefit administrators, teachers, and children.

To illustrate recent technology changes, consider how, in 10 to 15 years, online access has progressed from slow and unreliable dial-up service, to speedy cable/DSL access, to virtully instantaneous wireless connectivity. Or think about how we take pictures today compared with 10, 15, or 20 years ago. Instamatic pocket cameras were cutting edge technology when I entered the classroom. We would mail film to be processed, and if we were lucky our pictures (3" × 3" snapshots) were returned in less than 2 weeks. What's more, a teacher's salary made it possible to take pictures only two or three times a year. Now digital cameras come in every price range. The photos and videos they take can be fine-tuned with the click of a mouse. They can then be emailed immediately to families so they can see a picture of their toddler's first trip down the slide or hear their kindergartener read the story he wrote that morning. Technology is a tool with tremendous potential to enhance documentation of classroom events and teacher-family communication.

When purchasing hardware or software, research cutting edge techology, tap into the expertise of a parent or friend of the center, and purchase equipment that meets your needs and is aligned with the program's goals.

When purchasing computers for children's use, be sure to investigate products designed to meet their particular needs. Assistive technology can help children with and without disabilities be more successful navigating a computer. Adaptations range from a smaller mouse or a larger track ball to computerized interactive language systems.

There are many software programs and Web sites for young children. When selecting computer activities for the classroom, you will want to evaluate the contribution they can make to children's learning, growth, and development, and their alignment with the program's goals and theoretical base. That is, you will apply the same kinds of criteria that you apply to any classroom activity.

Particular issues to consider when evaluating a computer-based activity are as follows:

1. Does it make effective use of the computer's capacity? Is it more than computerized flashcards?
2. Is it easy to use? Can children understand how it works and navigate through it independently?
3. What happens when you make a mistake? Is there violence, like an explosion, or simply a signal to try again?
4. Is it accurate and free from gender, racial, or other stereotypes?
5. Can it be played at various levels of difficulty to provide for differences in children's interests and abilities?

Shade (1996) summed up these criteria by asking this question about software for children: "Can the child make decisions about what he wants to do and operate the software to accomplish that task, with minor help from the adult?" (p. 18). You need to be certain that computers with Internet access that are available to children are equipped with filters that control where they can go on the Internet. Web sites with recommendations for keeping children safe online are listed at the end of the chapter.

Adults at the center also need to use computer technology. Many administrators purchase a *database management system*—software that allows them to create, maintain, and access a database for administrative functions. Common applications manage children's records; accounts receivable/payable; payroll; meal planning (USDA); personnel management; general ledger; scheduling children and staff; online check-in and check-out; and report, letter, and label writing. Many software packages are now available. Small early childhood programs often use word processing programs, spreadsheet programs, or both to do their administrative record keeping.

Teachers and caregivers also need, more than ever, technology tools to help them with planning and implementation, to keep assessment records, and to communicate with families. That means the computers located in the teachers' lounge and/or workroom should have access to the Internet and email, should be connected to printers, and that teachers should be able to use word processing to make them more efficient. Teachers also need access to quality digital cameras to document the growth, development, and learning of the children in their care.

Caring for Equipment and Materials

Caring for equipment and materials teaches children good habits and helps prevent expensive repairs and replacements. The following routines will help create and maintain an orderly and safe center environment:

1. Equipment and materials should be stored close to where they will be used. Storage areas should be arranged to minimize accidents and to maximize efficiency.
2. Teachers and caregivers should set a good example by using equipment and materials with care and returning them to their storage place when they are finished.
3. Children should be expected to help care for toys, equipment, and materials and to help keep the classroom, playground, and other areas of the center clean and tidy.
4. Spills should be cleaned up immediately. Children should be involved with the cleanup if it is safe, for example, if there is no glass that might hurt them.
5. An employee should be assigned to periodically check toys, equipment, and materials to make sure they are clean, to make needed repairs, and to discard items that are broken or have missing parts.

Purchasing Insurance

It is very important that child care programs run as a small business in their own facility carry adequate insurance on the building as well as its equipment and materials. This coverage is required for mortgaged buildings. It is recommended for all programs that own their buildings and for the contents of rented buildings.

While states' laws are different, and this is one area where one size definitely does not fit all, we recommend that you discuss the coverages listed below with your personal insurance provider. If he does not offer child care insurance, he can probably put you in touch with someone who does. Explore the cost of purchasing these protections:

- **Building and related structures**   This insurance covers materials, equipment, supplies, additions, and new construction on the premises from fire and lightning. Most policies can also cover losses from wind, hail, explosion (except from steam boilers), civil commotion, aircraft, vehicles, smoke, vandalism, and malicious mischief.
- **Business income and extra expense**   This coverage protects you if you are not able to continue the business because of a loss of property.
- **Glass breakage**   A nondeductible option may be available with this coverage.
- **Sign coverage**
- **Fences and walls within and surrounding the property**
- **Sewer and drain backup**
- **School bus insurance**

The director may be required to provide documentation of the building's value and the value of the equipment and supplies therein.

You will want to explore insurance on other types of property such as vehicles. You will want van or bus insurance to protect against losses from damage or the destruction of the vehicle and its contents. Accident liability insurance is usually required by law. Theft insurance may also be desirable.

Programs that are part of a chain or franchise, are operated by Head Start or a public school, or are a nonprofit organization run by a religious entity or community organization may have different insurance needs. You will want to inquire about existing insurance and consider if additional coverage is desirable.

TRENDS AND ISSUES

The current issue most likely to have an impact on child care facilities relates to accountability, testing, and the troubling trend to replace time for free play with direct instruction and preparation for high-stakes tests. Child care administrators who are leaders in their communities need to be advocates for children and childhood. They must be prepared to stand their ground if this movement threatens programs that have traditionally been committed to a childhood with time for play—both indoors and out. Trends to eliminate free play threaten to undermine early childhood educators' efforts to keep child care a place for free play and exploration.

SUMMARY

Environments, more than what anyone says, or what anyone does, teach young children about the world and help them find their place in it. Environments create routines and predictability, signal children how they are expected to behave, and can either instill children with hope or bury them in despair. Successful early childhood facilities require careful planning. The program's theoretical orientation, goals, and objectives should be reflected in every aspect of the facility's design.

If the child care facility is thought of as the stage upon which child–child, child–adult, and child–material interactions take place, then we can see the director's hand evident at the front door—this is where the curtain rises and expectations are set. The facility's public areas and each classroom are where the action is. They are the first act, where the actors are engaged in teaching and learning; working and playing; eating and sleeping; reading, writing, singing, and laughing every day.

The outdoor playground is the second act. It is very different from the first, but no less important for the learning and living that goes on there. Adults working together are the stagehands. Families and teachers, behind the scenes, are working together to make sure the performance goes well. They are there to smooth small concerns before they become big ones, to cheer successes, and to resolve difficulties before the curtain comes down.

The materials and equipment teachers and caregivers use in their work with children are the set. It is safe and beautiful, full of interesting and sometimes unexpected details that delight. Everything has been thoughtfully and intentionally selected to help the players reach their goal. The set, along with the players, director, first and second acts are what make this play unique, unlike any performance that has ever been presented before, anywhere else, any time in history.

USEFUL WEB SITES

Playground Safety

The Consumer Product Safety Commission Handbook for Public Playground Safety can be found at

www.cpsc.gov/CPSCPUB/PUBS/325.pdf

A Guide to the ADA Accessibility Guidelines for Play Areas can be found at

www.access-board.gov/play/guide/intro.htm

The National Center for Boundless Playgrounds is another guide to making playgrounds accessible for all children. It can be found at

www.boundlessplaygrounds.org

Internet Safety

This Web site provides information about protecting children's safety on the Internet of

Safekids.com

TO REFLECT

1. A carefully planned physical environment can help a program achieve its goals. Identify three or more goals you have for children in your care. How could each goal be promoted through a carefully created environment? For example, if your goal is to help children become good decision makers, a classroom with learning centers would give children opportunities to make meaningful decisions about what they will do each day.

2. Planning often involves compromises. For example, how can a director plan (a) for physical challenges on the preschool playground without creating undue risks for the young children and (b) for a hygiene yet soft environment for infants?

7

FINANCING AND BUDGETING

NAEYC Administrator Competencies addressed in this chapter:

Management Knowledge and Skills

2. Legal and Fiscal Management
   Knowledge of various federal, state, and local revenue sources. Knowledge of bookkeeping methods and accounting terminology. Skill in budgeting, cash flow management, grantwriting, and fundraising.

Early childhood programs are expensive. Because of the amount that typical families can afford to pay and the high costs of providing high-quality services, many centers find it difficult to cover the full costs of quality services through tuition charges alone. The total revenue base for early childhood care and education programs is about $56 billion (Casper, 1995; Hill-Scott, 2000). Preschool early childhood programs are mostly a private-market approach with families paying 60%, the government paying 39%, and the private sector paying 1% of the overall costs (Mitchell, Stoney, & Dichter, 1997; Olson, 2002).

Due to the fact that many parents cannot afford to pay the full cost of quality early care and education services, and early childhood programs cannot operate at a financial deficit and remain in existence, program administrators are faced with the difficult task of finding ways to either cut costs, or generate additional income. This difficult balance requires knowledge of basic budgeting, financial management, and the ability to make informed decisions to ensure the fiscal health of the organization.

Both the scope and the quality of services are related to the financial status of a program. To maintain quality experiences for children and their families, a program must generate at least as much income as it expends; otherwise the program will cease to exist. Because directors must manage local programs' resources, they need financial management skills.

Greenman and Johnson (1993) indicated that directors are weak in financial management ability and have very limited skills in market assessment. Few early childhood administrators receive adequate training in fiscal management. Such training is important for two reasons. First, fiscal tasks take about 50% of a director's time (Cost, Quality, and Child Outcomes Study Team, 1995). Second, families, funding agencies, and taxpayers who believe that their early childhood programs are properly managed are more likely to subsidize the program.

As is true of all other aspects of planning and administration, fiscal planning begins with the goals of the local program. Unless the proposed services and the requirements for meeting those services (in the way of staff, housing, or equipment) are taken into account, a budget cannot be adequately planned. And although program objectives should be considered first, probably no early childhood program is entirely free of financial limitations.

Fiscal planning affects all aspects of a program; consequently, planning should involve input from all those concerned with the local program (e.g., the board of directors or advisory board, the director, staff members, families). By considering everyone's ideas, a more accurate conception of budgeting priorities, expenditure level, and revenue sources can be derived. Furthermore, planning and administering the fiscal aspects of an early childhood program should be a continuous process. Successful financing and budgeting will come only from evaluating current revenue sources and expenditures and from advance planning for existing and future priorities.

Not-for-profit programs are responsible to their funding agencies, for-profit programs are accountable to their owners and stockholders, and all programs are accountable to the Internal Revenue Service. Even if the average citizen does not understand the problems of fund management, any hint of fund misuse will cause criticism. Administrators must budget, secure revenue, manage, account for, and substantiate expenditures in keeping with the policies of the early childhood program in a professional and businesslike manner.

COSTS OF EARLY CHILDHOOD PROGRAMS

High-quality early childhood care and education programs are labor intensive and expensive. Most programs, except publicly funded ones, operate in a price-sensitive market. They are financed primarily by working parents and are only supplemented by public and private contributions.

Estimates of Program Costs

Reported costs of early childhood programs show extensive variation. Costs may vary with the type of program, the level of training and size of the staff; sponsorship (whether it is a federal program, a public school, or a parent cooperative); the delivery system (center based, home visitor); and the needs of the children enrolled (their ages and whether or not they have disabilities).

Another factor contributing to variations in cost is whether the program is new or is offering new, additional services and thus has start-up costs or whether the program is already under way and has continuing costs. Geographic location, the amount of competition, and the general economy also contribute to the varying streams of revenue.

Varied Costs of Different Programs.   Different types of programs vary in their operation costs. Neugebauer (1993b) conducted a national survey of fees charged to parents. He used as the baseline the fees charged for 3- and 4-year-olds attending centers full time (all day 5 days per week). For full-time care, the fees for toddlers were 15% higher and the fees for infants were 28% higher than the baseline. The percentages were rather consistent from center to center. School-age child care (SACC) fees for before- and after-school care were 26% lower than the baseline, and fees for after-school care were 55% lower than the baseline. SACC fees, however, were reported to vary "dramatically" from center to center; thus, the percentages are less meaningful. Facilities in continuous use (e.g., preschool child care) are cost effective in comparison with facilities with downtime (e.g., half-day nursery schools, SACC programs).

Meeting the needs of children with disabilities is also expensive. Costs are functions of the type and degree of a child's individual needs and the type of services provided (e.g., transportation for children with physical disabilities is often more expensive than tutors for children identified as having learning disabilities). On the average, costs for centers that enroll children with disabilities are about 15% higher than those for centers that do not enroll children with disabilities (Powell, Eisenberg, Moy, & Vogel, 1994). However, the total costs per service hour is about 8% less for inclusive programs than for traditional special education programs (Odom, Wolery, Lieber, & Horn, 2002).

Program Quality and Costs.   The costs of high-quality programs have also been considered. The Cost, Quality, and Child Outcomes Study Team (1995) estimated that the difference in today's market price for child care and the costs of going from minimal to quality services was 10% (from $4,940 to $5,434 per child year). This percentage assumes that 10% is spent on items related to quality enhancement. Willer (1990) estimated the full cost of high-quality center care to be $8,000 per child year for children under age 5. The National Institute of Early Education Research has similarly estimated the cost of providing quality care and education services to 3- and 4-year-old children at $8,700 per child. (Barnett, Hustedt, Friedman, Boyd, & Ainsworth, 2007).

The price that the child care market will bear, however, seems to remain low at the expense of program quality. Some of the reasons for this include the following:

1. The government contributes to low-quality care when its agencies impose payments at *market rate* (i.e., subsidies are capped at levels determined by what families with average incomes are supposedly willing to pay) for child care services or fail to provide higher reimbursement for higher quality care. Generally speaking, governmental agencies use estimated cash costs to determine what they will pay for services, and thus, to some degree, circularity results. In other words, because agencies pay a certain number of dollars, program designers plan their programs on the basis of expected amounts of money. If funded the first year, program designers write a similar program the next year in hopes of being refunded. Thus, the agency pays approximately the same amount again, and the cycle continues. The program is thus designed around a specific dollar value whether or not it makes for the "best" program.

2. Labor is the most expensive aspect of early childhood programs. In high-quality programs, about 70% of the budget is in salaries and benefits. The easiest way to make a program more affordable and to ensure profit/surplus is to decrease wages and increase the number of children per staff member. Low wages result in less qualified employees at the point of entry, less incentive for employees to increase skills because of the lack of significant monetary compensation, and greater employee turnover rates. The trade-off for low salaries and benefits is typically a low-quality program. Yet, research points to a positive relationship between program quality and budget allocations for teacher salaries and benefits; that is, programs that spent approximately two thirds of their budgets on salaries and staff benefits tended to be of high quality, and quality diminished considerably in programs spending less than one half of their budgets on salaries and staff benefits (Olenick, 1986). More recent research has supported the link between staff salary and program quality. In a recent comparison of nonprofit-versus profit-generating child care programs, Sosinsky, Lord, and Zigler (2007) found that centers that paid higher wages tended to provide higher levels of quality care and education services.

The real earnings by child care teachers and family child care providers have decreased by nearly one fourth since the mid-1970s (Bellm, Breuning, Lombardi, & Whitebook, 1992; Willer, 1992). Family- and center-based teachers pay about 19% to 20% of the full costs of child care through foregone earnings (Cost, Quality, and Child Outcomes Study Team, 1995; Helburn, 1995). More specifically, the U.S. Bureau of Labor Statistics (1996) reported that the average hourly wage of child care workers was $6.12 and that of family child care providers was $3.37. The Center for the Child Care Workforce (2000) found that family child care providers earned about $10,500 annually, and center child care teachers earned about $15,000 annually. Salaries of center teachers in the NAEYC-accredited programs are one half those of public elementary school teachers. The gap widens as the years of experience increase (Powell et al., 1994). Furthermore, non-public-school programs seldom provide pension plans or health benefits for staff.

3. As discussed in chapter 1, inadequate consumer knowledge on the part of families reduces incentives for centers to provide high-quality programs. Families should not only seek quality programs but also understand the full costs of such programs and become advocates for subsidies that move program incomes closer to full costs.

4. Directors also rely on volunteer help and other donations to help absorb the differences between the cash costs and the full costs of their programs. Volunteer services and donated goods absorb about 2% of full costs, and donated occupancy (e.g., programs using facilities of religious organizations) absorbs about 6% of full costs (Cost, Quality, and Child Outcomes Study Team, 1995).

Costs to Families

Programs primarily supported through user fees are expensive for families. Families pay about 60% of all expenditures for child care, with the federal, state, or local governments paying most of the remaining expenses (Stoney & Greenberg, 1996). In constant dollars, the average cost of family child care has increased steadily since 1990 (Casper, 1995), and family child care is almost totally paid through family fees. In 49 of the 50 states, the annual cash cost for child care was more than the annual tuition fees at a public college, and in cities in 15 states, child care costs twice as much as public college tuition (Schulman & Adams, 1998).

Because child care costs have risen to compensate programs for their loses in subsidies (Willer, 1992), child care has become less affordable for most families. Families do not have equitable financing either. Child care expenses are often the second or third largest item in a low-income working family's household budget. The average monthly costs for nonpoor families were higher in absolute terms, but lower in terms of the percentage of the household budget; that is, 18% to 25% for lower income families and 7% for higher income families (U.S. Bureau of the Census, 1997; U.S. Department of Health and Human Services, 1999).

Because families living in poverty can have their child care fees subsidized, their children are as likely to be enrolled in high-quality early childhood programs as those children coming from high-socioeconomic families. Struggling families whose incomes are just above the poverty level are often priced out of quality programs. Subsidies that lower the price of child care often induce low-income families to work. However, as their incomes rise, assistance with child care is decreased or cut off. Even if assistance were available, most states do not have enough child care program openings available to serve families eligible for assistance (Adams, Schulman, & Ebb, 1998).

Affordable programs for low-income families are of lower quality than government-subsidized ones (Blau & Hagy, 1998). Besides income, other factors also preclude low-income families from higher quality programs, such as nonday shifts (41% of low-income mothers work these shifts) and residence in low-income neighborhoods that do not have high-quality programs (Queralt & Witte, 1998; U.S. Bureau of the Census, 1997).

Costs to families differ for the following reasons:

1. Programs differ in costs because of the quality of services, geographic location, age of the children served, and ability of the program to take advantage of scale economics (i.e., serve more children or provide more hours of service than competing programs).

2. Even in programs that charge similar fees per child hour, the costs per family may vary because of various types of subsidies. The subsidies include the following:

   a. **Multi-child discounts.**   About half of for-profit centers offer multichild discounts; however, the fee discount varies greatly (Neugebauer, 1993b).

   b. **Fees subsidized by public funds.**   Some programs provide care for children whose fees are subsidized mainly through public funds. These government-funded subsidies are provided for children of low-income working families through the Child Care and Development Fund (CCDF) and Temporary Assistance to Needy Families (TANF). Rohacek and Russell (1998) found that (a) child care subsidy acts to keep families from ever needing welfare; (b) moves families from welfare to work; (c) pays for itself in real dollars; and (d) helps develop the regulated child care system. They found that the best subsidy system gives more help to families with the lowest incomes—those with the greatest risk of returning to welfare.

   c. **Tax credits and deductions.**   At both the state and federal levels, *tax credits* (taken against taxes owed) and *deductions* (amounts subtracted from income before computing taxes owed) reduce child care costs for eligible families who claim them. Families should determine their eligibility to claim the Dependent Care Tax Credit, Child Tax Credit, Earned Income Tax Credit, and the Dependent Care Assistance Program (DCAP). Because few eligible families claimed their tax credits, the National Women's Law Center launched the Child Care Tax Credits Outreach Campaign.

Although child care is expensive, not working can also be expensive because of a family's foregone income. The amount of foregone income when a family member provides child care services rather than obtains outside employment is another expense that varies from family to family. The income is considered foregone when a family member provides child care services either without payment or on an intrafamilial income transfer. In either case, the amount of foregone income depends on the caregiver's employable skills and the availability of employment or on the caregiver's potential income. (Calculating foregone income also requires considering the cost of outside employment, such as transportation, clothing, organization or union dues, and higher taxes.)

Costs of Local Programs

Local program administrators often think of costs in terms of budget items. Budget items are usually the program functional items used in cost-efficiency analysis. The following distinctions must be made in an analysis:

1. **Start-up costs.** Start-up costs are the monies that must be available before a program is under way. Even after the program begins, most programs underenroll for 6 months of operation, and monies from promised funding sources are often delayed. Start-up costs include monies for the building, equipment and supplies, 3 months of planning, and the first 6 months or longer of operation.
2. **Fixed and variable costs.** Fixed costs (e.g., program planning) do not vary with the number of children served, but variable costs (e.g., building, teacher salaries, equipment) vary with the number of children served.
3. **Marginal costs.** Marginal costs are the increased cost "per unit" (total program costs divided by the number of recipients) of expanding a program beyond a given enrollment. Marginal costs may decrease to a given point and then increase when additional staff or facilities is required.
4. **Capital versus operating costs.** Capital costs (e.g., building) are basically one-time costs, whereas operating costs (e.g., salaries, consumable materials) are recurrent.
5. **Hidden costs.** Hidden costs are costs free to a program but paid by someone else (e.g., the donor of a facility). **Joint costs** are somewhat "hidden" too because they are shared costs (e.g., two separately funded programs that share a staff workroom or audiovisual equipment). **Foregone income costs** (e.g., income foregone because of services or goods provided a program) are difficult to calculate.

FINANCING EARLY CHILDHOOD PROGRAMS

The specific ways early childhood programs are paid for by families, government, and corporations are referred to as **financing mechanisms.** The way the financing mechanism is administered (e.g., grants, contracts, loans, vouchers) is called an **administrative mechanism.** An administrative mechanism is governed by policy concerning the eligibility for and use of any funds (Brandon, Kagan, & Joesch, 2000). Although the majority of early childhood programs receive funds from parents (e.g., fees, tuition, and donated goods and services), some programs are subsidized with funding from government, philanthropic organizations, and corporations. These subsidies can be *direct* (i.e., paid directly to a given program, such as a grant) or *portable* (i.e., paid by users who had choices among programs enrolling children whose fees are subsidized—child care voucher, for example).

Various regulations govern (a) a program's eligibility to receive revenue from a source such as the federal government; (b) procedures for obtaining revenue; (c) the use made of the revenue; and (d) which personnel are accountable for the expenditure. Because of the many types of programs and the intricacies and variations involved in funding, only a brief description of the sources of financing is given here.

Government and Foundation Financing

Financing strategies for early child care and education programs are embedded in the rationale for high-quality programs, such as school readiness, brain development research, economic development, and welfare-to-work reforms. Thus, early childhood programs are becoming more publicly supported. To expand their current financing mechanisms for early childhood programs, the federal, state, and local governments are using these two revenue sources:

1. **Direct revenue sources.**   Direct revenue sources are primarily monies from tax sources—sales, income, and other taxes—planned for government spending. Although most states subsidize early childhood programs through general revenue dollars, some are funding through "sin tax" revenues, such as taxes on alcohol sales and the gambling industry and from tobacco company settlements (Sandham, 2002).
2. **Indirect revenue sources.**   Indirect revenue sources are foregone government monies due to claims made by individuals or corporations through the tax system (i.e., tax exemptions, deductions, and credits).

Government funding results in several ongoing concerns. Funds are not stable and fluctuate with government budget as choices are made among many needs. Another concern is the bewildering array of funding agencies and assistance programs. Because, at present, no federal centralized program of child care exists, the extent of federal involvement in early childhood programs is not easily determined. Along with the problem of dealing with the number of federal sources, a jumble of rulings from agencies results in many different standards. Assistance programs are constantly being deleted and added, and appropriations may fall below congressional authorization.

A final concern has to do with the regulations that accompany funding, especially federal funding. Federal funds can be **categorical grants** (grants used for specified, narrowly defined purposes) or **general revenue sharing** (funds provided on a formula basis to state and local governments, with few or perhaps no limits to how the money is spent). The trend has been toward federal "deregulation." The middle ground is achieved through **block grants.** In a block grant, federal aid is provided for more broadly defined activities so that state or local groups can have greater discretion in designating programs to meet local needs. Recipients must comply with some federal regulations (e.g., fiscal reporting and nondiscrimination requirements).

Public School Financing of Kindergartens and Primary Programs.   Public school programs are supported by local, state, and federal monies. Taxation is the major source of monies available for funding; consequently, revenues for public school programs are closely tied to the general economy of the local area, the state, and the nation.

Local Support.   Tax funds, usually from real and personal property taxes, are used to maintain and operate the schools, and the sale of bonds is used for capital improvements and new construction expenses. According to the National Center for Education Statistics (1997), the richest districts spend 56% more per student than do the poorest. These "poor fewer" have fewer qualified teachers, fewer resources, and more distressed housing. The local school board's authority to set tax rates and to issue bonds for school revenue purposes is granted by the state; that is, authority is *not* implied. When granted the power to tax, the local school board must follow state laws concerning tax rates and procedural matters in an exacting manner. In this way, the state protects the public from the misuse and mismanagement of public monies.

State Support.   The amount of state support for public schools varies widely from state to state. Almost every state has some form of foundation program designed to equalize the tax burden and educational opportunities among school districts. Generally, the foundation program begins with a definition of minimum standards of educational service that must be offered throughout the state. The cost of maintaining the standards is calculated and the rate of taxation prescribed. The tax rate may be uniform or based on an economic index ability—the ability of a local school district to pay.

If local taxes do not cover the cost of maintaining minimum standards, the balance of the costs is provided via state monies. States vary considerably in the machinery they use for channeling state monies to local school districts, the most common plans being flat and equalization grants. In the last decade, the issue of equalizing funding among school districts within a state has resulted in a rash of school finance litigation (Verstegen, 1994).

Federal Support.   Since the 1940s, the federal government has become the chief tax collector. Until recently, the trend was toward unprecedented expenditures for education. Consequently, public schools (as well as other institutions, agencies, and organizations) relied more and more on federal assistance programs to supplement their local and state resources.

Federal funding of public schools is used for two purposes: (a) to improve the quality of education (e.g., research, experimentation, training, housing, and equipment) and (b) to encourage greater effort by state and local districts to improve the quality of education by providing initial or matching funds for a program. Federal expenditures in education declined because of reductions in the types of programs funded or the amount of funds available in retained programs.

However, the No Child Left Behind Act of 2001 (NCLB), signed into law on January 8, 2002, is a major reform of the Elementary and Secondary Education Act (ESEA) and redefines the federal role in K to 12 education.

State Financing of Prekindergarten Programs.   Beyond commitment to financing kindergarten and primary grade programs in public schools, state investment in the financing of other early childhood programs is greater than ever before. States have long been involved in programs for young children. With the passage of welfare legislation, the Personal Responsibility and Work Opportunity Act of 1996, the state's role in early childhood services greatly expanded. According to the National Institute of Early Education Research, public support for pre-K programming has resulted in 38 states funding pre-K services and an increase in the quality standards for prekindergarten services for many publicly funded programs. Among the children receiving public supported prekindergarten services, two thirds were in public school settings while one third were receiving services through private and Head Start Programs (Barnett, Hustedt, Hawkinson, & Robin, 2006).

Although state commitment to support early childhood programs is growing, the support is far from adequate. Adams and Poersch (1997) measured state commitment to early childhood by looking at state funding practices. They found that

a. The amount of commitment varied widely across the nation and even between neighboring states
b. Many states with high rates of poverty did not secure available funds
c. State wealth was not associated with commitment
d. Early childhood programs were not high on the list of priorities to receive state funds.

Similarly, the National Institute for Early Education Research (Barnett et al, 2006) reported an overall increase in state investments, yet identified uneven progress across states. This increase, however, wasn't enough to compete with increasing enrollment and inflation. After adjusting for these factors, public funding for prekindergarten services is at an all time low (Barnett et al.).

The cost per child in state-sponsored early childhood programs varies considerably, too. Sandham (2002) reported that the variables that determine the cost are (a) the maximum income level at which a family is eligible, (b) the age at which a child is eligible, (c) the relationship between the family's income and the level of the subsidy, and (d) teacher salaries.

States are attempting to tie financing with the quality of programs. For example, 4% of a state's allocation under the CCDF block grant and 25% of all new Head Start dollars must be spent on initiatives to enhance quality (Olson, 2002). For the most part, state standards for quality are weak. For example, only 26 states require a college degree for teachers of prekindergarten children; 35 require specialized training in early childhood education, 37 have adopted group size limits of 20 children or less, and 37 have adopted comprehensive early learning standards.

Federal Financing.   In addition to providing some federal fiscal support to certain programs, such as the public schools, the federal government remains the primary source of support for some comprehensive early childhood programs. The federal government pays for early childhood services in two ways:

1. **Contracts and grants.**   Monies from contracts and grants flow directly to the program. The funds are awarded based on a specific service to be provided and a given number of recipients or targeted level of enrollment. Government agencies typically negotiate contract rates with a specific provider or group of providers. Rates are based on the amount of money that is available to purchase care and an assessment of the cost of providing the service (i.e., cash costs incurred in running the program).
2. **Vouchers.**   A voucher is a payment mechanism whereby funds are given to the family rather than the program and follow the child to the family-selected program. Vouchers include both purchase-of-service systems and cash payments. Voucher systems base reimbursement on the market rate.

The modern era of federal support for early childhood care and education began with Head Start in 1965. Other programs soon followed. Federal funding, targeted primarily for low-income families and including programs for young children, continued to grow until 1977. Although federal support for social programs declined from 1977 to 1988, federal support for early childhood programs (e.g., Head Start) remained rather constant in dollar amounts; in actuality, federal support declined because the number of children living in poverty increased (Einbinder & Bond, 1992) and inflation took its toll on the value of the dollar. After 1988, federal support increased. At the current levels of federal spending, about 50% of all children eligible for Head Start are being served, about 12% of all eligible children are receiving assistance from Child Care and Development Block Grant (CCDBG), and about 66% of children eligible for Title 1 are being served (Washington Update, 2001).

Federal Assistance Programs.   Throughout the modern era of federal financing, the purpose of most federal assistance programs has been to accomplish particular educational objectives or to meet the needs of specific groups. Most federal assistance programs (a) require early childhood programs to meet specified standards; (b) give priority or restrict services to certain client groups; (c) require state or local support in varying amounts; and (d) specify funds to be used for certain purposes (e.g., food, program supplies), which in turn curtail programs' flexibility.

Some of the major federal assistance programs, whose total funds dwarf state financing, include Head Start and Early Head Start, CCDBG, TANF, the Early Learning Opportunities Act, the Children's Day Care Health and Improvement Act, IDEA, and various food programs. The NCLB Act of 2001 is a $19 billion investment. Seven of the 10 title programs under the NCLB are described as follows:

1. **Title I—Improving the Academic Achievement of the Disadvantaged.**   The stated purpose of Title I is to ensure that all children have fair, equal, and significant opportunity to obtain a high-quality education and reach a minimum proficiency level on challenging state academic standards and assessments.

2. **Title II—Preparing, Training, and Recruiting High-Quality Teachers and Principals.**   The purpose of Title II is the preparation and training of principals and teachers.
3. **Title III—Language Instruction for Limited English Proficient and Immigrant Students.**   The purpose of Title III is to help students attain English language proficiency to meet the challenges of Title I.
4. **Title IV—21st Century Schools.**   Title IV funds programs to prevent school violence and to foster drug-free environments. Title IV also funds the creation of Community Learning Centers (before- and after-school opportunities) to complement the school academic program.
5. **Title V—Promoting Informed Parental Choice and Innovative Programs.**   Title V includes educational block grants, charter schools, magnet schools, and funds for the improvement of education in local areas.
6. **Title VI—Flexibility and Accountability.**   Title VI funds are designed to enhance state and local assessment systems and to improve the dissemination of information on student achievement and school performance to families and community members.
7. **Title VII—Indian, Native Hawaiian, and Alaska Native Education.**   Title VII authorizes expenditures to meet the unique educational needs (e.g., language) of these groups.

Obtaining Federal Assistance.   Federal funding sources are in a state of constant change. The latest edition of the *Catalog of Federal Domestic Assistance* describes the federal agencies administering various assistance programs and the projects and services funded under these agencies. (See the "Useful Web Sites" section at the end of this chapter to help you begin the search for external funding.)

Securing Federal Funds

Most federal funds are obtained by writing and submitting a grant proposal and having the proposal approved and funded. One person on the early childhood staff can best oversee the entire writing of the proposal, although input should be obtained from all those involved in the program. In fact, early childhood programs that plan to seek regular federal assistance may find it advantageous to hire a staff member with expertise in the area of obtaining federal as well as other funds, such as foundation grants, that require proposal writing. Proposal writing can vary according to an assistance program's particular requirements, but most use a similar format.

Certain terminology is used in obtaining federal funds and must be understood by those involved in locating appropriate grants and writing proposals. The following terms are frequently used:

1. **Assets.**   The amount of money, stocks, bonds, real estate, or other holdings of an individual or organization.
2. **Endowment.**   Funds intended to be kept permanently and invested to provide income for support of a program.
3. **Financial report.**   A report detailing how funds were used (e.g., a listing of income and expenses).
4. **Grant.**   A monetary award given a program. Grants are of several types:
   a. **Bricks and Mortar Act.**   An informal term for grants for building or construction projects.
   b. **Capital support.**   Funds for buildings (construction or renovation) and equipment.
   c. **Declining grant.**   A multiyear grant that grows smaller each year in the expectation that the recipient can raise other funds to make up the difference.

    d. General-purpose grant.   A grant made to further the total work of the program, as opposed to assisting a specific purpose.

    e. Matching grant.   A grant with matching funds provided by another donor.

    f. Operating-support grant.   A grant to cover day-to-day expenses (e.g., salaries).

    g. Seed grant or seed money.   A grant or contribution used to start a new project.

5. **Grassroots fund-raising.**   An effort to raise money on a local basis (e.g., raffles, bake sales, auctions).

6. **In-kind contribution.**   A contribution of time, space, equipment, or materials in lieu of a monetary contribution.

7. **Proposal.**   A written application for a grant.

Proposal Planning

Proposal planning is, in essence, research. And as is true with any other research, problem identification is the first step. What is needed? If the assistance program sends out a request for a proposal (RFP), the need is already defined in broad or general terms.

The second step is gathering documented evidence in the population or potential population served by the early childhood program. Also, assessment must be made as to how critical or extensive the need is. Most proposals require that needs and the degree of these needs be described in terms of demographic, geographic, and socioeconomic distribution as well as racial and ethnic makeup. Because proposals often have to be written quickly (perhaps in 2 to 4 weeks), a notebook should be kept with current data available. Data may be secured from the following and other sources:

- Community action associations (local)
- Department of Health and Human Resources (local and state) federal publications (found in the *Monthly Catalog of U.S. Government Publications*)
- U.S. Department of Commerce, Bureau of the Census
- U.S. Department of Labor, Bureau of Labor Statistics
- U.S. Department of Labor, Employment and Training Administration

The literature must be reviewed to see whether others have handled the problem and with what results. To prevent duplication of services in a local area, the administrator must also present evidence as to whether the same or similar needs are being met by other local programs. The duplication check needs to be made with local social services organizations, which can be identified through the telephone directory, the Department of Health and Human Services, and agencies served by the United Fund or Community Chest.

The final step is writing a two- or three-page proposal prospectus. The prospectus should contain a statement of the proposed problem, what will be done about the problem, the target group to be served, the number of people to be served, and whether the proposed early childhood program is needed. The prospectus is helpful in clarifying thinking and in getting the opinions of others, including reviewers of funding agencies. (Some federal agencies require a prospectus before accepting a complete proposal.)

Writing the Proposal

Federal agencies have their own guidelines for writing a proposal; they differ from agency to agency, but the guidelines should be followed exactly. Most guidelines want the following points to be covered in the body of the proposal:

1. **Title page.**   Title of project; name of agency submitting application; name of funding agency; dates of project; and names, addresses, and signatures of the project director and others involved in fiscal management.

2. **Statement of problem.**   General and specific objectives, documentation of needs and degree of needs, review of literature of programs that have tried to meet the specified needs, and description of any local programs currently involved in meeting specified needs.

3. **Program goals and objectives.**   Description of broad program goals and specific, measurable outcomes expected as a result of the program.

4. **Population to be served.**   What qualifications will children and families need for inclusion in the program? Will all who qualify be accepted? If not, how will the participants be chosen from those who qualify?

5. **Plan of procedure.**   Were several alternative approaches available for solving the problem? If so, why was a particular alternative selected? How will each objective be accomplished?

6. **Administration of project.**   What staffing requirements are being proposed? How will the program be managed? What is the program's capability to conduct the proposed project? Does the program have community support? Show a time schedule of activities that will occur from the day of funding until project termination.

7. **Program evaluation.**   What assessment devices will be used? Who will conduct the assessment? How and in what format will the evaluation be submitted?

8. **Future funding.**   How will the operation of the program be continued at the conclusion of federal assistance?

9. **Budget.**   Must show sound fiscal management.

10. **Appendixes.**   Include job descriptions, director's curriculum vitae, and organizational structure of the early childhood program.

Some agencies also require completion of an application form that usually asks for information about the general subject; to whom the proposal is being submitted; the legal authorization; the project title; the name of the person submitting the proposal; the program director's name, address, and telephone number; the probable budget; the amount of funds requested; and the date the application is transmitted.

Some agencies have a form for a proposal abstract, and usually agencies require that this summary be no longer than 200 words. Forms assuring protection of human subjects and nondiscrimination may be required.

Foundation Support.   Many fields, including education, have benefited from foundation giving. Foundations are one of several kinds of nongovernmental, not-for-profit organizations that promote public welfare, including that of young children, through the use of private wealth operated under a federal or state charter and administered by trustees. Other similar organizations are trusts and endowments. Foundation aid is typically given to support research.

Because of increased federal support of education, foundation grants to education have decreased in the past few years. Large foundations have many goals that change periodically. Smaller foundations are often limited to specific goals or specific geographic areas. A good source of support may be foundations from local corporations. Nevertheless, administrators of early childhood programs should investigate foundations as potential sources of funds.

As with federal funds, foundation funds are obtained through submission and approval of a proposal. The foundation's board of directors determines the guidelines for submitting proposals, sets a deadline for application, reviews proposals, and selects recipients.

Employer Assistance

Employers can provide child care assistance to their employees. Employer assistance includes some of the following methods:

1. Employers may contract with individual vendors to create a discount rate for specific programs.
2. Employers may subsidize costs by providing vouchers to employees.
3. Employees may receive assistance through a Dependent Care Assistance Plan (DCAP). DCAPs can enable employees to use pretax dollars to purchase dependent care services if they are offered through a flexible benefit program (i.e., employers offer a choice of benefits from which employees choose). The federal Internal Revenue Code allows employers who have established a DCAP to exclude child care benefits provided to their employees in an amount up to $5,000 per employee from federal income, FICA, and unemployment taxes and often from state income taxes. Benefits may come as cash, a voucher, or free or subsidized care in a child care facility. Usually the DCAP is a salary reduction that is returned to the employees as a reimbursement for child care expenses. (Any money *not* used for child care is *not* returned to the employee.)

   In short, a DCAP makes child care a nontaxable benefit. As a nontaxable benefit, salary reduction under a DCAP is more beneficial to higher income employees. To be beneficial to lower income employees, employers need to create a matching amount reduced from the employee's salary or to provide child care vouchers. Administrative costs of DCAPs are paid by employers.

Fees, Tuition, and Miscellaneous Sources of Funds

For-profit programs operate almost exclusively on tuition and fees and are usually the most expensive. Families who must pay more than 10% of their gross income for one or more children need subsidies. Directors should also inform families on how to apply for tax credits.

Although child care is costly, for-profit independent centers do not make substantial profits. Financial problems are often the result of overestimating income from fees and tuition.

Collecting tuition fee payments from families is essential for program survival.

Optimal fees and tuition for early childhood programs may be determined in several ways. One method is to determine costs and the amount of profit (or surplus) needed. The cost is distributed among the children on a fixed fee, a sliding scale fee, or two fixed fees for different income brackets. Because programs are not usually fully enrolled for an entire fiscal year, the tendency is to overestimate income from fees. Budgets must allow for a 3% to 8% vacancy rate. The administrator may also compensate by using G. Morgan's (1999) method of calculating last year's **utilization rate** (i.e., divide last year's actual income by the maximum potential income from fees).

A well-run center operates at 95% or greater utilization rate; thus, the utilization rate is a good estimate to use even if fees are increased. A more accurate **break-even analysis** (a managerial tool that identifies the point at which a program generates enough revenue to cover expenses) is also explained in detail by Morgan (1999). Essentially this is done by accounting for all of a program's annual expenditures, then identifying what level of income is necessary to meet all these expenses. A director should use the break-even point to evaluate the impact of various changes, such as enrollment trends and the need to either raise or lower tuition.

Application Activity

Based on your current enrollment and staffing patterns, how much would you have to raise individual child tuition to provide all staff members with a 3% wage increase? Using the same staffing and enrollment figures, how much would you have to increase tuition to compensate teachers at a salary comparable to early childhood public school teachers in your area? (Be sure to use salaries for teachers with similar education and experience.)

In addition to carefully calculating fees and tuition, an early childhood program must have definite policies on fee payment. Loss of income may occur as a result of absenteeism or child turnover. The following suggestions might be considered in establishing a fee policy:

1. Set a deposit fee at the time of enrollment, to be returned at the time of withdrawal if all monetary policies have been met. Two or 3 weeks' tuition or fees is reasonable.
2. Several weeks' notice should be given to withdraw a child. (The fee deposit covers this if notice is not given in advance.)
3. Children on the waiting list must be enrolled within a stated period of time after notification or their place on the waiting list will be forfeited.
4. Payments may be no more in arrears than the amount of the initial deposit.
5. Payments must be made when a child misses a few days, or a withdrawal notice should be given for an extended absence.

Some funds for early childhood programs can come from several miscellaneous sources. A few examples of these sources are as follows:

1. Public support via a community campaign can help make up the difference between the program's anticipated income and its expenses. For example, some programs qualify for United Way funds (which may be called by some other name). Specific eligibility requirements must be met to qualify for such local funds.
2. In-kind contributions are often available through some community resource, such as a charitable organization.
3. Endowments may be given in someone's memory, or scholarships may be awarded.

4. The early childhood program may engage in fund-raising projects to supplement income from other sources such as a community bake sale, or contracting with a vendor to sell goods to families with a portion of the profits coming back to the program. A cost-benefit analysis should be done before mounting a fund-raiser. Yields from $10 to $25 per hour, after expenses, are of marginal value; raising funds above $25 per hour is worthwhile. In addition to analyzing the monetary yield, the program must also determine if the promotion of certain products is aligned with the philosophy and values of the organization.

BUDGETING

A **budget** is a list of all goods and services for which payment may be made. Because the budget determines the planned allocations of a program's resources, Morgan (1999) stated, "Budget is policy" (p. 11). Budgets are important because no matter how good a program is, it cannot continue to operate if it is not on a sound fiscal foundation. Limited funds require making decisions about priorities, and funding and regulatory agencies require information about monetary functions.

Regulations Governing Budget Making and Adoption

Budgets of small, privately owned programs are developed by their owners/directors and are not subject to regulations unless the program receives some subsidies from public funds. Budgets of larger private and publicly funded programs are usually developed by local program directors or the superintendents of schools for public school programs. Efforts are usually made to include the opinions of various personnel in the first draft of the proposed budget.

However, in some of these large programs, such as a corporate chain or community action association, the budget is often created at the level of the larger organization, and the director only monitors expenditures and submits financial reports.

Budgets of larger private and publicly funded programs are subject to many budgetary regulations. Once created, the budgets are presented to their respective boards of directors or advisors for approval. In addition to requiring the board's approval, regulations may require that the budget be presented to licensing or funding agency personnel before approval. In publicly funded programs, funds and thus fiscal control, may come from several governmental agencies that will be involved before the adoption process ends.

Developing a Budget

The budget serves as a financial plan for a given period of time. Budgets itemize income (revenues) and expenses (expenditures). Directors often prepare several types of budgets.

Types of Budgets.   Directors of early childhood programs often work with two types of budgets. A budget projection and start-up budget are used in the beginning of the budgeting process. Operating budgets are used after a program is under way.

Budget Projections and Start-Up Budgets.   A *budget projection* (also called a *pro forma budget*) projects how the operation of a business will turn out based on certain assumptions. Often loans from banks or start-up grants require that a financial plan be submitted. Although a *financial plan* requires a description of the program, a management summary, and many supporting documents (e.g., licensing status, insurance coverage, tax status, contracts), the major aspect is the financial data. Financial data will include a projected start-up budget, funding requests and repayment plans if applicable, a break-even analysis, a projected monthly cash flow for a year, and a projected timetable for self-sufficiency.

A **start-up budget** includes all the income and expenses incurred in starting a program. Morgan (1999) listed the following categories of items in a start-up budget:

a. The capital cost of land, building, and equipment
b. Personnel costs for planning and implementing program
c. *Lag costs* (costs between the time one provides the service and gets paid)

Other start-up expenditures may include training, meetings, publicity, and repayment of the loan. Start-up budgets vary depending on whether one initiates a completely new program or buys a currently operating program. Morgan put dollar amounts to categories of start-up expenses.

Operating Budget.   An **operating budget** includes items on which money will be spent once a program is operating near the planned capacity. The operating budget includes all the income and expenses for one calendar year (January 1 through December 31) or for one fiscal year (often July 1 through June 30 or September 1 through August 31). Operating budgets usually have three components:

a. A synopsis of the program
b. Specifically itemized expenditures for operating the program, including direct costs (items attributed to a particular aspect of the program, such as personnel salaries) and indirect costs (overhead items not attributed to a particular aspect of the program, such as interest on bank loans, utility costs, and advertising)
c. Anticipated revenues and their sources, including in-kind contributions.

Before writing the budget, the administrator should list the program's objectives and needs. The program's goals and needs and the fiscal plan should be carefully related and reflected in the written budget.

Budget Formats.   Proposed revenues and expenditures must be presented in an effective way. Budgets are organized by headings, either determined by the funding agency or the local program. The headings are referred to as the **budget format.** Two types of format are as follows:

1. **Functional classification.**   This format assembles data in terms of categories for which money will be used, such as administration, child instruction, family education, food and health services, and transportation. The advantage of the functional classification format is that one can readily link expenditure categories to program purposes. One disadvantage to this approach is that functional categories tend to be somewhat broad and thus raise questions regarding the expenditures within a classification. Another disadvantage is the lack of distinct classifications for some items; for example, health services may be listed under several classifications.

2. **Line-item classification.**   This format lists the sums allocated to specifics of the program (e.g., salaries of designated personnel, gas, electricity, water, telephone, postage). The major advantage of this approach is that it shows specific accountability for expenditures. A disadvantage occurs if the categories are narrow because the director has little power to exercise changes in expenditures.

Many computer-assisted finance programs are available for use in preparing budgets and in performing and recording financial transactions. Often these have to be adapted to fit local needs.

Writing the Budget.   The first step in writing a budget is to create an estimate of income or receipts. This section should clearly indicate expected monies from specified services, such as tuition, fees, contributions, and fund-raising projects. Morgan (1999) offered excellent examples of how to maximize a program's income by balancing full-time and part-time children, monitoring enrollment and attendance, having waiting lists, and determining fees and collecting them. For purposes of income calculations, in-kind donations should be recognized only when the good or service would have had to be purchased if it were not given. (Some programs, such as Head Start, however, must recognize nonessential donations.)

The next step is to estimate costs. Estimated costs given as percentages of the total operating budget for the highest quality programs are as follows:

- Salaries—65%
- Rent or mortgage—11%
- Food—7%
- Educational equipment and materials—3%
- Insurance—2%
- Telephone, utilities, office supplies, maintenance and repairs, and health and social services—14%
- Supplementary services (screening/referral for children; family education and support)—3% (Powell et al., 1994).

Of the total operating budget for salaries, which may vary from 60% to 85% of the total budget in high-quality programs, 74% is for instructional staff, 13% is for noninstructional staff, and 13% is for benefits for all employees (Hayes, Palmer, & Zaslow, 1990). As shown, salaries account for the major part of the budget. In reality, for-profit centers making the most profits spend a lower percentage of their revenues on salaries (53.7%) than do centers making the least profits (62.4%; Stephens, 1991). Yet, as previously discussed, the quality of programs and salaries are highly correlated. Income must increase dramatically to provide the recommended level of compensation for early childhood professionals.

For a quick estimate of operating costs, begin by considering salaries at least equal to 50% of the budget. The full cost per child is then calculated by this formula:

$$\text{Full cost per child} = \frac{\text{Teacher's annual salary}}{\text{Number of children in the group}} \times 2$$

After completing the expenditure section, the administrators should furnish actual figures for the current fiscal year. Any significant difference between current services and expenditures and those proposed should be explained. In planning the expenditure section, directors should keep the following points in mind:

1. Wages or salaries must be paid on time.
2. A desirable inventory level is one that will carry a program through 2 months of operation.
3. A program may have cash flow problems. Federal funds do not pay ahead of time for expenses; receipts and proof of money spent are required for reimbursement, and even reimbursement checks may come irregularly.

To prevent cash flow problems, the director should observe the following practices:

1. Initial enrollment should not be overestimated.
2. Equipment estimates should be calculated on cost per use rather than on the purchase price. For example, it is more expensive to spend $100 on equipment and then not use it than it is to spend $500 on equipment that will be in constant use.

3. The number of staff hired should correspond to initial enrollment projections.
4. Enrollment variations—for example, a summer lull—should be expected and budgeted for.
5. The director should check with the governmental agency for its reimbursement schedule, which may be 6 months or longer, and then determine whether the local bank will give credit or a short-term loan to state or federally funded centers that receive governmental reimbursements.
6. Accrual accounting is the best. Expenses should be reported when monies are encumbered rather than when paid.

A budget may be written in many ways, with only one absolute rule of budget formulation: Planned expenditures cannot exceed projected income. An example of an annual budget format is given in Figure 7.1.

Application Activity

Review the operating budget for your program. Based on your reporting of current expenditures, what percentage of your budget is allocated for staff wages? What budget categories might be reduced to enable your program to allocate a higher percentage to staff compensation?

Reporting the Budget

Directors are required to give budget reports. Some common types of reports are

a. A *budget comparison report,* in which one compares the previous month to the current month in each category
b. An *annual report,* which lists the amount budgeted and the amount spent during the calendar or fiscal year
c. A *statement of financial position,* which reflects revenues earned and expenses incurred for a calendar or fiscal year

To prepare reports accurately, all financial transactions should be recorded immediately. A checking account is the safest way to handle financial transactions and provides the audit trail. Directors need to be aware of the financial accounting standards required for not-for-profit organizations.

TRENDS AND ISSUES

Although most people agree that early childhood care and education yield direct benefits to young children and their families as well as public benefits, there is a current problem in the disparity between what the public are willing to pay versus what high-quality care and education really costs. The problem is simply defined: If quality goes up in terms of wages, child–staff ratios, and program services, programs become less affordable, and vice versa.

All professionals agree that no trade-off should exist between quality and affordability; however, the reality is that trade-offs are occurring and that quality is, more often than not, the loser. The Carnegie Institute (Carnegie Corporation of New York, 1996) reported that the United States provides some of the worst services for children in Western society. As more and more programs fail to meet even minimum standards, a new question arises: Will the money not spent today, along with major interest, be used to pay the piper in a not so distant future?

ANNUAL BUDGET FORMAT

Income

   Annual tuition (tuition for each X number of children)   _____

   Application/registration fees   _____

   Government monies   _____

   Investment income   _____

   Cash donations and funds raised   _____

   Volunteer work and in-kind donations calculated as income   _____

   Other: _____   _____

   _____   _____

      Total income   _____

                     ****

Staffing Expenses

   Salaries

      Director or director/teacher   _____

      Teachers and assistants   _____

      Workers' Compensation, retirement, and other fringe benefits   _____

      Substitutes   _____

      Food service personnel   _____

      Secretary/receptionist   _____

      Custodian   _____

      Others: _____   _____

   Taxes   _____

   Payroll-related expenses   _____

   Bank charges and loan payments   _____

   Licensing and accreditation fees   _____

   Staff training including consultant fees   _____

   Professional memberships and fees   _____

   Health insurance   _____

   Advertising (for enrollment)   _____

   Loss of property and uncollectable accounts   _____

(Continued)

Figure 7.1
Example of an Annual Budget Format

Providing Adequate Subsidies

In child care and education, portable aid substitutes for, rather than supplements, any direct support to a program (Stoney, 1999). The opposite is true in other consumer areas, such as paying for housing or higher education; in these areas, support is provided through

Other: _____

_____   _____

Total staffing expenses   _____

****

Operating expenses

  Rent/mortgage   _____

  Building insurance   _____

  Children's equipment/materials/supplies (excluding food)   _____

  Field trips   _____

  Food and snacks   _____

  Meetings, special events   _____

  Vehicle purchase and maintenance   _____

  Utilities   _____

  Communication (telephone, fax, Internet service provider, and postage)   _____

  Business expenses:

    Office machines: computers, copiers, etc.   _____

    Service fees on office machines   _____

    Office supplies   _____

    Accounting and bookkeeping   _____

  Building repairs and maintenance costs   _____

  Publicity and fund-raising   _____

  Hygienic, health, and custodial supplies _____

  Laundry   _____

  Other: _____

_____   _____

Total operating expenses   _____

****

Total expenses before contingencies

Allowance for contingencies (3% of budget)   _____

Total expenses   _____

Net cash flow from operations   _____

_____

Figure 7.1 (Continued)

direct financial assistance to programs and through portable subsidies that are made available to help users purchase the needed goods and services (Barbett & Korb, 1999; Stoney, 1999). To enhance program quality and to serve all children, both direct and portable subsidies are needed by child care and education programs (Mitchell & Morgan, 2001).

Problems exist with portable subsidies, too. First, government portable subsidies for child care and education are based on the going market price rather than on the full costs per child. Quality improvements require paying above the market rate. Differential subsidy rates should be based on the child (i.e., program costs are higher for infants and toddlers and for children with special needs) and on the overall quality of the program (i.e., accredited programs should have the highest subsidy rates).

Second, gaps also exist in every state's subsidy system (Schulman, Blank, & Ewen, 2001). Because of restrictive eligibility, many families do not qualify for subsidies. Many eligible families do not receive aid because 33% of the states do not have the funds needed to serve all eligible families (Schulman & Blank, 2002). As previously explained, even families who receive aid often lose eligibility as soon as their income changes.

Without experiences in high-quality programs, children from low income families are at an increased risk for school failure. The Committee on Early Childhood Pedagogy recommended that the federal government fund high-quality center-based programs for all children who are at high risk for school failure (National Research Council, 2001).

Compensating a Skilled and Stable Workforce

Because early childhood care and education are essentially services, high-quality programs depend on a skilled and stable workforce (Howes, Smith, & Galinsky, 1998; Vandell & Wolfe, 2000). Stagnant, low wages result in a nonstable supply of workers with inadequate skills and education. Funds to support professional training are limited. Most funds provide entry-level training only. Some potential sources include the following:

- Child and Adult Care Food Program
- Child Care and Development Block Grant
- Child Care Improvement Grants (Family Support Act)
- Job Training Partnership Act
- Title II (NCLB)

Although investments in education have a positive effect on program quality, investments in education have not had the same effect on compensation. As previously discussed, teachers subsidize early childhood programs with foregone wages. Now that the link between the staffing crisis and teacher compensation is understood, *compensation initiatives* (initiatives that result in dependable and ongoing wage increases) are under way (Whitebook, 2002).

Initiatives vary with respect to the emphasis on the link between compensation and education/training (Whitebook & Eichberg, 2002). Some initiatives focus on wage increases or benefits tied to individual education/training; others focus on program eligibility to participate; and a few are system-based initiatives (e.g., U.S. Military's Personnel Pay Plan; Head Start Quality Improvement Act). (See the last section of this chapter for sources of summaries of some of those initiatives.)

Financing a System of Early Childhood Education

Without a coordinated system of services supported by financing strategies that provide needed resources, the goal of accessible, affordable, and high-quality programs for all children will not be fulfilled. The NAEYC (NAEYC Policy Brief, 2001) called for financing a system of early childhood education that includes (a) providing direct services to children in families with low incomes, (b) compensation for staff as a reward for additional education and a commitment to remain in a program for a longer period of time, and (c) funding the *infrastructure* (functions that support direct services).

Today, a major problem is the lack of financing coherence. The lack of coherence begins at the federal level, where the government cannot decide on one funding mechanism (e.g., tax credit or expansion of direct funding to early childhood programs). Thus, it has compromised by doing a little bit of everything. This lack of coherence in funding is perpetuated by the literally countless federal agencies that administer federal funds and by the two major state divisions (Department of Health and Human Resources and the Department of Education) that administer some of the federal funds and handle state supplementary revenues. By the time the paltry funds reach the local level, there is often no longer a good match between local needs and the goals of programs and no connection (transition) among programs. In all likelihood, there will be duplication of many program services, confusion for families who will find either too many program options or no viable program for their children, and children who will be placed in programs with inappropriate practices.

A tripartnership among the federal, state, and local levels is needed to create a coherent funding policy that can make the most out of these bits and pieces. Kagan (2000) stated that financing an early childhood education system begins with obtaining concrete data on how much it will cost; how revenues should be generated and disbursed; and the appropriate balance of contributions from public, private, and family sectors.

SUMMARY

Programs for young children are expensive. A quality program will cost $8,000 or more per child per year. Although families seldom pay the full costs, early childhood programs can be a large expenditure of the family budget, especially for middle- and low-income families. For many families, high-quality early childhood programs are simply not affordable.

Public early childhood programs are financed through local, state, and federal funding sources. For-profit early childhood programs are supported primarily through tuition and fees.

Budgets must be carefully made in keeping with program goals; that is, expenditures should reflect the goals of the program. The fiscal planning of the program administrator is one of the most important responsibilites. If there isn't a healthy balance between program income and expenditures, the program will be forced to close.

A major crisis centers on financing. Decisions about funding are decisions about program quality. Any trade-off between affordability and quality will result in a loss of benefits to young children, their families, and all segments of society. Without adequate staff compensation linked to training and experience, early childhood programs will continue to be of mediocre quality and experience high staff turnover rates. Funding diversity outside some framework of coherence, such as a system of early childhood education, further erodes the judicious use of funds for the creation and maintenance of high-quality programs for all children.

USEFUL WEB SITES

U.S. grant and funding sources at
    www.childcare.net/grantsusa.shtml

NOZA Search Inc.
Searchable database of philanthropic individuals and organizations at

    www.nozasearch.com/

PreK Now
Nonprofit organization advocating for increased funding to support prekindergarten services for young children at

    preknow.org/

TO REFLECT

1. Parent X has had her child enrolled in your program for 3 years. Her child's tuition has always been paid on time. Recently, the parent lost her job when a local plant closed. Although you have a fee policy, she asks if you will make an exception for her child until she can find another job. You also note that you have a waiting list of three other families who have steady employment. What should you do—keep the child whose parent cannot pay or follow your fee policy and enroll a child whose parents can pay?

2. Teachers subsidize early childhood programs with foregone wages. For example, the Cost, Quality, and Child Outcomes Study Team (1995) found that center-based teachers' foregone income was $5,200 a year, and a national report (Education Week, 2000) stated that public school teachers' foregone income was $7,894 per year. What would this amount to in a lifetime of earnings? Many teachers work (e.g., planning, assessing, recording, attending meetings) beyond paid hours and spend out-of-pocket money on equipment and materials for their classrooms. As a professional advocate, how would you face the perverse equation of care costing too little to achieve worthy staff compensation and too much to be affordable for many families? Do you think capable teachers who like teaching are justified in leaving the profession for better pay? In striking for better pay?

3. With many government budget crunches, funding sources for early childhood programs are limited. Under these circumstances should more affordable (and hence minimal quality) programs be offered to more children and families or should high-quality (and hence more costly) programs be offered to fewer children and families?

8

MARKETING YOUR CHILD CARE AND EDUCATION PROGRAM

NAEYC Administrator Competencies addressed in this chapter:

Management Knowledge and Skills

Marketing and Public Relations

Knowledge of the fundamentals of effective marketing, public relations, and community outreach. The ability to evaluate the cost-benefit of different marketing and promotional strategies. The ability to communicate the program's philosophy and promote a positive public image to families, business leaders, public officials, and prospective funders.

Marketing is about much more than simply advertising or publicizing your program. Marketing is the type of services that you provide and to whom, the extent to which your customers are satisfied with your service, and the public image of your program. While making coffee and providing an enriching experience for young children are vastly different occupations, we can learn a lot from companies like Starbucks. Successful companies effectively identify for whom they wish to provide services, how they intend to serve them, and then use various strategies to publicize the benefit of their service. In this chapter, we discuss ways you can make your clients' experiences more rewarding than my simple stop at a coffee shop.

Application Activity

Think about your favorite experience as a consumer. What business do you thoroughly enjoy visiting? What is it about this business that continually brings you back? How does your interaction with this business make you feel? If the product or service that you purchase from this business were to increase in price, would you still purchase it?

As I think about my favorite experiences as a consumer, an experience that immediately comes to mind is my experience with Starbucks Coffee.

I am a semiregular at Starbucks Coffee. My attraction to this establishment is based not only on the fact that I enjoy the taste of the coffee that they make, but also because I enjoy the experience of buying coffee at the particular location that I frequent. Some of the things that this location provides that I find attractive are (1) fast, reliable service (I am usually in a hurry when I stop in for a cup of coffee); (2) consistently good flavor; and (3) the feeling that I am part of a "cultured" group (I know the lingo).

When I first walked into a Starbucks Coffee store about 10 years ago, I felt a bit awkward. In line in front of me were several folks who didn't need a menu and seemed to order their coffee using a language that I didn't fully comprehend. The lady who ordered immediately before me requested a "half-caf, no whip, mocha with room." After learning the coffee lingo, I now feel as if I am part of a special group of coffee drinkers, a feeling that I get only when purchasing coffee at Starbucks, since other coffee shops don't tend to respond well to the same lingo.

My experience at Starbucks illustrates how this company, through a well-thought-through marketing plan, has effectively communicated what goods and services they will provide, established a unique culture that is attractive to their intended customer base, and developed systems to effectively deliver exactly what the customer expects. How can *you* translate this experience at Starbucks to operating an early care and education program?

MARKETING IS IMPORTANT

Up to this point in the text we have discussed the importance of defining your vision and mission for providing care and education services to young children and their families. We have also presented management strategies, aspects of facility planning, and finance and budget planning that are important considerations for the successful operation of an organization focused on the care and education of young children. While these topics are important to consider, arguably the most important aspect of your operation is your **marketing plan.**

Through this chapter we will bring together the topics discussed in Chapters 5, 6, and 7 and tie them to the importance of your program vision and the mission. In doing so, we will help you think about your program and identify ways you can make the experience of your clients fulfilling.

While there are a plethora of books that define marketing for the general business world, there are very few resources that have been designed to explicitly apply basic marketing concepts to the practice of early care and education. Through this chapter we present the best thinking from the business world and apply it to the context of early care and education. The ideas and strategies presented in this chapter will apply to a center in development as well as a center that is currently in operation. It is essential, however, that prior to engaging with the content in this chapter, you *have an established vision and mission for your early care and education program*. Through this chapter you will be encouraged to review this mission to identify the extent to which all aspects of your program and marketing plan align.

WHAT IS MARKETING?

According to the American Marketing Association (2007), "**Marketing** is the activity, set of institutions, and processes for creating, communicating, delivering, and exchanging offerings that have value for customers, clients, partners, and society at large" (AMA, 2007, About Us section, para. 1). In other words, marketing encompasses much more than advertisements (contrary to popular perception). It includes deciding on the type of product you will offer, deciding what consumer (client) you will target (**market segmentation strategy**), identifying that client's needs and desires, and then designing and refining your product to meet the needs of your client.

Following this line of thinking, the service that you provide to your clients (families and children) is marketing. The feeling that your customers derive from the service that you provide is marketing. The appearance and functionality of the physical facility that you have designed or are operating in is marketing. All the materials that bear your organizational logo, or bring your organization to the mind of clients or potential clients is marketing. In this way almost everything that your organization does or is perceived as doing might be considered part of your program's marketing strategy. Before we present the specific programmatic features that you focus on in developing your marketing plan, there is a principle of marketing that you must first understand.

This principle is best summarized through a common axiom within the marketing field: **Perception is reality.** This statement communicates the importance of almost everything that occurs in relation to your organization. What this saying really means, as it applies to the practice of working with young children and their families, is that whatever your client perceives to occur is what they react to and results in the truth as they see it.

For example, I was recently consulting with colleagues who own and operate a child care facility in Florida. Their concern was that despite the fact that they provide a robust curriculum that is nurturing and educationally beneficial, many parents who attend their program view the service that they receive as primarily custodial. This perception has led to child and family attrition. When children turn 4 years old, parents withdraw their children from the center and enroll them in "preschool" to prepare them for kindergarten. This is a common perception in the field of early care and education—that there are two distinct types of service providers: those that are considered primarily education service providers (preschools) and those that primarily provide custodial services to children (child care centers).

While many child care centers view their role as a combination of care and education, families who use these services as well as the general public might not recognize the educative value of these organizations based on their perception of what is occurring with the children during the day. This perception is in all likelihood fostered by the fact that child care centers tend to accommodate their provision of services to meet the needs of working families (i.e., open for extended hours and closed only a few days of the year).

Centers that are perceived by families as schools rather than child care offer limited hours of operation and follow the local school schedule. While the most effectively operated centers, preschool or child care, are likely to offer similar educative benefits to the children they serve, parents and the general public don't always recognize this to be true.

Through our brainstorming session, my colleagues identified some potential strategies they could employ to actively change the public perception of their program as primarily custodial (See Table 8.1 for further elaboration).

It is in the best interest of your organization to learn to anticipate how your clients might perceive the types of services and interactions that they have with your center and then behave in ways that are likely to foster favorable perceptions. Thus, the essence of marketing your program is actively working to cultivate a positive perception of the service(s) you provide among potential and current clients.

This will be done most effectively by living up to the promises that you make to your clients through your mission and your articulation of the types of services that you provide. Through thoughtful planning of the environment and program management, you can work to set the stage to create a positive perception. With this in mind we now turn to the impact that facility design and service delivery have on the perception that clients may form about your program.

Table 8.1
Child Care versus Preschool: Possible Influences on Perception

Program Characteristic	Child Care	Preschool
Days of Programming	Monday through Friday	M, W, F or T, TH Possibly Monday through Friday
Daily Hours of Operation	*7:00 A.M.–7:00 P.M.*	*9 A.M.–2 P.M.*
Annual Closings	Closed only on typical days of low enrollment; Thanksgiving, Christmas, New Years.	All nationally recognized holidays; closed several weeks during winter holidays; follows public school closings; also closed for teacher professional development days and for parent teacher conferences.
Daily Schedule	Large amounts of time for play, in centers, outside; may have craft activity daily.	Daily schedule, while it may include significant time for play, is labeled specifically to include typical curriculum subject areas (math, reading, science, social studies).
Curriculum	Described as eclectic or play based, with teachers emphasizing the importance of socialization, bodily functions, and self-help skills.	Again, while many of the same values may be in place, the center clearly articulates a specific curriculum and is able to describe how the planned engagements support children's learning in traditional subject areas.
Teacher Credentials/ Experience	Teachers/caregivers have limited professional education; limited experience in the field prior to joining the faculty or being placed in the charge of a group of children.	Teachers have some formal training in early childhood education; hold a CDA, AA, BA, or higher; hold a teaching certificate; have been working in the field for an extended period of time.
Cost	Economical, affordable for most families.	Higher cost for fewer hours of service.

Facility Design

A word of caution: For illustrative purposes, we will present examples in the following sections that are on different ends of a continuum. While we label some settings as institutional versus centers that are homelike to help make our point concerning the connection between the environment of your center and the messages that might be interpreted by families, we are not attempting to endorse a stark institutional environment.

The physical appearance of your facility sets the tone of your facility and communicates volumes to your current clients and potential clients regarding the culture of your organization, the quality of your program, and the type of service you provide. A center that has a large entryway equipped with comfortable chairs, decorative plants, magazines that might be of interest to families, and brochures highlighting community resources available to families with young children is likely to send the message to parents that they are welcome at the center. This might even foster a perception of the center as a warm and homelike place. While a detailed description of facility design was presented in chapter 6, take the time now to consider the messages that you are sending your clients through your current or planned facility.

To help illustrate the many messages that may be sent to clients and prospective clients through the physical environment of your center, look at Table 8.2 that identifies messages that might be associated with common child care physical environmental features.

When designing the physical facility, or if you are currently operating a program, think about the message you want to send to your client regarding the type of center you are. If, for example, you are focusing on attracting and maintaining a clientele base that needs a professional/institutional feel, consider hard surfaces for flooring, limited wall decorations, open and uncluttered classroom storage of materials.

If, on the other hand, part of your organizational mission is to facilitate a homelike setting, you should have softer flooring and wall colors, ample comfortable seating, fresh flowers, children's artwork, and maybe even a family message board. While a soft and comfortable environment is conducive to projecting a positive message to families, it is important to not get so comfortable that the facility appears disorganized or unclean.

The wall adornments in your center send a powerful message to families regarding the nature of your program. The staff information posted on the wall of this center might effectively communicate to families that the teaching staff are qualified and highly valued.

Table 8.2
Potential Messages from Child Care Facilities

	Positive Messages		Negative Messages
Electronic keypad at the front door; code or visitor button must be entered for access to be granted.	"This is a secure facility."	Soiled diaper or used fast-food wrappers in the parking lot.	"This place is dirty."
Brief biography of letter of introduction for each of the staff members prominently posted.	"The staff are: (depending on the content) highly qualified, friendly, stable."	Biographies not maintained and updated with staff changes.	"This center must have a lot of turnover."
Posted daily schedules that detail the activities and engagements planned for that day.	"The teachers have a planned curriculum," or Children are learning here."	Generic daily schedule posted that includes bland titles such as Morning Circle, Center Time, Lunch.	"They are organized and are likely to keep the class under control."
Recently completed children's artwork adorning the walls.	"The children are valued."	It is now January and Halloween artwork is posted on the wall.	This once positive message has now become negative: "The teachers aren't attentive."
Facility smells of finger paint, crayons, and so on.	"This is a school."	Classroom smells of a freshly soiled diaper (immediately following a diaper change).	"This is an unclean environment."
Certificate of Accreditation displayed.	"This is a quality program."	Certificate of GED, or high school diplomas of staff.	"Teachers are not well educated."
From the classroom entryway, contents of bookshelves may be seen.	"This is a fun and engaging place."	Toys and equipment not placed on shelves in an organized fashion.	"This place is chaotic."
Outdoor equipment is freshly painted and grounds are free of debris.	"This is a fun and safe environment."	Paint on outdoor equipment is faded (sun bleached); some debris is present on the grounds.	"This is not a safe place to play."

This would then project a very negative image to families regarding your ability to meet the basic health and safety needs of the children.

Service Delivery

The most important thing you can do to market your program is to actually provide the services that you promise. While the specific services offered to clients will vary from program to program, all centers have one thing in common: They primarily provide services to young children, for which parents or other family members pay. The care and education services that we provide children include tending to the basic health and safety needs, opportunities to foster growth and development, and achievement of some academic gains.

The primary outcomes some parents seek are happy healthy children, while others are primarily interested in their children's academic preparation for school. It is our responsibility as service providers to determine what we will aspire to deliver, work to ensure that families understand the outcomes we are attempting to achieve, and then provide consistent evidence to families that we are indeed achieving these outcomes. The ways in which we do that may take many forms and will vary depending on the desired outcomes.

For families who are primarily interested in custodial care, the most important message we can communicate to them is that when their children are in our care, they are safe, cared for, and healthy. We actively communicate this message by maintaining an environment where children are rarely injured, the facility is clean and organized, and the children are clean, nourished, and happy to attend.

When providing written communication to families, we might focus on describing the frequency and quantity of food consumed, the frequency and consistency of diaper changes, and a description of any special attention that a child was given to support emotional security. When family members arrive to either drop the children off or pick them up at the end of the day, they expect to see the children safely engaged in activity, and the teacher interacting in a nurturing way with the children.

When working with families whose primary goal is academic preparation, we should focus on sharing information with families that provides evidence that their children are "getting ready for school." While we are not advocating having the children engage in activities that are inappropriate for young learners, such as worksheets, we are encouraging teachers to actively describe the educational benefit of the children's experiences while at school. For example, if a child spent a significant amount of time drawing a picture illustrating a recent trip to the circus, the teacher can share with the parents how this use of symbols is related to early writing development.

Through written communication to families the teacher may highlight the specific skills the children have been working to acquire, describe upcoming content, and may even suggest activities that parents can engage in with their children at home to support the learning that has been occurring in the classroom. During classroom observations (drop-off and pickup) parents interested in academic development of their children will be looking to see the teacher engaged with the children in ways that appear to support learning, for example, asking a child to elaborate on his description of the difference between cats and dogs, or seeing the children independently engaged in activities that can be described as educative.

For all families, regardless of their specific reason for seeking a center-based experience for their children, it is important that we acknowledge that all parents want their children to be safe, and all parents want their children to be successful. Considering this, it would be wise to ensure that you send a message to parents that communicates that the children are safe and meaningfully engaged in learning.

Above all we need to work to communicate to the families who bring their children to us that we care about and know their children as individuals. We can set the stage for fostering this perception by sharing simple child specific anecdotes (that address individual parent-desired outcomes) with families when they arrive at the end of the day to retrieve their child. An example of such an anecdote follows:

Mr. and Mrs. Johnson, parents of Joey, are primarily interested in their child's ability to make friends and develop social skills. When they come to pick up Joey this afternoon, you share the following story that chronicles a brief interaction between Joey and a new child to the class, Stephen.

"Mrs. Johnson, I must share with you the wonderful thing that Joey did today while on the playground with the other children. Today was another little boy's first day in our classroom and during recess this new little boy was having a difficult time adjusting to time away from his parents and was sitting by himself crying by the sandbox. Well, you know how much Joey loves that little red dump truck. He pushed the truck over to the new child, sat next to him, and gave him the truck saying, 'I know you're sad right now. Would this dump truck help you feel better? It is my favorite.' After that, the new little boy wiped the tears from his eyes and began playing with Joey. Your boy really is a special friend to the children here at school. Make sure that you tell him what a good friend he is."

This story did something very special for Mr. and Mrs. Johnson. Not only did it communicate that their son is indeed learning the social skills that they value, but it also communicated to them that their son's teacher really pays attention to Joey. She cares enough about the parents to share this precious story with them and helps the parents become engaged in the educational process by providing them the opportunity to praise their child for exhibiting desired behavior.

Marketing Plan

The process of developing a marketing plan is essential to maximize program potential. Through the identification of your program mission, the articulation of specific objectives, an analysis of internal strengths and weaknesses and external threats and opportunities, and development of strategies designed to meet the objectives, you increase the likelihood that the message you send to clients is consistent and portrays the desired image of your program. A marketing plan includes the following elements: program mission, marketing objective, situation analysis, target market selection, marketing mix, and implementation plan (Lamb, Hair, & McDaniel, 2006).

According to McNamara (2007), the process of developing a marketing plan begins with **market research** to find out

1. What specific groups of potential clients might have which specific needs
2. How those needs might be met for each group (or target market), which suggests how a program might be designed to meet the need
3. How each of the target markets might choose to access the service
4. How much the customers/clients might be willing to pay
5. Who the competitors are
6. How to design and describe the product so clients will buy from the organization, rather than from its competitors (its unique value proposition)
7. How the product should be identified—its personality—to be most identifiable (its naming and branding)

Once you have done this research and evaluation, you must next turn to the important task of identifying goals and a marketing strategy that will accomplish these goals. A professional marketing firm might be helpful in conducting a market survey and providing insight regarding specific media and other strategies to advertise and publicize your program to potential clients.

It is up to the program to inform the firm about your program vision, mission, and the specific services you provide. For this reason it is wise for your organization to sketch out a marketing plan prior to contracting professional advertising firms. While different organizations use different formats to articulate their marketing plan, almost all contain the same basic elements: mission statement, objectives, present situation, target market strategy, marketing mix, and implementation and evaluation plan. To help your program begin development of a marketing plan, use the outline provided in Figure 8.1 as a guide.

Strategies to Publicize Your Program: Internal and External Marketing

As part of your marketing plan, you will need to identify specific media outlets and other means of making potential clients aware of your program and the benefits that might be obtained as a result of enrollment in your program. In order to be effective and to maximize

I. Program Mission Statement: A statement of the program's ultimate goal based on the identified services and careful analysis of benefits sought by present and potential clients.
   a. Refer to Chapter two for further discussion on the development of a program mission statement.

II. Marketing Objective: A statement of what is to be accomplished through marketing activities.
   a. The objectives that you identify should be realistic, measurable, and time specific. Objectives must help move the organization toward achievement of the program vision and mission.
   b. Example: Our objective is to retain 85 percent of our current families during the transition from summer to fall enrollment and begin the 2008–2009 session at 95 percent of our full capacity for enrollment.

III. Present Situation: Evaluating the context that your program will be marketed in.
   a. Internal Features: These are aspects of your program that the director has an influence on. When analyzing the present situation as it pertains to your marketing plan you are looking for strengths that should be "shouted from the roof tops and weaknesses that should be shored up. Determine the relative strength of organizational resources such as costs of services, marketing skills, financial resources, company image, employee capabilities, and available technology.
      i. Strengths:
      ii. Weaknesses:
   b. External Features: These features are present in the environment you are operating in but are not easily influenced or changed by a single person or organization. These external features include market forces, events, and relationships in the external environment that may affect the future of the organization or the implementation of the marketing plan.
      i. Opportunities:
      ii. Threats:

IV. Market Segmentation: Selection of the specific clientele that you intend to attract through your market strategy.
   a. Should be based on a recently conducted market survey which is a description and estimation of the size and sales potential of market segments that are of interest to the program and an assessment of key competitors in these market segments.

V. Marketing Plan: The composition of program features that are selected to create a mutually beneficial arrangement between the clientele and the program.
   a. Product: Description of the services that you are providing
   b. Place: Location of the facility, making the services available in the place the clientele wants them
   c. Promotion: The strategies that you will use to educate and/or remind your clients of the benefits that your services provide
   d. Price: What the client must pay to receive the service; this must be affordable, yet high enough to ensure financial health of the organization

VI. Implementation: A description that identifies who, what, where and when of the actualization of this marketing plan. Two essential elements that must be included are:
   a. Tasks: An identification of the specific tasks that will be accomplished to achieve the marketing objectives
   b. Evaluation: Formal assessment of the effectiveness of these activities and progress monitoring of the achievement of the marketing goal

Figure 8.1
Marketing Plan Outline

the financial resources that you dedicate to this, it is advisable that you include both **internal and external marketing strategies.**

Internal marketing strategies are the things you do to satisfy and retain current clients, which will likely result in word-of-mouth recommendations. External marketing strategies include the use of media advertisements, signs, brochures, and other printed materials to inform potential clients about the services you provide. According to the Wisconsin Child Care Improvement Project (2007) (WCCIP) over 90% of parents rely on recommendations from friends and family to decide on their selection of child care. This is consistent with the common business claim that it is much more expensive to attract a new customer than it is to keep a current customer satisfied (Hiam, 2004).

As you decide on your final marketing plan, it is important that you attend to both your internal and external marketing strategies, but be wise in how you allocate both human and financial resources. It is typically the internal marketing strategies you use that will have the most impact on maintaining a program with full enrollment.

The Wisconsin Child Care Improvement Project (WCCIP) (2007) has identified specific strategies that might be used by child care providers to attract and retain clients. They have categorized the strategies into three groups: internal strategies, external strategies, and initial point of contact strategies. See Figure 8.2 for a tip sheet outlining these strategies developed by the WCCIP.

Guidelines for Print Media

One important way you will communicate with the families you serve and families you might be able to attract to your center is with print media. Print media most commonly used by child care centers include letters, flyers, brochures, postcards, business cards, and signs. While it is wise to consult a visual artist or graphic designer to create a logo and format for print materials, this is not always something that the typical child care center is able to afford. Fortunately, with the application of a few basic principles and thoughtful consideration of the following questions, you can create documents that will effectively communicate with potential clients.

General Rules for Readable Print Media

- Use a font (no more than three per document) that is easy to read (avoid scripted or elaborate fonts and anything smaller than an 11-pt font)
- Include your logo on everything you distribute to families
- Carefully edit for content and grammar before distributing
- Use headings that attract the reader's attention and convey a meaningful message

General Questions to Consider

- What image of your program do you want to convey?
- What will draw their attention, hold their interest to read entire brochure, and then call you?

Content to Include in a Brochure

- Location, contact information (if possible list the name of the individual who will be talking with first-time visitors), Web site address
- Program mission and philosophy
- Specific hours of operation
- Benefits of your program
- Special services offered to children and families
- Staff qualifications and other professional affiliations

Internal Marketing Strategies

- Welcome parents at all times
- Invite feedback
- Respond positively to suggestions
- Include parents in activities and field trips
- Display photos of children at play
- Have evening family events
- Hold parent conferences regularly
- Be sensitive to diverse family structures

External Marketing Strategies

Advertising will be a significant part of your marketing plan and budget. Advertising costs can range from free to very expensive.

Child Care Resource and Referrals (CCR&Rs)

- Serve all areas of the state; maintain databases on *all* regulated child care in their region.
- At no cost to child care providers, parents contacting CCR&Rs receive a list of all regulated child care programs which meet their needs.

Printed Materials

- Business cards
- Outdoor sign
- Newspaper advertising
- Imprinted tee shirts, caps, totes, and so on
- Brochures
- Posters/flyers

News Media

- Radio
- Television
- News releases
  - Hiring of a new director or teacher
  - Staff attendance at a national seminar
  - Announcement of a new site or service
  - Special activities, unusual field trip
  - Free health screening offered at center

Special Events

- Participate in local parades
- Maintain a booth at a community fair
- Volunteer for a local fund-raising marathon

Other Marketing Ideas

- Invite elected officials to visit
- Invite news media
- Display children's art in the community
- Partner with technical schools and other training programs

Figure 8.2
Internal and External Marketing Strategies

Source: This tip sheet was developed by Wisconsin Child Care Improvement Project, March 1998, with funding from the Wisconsin Dept. of WFD, Office of Child Care, and DHFS. Available from www.wccip.org/tips/business/marketing.html\#Marketing

Web Site Design

In the current age of technology, having a "Web presence" has become an essential part of any marketing plan. Web site design can be somewhat tricky. It requires a fair amount of skill to create a Web site that not only functions properly but also has a high "hit rate" when folks use a search engine such as Google or Yahoo! to locate your center on the Web.

It is highly advised that you elicit the assistance of an individual who is knowledgeable in this area, since a poorly constructed or malfunctioning Web site can do more harm than good. At the end of the chapter we have included a couple of free Web sites that might help get you started.

When considering content that you might like to include on a Web site, you will want to include anything you would include in a brochure (possibly in expanded format) and then add additional content that will encourage individuals to return to your Web site. This "hook" might be descriptions of appropriate engagements that parents/family members might participate in with their child, a weekly blog describing what the children in your program are doing or learning about, or an announcement of community events.

Strategies for the Initial Point of Contact

As the adage goes, you get only one chance to make a first impression. A negative first impression will quickly help a potential client choose to enroll their child elsewhere. While a consistently high-quality and well-operated program will speak for itself, it is important to identify a plan for how you will handle a potential family's initial point of contact with you to ensure that their perception is positive. Figure 8.3 provides some strategies that we have employed and are also recommended by the WCCIP (see their Web site at the end of this chapter).

The Power of the Purple Cow

Godin, a highly esteemed marketing and business consultant and author of *Permission Marketing* and *Purple Cow,* eloquently defines the recent changes in the field of marketing. Through his work he has accurately portrayed conventional marketing strategies that rely primarily on external marketing strategies to be expensive and ineffective. One of the main points he makes is that with advancing technology and the constant bombardment of advertisement potential clients receive in the marketplace, we have learned to effectively ignore this type of advertisement. As a result of our ability to tune out external marketing, successful businesses and organizations focus more of their resources (human and financial) on internal marketing strategies. Through this, Godin presents the importance of offering a truly remarkable product or service—what he calls the Purple Cow.

An example of a Purple Cow that has recently entered the market is the iPod produced by Apple. Prior to its release, a relatively small group of individuals were downloading music from the Internet and listening to it via mp3 players. Once Steve Jobs and his creative crew at Apple created not only a unique and attractive mp3 player that is easy to use, but also a Web-based store to legally purchase music, an electronic music revolution was born. Now, several years after the initial release of the iPod, this device is everywhere, and the use of a lowercase "i" has become synonymous with an innovative product, even if the device is not released by Apple.

As you begin to develop your marketing plan and consider any revisions to the care and education services you provide, you must also think about how your program might become truly remarkable. Is there a service that families would value that you don't currently provide? Are there benefits that children gain from your program that you haven't effectively communicated to others?

Initial Phone Contact
- Have phone located in an area with a minimum of noise
- Answer promptly, three rings or less
- Use an answering machine with a friendly message
- Check for messages regularly
- Return calls promptly
- Maintain a phone log of inquirers
- Follow up inquiries

Initial Visit

- The visit begins outside; pay attention to the building's exterior and the entryway.
- Are outdoor play areas clean and appropriately staffed?

- Locate office where you can see visitors entering.
- What do parents hear when they enter?
- What do parents smell?
- What do parents see?

Greeting Parents and Children
- Greeting begins with your appearance
- Welcome the child by bending down to eye level.
- Use visitors' names several times during the conversation
- Listen to visitors' questions
- On a tour, describe typical activities and point out signs of quality:
  - High level of staff training
  - Accreditation certificate
  - Absence of serious noncompliance notice beside license
- Sell your program
  - A photo album of past events
  - Collection of past newsletters
  - Letters of testimonial from other parents
- Get information from the visitors
  - Name
  - Address
  - Phone number
  - Child's birth date
  - Schedule needed
- Follow up with a thank you note immediately and a phone call later.

Figure 8.3
Strategies for the Initial Point of Contact

Source: This tip sheet was developed by Wisconsin Child Care Improvement Project, March 1998, with funding from the Wisconsin Dept. of WFD, Office of Child Care, and DHFS. Available from: www.wccip.org/tips/business/marketing.html\#Marketing

SUMMARY

Through this chapter we have presented some key points that you must consider regarding the marketing of your early care and education program. In bringing your service of child care and education to market, it is your job to make sure you identify your intended market, understand the needs of the selected market, and monitor your provision of service to ensure that your clientele are satisfied. Through this process you will need to design an internal marketing plan that effectively communicates to your current clients and an external marketing plan that informs potential clients exactly what service(s) you provide and the benefits that might be derived from enrollment in your program.

USEFUL WEB SITES

Wisconsin Child Care Improvement Network, Inc.
www.wccip.org/tips/business/marketing.html

All About Marketing from the Free Management Library
www.managementhelp.org/mktng/mrltng.htm

Wise Geek: How to start your own Webpage
www.wisegeek.com/how-do-i-create-my-own-website
.htm

The SiteWizard.com: How to Start/Create your own website: The Beginners A-Z Guide
www.thesitewizard.com/gettingstarted/startwebsite.shtml

TO REFLECT

1. What is the public perception of your program? Is the public perception aligned with the vision and mission you have for the program?

2. What is your program currently doing to actively cultivate a positive perception among clients you already serve as well as the community at large? Are there things about your facility or your provision of service that are likely to foster the development of a negative perception of your program? What can or should you do to change?

3. In your community what type of marketing strategies do early childhood care and education programs typically use? Peruse the Internet and try to locate child care programs in your area. What content is presented on the Web? How easy is it to find information that you might be interested in?

4. What are the needs and desires of the parents and families in your community? Are there needs that are presently not being addressed by programs in your area?

9

PLANNING THE CHILDREN'S PROGRAM

NAEYC Administrator Competencies addressed in this chapter:

Early Childhood Knowledge and Skills

4. Curriculum and Instructional Methods
   Knowledge of different curriculum models, appropriate curriculum goals, and different instructional strategies for infants, toddlers, preschoolers, and kindergarten children. Ability to plan and implement a curriculum based on knowledge of individual children's developmental patterns, family and community goals, institutional and cultural context, and state standards. Ability to design integrated and meaningful curricular experiences in the content areas of language and literacy, mathematics, science, social studies, art, music, drama, movement, and technology. Ability to implement anti-bias instructional strategies that take into account culturally valued content and children's home experiences. Ability to evaluate outcomes of different curricular approaches.

5. Children with Special Needs
   Knowledge of atypical development including mild and severe disabilities in physical, health, cognitive, social/emotional, communication, and sensory functioning. Knowledge of licensing standards, state and federal laws (e.g., ADA, IDEA) as they relate to services and accommodations for children with special needs. Knowledge of the characteristics of giftedness and how educational environments can support children with exceptional capabilities. The ability to work collaboratively as part of family-professional team in planning and implementing appropriate services for children with special needs. Knowledge of special education resources and services.

The focus of planning and administering an early childhood program is on planning and implementing children's activities. All other administrative tasks—meeting regulations, establishing policies, leading personnel, planning the physical facilities, and financing—are performed in coordination with planning and implementing the children's program. The role of the director is to serve as the local program leader by

- Working toward fulfillment of the program vision and mission (by considering the knowledge and interests of children, the physical and social environments including the concerns of families and staff members, and standards for curriculum content)
- Ensuring that the program pedagogy is aligned with the vision and mission (being knowledgeable and sensitive to program implementation)
- Collaborating with community agencies that provide support services (e.g., health care, family support, social services)

PROGRAM PLANNING

Curriculum, when thought of in its broadest sense, is an all-encompassing plan for learning. When clearly articulated, the planned curriculum serves as a way of helping teachers think about children and organize children's experiences in the program setting. Young children learn from every experience; thus, curriculum involves individual and group activities, physical care routines, supportive relationships, and all other aspects of a child's day in the program. In short, everything in the program that children experience has the potential to impact children's learning. With this in mind, we turn to the process of deciding how you might go about structuring the curriculum to meet the needs of the children and their families.

Through the process of collaborative planning, teachers are more effective at identifying plans that are relevant and appropriate for the children they are working with.

Starting with the Program Vision and Mission

In chapter 2 we engaged in the process of developing your program vision and mission. Through this process you considered the needs of the children, families, and community stakeholders you hope to serve and examined the theoretical and philosophical foundations of child development and learning. As a result, you identified the goals you hope your program will achieve.

As you now move ahead to establishing or revising the program curriculum, it is imperative to keep in mind the decisions you made in developing your program mission. All aspects of your curriculum (e.g., planned engagements, available equipment and materials, daily routines) should help you accomplish the goals set forth in your program mission.

Developmentally Appropriate Practices: The Foundation of Excellence

While many early childhood programs select a specific early childhood curriculum model or approach to guide the program they implement, most experts in the field agree that the single most influential document guiding the practice of high-quality early childhood programs is the Developmentally Appropriate Practices (DAP) position statement adopted by the NAEYC (Bredekamp & Copple, 1997). The DAP position statement is not a program-based prescription; rather, it is an assertion that programs for young children should consider (a) present knowledge about child development and learning; (b) what we know about the strengths, needs, and interests of enrolled children; and (c) knowledge about the social and cultural contexts of the local community (Bredekamp & Copple, 1997).

Because these three dimensions of knowledge are dynamic, the stated program base will change as knowledge changes. Besides resources from model programs and position statements about DAP, curriculum standards, developed by various regulatory and funding agencies, are being used to guide the programming developed for young children.

Knowledge of Children.   Although a lack of consensus exists about whether child development and learning can be used as a conceptual basis for curriculum planning, most professionals believe that knowledge of children should inform program curriculum planning. The NAEYC identified 12 principles of child development and learning that inform practice (Bredekamp & Copple, 1997). Age-related human characteristics lead proponents of DAP to assert they can make general and reliable predictions about achievable and challenging curriculum for most young children in a given age/stage range (Katz, 1995b). For knowledge of children to be relevant, research must be current (e.g., National Center for Education Statistics, 2000) and be conducted in different cultures (Lynch & Hanson, 1998).

Interests and Needs of Children.   All educators realize that children have different needs and interests, and that these differences must be considered in planning. Teachers in traditional early childhood programs use continual observations of each child to determine challenging content and encourage child-initiated activities to implement much of the curriculum. Limited direct instruction is implemented with individuals or small groups rather than with whole groups, for the most part.

In addition, the education of young children with special needs must be considered. Today over half of all preschool children with identified developmental delays are included in some form of child care that serves typically developing children. The roots for the practice of inclusion began with the 1975 PL. 94–142 legislation which eventually became the Individuals with Disabilities Education Act or IDEA.

Children with special needs are diverse, as are all young children, and planning to meet the needs of a diverse group of children is challenging (Ferguson, 1995; Fuchs & Fuchs, 1998; Hunt & Goetz, 1997; Smith & Dowdy, 1998). The Individual Family Services Plan

(IFSP) or Individual Education Plan (IEP) is composed of tailor-made goals and requires supports that will help a child with disabilities benefit from the general education curriculum. According to Wolery, Strain, and Bailey (1992), these goals must be very specific and will usually require adult assistance for children to attain them.

Services focusing on measurable, specified outcomes, while required for an IEP, can be beneficial for all young children. When special education services and interventions are embedded in the natural environments of typical high-quality early childhood programs, the child receiving services is likely to generalize knowledge and skills across settings. Several early childhood special educators have designed strategies that combine DAP of the early childhood care and education programs with the more teacher-determined environment of the special education classroom (Hemmeter & Grisham-Brown, 1997; Mallory, 1998; Russell-Fox, 1997). Under the IDEA amendments of 1997, professionals are calling for a developmentally appropriate framework for writing IEPs (Edmiaston, Dolezal, Doolittle, Erickson, & Merritt, 2000; Yell & Shriner, 1997).

Environment of Local Programs.   The child has to be seen in terms of him- or herself (the *microsystem);* the child's immediate or extended family (the *mesosystem);* and the child's neighborhood, school, and community (the *macrosystem*). The United States is becoming a more diverse nation, and children come to early-childhood programs from all cultural backgrounds. Children are being socialized in home and classroom settings that are a microcosm of the world. Now, more than ever before, curriculum must mirror *all* young children (King, Chipman, & Cruz-Jansen, 1994). Thus, diversity is a hallmark of quality early childhood programs.

Physical Environment.   Young children's experiences are tied to their local physical environment. Successful curricular activities are based on prior experiences and are more likely to be successful when they involve an abundance of firsthand, direct experiences and real objects to manipulate. For example, the theme "winter activities" is not a good long-term topic in some climates. Furthermore, nearby sites are essential for conducting investigations when using the project approach.

In quality programs, the social and cultural environment is closely tied to the program's physical environment. The general decor of the space should look "homey," not "foreign." For example, the visuals displayed, music listened to, literature read, and dramatic play props should reflect the social and cultural composition of the families, staff, and community of the local program.

Social Environment.   Directors must also analyze the strengths and needs of families in the local programs. Cultural manifestations include

- Language (verbal and nonverbal) and conventions about its use
- Intellectual modes, such as learning styles
- Social values, such as daily child-rearing tasks, skills nurtured in children, guidance ("discipline") practices, and attitudes about delays and exceptionalities seen in children

Early childhood programs are becoming more culturally sensitive and responsive to the families they serve (Mallory & New, 1994). Three documents were especially influential in creating a greater sensitivity to the social environment of early childhood programs:

1. Bias was brought into the spotlight through the publication *The Antibias Curriculum: Tools for Empowering Young Children* (Derman-Sparks and ABC Task Force, 1989).
2. The NAEYC's (1995) recommendation that "the nation's children all deserve an early childhood education that is responsive to their families; communities; and racial, ethnic, and cultural backgrounds" (p. 1).

3. The NAEYC's revised statement concerning DAP, which included basing program practices on what is culturally appropriate in addition to what is developmentally and individually appropriate (Bredekamp & Copple, 1997).

The local program rationale should reflect the needs and strengths of families and the views of the staff. For example, Chipman (1997) called for

- Using various cultural learning styles (e.g., cooperative rather than competitive environments)
- Assessment that focuses on potential as well as performance and relies on multiple measures
- Awareness of multiple intelligences
- Greater cultural sensitivity when disciplining
- Acceptance and inclusion of children with special needs
- Correcting subtle stereotypical messages.

Program directors must realize there may be more than one path to high-quality programming (Bromer, 1999; Modigliani, 1990). Wardle (1999) believes that some culturally embedded practices might never be considered DAP, yet he sees some practices that might be developmentally inappropriate in some cultures, but appropriate in others.

Besides developing program philosophy influenced by the culture of the local community, all children need multicultural/antibias education. Local programs are often uncertain about which goals to pursue (Derman-Sparks & A.B.C. Task Force, 1989). Many experts realize that merely adding multicultural content to a traditional curriculum is not enough; they believe that what is needed is content approached from many cultural perspectives. The Quality 2000 Initiative (Kagan & Neuman, 1997) called for programs that promote cultural sensitivity and pluralism (Phillips, 1994b; Phillips & Crowell, 1994).

Derman-Sparks (1992) sees the following four goals for a multicultural/antibias curriculum for young children:

- Developing personal and group identity
- Seeing similarities as well as differences
- Identifying unfair or untrue images, speech, or behaviors and realizing that such things hurt
- Confronting bias by "speaking up."

Phillips (1994a) described three distinct ways to plan: (a) Programs can focus on changing negative responses to cultural diversity (b) programs can begin with the culture of the home and build transitions to mainstream lifestyle; and (c) programs can embrace biculturalism by asking family assistance in maintaining home cultural values and lifestyles.

Swick, Van Scoy, and Boutte (1994) suggested several appropriate opportunities for promoting multicultural sensitivity:

- Educating families about building children's self-esteem
- Helping children explore their own culture through family and school activities
- Training families and teachers to assess their multicultural competence
- Supporting the development of skills needed to promote multicultural understandings
- Promoting intense teacher education concerning multicultural education.

Directors must realize that programs cannot be totally preplanned without considering the abilities and interests of a particular group of children. Vygotsky (1978) pointed out that children's cognition is contextualized; that is, it emerges out of and derives meaning from particular activities and social experiences. He felt that learning experiences that do not make use of the social histories of particular children result in difficulties. Using the observations of children engaged in program activities as a resource for program planning has been called *emergent curriculum* (Jones & Nimmo, 1994).

Application Activity

Review your program vision, mission, and goals. Based on your review, to what extent does your program align with the DAP guidelines presented by the NAEYC?

Standards.   As a result in increased political interest, early childhood programs have recently become a standards-based environment. In general, *standards* can be defined as expectations for learning and development. More specific terms used to refer to standards include the following:

- **Program standards:**   Expectations for the quality of a program
- **Content standards:**   What a child should be able to do within an academic area, such as mathematics
- **Benchmarks:**   The knowledge and skills a child should have by a given time in school, such as the first semester of kindergarten
- **Performance standards:**   Quality levels of performance with respect to the knowledge or skill described in a benchmark

Program standards have been part of early childhood care and education for many years. For example, program standards were written for nursery education in 1929. More recently, program funding standards were written for Head Start (called "Head Start Performance Standards") and for other grant-funded programs. Several professional early childhood associations have published accreditation standards for early childhood programs for several years.

Early Learning Standards.   The NAEYC refers to content standards for young children as *early learning standards.* Early learning standards are relatively new to early childhood care and education. The standards movement, in which student outcomes on performance standards were linked to placement and retention decisions and to a program accountability, began in elementary and secondary education in the 1980s. The development of the National Education Goals of 1989 led to a standards movement affecting all levels of education (Bredekamp & Rosegrant, 1995a).

The No Child Left Behind legislation has continued to fan the flames of the standards-based movement in early childhood education. As a result of this legislation, many states have developed or are in the process of adopting early learning standards (sometimes referred to as early learning guidelines). Head Start has also developed new standards, called the "Head Start Child Outcomes Framework," intended to guide the assessment of 3- to 5-year-old children enrolled in Head Start (Head Start Bureau, 2001).

According to the National Child Care Information Center (NCCIC) the following statistics are relevant to early learning guidelines (ELGs):

- Twenty-eight states have ELGs for children from 3 through 5 years (Alabama, Arizona, Colorado, District of Columbia, Hawaii, Idaho, Illinois, Massachusetts, Mississippi, Missouri, Montana, Nevada, New Jersey, New Mexico, New York, North Carolina, Oklahoma, Oregon, Rhode Island, South Carolina, South Dakota, Texas, Utah, Vermont, Virginia, West Virginia, Wisconsin, and Wyoming).

- Nine states and two territories have ELGS for children from birth through 5 years (Alaska, California, Indiana, Iowa, Kansas, Kentucky, New Hampshire, Tennessee, and Washington; Commonwealth of the Northern Mariana Islands and Puerto Rico).
- Thirteen states and one territory have ELGs for children from birth through 3 years and ELGs for children from 3 through 5 years (Arkansas, Connecticut, Delaware, Florida, Georgia, Louisiana, Maine, Maryland, Michigan, Minnesota, Nebraska, Ohio, and Pennyslvania; Guam).
- One state is in the process of developing ELGs (North Dakota).

Application Activity

Has your state adopted early learning standards or guidelines for the ages of children your program serves? If so, locate these standards, review them, and determine the extent to which your program mission and goals align with the state curriculum expectations.

Several factors have contributed to the movement for early learning standards, including the following:

- Many states want their kindergartens and prekindergartens to have standards in alignment with state standards for older children as part of an effort to improve school readiness.
- Studies of brain development have increased the understanding of young children's capacity for learning (Bergen & Coscia, 2001).
- A recent longitudinal study showed that many children had learned traditional kindergarten subject matter in literacy and mathematics in preschool programs (National Center for Education Statistics, 2000) and were thus prepared for more challenging content in kindergarten.
- The Committee on Early Childhood Pedagogy recommended that federal and state departments of education develop, field test, and evaluate curricula and companion assessment tools based on what is known about children's development. They recommended that content standards for the early years address these often omitted areas: phonological awareness, number concepts, methods of science investigations, and cultural knowledge and language (NRC, 2001).

Literacy and Mathematics Standards.   The early childhood years are the most important period for literacy development. The NRC (1999) stated that *functional literacy* is now defined as reading for information and interpreting ideas. This definition has increased literacy expectations. The International Reading Association (IRA) and the NAEYC (IRA & NAEYC, 2000) adopted a joint position statement in 1998 on literacy development in young children. This statement included

- A call for developmentally appropriate goals and expectations
- A developmental continuum for reading and writing development to be used for identifying literacy goals
- A cautionary reminder for program designers to take into account developmental variation

The emphasis on early learning standards for literacy development has resulted in state involvement in literacy initiatives not only for kindergartens and primary grades, but also for younger children. Some of these initiatives are family literacy programs, but others are focused on the training of preschool and child care teachers (Jacobson, 2002). These initiatives are being funded by a mix of federal, state, and private monies.

Similar to the joint position statement on literacy, the National Council of Teachers of Mathematics (NCTM) and the NAEYC (2002) adopted a joint position statement in which the associations affirmed that high-quality and challenging mathematics for 3- to 6-year-old children is a vital foundation for later learning. Although the statement has many recommendations, a goals continuum was not developed. However, the NCTM (2000) had developed standards for prekindergarten through second-grade children prior to the position statement.

Stating Goals

Goals for a local program are typically broad and general statements about what the program hopes to achieve. Katz (1995a) believes curricula at every level should address the acquisition and strengthening of the following dimensions of growth:

- **Knowledge.**   Children should have knowledge the culture deems important. Knowledge includes representational knowledge (ideas, concepts, constructs) and behavioral knowledge (how to perform certain skills or enact certain procedures).
- **Skills.**   Children should develop general intellectual skills (observing, gathering information, problem solving), more specific academic skills (decoding words, writing letters), and social skills (communicating, negotiating).
- **Dispositions.**   Children should acquire positive dispositions or enduring habits of the mind (a desire to understand, a striving for accuracy, persistence, open-mindedness).
- **Feelings.**   Children should develop positive feelings, which are subjective emotional or affective states (feel competent, feel accepted).

Only a few statements will constitute the goals of a program. An example of a **goal statement,** the collection of written goals, is provided by the National Association for the Education of Young Children and the National Association of Early Childhood Specialists in State Departments of Education (1991).

Translating Goals into Child Outcomes

Local programs further delineate goal statements by identifying *child outcomes* (competencies children need to acquire or strengthen) that will result from program completion. Curricular competency lists may also include actions teachers may take to assist children.

Generally speaking, the competencies most often identified by highly prescriptive approaches to curriculum are limited to addressing academic content knowledge and skills. For example, competencies may include physical knowledge concepts, visual and auditory skills, language development, number concepts, and small-motor coordination skills. Competencies may also concern attitudes, such as persistence and delay of gratification.

Broad competencies are often further defined by writing as narrower concepts and skills which are then sequenced for implementation. Table 9.1 is an example of one of these concepts written in a competency format. In this example, "identify eight basic colors" is the broad concept, and the six narrower concepts are numbered and listed in sequential order of difficulty.

Competencies in traditional early childhood programs are often broad in comparison with more narrowly focused prescriptive approaches. Competencies cover all domains (i.e., physical, cognitive, language, social, and emotional) and may also cover Katz's (1995a) dimensions of development. Broad competencies permit the offering of a wide range of activities.

Table 9.1

Sample Competency Writing for a Prescriptive Curriculum Approach, Age Group: Preschoolers

Needed Competencies	*Sample Curriculum for Preschoolers*
Preschoolers need to	*For preschoolers, adults need to*
Identify eight basic colors (red, orange, yellow, green, blue, purple, black, and brown) by	
(1) matching	Provide materials for matching like colors.
(2) pointing to (3) naming	(a) Name colors (using colored paper) and ask child to point to color and (b) point to colors and ask child to name them.
(4) making secondary colors	Ask child to name primary colors and then secondary colors. Provide paints, color paddles, or crayons and paper and ask child to make secondary colors.
(5) coloring/painting with colors as directed	Provide a color sheet with directions for child to follow (e.g., color the ball "red").
(6) sorting color "families"	Provide materials showing various shades/tints of each of the eight basic colors. Ask child to group these into color families or to seriate shades/tints into color families.

Varying levels of skills and interests are accommodated through a range of performance criteria. Tables 9.2, 9.3, and 9.4 show examples of some of the competencies that might be used in these programs. Another example of competencies is the "Head Start Child Outcomes Framework" (Head Start Bureau, 2001).

Organizing the Curriculum

Curriculum activities must be organized in some manner. Children want to make sense of their physical and social world and to do so must build on their prior knowledge and skills. Thus, children cannot profit from a "grab bag" of experiences. Curriculum organizers are either separate concepts and skills or integrated approaches. Because the advantages of one organizer becomes the disadvantages of the other, only advantages will be discussed.

Separate Concepts and Skills.   To organize a curriculum by separate concepts and skills, key concepts are identified and carefully sequenced. (The sequenced key concepts, along with teaching suggestions, are often provided in manuals.) Teachers help develop the concepts in the prescribed sequence using the children's acquired competencies as the bridge to the next concept. For example, teaching number concepts may begin with rote counting followed by activities involving one-to-one correspondence, rational counting, recognition of written numerals, and number combinations (adding by using objects only, objects and symbols, and symbols only).

Curriculum organization by separate concepts and skills has long been used with older children who are often taught separate academic content even by different teachers during the school year. Early childhood program designers of both direct instruction approaches and curriculum guides focused on a single academic area often incorporate this method of organizing the curriculum.

Table 9.2
Sample Competency Writing for Traditional Early Childhood Programs Age Group: Infants and Toddlers

Needed Competencies	Sample Curriculum for Infants and Toddlers	
Infants and toddlers need to	For infants, adults need to	For toddlers, adults need to
Develop a sense of trust and a loving relationship.	Read infant cues and meet infants' physical and psychological needs quickly and warmly.	Support attempts to accomplish tasks, comfort when tasks are frustrating, and express joy at successes. Respect security objects, such as a favorite toy.
Develop a sense of self.	Call infant by name. Place mirrors at eye level, including near the floor.	Name body parts. Respect children's preferences (e.g., toys and food). Support attempts at self-care.
Have social contact.	Engage in face-to-face contacts, use physical contact, and have vocal interactions.	Help children control negative impulses and comfort when they fail. Help children become aware of others' feelings. Model interactions for children to imitate.
Explore their world.	Take children to their world of experience or bring objects and activities to them.	Provide support for active exploration (be near but refrain from too many adult suggestions for play).
Sample sensory experiences.	Provide pictures and objects to touch, taste, and smell.	Place books and objects on shelves. Decorate room with pictures and objects.
Undertake motor experiences.	Provide safe places for movement. Encourage movement (e.g., place objects slightly beyond reach). Express joy at successes.	Provide safe places and equipment and materials that aid large-muscle development (e.g., stairs, ramps, large balls, push/pull toys). Express joy at successes.

Organizing the curriculum by separate concepts and skills has its advantages, including the following:

- For some subject matter, researchers have identified a sequence of how particular concepts and skills build on others (Clements, Sarama, & DiBiase, 2003).
- Children develop concepts in a coherent manner (according to academic logic).
- In this age of standards and accountability, this method of organizing the curriculum ensures engagement with and hopefully mastery of important ideas. (The method is often seen as an efficient way to master standards that are important for program accountability.)

Integrated Curriculum Approaches.   An **integrated curriculum approach** involves choosing a topic or concept for extended investigation from which activities that draw from one or more academic disciplines (e.g., mathematics, science) can be planned. Several strategies can be used in the integrated approaches: (a) choosing topics that permit the exploration of content across subject-matter disciplines; (b) identifying concepts that are meaningful across the disciplines (e.g., literacy, patterns); and (c) identifying processes that are applicable to many disciplines (e.g., representation, scientific method). Many resources are available on the integrated curriculum (Dodge, Jablon, & Bickart, 1994; Hart, Burts, & Charlesworth, 1997; Hohmann & Weikart, 1995; Mitchell & David, 1992).

Table 9.3

Sample Competency Writing for Traditional Early Childhood Programs Age Group: Preschoolers and Kindergartners

Needed Competencies	Sample Curriculum for Preschoolers and Kindergartners
Preschoolers and kindergartners need to	For preschoolers and kindergartners, adults need to
Feel reassured when fearful or frustrated.	Use positive statements.
	Provide comfort when frustrated and repeatedly demonstrate needed rules.
Become more independent.	Provide opportunities for practicing self-help skills, such as having dressing dolls and providing time and just the needed assistance in toileting and eating.
Make friends.	Permit children to form their own play groups.
	Encourage onlookers to join a play group by suggesting roles for them (e.g., a grandmother in housekeeping center in which the other roles are already taken).
	Model positive social interactions for them to imitate.
Explore their world.	Provide many materials that children can manipulate (e.g., water, sand, blocks, latches) in order to discover relationships.
	Provide dramatic play props for children to use in trying on roles.
Exercise their large muscles and control their small muscles.	Provide equipment to climb on, "vehicles" to ride on, and balls to throw and catch.
	Provide materials to manipulate (e.g., art tools, puzzles, pegs and pegboards, beads to string).
Engage in language experiences.	Talk to, read to, sing to, tell and dramatize stories, and play singing games (e.g., Farmer in the Dell).
	Write children's dictated stories.
	Have classroom charts and other printed materials in view.
	Provide materials (e.g., paper and writing tools) for children to draw, scribble, write, copy signs, and so on.
Express themselves creatively.	Provide a variety of art media and various forms of music for creative expression.
Develop concepts of themselves and the world around them.	Provide opportunities to learn skills (e.g., mathematics) and content areas (e.g., social studies, science) in integrated ways (while working on projects instead of times set aside to concentrate on each area).
Become familiar with symbols.	Provide props for dramatic play.
	Provide books for "reading."
	Write children's dictated stories.
	Provide art and writing materials.
Make choices and implement their ideas.	Permit children to select many of their own activities.
	Provide a physical setting that encourages individual or small, informal groups most of the time.

Integrated curriculum approaches are not new. Correlated curriculum approaches and the project approach have long been used for school-age children. Integrated curriculum has been more or less *the* approach used in early childhood programs with only few exceptions. As such, the integrated curriculum has a rich history in early childhood education and

Table 9.4

Sample Competency Writing for Traditional Early Childhood Programs Age Group: Primary Grades/Levels

Needed Competencies	Sample Curriculum for Children in Primary Grades (Levels)
Children in primary grades (levels) need to	*For children in primary grades (levels), adults need to*
Show more self-control.	Prevent overstimulation when possible and help children deal with fears and excitements (e.g., talking about them).
	Set clear limits in a positive way and involve children in rule making.
	Use problem solving to manage discipline problems.
Gain more independence.	Permit children to identify areas needing improvement.
	Support children in their work toward mutually established goals.
Work with other children.	Provide opportunities through small groups for children to cooperate with and help other children.
Explore their world.	Provide materials that are concrete and relative to ongoing projects.
	Plan for field trips and resource people to enhance classroom projects.
Use large and small muscles.	Provide appropriate materials.
Use language as a way of both communicating and thinking.	Provide materials for both reading and writing that will enhance ongoing projects.
	Provide quality literature.
	Read aloud stories and poems each day and ask child readers to share in the oral reading.
	Plan projects, such as preparing a class newspaper or making books.
Express themselves creatively.	Plan ways to integrate art, music, dance, and drama throughout the day.
Develop concepts.	Integrate curriculum (skill and content areas) in such a way that learnings occur through activities such as projects rather than in an isolated format.
Use symbol systems.	Provide manipulatives.
	Assist children in developing skills in reading, writing, and mathematics when these are needed to explore or solve meaningful problems.
Make choices.	Provide opportunities to work individually and in small groups with self-selected projects and materials for a greater part of the time.
	Involve children in their own self-management (e.g., setting their own goals, budgeting their time, evaluating their own efforts, cooperating with others).

is closely aligned with the guidelines provided by the NAEYC through the position statement on Developmentally Appropriate Practices (Bredekamp & Copple, 1997).

Integrated curriculum approaches have many advantages, including the following:

1. Young children are active, self-motivated learners who learn best through self-initiated experiences rather than decontextualized teaching (Fromberg, 2002; Isenberg & Quisenberry, 2002).

2. Cognitive learning efforts foster the construction of knowledge and skills (Chaille & Britain, 1997), promote more social interactions (DeVries, Reese-Learned, & Morgan, 1991), and encourage children to take more responsibility for their own work (Jones, Valdez, Norakowski, & Rasmussen, 1994).

3. Children learning through integrated curriculum approaches showed high-level mastery of basic reading, language, and mathematics skills (Marcon, 1992). This

finding was particularly significant for boys (Marcon, 1992) and for children from low-income families (Knapp, 1995).

4. High-involvement and low-stress activities promote the best learning (Rushton & Larkin, 2001; Santrock, 2003; Wolfe & Brandt, 1998).

5. In integrated approaches, children can use different combinations and degrees of each of the eight intelligences or avenues for learning (Carlisle, 2001; Gardner, 1993).

6. Children develop social competence best through cooperative efforts (Katz & McClellan, 1997) and feel successful when they engage in meaningful learning and learn in a safe way (Fromberg, 2002; Isenberg & Jalongo, 2000).

7. Integrated approaches permit the curriculum to be based on the needs and interests of children in the group and thus would not look the same from year to year or from one classroom to another. Rather than be preplanned, curriculum is said to emerge from children's needs and interests, teachers' interests, things and people in the environment, unexpected events, and values of the culture (Jones & Nimmo, 1994; Williams, 1997).

8. Making conceptual connections across diverse academic disciplines reduces the volume of standards.

Themes Versus Projects: Authentic Learning Opportunities

When it comes to integrated curriculum in settings for young children, common approaches are theme-based curricula and project curricula. The main difference between these two is that project- or inquiry-based learning involves the children more integrally in the planning process. While themes may help to organize the learning engagements planned for young children, if careful thought is not given to the individual and collective experiences and interests of the children, what results is little more than a collection of cute, yet ineffective learning opportunities.

Units and Themes.   Two approaches to integrating the curriculum are units and themes. Both are teacher planned, for the most part, although children may participate in the planning and in choosing some activities. Usually, the *unit* has a narrower or more focused topic with more specific learning objectives than the *theme*. However, the approaches are so similar that many programs call this approach a *thematic unit*.

Thematic units often last 1 to 2 weeks. Teachers choose the topics, plan the activities, and prepare the materials for various learning centers and other activities to correspond with the topics. During implementation, information on the topic is given by the teacher to the whole group in a daily unit lesson. Usually, art, music, cooking, and literature, as well as other activities, tend to reflect the unit theme. Because teachers design these activities, children may not see the connection. Often, literacy and mathematics competencies are presented as contrived thematic activities. For example, during a "Fall" unit, children may match capital and lowercase letters written on laminated paper pumpkin shells and on "detached" laminated paper pumpkin stems, respectively. The child places the correct stem on each pumpkin. Matching is seldom learned in a week or even in a semester; thus, the matching will continue, but the patterns will change to correspond with the new thematic units.

Teachers may be tempted to repeat units year after year. In some schools, all the teachers on a given level (e.g., kindergarten) teach the same unit lessons, using many of the same materials. Teachers could make thematic units more DAP by carefully observing the needs and interests of the children who are currently enrolled and by allowing ideas to emerge from the children as well as the teachers.

Projects.   The *project approach,* an integrated curriculum approach, involves choosing an area of interest or a problem and incorporating curriculum areas into it (Katz & Chard, 2000). The project approach had its roots in progressive education (Dewey, 1916; Kilpatrick, 1918).

When learning engagements are relevant and authentic, children are likely to be fully engrossed in the activity.

Ideally, project ideas emerge as opposed to being preplanned. Project ideas can result from children's natural encounters with the real environment, the mutual interests of children and teacher, and the teacher's response to an observed need in children (Helm & Katz, 2001; Jones & Nimmo, 1994). The topic of the project is written as a narrative line used to convey the direction of children's investigation (e.g., instead of using the broad thematic unit topic of "Water," a project topic might be "How We Use Water" or "The River in Our Town"; Katz & Chard, 2000). Criteria used for determining project topics include the following:

- Topics must be related to children's own everyday experiences.
- The study must involve real objects.
- Opportunities must exist for collaboration, problem solving, and representation (e.g., artwork, block building, dramatic play).
- Competencies in all domains must be applied as needed.

According to Helm and Katz (2001), projects go through three phases. In Phase 1, teachers begin thinking about a project topic and may even "web" to see the possibilities. A **web** is a visual representation (a diagram resembling a spider web) of curriculum possibilities. An *anticipatory web* is one to which children add their own ideas. If the program has early learning standards, expected child outcomes may be added to the web or just listed (see Figure 9.1 and 9.2). The teacher checks for children's knowledge and interests by having the children verbally share their experiences about a topic and express them through representation. Phase 1 lasts about 1 week and forms the basis for modifying plans.

During the second and third weeks, Phase 2 occurs. Children gain new information. They get firsthand, real-world experiences and are led to recall and represent details. Children have many opportunities to reflect on their expanding and refining knowledge through multiple representations. A project grows from the input of children, teachers, and families and through the introduction of materials.

Phase 3 allows children time to further assimilate their ideas through play or share their understandings. Often, Phase 3 leads to new ideas and new projects. (See the end of this chapter for key books on project planning.)

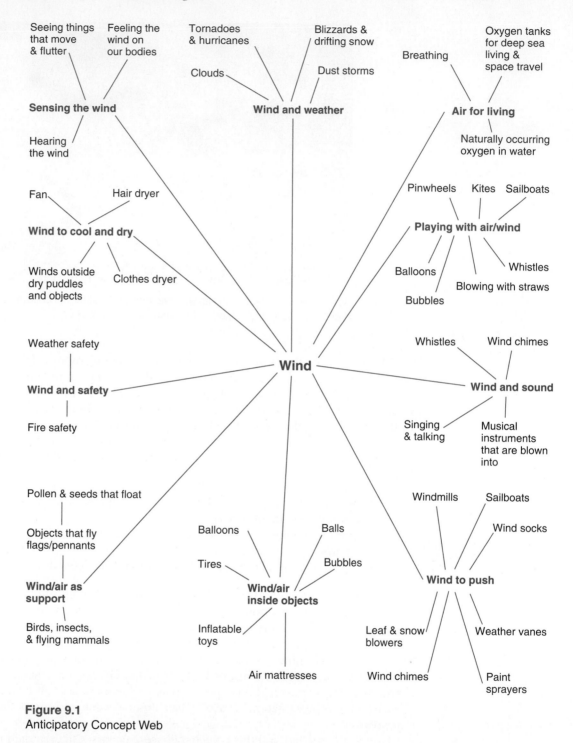

Figure 9.1
Anticipatory Concept Web

IMPLEMENTING THE CURRICULUM

After identifying and planning the basic approach of the local program, the director and staff must implement the program (i.e., decide how the specific features of the program will be carried out). To help all children reach their potential, planning must be done for a particular group of children, in a particular place, and at a particular

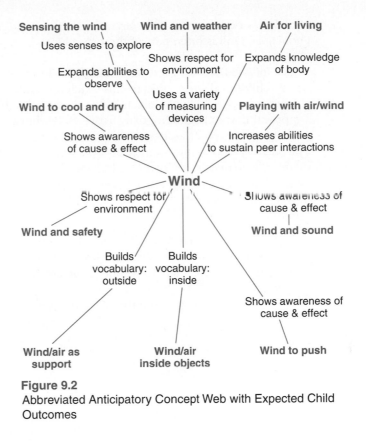

Figure 9.2
Abbreviated Anticipatory Concept Web with Expected Child Outcomes

time. Planning requires constant observation of children and a willingness to adjust program implementation.

Designing Teaching Strategies

Teaching strategies have to do with how teachers interact with children during instructional time. Similar to the lack of consensus on content, a lack of consensus on the best pedagogical strategies also exists. While there is great variation in the structure of teaching strategies that might be considered, continued research will help teachers identify strategies that are effective to attain specific learning outcomes in specific learning contexts. Typically, early childhood programs and curricula that have been most effective tend to be child centered and responsive to individual needs and interests. While a variety of teaching strategies have been found to be effective, most curriculum theorists and researchers advocate for a balance among the wide variety of strategies and learning structures.

Teacher-Directed Activities.   Teacher-directed activities take a variety of forms and are commonly used in early childhood programs, kindergartens, and programs for school-age children. Direct instruction is an effective method to convey content and information that is specific and is not likely to result simply from a child-initiated activity. For example, providing a 3-year-old child with the opportunity to explore and manipulate a pair of scissors without any instruction in their appropriate use might result in injury. To learn the appropriate use and safety precautions, the child must be taught directly.

For more complex content, the instructional plan, often written as a lesson plan, usually includes clearly stated performance objectives, a procedure, and an assessment of the children's performance. Objectives and corresponding materials are based on sequenced concepts. Drill is often part of the procedure.

Child-Initiated Activities and Scaffolding.   Child-initiated activities occur mainly in traditional early childhood programs. In this teaching strategy, children engage in child-initiated activities approved by the teacher. For example, High/Scope children plan and get teacher approval before beginning daily activities (Hohmann & Weikart, 1995).

Another type of assistance comes from Vygotsky's theory. Children are aided in their pursuits by scaffolding, a direct support system provided to a child to perform in his or her *zone of proximal development* (ZPD; the distance between where the child is functioning and where he or she can profit from assistance by an adult or more advanced peer).

Program planners who prefer child-initiated activities cite these reasons for their preference:

- Teacher-directed activities on a large- or whole-group basis make it almost impossible to provide for various developmental levels, interests, or learning styles.
- Child-initiated activities enhance all areas of development (Frost, Wortham, & Reifel, 2001).
- Teachers can provide the needed structure for children's learning by (a) structuring materials, space, and time; (b) engaging in coplanning with children; and (c) providing scaffolding or short periods of direct instruction.

Using Computers and Other Technologies

Computers have been in early childhood programs for over 2 decades, and many young children have computers in their homes. Program designers often debate whether the gains in children's development justify the costs (Healy, 1998). Undoubtedly, technology is here to stay, and if used appropriately, will impact children's learning by extending and enriching many concepts being offered in the classroom.

Connecting Technology to Young Children's Development.   Because development changes over the early childhood years, DAP with technology also changes. Because computers do

Effective early childhood curricula maintain a balance between teacher-initiated and child-initiated activities.

not match the way infants and toddlers learn, computer use is not recommended for this age group (Elkind, 1998; Haugland, 1999). Three- and 4-year-olds need to explore computers. Teachers may ask questions and propose problems to expand children's computer experiences but should provide minimal help. For these preschool children, computer activities should be one of many classroom experiences.

Kindergarten and primary-age children need to continue to make choices about computer activities but should also have some teacher-planned activities that match desired program outcomes. For this age group, important skills include learning how to seek out information and gathering and integrating knowledge from various sources, including appropriate use of the Internet (Haugland, 1999; Haugland & Wright, 1997).

Noting the Benefits.   Research indicates that computer activities can supplement other activities and also provide unique avenues for learning. Program designers must understand the connection between the types of computer activities and their benefits.

General Benefits.   Regardless of the program orientation, computers and other technologies will provide several benefits. First, children will learn about technology (e.g., people control technology by making up rules that in turn control how technology works; different programs work by using different rules; technology is part of the everyday world).

Second, new hardware and software features are permitting children with disabilities to use these technologies to enhance their ability to interact with peers and others in their environment (Behrmann & Lahm, 1994).

Third, some objects (e.g., shapes, pictures) can be manipulated more easily on the computer than their concrete counterparts (e.g., actual blocks) in a child's hand (Thompson, 1992). Fourth, technologies allow teachers to meet the diverse needs of children (Haugland & Wright, 1997).

Finally, computers can aid social competence, such as communication, cooperation, and leadership and help develop positive attitudes about learning (Cardelle-Elawar & Wetzel, 1995; Denning & Smith, 1997; Haugland & Wright, 1997).

Benefits of Selected Software and Integration.   Because computers can also be misused, educators must take responsibility for using this learning tool to the advantage of children. To help teachers in making critical judgments, the NAEYC developed a position statement on technology and young children (NAEYC, 1996). The statement calls for teachers to carefully evaluate software, integrate technology into the regular learning environment as only one tool of learning, and provide equitable access to technology.

The curricular values of these technologies are dependent on the selected software and the degree of technology integration into the curriculum. Thus, program orientation must be considered in all decisions. Programs with a narrow academic focus have primarily used **drill-and-practice software,** a form of software that resembles a ditto sheet or workbook page and is sometimes referred to as an "electronic ditto sheet." Some drill-and-practice software programs are small separate programs, but others are drill-oriented **integrated learning systems (ILSs),** a supersoftware package that provides a complete curriculum in a subject, especially reading or mathematics, through an extensive sequence of lessons.

Research has been conducted on the effects of using drill-and-practice software. Children who used these programs increased their reading skills (Hess & McGarvey, 1987) and showed even greater gains in mathematics (Clements & Nastasi, 1992). On the negative side, drill-and-practice use may diminish children's feelings that they control technology (Papert, 1993), may cause a loss of creativity (Haugland, 1992), and will not improve children's conceptual skills (Clements & Nastasi, 1993). In the affective domain, drill-and-practice software encourages turn taking (*not* collaboration) and competition (Clements & Nastasi, 1992).

Those who advocate traditional early childhood programs prefer **open-ended software,** software in which children are free to do many different things (e.g., drawing, but not "coloring in" predrawn pictures, word processing, and programming in Logo). Because children do not accomplish much when asked to "freely explore" (Lemerise, 1993), distinctions must be made between open-ended projects and "freely exploring" the computer; however, research has shown that the use of open-ended software results in gains in intelligence quotients, nonverbal skills, structural knowledge, long-term memory, manual dexterity, and self-esteem (Haugland, 1992).

Haugland also found that the gains were greater when children used supplemental activities (activities beyond the computer). For example, when compared with a drill-and-practice group of children, the "off-and-on" group showed gains of more than 50% over the drill-and-practice group in verbal, problem solving, and conceptual skills, although the drill-and-practice group had worked on the computer three times longer.

Research has also shown that open-ended software aids critical thinking (Clements & Nastasi, 1992; Kromhout & Butzin, 1993; Nastasi & Clements, 1994) and allows for the connection of ideas from different content areas (Bontá & Silverman, 1993). Unlike drill-and-practice software, open-ended programs encourage collaboration (Clements, 1994). Nastasi and Clements (1994) also reported higher scores on *effective motivation* (believing one can affect the environment).

Facilitating Effective Classroom Transitions

Transitions occur with changes of activity, location, or caregiver (e.g., when a parent leaves or picks up a child). The way transitions are handled either makes the day go smoothly and positively for children or causes chaos and negative reactions. Well-executed transitions incorporate the teachers' knowledge of individual and group needs (Taylor, 1999). Some general suggestions are as follows:

1. Begin the day on a calm and happy note. Early morning greetings and sharing are important.
2. Have a consistent daily routine and reduce the number of "between activity" transitions with large blocks of time.
3. When making a transition, do the following: (a) Prepare children by announcing the upcoming transition; (b) keep signals low-key (e.g., soft bell or quiet voice) and make the transition activity interesting but not too stimulating (see resources at the end of the chapter); (c) position oneself appropriately to offer assistance; and (d) begin new activities right away.
4. Use realistic expectations and provide some choices to diminish child resistance.
5. Prepare children in advance of moving them to a new location.
6. End the day pleasantly and calmly. Plan easy and quick ways to distribute notes or items to be sent home. Warmly acknowledge the departure of the group or each child.

Providing for Physical Care Routines

In traditional early childhood programs, physical care activities are used for socialization (e.g., table manners are emphasized during eating) and for cognitive enrichment (e.g., children discuss nutrition and the properties of foods—color, size, texture, and shape).

Planning for Special Times

Special plans must be suitable to children's needs and be as carefully developed as daily plans, although they require even more flexibility. Certain routines—especially eating, toileting, and resting—should always be followed as closely as possible.

First Days.   Whether the first days represent children's first experiences in early childhood programs or denote their entry into different programs, children view the first days with mixed feelings of anticipation and anxiety. The first days should be happy ones because they may determine children's feelings of security and their attitudes toward programs.

A baby or a toddler needs a week to make a gradual transition to a program (Miller & Albrecht, 2000). This time is called *inserimento* in the Reggio Emilia program (Bove, 1999). Initiation of preschool and even kindergarten children is best done gradually, too. This time allows for the preliminary orientation of children to the program. If all children enter on the same day, additional adult assistance should be secured for the first days.

Generally speaking, planning for first days requires that more time and individual attention be given to greeting children and their families, establishing regular routines, and familiarizing children with teachers and the physical environment. For the first days, use equipment and materials and plan activities that most children of the particular age group are familiar with and enjoy and that require minimal preparation and cleanup time. Teachers need to enjoy this time of becoming acquainted with the children.

Field Trips.   A field trip is a planned journey to somewhere outside the school building or grounds. Early childhood programs have long used community resources. Field trips and resource people are used extensively in projects. Thoughtful planning of field trips and for resource people is important both because of benefits to children's learning and because of the added dangers of taking children beyond the building and grounds. The teacher must do the following:

1. Help children achieve the goals of the program.

2. Make arrangements with those in charge at the point of destination. Staff should keep a perpetual inventory of local places to visit and resource people suitable to their program's needs. In compiling such an inventory,

- List the name of the place, the telephone number, the person at the location in charge of hosting visitors
- Age limitations
- The time of day visitors are welcome
- The number of children the place can accommodate
- How long a tour takes
- Additional comments

Preferable apparel, whether advance notice is required, what children can see or do, what the host provides for children, and the number of adults requested to accompany the group should also be stated. Refer to this inventory in making plans. Make arrangements for the visit, and if the host is to give explanations, make sure he or she can communicate with young children. Make arrangements for the care of the physical needs of children, staff, and other adults assisting with the field trip, such as locations of places to eat and rest rooms. One staff member should visit the destination before final plans are made.

3. Provide enough qualified volunteer aides to supervise. Good judgment and experience in working with young children are qualities to look for in volunteers. Volunteers should have a list of the names of the children under their care; when they do not know the children, name tags should be worn for easier identification.

4. Obtain written parent consent for each field trip and keep the signed statement on file. Notice the example of a field trip form in Figure 9.3. The signed form is essential because the parent's signature serves as evidence that the parent has considered the potential dangers of his or her child's participation in the field trip. No statement on the form should relieve the teacher and director of any possible liability for accidents. Such a statement is

Dear _____ ,

Our class will be making a field trip to the _____ bakery on May 13. A baker will take us on a tour of the bakery. We hope to learn how bread and rolls are made. We will be leaving school at 9:00 a.m. and will be returning in time for lunch. We will ride on a bus to the bakery and back to our school. We all think it will be fun to ride on the bus with our teacher, Mrs.Smith, and three mothers. Please sign the form below to give your permission for me to take the trip.

                                                                                    Jody

- -

I, _____ , give my permission for
              (Name of parent)

_____ to attend a field trip to
              (Name of child)

_____ .
              (Destination)

My child has permission to travel _____ .
                                          (In a parent's car, on a school bus)

I understand that all safety precautions will be observed.

Date _____ Signature _____

Figure 9.3
Field Trip Form

worthless because a parent cannot legally sign away the right to sue (in the child's name) for damages, nor can staff escape the penalty for their own negligence, as shown in judicial decisions (*Fedor v. Mauwehu Council of Boy Scouts,* 1958; *Wagenblast v. Odessa School Dist.,* 1988).

5. Obtain permission from the director or building administrator for the children to participate in the field trip. Policies of early childhood programs often require that teachers complete forms giving the specifics of the field trip.

6. Become familiar with the procedures to follow in case of accident or illness. Take children's medical and emergency information records in case emergency treatment is required during the field trip.

7. Make all necessary arrangements for transportation and determine whether all regulations concerning vehicles and operators are met.

8. Prepare children by helping them understand the purposes of the field trip and the safety rules to be observed.

9. Evaluate all aspects of planning the field trip and the field trip itself.

Class Celebrations.   Class celebrations are traditional in early childhood programs and require special planning. Celebrations should relate to the program's objectives because "tacked on" celebrations could be counterproductive. Directors need to consider the beliefs and preferences of families and staff members and local community customs concerning various celebrations. If celebrations are to be observed, specific policies should be written and provided to families.

Developing Supportive Relationships

Although many directors are aware of the importance of early brain development, fewer realize the importance of social and emotional competence. Recent research has confirmed that social and emotional competence is critical for a child's early school success and for later accomplishments in the workplace. Lack of social and emotional competence is linked to behavioral, social, and emotional problems.

School involves social relationships with adults and peers. Children who are successful in school are confident, use friendly approaches with peers, can communicate emotions, are able to concentrate on and persist in tasks, can follow directions, and are attentive. Yet data from a recent survey showed that up to 46% of kindergarten teachers reported that half their class or more had specific problems in a number of areas in making the transition to school (Peth-Pierce, 2001).

Because the early childhood years, beginning in infancy, are critical to the development of social and emotional competence, directors must give a great deal of attention to this aspect of children's development in their programs. The quality of the adult–child relationships is the most important aspect of the quality of the children's program. Children whose teachers are sensitive and responsive and who give them attention and support are more advanced in all areas of development compared with children who do not have these positive inputs (Lamb, 1998; NICHD Early Child Care Research Network, 1998, 2000).

Caring as Infant/Toddler Curriculum.   Close and caring relationships between very young children and significant adults provide the context for all aspects of growth, development, and learning (Thompson, 1997). Programs must stress continuity of care (Essa, Favre, Thweatt, & Waugh, 1999). Continuity can be accomplished by assigning each child to a primary and secondary caregiver and having these caregivers stay with a group of infants and toddlers until the preschool years. Caregivers must also build a supportive relationship with families to provide for continuity of care. Because culture is so involved in early child-rearing practices, cultural issues are becoming more important as programs enroll infants (Lally, 1995).

For infants, the development of a secure attachment with their mother, father, and/or other primary caregiver is the major social and emotional milestone (Raikes, 1996). To facilitate this attachment, caregivers must be able to show empathy and develop rapport with babies. Babies share their emotions, and adults must be able to read the cues, engage in mutual gazes, and communicate with gurgles and coos and with language, including happy and lulling songs (Honig, 1995). Reciprocal responsiveness between the adult and the baby has been likened to a dance (Honig, 2002; Thoman, 1987).

By age 2, toddlers become more self-aware and want to gain some independence and self-control. Good teachers show an attitude of total presence ("I am interested in you; I am here for you."). Teaching and caring for emotionally fragile toddlers require calmness and a sense of knowing when to do "more" and when to do "less" (Rofrano, 2002). Additional resources are listed at the end of the chapter.

Nurturing Emotional Literacy.   Peth-Pierce (2001) noted that young children, especially boys, enter school with emotional illiteracy. These children often misinterpret their own emotions and those of others. They often lack the ability to manage their emotions properly. Emotional literacy (intelligence) is based on three skill levels—perception, understanding, and managing (Salovey & Sluyter, 1997).

Although a universality of emotions exists, the culture affects the expression of emotions and the contexts in which they are expressed (Small, 1998). Thus, families and teachers often see "problem" behaviors and temperaments in different ways (National Center for Education Statistics, 2000). In talking about some behaviors, teachers and families may see that emotional literacy is using the appropriate emotional expression for a given social context.

To be effective, emotional literacy skills must be interwoven into the daily curriculum. Some ideas include the following:

1. Empower children by helping them feel successful. Teachers can begin empowering by
   a. Using both child-initiated and teacher-determined activities
   b. Encouraging both interdependent and independent activities
   c. Recognizing the uniqueness and contributions of each child
   d. Focusing on achievements in all domains
   e. Working individually with children
   f. Saving and displaying products of achievement
   g. Encouraging peers to say positive things about class members

2. Read stories that discuss emotions. Follow up with reflective questions (e.g., "How did _____ feel when _____?"). Relate the stories to children's lives (Sullivan & Strang, 2002/03).
3. Extend children's vocabulary of "feeling" words.
4. Help children make inferences about expressions, body language, and tone of voice.
5. Create a "comfort corner" in which children can express feelings by writing, drawing, using puppets, and dictating into a tape recorder (Novick, 1998). Other resources are listed at the end of this chapter.

Encouraging Social Competence.   **Social competence** is the ability to initiate and maintain good relationships with peers (Katz & McClellan, 1997). Children who are not competent are often labeled as aggressive or loners. Competent participation in a group is developmental and can be encouraged in the preschool years. Emotional literacy is tied to social competence. Understanding one's emotions and those of others as well as the ability to regulate one's emotions allows for the development of social competence. Beyond nurturing emotional literacy, teachers can aid social competence by reducing external controls and building a sense of community.

Reducing External Controls.   *Discipline* and *punishment* are terms that focus on external control by adults. Child development specialists and early childhood professionals have warned of the harmful effects of punishment, especially corporal punishment (Hyman, 1997). Any form of shame reinforces a negative self-label and leads to a self-fulfilling prophecy (Gartrell, 1995). Regrettably, external control is still used by many teachers.

Today, "time-out" has become the major means of dealing with class problems. The rationale for time-out is that children need to be separated from peers to regain emotional control and to think about the effects of their behaviors. Time-out is a technique that punishes rather than teaches strategies for handling impulsive behaviors (Gartrell, 1998). Using time-out diminishes the child's feelings of self-worth and deprives the child of group membership (Marion, 1999). In fact, the threat of time-out makes the class apprehensive and leads to a feeling of conditional acceptance (Clewett, 1988).

Although praise is not punishment, it is a form of external control. Teachers praise when children "jump through their hoops" (Kohn, 2001). Praise is ineffective and harmful for the following reasons:

1. Children may stop positive activities once attention is withdrawn.
2. Praise creates stress because one must continue doing good to maintain love.
3. Praise occurs only for observed actions (some actions are missed).

4. Praise makes children dependent on adult appraisal, as opposed to self-appraisal, of their efforts.
5. Praise may be used to control others (e.g., "I like the way _____ is sitting" means that others are not doing what the adult wants).

Effective praise can be used to promote self-confidence. Effective praise is delivered privately (Marshall, 1995) and focuses exactly on what the child did as opposed to a generalization of "goodness" (e.g., "Thank you for picking up your books" rather than "You are a good helper"; Hitz & Driscoll, 1988).

Building a Sense of Community.   Teachers need to build a sense of community instead of using practices that single out individual children or small groups of children for punishment or praise. Building a sense of community involves facilitating the learning of democratic life skills (i.e., seeing oneself as a worthy individual, working cooperatively as a member of the group, expressing emotions in nonhurtful ways, seeing the viewpoints and feelings of others, and solving problems in ethical ways; Gartrell, 1998). Some suggestions for building a sense of community are as follows:

1. Form teacher–child attachments to build trust (Betz, 1994).
2. Model openness and empathy. Champion all children as equal participants including those who may be stigmatized.
3. Work on projects and other small-group activities in which all children plan together, share responsibilities, and acknowledge each other's contributions.
4. Use class meetings to (a) make agreements that ensure an atmosphere free from exclusionary practices and ridicule, (b) work on biases, and (c) problem-solve (Vance & Weaver, 2002).
5. Be a facilitative coach for conflict resolution. Gartrell (2000) recommended this five-step approach to resolving conflicts: (a) Cool down, (b) help children state problem, (c) brainstorm for ways to resolve the issue, (d) try one alternative, (e) and follow up.
6. Use guidance talks with individual children. Discuss how their behaviors affect others, how positive approaches should work better for all concerned, and ways to make amends (Marion, 1999).

Other resources for encouraging social competence are listed at the end of the chapter. For children who have exceptionally challenging emotional or behavioral difficulties, special interventions are needed (see chapter 8).

Supporting Children Who Experience Stressful Events.   Young children experience *stressors* (situations and events that cause stress) in their lives. Some stressors involve illnesses; others involve loss, such as parental separation or the death of a loved one; and others involve violent acts. Even school activities, especially program transitions and assessment, can be stressful.

New information coming from brain research shows that all information is sent not only to the functionally appropriate place in the brain (e.g., the speech center), but also to the lower brain, which sorts its emotional significance. If the information is threatening, the normal thinking abilities are blocked (Wolfe & Brandt, 1998).

Teachers can work to create low-stress activities in the classrooms and to support children during stressful events in their lives. Some suggestions are as follows:

1. Acknowledge children's feelings and accept reactions that may seem "wrong." (A child's developmental stage affects reactions.)
2. Provide caring words to defuse upsetting things (Rushton & Larkin, 2001) and physical contact to help reassure children ("Helping Young Children in Frightening Times," 2001).

3. Emphasize familiar routines at home and at school.
4. Avoid letting children see the stressful event replaying many times. For example, turning off the television or getting children involved in activities away from the television can prevent them from seeing replays of certain events.
5. Express your own fears and sadness. Remain calm while talking to children and assure them that people are there to help those in need (Greenman, 2001).
6. Engage in classroom activities that release stress (discussions; physical activities; storytelling and dramatic play; sand, water, and block play; playing with clay; and reading books that deal with these stressors).
7. Communicate with families about any changes noted in a child's development and provide suggestions concerning what families may do. Other resources are listed at the end of this chapter.

Considering Other Aspects of Implementing the Curriculum

Regardless of the program goals, several other points need to be considered before implementing the curriculum. For each planned activity, adequate staff, space (and its arrangement), materials and equipment, and time must be provided. Plans must consider the needs of all children. For some children, activities may need to be modified by using a different learning modality or by changing the challenge level. McCormick and Feeney (1995) provided an example of a checklist form for "activity customization." Finally, planning also requires considering alternative activities to forestall problems that result from a lack of interest, inclement weather, unforeseen scheduling changes, or breakage of materials or equipment.

CREATING APPROPRIATE PROGRAM SUPPORTS

Decisions about grouping, scheduling, and staff responsibilities are the backbone or support of planning and implementing the local program. These decisions involve management within a group and thus directly affect how care and education services are delivered.

Grouping

U.S. society acknowledges the importance of the individual, yet, a chaos-free society must have some conformity—some group-mindedness. From birth until a child enters an early childhood program, the child's individuality is fostered, tempered only to some extent by the "group needs" of the child's family. In contrast, because of the number of children involved and the time limits imposed, the early childhood program is forced to put some emphasis on group needs except in infant and toddler programs. (Infants and toddlers function totally as individuals in quality programs.) Although the individual is most important throughout the early childhood years, group needs become more important as children advance in age. In fact, it is often said that a child enrolling in an early childhood program is entering a "group setting."

The NAEYC (1998) defines **group** as the number of children assigned to a staff member or to a team of staff members occupying an individual classroom or a well-defined physical space within a larger room. All grouping decisions are used to facilitate adult–child and child–child interactions in the program.

Size of Group.   Regardless of the program philosophy, the literature is replete with the benefits of small groups. Small classes are associated with more adult–child interaction, more individual attention, more social interactions, more complex play, and more teacher time given to fostering children's language and problem-solving skills (Howes, 1997; Kontos, Howes, & Galinsky, 1997).

Small class size increases school-age children's achievement in reading, mathematics, and science; decreases grade repetitions; and increases graduation rates (Krueger, 1999). Small group size is critical to children needing more individual attention—infants and toddlers, children with special needs, and children who are experiencing a lack of continuity in their lives.

The National Academy of Early Childhood Programs recommends a maximum group size of 8 for infants; 12 for toddlers up to 30 months; 14 for toddlers between 30 and 36 months; 20 for 3-, 4-, and 5-year-olds; 30 for 6- to 8-year-olds; and 30 for 9- to 12-year-olds in SACC programs (NAEYC, 2005). To determine the size of the group, the director must also consider the needs of the children, the skills of the staff, the housing facilities, and the grouping plan.

Adult–Child Ratios. The **adult–child ratio** is the number of children cared for by each adult. Data from Howes, Phillips, and Whitebook (1992) showed that programs that met the NAEYC-recommended adult–child ratios were more DAP than programs not meeting the NAEYC recommendations. The NAEYC (2005) concluded that smaller group sizes and lower adult–child ratios are strong predictors of program compliance with indicators of quality, especially appropriate curriculum and positive adult–child interactions.

Improving the ratio without reducing group size yields less positive results (Mosteller, 1995). In achieving quality in programs, the adult–child ratio is more important than the educational level of staff in infant and toddler programs; conversely, the educational level of the staff is more important than the adult–child ratio in programs for preschool and school-age children (NICHD Early Child Care Research Network, 1996).

The recommended adult–child ratio within group size is detailed in Table 9.5. Preschool model programs rarely exceed 1:7, but most states use a ratio of 1:10 to 1:20 for preschoolers, and kindergarten and primary classes often exceed 1:20 (Gormley, 1995). Even minor changes in group sizes and adult–child ratios affect program quality (Burchinal, Roberts, Nabors, & Bryant, 1996; Howes & Norris, 1997).

Table 9.5
Recommended Adult–Child Ratios Within Group Size[*]

Age of Child	Group Size										
	6	8	10	12	14	16	18	20	22	24	30
Infants (birth to 12 months)	1:3	1:4									
Toddlers (12 to 24 months)	1:3	1:4	1:5	1:6							
2-year-olds (24 to 30 months)		1:4	1:5	1:6							
2-1/2-year-olds (30 to 36 months)			1:5	1:6	1:7						
3-year-olds					1:7	1:8	1:9	1:10			
4-year-olds						1:8	1:9	1:10			
5-year-olds						1:8	1:9	1:10			
Kindergartners								1:10	1:11	1:12	

[*]Smaller group sizes and lower adult–child ratios have been found to be strong predictors of compliance with indicators of quality such as positive interactions among staff and children and developmentally appropriate curriculum. Variations in group sizes and ratios are acceptable when the program demonstrates a very high level of compliance with criteria for interactions, curriculum, staff qualifications, health and safety, and physical environment.

Source: Accreditation Criteria and Procedures of the National Academy of Early Childhood Programs, National Association for the Education of Young Children, 2005, Washington, DC: Author. Reprinted with permission.

Grouping Patterns.   **Grouping,** or organizing children for learning, is an attempt to aid individual development in a group setting; that is, to make caring for and teaching children more manageable and effective. Once curricular plans are formulated and the basic delivery system is chosen, decisions about grouping patterns follow.

Moving Children from Program to Program.   Two approaches are used to move children from program to program. The **graded** system, which began at the turn of the 20th century, is based on the concept that children of similar ages are homogeneous in ability. The graded system in which children enter at a legally specified age is the most typical practice of elementary schools. Many nonpublic early childhood programs group children in the same way based on the assumption that children should be grouped according to their stage and that age is the best predictor of stage.

Recognizing that children of similar ages are not necessarily homogeneous in achievement, other educators called for a **nongraded** approach, a plan that enables children to advance in the sequenced curriculum at their own rate. Self-pacing simply refers to the fact that some children will progress through the required curriculum either faster or slower than their age peers in all or some of the curriculum areas.

Grouping Within the Classroom.   **Ability grouping** is really achievement-level grouping. It is based on the assumption that both children and teachers profit from a homogeneous achievement group. Ability grouping is common in programs focusing on a targeted skill or intervention. Even nongraded approaches may use ability grouping, although the children in the group could be of different ages (Bingham, 1995).

In an attempt to get their instructional groups even more alike, some teachers place children in three or four intraclass groups for prereading, reading, or mathematics instruction. Recent research, however, is indicating that mixed grouping strategies are likely to have more educational benefits than homogeneous strategies commonly used in the past (Henry, Rickman & Dana, 2007).

In opposition to the homogeneity of ability groups, a resurgence of interests in mixed-age grouping is occurring. **Mixed-age grouping,** also called **multiage grouping** and **family grouping,** is defined as placing children who are at least one year apart in age in the same classroom group. Mixed-age grouping appears to be identical to the nongraded concept, which also groups children of mixed ages; however, unlike the nongraded approach, which may group according to ability, mixed-age grouping is designed to keep the groups heterogeneous in all ways (Bingham, 1995). In fact, the rationale for such programs rests on the benefits of heterogeneity itself.

Multiage grouping is more common at the preschool level than at the elementary level, although it was the "dominant model of education until the arrival of the industrial revolution and urbanization" (Veenman, 1995, p. 366). Early childhood programs using mixed-age groupings include Froebelian kindergartens, Montessori schools, the more recent "open education" models (e.g., British Infant Schools, the New Zealand schools), some child care centers, family child care homes, and the Reggio Emilia schools.

Traditional early childhood programs note that Piaget (1959) and Vygotsky (1978) both saw mixed-age peers as important for the learning process. DAP are based on the concept that curriculum is matched not only to the child's stage but also to the child's individual needs. Katz (1991) believes that early childhood programs must be responsive to a wide range of developmental levels and to the individual backgrounds and experiences of children. Individual needs can be met more readily in mixed-age groups.

A great deal of research has been conducted on mixed versus ability grouping. The cognitive and social advantages of mixed-age grouping over ability grouping are given by Bailey, Burchinal, and McWilliam (1993); DeBord and Regueros-de-Atiles (1991); Katz, Evangelou, and Hartman (1990); and Theilheimer (1993).

Mixed age/ability grouping does have some difficulties that must be worked out. Mixed grouping requires more skill on the part of the teacher as a diagnostician of what children need to enhance their development, more planning in terms of managing schedules and equipment and materials, and a greater ability to operate in a team-teaching situation. Mixed grouping also requires family education because many families think their older children are not being stimulated because of the presence of younger children in the group. Several excellent readings on strategies for programs implementing mixed-age groups are available (Katz et al., 1990; Moore & Brown, 1996).

Scheduling

Decisions about scheduling greatly influence children's feelings of security, the accomplishment of program goals, and the staff's effectiveness. **Scheduling** involves planning the length of the session and timing and arranging activities during the session.

Length of Session.   Early childhood programs traditionally have been half-day sessions with the exception of child care programs. Because of the awareness of the needs of young children who are considered at risk, Head Start and other preschool programs for at-risk preschool children are often full-school-day programs. As noted, more kindergartens are opting for a full-day schedule.

Although controversy has surrounded the length of the session, maternal employment and the growing emphasis on early learning standards will result in the continued increase of full-day programs. It is important to note, however, that the quantity of time spent in school is not as significant as the quality of the experience.

Timing and Arranging Activities.   Regardless of whether the session is half-day or full-day, good schedules for early childhood programs have the following characteristics:

1. A good session begins with a friendly, informal greeting of the children. Staff should make an effort to speak to each child individually during the first few minutes of each session. A group activity, such as a greeting song, also helps children feel welcome. This is also a good time to help children learn to plan their activities.
2. The schedule should fit the goals of the program and the needs of the children as individuals and as a group. A balance should be maintained between physical activity and rest, indoor and outdoor activities, group and individual times, and teacher-determined and child-initiated activities.
3. The schedule must be flexible under unexpected circumstances, such as inclement weather, children's interests not originally planned for, and emergencies.
4. A good schedule should be readily understandable to the children so they will have a feeling of security and will not waste time trying to figure out what to do next.
5. A good session ends with a general evaluation of activities, straightening of indoor and outdoor areas, a hint about the next session, and a farewell. Children need to end a session with the feeling of achievement and with a desire to return. These feelings are important to staff, too!

Schedules must fit the length of the program day, week, and year. However, *scheduling* usually refers to the timing of daily activities. Local programs should devise their own schedules. Programs that serve children of different age groups must prepare more than one schedule to meet each group's needs.

In general, schedules are often referred to as fixed or flexible. Programs place more emphasis on group conformity through using **fixed schedules;** that is, by expecting children to work and play with others at specified times and by taking care of even the most basic human differences—appetites and bodily functions—at prescribed times except for "emergencies." Often, programs for kindergarten and primary-grade (level) children have fixed schedules. (State departments of education/instruction often specify the total length of a school day and the number of minutes of instruction in each of the basic subjects).

Conversely, **flexible schedules** allow for individual children to make some choices as to how to spend their time and require children to conform to the group for only a few routine procedures (e.g., the morning greeting and planning session) and for short periods of group "instruction" (e.g., music, listening to stories).

Infant programs have perhaps the most flexible schedules of all early childhood programs because infants stay on their own schedules. Child care programs often have flexible schedules because of their longer hours of operation, children's staggered arrivals and departures, and the varying ages of children the center serves.

Flexibility is a must for children with special needs, too. McCormick and Feeney (1995) provided excellent suggestions for helping these children prepare for program transitions and follow transition directions. Furthermore, the health care services provided for children with special needs (e.g., ventilating, breathing treatments, tube feeding) should be planned to meet the individual needs of these children and when it causes least disruption to peers. Programs adhering to the traditional early childhood approach, including open education primary-level programs, also have long, flexible time periods.

Flexible schedules are more appropriate with emergent and integrated curricula (Jones & Nimmo, 1994; Rosegrant & Bredekamp, 1992). Rigid schedules undermine children's decision making and play (Wien, 1996). Of course, children need guidance in programs with flexible schedules; Wien and Kirby-Smith (1998) showed how two teachers used collaborative reflection to know when an adult-imposed change in activities is and is not appropriate.

Because almost all programs use schedules, a few examples for different age groups follow. Examples are not given for infants, who follow their own schedules, or for public school kindergarten and primary programs because they adhere to state and local regulations regarding scheduling. Feeding, toileting, and resting were placed on all the foregoing schedules; however, health needs should be provided on an as-needed basis but also should be offered at regularly scheduled times. The schedules are only suggestions; they are not prescriptive.

1. **Toddler schedules.**   Toddler schedules usually revolve around the children's feeding and sleeping periods but should include lots of time for play activities both inside and outside. An example of a schedule for a full-day session is shown in Figure 9.4.
2. **Child care center schedules.**   Child care centers have perhaps the most flexible schedules of all early childhood programs. An example of a child care center schedule is shown in Figure 9.5.
3. **School-age child care program schedules.**   School-age child care (SACC) programs usually follow very flexible schedules. An outline of an SACC program is shown in Figure 9.6.

Determining the Responsibilities of Staff

In making daily plans, coordination of the responsibilities of staff is essential. Without careful planning, the program will have duplication of tasks, omissions in services, and a general lack of staff efficiency. Following are some criteria to consider in planning the responsibilities of the staff:

1. The goals of the local program
2. Specific organizational policies (the way children are grouped for care or instruction)

Daily Schedule

7:00–8:30 a.m.	Arrival, changing or toileting, dressing babies who are awake, and individual activities
8:30–9:00 a.m.	Breakfast snack, songs, stories, and finger plays
9:00–10:00 a.m.	Manipulative toy activities conducted by staff, and changing or toileting
10:00–11:00 a.m.	Naps for those who take morning naps and outside play for others. (Children go outside as they awaken.)
11:00–11:45 a.m.	Lunch and changing or toileting
11:45–1:00 p.m.	Naps
1:00–2:00 p.m.	Changing or toileting as children awaken and manipulative toy activities
2:00–2:30 p.m.	Snack, songs, stories, and finger plays
2:30 p.m. until departure	Individual activities

Figure 9.4
Toddler Schedule

Daily Schedule

7:00–9:00 a.m.	Arrival, breakfast for children who have not eaten or who want additional food, sleep for children who want more rest, and child-initiated play (which should be relatively quiet) in the activity centers
9:00–9:30 a.m.	Toileting and morning snack
9:30–11:45 a.m.	Active work and play period, both indoor and outdoor. Field trips and class celebrations may be conducted in this time block
11:45–12:00 noon	Preparation for lunch, such as toileting, washing, and moving to dining area
12:00 noon–1:00 p.m.	Lunch and quiet play activities
1:00–3:00 p.m.	Story, rest, and quiet play activities or short excursions with assistants or volunteers as children awaken from naps
3:00–3:30 p.m.	Toileting and afternoon snack
3:30 p.m. until departure	Active work and play periods, both indoor and outdoor, and farewells as children depart with parents
5:00 p.m.	Evening meal for those remaining in center, and quiet play activities until departure

Figure 9.5
Child Care Center Schedule

Daily Schedule

6:30–7:00 a.m.	Arrival, and activities such as quiet games or reading
7:00 a.m. until departure for school	Breakfast, grooming, and activities such as quiet games or reading
3:00–3:15 p.m.	Arrival from school
3:15 p.m. until departure	Snack, and activities such as homework, tutorials, outdoor play, craft projects, table games, and reading

Figure 9.6
School-Age Child Care Schedule

3. The number of staff involved and the qualifications and skills of each individual
4. The layout of the building and grounds and the nature of equipment and materials
5. The specific plans for the day

The responsibilities of staff must be in keeping with legal authorizations (e.g., certification) and with the policies of the governing board. The director usually determines the responsibilities of staff, although in some cases, teachers may assign duties to assistant teachers and volunteers. Specific responsibilities may be delegated by the director or lead teacher, but mutually agreed-on responsibilities in keeping with the basic job descriptions are usually more satisfactory.

A periodic exchange of some duties lessens the likelihood of staff burnout and the frustration of always having less popular responsibilities, such as straightening the room. Staff morale will be higher and the program will function more coherently and smoothly when all staff members are involved in the program from planning to implementation.

TRENDS AND ISSUES

Three major trends and issues seem to be occurring in planning the children's program. One concern is planning a quality curriculum within today's standards-based environment. A second concern, closely tied to the first, is how to implement the curriculum using balanced teaching strategies. The third concern is the debate about inclusion.

Defining Quality Curriculum: The Standards Movement

As discussed in Chapter 1, concern about quality programs, including quality curricula, has been growing. Release of data from several national studies showed the poor to mediocre quality of early childhood programs (Friedman & Haywood, 1994; Helburn, 1995; Kontos, Howes, Shinn, & Galinsky, 1995). The importance of curriculum quality as a foundation for lifelong academic and social competence was confirmed by two reports: *From Neurons to Neighborhoods: The Science of Early Childhood Development* (Shonkoff & Phillips, 2000) and *Eager to Learn: Educating Our Preschoolers* (National Research Council, 2001). Additionally, a call for early learning standards became part of an effort to improve school readiness by improving content and pedagogy in the early years.

Seeing the Benefits.   Early learning standards can be part of a high-quality system of program services to children. Curriculum standards can help identify important educational outcomes and can help build a coherent system of learning opportunities for children, even resolving some of the barriers to program transitions (Caldwell, 1991). Developing local curriculum standards can also be a means of building consensus between schools and families.

Noting the Risks.   Although every professional agrees on "quality," curricular issues are far from resolved. Adopting standards can be beneficial, but doing so can be risky because standards reflect preferences. Several professional associations see the risks of early learning standards as being basically the same as the risks expressed about the trend toward "academic" programs that led to position statements about DAP. Following are some of the concerns about early learning standards:

- Standards may focus on children's achievements rather than content and pedagogical improvements (Hatch, 2002).
- Test scores can be used to penalize children (Shepard, Kagan, & Wurtz, 1998).
- Because of developmental variability and heightened risks for some children, benchmarks are an added risk (Neuman, Copple, & Bredekamp, 2000).
- Standards themselves can be too narrow if they are a fact- and skill-driven approach. Nonacademic strengths, such as emotional literacy, social competence, and positive approaches to learning, also predict success in school and in later life (Peth-Pierce, 2001; Raver, 2002).
- Standards are not beneficial without highly qualified teachers and comprehensive school resources.

Issuing Standards on Standards

Because of the risks of early learning standards, the NAEYC and the National Association of Early Childhood Specialists in State Departments of Education (2002) approved a joint position statement, "Early Learning Standards: Creating the Conditions for Success." These associations recommend that early learning standards be

- Significant, developmentally appropriate content and outcomes
- Informed by research and developed and reviewed by all stakeholders
- Implemented and assessed by ethical and appropriate means
- Supported by adequate program resources, professional development, and a partnership with families and other community members.

Balancing Teaching Strategies

As previously discussed, prescriptive models and traditional early childhood programs use different teaching strategies, as shown in Table 9.6. The prescriptive curriculum approaches use more teacher-determined and whole-group activities to teach separate concepts and skills. Conversely, the traditional early childhood approach emphasizes child-initiated and small-group activities presented as integrated content. Guidelines for DAP emphasize self-directed learnings. However, DAP also recognizes some direct instruction; for example, teachers may use direct instruction as a scaffolding strategy for individuals or small groups.

The benefits of DAP are well researched, but the implementation of DAP is more of a goal than a reality. Some professionals who work with at-risk children see DAP as inappropriate (Stipek & Byler, 1997); however, others do not agree, saying that "children destined to be leaders of tomorrow are not being educated in skill and drill" (Hale, 1994, p. 207). Many teachers are simply not implementing DAP. For example, over 67% of teachers questioned in one study thought that what they did each day was in conflict with their personal beliefs favoring DAP (Hatch & Freeman, 1988). Many researchers felt that full-day programs, especially full-day kindergartens, would offer more child-initiated activities; however, the greatest percentage of time in both full-day and half-day programs is

Table 9.6

Teaching and Learning Activities in Prescriptive and Traditional Early Childhood Programs

Prescriptive Approaches	Traditional Early Childhood Approaches
Content is often written in lesson plan format.	Content is written as units/themes and projects.
Curriculum is compartmentalized (taught as separate subjects).	Curriculum is integrated.
Content or skills presented in teacher-prescribed lessons are often foreign to children.	Understandings are built as children recall past events to understand new ideas.
Skills often do not meet individual needs because the same competencies are deemed necessary for all children and the lessons are teacher prescribed without child input or choice.	Projects are collaboratively planned. Children choose among the activities.
Competencies learned through separate subject lessons may seem useless beyond the classroom doors.	Competencies gained through projects are learned in the real-world setting and thus seem more relevant now and in the future.

consumed by teacher-determined, whole-group activities (Elicker & Mathur, 1997; Morrow, Strickland, & Woo, 1998).

Several causes contribute to the lack of implementation of DAP. Teachers admit that their practices are influenced by families and school administrators (Stipek & Byler, 1997). Other causes for the lack of implementation of DAP may include (a) the national mania for accountability, (b) inexperienced staff whose feelings of insecurity lead to dependence on prescribed activities (Galley, 2002), and (c) the cost of quality programs.

Considering Inclusion

It is important to first recognize that federal legislation (IDEA) mandates that young children with special needs receive special education services in the **least restrictive environment** (LRE). This, for the vast majority of young children with special needs, will be a general education classroom. Placement decisions should be made based on the individual needs of the child, not based on categories of eligibility or diagnostic labels. Unfortunately, within the field of early childhood education there are limited models for successful inclusion. As a result, early childhood professionals are continuing to debate the best practices for including children with disabilities in general community educational settings.

Inclusion means many things and can be seen on a continuum. **Full inclusion** has come to mean that *all* children are served in a general education classroom setting with both general and special educators working collaboratively. **Partial inclusion** means that children with special needs may be included in general education settings for part of the day. **Self-contained special education** means that children with special needs are in self-contained classrooms with little or no interactions with typically developing peers. Shonkoff and Phillips (2000) indicated that the individualization of service delivery and making the intervention a coordinated family-centered one are essential features of intervention.

Full inclusion seems to be easier to implement at the preschool level than at any other level because (a) the educational goals recommended for early childhood and special education are similar (NAEYC, 1996a); (b) early childhood and special education teachers have used team teaching (Bergen, 1994); and (c) some teachers hold dual certificates or have had some course work in both areas.

At the kindergarten and primary levels, partial inclusion may work best for all concerned because of (a) a lack of additional personnel; (b) higher adult–child ratios; (c) inadequate housing; and (d) state-mandated curriculum standards that do not conform to DAP and are thus inappropriate for young children with disabilities.

SUMMARY

Curriculum is a way of helping teachers think about children and organize children's experiences in the program setting. The first step in program planning is to establish the program vision and mission. The director must then make statements concerning the local program's curriculum, which is often called the "program philosophy." The philosophy should be based on knowledge of children, the interests and needs of children, and the physical and social environment of the local program. Often, early learning standards have to be considered as well. From these sources, goal statements must be generated. Goal statements are then translated into written program competencies that further refine the broad goal statements. The basic organization of the curriculum must be determined.

Plans must be made for implementing the curriculum. Deciding on the basic teaching strategies is most important. Other aspects of implementation include decisions about how computers will be used, classroom transitions, physical care routines, and special times. Plans for developing supportive relationships, both adult–child and child–child, are necessary to aid children in reaching program goals.

Directors and teachers must make decisions about group size and adult–child ratios, grouping children, and scheduling activities. These plans must conform to regulations and should be compatible with program goals. Finally, equitable staff responsibilities must be determined.

Three trends and issues seem to be occurring in program planning:

1. Defining program quality in light of the standards movement
2. Implementing curriculum activities through balanced teaching strategies
3. Planning the best settings for children needing special interventions

Attempts are being made to resolve all these issues, but many barriers are still to be removed.

USEFUL WEB SITES

Institute of Education Services What Works Clearinghouse

www.ies.ed.gov/ncee/wwc

This resource presents research based recommendations regarding the effectiveness of early childhood curricula and teaching strategies.

High/Scope Educational Research Foundation

www.highscope.org/

This resource provides information relating to the philosophy and the pedagogy of the high/scope curriculum.

American Montessori Society

www.amshq.org/

Provides information about the Montessori Curriculum as it has been modified for American society.

Association Montessori Internationale

www.montessori-ami.org/

Founded by Dr. Maria Montessori, this Web site outlines the philosophy and principles of the Montessori approach to early childhood education.

Creative Curriculum

www.creativecurriculum.net

Provides basic information about the Creative Curriculum

Project Approach

www.projectapproach.org/

Official Web site for the project approach as described by Sylvia Chard. This site provides a detailed description of the approach and links to project examples and research on their effectiveness.

TO REFLECT

1. An early childhood director is faced with many families wanting a limited academic program for their children. What can the director say to explain the risks and lack of benefits of such a program? If the director's explanation is not accepted, what should the director do? Should the director do as the families wish as a way of possibly ensuring the enrollment for the program? Should the director follow what he or she feels is "best practices" and hope that most families will stay with the program?

2. The director of a preschool center has called a meeting of the lead teachers for each of the five classrooms. According to their job description, lead teachers must take the responsibility for the development of curriculum plans that will be implemented in their own classrooms. The director wants the group to develop a list of criteria that they can use in deciding on the appropriateness of themes or projects and the corresponding activities. What criteria could be used? (Be specific enough to be helpful.)

10

PROVIDING NUTRITION, HEALTH, AND SAFETY SERVICES

NAEYC Director Competencies addressed in this chapter:

Management Knowledge and Skills

5. Program Operations and Facilities Management
   Knowledge of nutritional and health requirements for food service.
6. Family Support
   Knowledge of community resources to support family wellness.

Early Childhood Knowledge and Skills

5. Children with Special Needs
   The ability to work collaboratively as part of family-professional team in planning and implementing appropriate services for children with special needs.
6. Family and Community Relationships
   Knowledge of different community resources, assistance, and support available to children and families.
7. Health, Safety, and Nutrition
   Knowledge and application of practices that promote good nutrition, dental health, physical health, mental health, and safety of infants/toddlers, preschool, and kindergarten children. Ability to implement practices indoors and outdoors that help prevent, prepare for, and respond to emergencies. Ability to model healthful lifestyle choices.

In recent years there has been an increased emphasis on ensuring young children the best possible nutrition and protecting their health and safety while at home and in out-of-home settings. You are probably sensitive to the fact that health, safety, and nutrition are interrelated. Think, for example, how inadequate nutrition during infancy and early childhood can have a lifelong impact on children's health. When children are poorly nourished, even for a short period of time, they are apt to be less alert and prone to accidents and injury. A comprehensive approach to nutrition, health, and safety services in early childhood programs requires you to:

- Provide children nutritious meals and snacks
- Make sure the environment for children's care and education is healthy and safe
- Educate children, staff, and families on the importance of health, safety, and nutrition. This includes emphasizing the importance of prenatal care and nutrition as appropriate.

This comprehensive approach is supported by the third objective of Goal 1 of *America 2000* (U.S. Department of Education, 2001), which states, "Children will receive nutrition and health care needed to arrive at school with healthy minds and bodies, and the number of low birth weight babies will be significantly reduced through enhanced prenatal health systems" (p. 61). It is also addressed by the fifth standard of NAEYC's Accreditation Standards (NAEYC, 2005).

PROMOTING GOOD NUTRITION

Adequate nutrition is essential for physical growth and development. A healthy diet also supports children's immune systems so they stay healthy and have energy to play and explore. As part of society's current heightened interest in nutrition, early childhood programs are becoming more focused than ever on ensuring that children are offered a variety of appealing foods with high nutritional value.

Children are especially vulnerable to harm from malnutrition during periods of rapid growth. These effects can be particularly devastating during the prenatal period when inadequate nutrition can interfere with the development of the brain and central nervous system as well as the liver, kidneys, and pancreas. Maternal malnutrition can also cause babies to be born prematurely with low birth weights (Berk, 2008; Morgan & Gibson, 1991; Strupp & Levitsky, 1995).

Good nutrition remains critically important during infancy when, pound for pound, children need twice the calories as adults because 25% of their total caloric intake is devoted to growth (Berk, 2008). Children's appetites tend to become unpredictable during the preschool years when they are growing more slowly. During this period it is particularly important to offer a variety of healthful choices and not to worry if they pick at their food and eat little at one meal because they are likely to make up for it by eating more later.

As a director of a program of early care and education, you will want to be sensitive to the fact that it is likely you will work with families who do not always have access to enough food to meet their basic needs. It is a sobering fact that reliable access to adequate food is an issue for 35.5 million Americans, including 12.6 million (or 17.2% of all children) (Nord, Andrews, & Carlson, 2007).

Hunger is of the greatest concern among African American and Hispanic populations. The U.S. Department of Agriculture reports that 21.8% of African Americans and 19.5% of Hispanic families experience hunger and are not assured access to enough food for an active lifestyle (Nord et al., 2007). This means that, particularly if you work in a low-income community, the chances are good that you will want to learn about community resources such as food pantries, food banks, soup kitchens, or emergency kitchens operated by churches and other community organizations. This will ensure all the children you serve have reliable access to the high-quality nutrition they need for optimal development.

Even while hunger and reliable access to nutritional food remain daily concerns for many families, the fact is that increased numbers of American children suffer from *misnourishment*—underconsuming important nutrients and overconsuming calories through high-fat and sugary foods (Bhattacharya & Currie, 2001). It is shocking that 73% of 2- through 5-year-old children and 87% of 6- through 9-year-old children have poor diets (Federal Interagency Forum on Child and Family Statistics, 2002). Critics blame much of this misnourishment on commercials for foods high in fat, sugar, and sodium and fast-food restaurants' menus that are full of high-fat and high-calorie offerings (Linn, 2004; Powell, Szczypka, Chaloupka, & Braunschweig, 2007).

Whether caused by the inability to access enough food or poor eating habits, the results of poor nutrition are the same. Children with poor diets are likely to have *stunted growth,* to suffer from *iron deficiency,* and to be overweight. Children with *stunted growth or wasting* (when a child is below the 10th percentile in height for age and/or below the 10th percentile in weight for height) often lag in cognitive development, specifically, visual motor skills, early mathematics skills, phonemic awareness, aural comprehension, and general knowledge (Karp, Martin, Sewell, Manni, & Heller, 1992).

Iron deficiency causes lower test scores on cognitive processes (e.g., spatial memory, selective recall), mental functioning (e.g., arithmetic achievement, written expression), and motor development (Lozoff Jimenez, Hagen, Mollen, & Wolf, 2000; Nokes, van den Bosch, & Bundy, 1998). Children with iron deficiency were shown to be fearful, anxious, and depressed. Similarly, families reported that these children had cognitive problems (i.e., shortened attention spans and failure to focus on tasks) and social problems (Lozoff et al., Lozoff et al., 1998). Importantly, these cognitive and behavioral problems tended to persist even with treatment (Lozoff, et al.).

Misnourishment and overconsumption of calorie-rich snacks high in fat and sugar, along with sedentary lifestyle where children spend over 2 hours each day watching TV or videos or using computers, often eat in front of the TV, and seldom walk or ride their bike to school, lead to childhood obesity (Anderson & Butcher, 2006; Bar-Or, 2000; Rideout & Hamel, 2006).

The definitions of *obesity* and *overweight* rely on the body mass index (BMI*), which is a measure of weight in relation to height. Overweight* is usually defined as being at or above the 85th percentile of weight-to-height, and *obesity* as being at or above the 95th percentile of weight-to-height. Experts note that children grow at different rates and caution that these calculations are estimates at best (Anderson & Butcher, 2006).

About 25% of children in the United States are now considered to be overweight, 11% are obese, and those numbers are growing (Dehghan, Akhtar-Danesh, & Merchant, 2005). The public was warned about the looming obesity epidemic over 20 years ago (Javernick, 1988), and rates of childhood obesity have now reached alarming levels (Gabbard, 2000).

Obesity and low physical activity have lifelong implications, including an increased risk of early hypertension and diabetes (Perry, 2001; Stoneham, 2001); increased incidence of cardiovascular and digestive diseases (Dehghan et al., 2005); and an increased risk for sleep apnea (brief cessation of breathing during sleep); gallbladder disease, joint and skeletal abnormalities; and other health problems (Huettig, Sanborn, DiMarco, Popejoy, & Rich, 2004).

Psychological risks include an increased prevalence of childhood depression (Dehghan et al., 2005), damage to children's self-esteem (Loewy, 1998), and social rejection and withdrawal (Huettig, Sanborn, DiMarco, Popejoy, & Rich, 2004).

It is important to remember the food preferences and eating habits established in childhood last a life time, so programs of early care and education have an important role to play in helping children develop healthy attitudes about food and good eating habits.

Application Activity

The Web site for the Centers for Disease Control and Prevention (CDC) BMI Calculator for Children and Teens is listed at the end of this chapter. Carefully weigh and measure a child over 2 years old and enter that data in this Web site. Bring the report to class with, if possible, a picture of the child. Consider whether the description on the CDC Web site—"underweight, healthy weight, at risk of overweight, or overweight"—seems accurate.

Providing and Serving Nutritious Meals and Snacks

Programs of early care and education have a responsibility to provide the children they serve high-quality meals and snacks. They also have an opportunity to educate families about the importance of high-quality nutrition in the early years and to serve as a resource to ensure all children access to appropriate quantities of nutritious foods.

Meals and snacks served in early childhood programs often provide the majority of children's daily nutrition. The specific proportion provided by the program will, of course, depend on the amount of time the child spends at the center.

The program's funding agency may also have specific requirements about its food services. It is not uncommon for full-day programs to serve children up to four-fifths, and possibly more, of the food they eat each day. Menu planning must take dietary guidelines into account, as well as children's particular dietary needs, including food allergies or sensitivities and families' religious or culturally determined preferences such as wanting their children to follow a vegetarian diet or to avoid certain foods, such as pork (Holland, 2004). Programs should provide menus to families in advance to keep them informed about what their children will be offered while in care and to guide them in making food selections for the remaining part of the child's day.

It is important to remember that mealtimes feed the spirit as well as the body (Murray, 2000). While meeting children's nutritional needs, the center's food program has an opportunity to provide children opportunities to learn about new foods (Birch, Johnson, & Fisher, 1995); to experience new ways of serving foods; and, particularly when meals are served family style, gives them opportunities to enjoy mealtime in a social setting where they can enjoy relaxed conversations and learn table manners.

Regulations and standards related to ensuring children's nutritional well-being while in out-of-home care come from several sources. All are based on the Recommended Dietary Allowances (RDA) published by the Food and Nutrition Board of the National Academy of Sciences. The RDA identifies needed vitamins and minerals. The interactive Web site at the end of this chapter makes it possible to determine how much of each nutrient typically developing children need for optimum health, growth, and development.

Many states' licensing regulations as well as NAEYC's Accreditation Standards (2005) require that food be prepared, served, and stored in accordance with the U.S. Department of Agriculture's (USDA) Child and Adult Care Food Program (CACFP) guidelines. These guidelines for meals and snacks are the basis for examples presented in this text. The meal and snack patterns are based on the USDA's MyPyramid food guidance system for children 2 to 6 years old. (U.S. Department of Agriculture, 2005) See Figure 10.1.

Food can be a substantial part of an early childhood program's budget. Programs serving children eligible for free or reduced lunch can reduce these costs by participating in the USDA's National School Lunch Program and all the Child Nutrition Programs. Generally speaking, not-for-profit programs and for-profit programs that serve a significant number of low-income children are eligible. Specific information about whom to contact in your state for information can be found at the end of this chapter.

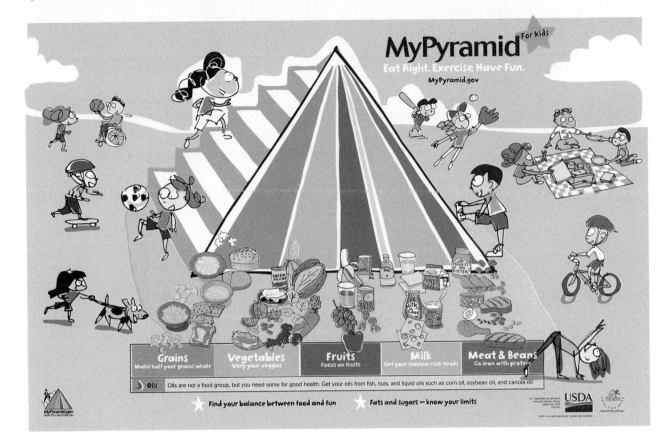

Figure 10.1
MyPyramid graphic from USDA

All programs participating in the school lunch program must participate in mandated training and must follow strict documentation requirements. It is imperative to check all regulations to avoid costly mistakes and delayed implementation. The guidelines that are summarized next provide an overview of food program standards.

Infants.   Because infants have such important nutritional needs, program directors and infant caregivers should work closely with families to create feeding routines that are relaxed, free from distractions, and focused on meeting the infant's physical and emotional needs. Since breast milk is the best possible food for most babies, child care programs can play an important role by encouraging and supporting mothers to continuing breast-feeding their babies after they return to work or school. Efforts to support breast-feeding are important because breast milk provides the nutrition infants need for optimum growth and development, "offers lifelong health advantages [for babies] … contributes to the health of mothers and enhances the economic well-being of society" (U.S. Breastfeeding Committee, 2002, p. 1).

There are several ways child care programs can support mothers' efforts to continue breast-feeding when their babies enter care. The first is to design a comfortable place for mothers to nurse their babies and/or express milk for use later. The second is to be certain that, as the program director, you welcome breast-feeding mothers and can connect them with support they may need, such as the services of a lactation consultant or where to rent an electric breast pump. And finally, you can increase caregivers' knowledge about breast-feeding and its importance to mothers and their babies and teach staff how to properly store, handle, and feed breast milk (U.S. Breastfeeding Committee, 2002).

Table 10.1
Child Care Infant Meal Pattern—CACFP

Birth–3 Months	4–7 Months	8–11 Months
Breakfast		
4–6 fluid ounces of formula[1] or break milk[2, 3]	4–8 fluid ounces of formula[1] or breast milk[2, 3]	6–8 fluid ounces of formula[1] or breast milk[2, 3]; and
	0–3 tablespoons of infant cereal[1, 4]	2–4 tablespoons of infant cereal[1]; and
		1–4 tablespoons of fruit or vegetable or both
Lunch or Supper		
4–6 fluid ounces of formula[1] or breast milk[2, 3]	4–8 fluid ounces of formula[1] or breast milk[2, 3]	6–8 fluid ounces of formula[1] or breast milk[2, 3]
	0–3 tablespoons of infant cereal[1, 4]; and	2–4 tablespoons of infant cereal[1, 4]; and/or
	0–3 tablespoons of fruit or vegetable or both[4]	1–4 tablespoons of meat, fish, poultry, egg yolk, cooked dry beans or peas; or
		1/2–2 ounces of cheese; or
		1–4 ounces (volume) of cottage cheese; or
		1–4 ounces (weight) of cheese food or cheese spread; and
		1–4 tablespoons of fruit or vegetable or both
Supplement (Midmorning or Midafternoon Snack)		
4–6 fluid ounces of formula[1] or breast milk[2, 3]	4–6 fluid ounces of formula[1] or breast milk[2, 3]	2–4 fluid ounces of formula[1] or breast milk[2, 3], or fruit juice[5]; and
		0–1/2 bread[4, 6] or
		0–2 crackers[4, 6]

[1]Infant formula and dry infant cereal must be iron-fortified.

[2]Breast milk or formula, or portions of both, may be served; however, it is recommended that breast milk be served in place of formula from birth through 11 months.

[3]For some breastfed infants who regularly consume less than the minimum amount of breast milk per feeding, a serving of less than the minimum amount of breast milk may be offered, with additional breast milk offered if the infant is still hungry.

[4]A serving of this component is required when the infant is developmentally ready to accept it.

[5]Fruit juice must be full-strength.

[6]A serving of this component must be made from whole-grain or enriched meal or flour.

Source: Building Blocks for Fun and Healthy Meals: A Menu Planner for the Child and Adult Care Food Program, United States Department of Agriculture, 2000, Washington, DC: Author.

The USDA Infant Meal Pattern in Table 10.1 describes accepted feeding practices with young children. Work closely with infants' families when beginning solid foods. Offer only one new food at a time and continue it for 3 or 4 days before introducing another. Start with 1 to 2 tsp and gradually work up to the recommended amounts. Introduce cereals first, then strained fruits and vegetables, and finally strained meats. Fruit juices must also be offered one at a time. Introduce mashed and finely chopped foods including finger foods when babies are ready for them.

Guidelines for Feeding Infants

Follow these procedures when feeding infants:

1. Keep breast milk or prepared formula in the refrigerator until just before feeding. Be certain to label each baby's bottle. It is important to give babies breast milk *only* from their mother.
2. Wash your hands before getting formula, food, or items used in feeding.
3. Heat bottles in hot (not boiling) water. Some centers use a crock pot to keep hot water ready for warming bottles. Shake well and test the temperature before giving to the baby. *Never microwave bottles to heat them.* Microwaving destroys nutrients in breast milk and creates hot spots that can burn babies' mouths and throats.
4. Change the infant's diaper. Then, wash your hands again.
5. Before feeding, place a bib under the infant's chin.
6. Hold infants under 6 months of age comfortably in a semisitting position. Eye contact and cuddling are essential to effective development. Never prop bottles. Babies taking bottles in a reclining position are more prone to choking and developing ear infections and dental caries than infants who take their bottles in a semisitting position. Older infants may be fed in low chairs. Adults must supervise children at all times.
7. If offering solid foods, offer them before the major portion of the formula or breast milk.
8. Discard opened or leftover formula or breast milk.
9. Keep infants upright for 15 minutes after feeding to help avoid regurgitation of formula, breast milk, or food.
10. Encourage older infants to explore and handle food and try to feed themselves.
11. It usually takes considerable patience to teach babies to eat from a spoon. Pushing food from their mouths is a reflexive reaction.
12. Clean the baby's hands, face, and neck after feeding.

Resources providing additional information on infant feeding are provided at the end of the chapter.

Young Children.   Young children should be encouraged to enjoy a variety of nutritious foods. Table 10.2 is a meal and snack plan developed by the USDA. Some studies show that staff members with little specialized training frequently plan the meals in child care settings (Drake, 1992; Pond-Smith, Richarz, & Gonzalez, 1992). Resources for menu planning are provided at the end of the chapter. They can help your program plan healthy, balanced meals. Licensing regulations often require centers to prepare menus in advance. They are also sometimes needed for auditing purposes.

Guidelines for Providing Enjoyable Meals and Snacks

When you are the program director, you have a responsibility to explicitly express your expectations that staff will model the same kinds of mealtime behaviors that children are to exhibit. They are to make nutritious choices, enjoy a wide variety of healthy foods, and welcome the opportunity to sample new and unfamiliar dishes when they are offered.

Table 10.2
Meal Pattern for Young Children—CACFP

Breakfast Meal Pattern

Select All Three Components for a Reimbursable Meal

Food Components	Children Ages 1–2	Children Ages 3–5	Children Ages 6–12[1]
1 milk			
fluid milk	1/2 cup	3/4 cup	1 cup
1 fruit/vegetable juice;[2]			
fruit and/or vegetable	1/4 cup	1/2 cup	1/2 cup
1 grains/bread[3]			
bread or	1/2 slice	1/2 slice	1/2 slice
cornbread or biscuit or roll or muffin or	1/2 serving	1/2 serving	1 serving
cold dry cereal or	1/4 cup	1/3 cup	3/4 cup
hot cooked cereal or	1/4 cup	1/4 cup	1/2 cup
pasta or noodles or grains	1/4 cup	1/4 cup	1/2 cup

[1]Children age 12 and older may be served larger portions based on their greater food needs. They may not be served less than the minimum quantities listed in this column.

[2]Fruit or vegetable juice must be full-strength. Juice cannot be served when milk is the only other snack component.

[3]Breads and grains must be made from whole-grain or enriched meal or flour. Cereal must be whole-grain or enriched or fortified.

Lunch or Supper Meal Pattern

Select All Four Components for a Reimbursable Meal

Food Components	Children Ages 1–2	Children Ages 3–5	Children Ages 6–12[1]
1 milk			
fluid milk	1/2 cup	3/4 cup	1 cup
2 fruits/vegetables			
juice,[2] fruit and/or vegetable	1/4 cup	1/2 cup	3/4 cup
1 grains/bread[3]			
bread or	1/2 slice	1/2 slice	1 slice
cornbread or biscuit or roll or muffin or	1/2 serving	1/2 serving	1 serving
cold dry cereal or	1/4 cup	1/3 cup	3/4 cup
hot cooked cereal or	1/4 cup	1/4 cup	1/2 cup
pasta or noodles or grains	1/4 cup	1/4 cup	1/2 cup
1 meat/meat alternate			
meat or poultry or fish[4] or	1 oz.	1–1/2 oz.	2 oz.
alternate protein product or	1 oz.	1–1/2 oz.	2 oz.
cheese or	1 oz.	1–1/2 oz.	2 oz.
egg or	1/2	3/4	1

Food Components	Children Ages 1–2	Children Ages 3–5	Children Ages 6–12[1]
cooked dry beans or peas or	1/4 cup	3/8 cup	1/2 cup
peanut or other nut or seed butters or	2 Tbsp.	3 Tbsp.	4 Tbsp.
nuts and/or seeds[5] or	1/2 oz.	3/4 oz.	1 oz.
yogurt[6]	4 oz.	6 oz.	8 oz.

[1]Children age 12 and older may be served larger portions based on their greater food needs. They may not be served less than the minimum quantities listed in this column.

[2]Fruit or vegetable juice must be full-strength. Juice cannot be served when milk is the only other snack component.

[3]Breads and grains must be made from whole-grain or enriched meal or flour. Cereal must be whole-grain or enriched or fortified.

[4]A serving consists of the edible portion of cooked lean meat or poultry or fish.

[5]One-half egg meets the required minimum amount (one ounce or less) of meat alternate.

[6]Yogurt may be plain or flavored, unsweetened or sweetened.

Source: Building Blocks for Fun and Healthy Meals: A Menu Planner for the Child and Adult Care Food Program, United States Department of Agriculture, 2000, Washington, DC: Author.

Supplement (Midmorning or Midafternoon Snack)

Select Two of the Four Components for a Reimbursable Meal

Food Components	Children Ages 1–2	Children Ages 3–5	Children Ages 6–12[1]
1 milk			
fluid milk	1/2 cup	1/2 cup	1 cup
1 fruit/vegetable			
juice;[2] fruit and/or vegetable	1/2 cup	1/2 cup	3/4 cup
1 grains/bread[3]			
bread or	1/2 slice	1/2 slice	1 slice
cornbread or biscuit or roll or muffin or	1/2 serving	1/2 serving	1 serving
cold dry cereal or	1/4 cup	1/3 cup	3/4 cup
hot cooked cereal or	1/4 cup	1/4 cup	1/2 cup
pasta or noodles or grains	1/4 cup	1/4 cup	1/2 cup
1 meat/meat alternate			
meat or poultry or fish[4] or	1/2 oz.	1/2 oz.	1 oz.
alternate protein product or	1/2 oz.	1/2 oz.	1 oz.
cheese or	1/2 oz.	1/2 oz.	1 oz.
egg[5] or	1/2	1/2	1/2
cooked dry beans or peas or	1/8 cup	1/8 cup	1/4 cup

(Continued)

Table 10.2 (*Continued*)

Food Components	Children Ages 1–2	Children Ages 3–5	Children Ages 6–12[1]
peanut or other nut or seed butters or	1 Tbsp.	1 Tbsp.	2 Tbsp.
nuts and/or seeds or	1/2 oz.	1/2 oz.	1 oz.
yogurt[6]	2 oz.	2 oz.	4 oz.

[1]Children age 12 and older may be served larger portions based on their greater food needs. They may not be served less than the minimum quantities listed in this column.

[2]Fruit or vegetable juice must be full-strength. Juice cannot be served when milk is the only other snack component.

[3]Breads and grains must be made from whole-grain or enriched meal or flour. Cereal must be whole-grain or enriched or fortified.

[4]A serving consists of the edible portion of cooked lean meat or poultry or fish.

[5]One-half egg meets the required minimum amount (one ounce or less) of meat alternate.

[6]Yogurt may be plain or flavored, unsweetened or sweetened.

Source: Building Blocks for Fun and Healthy Meals: A Menu Planner for the Child and Adult Care Food Program, United States Department of Agriculture, 2000, Washington, DC: Author.

These are some practices that will help your program provide enjoyable meals and snacks:

1. Avoid foods that can be choking hazards, such as whole grapes, nuts, popcorn, raw peas, hard pretzels, spoonfuls of peanut butter, or chunks of raw carrots or meat larger than can be swallowed whole. Cut food into pieces no larger than 1/4-in square for infants and 1/2-in square for toddlers to 2-year-olds. Children's ability to chew and swallow should guide feeding practices (NAEYC, 2005).

2. Offer children small servings, with second helpings available if they are still hungry.

3. When serving a new or unpopular food, try the following:
   a. Serve a tiny portion with a more generous portion of a popular food
   b. Introduce only one new food at a time
   c. Introduce a new food when children are hungry
   d. Eat the food yourself
   e. Have children prepare the food
   f. Keep offering the food because the more often children are offered a food, the more they are inclined to try it

Before putting foods on the menu, teachers might want to introduce them as snacks.

4. Children are likely to enjoy special foods for holidays and birthdays, but holidays do not mean children are taking a break from nutrition. Festive foods can still be healthy choices (Wardle, 1990).

5. Do not serve the same food, or virtually the same food, such as meatballs and hamburgers, on consecutive days.

6. Make an effort to serve children the same kinds of foods they eat at home. This may require you to learn more about families' food preferences and can be a good way to strengthen home-school relationships.

7. Take children's likes and dislikes into account when preparing and serving foods. Young children generally like a variety of foods (different sizes, shapes, colors, textures, and temperatures); foods prepared in different ways, foods served in bite-sized pieces or as finger foods; vegetables with mild flavors; fruit (but not vegetable) combinations; pleasing textures (fluffy, not gooey, mashed potatoes); and foods that are not too hot or cold.

8. Provide a pleasant physical environment and positive emotional climate for meals and snacks. The lunch room or the section of the room used for eating should be quiet enough for children and adults to easily engage in conversation. It should be attractive, with furniture, dishes, silverware, and serving utensils that are easy for the children to handle. Adults should join children at meals rather than hover over them while they eat. They should give children opportunities to make choices and recognize that it is not unusual for preschoolers to go through phases when they are picky eaters or even go on **binges** where they will want to eat only a certain food for a week or two.

Children with Special Needs.   Programs serving children who have special needs have a responsibility to make the accommodations necessary to ensure them access to nutritious meals and snacks. For example, some children may need special help feeding themselves, and children with metabolic disorders will need a carefully planned diet. Ask families and the child's health care provider to provide specific dietary information in writing when children's special needs require accommodations at mealtimes.

Toddlers enjoy mealtimes when they can feed themselves in relaxed and social settings.

Application Activity

Use the menu ideas above to plan a week of lunches for a group of toddlers or preschoolers. Prepare a shopping list that indicates how much of each item you would need to serve a class and two teachers for a week. Use NAEYC group sizes to determine how many children you will need to plan for.

Hiring Staff and Meeting Requirements for the Food Service Program

Directors must consider more than the nutritional needs of children when planning the program's food services. They must also consider how food will be ordered, stored, prepared, served, and how the food service area will be kept clean and sanitary. That means they need to determine their staffing needs as well as the availability of storage for food and supplies, and space and equipment for food preparation and cleanup. They must also ensure compliance with applicable sections of licensing, health department, and accreditation regulations and standards. All these decisions have financial implications. Some food service options to consider follow:

1. Catered meal services are often an expensive option but may be desirable if the program does not have a kitchen.
2. Prepackaged convenience foods may be nutritionally inferior, are expensive, and require large freezers for storage and large ovens or microwaves for preparation.
3. On-site meal and snack preparation requires hiring qualified staff, adequate storage space, and food service equipment.

Hiring Staff.   It is important to have enough help so that meals and snacks can be prepared and served in a reasonable length of time. Some staffing requirements for food service in different child care arrangements follow (AAP/APHA/NRCHSCCEE, 2002):

1. The caregiver in a family child care home
2. One full-time child care food service worker in centers enrolling up to 30 children
3. One full-time child care food service worker and a part-time aide in centers enrolling up to 50 children
4. One full-time child care food service worker and a full-time aide for centers enrolling up to 125 children
5. One full-time food service manager, one full-time cook, and a part-time aide for centers enrolling up to 200 children
6. One part-time or full-time staff member if vendor services are used

Your state's licensing standards or applicable federal regulations are apt to identify the qualifications of food service personnel. If you are not able to hire a registered dietitian, you may want to arrange for one to serve as a consultant.

Providing Facilities and Equipment.   A local child care nutrition specialist or food service expert should work with the architect on the design of the food service areas of the facility. Food service equipment must be purchased, installed, and operated according to the standards of the National Sanitation Foundation (NSF), applicable public health regulations, or the USDA.

Purchasing Food.   Planning food purchases helps control costs and reduces waste. Consider these suggestions:

1. Check several food companies or stores in the area for quality food at reasonable prices and for services you need, such as a line of credit and regular delivery.
2. Look for high-quality products. Your state's licensing regulations are likely to specify that you purchase only government-inspected meats, fish, and poultry; pasteurized grade-A milk and milk products; frozen foods that are kept hard-frozen; and perishable and non-perishable foods that are wholesome, unspoiled, free from contamination, properly labeled, and safe for human consumption.
3. Fresh fruits and vegetables and minimally processed prepared foods are likely to have higher nutritional value; will help you avoid serving children foods high in transfats, sugars, and salt; and are likely to be appealing to children and adults alike.

A qualified cook will create menus and prepare foods children enjoy.

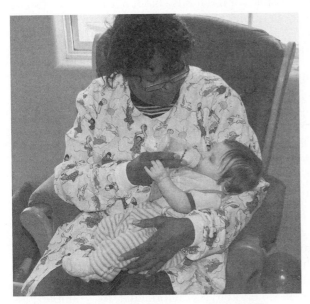

Mealtimes for infants should be time for intimate one-on-one interactions with their caregivers.

4. Carefully calculate the quantities of food needed. Use standardized recipes that can be adjusted to provide the appropriate number of servings. See the resources at the end of the chapter for sources for recipes and menus.

5. Carefully consider the types of food (perishable or non-perishable) and the amount of storage space when deciding when and how much food to purchase.

6. Keep accurate records about the food purchased, when and how it was used, its cost, and any other notes that will help you make future purchases.

Meeting Sanitation Requirements. You can help to prevent disease by carefully following all sanitation guidelines. Cleanliness must be considered in all aspects of food service. These are some recommended food service practices:

1. All food service employees must meet state and local health requirements, must wash hands thoroughly, wear clean clothes, take measures to keep their hair out of the food, be free from skin infections, and must not have a contagious disease when they prepare or serve food.

2. Preparation and serving utensils and dishes must be thoroughly washed, sanitized, and properly handled. Most state's licensing regulations describe specific procedures. They might say, for example, that the dishwasher should be set for a water temperature of 160–165 °F (66–74 °C), using 0.25% detergent concentration or 1 oz of detergent per 3 gal of water. These are typical instructions for washing by hand:

   a. Wash with soap or detergent in hot water (110–120 °F or 43–49 °C).

   b. Rinse in warm water.

   c. Sanitize by immersing for at least 1 minute in clean, hot water (at least 170 °F or 76 °C) or by immersing for at least 3 minutes in a sanitizing solution of 1 tbsp household bleach per 2 gal of water.

   d. Air dry; do not wipe.

3. Foods should be checked on delivery, protected in storage, used within the specified time, and kept at appropriate serving temperatures: hot foods at 140 °F (60 °C) or above and cold foods at 45 °F (7 °C) or below.

4. Wash raw foods carefully and cook prepared foods properly.

5. Dispose of all foods served and not eaten.

6. Help children learn how to wash their hands thoroughly and get them into the habit of washing their hands before eating.

Planning Nutrition Education

Programs of early care and education have an important opportunity to educate children and families about the importance of good nutrition. They can also help children develop healthy lifelong habits and attitudes about food.

Integrating Nutrition Education into the Curriculum.   Early childhood programs should intentionally plan how they will teach young children about the importance of good nutrition and help them learn to identify the foods that will help to keep them strong and healthy. These activities can easily be integrated across content areas in classrooms that actively engage children in meaningful activities. These are some ways to integrate nutrition education into the curriculum.

1. Teach children how foods support health, growth, and development and help them develop positive attitudes about food and healthy diets.
2. Give children opportunities to learn about where food comes from and how it is prepared. This means children might participate in planting, caring for, and eating vegetables from an on-site garden, or visit a farm, farmer's market, greengrocer, or supermarket to purchase foods to prepare in the classroom.
3. Plan, prepare, and serve nutritious snacks. Cooking experiences will help children learn to measure, follow directions, cooperate with others, coordinate eye–hand movements, use language as a means of expression, appreciate differences in food preferences, and eat foods prepared in different ways. Cooking will also foster creativity using food products (Cosgrove, 1991; Dahl, 1998; Howell, 1999; Klefstad, 1995). There are many cookbooks for young children.
4. Provide opportunities for children to socialize during meals and snacks and develop good manners. This will help them enjoy meals in a variety of settings—home, child care, restaurants, or picnics.

Serving Families' Needs.   Families have a much greater lifelong impact on children's nutrition habits than do schools (Swadener, 1995). Although children decide how much (or even whether) to eat, adults are responsible for the foods children are offered. Family members can help their children learn about nutrition and can help them develop positive attitudes about healthy foods (Nahikian-Nelms, Syler, & Mogharrehan, 1994). They need to be informed about various nutrition-related topics including:

a. Foods children need for optimum health, growth, and development
b. Planning, buying, storing, and preparing varieties of foods
c. Eating problems that children are apt to develop
d. Meeting the needs of children who require special diets
e. Strategies to help families manage their budgets so they can count on having an appropriate supply of nutritious food for their growing family

Staff should make efforts to become acquainted with families' lifestyles: Do they frequently eat in restaurants? Do they cook at home, preparing foods "from scratch," or do they rely on prepared foods to make food preparation easier? Do they make it a priority to provide children organic foods, or grow much of their family's foods themselves?

Consider adapting the form in Figure 10.2 to let families know that enjoying a variety of foods is part of your curriculum. This form also invites families to share foods that are favorites in their home with their child's classmates.

Child care personnel should also make an effort to stay informed if, for example, parents should become unemployed, or face particular challenges providing for their family's basic needs. Programs can reach out to families by offering information about children's nutritional needs and how to meet them in meetings, demonstration classes, home visits and through newsletters. Consider the following specific suggestions:

1. Staff can help families plan nutritious meals by providing them with copies of the MyPyramid food guidance system and by conducting workshops to help them apply these guidelines when planning family meals. The MyPyramid Web site at the end of the chapter has helpful information to help plan presentations.

Child's name _____

Our center provides children many opportunities to experience a wide variety of healthy foods. We hope you'll join us in encouraging your child to enjoy tasting unfamiliar fruits, vegetables, and other healthy offerings.

Perhaps you would like to send a snack, fruit, or vegetable that you enjoy at your home for your child to share with his/her classmates. This can be a good way to share your family's special traditions with your child's classmates.

Does your child have any identified food allergies? *Please let us know if they are so severe that we need to restrict foods (such as nuts) that come into the classroom.*

What are some of your child's favorite foods for breakfast, lunch, and healthy snacks?

Please let me know if you would like to share something that is a favorite at your home with our class.

Figure 10.2
Sample Favorite Foods Form

2. Newsletters can include ideas for healthy kid-friendly meals, recipes that can help nurture young children's interest in healthy foods and snacks, and nutritional information for offerings at local fast-food restaurants to help families make healthy choices when eating out.
3. Printed program menus should be sent home so families can plan meals that supplement rather than duplicate school offerings.
4. Ask family members to participate in cooking activities.
5. Put families who may need assistance gaining access to adaquate food in touch with appropriate social service agencies. Follow up to be certain their needs were met.

PROMOTING GOOD HEALTH

Programs for young children began focusing on children's health in the mid-1940s (Child Welfare League of America, 1945). Although interest in issues related to children's health has fluctuated over the years, efforts to enhance children's health status were brought front and center by the Goals 2000 legislation enacted in 1994. The first of these goals challenges America to guarantee that "all children in America will start school ready to learn [and will] receive the nutrition, physical activity experiences, and health care needed to arrive at school with healthy minds and bodies, and to maintain the mental alertness necessary to be prepared to learn...." (Goals 2000, 1994). Progress toward that goal continues to motivate advocates and policy makers focused on children's issues.

Today, the definition of *health* has shifted from the absence of disease to a state of total physical, mental, and social and emotional well-being. Each of the three aspects of health contributes equally to a person's overall health. For example, physical health problems often cause young children to be listless, which results in less exploration and play. This decreases interaction in one's physical and social worlds and adversely affects cognitive, social and emotional development.

Conversely, a stressful cognitive, social, or emotional environment can lead to physical health problems. As a result of our increased understanding of this interactive relationship, early childhood professionals are giving increased attention to children's health and physical well-being.

Program directors must be concerned about the health of all those involved in early childhood programs. More specifically, directors must develop health policies for children and staff in keeping with current information and must plan and oversee the implementation of the policies.

Assessing Health Status

Assessment of health is an appraisal of an individual's health status. Because an individual's health status is changing and dynamic, this appraisal should include a periodic in-depth assessment by a specially trained health care professional as well as continuous observations conducted during various day-to-day activities.

Staff.   Working in an early care and education program is physically demanding, exposes employees to infectious illnesses, can put individuals at risk for back injuries from frequent lifting, and can be emotionally stressful. The health of adults is a key element in the quality of an early childhood program. A staff member's illness can become a health hazard to children and other staff members, can interfere with the program's efforts to provide continuity of care, and can be costly if substitutes are frequently needed.

Planning to assess each staff member's health begins with the wording of the program's job descriptions. Each needs to be explicit about the physical demands required to successfully complete required tasks. Without this level of specificity, hiring or dismissal decisions may appear to be discriminatory. Although all employees must meet some requirements (e.g., being free from contagious diseases), others are more job specific (e.g., the ability to lift or visually supervise the children in their care).

Policies should be established concerning:

a. The extent of the health history and medical examination required for employment including specific requirements for employees in particular positions
b. Who can conduct the required physical examination and who can sign the required form (i.e., Is it acceptable for the form to be signed by a nurse practitioner or physician's assistant?)
c. Who pays for the preemployment physical exam?
d. Who at the local program receives the information?
e. When must the report be received for the applicant to be considered for a specific position?

The medical assessment should be completed and reviewed before the job offer is made final and before the hiree comes into contact with children. Samples of staff health assessments can be found by following links to online resources at the end of this chapter.

Children.   Children's health status must be documented before they can participate in a program of early care and education and is assessed continuously while they are participating in the program. As discussed in chapter 3, most states' licensing regulations require that children have a medical examination and that they submit a doctor's report including documentation that they have received the required vaccinations.

Samples of child health assessments can be found by following links to online resources at the end of this chapter. These sample forms ask for pertinent information on the child's health history, current medical examination results, allergies, immunization record, results of screening tests, and the date of the child's last dental examination. The physician is also asked to list any health problems or special needs and recommended care.

Children sometimes become ill while in care. When that happens you need to have a systematic way to record symptoms and report them to the child's family. See Figure 10.3 for an example of a symptom record.

Child's Name _____

Date _____

SYMPTOMS

Major Symptoms

    Respiratory: runny nose; sore throat; difficulty in breathing; cough; other

       (Please describe) _____

       _____

    Skin: itch; rash; oozing; lesion; other

       (Please describe) _____

       _____

    Gastrointestinal: nausea; vomiting; diarrhea; trouble urinating; frequent urinating with pain; other

       (Please describe) _____

       _____

    Body movement: stiff neck; limp; other

       (Please describe) _____

When symptom began _____

CHILD'S REACTIONS

    Food/fluid intake

       (Please describe) _____

       _____

    Urine, bowel, and/or vomiting

       (Please describe) _____

       _____

    Crying, sleeping, other behavior

       (Please describe) _____

       _____

EXPOSURE

    Ill children or staff

       (Please describe) _____

       _____

    Ill parent or sibling

       (Please describe) _____

       _____

    New foods

       (Please describe) _____

       _____

Ingestion of or contact with potentially harmful substance (e.g., art materials, cleaning materials, room paint, plants, animals)

(Please describe) _____

_____

Figure 10.3
Symptom Record

CARE AND ADVICE
First aid, emergency care, or other care

(Please describe) _____

_____

Health provider advice

(Please describe) _____

_____

Parent consultation

(Please describe) _____

_____

_____
(Signature of person completing form)

Figure 10.3 (*Continued*)

Advocating for Preventive Health Care

Early childhood programs can have considerable influence on participating children's health. There may be opportunities to help families secure health care including dental services and to educate children, families and caregiviers about how to prevent infections in the program.

Securing Health Services.   Health care professionals advise that all children should have a medical home providing "primary care that is accessible, continuous, comprehensive, family-centered, coordinated, compassionate, and culturally effective" (American Academy of Family Physicians, American Academy of Pediatrics, American College of Physicians, & American Osteopathic Association, 2007). Early childhood programs are often in a position to help families establish a medical home including dental care for their children. For this reason, connecting families with quality primary care should be a focus of the outreach and advocacy efforts for programs enrolling children in need of these primary health care services.

Program directors should familiarize themselves with resources available in their communities so they can assist families who may need their help. Directors might begin by checking with their local health department; clinics operated by hospitals and medical schools, voluntary groups such as the United Way, the American Red Cross, civic clubs, religious groups, and family service associations; medical assistance under Medicaid (Title XIX); armed forces medical services; and insurance and other prepayment plans so they can knowledgeably guide families toward services they may need.

NAEYC Accreditation Criteria and regulations in many locales also require early childhood programs to provide some health services, such as health consultation (Dooling & Ulione, 2000; NAEYC 2005).

Preventing Infections in Programs.   Protection from infectious diseases is a daily concern of early childhood staff, families, and health care professionals. Although it is impossible to prevent the spread of all infectious diseases in any group (including a family), much can be done to reduce the risk of transmission.

Vulnerability of Children.   Infections are transmitted through direct contact (touching) with blood, mucus, or other fluids from the respiratory tract and stool. Children are highly vulnerable for many reasons:

1. Child care routines create opportunities for close physical contacts among children and adults such as those that naturally occur during feeding; diapering and

toileting; sharing toys, art materials, and water tables; and the expressions of affection that bring children into close contact with peers and adults.

2. Children's immunity systems are immature. They are typically very vulnerable to infection.

3. The scrapes children often have on their skin make it possible for germs to enter their bodies.

4. Children often do not know how to protect themselves from exposure to risks of infection.

Health concerns are greatest for infants and toddlers cared for in group settings. These very young children show an increased incidence of respiratory illness and diarrhea as compared with infants and toddlers not in group settings (Harms, 1992). It is important to take extra precautions to keep them healthy.

Strategies to Keep the Environment Healthy.   When accepted practices are carefully followed, child care environments will be safe and healthy for both children and adults. Researchers have found that caregivers in many infant and toddler programs do not follow recommended practices when diapering, toileting, washing hands, or grooming children (Cost, Quality, and Child Outcomes Study Team, 1995). Those findings highlight how important it is to help caregivers become informed about practices that support children's health and that caregivers reliably follow these recommended practices. The following practices help keep children and adults healthy:

1.   Food service must strictly follow all recommended practices. The food supply must be safe and all foods and beverages must be stored, prepared, and served properly. Rely on appropriate agencies, licensing and accreditation standards to establish routines that will keep children and adults healthy.

2.   Dangerous microorganisms can thrive in the diapering area. The following practices will help reduce the risks associated with diapering. Refer to licensing and accreditation standards for specifics.

   a. Change children on a table with a plastic-covered pad that has no cracks. The table should have an edge to help prevent falls.

   b. Disinfectant the diapering surface after every diaper change by spraying with a solution of 1 tablespoon chlorine bleach to 1 quart of water. The sanitizing solution must be made fresh daily. Leave the solution on the surface for at least 10 seconds, and ideally 2 minutes, to air dry or wipe down with a dry paper towel. Many centers line the changing table with paper that is changed after each diaper change.

   c. You may use disposable gloves to change diapers (a fresh pair for each diaper change), but gloves do not eliminate the need for careful hand washing.

   d. Dispose of used diapers, wipes, and changing table paper in a hands-free covered trashcan such as one with a foot pedal to control the lid.

   e. Post procedures for diapering in the diapering area.

3.   Proper hand washing is the best way to stop the spread of germs. Children and adults should wash their hands when

   - They arrive for the day
   - After diapering or using the toilet
   - After blowing or wiping a nose or touching mucus, blood, or vomit
   - Before preparing, eating, or serving food, or after handling raw food that needs to be cooked (i.e., meat, eggs)
   - After handling animals or any surfaces such as dirt or sand that might have been contaminated by animals

Adults must also wash their hands

- Before and after feeding a child
- Before and after administering medication
- After assisting a child blow her nose or use the toilet
- After handling garbage or cleaning

Proper hand washing procedures require the use of liquid soap and running water. You need to rub your hands together vigorously for at least 10 seconds. You might remind children to wash their hands for as long as it takes them to sing the alphabet song or "Row, Row, Row Your Boat" so they don't rush through the process. Be sure to include the backs of your hands, your wrists, between your fingers, and under your fingernails; rinse well; dry your hands with a paper towel or a blow dryer. Avoid touching the faucet with just-washed hands by using a paper towel to turn off the water (Cryer, Harms & Riley, 2003; NAEYC, 2005).

Alcohol-based hand sanitizing gels do not replace routine hand washing but can be very helpful when soap and water are not readily available. Not all hand sanitizer products are created equal, however. Be certain to select a product with at least 60% alcohol. Apply about 1/2 teaspoon directly to the palm of your hand, rub hands together to cover all surfaces, and keep rubbing until your hands are dry (Mayo Clinic, 2007). These substances are toxic and flammable so it is important to use them with care and to follow directions.

4. Even though the risk of exposure to blood-borne pathogens in child care settings is small, most states' child care licensing regulations require teachers and caregivers to have regular Occupational Safety & Health Administration (OSHA) approved training on universal precautions to prevent transmission of blood-borne diseases (e.g., HIV/AIDS and Hepatitis B).

These are some of the basic principles of universal precautions:

a. Avoid touching blood and bodily fluids that might contain blood.

b. Wear disposable latex gloves when you encounter blood or bodily fluids that might contain blood; remove and dispose of the gloves carefully to avoid contaminating clean hands and surfaces; and wash your hands well when you remove the gloves.

c. Use disposable absorbent materials (e.g., facial tissue, paper towels) to stop bleeding. Discard blood-stained materials in a sealed plastic bag and place in a lined, covered garbage container.

d. Put blood-stained laundry in sealed plastic bags. Machine wash separately in cold soapy water and then wash separately in hot water.

e. Clean blood-soiled areas and disinfect with a solution of 1 part chlorine bleach and 9 parts water.

5. A clean facility will help children and adults stay healthy. Table 10.3 summaries guidelines for cleaning and sanitizing floors, furnishings, and toys. The recommended sanitizing solution is made by mixing 1 tablespoon chlorine bleach with 1 qt of water and must be mixed fresh daily.

You will want to create a cleaning and sanitation schedule and a checklist that makes employees responsible for keeping up-to-date with needed cleaning. Establish a regular day to perform weekly tasks, such as washing all linens on Friday, and a regular time to perform monthly tasks, like the first Monday of the month.

Communicating with Families.   Centers should communicate with families regularly about issues related to children's health and well-being. Some of the topics that should be addressed in these communications follow:

1. Describe the program's exclusion policies, identifying symptoms of frequently occuring childhood illnesses and other symptoms such as fever or vomiting that indicate that children should not come to school. When appropriate, share information about community programs providing care for mildly ill children.

Table 10.3
Cleaning and Sanitation Frequency Table

Area	Clean	Sanitize	Frequency
Classrooms/child care/food areas			
Countertops/tables	X	X	Daily and when soiled
Food preparation and service surfaces	X	X	Before and after contact with food activity; between preparation of raw and cooked foods
Floors	X	X	Daily and when soiled
Door and cabinet handles	X	X	Daily and when soiled
Carpets and large area rugs	X		Vacuum daily when children are not present. Clean with a carpet cleaning method approved by the local health authority. Clean carpets only when children will not be present until the carpet is dry. Clean carpets at least monthly in infant areas, at least every three months in other areas and when soiled.
Small rugs	X		Shake outdoors or vacuum daily. Launder weekly.
Utensils, surfaces, and toys that go into the mouth or have been in contact with saliva or other body fluids	X	X	After each child's use; or disposable, one-time use utensils or toys.
Toys	X		Weekly and when soiled
Dress-up clothes not worn on the head	X		Weekly
Sheets and pillowcases, individual cloth towels (if used), combs and hairbrushes, washcloths, and machine-washable cloth toys	X		Weekly and when visibly soiled (used only by one child)
Blankets, sleeping bags and cubbies	X		Monthly and when soiled
Hats	X		After each child's use (or use disposable hats that only one child wears)
Cribs and mattresses	X		Weekly or before use by a different child
Mops and cleaning rags	X	X	Before and after a day of use, wash, rinse, and sanitize mops and cleaning rags.
Toilet and diapering areas			
Hand-washing sinks, faucets, surrounding counters	X	X	Daily and when soiled
Soap dispensers	X	X	Daily and when soiled
Toilet seats, toilet handles, cubicle handles and other touchable surfaces, floors	X	X	Daily or immediately if visibly soiled
Toilet bowls	X	X	Daily
Doorknobs	X	X	Daily
Changing tables	X	X	After each child's use
Potty chairs	X	X	After each child's use. (Use of potty chairs in child care is discouraged because of high risk of contamination.)
Any surface contaminated with body fluids: saliva, mucus, vomit, urine, stool, or blood	X	X	IMMEDIATELY

Support Document for NAEYC Program Standards (2005), *A Manual for Programs,* NAEYC Accreditation Criteria, 2005, NAEYC, 2002. Used with permission.

2. Provide strategies for caregivers and families to share information as children are passed from family to center care. The program should provide forms for daily written communication between families and infant and toddler caregivers. There should also be plan for teachers and caregivers of preschoolers and young school-age children to communicate with families if symptoms of illness appear.

3. Inform families when their chidren have been exposed to a communicable disease. Describe the symptoms of the disease, how it is spread, how it is prevented or controlled, what the program is doing to prevent its spread, and what the family can do to stay healthy. A note on the door (See Figure 10.4) is sufficient for minor illnesses, but you need to send a letter for more serious contagious diseases.

Some communicable diseases must also be reported to your licensing agency or the local health department, which in turn will make recommendations for informing families of children who may have been exposed.

Providing Health Care

Most child care programs will not be able to serve children who are ill. If you are interested in learning about recommended policies and procedures for serving children who are mildly ill or children with chronic health conditions that make it inadvisable for them to participate in programs for typically developing children, you will want to consult specialized resources and your state's child care regulations that apply to these special circumstances.

Caring for Children with Noninfectious Chronic Illnesses and Disabilities

It is often appropriate and desirable for children who have a chronic noncontagious condition or an identified disability to participate in programs with their typically developing peers. These children may be eligible for support services under Part C or Part B of

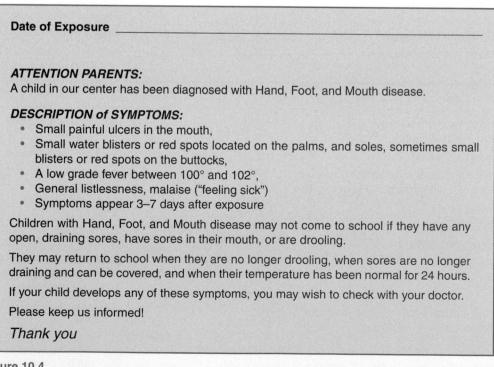

Date of Exposure _____

ATTENTION PARENTS:
A child in our center has been diagnosed with Hand, Foot, and Mouth disease.

DESCRIPTION of SYMPTOMS:
- Small painful ulcers in the mouth,
- Small water blisters or red spots located on the palms, and soles, sometimes small blisters or red spots on the buttocks,
- A low grade fever between 100° and 102°,
- General listlessness, malaise ("feeling sick")
- Symptoms appear 3–7 days after exposure

Children with Hand, Foot, and Mouth disease may not come to school if they have any open, draining sores, have sores in their mouth, or are drooling.

They may return to school when they are no longer drooling, when sores are no longer draining and can be covered, and when their temperature has been normal for 24 hours.

If your child develops any of these symptoms, you may wish to check with your doctor.

Please keep us informed!

Thank you

Figure 10.4
Sample Exposure Notice

IDEA. You will want to coordinate with the Individual Family Service Plan (IFSP) or Individual Education Plan (IEP) case manager to plan for how you will accommodate these children's special needs before they begin to attend your program. These are some issues to consider:

1. Will you need to adapt your program or routine activities to accommodate children with identified special needs?
2. Will you need to adapt the facility or acquire special equipment?
3. Do you need to anticipate the child's special dietary needs? Will she need to be fed or need other special help?
4. Do you have a plan in place to coordinate the administration of medicine with the child's family?
5. Do staff members need training in providing specialized care and emergency procedures (e.g., replacement equipment should failure occur, backup power source, supplemental oxygen, resuscitator bag, and suctioning catheter)

Although some children require intensive services beyond those typically provided by an early childhood program, most children with a chronic illness or a disability will require only minor adaptations and will make a significant contribution to your program, children, and teachers.

Administrating Medication.   As discussed in chapter 4, your program needs to establish policies describing how you will administer over-the-counter and prescribed medicines to children in your care. These procedures are likely to be part of your state's child care licensing regulations. They will address what medicines can be administered (i.e. prescription medications labeled for the specific child enrolled, over-the-counter medicines when ordered by a physician). Regulations will also describe appropriate storage, record keeping, and what to do if there is a medication error such as a missed dose. See Figure 10.5 for an example of a medication administration log that satisfies most states' requirements.

Promoting Children's Mental Health.   Mental health is, perhaps, the most important health-related issue you will address while caring for young children. We know that many of children's challenging behaviors are the result of biological factors, such as prenatal stress, birth trauma, and congenital defects (Brennan, Mednick, & Kandal, 1991; Shore, 1997), or

| Child's name _____ |
| Date _____ |

Time	Safety Check of Label and Storage	Notes	Staff Member's Initials

(Give copy to parent when child is picked up.)

Figure 10.5
Medication Administration Log

they can be environmental, such as the social conditions arising from poverty, exposure to violence, and even the lack of a caring environment in low-quality programs (Kaplan, 1998; Simmons, Stalsworth, & Wentzel, 1999; Slaby, Roedell, Arezzo, & Hendrix, 1995; Stanford & Yamamoto, 2001).

The emotional domain is perhaps the most compelling aspect of development in young children, so much so that we know the problems facing infants and toddlers are most likely to "lie in the domain of social/emotional functioning" (Honig, 1993, p. 69). During these early years, children must build secure relations and develop independence. Family and staff education, professional resources, and environmental changes aimed at reducing stress are all effective strategies for ensuring young children's mental health (Honig, 1993). Even for preschoolers, group programs can be sources of great tension. Young children often feel "one among many" for very long hours and are apt to feel lonely and stressed when away from their families (Vermeer & IJzendoorn, 2006). Primary-age children are coping with the stress of "school" and often with the daily transition of school to child care programs or school to "home alone."

Promoting children's mental health both at home and in out-of-home programs must be a top priority as you work with young children. Directors and staff may find these strategies helpful:

1. Provide staff in-service education about stressors that adults may confront in early childhood programs. For example, family members are likely to feel anxious when their child enrolls in child care for the first time, and they are frequently stressed by their efforts to balance the sometimes conflicting demands of the home and the workplace. Staff often feel stressed when trying to meet the needs of distressed infants, demanding toddlers, and aggressive or withdrawn preschoolers; when negotiating differences with family members; and with the challenges of the workplace. Finally, some children and adults are also experiencing difficult and possibly even abusive home lives; these "from home" stressors will be played out on the stage of the group setting.

2. Address children's exposure to violence. Directors and staff should work with families, civic leaders, and social agency professionals to promote activities aimed at reducing the risks of violence within the community and children's exposure to violent media.

3. Recognize the risk factors (see Figure 10.6) and signs of possible neglect and abuse (see Figure 10.7) in children. Know how to respond to child disclosures of neglect or abuse (Austin, 2000) and have written policies on reporting suspected child neglect or abuse that are in line with your state's laws related to mandated reporters.

4. Develop strict program policies describing appropriate discipline and guidance. Directors must be vigilant in the implementation of these policies and in protecting children from abuse or neglect while they are in out-of-home settings (Mikkelsen, 1997; NAEYC, 1997).

5. Work with families to create partnerships designed to maintain consistent expectations for children's behaviors.

6. Provide families with strategies for resolving conflicts and reducing violence in the home including information about professional and emergency assistance.

7. Equip families with a rationale and strategies for limiting children's "screen time," that is, their use of electronic media including television, videos, and online and software games (Levin, 2003).

8. Equip staff with constructive coping strategies for dealing with children's challenging behaviors by
   a. Using positive guidance (see chapter 9)
   b. Implementing strategies for dealing with persistent and very challenging behaviors (see the resource list at the end of the chapter)

Society

- Poverty
- Overcrowding
- Illegal drug culture
- High crime area
- High unemployment rate
- Few social services
- Unaffordable health care

Parent/Family

- Unwanted pregnancy
- Single parent
- Teen parent
- Physical, sexual, or emotional abuse as a child
- Emotional neglect as a child
- Use of violence to express anger
- Lack of self-esteem
- Emotional immaturity
- Poor coping skills
- Alcohol or illegal drug abuse
- Marriage problems
- Financial stress
- Recent stressful events (divorce, recent move, death in family)
- Illness (physical or mental health, especially depression)
- Lacks parenting skills including no preparation for the extreme stress of a new baby
- Lacks knowledge of child development; thus has unrealistic expectations for the child
- Heavy parenting responsibility (multiple births or single children less than 18 months apart in age)
- Weak bonding or attachment to a child (often due to child's care in ICU after birth)
- Use of physical punishment (called corporal punishment)
- Isolation (lack of family or friend support)

Child

- Under the age of five years, especially under age of one year
- Low birthweight or premature
- Looks like or has traits like a disliked relative
- Irritable or cries a great deal (colic; ADHD)
- Disobeys parents or argues a great deal (older child)

Figure 10.6
Risk Factors for Neglect and Abuse
Source: Children: The Early Years (p. 676), by C.A. Decker, 2004, Tinley Park, IL: The Goodheart-Willcox Company, Inc. Reprinted with permission.

    c. Recognizing children's behaviors that indicate the child may need to be screened by a health professional (Division of Early Childhood of the Council for Exceptional Children, 2006)

Protecting the Health of Children and Staff.   Most states' child care regulations require staff to have training in pediatric first aid including rescue breathing and CPR and to participate in an OSHA-approved session on universal precautions that prevent the spread of blood-borne pathogens. This training protects children and adults alike.

Neglect

A child may be physically neglected when he or she
- is malnourished
- fails to receive needed health care without a parental objection
- fails to receive proper hygiene (is not washed or bathed; has poor oral hygiene; has ungroomed skin, nails, and hair)
- has insufficient clothing or clothing that is dirty, tattered, or inappropriate for the weather
- lives in filthy conditions and/or inadequate shelter

A child may suffer mental or educational neglect when he or she
- lacks moral training
- lacks constructive discipline
- fails to receive positive examples from adults
- fails to have adequate supervision
- is left alone for hours
- fails to attend school regularly because of parents
- fails to receive parent stimulation toward learning or education suited to his or her ability
- is not allowed to take part in wholesome recreational activities

A child may be emotionally neglected if he or she
- experiences constant friction in the home
- is denied normal experiences that produce feelings of being wanted, loved, and protected
- is rejected through indifference
- is overly rejected, such as through abandonment

Abuse

A child may be physically abused if he or she
- seems fearful or quiet around parents but has no close feeling for them
- is wary of physical contact initiated by an adult
- has little or no reaction to pain and seems much less afraid than most children the same age
- has unexplained injuries or shows evidence of repeated injuries, such as having bruises in various stages of healing or repeated fractures
- is dressed inappropriately, such as an injured child dressed in pajamas who was reportedly injured on a bicycle or a child dressed in a turtleneck in the summer to cover bruises
- has long bones that, when x-rayed, show a history of past injuries
- has injuries not reported on previous health records
- has parents who have taken the child to many hospitals and doctors without appropriate explanation
- has parents who refuse further diagnostic studies of their child's injuries
- has parents who show detachment or see the child as bad or "different" during medical treatment
- has parents who give too many minute details about the cause of injury
- tries to protect parents when they are questioned about the child's injuries

A child may suffer verbal abuse if he or she
- lacks self-esteem
- is either too quiet and polite or uses harsh and improper language when dealing with others, especially those who are smaller or younger
- expresses long-term feelings of damage and isolation

Figure 10.7
Signs of Child Neglect and Abuse

Source: Children: The Early Years (pp. 679–680), by C.A. Decker, 2004, Tinley Park, IL: The Goodheart-Willcox Company, Inc. Reprinted with permission.

A child may be sexually abused if he or she
- has extreme and sudden changes in behavior, such as loss of appetite or sudden drop in grades
- has nightmares and other sleep problems
- regresses to previous behaviors, such as renewed thumb sucking
- has torn or stained underwear
- has infections (with symptoms like bleeding or other discharges and itching) or swollen genitals
- fears a person or shows an intense dislike of being left alone with that person
- has an STD or pregnancy
- has unusual interest in or knowledge of sexual matters

Figure 10.7 (*Continued*)

Employees also need to know how to protect themselves from injuries and illnesses they might encounter at their work. Child care workers are constantly lifting, bending and carrying and so are at risk of injuring their backs. Back injuries can be avoided by having changing tables at adult height, installing steps so children can climb onto the changing table, and by providing adult-sized furniture so employees do not have to routinely use child-sized chairs or sit on the floor (AAP et al., 2002). They are also frequently exposed to colds, coughs, and intestinal upsets that children bring to school. It can be hard to stay healthy when feeding, changing, and caring for children.

Adequate paid sick leave protects the health of both children and adults. When staff have a reasonable number of paid sick leave days, they more likely to stay out of work when they are ill and to stay home until they are able to resume their duties without putting themselves, chidren, or adults at risk of exposure to communicable diseases (AAP et al., 2002). Fully paid health insurance in child care programs is rare, however, and remains a focus of advocacy efforts in the field. (Whitebook, Howes, & Phillips, 1998).

BEING SAFE

Protecting children's safety involves eliminating risks in the environment, preparing for emergencies, and being alert to unanticipated and yet-to-be identified risks. That means safety is a day-to-day concern for those who educate and care for children.

Addressing Environmental Safety

Ensuring children's safety in the environment includes setting appropriate limits; keeping the facility free from structural, chemical, electrical, and other potential hazards; protecting children when they travel to and from the center; and keeping them from dangers created by near-by vehicular traffic.

Setting Limits for Children.   Children learn about themselves and the world around them by taking risks. But children need to be protected from hazards that put them into potentially harmful situations. It takes maturity for children to be able to identify the difference between a manageable risk and a dangerous hazard. That is why it is the adult's responsibility to protect children from danger.

The facility must, for example, have sturdy and reliable gates and fences that keep children away from traffic. Teachers must, on a day-to-day basis, assess the safety of their classrooms and keep, for example, small magnets away from children who might put them in their mouths.

It is best to have a limited number of rules that have been thoughtfully developed to protect the children you serve from hazards that may be present in your environment. As discussed in chapter 6, your environment should say "yes" to children's explorations, but you will inevitably need to set some limits to keep children safe. Rules should always be stated positively, emphasizing the desired behaviors rather than the prohibited ones. Say, for example, "Fences are to keep us safe. Climbing is fun. If you want to climb, play on the climbing wall."

Keeping Your Facility Safe.   Each program needs to establish safety policies and procedures to address their particular circumstances. They should develop a safety checklist based on their facility and establish a system of accountability so individual staff members are responsible for checking particular parts of the building. For example, who is responsible every day for making certain all doors are secured so children cannot wander off, and unauthorized individuals do not have access to your center? Checklists and systems of accountability are essential so you can be certain these tasks are done regularly.

We recommend that teachers be expected to check their classrooms at least weekly for hazards such as loose carpets that could be tripping hazards, broken furniture or toys, chipped paint, and missing outlet covers. Some repairs need to be made immediately; others can be corrected as part of the facility's routine maintenance.

The important thing is to have a system in place to be certain that issues needing attention are identified and addressed. This can be done by developing a checklist so individuals are accountable for keeping their rooms safe and identifying repairs that need to be made. Staff should also be expected to be continually alert to safety hazards and notify administrators of repairs that must be made immediately, or actions that should be taken to prevent children's contact with the hazard.

As the administrator you should also monitor the U.S. Consumer Product Safety Commission (CPSC) Web site listed at the end of this chapter. You also need to be alert to recalls publicized in the media. The CPSC recalls toys and equipment found to have defects that could harm or even kill consumers. For example, in recent years millions of toys have been recalled because they contained excessive levels of lead. Lead poisoning, which lowers intelligence, creates behavioral problems, and diminishes school performance has been reported in 1 of every 30 children in the United States (Lanphear, 2001).

By following the advice of the CPSC, you would be able to remove toys found to put children's health at risk. You should not only remove toys and materials identified as being defective or harmful, but you should also notify families when recalls might involve toys and materials they are likely to have in their homes.

Vehicular Safety

If your program transports children, there are a number of precautions you must take to keep children safe from harm. Staff eligible to drive children must:

- Have a valid driver's license for the vehicle they will be driving
- Provide evidence of a safe driving record
- Have no record of substance abuse, violent crimes, or child abuse or neglect
- Not have recently used alcohol or drugs (including prescribed and over-the-counter medications) that could impair their ability to drive safely

You should keep a record of "the driver's license number, vehicle insurance information and verification of current state vehicle inspection on file in the facility" (AAP et al., 2002, p. 60). All but four states address transportation in their child care licensing regulations (NARA/NCCIC, 2006). Standards typically address child-staff ratio, describe required supervision, and may require the vehicle be equipped with age-appropriate car seats.

Ammonia (for bee stings)
Antiseptic (solid packages)
Bandages (assorted sizes, including triangular and eye dressing)
Cash for emergencies
Cold pack
Container for carrying insect, plant, or spider specimens (for medical identification)
Cotton balls (for applying pressure)
Emergency information forms and medication for children with chronic problems
Eye irrigation solution
Facial tissues
First aid books and charts
Gauze (pads—2" × 2" and 4" × 4"; flexible roller gauze—1" and 2" widths)
Gloves (disposable latex)
Injury report forms (see Figure 10.9)
Insect sting bronchodilator inhaler or epinephrine kit (if needed by anyone in program) and
baking soda (to soothe insect stings and bites)
Notepad and pen/pencil
Plastic bags
Pocket mask for CPR
Safety pins
Scissors and tweezers
Soap (preferably liquid)
Splints (plastic or metal)
Tape (adhesive—1/2" and 1" widths)
Telephone numbers for emergency aid and local poison control center and cell phone
Thermometer (nonglass)
Towels (1 large and 1 small)
Water

Figure 10.8
Contents of First Aid Kit

Plan carefully for field trips that take children away from your carefully designed facility. Decide in advance where and how children will be loaded into vehicles and where they will be unloaded. There must be at least two adults with each group of children, but some trips will require closer supervision. Teachers should work with their director to determine how many extra adults are needed to safely take the children away from the center. Whenever children leave the school premises, teachers should take along children's emergency information blank injury report forms, a first aid kit (see Figure 10.8), and a cell phone.

Preparing for Emergencies

Emergencies occur even when early childhood programs take every possible precaution to protect children's health and safety. You should develop emergency procedures in advance and train all staff so they are familiar with the plans. Consider the following issues when developing emergency plans for your program:

1. Plan how you will evacuate the building in the event of a fire or explosion. Post exit routes and emergency procedures near or on exit doors. Have completed emergency information forms and class lists on a shelf by each exit door. Identify a designated meeting place to be certain everyone is accounted for. Conduct regular fire drills to practice these routines and to be certain everyone knows how to respond.

2. Identify where you will go if you must leave the premises and inform families of this evacuation location. Plan how you will notify families if the center needs to be evacuated.

3. Plan how you will protect children and notify families in the case of a natural disaster such as a tornado, flash flood, earthquake, or other emergency such as a chemical spill, terrorist attack, or other violent incident in your vicinity.

Have flashlights, a first aid kit (see Figure 10.8), a cell phone, a battery-operated radio, food and water, blankets, children's books, paper and crayons readily available nearby. Your local fire marshal and Homeland Security Office can help you make plans for these emergencies. Refer to the Web sites at the end of this chapter for specific recommendations.

Assessing Risks and Protecting Children.   Early childhood professionals must never become complacent about safety. Each staff member must learn to constantly assess current risks by considering what their children are doing, where they are doing it, and how specific children respond to different experiences. Remember, little things can be the difference between a safe environment and a dangerous one. Young children can drown in even a small amount of standing water, strings on jackets can get trapped on slides or climbing equipment and become choking hazards, an improperly closed door or gate may let children get into traffic or other hazards.

Professionals are expected to ensure children's safety. They need to be vigilant to avoid both acts of omission and acts of commission:

1. **Acts of omission:**   Adults fail to take precautionary measures needed to protect children (e.g., failure to inspect facility for safety, failure to supervise or provide adequate supervision)

2. **Acts of commission:**   Adults' actions or decisions put children at risk (e.g., taking a field trip even though several needed volunteers did not show up to accompany the children)

Directors can protect children and limit the center's liability by carefully writing job descriptions; being certain all staff have appropriate training in all areas of health and safety; maintaining appropriate records, especially accident reports; and securing liability insurance. Although safety management is challenging, creating a culture of acting responsibly can save lives and prevent accidents and injuries. When an accident occurs you will want to use an injury report form similar to the one in Figure 10.9 to gather the documentation you need.

Teaching Children to be Safe.   Everyday interactions are the best way to teach children how to protect their health and to be safe. Bus safety, for example, is a natural part of riding the bus; and kitchen safety will naturally be integrated into classroom cooking activities. These authentic experiences are more meaningful than educational programs such as "Eddie Eagle" designed to teach gun safety or "Stranger Danger" designed to warn children against talking to strangers (Himle, Miltenberger, Gatheridge, Flessner, 2004; McBride, n.d.). While these packaged programs have been shown to teach children what to *say,* they have proven to be minimally effective teaching them what to *do* in real-life circumstances. It is important to appreciate that ultimately adults, not children, are responsible for creating safe and healthy environments. Families and teachers should join together in their efforts to create safe environments for their children and their community.

Child's name _____

Birth date _____

Parent location information _____

_____

Child's physician _____

(Telephone) _____

- -

Injury

Date _____ Time _____

General description (e.g., bite, burn, cut) _____

_____

Where/how injury occurred _____

_____

Staff supervisor (at time of injury) _____

Other adult witnesses to the injury _____

_____

Action Taken

Child's apparent symptoms and reaction _____

_____

First Aid (if any)

Nature of _____

_____

Administered by _____

Assisted by _____

Medical Help Sought (if any)

From whom _____

Time of contact _____

Advice _____

Parent Contact

Attempts _____

Parent advice _____

Follow-up Care

Description _____

_____

Condition of Child at Time of Release

Description _____

_____

(Signature of person completing form)

Note: For quick reference and as a time saver, always have a form with information above the dotted line completed on each child.

Figure 10.9
Injury Report Form

SUMMARY

Providing for children's nutrition, health, and safety are essential ingredients of quality early childhood programs. Nutrition is very important for two reasons: (a) Early childhood programs are apt to provide up to 80% of a young child's total nutrition requirements during their formative early years, and (b) children develop lifelong attitudes and habits during early eating experiences. For these reasons teachers and caregivers of young children need to be informed about the nutritional requirements of young children, offer children nutritious foods, and create a relaxed and inviting environment at mealtimes and during snacks.

Health affects each area of development. An early childhood program's goals related to health include assessing the health status of staff members and children, advocating for preventive health care including a medical home for every child, communicating with families about their child's health, and serving as a resource to help families access the resources they may need.

Child safety includes planning a safe environment, preparing for emergencies, protecting children from injury, and promoting safety consciousness and education.

In short, nutrition, health, and safety are components of early care and education that require attention every day. They are on-going concerns for teachers, caregivers, and those in administrative positions.

Trends and issues related to health, safety, and nutrition include concern about the control of infectious diseases in early childhood programs, ensuring the safety of children at home and in out-of-home settings by being sure that the foods they eat, the toys they play with, and the facilities where they spend their days are free from toxic chemicals or other harmful additives. Many also identify the importance of ensuring each child access to health care their family can afford, beginning during their advocacy prenatal period, through their early childhood years.

USEFUL WEB SITES

Nutrition Resources

Interactive Nutrition Web sites

Body Mass Index (BMI) Calculator for Children and Teens at www.cdc.gov/nccdphp/dnpa/bmi/.

Interactive My Pyramid Plan that applies the food pyramid based on age, gender, and other information at

www.mypyramid.gov/mypyramid/index.aspx

Recommended Dietary Allowance (RDA) calculator at

www.dietandfitnesstoday.com/rda.php

Other Nutrition Resources

United States Department of Agriculture (USDA) Food Pyramid and Toddlers at

www.wholesometoddlerfood.com/pyramid.htm

U.S. Department of Agriculture Tips for Using the Food Guide Pyramid of Young Children 2 to 6 years old at

www.cnpp.usda.gov/Publications/MyPyramid/Original-FoodGuidePyramids/FGP4Kids/FGP4KidsTipsBook.pdf

USDA Healthy Meals Resource System

Click on information for child care providers. Topics include nutrition information, recipes, menu planning, and special diets. These areas are collections of materials from many agencies and institutions.

healthymeals.nal.usda.gov

The National Food Service Management Institute (NFSMI) This organization offers staff training in food service management and posts other resources on their Web site at

www.olemiss.edu/depts/nfsmi/index.html

For information on the operation of the National School Lunch Program and all the Child Nutrition Programs, contact the state agency responsible for the administration of the programs. A listing of all the state agencies may be found at the USDA Web site at

www.fns.usda.gov/

Select "School Meals." You may also contact the USDA School Lunch Program in your state by going to www.fns.usda.gov and clicking on "Contact us" and "Child Nutrition Services."

Health Resources

The National Resource Center for Health and Safety in Child Care and Early Education is a collaborative effort that brings together many organizations. They have developed two publications that are indispensable resources for program administrators. Both are available by following links found at

nrc.uchsc.edu/

1. *Caring for Our Children,* 2nd ed. is a comprehensive guide that includes 659 standards related to health and safety. See the appendices for sample Child Care Staff Health and Child Health Assessment forms, a Recommended Childhood Immunization Schedule, and other helpful information.
2. *Stepping Stones for Using Caring for Our Children* includes the 233 most critical standards. It includes just the standards without the rationales to keep the document a more manageable size.

The American Academy of Pediatrics (AAP) offers many resources for parents and early childhood educators. In collaboration with the Department of Health and Human Services, the Child Care Bureau, and the Maternal and Child Health Bureau. AAP sponsors the Healthy Child Care America Campaign at

www.healthychildcare.org

Safety Resources

The Consumer Product Safety Commission is a governmental agency that monitors the safety of consumer products. Recalls are posted continuously on its Web site at

www.cpsc.gov/

TO REFLECT

1. Some foods are difficult for "little hands" to handle. What are some reasonable things that teachers who are eating with young children, and even school-age children, can do to assist them at mealtime? Consider both meals that are provided at the center and lunches or snacks that children bring to the center.
2. You have just attended a workshop on nutrition and foods in early childhood programs. The presenter made the following points: (a) Providing nutritious meals and snacks is not enough, children have to eat the foods to get the benefits; and (b) children learn many things during meals and snacks. They learn, for example about good nutrition,

develop their vocabularies, have rich sensory experiences, develop good table manners, and so on. As a novice teacher, you are eager to implement all you've heard. However, your mentor colleague suggests that cooking activities can be overwhelming. What does the mentor mean? Who is right? Can teachable moments create stress?
3. As a director of a preschool program, you are writing a policy describing when children must be excluded because of illness, and when they can return. What criteria should you use to achieve the balance between a child's need to be cared for by a family member and the family member's need to meet the demands of a job?

11

ASSESSMENT: AN ESSENTIAL COMPONENT OF EFFECTIVE EARLY CHILDHOOD PROGRAMMING

NAEYC Administrator Competencies addressed in this chapter:

Management Knowledge and Skills

1. Personal and Professional Self-Awareness
   The ability to be a reflective practitioner and apply a repertoire of techniques to improve the level of personal fulfillment and professional job satisfaction.

Early Childhood Knowledge and Skills

3. Child Observation and Assessment
   Knowledge and application of developmentally appropriate child observation and assessment methods. Knowledge of the purposes, characteristics, and limitations of different assessment tools and techniques. Ability to use different observation techniques including formal and informal observation, behavior sampling, and developmental checklists. Knowledge of ethical practice as it relates to the use of assessment information. The ability to apply child observation and assessment data to planning and structuring developmentally appropriate instructional strategies.

Evaluation is the process of making judgments about the value or quality of outcomes achieved through the provision of services. **Assessment,** an essential component of the evaluation process, is a process through which professionals collect and analyze data to help gain an understanding of children's development and program effectiveness. By using assessment and evaluation information effectively, program directors can enhance program functioning as related to meeting the collective and individual needs of the children and families served through their programs. When assessment is conducted appropriately, the process is linked to program goals.

Assessment involves several different activities that coalesce to establish a method for systematically asking and then answering questions regarding individual child progress as well as collective program effectiveness in helping all children and families achieve desired outcomes.

This chapter presents four processes that will help facilitate the development of an effective assessment and evaluation plan for an existing center or one that is still in the planning stages. The processes described through this chapter include

1. Determining the need for and thus the purpose of assessment
2. Selecting assessment practices and identifying strategies for gathering evidence that are aligned with the stated purposes
3. Processing the information to permit evaluation and the formation of judgments
4. Making professional judgments, that is, using assessment results as a tool in the decision-making process

CALL FOR "RESPONSIBLE ASSESSMENT"

Professional reactions to high-stakes testing and calls for appropriate assessment began to emerge in the 1990s. The following professional associations have issued position statements supporting appropriate assessment:

American Educational Research Association (2000)

American Educational Research Association, American Psychological Association, & National Council on Measurement in Education (1999)

Association of Childhood Education International (1991)

Southern Early Childhood Association (1990/1996/2000)

National Association for the Education of Young Children & National Association of Early Childhood Specialists in State Departments of Education. (2007)

National Association of Early Childhood Specialists in State Departments of Education (2001)

National Association of School Psychologists (1999)

The NAEYC (2001) has called assessment that is ethically grounded and supported by sound professional standards *responsible assessment*. Some specific characteristics of responsible assessment are as follows:

1. The overall purpose of assessment is to benefit children and families, help teachers in their work, and aid the improvement of programs.
2. Assessment instruments and data use should be tailored to a specific purpose and be valid, reliable, and fair for that use.
3. Assessment practices should be collaborative. Teachers and families need to be involved in decisions about assessment practices.

4. Assessment needs to be "developmentally valid" (Meisels & Atkins-Burnett, 2000). To be developmentally valid, assessment practices must be
   a. Age and stage appropriate in content and method of collection
   b. Culturally and linguistically appropriate
   c. Adapted as needed
   d. Focused on children's strengths and best performances

5. Assessment must be closely connected or aligned with the goals of the local program. If appropriate, assessment practices will be
   a. Broad based (i.e., covering all domains of development and learning)
   b. Performance oriented
   c. Embedded in classroom activities
   d. Drawn from multiple sources over many points in time (Shepard, Kagan, & Wurtz, 1998b)

PURPOSES OF ASSESSMENT AND DOCUMENTATION

The purposes for which you will be using assessment information should inform all other aspects of your evaluation plan and the format of your documentation. Purposes will inform what is measured, how it is measured, and even the acceptable levels of validity and reliability (Shepard et al., 1998b).

According to the Joint Position Statement of the National Association for the Education of Young Children (NAEYC) and the National Association of Early Childhood Specialists in State Departments of Education (NAESC/SDE) adopted in 2003, assessment on children from birth through the primary grades should be guided by the ethics of the profession, informed by what is known to be age appropriate, and should play a central role in all early childhood programs. In the most recent Code of Ethics adopted by the NAEYC (2005) new elements were added specifically addressing the ethical use of assessment in early childhood settings.

There are two main purposes for which child care directors will use assessment and evaluation within their programs: (1) to promote children's development and learning and (2) evaluate program effectiveness.

Promoting Children's Development and Learning

Assessment and evaluation systems designed for the purpose of promoting children's learning and development include **formative assessment** and **developmental screening.** Formative assessment is used to

a. Determine a child's progress in attaining program goals and objectives
b. Serve as a tool in family–staff communication (e.g., families learn about the curriculum, appropriate expectations for children, and their child's performance in the program)
c. Improve the quality of the program by helping teachers determine what is working and not working

Through the identification of the aspects of a teacher's practice that is effective and those practices that are less effective, teachers can make better decisions regarding curriculum and teaching strategies that are appropriate for an individual child or an entire classroom of children. This might also lead a teacher to identify specific professional development topics he or she might need to make necessary improvements.

Developmental screening is another form of assessment that is essential in that it is a systematic tool that provides a quick snapshot of an individual child's development to help determine if a child should be referred to a specialist for further evaluation and/or diagnosis.

Effective assessment requires teachers to understand each child's performance through knowledge of child development, cultural and linguistic competencies, and age and grade expectations (i.e., know when a given response is precocious performance, expected performance, or below expected performance) (Bredekamp & Copple, 1997). **Validity** (the degree to which an assessment measures what is intended) and **reliability** (the accuracy of the assessment tool) can be achieved when teachers are well informed regarding the importance of objectivity and accuracy when assessing young children and when they collect assessment data using multiple strategies over various points in time (Grisham-Brown, Hemmeter, & Pretti-Frontczak, 2005; Shepard et al., 1998b).

The importance of collecting data to inform caregiver assessment and evaluation leads us to a brief discussion of authentic assessment and ways to document children's performance in the context of the children's daily lives in child care and education programs.

Authentic assessment and **documentation methods,** also called *performance assessment and documentation,* require the teacher to observe and document children's demonstration of what they know and what they can do; that is, they apply knowledge within the context of a real or simulated situation (Bergen, 1993/94; Meisels, Dorfman, & Steele, 1995). High-quality assessment of young children includes the following characteristics:

1. It is closely aligned with the learning goals identified by the program.
2. It is conducted in natural environments.
3. It uses multiple observation and documentation strategies.
4. It includes participation from multiple stakeholders (including families and other early childhood professionals) (Grisham-Brown, Hallam, and Brookshire, 2006; Grisham-Brown et al., 2005).

In essence, authentic assessment is the process of identifying desired results or learning objectives you hope that children will achieve and then looking for opportunities to

A key characteristic of authentic assessment is the collection of child created artifacts that demonstrate their knowledge and skills.

see the children demonstrate these competencies through their daily interaction with other children and their environment. When the children demonstrate these behaviors and skills, it is then the teacher's responsibility to document them.

Learning objectives that typically inform our authentic assessment of young children are often informed by state early learning standards (where they exist), program goals, family goals and values, and a general understanding of the typical developmental progression of young children. The next section provides a brief overview of strategies that are commonly used to authentically assess young children in early care and education programs.

Observations.   Observations entail systematically focusing on a child or small group of children to see their behavior, which will lead to an ability to make judgments of individual child competence. This is a fairly popular method of assessing young children's development and learning because it allows a caregiver to see what children are capable of doing as they play and interact with their peers. Other reasons for the popularity of observation may be the following factors:

1. A person can simultaneously work and observe children (regrettably, many look and do not see!).
2. Observations may be conducted by teachers as well as by researchers.
3. Observations may be conducted for long or short intervals of time.
4. Observations may be used in conjunction with any other assessment method.
5. Observations are suitable for use in any type of program because one child or a group of children may be observed and any aspect of development can be assessed.

Disadvantages in using observations for assessment are as follows:

1. The validity of observation depends on the skill of the observer.
2. The observer's biases are inherent in observations.
3. The soundness of observations may depend on the behaviors observed because some aspects of development (e.g., motor skills) are easier to observe than others (e.g., thinking processes).
4. When a person is simultaneously working with children and observing them, it can be difficult to "see the forest for the trees."

The purposes of the observations determine the method of observation and the recording system. Several popular methods of observing young children and some of the recording possibilities used by teachers (and researchers) are described in the following sections. Figure 11.1 illustrates how an anticipatory planning web can be used to plan for assessment and documentation.

Naturalistic Observations

Naturalistic observations are observations of a child engaged in regular day-to-day activities within the natural setting. These open-ended observations allow the child options that in turn permit the teacher (or researcher) to see the uniqueness of the child more clearly (Rhodes & Nathenson-Mejia, 1992). These researchers refer to it as a "story of an individual" (p. 503). However, biases occur in what we record.

Naturalistic observations may be recorded as an anecdotal record or a running record. An **anecdotal record** is a record of an incident in a child's life that occurred during participation in program activities or during a home visit. Characteristics of a good anecdote are as follows:

1. It gives the date, the place, and the situation in which the action occurred. This is called the *setting*.

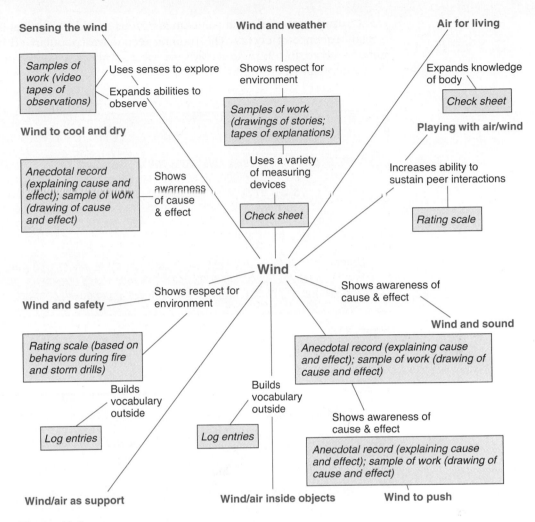

Figure 11.1
Assessment and Documentation Methods Included on Anticipatory Web (Review Figures 9.1 & 9.2)

2. It describes the actions of the child, the reactions of other people involved, and the responses of the child to these reactions.

3. It quotes what is said to the child and by the child during the action.

4. It supplies "mood cues"—postures, gestures, voice qualities, and facial expressions that give cues to how the child felt. It does not provide interpretations of the child's feelings but provides only the cues by which a reader may judge what the feelings were.

5. The description is extensive enough to cover the episode. The action or conversation is not left incomplete and unfinished but rather is described until a little vignette is created.

Below the narrative account, space should be left for comments. These comments may be interpretive (what the observer believes about the incident) and/or a written professional judgment (what the observer believes should be done to help the child developmentally). See an example of an anecdotal record in Figure 11.2.

A **running record** is similar to an anecdotal record except that it is more detailed with a total sequence of events. The running record was popularized by Piaget (1952). In a running record, the observer records everything without screening out any information. See the example in Figure 11.3.

Child's name: _Susie_   Date: _2/12/2008_

Setting: _Block center in a child care center: activity child-chosen. Incident: Susie was building a block tower. When the seven-block tower fell, she tried again. This time, she succeeded in getting only six blocks stacked before they fell. She kicked her blocks and walked over to John's nine-block tower and knocked it over. When the teacher approached, she cried and refused help with the tower. (John left the center after his tower was knocked over.)_

Comments: _Susie is showing more patience by rebuilding—a patience not seen last month. However, her crying and destructive responses are not as mature as they should be for a 5-year-old. She must be shown ways to cope with common frustrations._

Figure 11.2
Anecdotal Record of Behavior

Child's name: _Susie_   Date: _5/5/2008_

Setting: _Block center in a child care center: activity child-chosen._

	Incident	**Comments**
9:25	Susie watches three or four children play with the blocks.	Susie is interested in the blocks.
9:30	She calls to John, "What are you doing?" John replies, "I'm building a tall, tall building, the biggest one ever." Susie says, "I can build a big one."	She especially likes John's tower.
		Susie is apparently challenged.
9:31	Susie stacks seven blocks. They fall. (She counts the blocks in John's tower.) She again starts stacking blocks—with the sixth block, they fall.	Susie knows she almost got the same height tower again.
		Susie is willing to try again.
9:35	She kicks at her blocks three times and then walks over to John's tower and strikes it with her hand.	Her aggression spreads to John.
9:37	Mrs. Jones approaches Susie. Susie turns her back on Mrs. Jones and cries. Mrs. Jones kneels and talks to Susie. Then Mrs. Jones picks up a block, but Susie runs away.	She is not yet willing to be comforted or helped.
		Teacher's approach was calming—no more aggression.
	(John left the center earlier.)	

Figure 11.3
Running Record of Behavior

Structured Observations

Structured observations are structured in terms of either bringing children into planned environments (e.g., how infants react when a stranger is present and the mother is present and then absent) or identifying a specific defined behavior, observing it in the natural environment, and keeping quantitative records (e.g., Sarah had two biting episodes on Monday and one biting episode on Tuesday). Two types of structured observations are event sampling and time sampling.

Event sampling is a narrative of conditions preceding and following a specified behavior. For these observations, a behavior is preselected (called a *target behavior)*, defined very specifically, and then observed. To record, the observer usually knows when to expect the behavior (e.g., time of day, during a certain activity, in a certain grouping pattern, with a given adult). In event sampling, the observer is trying to confirm a hypothesis about what triggers the behavior. Thus, three items are recorded: (a) the antecedent behavior (what led to the target behavior); (b) the targeted behavior (complete description of the incident); and (c) the consequent event (reactions of the child, such as crying). Describing the event in detail is most important. See Figure 11.4.

Time sampling is tallying a specified behavior while it is occurring. In time sampling, a target behavior is preselected, carefully defined, and then observed at specified intervals. These time intervals may be preset at uniform time periods or at randomly selected time intervals. For discrete behaviors, a simple frequency tabulation is recorded. Several types of coding systems may be used (Irwin & Bushnell, 1980). The observer can write a narrative in addition to coding. See Figure 11.5. Other examples are given by Beaty (2002), Bentzen (2000), and Nilsen (2000).

Because the amount of writing is reduced, the observer can record observations on several children in one session by rotating observations in a predetermined and consistent manner among the children. Using the time periods in the example in Figure 11.5, Child A would be observed during the first minute of each time frame—9:00 to 9:01, 9:05 to 9:06, and so on; Child B would be observed during the second minute of each time frame—9:01 to 9:02, 9:06 to 9:07, and so on; and in a similar way, three other children would be observed.

| Child's name: | Mike | Date: | 2/1/2004 |

Behavior: *Biting a child on exposed skin areas*

Time	Antecedent	Behavior	Consequent Event
8:00	Children eating breakfast as they arrive. Ann has finished breakfast but takes a piece of apple off Mike's plate	Mike tries to get it back. When unsuccessful, he bites Ann's hand.	Ann cries, and Mike calls out, "I didn't bite."

NOTE: Other behaviors are recorded as they occur.

Figure 11.4
Event Sampling Behavior Record

Child's name: _____   Date: _____

Target Behavior: *Types of interaction in the housekeeping center.*

	Time 1	Time 2	Time 3	Time 4	Time 5
	9:00	9:05	9:10	9:15	9:20
	V+	V+	NV–	V–	0

V = verbal interaction
NV = nonverbal interaction
0 = no interaction
+ = positive
– = negative

Figure 11.5
Time-Sampling Behavior Record

Child's name: _____   Date: _____

Behavior: Wandering from center to center. (Child stays less than 2 minutes at an activity in one "stretch.")

Days	Time	Subtotal	Total
1	9:04–9:08	4	
	9:12–9:13	1	5
2	9:01–9:04	3	3
3	9:04–9:07	3	
	9:13–9:15	2	5
4	9:01–9:05	4	
	9:12–9:13	1	5
5	9:02–9:07	5	
	9:10–9:11	1	6

Average: 4.8 minutes per day

Figure 11.6
Duration Record of Behavior

For nondiscrete behaviors (e.g., crying, clinging to adult, wandering around the room), the length of occurrence or duration is often recorded (see the example in Figure 11.6). Both frequency and duration recordings may be summarized in graphs, which give visual representations. Even two complementary behaviors may be plotted on the same graph for a better picture of a child (e.g., daily totals of aggressive and sharing acts).

Interviews.   Interviews with families are now used with greater frequency in early childhood programs. The interview method permits a more comprehensive picture of the child's life at home and with peer groups. The *interview method of assessment* generally has the following characteristics:

• Questions used in an interview are usually developed in collaboration with staff and center administration.

- Family members of the child are usually interviewed; others familiar with the child are occasionally interviewed.
- Specific questions in the interview commonly include background information about the child and sometimes the family. Interview data help in assessing needs and potential program services.

Advantages of the interview as an assessment technique are as follows:

- Valuable information—both verbal and emotional—may be gleaned.
- Interviews can be used in conjunction with other assessment methods.
- Interviews are suitable for use in any type of early childhood program.
- Interviews can help clarify and extend the information found on written forms.

The interview method also has disadvantages:

- The information obtained may not be comprehensive or accurate because the questions were unclear or not comprehensive or because the interviewee was unable or unwilling to answer.
- The interviewee's and interviewer's biases are entwined in the information given and in the interpretation of the information, respectively.
- The interview method is very time consuming.

Samples of Children's Work.   Collecting artifacts that illustrate children's knowledge and skill is a particularly informative strategy to gather data for assessment purposes. Samples of children's work serve as an excellent authentic method of assessment if they meet the following criteria:

- Samples of various types of children's work should be collected: dictated or tape-recorded experiences told by children; drawings, paintings, and other two-dimensional art projects; photographs of children's projects (e.g., three-dimensional art projects, block constructions, a completed science experiment); tape recordings of singing or language activities; and videotapes of any action activities.
- Samples are collected on a systematic and periodic basis.
- Samples are dated, with notes on the children's comments and attitudes.
- A systematic method of organizing children's work is established and aligns with program goals and objectives.

Advantages to using samples of children's work as an assessment technique are as follows:

- The evidence is a collection of children's real, ongoing activities or products of activities and not a contrived experience for purposes of assessment.
- Collecting samples is not highly time consuming.
- Collecting samples works for all aspects of all programs.
- Samples can be used as direct evidence of progress.
- If samples are dated and adequate notes are taken about them, interpretations can be made later by various people.
- Some samples can be analyzed for feelings as well as for concepts.
- Samples can be used in conjunction with other assessment methods.

Disadvantages of using samples of children's work are as follows:

- Samples may not be representative of children's work.
- Samples of ongoing activities are more difficult to obtain than two-dimensional artwork.
- Some children do not like to part with their work.

- Storage can be a problem (although, with advances in technology this may become less of an issue in the future as we are better able to collect video and photographs of children's work through the use of digital cameras).
- Photographs, magnetic tapes, and videotapes are relatively expensive.

Tools for Structuring Authentic Assessments

Although authentic assessment resolves the conflict between program goals and what is measured, a gap does exist between idealized portrayal of authentic assessment and its implementation. Teachers need a framework for systematically collecting and documenting children's performance aligned with program goals. Such a framework allows assessment to be worthwhile for promoting children's learning and development and to be understood by family members and policy makers.

Over the years, several assessment tools have been developed to guide teachers in the collection and analysis of authentic assessment information. Because researchers have identified the important constructs of children's learning and development, the tools mesh assessment procedures with the educational goals of many quality early childhood programs. Both tools provide a comprehensive picture of how the child is performing in the program and thus allow teachers to connect assessment results to decision making about curriculum content and teaching strategies. This family of assessment tools is commonly referred to as curriculum-based measures; as such they focus on demonstrated knowledge and skill achievement.

High/Scope Child Observation Record (COR).   The Infant Toddler Child Observation Record (High/Scope Educational Research Foundation, 2001) and the Revised Preschool Child Observation Record (High/Scope Educational Research Foundation, 2002) are used to assess children from birth to age 6. While these were developed specifically to align with the High/Scope curriculum, the developers report that this assessment can be used in most developmentally appropriate early childhood care and education programs.

Using notes taken over several months that describe episodes of a child's behavior in six COR categories (initiative, creative representation, social relations, music and movement, language and literacy, and logic and mathematics), the teacher rates the child's behavior on 28 (Infant and Toddler) and 32 (Preschool) five-level COR items. Teachers score the COR two or three times each year, with the initial ratings given after children have been in the program 6 to 8 weeks.

The Work Sampling System.   The Work Sampling System (Meisels et al., 1994) is a performance assessment system designed for children from preschool through Grade 5. The approach is used to assess and document children's skills, knowledge, behavior, and accomplishments in seven domains (personal/social development, language and literacy, mathematical thinking, scientific thinking, social studies, the arts, and physical development) performed on multiple occasions. The Work Sampling System comprises the following components: developmental guidelines and checklists, portfolios of children's work, and summary reports completed by teachers. Assessment takes place three times a year.

Creative Curriculum Developmental Continuum.   Trister-Dodge, Colker, and Heroman (2003) have developed a curriculum-based assessment tool aligned with the goals and intended outcomes of the *Creative Curriculum.* This tool is organized to evaluate children's development in four domains (social/emotional, physical, cognitive, and language) which are addressed through 50 items (Lambert, 2003). While, as designed, the developmental continuum evaluation is completed three times annually, teachers and caregivers are encouraged to collect artifacts and observation notes to document children's development continually.

Assessment, Evaluation, and Programming System for Infants and Children (2nd Edition).   This assessment, edited by Diane Bricker (2002) is designed as a comprehensive system to link assessment with the daily planning to help facilitate optimal development of children. This tool spans from birth to age 6 covering six developmental domains (fine motor, gross motor, adaptive, cognative, social-communication, and social). This assessment is in the form of a rating checklist and allows the caregiver to identify the child's level of performance. This tool is designed to be used either during naturalistic observation of children, but if time is limited, also suggests small group engagements that would allow the caregiver to complete the assessment of several children in a relatively short period of time (over a couple of days).

Identifying Children Needing Additional Intervention Services

The identification of children needing additional intervention services is a two-stage process. The first stage, usually called **screening,** involves a brief assessment to determine whether referral for more in-depth assessment is needed. The second stage, usually called **diagnostic assessment,** consists of a more complete assessment. If the child is identified as needing intervention, special plans are made.

Screening Assessments.   Developmental screening is the first step in an assessment/ intervention process (Nuttall, Romero, & Kalesnik, 1999). Screening is performed individually on large numbers of children and can be done by nonspecialists (general education teachers/caregivers or parents). Since the intent of a screening test is to determine only if further evaluation is warranted, results should be interpreted with care, and neither child placement decisions nor major program decisions should be made based on their results. Screening tests must be valid for the purpose with which they are used and reliable (Meisels & Atkins-Burnett, 1994).

Diagnostic Assessments.   According to federal law, diagnostic assessments, administered following screening, must be conducted in a team setting that uses multiple sources of assessment data and must be a part of a system of intervention services. Diagnostic assessments should consider the child's biology, interactions with others, and patterns of cultural and linguistic environment (Greenspan & Weider, 1998). These criteria should be rigorously used to prevent children from being misclassified and receiving intervention that do not meet their needs (Burnette, 1998). Although diagnostic assessment data are used to create IFSPs and IEPs, monitoring the provision and effectiveness of services is a must.

Determining Program Effectiveness and Making Policy Decisions

Assessment designed for the purpose of determining program effectiveness and making policy decisions is called **summative assessment.** More specifically, summative assessment is the evaluative process that is used to determine the effectiveness of curriculum and methodology and to provide a product measurement (i.e., a judgment about the overall worth of a program). Program evaluation permits the planning of additions to or revisions of services and even determines changes in program rationale. It is the responsibility of the program administrator to identify a systematic process for continuously evaluating the effectiveness of the program.

For the purposes of program evaluation, the assessment system should include information from all clients being served, which might include families, teachers, community members, and children. The process of program evaluation must also include objective information regarding the extent to which a program is meeting its goals. This might include systematically compiling classroom-level assessment information to determine the extent to which all children's learning goals are being achieved. In this way, caregivers' assessment of individual children's learning will be summarized by classroom teachers and reviewed. Through this analysis process, the program director will identify goals that are not consistently being met and then engage in the process of identifying ways to strengthen the program to address these needs.

Since the mid-1990s, a shift toward summative evaluation has occurred. Researchers are looking at the results of quality early childhood programs (Council of Chief State School Officers, 1995; Schorr, 1994). Information about the connection between effective services and desired outcomes for young children and their families can assist in holding decision makers accountable for investing in quality early childhood programs and meeting specified outcomes (Kagan, Rosenkoetter, & Cohen, 1997). However, high-stakes testing is not beneficial for informing individual center or programmatic changes (NRC, 1997, 1999). Damage is not distributed equitably across the population because the vast majority who fail the tests are poor, minority, and male (Meisels & Atkins-Burnett, 2000).

For purposes of determining program effectiveness and making policy decisions, children, teachers, and schools are increasingly measured through standardized achievement tests (this is particularly true for publicly funded educational services). Unfortunately, when used in isolation, this tool is essentially meaningless. While a global report of children's performance might be helpful in determining the extent to which children achieved academic outcomes, this information doesn't provide authentic information regarding an individual child's knowledge and skill.

Description of Standardized Tests.   **Standardized tests** can be thought of as tests developed by people familiar with test construction and as more formal assessment devices than authentic assessments. This form of assessment can be useful when used in conjunction with authentic data collection and analysis, but when used in isolation it is not particularly informative. Standardized tests have the following characteristics:

1. Specific directions for administering the test are stated in detail, usually including even the exact words to be used by the examiner in giving instructions and specifying exact time limits. By following the directions, teachers and counselors in many schools can administer the test in essentially the same way.

2. Specific directions are provided for scoring. Usually, a scoring key is supplied that reduces scoring to merely comparing answers with the key; little or nothing is left to the judgment of the scorer. Sometimes, carefully selected samples are provided with which a student's product is to be compared.

3. Quantitative data are usually supplied to aid in interpreting the part and composite scores. Generally, the test is referred to as a **criterion-referenced measure** (a measure in which a person's behavior is interpreted by comparing it with a preselected or established standard or criterion of performance) or a **norm-referenced measure** (a measure in which a person's behavior is interpreted against the behavior of others—one would hope, but not always—of similar backgrounds on the same testing instrument).

4. Information needed for judging the value of the test is provided. Before the test becomes available for purchase, research is conducted to study its reliability and validity.

5. A manual that explains the purposes and uses of the test is supplied. The manual describes briefly how the test was constructed; provides specific directions for administering, scoring, and interpreting results; contains tables of norms; and provides a summary of available research data on the test.

Concerns About Standardized Assessment Practices.   With the explosion of standardized tests and testing, professionals, especially those in the holistic/developmental camp, became vocal concerning how some assessment uses and practices have the potential for doing harm. The following recent concerns should be taken seriously by early childhood program directors:

1. The assessment instrument may not match the program's rationale. One of the greatest dangers is that assessment itself can determine a program rather than a program determining the how and why of assessment. It is almost as though the cart is placed before the horse. For example, some program planners take the content of standardized tests and plan activities to teach these items. Teaching to a test encourages a narrow academic program (Peel & McCary, 1997). "Curriculum based on tests is narrow and fails to embed knowledge in meaningful contexts, thus making it virtually unusable for the learner" (Bowman, 1990, p. 30).

Warnings that standardized tests are altering the curriculum continue to be given (Dahlberg & Asen, 1994). Kohn (2000) stated that when high-stakes testing is employed, instruction becomes less DAP. He explained that important practices and policies (e.g., caring communities, emergent curriculum) are threatened by "top-down, heavy-handed, corporate-style, standardized version of school reform that is driven by testing" (Kohn, 2001, p. 20). The order should be reversed. A program should be rationally planned and based on current and accurate information about children; tests should be selected to fit the program's goals and objectives.

2. Tests may not meet the standards given in the current editions of reference books providing technical qualities of tests (e.g., acceptable levels of validity and reliability, statistics appropriate to the program's purpose, lack of inherent cultural and linguistic biases; NRC, 1999). The psychometric quality of most standardized measures designed for young children has been and continues to be inadequate (Langhorst, 1989). Scoring errors can also occur (Meisels & Atkins-Burnnett, 2000).

3. Testing can be stressful and/or inappropriate for all those involved.

   a. Testing may be stressful for children (Charlesworth, Hart, Burts, & DeWolf, 1993; Greenspan & Weider, 1998). Testing itself is always a problem with young children because young children do not have a repertoire of test-taking skills. Some of the problems these children have are inadequate motor skills for taking paper-and-pencil tests; short attention spans; problems in following directions; and the problem of being influenced by the tester, the physical setting, or both. Staff need to be aware of children's feelings.

   b. Family members are also under a great deal of stress. Many families are apprehensive of decisions based on testing and on labels that may be placed on their children if "inadequacies" are noted. Placement and retention decisions should not be based on data from one assessment source. Stiggins (1991) referred to this use of tests as the "ultimate sorting tool" (p. 2). Darling-Hammond and Falk (1997) stated that retention is not appropriate if children do not learn the material when it is first taught.

   c. Teachers are under stress when testing is the predominant indicator of teachers' accountability. Regrettably, this situation has led to teachers' basing their curriculum on certain tests and, in some instances, teaching the test items themselves, helping children with the answers during the testing session, and even tampering with recorded responses.

   d. Directors of programs are often stressed, too. Testing drains learning time and funds. Some school systems and states use aggregate scores as a way of comparing schools. Standardized tests are designed to produce variances. Thus, statistically, some children and some schools will fall at the lower end of the performance range. High scores are most often correlated with high family incomes.

Position Statements on Standardized Testing.   As discussed, various professional associations issued strong statements about standardized testing because of these concerns in assessment practices. The goal is not to prohibit all standardized testing but for early childhood directors to recognize the following:

1. Assessment instruments should be used only for their intended purposes.
2. Assessment instruments should meet acceptable levels of quality (e.g., validity, reliability).
3. Placement and retention decisions should be made from multiple sources of data.
4. Assessment instruments should be used only if children will benefit and the benefit does not come from reduced group variation. (Schools must be more adaptive to normal variance.)

Shepard (1994) added two principles to the NAEYC's guiding principle of assessment—that any assessment practice should benefit children or else it should not be conducted: (a) "the contents of assessments should reflect and model progress toward important learning goals" (p. 208), and (b) the methods of assessment must be developmentally appropriate.

To understand how these principles are applied, 30 questions for program administrators to affirm in making assessment decisions were included in the position statement of the National Association for the Education of Young Children and the National Association of Early Childhood Specialists in State Departments of Education (2003).

Shepard and colleagues (1998b) stated that if standardized testing is mandated, early childhood programs should make efforts to use sampling methods rather than subject all children to testing. For example, the use of *matrix sampling,* a statistical technique whereby each child takes only part of the test, is helpful because the method lessens the testing burden on each child and makes it impossible to use individual scores to make high-stakes decisions. They stated, "Before age eight, standardized achievement measures are not sufficiently accurate to be used for high-stakes decisions about individual children and schools" (p. 53). Kohn (2001) suggested various short-term and long-term responses to the current assessment situation.

RECORDING

Record keeping, the documentation of assessment, has always been an important aspect of a staff member's duties; today, record keeping is becoming even more important and prevalent. Many advantages come from record keeping, such as the following:

1. Teachers who document children's learning make more productive planning decisions; documentation informs teaching.

2. Records can help staff see each child's progress. Staff who work daily with a child may better see progress through a review of the records. By documenting, the teacher can tell whether expected skills and concepts are emerging as they should or whether significant lags without progress are occurring in which specialized professional assistance may be needed. Through records, specialists can determine whether a problem is transient or continuous, when a problem began, and how pervasive its effects are on the child's development. On the basis of the evidence found in the records, specialists can suggest possible solutions to the problem. Good records also permit the independent assessment of a child by more than one person.

3. Documentation communicates to children that their learning is important. Thus, children become more evaluative of their own work. They can see their own progress in records—especially in collected, dated, and sequenced samples of work.

4. Documentation is needed because of greater involvement with families. Records can be used as a basis for discussions with family members.

5. Records are also beneficial to a child who changes programs frequently. Records of a recently transferred child make it easier for staff to assist the child in the new situation.

6. Because funding agencies, citizens' groups, boards of directors or school boards, and parents often require "proof" of the early childhood program's effectiveness in meeting its goals, the evidence is often best demonstrated by the records that have been kept. The local program's regulatory agency requires various records as a basis for subsequent funding.

7. Records also help teachers see the results of new teaching techniques or services. Records can also be used as data for research.

Possible disadvantages to record keeping are as follows:

1. A staff member can spend more time keeping records than planning and working with children.
2. A staff member can make a prejudgment based on records and become positively or negatively biased toward a child.
3. Because of the requirements of the Family Educational Rights and Privacy Act, staff need special training in developing accurate, appropriate, and relevant records and in developing record protection and handling procedures.
4. Record keeping may become a meaningless activity because the types of data required to be kept may not be congruent with the goals of the local program or because records may be filed and forgotten or may not be used effectively.

Computers are helping programs overcome some of these problems. For example, microcomputers can store information, maintain and generate files, and ensure privacy of records (by coding the computer so that only specified people have access to certain parts of a child's file). Producers of software have noted teachers' needs for quick and accurate record keeping.

Types of Records

Records may be classified in many ways. For purposes of this book, we classify records as background information records, performance records, referral records, and summary records.

Background Information Records.   **Background information records** include information gathered from various sources outside the local program. Early childhood professionals are realizing that early experiences in the home and neighborhood and previous early childhood program (or school) experiences provide important "pictures" of a child. Many programs now ask for considerable information from families. Sometimes, these records are supplemented by additional information obtained by a caseworker or specialist or are volunteered at a later date by the family members or the child.

Basic information about a child and the child's family is always part of background information records, including the child's legal name, home address, and telephone number; birth date, birthplace, and birth certificate number; number of siblings; and parents' or guardians' legal names, home address and telephone number, occupation(s), place(s) of business, and business telephone number(s).

Medical information is also included in the background information records, and completion of medical information records is required before a child is admitted to a program.

Finally, records on the child's personal and social history are frequently included as part of the background information records. This information may be supplied by a family member or by another adult who knows the child. Family members may record the information on forms, or a staff member may record the information during an interview. The child's personal and social history is likely to include information about

- Birth history (birth weight, problems associated with birth, or birth defects)
- Self-reliance
- Development, especially affective development and motor skills
- Previous experiences that aid concept development, such as places the child has visited in the community, trips taken beyond the community, and previous group experiences
- Problems, such as disabilities and illnesses, fears, and accident proneness
- Interests, such as television programs, computers, books, toys, pets, and games

Occasionally, questions are asked about the family situation, family relationships, and family member attitudes. Questions may also encompass family income, housing, occupations, educational level, aspirations for their children, and views of child rearing, including guidance methods family members have found to be effective. Martin (1998) provided an example of such a questionnaire.

Performance Records.   Performance records include any documentation regarding children's development and learning. A given performance record may be used as an entity, such as a composite score on an achievement test. Conversely, a performance record may be used as a professional note, such as an anecdotal record, contributing only one piece to the child's blueprint.

Most early childhood programs keep performance records, and these records are mandated in many programs. The contents of performance records differ according to the goals of the local program. In traditional early childhood programs, professionals want to assess knowledge, skills, dispositions, and certain affective expressions in all domains and in many contexts. These programs find authentic assessment techniques and the performance records generated from these techniques compatible with their beliefs.

Performance records take several forms. The chosen form depends on the nature of the observation. For example, if a teacher wants to assess whether a child can name certain colors, a check sheet makes a more appropriate record than a rating scale. Conversely, a social competence, such as "getting along with others," exists on a continuum and thus is better described by using a record that has a continuum format, such as a rating scale. Common forms of performance records include the following:

1.   Log entries are short, dated notes. A single entry may not be significant, but multiple entries in one area of development spanning weeks and months often provide useful information. Many teachers find it easier to write logs on several children (and possibly in several domains) on pages that have been divided into eight rectangles or on pages of white, adhesive labels. (The log notes will measure approximately 1 1/2" to 2 3/4" × 4".) Each note or label is then transferred to an individual child's record sheet devoted to a specific domain of development (see Figure 11.7). The COR uses log entries (High/Scope Educational Foundation, 2002).

2.   Anecdotes often give more information than logs. Similar to a series of log entries, a series of well-written anecdotes in one domain can reveal patterns of development. As previously discussed, a running record is an even more thorough account of performance. Figure 11.8 is an example of an anecdotal record.

3.   A checklist is a prepared list of behaviors based on program goals. The teacher simply indicates the presence or absence of these behaviors in a child. Dating (rather than merely checking) observed behaviors provides more information. Check sheets may be completed while actually observing children because information can be recorded rather

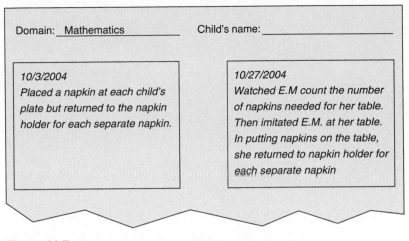

Domain: __Mathematics__   Child's name: _____

10/3/2004
Placed a napkin at each child's plate but returned to the napkin holder for each separate napkin.

10/27/2004
Watched E.M count the number of napkins needed for her table. Then imitated E.M. at her table. In putting napkins on the table, she returned to napkin holder for each separate napkin

Figure 11.7
Individual Child's Log Entries

Sept. 27 Tim and two other boys (Stefan and Binh) were in the sandbox using dump trucks for hauling sand. Stefan remarked that his lot needed more sand than the lot to which they had just delivered one dump-truck load. Tim looked and asked, "How much more sand?" "Twice as much," replied Stefan. "Then I'll drive my truck up once and give them a load and come back for one more load of sand," Tim commented.

Figure 11.8
Anecdotal Record

quickly, or check sheets with more summary types of statements (e.g., "Uses physical one-to-one correspondence") can come from narrative records, such as a series of log entries. Some records, called *checklists* by some professionals, are really more like rating scales because teachers are given the behavioral descriptors and then are asked to check on a continuum (e.g., "no evidence, beginning, developing, or very secure"). An example of a checklist in shown in Figure 11.9.

4. **Ratings** assess the quality of an attribute with the judgment indicated on a quality-point scale. Only behaviors that can be described according to the degree to which the competence or trait exists can be recorded on rating scales. Judgments are based on either observations or impressions; thus, the validity of rating scales is based mainly on the adequacy of the observations. Three popular rating scales are as follows:

    a. **Forced-choice.**   Observers must choose among predetermined (spelled-out) behaviors on a continuum (see Figure 11.10).

    b. **Semantic differential.**   The observer is given descriptions of the two extremes, which are opposites on the continuum. The observer chooses any marked point between the extremes. Often, the number of points between the extremes (see Figure 11.11) is an odd number (3, 5, 7, or 9).

    c. **Numerical.**   Numerical scales use numerals on a continuum (often 1–3, 1–4, or 1–5). Each numeral may be verbally described, or only certain numerals may be described (e.g., endpoints or endpoints and middle numerals; see Figure 11.12). Other examples of rating scales used in early childhood programs are given by Beaty (2002), Martin (1998), Nicholson and Shipstead (2002), and Nilsen (2000).

_____
(Child's name)

Art Concepts

Can recognize these colors: red   _____

yellow   _____

blue   _____

green   _____

orange   _____

purple   _____

black   _____

brown   _____

Can arrange four varying grades
of sandpaper from rough to smooth.   _____

Can name the colors and point to
rough and smooth fruit in a
reproduction of Cezanne's painting
Apples and Oranges.   _____

Figure 11.9
Checklist

_____
(Child's name)

1. Can put on his or her outdoor clothes

Not   Sometimes   Always
Yet

Figure 11.10
Forced-Choice Rating Scale

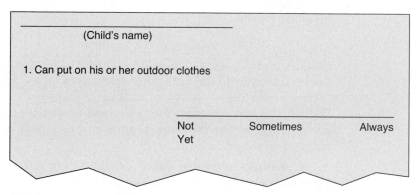

_____ can be seen as
(Child's name)

Happy — — — — — — — — — Sad
Active — — — — — — — — — Passive

Figure 11.11
Semantic Differential Rating Scale

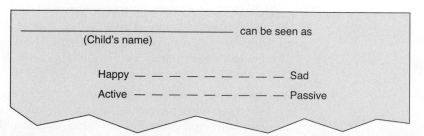

```
   _____
        (Child's name)


1. Motor skills can best be described as:

                              1 = Poor skill < — — — — —> 5 = Excels in skill

      hops                        1      2      3      4      5

      skips                       1      2      3      4      5

      climbs steps (ascending)    1      2      3      4      5
```

Figure 11.12
Numerical Rating Scale

5. Samples of children's work. Samples of children's work can take many forms. Common samples are drawings and paintings and papers showing language and mathematics skills. Less common but very important samples are (a) pictures of three-dimensional art products, block structures, and even two-dimensional materials too large to keep easily; (b) printouts from computer work; (c) audiotapes of verbal performances; and (d) videotapes of other performances (e.g., motor skills, interactions with others in the program). Helm, Beneke, and Steinheimer (1998) and Nilsen (2000) provided many ideas for documenting samples of children's work.

6. Test scores and diagnostic profile information. These records are often raw or converted scores or other graphic or descriptive information coming from performance on staff-constructed or standardized instruments.

Referral Records. All early childhood programs that employ specialists to work with children who need unique assistance need **referral records.** Specialists hired as full-time staff or as part-time consultants may include medical professionals, psychometrists, counselors, speech pathologists, and physical therapists. If the program does not employ specialists for support services, the director should develop a community resource directory. In some cases, a directory may be available through the local Chamber of Commerce, the United Fund, the Community Council, or the state's Department of Social Services.

Directors who must compile their own file of community resources should include in each description the basic service: whether it is physical health, mental health, or recreation; the name of the agency, its address, and telephone number; the days and hours of operation; and a detailed explanation of the services it provides, eligibility requirements, and the name of the person to contact.

The contents of referral records must be in keeping with the law. Local early childhood programs should develop a separate referral form for each type of referral (different forms for referral to medical specialists, speech pathologists, and so forth). The items on each form differ, but each type should include

- The signed permission for referral from a parent or legal guardian
- The date and the person or agency to which the referral is being made
- The name of the staff member referring the child
- The specific reasons for the referral
- Either a digest of or the complete reports from other referrals
- The comments or attitudes of family members, peers, or the child him- or herself if they are available

- The length of time the staff member has been aware of the problem
- What staff or family members have tried and with what success

Many referral records allow space for the specialist's report after assessment and support services are provided.

Summary Records.   **Summary records** are records that summarize and interpret primary data. No new information is added, but primary data are studied and interpreted. Background information records and referral records, on the one hand, are kept intact and updated but are rarely summarized. Performance records, on the other hand, written or collected by using various formats and encompassing a length of time, must be reviewed and reduced to a summary format in order to analyze them for either formative or summative purposes.

Summary records are completed several times a year to aid teachers in better understanding each child's progress and interests for the purposes of curriculum planning and communicating with families. Summary records are used to abstract aggregate data (with individual children's identification removed) for aiding program directors in their periodic reports to their funding or sponsoring agencies.

Thus, summary performance records often use broad descriptors of behavior, such as "Likes to write" or "Knows that print is read left to right and top to bottom." These summary statements can be developed from the program's goals for children's development and learning in each domain. Roskos and Neuman (1994) gave an example of this type of summary record.

In a way, check sheets and report cards given to parents are also summary records. Other summary instruments, designed to assess many domains, are called *developmental assessment systems* (discussed in detail by Cohen, Stern, and Balaban, 1997). The Work Sampling System (Meisels et al., 1994) uses summary records.

Record Collections

Most family child care programs and small child care centers have not kept any record collections. Public school programs have kept cumulative records on children from entrance to graduation. Head Start and other government-funded programs keep records on children from year to year. The most common type of record collection is the cumulative record. The portfolio is now becoming a recommended method for documentation collection.

Cumulative Records.   A **cumulative record,** a summary record of the entire school career, was often reduced to a card the size of a file folder. The cumulative record was limited to the child's name, birth date, and birth certificate number; parents' or guardians name's and addresses; the child's immunization records; and each year's attendance record, summary grades, standardized test information, and a digest of any major actions taken by the school or family (e.g., referrals). Many university-sponsored child study and teacher training programs and some government- and foundation-supported early childhood programs have kept voluminous records on young children's growth and development.

Portfolios.   Danielson and Abrutyn (1997) identified three types of portfolios:

1. **Display portfolios** are photographs and general descriptions of what children do in the classroom, but these portfolios do not focus on an individual child.
2. **Showcase portfolios** show an individual child's best work; however, because the work is only the "best" work, the portfolio may not be an accurate picture of that child.

3. **Working portfolios** show the individual child's process of learning skills and concepts; evidence of typical work with both the strengths and weaknesses is included, with all samples clearly connected to program goals.

In this text, the **portfolio,** defined as a method of gathering and organizing evidence of a child's interests, skills, concepts, and dispositions over time with documentation clearly connected to program goals, is a summary record. Thus, the text definition fits Danielson and Abrutyn's definition of a working portfolio. Most programs will use both **process portfolios** (several items collected to document each goal) and **archival portfolios** (final item or items put in the portfolio) for each predetermined sampling date (e.g., September, January, and April).

Constructing a portfolio involves the following steps:

1. Plan with all staff members the types of data that can document specific criteria being used as the learning goals of the local program. Each child's work sample may be different because children can demonstrate their understandings and skills in many ways. A chart could be made of program goals, typical activities, and types of authentic assessment samples that would fit each type of activity. Some excellent samples were suggested by Trister-Dodge, Colker, and Heroman (2003) and Meisels, Dichtelmiller, Jablon, Dorfman, and Marsden (1997). A general listing of types of contents for working portfolios is given in Figure 11.13. Samples and documentation should come from many sources, including teachers and other professionals, family members, and the children (who should be encouraged to select some of the items).

Background information
Health information
Teacher observations
    Logs, anecdotal records, running records, etc.
    Check sheets
    Rating scales
    Samples of child's work, such as writing,
        drawing, painting, scissor work,
        audiotapes (storytelling, show and tell, etc.),
        videotapes (projects, gross-motor activities, fine-motor activities,
        dramatic play, etc.), and photos (artwork—especially 3-D, block
        building structures, etc.)
Test scores
Activity chart (shows centers child chose)
Interviews with child
Parent information
    Parents' observations
    Parent–teacher and parent–teacher–child conference summaries
    Parent questionnaires
    Parent notes

Figure 11.13
Contents of Working Portfolios

2. Document each item collected. Collection alone is not enough. The documentation should contain the date, whether the child worked independently or with others, and the amount of work required. Gronlund (1998) offered an example of a Portfolio Documentation Checklist (p. 6), which saves time documenting each item.

3. Decide how frequently samples should be taken. Samples are often taken in September (baseline documentation), January, and April.

4. Identify criteria for judging samples as evidence that children are progressing toward goals. For example, neatness of handwriting should not be a criterion of creative writing.

5. Decide how the portfolios will be used. A portfolio from the previous year with the name and other identifying information removed can be used to explain the working portfolio to family members, teachers, and board members: Portfolios can be used in conjunction with family–teacher–child conferences: A few pages of the portfolio can be removed and sent to the family member along with a note for families not attending conferences or for nonconference times (the pages are to be returned). Portfolios can be sent to the next teacher and can also be used to prepare various reporting documents.

6. Decide how both a process and an archival portfolio will be "housed." Process portfolio materials are initial records usually kept in several folders or an expandable file folder with about 12 pockets for each child. (The file folders or pockets should be labeled background information records, anecdotal records, artwork, and so forth.) Archival portfolio materials are perhaps best kept in an individual three-ring binder with materials displayed in clear vinyl page-sized pockets. Confidential information should be stored in a secure place elsewhere.

Family Educational Rights and Privacy Act (FERPA)

Children's records are protected under the Family Educational Rights and Privacy Act (FERPA). This law provides the following:

1. Parents or legal guardians of children who attend a program receiving federal assistance may see information in the program's official files. This information includes test scores, grade averages, class rank, intelligence quotient, health records, psychological reports, notes on behavioral problems, family background items, attendance records, and all other records except personal notes made by a staff member solely for his or her own use.

2. Records must be made available for review within 45 days of the request.

3. Parents may challenge information irrelevant to education, such as religious preference or unsubstantiated opinions.

4. Contents of records may be challenged in a hearing. If the program refuses to remove material challenged by parents as inaccurate, misleading, or inappropriate, the parent may insert a written rebuttal.

5. With some exceptions (e.g., other officials in the same program, officials in another program to which the student has applied for transfer, some accrediting associations, state educational officials, some financial aid organizations, the courts), written consent of parents is required before program officials may release records. Programs must keep a written record as to who has seen or requested to see the child's records.

6. Parents have the right to know where records are kept and which program officials are responsible for them.

7. Unless a divorced parent is prohibited by law from having any contact with the child, divorced parents have equal access to official records.

8. Most of the foregoing rights pass from parent to child when the child is 18 years of age.

9. Program officials must notify parents (and 18-year-olds) of their rights.

REPORTING

Reporting is becoming a more important aspect of early childhood programs as programs seek to involve family members in their children's development and as the programs become more accountable to families, citizens' groups, and funding and regulatory agencies. As is true of all other aspects of an early childhood program, reporting practices should be based on program goals.

Planning reporting requires administrators to think in terms of four steps in developing a reporting practice:

1. Determining the purposes of reporting
2. Facilitating reporting through assessment data
3. Selecting the methods of reporting
4. Rethinking reporting practices

Because reporting is so tied to the assessing and recording process, it is best considered before assessment plans are completed.

Determining the Purposes of Reporting

The first step in developing a reporting practice is to determine the purposes of reporting. For most early childhood programs, a major purpose of reporting is to provide information to family members about their child's progress. Families and staff jointly discuss the child's strengths and needs and plan the next steps in the educative process.

Another major purpose of reporting is to meet the requirements of funding and regulatory agencies. Although funding and regulatory agencies require reports on many aspects of programs, program success as measured by children's progress is a major component in the reports made to all regulating and sponsoring agencies.

Facilitating Reporting Through Assessment Data

Once the specific purposes of reporting have been determined, the next step is to make a connection between assessment data and purposes. Several important questions are as follows:

1. **What type of assessment meets the purposes of reporting?** More specifically,
   a. What information do family members need to know about their child's progress? (Likely, much of this information will be the same as teachers need for curriculum decisions)
   b. What information does the regulatory or funding agency expect to know about the collective progress of children that in turn will demonstrate the program's value? (These data can be used in rethinking program goals, too.)

Basically, the desired information for both families and agencies should be directly linked to the program goals. Programs with narrower, academic goals will assess and report children's progress in academic areas; programs with more holistic/developmental goals will gather and report data in many domains of children's development and learnings.

2. **In what format will assessment data be recorded?** Generally, standardized tests yield quantitative data—numerical raw scores (e.g., number correct) and numerical converted scores (e.g., percentiles, stanines, developmental ages). Authentic assessment techniques yield qualitative data (e.g., anecdotes, samples of children's work). If one considers assessment data from the standpoint of the ease of reporting only (not in terms of their appropriateness for program goals and the ages of children involved, although these are critical criteria), quantitative data are more difficult to explain to families, who want to

know what the scores mean. Furthermore, composite scores yield no information about the specific strengths and weaknesses in each child's progress; thus, reporting requires a careful interpretation of subscore data.

Quantitative data, however, lend themselves to the concise summary data often expected by funding and regulatory agencies; in fact, many standardized achievement tests provide class record/profile data that can easily be incorporated into agency reports. In some cases, however, quantitative scores may not be understood by those reading the agency reports.

Conversely, qualitative data are much easier for families to understand but are more difficult to summarize and definitely do not lend themselves to tables and graphs. If both quantitative and qualitative assessment data have been collected, the teacher must explain each type of data and also show how the data relate to each other.

3. Against what criterion will assessment outcomes be measured? For example, Is progress being compared with that of a norming group? Is progress measured against specific program goals? Is progress being compared with developmental landmarks? This information must be reported.

4. How will data be assembled? The ways data are assembled determine the ease of access and the need to summarize before reporting.

Selecting the Methods of Reporting

The third step in planning reporting is to determine the method or methods of reporting, especially to families. (Agencies usually have their own reporting formats.) Reporting methods are diverse. The types of methods are both oral and written. Most families prefer some of each type. Common methods include informal reports, report cards, check sheets, narrative report letters, and individual conferences.

Informal Reports.   Informal reports are perhaps the most common way of reporting—so common that staff may not even be aware they are communicating information about children's progress. This kind of report may be a casual conversation with a family member in which a staff member mentions, "Lori excels in motor skills," or, "Mark is learning the last step in tying his shoes."

Family members may note their child's progress while volunteering in the program. Samples of children's work with or without teachers' comments are often sent home. Children, too, report on themselves, such as, "I learned to skip today," or, "I shared my boat with everyone at the water table."

Narrative Report Letters.   Programs using **narrative report letters** usually provide forms on which teachers write a few brief comments about a child's progress under each of several headings, such as psychomotor development, personal and social adjustment, cognitive development, language growth, work habits, problem-solving growth, aesthetic growth, self-reliance, and general evaluation. An example of a narrative report letter form is shown in Figure 11.14.

Narrative report letters are highly appropriate for summarizing authentic assessment records. The advantage of report letters is that teachers can concentrate on a child's specific strengths and needs without giving letter grades or marking "satisfactory/unsatisfactory" and without noting progress in highly specific areas, such as "knows his address" or "ties her shoes."

The two disadvantages to report letters are that (a) report letters are highly time consuming, but the use of computers lessens the time spent in preparing them (the computer generates the report form and permits the word processing of the narrative itself); and (b) unless teachers carefully study their records on each child, they may slip into writing stereotypical comments, especially after writing the first few reports.

Your Child's Progress

Name _____ Level _____

Psychomotor development (motor skills):

George can gallop, skip, run, and throw and catch a rubber ball. He enjoys all games that use movement, and his skills indicate that his attainment is high in this area of development.

Personal/social adjustment:

George does not initiate many aggressive acts; however, he still has trouble keeping his hands to himself. He responds to negative overtures from his classmates by hitting.

Language growth:

George appears to enjoy new words. He uses rhyming words and makes up words to fit the rhymes. He has not been able to express negative feelings toward others with words, however.

General evaluation:

George is progressing nicely. More opportunities to talk with others would help him learn to express himself. He performs well in the room and on the playground as long as he is kept busy and as long as others leave him alone.

Figure 11.14
Narrative Report Letter

Individual Conferences.   Many programs schedule **individual conferences** with each child and the child's family members. Conferences permit face-to-face communication among children, families, and teachers. A teacher must plan intensively for a successful conference. (General guidelines for planning the conference are given in chapter 10.)

To effectively discuss children's progress, teachers need to plan the conference by using a written guide sheet that lists the topics and main points to be discussed. The

By posting the work of children this program is able to effectively communicate to families the knowledge and skills their children have demonstrated.

teacher should consult all records on the child and carefully transfer to the guide sheet any information to be shared with family members. A report card, check sheet, developmental profile, or selected materials from the portfolio given to family members can be used as the guide sheet. Time is provided for family members to express their concerns as topics listed on the guide sheet are covered. Additional concerns of family members need to be addressed, too.

Conferences should end on a positive note, with plans for follow-up in areas of concern at home and at school. Family members and children can look at the other items in the portfolio at the end of the conference. Many program directors are finding that if teachers give a copy of the guide sheet to each family member a few days before the conference, family members have time to think about the contents and to prepare questions and comments for the conference.

Rethinking Reporting Practices

The final step in developing a reporting practice is to experiment with the reporting plans and revise them if necessary. Reporting practices must not only work for program personnel but also open dialogue between staff and the recipients of reports, especially families. In short, the only purpose of reporting to families is to establish collaboration on behalf of children.

TRENDS AND ISSUES

Assessment reform seems to be lagging behind the push to modify the curriculum. Kagan (2000) believes that early childhood professionals must design an assessment system that will determine children's full range of development and learnings (i.e., physical well-being and motor development, social and emotional development, approaches toward learning, communication and language development, and cognitive development). It must also provide needed safeguards (e.g., unnecessary assessment, improper techniques, misuse of data).

In 1994, the National Education Goals Panel convened the Goal 1 Early Childhood Assessments Resource Group. The following purposes for assessment in early childhood were identified

a. To promote children's learning and development
b. To identify children for health and special learning services
c. To monitor trends and evaluate programs and services
d. To assess academic achievement and hold individual students, teachers, and schools accountable

Shepard, Kagan, and Wurtz (1998a) outlined how appropriate uses and technical accuracy of assessments for the foregoing purposes change across the early childhood age continuum.

Many directors and teachers agree with the concept of authentic assessment. Teachers need help in using authentic assessment and will need intense training in purposeful observation, documentation, and analysis of assessment data. Furthermore, many teachers are not familiar with making professional judgments based on broader pictures of children and may even be hesitant in assuming this responsibility.

Several authentic assessment systems, such as COR and the Work Sampling System, provide a structure for the assessment data and inform teachers of criteria that may be used in making inferences about what children can do. In addition, the systems have the qualities of strong standardized tests, that is, a strong reliability and predictive validity.

Many professionals are questioning screening practices and the use of the data. Teachers need training in recognizing whether a child's departure from a typical developmental trajectory is a sign of a learning problem or is consistent with cultural and linguistic differences. Perhaps programs should provide more high-intensity intervention to *all* children coming from high-risk backgrounds.

Another problem in assessment comes from trying to combine the purposes of assessment and use the data in many ways. Often, standardized achievement tests are used for assessment. Although combining purposes saves money and time, such combining often results in the misuse of data, such as using readiness tests for screening or using assessment for determining program effectiveness and also for holding individual children accountable. This is an unethical practice that must be avoided.

Finally the most recent educational reform initiative in the field of early childhood care and education is the process (discussed in chapter 9) termed Recognition and Response by Mary Rith Coleman, Virginia Buysee, and Jennifer Neitzel (2006). This process of providing a sound general education curriculum, engaging in the process of systematic and continuous assessment and progress monitoring, and then responding to individual child needs according the results of the assessment and evaluation will continue to evolve as more research is conducted on its impact on achieving student outcomes.

The point to be made here is that assessment is continuing to become even more important to the provision of high-quality early childhood care and education services. To meet this challenge we must continue to enhance our knowledge and understanding of effective assessment and evaluation.

SUMMARY

Assessing, recording, and reporting are integral parts of an early childhood program. Thus, these components must be thoughtfully and carefully planned in keeping with program goals. Providing quality assessment and recording and reporting assessments are not a simple matters but require a highly trained staff and leadership by directors.

Similar to the professional concerns about inappropriate curriculum content and teaching strategies are concerns about assessment. Assessment can support children's development or undermine it. Abuses and misuses have occurred in how assessment methods have been selected and administered (e.g., a disconnect between curriculum/teaching strategies and assessment practices); by the lack of a user-friendly format for young children (e.g., the use of the paper-and-pencil format); by the misassessment of young children with disabilities and those from culturally and linguistically diverse families; by the use of single measurements for making high-stakes decisions about children, staff competencies, and program effectiveness; and by the way scores have been interpreted to family members.

Professional associations have called for many changes in assessment, recording, and reporting practices. The major changes recommended include the following:

1. The increased use of ongoing observations of children in actual classroom situations (authentic or performance assessment), and the use of special sampling techniques when standardized tests are mandated to determine program effectiveness.

2. Documentation of authentic performance assessment done by the writing of logs and anecdotes, the checking and rating of certain specified behaviors, and the gathering of samples of children's work. Other records can include notes taken during interviews and home visits and the summaries of assessments and services provided by specialists.

3. The development of reporting purposes and practices that mirror local program goals and that are verified by authentic performance assessment and appropriate observation records. Usually, the contents of reports are summarized performance records with samples of actual performance used to document the summary data and collected to form a portfolio. The format for reporting may be written, oral, or a combination of the two.

Several trends and issues were noted. Assessment reform seems to be lagging behind curriculum reform. Professionals are calling for an appropriate assessment system to fulfill the various purposes of assessment and to provide needed safeguards.

USEFUL WEB SITES:

Early Childhood Assessment Resources:

> www.newassessment.org/Public/Assessments/
> selecttool.cfm?CategoryID=20

Provides links to information regarding different assessments appropriate for young children.

NCCIC Annotated Resources on Early Childhood Assessment Systems:

> www.nccic.org/poptopics/annores-assess.html

TO REFLECT

1. The ethical use and engagement in assessment is of utmost importance when working with the highly vulnerable early childhood population. Using the *NAEYC Code of Ethical Conduct* (www.naeyc.org/about/positions/pdf/PSETH05.pdf), evaluate the extent to which your center's assessment and evaluation plan might be considered appropriate. If your center doesn't yet have an evaluation plan, design a sample evaluation plan that would be considered ethical.

2. A primary school principal changed the program policy of giving letter grades (A, B, C, etc.) to authentic assessment and portfolio documentation. Several of the children's family members were upset at the change. What could have been done to prevent some of the conflict from arising? Specifically, what rationale could the principal have used to support this change in policy?

12

WORKING WITH FAMILIES AND COMMUNITIES

NAEYC Director Competencies addressed in this chapter:

Core Competencies

6. Family Support

Knowledge and application of family systems and different parenting styles. Knowledge of community resources to support family wellness. The ability to implement program practices that support families of diverse cultural, ethnic, linguistic, and socio-economic backgrounds. The ability to support families as valued partners in the educational process.

Early Childhood Knowledge and Skills

6. Family and Community Relationships

Knowledge of the diversity of family systems, traditional, non-traditional and alternative family structures, family life styles, and the dynamics of family life on the development of young children. Knowledge of socio-cultural factors influencing contemporary families including the impact of language, religion, poverty, race, technology, and the media. Knowledge of different community resources, assistance, and support available to children and families. Knowledge of different strategies to promote reciprocal partnerships between home and center. Ability to communicate effectively with parents through written and oral communication. Ability to demonstrate awareness and appreciation of different cultural and familial practices and customs. Knowledge of child rearing patterns in other countries.

Also addressed are parts of Management Knowledge and Skills

9. Oral and written communication

Knowledge of oral communication techniques including establishing rapport, preparing the environment, active listening, and voice control. The ability to communicate ideas effectively in a formal presentation.

Knowledge and Skills

10. Professionalism

Application of the *NAEYC Code of Ethical Conduct* and its *Supplement for Program Administrators* is also stressed.

Early childhood programs play an important role in the lives of young children and their families. We hope this chapter will help you develop a greater appreciation for the ways families, programs of early care and education, and communities can join forces to improve the quality of life for young children while enhancing children's chances for success in school and beyond.

These linkages are essential—neither families nor programs for young children exist in a vacuum. The coordinated interface between home, school, and community creates an essential network of support each child deserves (Bronfenbrenner, 1979). Program administrators, teachers, and caregivers who spend their days with young children have the opportunity to create and nurture relationships with families and begin the process of linking families to their community's educational and social service resources. It is our goal to help you take the lead in strengthening connections between your early childhood program and the families and communities you serve.

EARLY CHILDHOOD EDUCATORS HAVE A LONG HISTORY OF PARTNERING WITH FAMILIES

The history of family involvement in early childhood programs goes back to the field's earliest days. Pioneering programs of the early 1900s recognized that families were children's first and most influencial teachers. They saw it as their responsibility to support family efforts to enhance and ensure children's physical, social, and cognitive well-being.

In spite of the fact that families face some very different challenges today than they did more than a century ago, many of the issues they confront remain the same. Teachers and families continue to work together with one shared goal—to give all children opportunities to pursue their dreams and to achieve success.

Collaboration: A Crucial Element of Quality Programming

Opportunities for programs, families, and communities to work together are a crucial component of quality early childhood programming (Larner, 1996; Raab & Dunst, 1997). The theoretical foundation for this three-way collaboration is based on Vygotsky's sociocultural theory (1978) and Bronfenbrenner's ecological systems theory (1979) of human development.

Findings reinforced by a growing body of research led the authors of the groundbreaking book *Eager to Learn* to recommend that "all early childhood programs build alliances with parents to cultivate mutually reinforcing environments for children at home and in early childhood programs" (NRC, 2001, p. 318). The centrality of the relationship linking families with programs for young children is illustrated by the following important professional guidelines that include creating partnerships with families as a key component of quality:

- Head Start Performance Standards (Administration for Children and Families, 2007)
- National Association for the Education of Young Children (NAEYC) Early Childhood Program Standards (2005) including the Program Administration Core Competencies that are part of the NAEYC Program Accreditation
- *NAEYC Code of Ethical Conduct* (NAEYC, 2005) and its *Administrator's Supplement* (NAEYC, 2006)
- Influential position statements including NAEYC's statements on *Developmentally Appropriate Practice* (Bredekamp & Copple, 1997), *Linguistic and Cultural Diversity* (NAEYC, 1995), *Violence in the Lives of Children* (NAEYC, 1993) and the position

statement of the Division for Early Childhood (DEC) of the Council for Exceptional on *Inclusion* (DEC, 1993) call for program–family–community collaboration

- *NAEYC's Early Childhood Professional Preparation Accreditation Criteria* that set standards for both associate and initial licensure (bachelor's or master's) degree-granting programs (NAEYC, 2003; NAEYC, 2001)
- Environment Rating Scales (Harms, Clifford, & Cryer, 2005; Harms, Cryer, & Clifford, 2003; Harms, Jacobs, & White, 1996) that are widely used as measures of program quality

---

Application Activity

The *NAEYC Code of Ethical Conduct* (2005) (see appendix 2) and its *Supplement for Program Administrators* (2006) (see appendix 3) provide guidance for programs striving to develop and maintain strong collaborative relationships with families and communities. Working in groups, discuss a difficult situation you have encountered while working with families. Identify the core values involved in this situation and the Ideals and Principles in the NAEYC Codes that guide your ethical decision making. Describe a defensible course of action that is true to these ethical principles.

BENEFITS AND CHALLENGES OF WORKING WITH FAMILIES

The fact that family involvement can help ensure positive child outcomes is now a generally accepted fact. However, in spite of influencial position statements; standards for teacher preparation; criteria for accreditation of early childhood programs; and, in some instances, legislation requiring family-school collaboration, the fact remains that early childhood educators are apt to describe working with parents as the most demanding part of their job (Gibbs, 2005).

Threefold Benefits of Family–School Collaboration

Families are their children's first and most important teachers. Today's families often rely on resources outside the family, such as early childhood programs and schools, to help them care for and educate their young children. Bronfenbrenner's ecological systems theory (1986) provides a framework for understanding the relationship between the child's home and his school or child care experience. Bronfenbrenner explained that children have distinct and separate relationships or "systems" at home and at school.

The connections between these systems can enhance or detract from children's social and emotional growth and development. When the home and child care program work in harmony, children and families are supported, benefiting from their shared purpose. If the home and school are at odds, however, viewing each other with suspicion or casting blame, then children's healthy development is in jeopardy.

Healthy collaboration requires dedication toward a common goal. This begins with a desire to work together, requires effort to develop trusting relationships, and patience to overcome the inevitable challenges along the way. When the connections between the home and school are strong, children, families, schools and child care programs, and communities benefit, offering support that none could provide if they were acting alone.

Involving families in children's early childhood experiences enhances the program's effectiveness and also, importantly, increases the likelihood that families will remain engaged in their children's education as they progress through elementary and secondary school (Henrich & Blackman-Jones, 2006). The following six kinds of parent involvement illustrate that there are many ways for families, schools, and communities to work together (Epstein et al., 2002):

- **Parenting.**   Early childhood programs can assist families in their efforts to create healthy homes that support children's physical, emotional, and cognitive development.
- **Home-to-School and School-to-Home Communication.**   Teachers and caregivers can use strategies such as newsletters, conferences, phone calls and, when appropriate, email, to create lines of communication between school and home and to keep them open.
- **Participation.**   Early childhood programs should work to develop effective strategies to recruit and involve families as classroom volunteers and to involve them in schoolwide special events.
- **Learning at Home.**   Early childhood programs can help families create home environments that are conducive to learning and support children's work at school.
- **Decision Making.**   Families should be invited to participate in the program's decision making and governance through vehicles such as the center's parent-teacher organization. Some families may become involved in advocacy activities outside the program. They may, for example, attend meetings of the school board or another body that oversees the program's operations.
- **Community Outreach.**   Early childhood programs and parent-teacher groups can engage community members and businesses in the education of young children by soliciting their financial or in-kind support.

Benefits for Children.   Children are at a tremendous advantage when families and teachers agree on what they expect children will learn and be able to do, and when they agree on how to help children achieve those goals (Powell & Gerde, 2006). When operating from these shared understandings, functioning as an extended family, early childhood programs are at their best (Caldwell, 1985). Benefits for children of these collaborative efforts include the following:

1. Recent demographic and economic changes have, in some instances, interrupted and undermined the relationships essential for families' healthy psychological development (Bronfenbrenner & Morris, 1998; Lee & Burkam, 2002). Children benefit when child care programs, schools, and communities can provide these supports.

2. Family involvement can enhance children's cognitive development; improve behavior; boost academic achievement; and increase language and problem-solving skills. It can decrease the chances that children will be referred into special education classes, be retained or eventually drop out of school, or be considered to be "juvenile delinquents" (Bermudez & Marquez, 1996; Henrich & Blackman-Jones, 2006; Marcon, 1994b; Pena, 2000).

3. Family involvement helps schools and teachers successfully advocate for the evaluation of children with suspected disabilities and helps involve families in securing special services when they are needed to enhance children's chances for success (Pena, 2000).

4. Family involvement gives children opportunities to see that family members and teachers are working together for shared goals. This relationship impacts children's affective functioning, leading to a positive self-image, a productive orientation to social relations (Marcon, 1994a), and to positive attitudes about school (Epstein, 2001).

Benefits for Families.   Parents benefit when they take advantage of opportunities to participate in their children's early childhood educational experiences. These are some of the benefits family members can enjoy:

1. Participation in early childhood programs can enhance family members' feelings of self-worth and contribute to increased educational and employment opportunities (Bermudez & Marquez, 1996; Epstein, 2001).

2. Family members benefit from observing teachers' interactions with young children. It increases their knowledge of child development and informs them about appropriate approaches to guidance in the early years. Adults who have spent time in their young children's classrooms have been shown to apply this knowledge to adult-child interactions in the home (Keyser, 2006; White, 1988).

3. When family members interact with children in an early childhood setting, they are likely to gain confidence in their own ability to nurture and educate their children (Epstein, 2001; Powell, 1989).

4. Parents who have a trusting and respectful relationship with their child's teacher can leave their child with confidence. They know they have a caring partner in care with whom to share the joys and challenges of parenthood, and to receive acknowledgement for the important yet often thankless work of being their child's first teacher (Keyser, 2006).

5. When family members are involved in their children's schools, they better understand the important role they play in their children's education. It helps them appreciate that they are their child's first and most important teacher (Epstein, 2001; Keyser, 2006).

6. When family members participate in their children's programs, they are likely to form friendships and to create networks of support. These affiliations often link families of participating children, including children with and without disabilities, enriching the lives of all (Powell, 1989).

Benefits for Programs.   Early childhood programs also benefit from family involvement. These are some of the ways:

1. When families are able to explain their family's makeup and culture to school personnel, caregivers and teachers are likely to become more empathetic and to be better able to work from their understanding of the family's strengths (Gonzalez-Mena, 2007, 2008).

2. Family members who are involved in the program are more likely to understand its rationale, curriculum, and teaching strategies. Designers of model programs launched in the 1960s found that participating parents had a unique ability to explain the program's services to other parents—they were advocates that helped the program build credibility in their community.

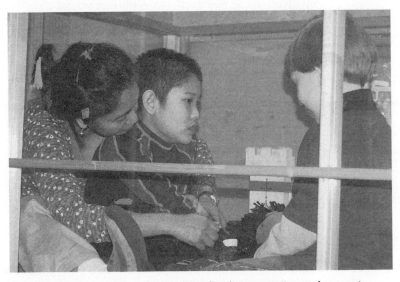

Parents, children, and programs benefit when parents are frequent visitors to the classroom.

3. Family involvement can make it possible for the center to comply with program requirements. For example, Head Start Performance Standards mandate that local advisory boards have parent representatives and that parents serve in the classroom as paid employees, volunteers, and observers. In another example, federal guidelines established for programs serving children with disabilities require parents to participate in developing Family Service Plans (FSPs) or their children's Individual Education Plans (IEP). If parents fail to "buy in" to these programs, they will not be able to meet their legislative mandates.

4. When family members volunteer in the classroom, there is a better adult-child ratio. That means children can benefit from adults' one-on-one attention for activities such as lap reading. The teacher may also be able to plan activities, such as cooking or special crafts, that require an extra pair of adult hands (Gonzalez-Mena, 2007).

5. Family members can serve as classroom resources. Their special talents and interests can make valuable contributions when children are studying particular hobbies, such as playing a musical instrument or gardening. They can also help teachers when children have questions about occupations, such as being a truck driver, a veterinarian, or a mail carrier (Gonzalez-Mena, 2007).

6. Program directors and teachers view family involvement as a sign of respect. It enhances staff morale (Epstein, 2001), and can motivate staff to initiate partnerships in return.

7. Involved family members are likely to become the program's biggest boosters. This kind of good publicity can increase enrollment and can help promote the program's reputation throughout the community.

8. Family members can serve as program decision makers. This contribution will be discussed later in this chapter.

In spite of evidence that family involvement benefits children, families, and the programs that serve them, the fact remains that not all families are actively involved in their young children's programs of early care and education. Families most likely to be involved in their children's school are well educated (Stevenson & Baker, 1987) and come from affluent communities (Epstein, 1995). That means that low-income and less well educated families, including families who are in crisis because of homelessness or another stress-producing situation, are less engaged, less involved, feel less welcome, and have fewer opportunities to become involved in the day-to-day lives of their young children (Swick & Williams, 2006).

These trends highlight the fact that not all programs are doing a good job of meeting the needs of all families. They should challenge those committed to family involvement to reach out in innovative ways that are likely to involve these hard-to-reach populations so all children can reap the benefits of robust family involvement.

Application Activity

Describe an activity that will give families an opportunity to participate in your center. Identify how children, families, and the center might benefit from this well-designed and effectively implemented event. Consider if this activity is likely to appeal to traditionally hard-to-reach populations.

Challenges to Family Involvement

Differences Can Create Barriers to Family-School Collaboration.   It is likely that there will be instances when families and program staff bring different values and beliefs to their interactions with young children. These differences reflect the influences of their culture, family, and personal experiences. They can mean families and caregivers have very different expectations about caregiving as well as children's behavior and development (Powell & Gerde, 2006).

Early childhood educators have a responsibility to work to understand these differences and to eliminate the barriers they create. Some likely sources of difference you may encounter in your work follow in the next sections.

Family Structure.   The children who come to your program are likely to have varied *family structures.* Some family structures have been shown to create stresses that make program involvement difficult or put children's physical, social, and emotional development at risk. For example, single mothers' responsibilities often make it difficult for them to be involved in their children's schools. In addition, children in single-parent homes often have fewer emotional supports, less cognitive stimulation, and may perform less well academically (Cherlin, 1999; Levine-Coley, 1998).

Advocates working with families headed by gay and lesbian couples report that if programs make them or their children feel like misfits, they will be reluctant to fully participate in school-sponsored events and activities (Clay, 2004). In addition, recent years have seen an increase in the number of grandparents who have become young children's primary guardians, often as a result of a family crisis of one sort or another. These families are likely to face unique stresses and to need particular kinds of outreach (Birckmayer, Cohen, Jensen, & Variano, 2005).

These examples illustrate some of the barriers family structures can create that make it difficult for some parents to support their children and participate in their schools and educational experiences.

Socioeconomic Status.   Families with higher socioeconomic backgrounds are more likely to be involved in their children's schools and their children are likely to perform better academically than are children from low-income families (Lee & Burkam, 2002; Smith, Brooks-Gunn, & Klebanov, 1997; Stevenson & Baker, 1987).

Low-income families, on the other hand, are more apt to have inflexible work hours and may not have access to reliable transportation. They are also more likely to be working in the early morning, late at night, and on weekends. These work-related responsibilities may make it impossible for them to participate in events at their child's school and may make scheduling conferences with teachers difficult. Furthermore, low-income families are more likely to experience stress-producing events such as homelessness and to have fewer resources for coping with those crises when they occur (Edkin & Lein, 1997).

Cultural Diversity.   Culture reflects families' beliefs, values, and ways of interacting. Children are enculturated by their families' day-to-day interactions. They are their family's investment in the future and are being prepared to perpetuate their culture (Christian, 2007; Gonzalez-Mena, 2008). Identifying culturally-determined values and ways of interacting helps you understand the families with whom you work.

One framework for developing this understanding is to consider the difference between low-context and high-context cultural patterns. In low-context cultures, the individual is valued over the group, independence of individuals is a virtue, individuals are encouraged to assert themselves, individual achievement is valued, and communication is verbal and precise. These characteristics usually describe Western Europeans and members of the mainstream, dominant United States culture.

By contrast, in high-context groups, interdependence, as shown by reliance on the extended family and the community, is valued; achievement within cooperative groups is encouraged and rewarded; contributions to the group are prized; and language is likely to include nonverbal and contextual cues. These characteristics are likely to describe individuals raised in Asian, Southern European, Latino, African American, and Native American traditions (Hall, 1977).

Child-rearing practices, particularly beliefs about "the right way" for children to sleep, eat, toilet, and play reflect culturally determined expectations. In low-context cultures, for example, even very young children sleep alone; they are encouraged to feed themselves at a young age, even if that means Cheerios are thrown on the floor or feeding is a very messy affair. Toilet training begins when children are able to get themselves into the bathroom and handle their clothes independently. Solitary play is encouraged by creating settings where there are enough toys, and duplicates of popular options, so that children have access to what they want when they want it.

Children reared in high-context cultures, on the other hand, are likely to sleep in the family bed at least during infancy, and with their parents or siblings throughout the early childhood years; are often fed by adults until they are about 4 years old (because this is seen as a way to foster interdependance); may be toilet trained during infancy (in part because their families are likely to believe children should always be held, which gives the caregiver the opportunity to learn the subtle signals indicating they are about to eliminate); and social play may be a necessity because toys are limited and sharing is viewed as a natural way of interacting (Freeman, 1998; Gonzalez-Mena, 2008).

When teachers and caregivers share the culture and language of the families they serve, home values are reinforced and the transition to school is often a smooth one. When there are significant differences between families and program personnel, there may be a mismatch between the program's goals, curriculum content, adults' interactional styles, and teaching strategies and families' expectations. This incongruity may mean that children's and families' strengths and competencies go unrecognized, causing children and families to feel isolated and alienated (García Coll & Magnuson, 2000; Greenberg, 1989; Keyser, 2006).

Early childhood educators have an important responsibility to bridge these cultural gaps when they occur. Culturally competent programs are able to negotiate cultural differences with families to help all children succeed at home and in out-of-home settings (Gonzalez-Mena, 2008).

Linguistic Diversity.   A child's home language is the language of nurture, emotion, and care. It is a child's link to her extended family, to her family's past, and family traditions. As America becomes more diverse, it is increasingly likely that you will work with families whose home language is not English, and it is more important than ever to find strategies for working with linguistically diverse children and families.

One way to reduce the language barrier that may make it difficult for some families to participate in your program is to tap into members of the community who may be able to provide translation services. Another option is to use computer software to translate school-home and home-school communications (Kirmani, 2007). This is an essential step if all participating families are to have access to information about your program. It will also make it possible for caregivers and teachers to learn from their children's families, and for families to benefit from the teacher's and caregiver's insights about their children's learning, growth, and development.

The most important contribution an early childhood educator can make to families whose home language is not English is to support their use of this language of emotion and nuture while, at the same time, preparing their child for success in English-speaking settings he will encounter during the school years and beyond (Kirmani, 2007).

Tension Between Families and Center Personnel Can Make Collaboration Difficult.   Collaborative efforts may also be difficult when home-school relationships are characterized by tension or conflict. Some families may feel inhibited or even inferior around staff members because of their family's structure, cultural, or linguistic differences, or because of their own limited or unhappy school experiences (Christian, 2007). When communication with staff members is difficult, these feelings are even more pronounced.

Early childhood educators who lack respect for all families may respond negatively to differences. They may discount what families do for their children. Their attitudes may make it unlikely that the families most in need of help navigating their child's educational setting will get the support they need (Greenberg, 1989; Kontos & Wells, 1986, Swick & Williams, 2006).

Conflicts may also arise over the curriculum content and teaching strategies. Families may expect early childhood experiences to be structured and academic, while best practices include hands on authentic experiences, an integrated curriculum, and instruction based on teachers' understanding of children's developmental needs. Although both families and teachers want children to achieve, conflicts can emerge about differences in opinions about appropriate academic goals (Gonzalez-Mena, 2008; Kostelnik, Soderman, & Shiren, 2007).

Family members and staff also bring particular perspectives and needs to the parent-teacher relationship. Stress can be created when family members expect staff to be sympathetic when they bring a mildly ill child to school because they were not able to arrange alternative backup care, to understand that the bus can be unpredictable and may make them late for afternoon pickup, and to be accommodating when they are not able to pay tuition the first of the month when it comes due (Galinsky, 1988; Leavitt, 1987).

From their perspective, staff members expect families to appreciate how physically and emotionally exhausting it can be to care for a group of active young children, to respect that they need to leave work on time so they can meet their own family and personal obligations, and to recognize how important it is that tuition payments be made on time so they can meet the center's payroll and and financial obligations.

The attitudes of program staff and families about collaboration itself may impede working together. The family's right to make decisions about the education of their children may be difficult for some staff members to accept, particularly if cultural differences lead the teacher to believe parents are not caring for their children as they think they should (Christian, 2007).

Perhaps these attitudes are the result of a long tradition in which family involvement threatened teachers and interrupted their work. Family members' critiques of the program's curriculum and methodology may also be seen as unqualified judgments of professionals by nonprofessionals. These are some reasons why, before the 1960s, working with parents usually took the form of parent education—the school communicated to parents, but parents were not seen as partners and were not involved in programmatic decision making.

Interestingly, a teacher's perspectives about parent involvement often reflects her stage of professional development. In the early stages of professional life, a teacher often views families from a deficit perspective. For that reason, when dealing with families, the teacher tends to be authoritarian or paternalistic. With experience, teachers develop an awareness of the importance of working collaboratively with families, and collaboration becomes easier (Vander Ven, 1988).

Similarly, family members' attitudes and actions can undermine collaboration. Sometimes families constantly call attention to the program's shortcomings. In other instances, family members take no initiative to work with the school. There are also families who show a pattern of abusing the teacher's time, and where a member of the family claims greater educational expertise than the teacher or caregiver, creating understandable resistance and resentment on the part of the early childhood professional (Kraft & Snell, 1980).

These observations point to the important role of the program administrator to lead novice teachers to see families as partners, and to help families acknowledge teachers' expertise and caring.

Teachers Are Often Not Well Prepared to Work with Families.   Beginning teachers often feel ill-prepared to work effectively with families (Feeney & Sysko, 1986; Freeman & Knopf, 2007). This remains the case even though standards of professional preparation include the expectation that teachers view families as partners and that they build strong school-home relationships to enhance children's chances for school success.

Preservice teacher preparation programs should work to provide students increased authentic opportunities to work collaboratively with families (Freeman & Knopf, 2007). In addition, in-service training should be designed to help staff become sensitive to all families' needs and to develop their abilities to communicate effectively across cultures, even when they have to have difficult conversations (Alexander & Entwisle, 1988; Galinsky, 1987; Christian, 2007; Powell, 1989; Stevenson & Baker, 1987; Stevenson, Chen, & Uttal, 1990).

Meeting the Challenges of Collaboration

Although directors and staff members experience challenges in working with families, many of these problems can be overcome. Professionals must develop understanding about the sources of these differences and show as much acceptance for differing family views as they do for differences in children. These suggestions may help your center achieve these goals:

1. Staff members need to develop positive attitudes about working with families, including families whose culture, language, or ethnicity is different from their own. They also need support in developing skills working with diverse families and need practice putting these ideals into action. Many programs are changing their approaches to working with families. For example, High/Scope no longer provides "knowledge" to families. Their materials now emphasize the importance of embracing diversity and developing respectful relationships with families (Hohmann & Weikart, 1995). See Figure 12.1 for more specific information on the concepts, skills, and attitudes teachers need to bring to their work with families.

2. Program expectations should be realistic (Epstein, 2001). All families will not want, or be able to, participate in every kind of activity. They need many activities from which to choose (Gonzalez-Mena, 2007; Stevenson & Baker, 1987; Workman & Gage, 1997). The important challenge is to offer a range of family involvement opportunities tailored to the needs of all families you serve.

3. Involving families can be a developmental process for programs of early care and education (Epstein, 2001). Programs committed to making working with families an intregal part of the program's offerings should develop specific goals and objectives to measure their success (Davies, 1991; Gonzalez-Mena, 2007; Powell, 1991). The following strategies will help you build collaborative relationships with families:
   - Develop a genuine understanding of, and a respect for, diversity.
   - Learn what the families you serve want for their children.
   - Learn how local agencies and organizations are involved with families and network with them to meet the needs of the families you serve.
   - Evaluate your program's family involvement program to measure its success. (Christian, 2007; Coleman; 1997; Gonzalez-Mena, 2007).

4. Professionals need to learn to work with "difficult" families just as they work with "difficult" children. It is important to remember that all families care deeply about their children. They are likely to feel bewildered, vulnerable, and sensitive about problems their children might be having at school. If you have developed a positive relationship with parents, you will have a storehouse of good will that will make it easier for them to accept concerns you might have about children's academic progress; physical, emotional, or cognitive

Teachers need to

—know more about the families they serve

Many variables influence families' values and needs. They have an important influence on communication between teachers and families. Teachers benefit when they know about

- Children's daily routines at home
- The communication style in the home
- Parents' beliefs about effective instructional strategies
- The family's approach to child guidance and discipline
- Expectations about age-appropriate self-help skills
- Relationships that are important to children including grandparents and other highly involved members of their extended family
- The family's involvement in the community, for example, if they are active in their church and if they have a broad network of support
- Challenges that confront families as a result of poverty, inability to understand or speak English, and the impact of stress-producing circumstances (including homelessness, joblessness, serious illness, death, divorce, single parenting, incarceration, parenting special needs children, and so on) (Murphy, 1997; Neuman, Hagedorn, Celano, & Daly, 1995; Powell, 1987; 1991)

—know potential challenges to family involvement

We know there are a number of barriers that can prevent parents' participation in their child's early childhood programs. They include the parents' work schedules, their access to reliable transportation, their need for child care for younger children, and their own school or training schedules. Barriers such as these may make it impossible for parents to volunteer in their preschooler's classroom or to attend evening events that do not include children (Henrich & Blackman-Jones, 2006).

Parents also need to know it is all right to choose *not* to be involved (Sciarra & Dorsey, 1998), although they should be encouraged to suggest ways involvement in their child's educational experiences may be possible.

—convey the similarities of goals

Both parents and teachers are committed to young children's healthy development and learning (Epstein, 1991; Stipek, Milburn, Clements, & Daniels, 1992). Both want the child to be cared for and educated in a program of early care and education that reflects the values and beliefs of their family, culture, and community (Comer & Haynes, 1991; Garbarino & Abramowitz, 1992; Powell, 1991; Zigler, 1989). That means that teachers and caregivers need to understand the families they serve. When differences emerge, early childhood educators have a responsibility to explore these differences with families. Often mutually agreeable solutions to problems can be found. When that is not possible, programs and families may respectfully agree to disagree—with the understanding that children's health, safety, and well-being will always be foremost in their minds (Gonzalez-Mena, 2002).

—convey the importance of the family

Parents should frequently be reminded that they play *the* most important role in their children's lives. Children's relationships in quality programs of early care and education can last throughout their early years, but the relationships between children and families last a lifetime. Not surprisingly, the quality of these lasting relationships are a stronger predictor of children's development than the quantity and quality of care in early childhood programs (NICHD, 1997). This is why an early childhood educator's role sharing insights about growth, development, and appropriate expectations for children's learning and behaviors with families is so important in both the short and long term.

Figure 12.1
Concepts, Skills, and Attitudes That Characterize Sensitive Programs of Family Involvement

development; or behavior (Boutte, Keepler, Tyler, & Terry, 1992). When teachers and caregivers have empathy for what families are feeling, even "difficult" parents can become allies working together on children's behalf.

COLLABORATION WITH FAMILIES

Families generally want to be involved in early childhood programs. They rely on program personnel to show them how (Daniel, 1996; Epstein & Sanders, 1998). Families are more likely to be involved if they believe the invitation for involvement is sincere. They feel welcome when the program's climate is an inclusive one that shows respect and empathy.

One way programs show their commitment to inclusion is by having men and women who represent the diversity of the community on its staff. Another way is by having artifacts and furnishings that reflect the cultural backgrounds, linguistic traditions, and family structures of participating families. A third way programs demonstrate a commitment to family involement is by offering a wide variety of ways to be involved (Coleman & Wallinga, 2000; Gonzalez-Mena, 2007; Hoover-Dempsey & Sandler, 1997).

Family–Staff Communication

Frequent and effective communication between families and teachers and caregivers is an essential characteristic of quality early care and education. While it can be difficult to keep lines of communication open with all families, the benefits are well worth the investment in time and energy. The following suggestions may help your program communicate effectively with families:

1. Be consistantly available to all families. Frequent communication helps program personnel and parents build trust. In fact, frequently communicating teachers and parents are more likely to respect each other than are teachers and parents who communicate infrequently (Kontos & Dunn, 1989).

2. Match your communication style to the family's linquistic, cultural, and educational background. Program personnel should make every effort to communicate in the family's primary language; should carefully avoid educational jargon; and should be conscious of their use of nonverbal communication such as personal space, eye contact, and touching (Gonzalez-Mena, 2008; Seplocha, 2004).

3. Promote comfortable exchanges. Show interest, respect, and caring for each child and family. Make every effort to begin every interaction with families by sharing something positive about their child—something new they have accomplished or an example of how they have helped or shown consideration for a classmate. If you need to discuss a problem or concern, describe the issue using anecdotes and specifics, listen to the family's perspective, and respond in a professional way that helps to develop a partnership with the family (Pogoloff, 2004).

4. Support staff in plans to communicate regularly with all families, using a variety of ways to stay in touch. Morning drop-off and evening pickup times are often perfect for short check-ins to share information about the child's health, eating and sleeping routines, or significant events at home or at school. If children are present, it is important to include them in these conversations. In the morning you might encourage parents to say something such as, "I'm telling your teacher about the fun you had on the swing at the playground on Sunday" and afternoon pickup might include a conversation such as, "Let's tell your mother how much you enjoyed playing in the mud this morning, and how we changed your clothes when we can in from the playground" (Keyser, 2006).

Drop-off and pickup are perfect opportunities for teachers and parents to share information.

When caring for very young children, daily logs describing the child's experiences and caregiving routines are essential. These logs should include specifics about when the baby's diaper was changed, when and what she ate, when and for how long she slept, and other noteworthy happenings parents would appreciate knowing about. Parents who will not see their baby's primary caregiver at drop-off time should be encouraged to include a short note describing the baby's overnight and early morning routines to help the caregiver meet her particular needs during the day. See Figure 12.2 for an example of a daily log for infants.

Parents of older children appreciate regular updates as well. These can be short notes to all parents, such as a reminder about an upcoming PTO meeting or a class trip, or individual notes sharing their child's special accomplishment or thanking them for a recent contribution to the class.

Accident reports are another kind of note you sometimes need to write to parents. Compose these notes carefully. Share facts as needed but take care to neither minimize a minor injury nor to alarm parents. Consider the OK and NOT OK examples in Figure 12.3.

Some programs use interactive journals exchanged between teachers and parents on a regular basis to "talk" when they are not able to check in daily. Email may be an appropriate communication tool if the families you serve have easy access on the Internet. In addition to these quick check-ins, regular newsletters let families know about centerwide events and classroom-specific happenings.

As the director, you or individual teachers might also lead special-topics meetings to share information about child development or to address parents' questions about toilet training, appropriate guidance, welcoming a new baby, or other issues they may be facing.

Caregivers should also plan time for in-depth one-on-one conversations with families to share specific information about children's growth, development, and learning. As the program director, you will create expectations about how and when teachers communicate with parents. When you model effective communication with families and set high expectations, program personnel are likely to follow your lead.

Family Area.   The program's family area is described in chapter 6. It should invite relaxed communication among families and between families and professionals. It should be well defined and inviting, with adequate lighting and ventilation, comfortable chairs, and a

Cuddly Cubs Daily Log

Date _____   Primary Caregiver _____

Name _____   Last Feeding _____

Arrival Time: _____

Diaper changes: (W=wet, BM=bowel movement, D=dry)
_____ W BM D   _____ W BM D
_____ W BM D   _____ W BM D
_____ W BM D   _____ W BM D

Feedings

Time	Type of Food and Amount/ Notes

Naps:

_____ to _____   Notes:_____

_____ to _____   Notes:_____

_____ to _____   Notes: _____

Your child needs:

___ Cereal   ___ Diaper Cream   ____ Wipes
___ Extra clothes   ___ Diapers   _____

Notes:

Figure 12.2
Example of a Daily Log for Infants

Displays in classrooms, foyers, and hallways help families stay informed about center events.

place to write. If it will be used for parent-teacher conferences, plan a private area where sensitive information can be shared confidentially.

Family members appreciate information about child development and about the early childhood program. Consider using bulletin boards and display shelves to share the following kinds of materials with the families you serve:

1. Information about the program's services, schedule, vacation calendar, names and responsibilities of all staff members, and upcoming special events
2. Materials or Web sites for parents prepared by organizations focused on young children such as Zero to Three and NAEYC. These materials might help parents prepare for an upcoming parent education event or might follow up on a past session led by program staff
3. Guidelines for helping families choose appropriate books, toys, media, and other materials for young children
4. Information about community resources and happenings designed for children and families
5. Directions and recipes for family projects and crafts, such as finger paint, play dough, lunchtime favorites
6. Words to children's favorite songs
7. Information on childhood diseases, safety in the home and on the playground, and Consumer Product Safety Commission recalls of products used by children. Free or inexpensive booklets are often available from the American Red Cross, local pediatricians, and insurance companies.

Family resources can also be incorporated into children's classrooms. A bench or small couch can provide a place for a family member to observe the program in action or to help their child transition between home and school. A family information bulletin board is also a good way to provide information about the daily routine, to provide resources to expand on a recent topic of study, age-specific information about child development, notices to ask parents for specific kinds of help, or to keep families informed about upcoming special events.

The Family's Initial Visit.   For child care programs with continuous enrollment, a family's[1] first visit is often to tour the center and perhaps to register their child. This is an important time of first impressions for the family and staff alike.

The director should provide (a) an overview of the goals of the program, (b) an explanation of major policies, and (c) application/enrollment forms. This visit might also include an "intake interview" during which the director learns about the child and the family (Hanhan, 2003).

An observant director can use this opportunity to learn about (a) the relationship between the parent and the child, (b) how the child reacts to new situations and how the parent feels about putting the child in the program, (c) the child's personal history, and (d) the parent's opinions of the child's developmental strengths and weaknesses.

If at all possible, the parent and child should be invited to observe in the child's classroom and to meet his teacher. It would be nice to invite the child to become involved in classroom activities, if appropriate. Observation and participation give the parent and child time to become comfortable in the setting and allow the teacher an opportunity to begin to form a relationship with the child and his family.

Spring or Autumn Orientation.   Many early childhood programs have an orientation meeting in the late spring or early autumn for families who will be enrolling children for

---

[1]We will use the word "parent" for clarity but appreciate that many families involve other primary caregivers including grandparents, foster parents, and other guardians.

NOT OK

Aaron fell off the tricycle and was bleeding all over the place. We applied ice and TLC ☺

OK

Arron was riding the trike and lost his balance. He cut his left arm just below the elbow. We stopped the bleeding, washed with soap and water, applied Neosporin and a band-aid. He got a smiley face for his bravery ☺.

NOT OK

Natasha was playing in the sand box and got some sand in her eye. She screamed for 15 minutes. We flushed with water but she screamed even more. We applied ice and TLC. She said she was OK ☺

OK

Natasha was building a sand castle when some of the sand flipped up from her shovel into her eye. We flushed with water and applied ice since she was trying to wipe her eye. The cool cloth seemed to calm her down. The whole experience upset her so we tried to comfort her as much as possible. After a few minutes she was back in the sandbox and enjoying herself again.

Figure 12.3
OK and NOT OK Accident Reports

the first time. The purpose of the meeting is to orient families to the program's services and requirements for admission. As director, you will want to use this opportunity to share information about strategies families might use to prepare their children for their transition into your program. This is also an excellent way to begin to establish trusting and cooperative relationships between families and center personnel.

After greeting family members, you might plan to showcase typical classroom activities with a Powerpoint presentation or share a video illustrating the program's hands-on active approach to learning. See the listing of videos to consider at the end of this chapter. If children have been invited, you might want to involve them in a read-aloud, songs, or finger plays.

You will also want to use the orientation to review information about food services, transportation, supplies, fees, and other essential policies. You may want to demonstrate how supplies are to be marked and indicate how fees are to be sent to school. This information should be included in the program's family handbook (which was described in detail in chapter 4).

Families want to know how to prepare their child for school success. Discourage them from taking an academic "superbaby" approach. You know that young children are unlikely to benefit from those kinds of skill and drill activities and they may extinguish children's love of learning. You want to stress, however, how important it is for families to be involved in their child's development and learning. You may want to suggest some hands-on activities they can do at home that will help prepare their children for school success. You will also want to invite general questions but should remind familes to save questions concerning their child for one-on-one conversations.

The meeting should last no longer than an hour. A social time following the meeting gives families a chance to visit with each other and with staff. This is a good time to offer a tour of the facility—families always appreciate seeing where their children will spend their days.

Open House or Curriculum Night.   An *open house* or *curriculum night* is another way for the program to inform families about their program. Unlike the spring or autumn orientation, the open house or curriculum meeting is held a few weeks after the beginning of the school year. Sometimes these are large group events, in other instances each classroom hosts the families of its children, and sometimes large-group and classroom-based activities are combined. As the program's director you will plan and lead these events. The following guidelines should help you be successful:

1. Select a date during the first weeks of school.   A meeting after the school year has begun will help you associate children with their families and will strenghten newly formed relationships.

2. Send invitations.   If you include an RSVP, you can follow up by telephone with families who do not respond. A night meeting is preferable because it is likely to make it possible for more working families to attend. Tuesdays, Wednesdays, and Thursdays are usually the best evenings for meetings, but consider other community events, like Wednesday night church services, before setting a date. Plan the meeting to last a maximum of 1 hour followed by a social period, or plan a simple family supper followed by the meeting for adults. You will want to start early enough to allow children to go to bed at their usual bedtime. Child care services almost always ensure a better turnout. See the Figure 12.4 for a sample open house invitation.

3. Give families time to visit their child's classroom.   Ask teachers to arrange their classroom so families will know how their children spend their days. They should describe the classroom's daily schedule, arrange materials and equipment as they would for children to use them, and display some of the children's work. This will be a good time for them to describe the curriculum and to illustrate what children learn when playing with blocks, at the water or sand table, in the dramatic play center, or when they are using art materials in creative ways.

4. Prepare an outline of your presentation.   For example,
   a. After most of the guests have arrived, greet them as a group.
   b. Introduce yourself and other staff members.
   c. Briefly describe your background and the program's history and express confidence in the coming year.
   d. Indicate that the purpose of this meeting is to share information about your program and the year ahead:
   • Welcome families to call or, if appropriate, email you or their child's teacher any time they have a question about the program or their child.
   • Describe your program's strategies for helping families and teachers communicate. You might invite parents to sign up for individual conferences or indicate when individual conferences will be scheduled.

Dear _____

We are looking forward to our Open House on Thursday, October 24th, at 7:30 P.M. You will learn more about our daily routines; the toys, materials, and equipment in our classroom; and the kinds of activities we do every day. We will also have examples of your child's work for you to take home. We hope you will come and see some of the things your child is doing in preschool.

We hope to see you soon!

Refreshments will be served in the multipurpose room after a short presentation in our classroom.

Sincerely,

_____
(Teacher's signature)

Figure 12.4
Open House Invitation

- Describe the program's goals by using specifics, for example, describe a typical day. A multimedia presentation of children actively engaged is often very effective.
- Review the program's policies. Point out any that are new or have been changed. You might ask families to bring their handbooks for reference—they should have been distributed at the very beginning of the school year.
- Remind families about the calendar, noting days the center will be closed.
- Describe any new services like gymnastics or music classes you will be offering on-site.
- Suggest ways families can help their children get the most out of each day.
- Have a short question-and-answer period, but remind families that particular concerns are discussed in individual conferences.
- Invite families to enjoy simple refreshments, to visit with each other, and to look around the facility.
- Thank them for coming.

Special-Topics Meetings.   As mentioned earlier in this chapter, families often have interests in particular topics like effective bedtime routines, potty training strategies that work, helping children prepare for the birth of a sibling, and so on. Articles, brochures, Web sites and videos are available from professional associations that provide quick, concise, down-to-earth messages for families on many of these frequently requested topics. Some of these materials are sold in multiple copies at reasonable prices.

Program directors should determine convenient times for meetings and topics that are of interest to their families. Sometimes, directors compile a list of possible topics and invite families to add to it. A small committee can help the director plan meetings that meet families' needs at times when interested families can participate.

Special-topics meetings may be for all families or they can be for small groups of interested family members. The topic for this kind of meeting is predetermined and announced in advance. Sometimes a local expert, perhaps a member of the early childhood faculty from a nearby college or university, might lead the meeting. It is a good idea to plan for a short presentation summarizing the "big ideas"—what families need to know. This overview might be based on resources parents have been provided in advance or distributed at the meeting.

A discussion should follow, giving families the opportunity to apply what they have heard to their own situation and to ask follow-up questions. These meetings should be scheduled for 60 to 75 minutes. Child care services are likely to make it possible for more families to participate, and refreshments always help to create a relaxed and collegial atmosphere.

Small-group meetings have several advantages over those involving a large group: (a) they are easier to schedule because fewer families are involved, (b) they make it easier for those who feel uneasy in an individual conference or large-group meeting to become involved, and (c) they meet the special needs and interests of families and reassure families that others have similar concerns. The major disadvantage is that they put demands on the director, creating work responsibilities in the evening or on weekends.

Regularly Scheduled Individual Conferences.   Individual family–staff conferences help families understand the program, learn how their child is developing, and what he is learning. When you schedule conferences early in the year, family members have an opportunity to help set specific learning goals and may help avoid problems later because they lay a foundation for teachers and families to work together toward common goals (Neilson & Finkelstein, 1993). Conferences are also important as children prepare to transition from one classroom to the next, and at the end of the year to review progress toward agreed-upon learning goals.

Although the conference setting may be informal, teachers should prepare carefully so they can describe how individual children are progressing across developmental domains. Consider sharing these recommendations when teachers are preparing for individual conferences. In many centers this would be a very good topic for a staff development training. Consider the training outline in Figure 12.5. Figure 12.6 provides a sample invitation to schedule a conference.

Specially Called Individual Conferences.   Unlike regularly scheduled individual conferences, which occur at scheduled intervals, specially called parent-teacher conferences may be initiated by a parent, teacher or caregiver, or director to address a specific concern. The

---

1.   Inviting families to make appointments for individual conferences   You want to be certain all families know how to schedule conferences and when they can expect those individual conferences to occur. Some programs schedule individual conferences for all children at the same time of the year. If that is the case in your center, remind families when that time is approaching. Other programs, particularly those with year-round admissions, schedule conferences throughout the year, for example, every 6 months on the anniversary of the child's enrollment. In either case, you will want to use your regular newsletter to remind families how important these meetings are, to ask them to come prepared to share insights about their child, and to indicate what teachers hope to accomplish during scheduled conferences.

It is important to intentionally invite both mothers and fathers to parent conferences. All too often men are unintentionally "disinvited" because they may not be able to participate at the times usually scheduled for conferences, or because the school subtly suggests that home-school relationships are "woman's work." (Gonzalez-Mena, 2007). In cases where the child does not live with both parents, it is important to include the noncustodial parent in conferences discussing the child's growth, development, and learning.

When there is a noncustodial parent who is involved with his or her child on a regular basis, you will want to communicate with both parents, even if that means sending home two sets of home-school communications or mailing materials to the parent with visitation rights. It is possible that conferences with parents who are separated or divorced will have to be held separately, but the effort is worth the payoff if these meetings will help to keep both parents involved in supporting their child's growth and development.

2.   Scheduling conferences   Your classroom should develop a schedule of conference times and should invite families to choose a time that fits their needs. If possible, schedule only a few conferences each day, perhaps some before the center opens in the morning, some during lunch/nap time, and others in the late afternoon or early evening. Be sensitive to families' individual needs, however, and indicate your willingness to make special accommodations for families who are not able to meet at the suggested times. Be certain to allow at least 30 minutes for each conference and to provide a break between appointments so you have time to jot down notes and prepare for the next family. It is very important to stay on schedule. This shows your respect for family members' time and their other commitments. Be certain to confirm the conference appointment the day before.

3.   The purpose of conferences.   Conferences enable you to better understand the children and families with whom you are working, to share information about children's progress across developmental domains, and to give family members an opportunity to ask questions or share information related to their child's performance and success. As noted in chapter 11, conferences are the perfect time to share insights gained when

Note: We use the word "parents" in this discussion but appreciate that conferences may include the extended family and other caring adults (Christian, 2007).

Figure 12.5
Staff Development: Guidelines for Effective Parent/Teacher Conferences

conducting individual assessments such as the Child Observation Record (COR; High/Scope Educational Research Foundation, 1992), Work Sampling System (Meisels et al., 1994).

4. Prepare for conferences carefully.

   a. In your letter requesting family members to make appointments, explain whether they may bring their enrolled child and other young children to the meeting. If child care is provided or if younger siblings can play quietly during the conference, more families may be able to participate.

   b. Provide an attractive, comfortable, private place for the conference. It is important to consider the nonverbal messages sent by the setting as well as by your body language. For example, tables and chairs should be adult-sized so everyone can be comfortable. The teacher should not sit behind a desk but should create a setting where she can sit next to parents, creating an atmosphere of cooperation and collegiality (Lawrence-Lightfoot, 2003).

   c. Provide families who arrive early a comfortable place to wait. It is thoughtful to have simple refreshments and appropriate reading material to make waiting easier.

   d. If you have conducted assessments such as the COR or Work Sampling System, have copies of the appropriate reports to give to parents. In addition, you will want to organize the child's portfolio to serve as your outline for the conference. Consider if there are any particular questions you want to ask the family and have them available so you do not forget to ask.

5. Conducting a successful conference.

   a. Greet each parent cordially by name.

   b. Set a positive tone by asking parents what they are particularly enjoying about their child at this age, and, in return, share a positive anecdote that highlights the child's successes, growth, and development.

   c. Describe the child's learning, growth, and development by sharing assessments, if appropriate, and by giving examples of the child's activities in the classroom. You should have developed a portfolio for the child with artifacts illustrating his progress to date. Point out the child's strengths and accomplishments and then note any areas of concern or that need particular attention.

   d. Invite the parents to comment, ask questions, and add to the information you have shared.

   e. Develop shared goals for the child in the coming months. What does the family and what do you hope he will learn and be able to do by the time of the next scheduled parent-teacher conference? Develop strategies for working toward these goals at home and at school. Following up on these plans should be the basis for the next planned conference and can also help guide informal day-to-day parent-teacher conversations.

   f. If the conference has included some difficult conversations, take care not to blame the family, avoid putting them on the defensive, and be careful not to react argumentatively if you encounter a difference of opinion. It is possible the family may blame the teacher or the program if the child is having difficulties or believe their child is simply going through a stage. Family members can be especially unprepared to hear or accept the fact that you recommend screening for a suspected disability.

   g. Invite parents to participate in the classroom and explore what kinds of involvment might be most appealing and appropriate.

Figure 12.5 (*Continued*)

h. Do not make family members feel rushed; however, in fairness to others who are waiting, it is important to stay on time. If appropriate, invite parents to make another appointment to continue the discussion.

i. Make notes on the conference to include in the child's folder. (Seplocha, 2004).

Sometimes older preschoolers and primary-age children are invited to participate in at least part of their family's conference with their teacher. This gives them a meaningful opportunity to develop reflective skills of self-assessment and decision making as they select items to include in their portfolio and explain to their parents why this represents their "best work." Children may also participate in setting goals for the coming weeks and months (Shores & Grace, 1998; Taylor, 1999).

Figure 12.5 (*Continued*)

Dear _____

It's hard to believe your child has been in our program for 8 months! It has certainly been a time of growing and learning!

Our center schedules regular family conferences during the month of March. I would like to plan to meet with you for about 30 minutes in the coming weeks.

I am available

- before school from 7:00 A.M.–8:00 A.M.
- during nap time from 12:00 noon–1:30 P.M.
- at the end of the day 5:00 P.M.–6:00 P.M.

Please suggest some days and times that would work for you, and I will be in touch to confirm a day and time soon.

We will meet in the Parent Resource Center—Room 114. We plan this as a meeting for adult conversation. Please let us know if you will have difficulty arranging care for any younger children.

I look forward to sharing what we have learned about your child's growth and development during the past months and I hope you do too.

Please return this form by **Tuesday, February 18th.**

I look forward to conferencing with you soon!

Ms. Elaine

- -

Name _____

I am available

Date	Time
_____	_____
_____	_____
_____	_____
_____	_____

What is the best way to contact you? _____

home phone   work phone   cell phone   email

please circle

Figure 12.6
Invitation to Schedule an Individual Conference

most common reasons for specially called conferences are problem behaviors such as biting, aggression, uncontrolled anger, and an unwillingness to cooperate. Concerns about other issues may, however, prompt a parent or teacher to schedule a meeting to discuss a child's progress. These specially called conferences should be seen as opportunities for collaborative problem solving. A systematic approach can help families and program personnel work together toward shared goals that will make the child's school experiences more successful and more pleasant for all.

Teachers often need their director's guidance when addressing problem behaviors. It may be helpful to guide teachers through the following steps when planning for a specially called conference. You may also want to offer to join the conversation to add insights based on your experience and training.

1. Define the behaviors that are causing you concern and provide documentation demonstrating when those behaviors occur in the school setting. Describe how the school setting has responded to these concerning behaviors.
2. Ask parents to share their observations. Have they observed the same behavior? Do they know of experiences or conditions that may explain these behaviors? How do they respond to these behaviors at home and other out-of-school settings?
3. Agree on behaviorial goals and strategies to reinforce desired behaviors.
4. Agree to follow up on these efforts after trying the agreed-upon strategies for a specified time, perhaps 2 or 4 weeks.
5. If parents and teachers are not able to report that they have made progress encouraging the desired behavior, it may be time to seek the advice of a specialist at the local school district, at a nearby college or university, or a practitioner recommended by the family's pediatrician.

Home Visits.   Home visits have had a long history in early care and education and are an extremely valuable way to learn more about the children and families you serve. Home visits provide teachers invaluable insights into the child's community, home, and family. They lay a foundation for the creation of positive relationships between children, families, and the program. They can also give teachers opportunities to explain the program's goals, to conduct an intake interview, and may present opportunities to share information about child development and developmentally appropriate expectations.

Additional ways home visits contribute to the creation of a quality program of early care and education are as follows:

1. Professionals are seen as people who care enough about the child to visit the family.
2. Family members are likely to be more comfortable in their own homes than at the program site. They may provide more information and discuss more of their concerns in this comfortable setting.
3. Transitions are often easier for children whose teachers visit them in their homes before their first day of school. Teachers might want to take along a digital camera so they can pose for a picture with their future student. This picture makes a nice addition to the classroom and is a meaningful keepsake to send home with the child.

As the program director, you will be responsible for helping teachers prepare for home visits and will want to help them be successful. Remind teachers to keep in mind that home visits require careful planning. They must always be prearranged so they can be planned for a time that is convenient for the family as well as the teacher. The teacher should confirm the appointment a day in advance to be certain the previously scheduled time is still convenient. It may be advisable for teachers to make home visits in pairs, or for the director to join the classroom teacher, particularly if the families participating in their program live in high-crime neighborhoods or if teachers are unfamiliar with the area.

Advise teachers that home visits should last no more than 1 hour. The first 5 to 10 minutes is a time for greetings and for teachers, family members, and the child to get acquainted. Then plan a 20- to 30-minute activity to do with the child in the child's room or another private place suggested by the family. That leaves 15 to 20 minutes for adult conversation when the teacher can learn more about the family, share information about the program, and answer questions. It is good to then have a parting ritual, such as taking a few photographs, offering the child a small gift she can use in school, or walking to the car together (Fox-Barnett & Meyer, 1992; Johnston & Mermin, 1994; Keyser, 2006).

It is possible that not all families will be comfortable inviting their child's teacher into their home. When this is the case, the teacher might suggest meeting at a near-by park or family-friendly fast food restaurant where they can have the same kinds of informal interactions with the child and the family.

Classroom Visits.   Parents are likely to appreciate the opportunity to experience your program first-hand and see their child interacting with peers and adults in their natural setting. Encourage parents to visit, either by appointment or to drop in unannounced, at any time—except when children are settling down for nap or when they are sleeping. It is sometimes helpful to send a personal invitation inviting parents to visit your program, or particular classrooms in your center. That extra step might encourage reluctant parents to come and may even initiate greater family involvement. See Figure 12.7 for a sample invitation to visit the classroom.

Workshops or Workdays.   Workshops and workdays can be popular family involvement events. They can provide an informal setting for families and staff to work together. There are two common types of workshops:

1. In **materials workshops** adults construct materials and equipment. This may involve making instructional materials and games for the classroom. It might also be an opportunity for families to help build a playground. Teachers should determine the types of activities families are willing to take part in and provide choices for participants (Dodd & Brock, 1994).
2. **Cleanup/fix-up workdays** may be held in the evening or on the weekend to clean and repair the building, classrooms, the grounds equipment, or materials.

Newsletters.   Newsletters give family members a vehicle for talking with their children about program activities, can provide them information about meeting their children's developmental and learning needs at home, and are a good way for staff and families to communicate.

Dear _____

There is always a lot going on in our classroom! We love to have family visitors. You can plan ahead—or visit on the spur of the moment. We'd love to have you either way.

Did you know we have new baby gerbils? They are just beginning to open their eyes. We'd love for you to come see them!

We also can show you what we've learned about planting and caring for a garden. We should have radishes soon. You can come for a snack any time.

Maybe you'd like to come and play—or you'd like to bring your guitar and let us sing along.

And we always welcome family members to join us at story time. We have a good selection of books on hand if you would like to read one to the group—or maybe you have a special book from home that you'd like to share.

___(teacher's signature)___   and Mr. Randall's Fantastic Four's

Figure 12.7
Invitation to Visit the Classroom

These are suggested topics to include in your newsletters:

1. Announcements about the program, including dates for registration, school closings, and other important events and deadlines
2. Information about new books, music, toys, Internet sites and software, and community events for children and families
3. Reprints of articles of interest to families with young children
4. Ideas for activities the family may enjoy during the summer or school vacations
5. Future plans for the program
6. Recipes from classroom cooking activities
7. Words to favorite songs and fingerplays
8. Updates on staff changes and profiles of staff and families
9. Notes of appreciation to family and community volunteers

Newsletters should be no more then two pages long. Be careful to avoid professional jargon and make sure they have a polished and professional appearance. Proofread carefully for accuracy and clarity. Like all other written communication, newsletters should be, if at all possible, provided to each family in their primary language and should take families' reading level into account.

There are a number of sources for ideas including short copy-ready articles to include in newsletters. NAEYC's new publication *Teaching Young Children* includes camera-ready handouts, and other sources have ideas and materials that can make the task of preparing a regular newsletter easier (Diffily & Morrison, 1997; Meisels, Marsden, & Stetson, 2000). Newsletters can be copied or, in some communities, emailed to all families on a regular basis—usually monthly.

Application Activity

Look at the suggested topics for newsletters listed above. Write a short newsletter article on one of these topics. Take care to have a friendly, but professional, tone and to avoid professional jargon. Exchange articles with a classmate. Evaluate each other's work using criteria identified above.

Telephone Conversations.   Telephone conversations may be initiated by the parent or a member of the staff. Parents are likely to use telephone conversations to provide teachers and caregivers insight into a recent event—perhaps the child came home from school worried, was particularly excited about a classroom activity, or is sad because a beloved pet is very sick. Some parents might prefer talking over the telephone rather than face-to-face communication. Telephone conversations allow for quick, unplanned contacts.

Teachers and caregivers should make certain their first telephone conversation is a positive one. They should plan to touch base with all parents regularly with good news, describing something interesting or successful their child has done. Families are also likely to appreciate a call to inquire how their child is if he has been out of school for a few days, or to congratulate them on the arrival of a new baby.

The telephone can also be useful when a child has had a difficult day. When based on the foundation of a trusting and positive relationship, telephone calls can alert families to issues you are facing with a child and might help prevent a small worry from becoming a major concern.

Even though almost everyone has a telephone, teachers and caregivers should be sensitive to the fact that they may have families who do not have ready access to a telephone. Be alert for signs that this may not be the best way to communicate with some families, particularly those living in poverty.

Other Methods of Communication.   Several other methods aid family–staff communication. These are some examples:

1. Informal notes.   Notes or short email messages are very effective and quick ways to communicate. These are some topics that may prompt you to write a short note home:

   a. Parents appreciate it when you can ask them to give their child a "Pat on the Back" for a job well done. Figure 12.8 is an example of a "Pat on the Back" note.

   b. Families appreciate thanks for a helping hand. Be sure to show your appreciation when families support the goals of your program.

   c. Families enjoy a photograph of an activity their child particularly enjoyed. Maybe Tyrone built an extra-tall tower in the block center or went down the slide alone for the very first time. His family would appreciate a snapshot with an interpretive note to share these kinds of every day accomplishments.

   d. You might create "Ask Me About" badges to let families know their children have accomplished a goal or reached a milestone. They prompt families to ask children about these important events (Stamp & Groves, 1994).

   e. Families know you care when you send cards or notes for children's birthdays or when family members are ill.

Please give _____ a pat on the back today
for _____

Figure 12.8
"A Pat on the Back"

2. Program Web Site.   A Web site can identify the program's goals and can include the family handbook, enrollment forms, menus, information about fees, the center's calendar, a newsletter, information about parent-teacher organization projects and events, contact information for the director, and other information you want available to the public. While pictures of the facility may be a good addition, avoid posting children's pictures to ensure their privacy. Guidelines for Web site development are discussed in chapter 8. You may want to consider a password-protected section of the Web site for information for participating families such as information about each classroom's activities.

3. Program videos.   Videos of program activities, including special events, can be shared with families and can also contribute to marketing efforts.

4. Social events.   Social meetings, such as picnics for the whole family, adult-child breakfasts or going-home snacks, or a recognition event for volunteers, stimulate good relationships between families and staff.

Family Participation

There is a long tradition of families participating in programs of early care and education. In parent cooperative programs, parents learn about child development and about developmentally appropriate activities by agreeing to lead activities in their children's classrooms. Head Start and other government-sponsored programs create the expectation that parents will be involved as employees and volunteers and to serve on advisory councils. Programs serving children with disabilities also often require families to be involved on a regular basis. The truth is that all children, families, and programs benefit when families are actively involved in their children's education.

Family Members as Volunteers.   In effective programs, all families are given opportunities to participate in a variety of ways and are given the freedom to determine the extent of their participation. Social activities and fund-raising projects are most likely to involve the greatest numbers of families, but there are many other ways families can volunteer on a regular or occasional basis.

For a volunteer program to work, an administrator must help plan and organize the volunteers. Once a volunteer program has been launched, volunteers should be able to operate the program themselves.

Unfortunately, fathers are often not as likely as mothers to be involved in their children's early childhood programs (Fagan, 1994). This may be because early childhood programs, often inadvertently, create barriers that make it difficult for fathers to participate, or make them feel unwelcome (Gonzalez-Mena, 2007). Activities planned by fathers and specifically designed to appeal to their interests and skills are more likely to engage men in their young children's school experiences (Cunningham, 1994; Fagan, 1994, 1996; Gonzalez-Mena, 2007).

Grandparents are another sometimes-hard-to-reach group. We know that grandparents are, increasingly, young children's primary caregivers. They bring particular needs and unique resources to your program. It is worth the effort to reach out to both custodial and noncustodial grandparents—your program will undoubtedly benefit from their contributions and special perspectives (Birckmayer et al., 2005).

Even when rolling out the welcome mat in as many ways as possible, there will always be some families who can not, or choose not to, participate (Sciarra & Dorsey, 1998). It is important to respect this decision, and to maintain the same kind of positive and productive relationship with all families, regardless of their interest in, or ability to, participate.

Appropriate Roles for Family Volunteers.   Family members are valuable volunteers because they (a) are likely to know and understand other families' working hours, transportation situations, and community mores; (b) can serve as cultural models for children; (c) help staff members understand children's likes and dislikes, strengths and weaknesses, and home successes and struggles; (d) can often serve as interpreters in bilingual programs; and (e) can assist staff in program activities, such as storytelling, art, music, and gardening. As volunteers they may also assist in the positive guidance of children, accompany staff members in home-visiting programs, and serve as ambassadors to the neighborhood.

Specific expectations of volunteers should be determined by the program's needs and the volunteers' abilities. These are some basic issues to consider:

1. Volunteers should have an orientation to the program's facility and staff, to applicable professional ethics, and to state and local laws regarding personnel qualifications and activities. Orientation could include a broad overview of the program's goals, rules, and regulations, specific tasks and limits of responsibility, classroom management (if involved with children), and a hands-on experience with materials. Volunteers' feedback about the usefulness of the orientation will help you plan orientations in the future.

2. Teachers and caregivers should be coached about appropriate ways to use volunteers' help. In most cases volunteers cannot be counted in staff-child ratios for licensing. Volunteers are not to be responsible for supervising children alone. This is important because the program is liable if a volunteer or child under a volunteer's supervision is injured. Teachers and caregivers should be able to decide if they want family volunteers in their classrooms and what they want them to do.

3. A handbook reiterating much of the information given during the orientation program is helpful for staff and volunteers.

4. Teachers and caregivers should have a specific plan for what volunteers are to do during their visits. It is important to avoid giving volunteers only menial jobs or tasks no one else wants to do because they are apt to develop a negative attitude and may lose interest in being involved if they do not feel their talents are being used (Greenberg, 1989). Volunteers need guidance if they are to lead a learning activity. They should typically work with individual children or small groups. The teacher should demonstrate what she expects the volunteer to do, provide a brief rationale for the activity, describe what children will learn during this activity, and show the volunteer where she will find the needed materials.

5. Volunteers' performance and effectiveness should be assessed by the director, with the teacher if appropriate. Tasks should be tailored to their strengths and interests. That kind of planning makes volunteering a win-win situation.

6. Family members can also volunteer in the program's support service areas: working in the lunchroom, assisting the school nurse, assisting in the library/media center, helping with the distribution of equipment and materials, working with transportation services, and providing general office support.

Occasional Volunteers.   Many family members cannot volunteer on a regular basis but enjoy helping out periodically during the year. Family members can be very valuable chaperoning field trips, working on fund-raising projects, and helping during special occasions such as the fall open house or class parties. Volunteers can also be valuable classroom resources, sharing their occupation or hobby with children as appropriate.

It is wise to survey family members to learn about their special talents and interests and to encourage them to share these talents and interests with young children.

Parent Education and Family Resource and Support Programs

The child study movement of the early 1900s made child rearing a science. In the 1960s and 1970s, parent education programs became part of almost all early intervention programs. Parents learned about child development and were encouraged to collaborate with their child's early childhood program or school to help them meet their child's needs.

A major movement toward family resource and support programs began in the 1980s and continues into the present.

Types of Parent Education and Family Resource and Support Programs.   There are many types of parent education, family resource, and family support programs (Epstein, 2001; National PTA, 2000). Their nature depends on program needs, families' needs and wishes, and program goals. Techniques may vary as well. Services for families may be either staff directed or family initiated; they may have one focus or be multifaceted; and they may be delivered through direct instruction, or indirectly, with family members observing teaching and guidance techniques while visiting in classrooms. Programs may be sponsored by school systems, universities, or various community agencies. They might also be cooperatively planned by agencies working together.

Orientation Programs.   Perhaps the most common service offered to parents of children enrolled in an early childhood program is an orientation which is provided through handbooks, newsletters, and meetings. Orientation programs are designed by the local program's staff.

Home-Visiting Programs.   Home-visiting programs help family members learn how to teach their young children. They often begin at birth and demonstrate to families how to talk to and interact with their baby, and how to use everyday household materials as educational toys. The exact nature of home-visiting programs depends on the program's objectives, the number of families to be visited, the number and frequency of visits per family, and the program's financial resources.

Family Discussion Groups.   The basic goals of family discussion groups are to help families learn more about positive parenting practices, child development, and learning. Discussion groups are sometimes led by a knowledgeable resource person. Sometimes they are led by parents. Peer support groups are often particularly popular among families of children with disabilities.

Resource Centers.   A common type of resource center is the toy-lending library designed to give families access to materials that help children develop concepts, enhance verbal fluency, and build problem-solving skills. Toy lending libraries offer families guidelines in the appropriate use of selected toys. Parent resource centers also provide child-rearing information. These kinds of resource centers are sometimes located in public libraries and are often sponsored by the state's or the community's comprehensive early childhood program.

Self-Improvement Programs.   Self-improvement programs are designed to empower adult family members to improve their own lives. Services may include instruction in basic adult education; English for second-language learners; consumer, nutrition, or health education; information about how to access community resources; how-to classes in home repairs; and other family life topics. This instruction may be in the form of formal courses for high school credit or informal workshops. They are usually offered by the public school system for the benefit of all adult residents of a community.

Family Resource and Support Programs.   Family resource and support programs are for all families. To be effective, however, the services must be individualized to support different stages in the family life cycle and to meet other particular needs (e.g., work/family issues, family crises). Services could include the following:

1. Programs for children, including a home-visiting program, a home-care program, or a center-based program
2. Programs for adults in areas such as family and consumer sciences, child development, adult education, and job counseling
3. Health and nutrition services, including medical services for children and adult family members, and classes in child care, safety, and nutrition
4. Social services, such as referrals, recreational activities, and assistance in finding adequate housing and in providing food and clothing

EARLY CHILDHOOD EDUCATORS HAVE A LONG HISTORY OF PARTNERING WITH THEIR COMMUNITIES

Communities in the United States have always played an important role in the support of families and the educational programs that serve their young children. Demographic and social changes, such as population growth, increasingly diverse communities, families' increased mobility, and fewer families with young children who live near their extended families, have diminished the feeling of community in some locales. Efforts to link families and early childhood programs with their community are particularly important in these rapidly changing and turbulent times (NAEYC, 1994).

Early childhood professionals have a unique opportunity to link the families they serve with their communities. This is because they are likely to work closely with families over a long period of time and are knowledgeable of, and visible within, the community.

Early childhood professionals can serve as advocates for families because they are often in a position to link families with services they might need such as Temporary Assistance for Needy Families (TANF) child welfare services; subsidized child care; child health services such as Medicaid, nutrition programs, local health clinics; and special child care needs such as Head Start, family violence prevention and treatment, adoption and foster care, homeless services (Allen, Brown & Finlay, 1992).

Increasingly, business leaders appreciate the need for employer-supported child care for their employees and for quality early childhood education as the basis for maintaining a competitive workforce for the future (Heckman, 1999; Rolnick & Grunewald, 2003).

Tapping into Family and Community Support Through Advisory Committees and Boards of Directors.

Many early childhood programs include representatives from participating families as well as other members of the community on their program-level *advisory committee,* which addresses issues related to the program's day-to-day operations, and on the agency level *board of directors* responsible for issues related to finances and legal obligations.

When planning whom to invite to serve on your advisory committee and governing board, it is important to look beyond individuals you already know and trust, such as friends or parents of current children. When current parents predominate, the board may act more like a parent-teacher organization than a governing board or may simply become a rubber stamp for the director (Gottlieb, 2005). Board members outside the program are also likely to have a longer view and are more likely to be willing to serve your organization for several years.

The first issue to address when establishing a board is to identify the issues it will address. The following tasks are typically assigned to advisory and/or governing boards:

- Creating statements of the organization's purpose, vision, and goals
- Evaluating the program's success meeting expectations stated in the statements of purpose, vision, and goals
- Hiring and evaluating the director
- Setting fees
- Creating salary schedules
- Negotiating fringe benefit packages for employees
- Overseeing the facility, including plans to build, remodel, and perform needed maintenance

The next issue to consider is how many members these governing bodies need. Many states require nonprofit governing boards to have at least 3 members. Experts recommend that effective boards usually have between 7 and 13 members. Group size may vary depending on what needs to be accomplished. A larger group will be needed when the program is being established; facilities are being built or remodeled; and policies, procedures, and handbooks are being created.

Organizations that have a history of running smoothly are likely to need smaller advisory commitees and governing boards, whose responsibilities can be characterized as keeping the ship running on course. Small groups are more flexible and members are more likely to have a feeling of unity and purpose. Larger committees and boards, however, bring more expertise to the tasks at hand and there are more people to do the needed work.

The third issue is, "What stakeholders and expertise do you need on your advisory committee and governing board?" Most state licensing laws require that a not-for-profit private early childhood organization operate under a governing board composed, at least in part, of the people it serves. Head Start has specific guidelines about stakeholders' participation on these kinds of governing bodies. Review the list in Figure 12.9 to determine which of these skills and expertise will best serve your organization.

Remember, it is possible that an individual may bring more than one kind of expertise to the table. Refer to appendix 6 for examples of how you can assess the contribution each potential member may bring to your organization. It is important to learn to identify the leadership potential of even shy and quiet individuals. Can you discover who has vision? Who wants to make something happen? Who can work both independently and interdependently? (Gonzalez-Mena, 2007). When you do, your program will be enriched

Stakeholders and Those with Specialized Skills and Expertise to Consider as Prospective Members of Your Advisory Committee and Governing Board.

Stakeholders

- Parent of child in your program
- Representative from the licensing agency or another representative from the government
- Community resident
- Business owner

Skills and Expertise

- Organizational and financial management
- Community development
- Administration
- Academic/education
- Business/corporate
- Accounting/ Banking/Investments
- Fund-raising (both experienced fund-raisers and those who may be able to generate substantial gifts)
- Laws/regulations
- Accreditation
- Representative from the licensing agency or another representative from the government
- Marketing/Public relations
- Personnel
- Physical plant (architecture, engineer)
- Strategic or long-range planning
- Real-estate

Figure 12.9
Makeup of Advisory Committee and Governing Board

by the inclusion of many voices. You will want to take demographic factors into account as well, striving for a group of men and women of various ages that reflects the ethnicity, cultures, and socioeconomic status of the community and families you serve.

And finally, create some expectations about how the advisory committee and governing board will operate. See appendix 7 for an example of a board director position description and statement of commitment.

It is wise to have terms of 2 or 3 years so that these governing bodies will have the benefit of some of the same members' experience each year. Candidates should also be informed of expectations for board membership. Provide a job description that includes:

- Purpose of the organization and the role of the advisory committee and board of directors
- Term of office including term limits
- How members of these governing bodies are expected to support the organization, including responsibilities for participating in events
- Estimate of the time required for this service (About how many hours per month or per year will participating on this committee/board require?)
- Frequency of committee/board meetings (How long are the meetings? Is there a set meeting time, such as noon to 2:00 P.M on the first Tuesday of the month?)
- List of subcommittees of this committee/board and a description of when they meet
- Orientation provided for members of the committee/board (Gottlieb, 2005)

It is important to prepare your governing bodies for the work at hand. This training should focus on strategies to help them work together to understand the regulations and accreditation standards (when applicable) within which your program operates, identify problems, generate possible solutions, learn decision-making and consensus-building strategies, and communicate recommendations to all stakeholders, including, when appropriate, parent organizations.

TRENDS AND ISSUES

Early childhood professionals are faced with the responsibility of responding to significant changes in their communities. America is becoming more culturally and linguistically diverse; more mothers of infants and toddlers are entering the workforce than ever before; increased numbers of families are headed by single mothers, including young women with low levels of education. Grandparents have, in increased numbers, become young children's primary guardians, often as a result of a family crisis; and increased life spans mean that many parents of young children face the challenges of being in the "sandwich generation"—responsible for caring for elders while at the same time raising their own families.

Many communities remain ill-prepared to provide families the safety net they need. As one of the first experiences many families of young children have with the helping professions, early childhood educators have a unique opportunity to support families in their efforts to nurture and care for their young children, preparing them for success in school and beyond.

Early childhood professionals' commitment to children and families can help them access needed related services. These efforts will, more than ever, make *partnership* and *collaboration* hallmarks of the profession.

Table 12.1 outlines of the principles and components of family-centered collaboration. Some programs with integrated services are Early Head Start, Head Start, and Even Start. Besides these federally funded programs, efforts are under way in local communities and states.

Table 12.1
Family-Centered Models

Principles Underlying Model	Components of Programs
Families are viewed within their community contexts, which promote or curtail family strength.	Target the overall development of parents as individuals by acknowledging the many roles and responsibilities they shoulder, by providing an empathic partner in care, and by encouraging their efforts to form supportive relationships with other adults.
Parents are seen as individuals with roles and responsibilities in which child rearing is only one role.	
The parent–child relationship is influenced by parenting knowledge, but, more importantly, by parents' self-esteem, family background, socioeconomic status and other cultural and linguistic factors, and the community setting.	See the parent–child relationship (rather than the child) as the primary client of the program and work to strengthen this enduring relationship. Seek input from families when planning and creating program policies. Take A "facilitator" role rather than "expert" role when appropriate.
A specific event that influences any member of the family has some effect on the entire family system.	Offer comprehensive services or provide community links to families and children needing services.

SUMMARY

Early childhood educators have a long history of working closely with the families of the children they serve. Parent involvment and parent education have taken many forms from the early 1900s to the present. Today's emphasis is on providing diverse families needed resources and support programs that serve not only as agents of family change, but also as support systems designed to prevent problems.

Today's, early childhood educators strive to form *collaborative partnerships* with parents that emphasize the strengths every family brings to its efforts to nurture and care for their young children. These efforts rely on the creation of respectful relationships that link early care and education professionals with the diverse families they serve. It requires teachers and caregivers of young children to invest the time and effort needed to develop effective strategies to involve all families with their children—for the benefit of children and the communities they will one day lead.

USEFUL WEB SITES

Videos to Help Children and Families Transition into School

Educational Productions. (2001). Kindergarten here I come! (in English and Spanish)

  www.kindergartenhereicome.com/home.shtml)

Best Life Videos. Preparing for Kindergarten: A parent's guide (in English and Spanish).

  www.bestlifevideos.com/videos.asp#kgv_english

TO REFLECT

1. Allan (1997) referred to the imaginary line that still separates schools and families and prevents families from truly participating in the school lives of their children. What is the symbolism inherent in that demarcation? How do professionals make hard-drawn lines even in subtle ways? How can we recognize and erase these barriers?

2. How can we decide when it is appropriate for families to have "the" say in policy decisions and when the director or board should have "the" say? How might staff members respect the delicate balance of shared family–program responsibilities?

3. Families often bring their own adult concerns (e.g., divorce, stress of being a single parent, financial problems) into formal and informal family–teacher conferences. As a director, how would you advise your teachers to address such concerns?

4. One of the most difficult situations for directors working with families is dealing with families who do not believe they have the time, abilities, and skills, or interests to help their children. When families lack confidence in their child-rearing roles, how does the program build on their strengths? Can all families be empowered? Can cooperation be defined in different ways to accommodate different family-life pressures?

13

CONTRIBUTING TO THE PROFESSION

NAEYC Director Competencies addressed in this chapter:

Management Knowledge and Skills

1. Personal and Professional Self-Awareness
   The ability to evaluate ethical and moral dilemmas based on a professional code of ethics
8. Leadership and Advocacy
   Knowledge of the legislative process, social issues, and public policy affecting young children and their families
   The ability to advocate on behalf of young children, their families and the profession.

Early Childhood Knowledge and Skills

10. Professionalism
    Knowledge of different professional organizations, resources, and issues impacting the welfare of early childhood practitioners
    Ability to reflect on one's professional growth and development and make goals for personal improvement.

Early childhood administrators are leaders. They have a responsibility to ensure the quality of the program they serve. They also have an opportunity to be an advocate. They can work toward ensuring all families access to quality early childhood programming by becoming active in their community or in a larger arena. Program administrators also have an opportunity to contribute to the field's efforts to move toward higher standards of practice and increased professionalism.

Some ways program administrators can accomplish these goals are by engaging in informed advocacy; mentoring novices, experienced practitioners, and emerging leaders; making the pubic aware of the field's reliance on a code of ethics; and, when appropriate, becoming involved in research to increase what we know about the characteristics and lifelong benefits of quality programming for young children.

PROMOTING PROFESSIONALIZATION[1]

Lilian Katz, one of the most influential voices in the field of early care and education, began discussions about the professionalism of the field in the mid-1980s. At that time she noted that "professionalism" generally denotes praiseworthy work, and she observed that professionals are typically rewarded with high pay and elevated social status (Katz,1995).

It is now generally agreed that early childhood education is an "emerging" profession. It is neither like the "paradigm professions" of law and medicine, nor are early childhood educators unskilled workers, such as day laborers or short-order cooks, who enter the workplace with little prior training or specialized knowledge and whose employers are likely to consider them to be interchangeable.

To understand where early childhood lies on the professional continuum, consider how it measures up in terms of the following attributes commonly used to determine whether an occupation is, or is moving toward becoming, a profession (See Figure 13.1 for a depiction of the professional continuum).

1. Professionals *possess specialized knowledge*. They acquire this knowledge and skill and in its application by following a course of *prolonged training*.
2. Professions have rigorous *requirements for entry* into professional training, and training is delivered in *accredited* institutions.
3. Members of a profession have agreed upon *standards of practice* that guide their efforts to carry out their duties and meet their professional obligations.
4. A profession has a commitment to meeting a *significant societal need*.
5. Professionals are *altruistic* and *service-oriented* rather than profit-oriented. Their primary goal is to meet clients' needs.
6. Professionals provide an *indispensable service* and are recognized as the only group in society who can perform its function.
7. A profession is characterized by *autonomy*—it has control over entry into the field, oversees the quality of the services offered by its members, and it regulates itself.
8. A profession has a *code of ethics* that spells out its obligations to society (Katz, 1995; Stonehouse, 1994; Feeney, 1995).

[1]Versions of this discussion have been published in "The New Face of Early Childhood Education: Who Are We? Where Are We Going?" by N. K. Freeman and S. Feeney, 2006, *Young Children, 61*(5), pp. 10–16 and also in "Professionalism and Ethics" by N. K. Freeman and S. Feeney, 2009, *Continuing Issues in Early Childhood Education,* 3rd ed., S. Feeney, A. Galpar, and C. Seefeldt, (Eds.), Upper Saddle River, NJ: Merrill/Pearson.

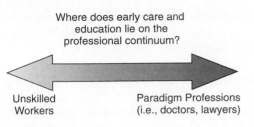

Where does early care and
education lie on the
professional continuum?

Unskilled   Paradigm Professions
Workers   (i.e., doctors, lawyers)

Figure 13.1
A Professional Continuum

The field of early care and education is making strides in some of these areas, but progress has been slow in others. The following discussion focuses on two particular dimensions of professionalism in which there has been notable progress in recent years. The first is the acquisition of *specialized knowledge* attained through *prolonged training* (number 1), and the second is reliance on a *code of ethics* (number 8).

Application Activity

Our discussion focuses on efforts to increase the professionalism of the field by setting higher expectations for professional preparation and by making our reliance on our *Code of Ethical Conduct* explicit. Select one of *the other* criteria of professionalism. Decide where the field of early care and education falls on the professionalism continuum that puts doctors and lawyers at one end and unskilled workers at the other. Provide a rationale for your conclusion.

Moving Toward Professionalism: Professional Preparation and Reliance on the *NAEYC Code of Ethical Conduct*

Professional Preparation.   It remains true that many states' licensing regulations are minimal. Some require child care teachers and caregivers to have only a high school diploma or GED and stipulate only that directors and master teachers hold a child development associate (CDA) credential (which is generally considered to be the equivalent of one year of postsecondary study) (NARA/NCCIC, 2006).

Publically funded programs have begun, however, to raise the bar for entry into the field. The *Improving Head Start Act of 2007* requires 50 percent of all center-based teachers to hold at least a bachelor's degree in early childhood or a related field by 2013 (Administration for Children and Families, 2007). Publically funded 4K is following suit. Most require teachers to hold at least a bachelor's degree or to be making progress toward graduation (Barnett, Hustedt, Hawkinson, & Robin, 2007).

NAEYC's Program Accreditation Standards also, over time, raise educational requirements across the board. They stipulate that by 2020 75% of the teachers in an accredited program must have a minimum of a baccalaureate degree in early childhood education or a related field. NAEYC accreditation also requires directors to hold at least a baccalaureate degree and stipulates that they must have specialized coursework in administration and management as well as child development and learning, or a plan to meet these requirements within 5 years (NAEYC, 2005a).

It is likely that the effects of these policy changes will be felt across the entire field of early care and education, raising expectations for educational attainment in nonprofit and for-profit programs operated under a wide variety of auspices. These developments point to progress the field has made in one criterion of professionalism: requiring early childhood practitioners to have specialized *knowledge gained by following a course of prolonged training.*

Reliance on the *NAEYC Code of Ethical Conduct.*   Reliance on a code of professional ethics is a second criterion of professionalism in which early childhood educators have made strides in recent years. The *NAEYC Code of Ethical Conduct* (2005) includes statements of the profession's Core Values and guides practitioners in their efforts to meet their responsibilities to children, families, colleagues, and society. It articulates Ideals (how we aspire to behave), and Principles (standards of conduct describing what we must and must not do). A Statement of Commitment accompanies the Code. It is not a part of the Code of Conduct but attests to members' resolve to abide by the Code as they work with young children and their families.

NAEYC first adopted its *Code of Ethical Conduct* in 1989 (Feeney & Kipnis, 1989) and revised it in 1992, 1997, and 2005. The field has taken steps to enhance practitioners' reliance on the Code and to make this reliance more apparent to those outside the profession.

One way reliance on the Code has been promoted is by making it an important criterion in NAEYC Accreditation Standards both for programs serving young children and for postsecondary programs preparing teachers for every rung of the professional ladder—from CDA through the terminal degree. These standards ensure that all practitioners in accredited programs are knowledgeable about the Code, and all who graduate from accredited postsecondary programs have demonstrated their knowledge of, and skill applying, it in their work.

Two supplements have been designed to be used with the original *Code of Ethical Conduct*. They extend the reach of the Code beyond those working directly with young children and their families. The first supplement addresses the particular needs of program administrators (2006). It provides guidance as you face situations with ethical dimensions unique to the director, such as filling a much-sought-after opening in the infant room, terminating a teacher because decreased enrollment is forcing you to downsize, and managing relationships with families in a way that lets you keep the needs of children paramount in your decision making.

The second supplement guides adult educators (2004). It extends the original Code to meet the needs of those providing training and education, whether in credit-granting institutions such as colleges or universities, or in informal professional development activities. As a program director, you are likely to provide professional development designed to meet the particular needs of your staff. This supplement reminds you, for example, to remain true to the approved training plan and helps you have the courage to deny credit to the caregiver who slept through the training activity instead of participating and learning from it.

Several efforts have helped to make the Code widely accessible. The original Code is now reprinted in many introductory textbooks; the Code and both supplements are posted on the NAEYC Web site, the original Code in both English and Spanish; and the Code is available from NAEYC in both English and Spanish in an inexpensive brochure format. NAEYC also offers an attractive laminated poster of the Statement of Commitment. Programs that display this poster attest to their pledge to abide by the field's ethical standards.

In addition to making the Code widely available, NAEYC has made efforts to support practitioners' efforts to apply the Code effectively in their work. NAEYC has published two books focusing on professional ethics: *Ethics and the Early Childhood Educator* (Feeney & Freeman, 1999/2005) provides a comprehensive introduction to the Code, describes its development, and offers guidance in applying each of its sections: responsibilities to children, families, colleagues, and the community.

The second book, *Teaching the NAEYC Code of Ethical Conduct* (Feeney, Freeman, & Moravick, 2000) describes many activities for teaching the Code and includes reproducible training materials that help you prepare for effective training sessions. Other materials to help you teach your staff to apply the Code are identified on the "Teaching the NAEYC Code updates" link from the NAEYC Web site listed at the end of this chapter.

You can help make the families you serve and others outside the profession aware of the field's reliance on the *Code of Ethical Conduct*. One way to accomplish this goal is to include the Code in your program's family handbook and to put families (and staff) on notice that they can expect your behavior and that of your staff to reflect your commitment to these ethical principles. Another is to prominently display the Statement of Commitment poster attesting to your program's reliance on the Code. You are likely to think of others that will work well in your particular setting.

Because it is an emerging profession with a rich and unique history, we believe it is more appropriate to satisfy some criteria of professionalism than others. It is unlikely, for example, that early childhood educators would want to abandon our commitment to making a place for novices eager to pursue their education while working in the field. This is why we embrace T.E.A.C.H.® scholarships that support employees' pursuit of their associate's degree while they are working with young children. This illustrates why we believe it is appropriate for early care and education to carve out a unique niche on the professionalism continuum that honors our roots while at the same time moving toward greater reliance on standards of practice shown to benefit young children and their families.

As we move toward increased professionalism, it is important that program administrators, as leaders in the field, be active in organizations that support their efforts to remain informed and engaged professionals. Consider the organizations listed in appendix 8. Participation in organizations that are of particular interest to you can enhance your practice and connect you with the larger community of early childhood educators and advocates.

Application Activity

Rely on the *NAEYC Code of Ethical Conduct* (appendix 2) and the *Supplement for Program Administrators* (appendix 3) to resolve one of the following dilemmas. Analyze each dilemma by identifying to whom you have responsibilities. Find guidance in the *NAEYC Code* and *Supplement for Program Administrators* (note item number[s]). Then decide what the "good director" should do in each of these situations.

An enrollment issue: The mother of the next child on your list for admission has told you that she has had her child in five different preschools in the last 6 months. She tells you very emotional stories about what she found wrong with each of them.

A personnel issue: Your enrollment is down. You must close a classroom and let a teacher go. Do you choose the last person hired who is an excellent teacher or the old timer who has never done a very good job?

A family issue: A parent who has been rude and abusive to staff withdraws her child but then wants to come back to the center.

ENGAGING IN INFORMED ADVOCACY

Advocacy is speaking out for, and taking action in support of, causes that protect and support vulnerable populations. Advocates sometimes take immediate action as they do when they lobby on behalf of specific legislation, or build a coalition around a specific issue. In other instances, advocates set goals for what they want to accomplish in the future. They engage in this kind of advocacy when they contribute to political action campaigns or vote for candidates who support their interests.

Early childhood advocates invest their efforts on behalf of young children, their families, and the profession. They can champion a wide variety of causes, all designed to improve the lives of the children and families. Our commitment to advocacy is established by *The Statement of Commitment* that accompanies the *NAEYC Code of Ethical Conduct*. It states that early childhood educators agree to "serve as advocate[s] for children, their families, and their teachers in community and society" (NAEYC, 2005b). The Code includes the following Ideals that should guide our work, both individually and collectively, on behalf of children, the community and society:

> *I-1.9—To advocate for and ensure that all children, including those with special needs, have access to the support services needed to be successful.*
>
> *I-4.3—To work through education, research, and advocacy toward an environmentally safe world in which all children receive health care, food, and shelter; are nurtured; and live free from violence in their home and their communities.*
>
> *I-4.4—To work through education, research, and advocacy toward a society in which all young children have access to high-quality early care and education programs.* (NAEYC, 2005b)

Advocacy can involve speaking up in a private or public setting or working on behalf of a particular child or family. Advocacy may also take you into a public arena where you have the opportunity to protect the well-being of children and families in your community, state, or in the nation.

Your personality, your passion, your available time and energy, and your stage of professional development are all likely to influence the kinds of advocacy that are right for you. When you are a novice in the field, advocacy on behalf of a particular child or family will probably be the best fit for your interests and abilities. As you become more experienced, and particularly when you move into an administrative role, it will be time to reevaluate your strengths and interests. You may be ready to assume a leadership role in your local community, and perhaps even on a larger stage. Consider the classifications of advocacy in Figure 13.2 and the following list to identify the kinds of advocacy that are right for you:

1. Individual Advocacy involves professionals in working on behalf of children or families. You engage in **personal advocacy** when you help a particular child or family gain access to needed services. An example of this kind of personal advocacy is pursuing speech therapy for the child whose poor articulation is making it difficult for him to have positive interactions with his peers.

Your individual advocacy efforts may also involve sharing your views with individuals or groups to raise their awareness about an issue. This kind of advocacy can be either spontaneous or planned (Robinson & Stark, 2002). Distributing information about the *Campaign for Commercial Free Childhood* to the families of the children in your program,

---

- Some advocates will be **leaders**—people who provide vision and keep the advocacy effort on track.
- Some advocates will be **advisors**—people who are willing to share their special expertise with advocates and the policy makers whom advocates are trying to influence.
- Some advocates will be **researchers**—people who can collect data and synthesize research reports into issue briefs and background papers.
- Some advocates will be **"contributors"**—those people who are willing to roll up their sleeves and participate in the nuts-and-bolts work of advocacy, from making phone calls to stuffing letters or marching in front of the state capitol.
- Some advocates will be **friends**—people who do not have the time or resources to participate in every aspect of the planning and implementation of advocacy, yet who care and can always be counted on to help when a push is needed.

Figure 13.2

What Kind of Advocate Do You Want to Be?

Source: Reprinted from NAEYC Affiliate Public Policy Tool Kit, 2004, p. 14. www.naeyc.org/policy/toolbox/pdf/toolkit.pdf. Used by permission.

and encouraging them to limit the number of commercial messages to which their children are exposed, is an example of individual advocacy.

2. **Collective advocacy** involves professionals working together on behalf of a group of people, for example, young children, working mothers, or individuals with disabilities. As an early childhood advocate you are probably focused on securing a "greater societal commitment to improving programs for young children and more support for early childhood educators" (Jacobson & Simpson, 2007, p. 92). There are two kinds of class advocacy targeting decision makers far removed from the daily lives of young children and their families:

   a. **Public policy advocacy** may involve you in efforts to influence public policies and practices to make them more responsive to the needs of children and families. Public policy advocates challenge those who receive public funds and who develop laws, regulations, and policies to enact policies that support young children and their families (Robinson & Stark, 2002). When professional organizations communicate their position to the state legislature, they are engaged in collective public policy advocacy.

   b. **Private-sector advocacy** includes efforts to make the workplace more family friendly. Successful advocacy efforts have increased the number of corporations that offer employees flexible schedules, job sharing, telecommuting, and part-time employment. Other advocacy efforts have increased the number of corporations that offer on-site employer-supported child care or invest in goods and services for children.

The field of early care and education has a long history of advocacy for children and their families. We hope that you will continue this tradition by seizing opportunities to speak out for those who are most vulnerable and unable to speak out for themselves.

Application Activity

Identify an issue facing your center, your community, or your state. Identify who might help you resolve this issue. Should the target of your advocacy be local policy makers, state-level legislators, or corporate leaders? Identify strategies likely to be most effective to bring attention and eventually action to remedy the problem or resolve the issue.

Becoming an Effective Advocate

Becoming an effective advocate is an important part of becoming a mature professional. But the fact is, many early childhood educators who enjoy their work with children find it very difficult to speak with authority to adults, particularly to policy makers. That may be because working directly with children requires a very different skill set than leading adults. We know, however, that if we are to attract the public support needed to create a robust and sustainable system of early care and education, we must be effective advocates.

One strategy that helps to ensure success is to create coalitions of support and to network with other groups or individuals who share your cause (Ellison & Barbour, 1992; Levine, 1992). That may mean making linkages with providers of special services like speech or occupational therapists, or working with mother-support groups such as *Mom's Rising,* a grassroots effort designed to support family-friendly policies and practices. Review Figure 13.3 which identifies characteristics of effective advocates.

> - **Are intentional.**   They know what they want to accomplish and create realistic long- and short-term plans.
> - **Are informed.**   They know the legislative or decision-making time line so that they make good use of policy makers' time.
> - **Are organized.**   They present compelling facts and figures accurately and concisely, keeping their audience in mind.
> - **Are solution oriented.**   They help their audience understand the problems and challenges facing children and families and provide realistic solutions.
> - **Are strategic.**   They take into account the current political and business climates and budgeting constraints and reach beyond the early childhood care and education community to create coalitions from many stakeholder groups including parents in influential positions.
> - **Are flexible.**   They are poised to move their issue forward when opportunities present themselves, know how to wait for that strategic moment, and use a variety of advocacy approaches to appeal to multiple audiences when the time is right.

Figure 13.3
Characteristics of Effective Advocates
Source: Blank, 1997; Muenchow, 1997; Robinson & Stark, 2002.

An Advocates' Toolbox

Effective advocates are very good communicators. They are clear about the message they hope to convey and keep their communications explicit and direct (Jacobson & Simpson, 2007). They have many tools in their toolbox. Each must be tailored to meet each particular audience's need for information about the problem you have identified and the solution you propose.

Position statements are a professional organization's formalized stance on issues related to its mission. NAEYC, the Southern Early Childhood Association (SECA), and the Association for Childhood Education International (ACEI) have each developed position statements addressing controversial or critical issues related to early childhood education practice, policy, and professional development. Sometimes two or more professional organizations develop position statements together. For example, *Early Childhood Mathematics: Promoting Good Beginnings* is a joint position statement of the National Association for the Education of Young Children (NAEYC) and the National Council of Teachers of Mathematics (NCTM). In other instances, allied organizations embrace each other's position statements, as ACEI did when endorsing the *NAEYC Code of Ethical Conduct*.

Position statements typically include extensive reviews of the literature and are a valuable foundation on which to base your advocacy efforts. They are not usually appropriate, however, for legislators or other decision makers because they are too in-depth and detailed for their purposes. They can be most helpful as you prepare to testify on behalf of legislation or to meet with policy makers in other settings.

A briefing paper typically describes one problem, describes the policy you propose, and gives an example of how the policy you propose is working in another locale. Legislators are particularly interested in policies in neighboring states, so provide a close-to-home example whenever possible (Robinson & Stark, 2002).

Talking points are short and to the point. They include "sound bites telling why you support or oppose a particular policy or decision" (Robinson & Stark, 2002, p. 82). Advocates can use talking points when meeting with policy makers or talking to the media.

Key facts handouts are a short and to-the-point advocacy tool intended for the public, policy makers, and the media. They are short (one-or two-page) summaries of the basic facts surrounding your issue. It is very important that any statistics you reference are accurate and up to date (Robinson & Stark, 2002). See Figure 13.4 for an example of a Key Facts Handout.

Advocating for Changes in South Carolina's Licensing Regulations
Lowering Ratios and Regulating Class Size

Many researchers and professionals consider a low child-adult ratio the *sine qua non* of high-quality child care. (NICHD, 1996, p. 271)

Large-scale research studies show that 88% of infants, 78% of toddlers, and 88% of preschoolers are in programs with *barely adequate* or *inadequate* numbers of adults for the children in their care (1993).

When programs lower the number of infants/toddlers/young children each adult cares for:
• Children imitate the language and gestures of others more often and at an earlier age
• Providers have more time for each child
• Children talk and play more often
• Children are less often distressed
• Children are less frequently exposed to danger

When group size is reduced:
• Infections and disease are less likely to spread
• Providers are able to give closer attention to individual children
• Providers spend more time interacting with children and less time "just watching" or disciplining them
• Children have more positive developmental outcomes and, importantly, the benefits persist into the elementary years
• Children are more cooperative and more responsive to adults and other children
• Children are more likely to speak spontaneously
• Children are less likely to wander aimlessly or be uninvolved
• Children score higher on standardized tests

Ratios and Group Sizes in South Carolina and Neighboring States

Age of Children	South Carolina Ratio/ Group Size	South Carolina Proposed	North Carolina	Georgia	Mississippi
0–12 months	5:1 / Not regulated	5:1 / 10	5:1 / 10	6:1/12	5:1/10
12–18 months	6:1 / Not regulated	5:1 / 10	6:1/ 12	6:1/12	5:1/10
18–24 months	6:1 / Not regulated	6:1 / 12	6:1 / 12	8:1/16	9:1/10
2 to 3 years	8:1 / Not regulated		10:1 / 20	10:1/20	12:1/14
3 years	12:1 / Not regulated	11:1 / 22	15:1 / 25	15:1/30	14:1/14

Figure 13.4
Key Facts Handout

Source: NAEYC (1993). Research into action: The effects of group size, rations, and staff training in child care quality. *Young Children*, 48 (2), 65–67.

Concrete examples are compelling and often very effective ways to demonstrate the importance of the policy or initiative you are recommending. If you are advocating for quality programs for 4-year-olds, for example, you will want to give policy makers a glimpse into a classroom full of authentic hands-on experiences and will need to make it clear to them what children learn when they build with blocks or dress up in the dramatic play center. You can do this by inviting policy makers to your center or by taking the center to them with photos and real-life success stories (Jacobson & Simpson, 2007).

Action alerts are tools advocates use to mobilize their network of support. They are often emailed or faxed to supporters urging them to call their legislators to urge them to vote in support of particular bills under consideration. Action alerts include phone numbers and email addresses of targeted legislators and specific facts advocates can use in their message (Robinson and Stark, 2002).

HELPING OTHERS FIND A PLACE IN THE PROFESSION

Helping others find their place in the profession of early care and education is an important responsibility of leaders in the field. This is a form of advocacy because it gives you an opportunity to support novices as they prepare to contribute to the care, education, and well-being of children and support more experienced practitioners as they become leaders. Early childhood educators can help others find their place in the profession by:

1. Being a resource for those who want to know more about a career in early care and education
2. Welcoming student teachers, interns, and other preservice personnel who need a field placement to complete practicum assignments
3. Mentoring novices to enhance their skills and knowledge of young children and early childhood education
4. Encouraging emerging leaders to enhance their professional knowledge by pursuing postsecondary degrees, enrolling in short courses, and participating in professional organizations including attending and presenting at local, regional, and national conferences.

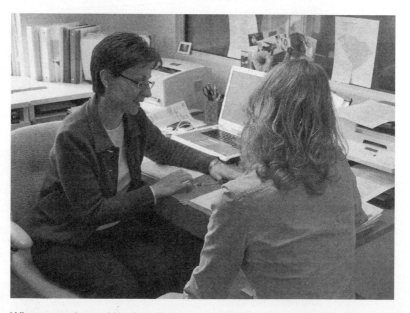

When experienced leaders find time to provide mentoring, they are contributing to the future of the profession.

BECOMING INVOLVED IN RESEARCH

As a program director, you and the children and families you serve may be asked to participate in research projects investigating some topic related to children, families, teaching, or learning. You will first want to be certain proposed projects meet the standards established by the *NAEYC Code of Ethical Conduct's* (2005) principle addressing research with young children:

> P-2.10—*Families shall be fully informed of any proposed research projects involving their children and shall have the opportunity to give or withhold consent without penalty. We shall not permit or participate in research that could in any way hinder the education, development, or well-being of children.*

Then you will want to ask researchers if their project has been approved by the appropriate institutional review board. This review requires researchers to have a plan to request participants' consent and to have procedures in place to protect the privacy of participating children and adults. Once you are convinced those requirements have been met, we advise you, whenever possible, to grant research requests and invite researchers involved in expanding the field's knowledge base into your program.

Teachers as Researchers

It is important to appreciate that research can be conducted not only by scholars, but also by teachers in their own classrooms (Cochran-Smith & Lytle, 1999). Teachers involved in this kind of **action research** explore practical questions within their own world of work. For them, research is an everyday event that informs their practice (Paley, 1981).

As a program administrator, you can create a culture that supports teacher research. This moves teachers away from the view that they transmit knowledge to children and toward the view that they construct knowledge and understandings with the children they teach (Moran, 2007). Action research can take teachers to the cutting edge of best practices and can give them opportunities to collaborate with colleagues, university researchers, and preservice teacher preparation programs (Charlesworth & DeBoer, 2000; Cooney, Buchanan, & Parkinson, 2001; Hankins, 1998; Moran, 2007; Stremmel & Hill, 1999).

TRENDS AND ISSUES

The field of early childhood care and education is more than 150 years old. While many have made contributions that have shaped our traditions, the field is in a period of rapid change and transition. This book has explored many aspects of leadership and management in early care and education. The first chapter provides a broad overview of the field and following chapters look closely at specific issues of concern to program administrators.

It is appropriate to revisit these issues regularly as you consider how you can pursue excellence across all segments of the profession. Consider the following three linked strategies that can move the field toward our shared goal of providing all children access to quality experiences in early care and education:

1. Move from "programs" to "systems."   Early childhood has a rich history. Through the years programs for young children have been developed under a variety of auspices for different purposes. From the early childhood profession's many program models, professionals have learned the elements and principles of quality programming. Most of these are now incorporated into standards adopted by various agencies and professional associations. Professionals now need a commitment to institutionalizing these standards while meeting the particular needs of the children, families, and communities they serve.

2. Move from a particularistic to a universal vision.   The diverse nature of our field has, too often, led to a lack of connections among programs, to confusion for policy makers, and to fragmented and inefficient services. *Conceptual or visionary leaders* plan for the long term and think in creative ways. They recognize the importance of thinking beyond their own programs and circumstances to creating linkages with allied fields such as psychology, medicine, public health, social work, and anthropology and to collaborate to meet current and future challenges (Clifford, 1997; Kagan & Neuman, 1997; Nanus, 1992).

3. Move from short- to long-term commitments.   We need to move from thinking about early childhood programs serving limited segments of our society or fulfilling short-term needs to seeing the field as a permanent part of our social fabric. That means that we should help the media, government, religious and civic groups, professional associations, and employers view early childhood programs as many children's and families' "extended family" (Perreault, 1991).

The hard work of making early childhood programs better must continue. We must contribute to the profession by coming together on behalf of our children and their families.

SUMMARY

Recent years have seen many calls for increased professionalism in early childhood education. Professionalism involves the use of professional knowledge and skills in maintaining, extending, and improving services to children and their families. Professionalism is enhanced when practitioners develop their professional skills and knowledge and commit to abiding by their code of ethics. Early childhood educators also affirm their commitment to professionalism by helping novices identify with, and become involved in, the profession.

Families and children are dependent on professionals who understand their needs and who can make their needs visible to decision makers. This is how advocacy efforts actualize our professional responsibilities.

The knowledge base of our profession is research based. It is important for program administrators to encourage and support researchers and teachers who are working together to increase what we know about young children and how they develop and learn. Researchers need to be aware of the realities of daily practice, and teachers need to learn from researchers' perspectives which can inform their work.

The long and diverse history of early childhood care and education has a tradition of impressive individual and collective accomplishments. It has involved professional associations; governmental agencies; private foundations; and religious, civic, and corporate groups in achieving its goals. At the current crossroads it is important to continue efforts to collaborate at national, state, and local levels so young children and their families can profit from the creation of a shared vision and a sustained effort toward shared goals.

Professionalism is dynamic. Early care and education will continue to change in positive ways as all of us who call ourselves early childhood educators become involved in promoting increased professionalism, helping others find a place in the profession, engaging in informed advocacy, and becoming involved in research. This profession needs administrators who take the leadership role and seize opportunities to make a difference in the lives of young children and their families.

USEFUL WEB SITES

Web Sites for Professional Ethics Resources

National Association for the Education of Young Children ethics resources are available by following links from naeyc.org/about/positions/ethical_conduct.asp

- *NAEYC Code of Ethical Conduct* (2005)
- El Código de Conducta Ética y Declaración de Compromiso (2005)
- Supplement for Adult Educators (2004)
- Supplement for Program Administrators (2006)
- "Teaching the NAEYC Code" updates

Web Sites for Advocacy Resources

Early childhood advocacy toolkit (2004) developed by the Minnesota Association for Family and Early Education available by following links from

www.mnafee.org/

Family and Work Institute, nonprofit research organization focused on issues related to the workplace, families, and community at

familiesandwork.org/site/about/main.html

Mom's Rising, a grassroots effort encouraging family-friendly policies and workplaces at

www.momsrising.org/

NAEYC Affiliate Public Policy Tool Kit (2004) available from

www.naeyc.org/policy/toolbox/pdf/toolkit.pdf

Supporting early childhood initiatives: Legislative strategies for everyday people (2003) available from

www.financeproject.org/Publications/LegislativeStrategies.pdf

TO REFLECT

1. Bowman (1995) pointed out that at professional conferences, sessions discussing public policy topics have the fewest participants whereas sessions featuring "Music for Monday Mornings" are filled to capacity. What do you think this says about our profession? How could this situation be changed?

2. A class in administration is discussing collaboration. One student commented, "We always talk about all we can accomplish through collaboration, but doesn't collaboration come with a price tag?" What are the price tags attached to collaboration?

SUPPLIERS OF MATERIALS AND EQUIPMENT FOR EARLY CHILDHOOD PROGRAMS

SUPPLIERS OF CHILDREN'S FURNITURE AND LEARNING MATERIALS

abc School Supply, Inc.
www.abcschoolsupply.com

The Angeles Group
www.angeles-group.com

Becker School Supplies
www.shopbecker.com

Busy Kids
busy-kids.com

Child Safe Products
www.childsafeproducts.com

Community Playthings
www.communityplaythings.com

Constructive Playthings
www.constructplay.com

Discovery Toys, Inc.
www.discoverytoysinc.com

Environments, Inc.
www.eichild.com

Insect Lore Products
www.insectlore.com

Jonti-Craft, Inc.
www.jonti-craft.com

Kimbo Educational
www.kimboed.com

Lakeshore Learning Materials
www.lakeshorelearning.com

Learning Resources, Inc.
www.learningresources.com/home.do

Music for Little People
www.musicforlittlepeople.com

Nienhuis for Education
www.nienhuis.com

Nursery Maid Furniture
www.nurserymaid.com

Puppet Partners
www.puppetpartners.com

Rhythm Band Instruments, Inc.
www.rhythmband.com

Spaces for Children
spacesforchildren.com

Tout About Toys, Inc.
www.toutabouttoys.com

Tree Blocks
www.treeblocks.com

SUPPLIERS OF PLAYGROUNDS AND OUTDOOR EQUIPMENT

Child Forms
www.childforms.com

Custom Playground Designs
www.customplayground.com

GameTime
www.gametime.com

Grounds for Play
www.groundsforplay.com/

Kompan
www.Kompan.com

Landscape Structures, Inc.
www.playlsi.com

SUPPLIERS OF CHILDREN'S VIDEOS AND SOFTWARE

Broderbund Software, Inc.
www.broderbund.com

MECC
www.mecc.com

Children's Software Online
www.childrenssoftwareonline.com

Micrograms Software
www.micrograms.com

Compu-Teach, Inc.
www.compu-teach.com

National Geographic
www.nationalgeographic.com

The Discovery Channel
www.discovery.com

Optimum Resource, Inc.
www.stickybear.com

Humongous Entertainment
www.humongous.com

Society for Visual Education Media
www.svemedia.com

Knowledge Adventure
www.knowledgeadventure.com

Tom Snyder Productions
www.tomsnyder.com

The Learning Company
www.learningco.com

SELECTING CHILDREN'S BOOKS

A World of Difference Institute: Recommended Multicultural and Anti-bias Books for Children
www.adl.org/bibliography/

The Children's Book Council
www.cbcbooks.org/—see particularly links from the Reading Lists tab

American Library Association/Association for Library Service for Children Recommended Book Lists
www.ala.org/ala/alsc/alscresources/booklists/booklists.htm

The Horn Book: Teachers and Parents
www.hbook.com/teachersparents/default.asp

RESOURCES/TOOLS FOR TEACHERS AND PROFESSIONAL DEVELOPMENT

Accu-Cut Systems
www.accucut.com

Program for Infant/Toddler Care
www.pitc.org

Educational Productions
www.edpro.com

Scholastic
www.scholastic.com

BUSINESS MANAGEMENT SOFTWARE

Child Care Office Pro
www.childcareoffice.com

Childcare Manager
www.childcaremanager.com/

Daycare Manager Software
www.daycaresoft.com

EZ Care 2 (SofterWare)
www.softerware.com/ezcare2/

KidKeeper
www.kidkeeper.com

Orgamation Technologies
www.orgamation.com

ProCare Software (Professional Solutions)
www.procaresoft.com

NAEYC CODE OF ETHICAL CONDUCT

PREAMBLE

NAEYC recognizes that those who work with young children face many daily decisions that have moral and ethical implications. The **NAEYC Code of Ethical Conduct** offers guidelines for responsible behavior and sets forth a common basis for resolving the principal ethical dilemmas encountered in early childhood care and education. The **Statement of Commitment** is not part of the Code but is a personal acknowledgement of an individual's willingness to embrace the distinctive values and moral obligations of the field of early childhood care and education. The primary focus of the Code is on daily practice with children and their families in programs for children from birth through 8 years of age, such as infant/toddler programs, preschool and prekindergarten programs, child care centers, hospital and child life settings, family child care homes, kindergartens, and primary classrooms. When the issues involve young children, then these provisions also apply to specialists who do not work directly with children, including program administrators, parent educators, early childhood adult educators, and officials with responsibility for program monitoring and licensing. (Note: See also the "Code of Ethical Conduct: Supplement for Early Childhood Adult Educators," online at http://www.naeyc.org/about/positions/ethics04.asp.)

Source: National Association for the Education of Young Children. 2005. *Position Statement. Code of Ethical Conduct and Statement of Commitment.* 2005 rev. Washington, DC: Author. Online: http://www.naeyc.org/about/positions/pdf/PSETH05.pdf. Reprinted with permission from the National Association for the Education of Young Children.

Endorsed by the Association for Childhood Education International.
Adopted by the National Association for Family Child Care.

CORE VALUES

Standards of ethical behavior in early childhood care and education are based on commitment to the following core values that are deeply rooted in the history of the field of early childhood care and education. We have made a commitment to

- Appreciate childhood as a unique and valuable stage of the human life cycle
- Base our work on knowledge of how children develop and learn
- Appreciate and support the bond between the child and family
- Recognize that children are best understood and supported in the context of family, culture,[1] community, and society
- Respect the dignity, worth, and uniqueness of each individual (child, family member, and colleague)
- Respect diversity in children, families, and colleagues
- Recognize that children and adults achieve their full potential in the context of relationships that are based on trust and respect

[1]Culture includes ethnicity, racial identity, economic level, family structure, language, and religious and political beliefs, which profoundly influence each child's development and relationship to the world.

CONCEPTUAL FRAMEWORK

The Code sets forth a framework of professional responsibilities in four sections. Each section addresses an area of professional relationships: (1) with children, (2) with families, (3) among colleagues, and (4) with the community and society. Each section includes an introduction to the primary responsibilities of the early childhood practitioner in that context. The introduction is followed by a set of ideals (I) that reflect exemplary professional practice and a set of principles (P) describing practices that are required, prohibited, or permitted.

The ideals reflect the aspirations of practitioners. The principles guide conduct and assist practitioners in resolving ethical dilemmas.[2] Both ideals and principles are intended to direct practitioners to those questions which, when responsibly answered, can provide the basis for conscientious decision making. While the Code provides specific direction for addressing some ethical dilemmas, many others will require the practitioner to combine the guidance of the Code with professional judgment.

The ideals and principles in this Code present a shared framework of professional responsibility that affirms our commitment to the core values of our field. The Code publicly acknowledges the responsibilities that we in the field have assumed and in so doing supports ethical behavior in our work. Practitioners who face situations with ethical dimensions are urged to seek guidance in the applicable parts of this Code and in the spirit that informs the whole.

Often, "the right answer"—the best ethical course of action to take—is not obvious. There may be no readily apparent, positive way to handle a situation. When one important value contradicts another, we face an ethical dilemma. When we face a dilemma, it is our professional responsibility to consult the Code and all relevant parties to find the most ethical resolution.

SECTION I: ETHICAL RESPONSIBILITIES TO CHILDREN

Childhood is a unique and valuable stage in the human life cycle. Our paramount responsibility is to provide care and education in settings that are safe, healthy, nurturing, and responsive for each child. We are committed to supporting children's development

[2]There is not necessarily a corresponding principle for each ideal.

and learning; respecting individual differences; and helping children learn to live, play, and work cooperatively. We are also committed to promoting children's self-awareness, competence, self-worth, resiliency, and physical well-being.

Ideals

I-1.1—To be familiar with the knowledge base of early childhood care and education and to stay informed through continuing education and training.

I-1.2—To base program practices upon current knowledge and research in the field of early childhood education, child development, and related disciplines, as well as on particular knowledge of each child.

I-1.3—To recognize and respect the unique qualities, abilities, and potential of each child.

I-1.4—To appreciate the vulnerability of children and their dependence on adults.

I-1.5—To create and maintain safe and healthy settings that foster children's social, emotional, cognitive, and physical development and that respect their dignity and their contributions.

I-1.6—To use assessment instruments and strategies that are appropriate for the children to be assessed, that are used only for the purposes for which they were designed, and that have the potential to benefit children.

I-1.7—To use assessment information to understand and support children's development and learning, to support instruction, and to identify children who may need additional services.

I-1.8—To support the right of each child to play and learn in an inclusive environment that meets the needs of children with and without disabilities.

I-1.9—To advocate for and ensure that all children, including those with special needs, have access to the support services needed to be successful.

I-1.10—To ensure that each child's culture, language, ethnicity, and family structure are recognized and valued in the program.

I-1.11—To provide all children with experiences in a language that they know, as well as support children in maintaining the use of their home language and in learning English.

I-1.12—To work with families to provide a safe and smooth transition as children and families move from one program to the next.

Principles

P-1.1—Above all, we shall not harm children. We shall not participate in practices that are emotionally damaging, physically harmful, disrespectful, degrading, dangerous, exploitative, or intimidating to children. This principle has precedence over all others in this Code.

P-1.2—We shall care for and educate children in positive emotional and social environments that are cognitively stimulating and that support each child's culture, language, ethnicity, and family structure.

P-1.3—We shall not participate in practices that discriminate against children by denying benefits, giving special advantages, or excluding them from programs or activities on the basis of their sex, race, national origin, religious beliefs, medical condition, disability, or the marital status/family structure, sexual orientation, or religious beliefs or other affiliations of their families. (Aspects of this principle do not apply in programs that have a lawful mandate to provide services to a particular population of children.)

P-1.4—We shall involve all those with relevant knowledge (including families and staff) in decisions concerning a child, as appropriate, ensuring confidentiality of sensitive information.

P-1.5—We shall use appropriate assessment systems, which include multiple sources of information, to provide information on children's learning and development.

P-1.6—We shall strive to ensure that decisions such as those related to enrollment, retention, or assignment to special education services, will be based on multiple sources of information and will never be based on a single assessment, such as a test score or a single observation.

P-1.7—We shall strive to build individual relationships with each child; make individualized adaptations in teaching strategies, learning environments, and curricula; and consult with the family so that each child benefits from the program. If after such efforts have been exhausted, the current placement does not meet a child's needs, or the child is seriously jeopardizing the ability of other children to benefit from the program, we shall collaborate with the child's family and appropriate specialists to determine the additional services needed and/or the placement option(s) most likely to ensure the child's success. (Aspects of this principle may not apply in programs that have a lawful mandate to provide services to a particular population of children.)

P-1.8—We shall be familiar with the risk factors for and symptoms of child abuse and neglect, including physical, sexual, verbal, and emotional abuse and physical, emotional, educational, and medical neglect. We shall know and follow state laws and community procedures that protect children against abuse and neglect.

P-1.9—When we have reasonable cause to suspect child abuse or neglect, we shall report it to the appropriate community agency and follow up to ensure that appropriate action has been taken. When appropriate, parents or guardians will be informed that the referral will be or has been made.

P-1.10—When another person tells us of his or her suspicion that a child is being abused or neglected, we shall assist that person in taking appropriate action in order to protect the child.

P-1.11—When we become aware of a practice or situation that endangers the health, safety, or well-being of children, we have an ethical responsibility to protect children or inform parents and/or others who can.

SECTION II: ETHICAL RESPONSIBILITIES TO FAMILIES

Families[3] are of primary importance in children's development. Because the family and the early childhood practitioner have a common interest in the child's well-being, we acknowledge a primary responsibility to bring about communication, cooperation, and collaboration between the home and early childhood program in ways that enhance the child's development.

Ideals

I-2.1—To be familiar with the knowledge base related to working effectively with families and to stay informed through continuing education and training.

I-2.2—To develop relationships of mutual trust and create partnerships with the families we serve.

I-2.3—To welcome all family members and encourage them to participate in the program.

I-2.4—To listen to families, acknowledge and build upon their strengths and competencies, and learn from families as we support them in their task of nurturing children.

---

[3]The term family may include those adults, besides parents, with the responsibility of being involved in educating, nurturing, and advocating for the child.

I-2.5—To respect the dignity and preferences of each family and to make an effort to learn about its structure, culture, language, customs, and beliefs.

I-2.6—To acknowledge families' childrearing values and their right to make decisions for their children.

I-2.7—To share information about each child's education and development with families and to help them understand and appreciate the current knowledge base of the early childhood profession.

I-2.8—To help family members enhance their understanding of their children and support the continuing development of their skills as parents.

I-2.9—To participate in building support networks for families by providing them with opportunities to interact with program staff, other families, community resources, and professional services.

Principles

P-2.1—We shall not deny family members access to their child's classroom or program setting unless access is denied by court order or other legal restriction.

P-2.2—We shall inform families of program philosophy, policies, curriculum, assessment system, and personnel qualifications, and explain why we teach as we do—which should be in accordance with our ethical responsibilities to children (see Section I).

P-2.3—We shall inform families of and, when appropriate, involve them in policy decisions.

P-2.4—We shall involve the family in significant decisions affecting their child.

P-2.5—We shall make every effort to communicate effectively with all families in a language that they understand. We shall use community resources for translation and interpretation when we do not have sufficient resources in our own programs.

P-2.6—As families share information with us about their children and families, we shall consider this information to plan and implement the program.

P-2-7—We shall inform families about the nature and purpose of the program's child assessments and how data about their child will be used.

P-2.8—We shall treat child assessment information confidentially and share this information only when there is a legitimate need for it.

P-2.9—We shall inform the family of injuries and incidents involving their child, of risks such as exposures to communicable diseases that might result in infection, and of occurrences that might result in emotional stress.

P-2.10—Families shall be fully informed of any proposed research projects involving their children and shall have the opportunity to give or withhold consent without penalty. We shall not permit or participate in research that could in any way hinder the education, development, or well-being of children.

P-2.11—We shall not engage in or support exploitation of families. We shall not use our relationship with a family for private advantage or personal gain, or enter into relationships with family members that might impair our effectiveness working with their children.

P-2.12—We shall develop written policies for the protection of confidentiality and the disclosure of children's records. These policy documents shall be made available to all program personnel and families. Disclosure of children's records beyond family members, program personnel, and consultants having an obligation of confidentiality shall require familial consent (except in cases of abuse or neglect).

P-2.13—We shall maintain confidentiality and shall respect the family's right to privacy, refraining from disclosure of confidential information and intrusion into family life. However, when we have reason to believe that a child's welfare is at risk, it is permissible to share confidential information with agencies, as well as with individuals who have legal responsibility for intervening in the child's interest.

P-2.14—In cases where family members are in conflict with one another, we shall work openly, sharing our observations of the child, to help all parties involved make informed decisions. We shall refrain from becoming an advocate for one party.

P-2.15—We shall be familiar with and appropriately refer families to community resources and professional support services. After a referral has been made, we shall follow up to ensure that services have been appropriately provided.

SECTION III: ETHICAL RESPONSIBILITIES TO COLLEAGUES

In a caring, cooperative workplace, human dignity is respected, professional satisfaction is promoted, and positive relationships are developed and sustained. Based upon our core values, our primary responsibility to colleagues is to establish and maintain settings and relationships that support productive work and meet professional needs. The same ideals that apply to children also apply as we interact with adults in the workplace.

A-RESPONSIBILITIES TO CO-WORKERS

Ideals

I-3A.1—To establish and maintain relationships of respect, trust, confidentiality, collaboration, and cooperation with co-workers.

I-3A.2—To share resources with co-workers, collaborating to ensure that the best possible early childhood care and education program is provided.

I-3A.3—To support co-workers in meeting their professional needs and in their professional development.

I-3A.4—To accord co-workers due recognition of professional achievement.

Principles

P-3A.1—We shall recognize the contributions of colleagues to our program and not participate in practices that diminish their reputations or impair their effectiveness in working with children and families.

P-3A.2—When we have concerns about the professional behavior of a co-worker, we shall first let that person know of our concern in a way that shows respect for personal dignity and for the diversity to be found among staff members, and then attempt to resolve the matter collegially and in a confidential manner.

P-3A.3—We shall exercise care in expressing views regarding the personal attributes or professional conduct of co-workers. Statements should be based on firsthand knowledge, not hearsay, and relevant to the interests of children and programs.

P-3A.4—We shall not participate in practices that discriminate against a co-worker because of sex, race, national origin, religious beliefs or other affiliations, age, marital status/family structure, disability, or sexual orientation.

B-RESPONSIBILITIES TO EMPLOYERS

Ideals

I-3B.1—To assist the program in providing the highest quality of service.

I-3B.2—To do nothing that diminishes the reputation of the program in which we work unless it is violating laws and regulations designed to protect children or is violating the provisions of this Code.

Principles

P-3B.1—We shall follow all program policies. When we do not agree with program policies, we shall attempt to effect change through constructive action within the organization.

P-3B.2—We shall speak or act on behalf of an organization only when authorized. We shall take care to acknowledge when we are speaking for the organization and when we are expressing a personal judgment.

P-3B.3—We shall not violate laws or regulations designed to protect children and shall take appropriate action consistent with this Code when aware of such violations.

P-3B.4—If we have concerns about a colleague's behavior, and children's well-being is not at risk, we may address the concern with that individual. If children are at risk or the situation does not improve after it has been brought to the colleague's attention, we shall report the colleague's unethical or incompetent behavior to an appropriate authority.

P-3B.5—When we have a concern about circumstances or conditions that impact the quality of care and education within the program, we shall inform the program's administration or, when necessary, other appropriate authorities.

C-RESPONSIBILITIES TO EMPLOYEES

Ideals

I-3C.1—To promote safe and healthy working conditions and policies that foster mutual respect, cooperation, collaboration, competence, well-being, confidentiality, and self-esteem in staff members.

I-3C.2—To create and maintain a climate of trust and candor that will enable staff to speak and act in the best interests of children, families, and the field of early childhood care and education.

I-3C.3—To strive to secure adequate and equitable compensation (salary and benefits) for those who work with or on behalf of young children.

I-3C.4—To encourage and support continual development of employees in becoming more skilled and knowledgeable practitioners.

Principles

P-3C.1—In decisions concerning children and programs, we shall draw upon the education, training, experience, and expertise of staff members.

P-3C.2—We shall provide staff members with safe and supportive working conditions that honor confidences and permit them to carry out their responsibilities through fair performance evaluation, written grievance procedures, constructive feedback, and opportunities for continuing professional development and advancement.

P-3C.3—We shall develop and maintain comprehensive written personnel policies that define program standards. These policies shall be given to new staff members and shall be available and easily accessible for review by all staff members.

P-3C.4—We shall inform employees whose performance does not meet program expectations of areas of concern and, when possible, assist in improving their performance.

P-3C.5—We shall conduct employee dismissals for just cause, in accordance with all applicable laws and regulations. We shall inform employees who are dismissed of the reasons for their termination. When a dismissal is for cause, justification must be based on evidence of inadequate or inappropriate behavior that is accurately documented, current, and available for the employee to review.

P-3C.6—In making evaluations and recommendations, we shall make judgments based on fact and relevant to the interests of children and programs.

P-3C.7—We shall make hiring, retention, termination, and promotion decisions based solely on a person's competence, record of accomplishment, ability to carry out the responsibilities of the position, and professional preparation specific to the developmental levels of children in his/her care.

P-3C.8—We shall not make hiring, retention, termination, and promotion decisions based on an individual's sex, race, national origin, religious beliefs or other affiliations, age, marital status/family structure, disability, or sexual orientation. We shall be familiar with and observe laws and regulations that pertain to employment discrimination. (Aspects of this principle do not apply to programs that have a lawful mandate to determine eligibility based on one or more of the criteria identified above.)

P-3C.9—We shall maintain confidentiality in dealing with issues related to an employee's job performance and shall respect an employee's right to privacy regarding personal issues.

SECTION IV: ETHICAL RESPONSIBILITIES TO COMMUNITY AND SOCIETY

Early childhood programs operate within the context of their immediate community made up of families and other institutions concerned with children's welfare. Our responsibilities to the community are to provide programs that meet the diverse needs of families, to cooperate with agencies and professions that share the responsibility for children, to assist families in gaining access to those agencies and allied professionals, and to assist in the development of community programs that are needed but not currently available.

As individuals, we acknowledge our responsibility to provide the best possible programs of care and education for children and to conduct ourselves with honesty and integrity. Because of our specialized expertise in early childhood development and education and because the larger society shares responsibility for the welfare and protection of young children, we acknowledge a collective obligation to advocate for the best interests of children within early childhood programs and in the larger community and to serve as a voice for young children everywhere.

The ideals and principles in this section are presented to distinguish between those that pertain to the work of the individual early childhood educator and those that more typically are engaged in collectively on behalf of the best interests of children—with the understanding that individual early childhood educators have a shared responsibility for addressing the ideals and principles that are identified as "collective."

Ideal (Individual)

I-4.1—To provide the community with high-quality early childhood care and education programs and services.

Ideals (Collective)

I-4.2—To promote cooperation among professionals and agencies and interdisciplinary collaboration among professions concerned with addressing issues in the health, education, and well-being of young children, their families, and their early childhood educators.

I-4.3—To work through education, research, and advocacy toward an environmentally safe world in which all children receive health care, food, and shelter; are nurtured; and live free from violence in their home and their communities.

I-4.4—To work through education, research, and advocacy toward a society in which all young children have access to high-quality early care and education programs.

I-4.5—To work to ensure that appropriate assessment systems, which include multiple sources of information, are used for purposes that benefit children.

I-4.6—To promote knowledge and understanding of young children and their needs. To work toward greater societal acknowledgment of children's rights and greater social acceptance of responsibility for the well-being of all children.

I-4.7—To support policies and laws that promote the well-being of children and families, and to work to change those that impair their well-being. To participate in developing policies and laws that are needed, and to cooperate with other individuals and groups in these efforts.

I-4.8—To further the professional development of the field of early childhood care and education and to strengthen its commitment to realizing its core values as reflected in this Code.

Principles (Individual)

P-4.1—We shall communicate openly and truthfully about the nature and extent of services that we provide.

P-4.2—We shall apply for, accept, and work in positions for which we are personally well-suited and professionally qualified. We shall not offer services that we do not have the competence, qualifications, or resources to provide.

P-4.3—We shall carefully check references and shall not hire or recommend for employment any person whose competence, qualifications, or character makes him or her unsuited for the position.

P-4.4—We shall be objective and accurate in reporting the knowledge upon which we base our program practices.

P-4.5—We shall be knowledgeable about the appropriate use of assessment strategies and instruments and interpret results accurately to families.

P-4.6—We shall be familiar with laws and regulations that serve to protect the children in our programs and be vigilant in ensuring that these laws and regulations are followed.

P-4.7—When we become aware of a practice or situation that endangers the health, safety, or well-being of children, we have an ethical responsibility to protect children or inform parents and/or others who can.

P-4.8—We shall not participate in practices that are in violation of laws and regulations that protect the children in our programs.

P-4.9—When we have evidence that an early childhood program is violating laws or regulations protecting children, we shall report the violation to appropriate authorities who can be expected to remedy the situation.

P-4.10—When a program violates or requires its employees to violate this Code, it is permissible, after fair assessment of the evidence, to disclose the identity of that program.

Principles (Collective)

P-4.11—When policies are enacted for purposes that do not benefit children, we have a collective responsibility to work to change these practices.

P-4-12—When we have evidence that an agency that provides services intended to ensure children's well-being is failing to meet its obligations, we acknowledge a collective ethical responsibility to report the problem to appropriate authorities or to the public. We shall be vigilant in our follow-up until the situation is resolved.

P-4.13—When a child protection agency fails to provide adequate protection for abused or neglected children, we acknowledge a collective ethical responsibility to work toward the improvement of these services.

Glossary of Terms Related to Ethics

Code of Ethics. Defines the core values of the field and provides guidance for what professionals should do when they encounter conflicting obligations or responsibilities in their work.

Values. Qualities or principles that individuals believe to be desirable or worthwhile and that they prize for themselves, for others, and for the world in which they live.

Core Values. Commitments held by a profession that are consciously and knowingly embraced by its practitioners because they make a contribution to society. There is a difference between personal values and the core values of a profession.

Morality. Peoples' views of what is good, right, and proper; their beliefs about their obligations; and their ideas about how they should behave.

Ethics. The study of right and wrong, or duty and obligation, that involves critical reflection on morality and the ability to make choices between values and the examination of the moral dimensions of relationships.

Professional Ethics. The moral commitments of a profession that involve moral reflection that extends and enhances the personal morality practitioners bring to their work, that concern actions of right and wrong in the workplace, and that help individuals resolve moral dilemmas they encounter in their work.

Ethical Responsibilities. Behaviors that one must or must not engage in. Ethical responsibilities are clear-cut and are spelled out in the Code of Ethical Conduct (for example, early childhood educators should never share confidential information about a child or family with a person who has no legitimate need for knowing).

Ethical Dilemma. A moral conflict that involves determining appropriate conduct when an individual faces conflicting professional values and responsibilities.

Sources for Glossary Terms and Definitions

Feeney, S., & N. Freeman. 1999. *Ethics and the early childhood educator: Using the NAEYC code.* Washington, DC: National Association for the Education of Young Children.

Kidder, R.M. 1995. *How good people make tough choices: Resolving the dilemmas of ethical living.* New York: Fireside.

Kipnis, K. 1987. How to discuss professional ethics. *Young Children, 42*(4), 26–30.

STATEMENT OF COMMITMENT[4]

As an individual who works with young children, I commit myself to furthering the values of early childhood education as they are reflected in the ideals and principles of the NAEYC Code of Ethical Conduct. To the best of my ability I will

- Never harm children.
- Ensure that programs for young children are based on current knowledge and research of child development and early childhood education.
- Respect and support families in their task of nurturing children.
- Respect colleagues in early childhood care and education and support them in maintaining the NAEYC Code of Ethical Conduct.
- Serve as an advocate for children, their families, and their teachers in community and society.
- Stay informed of and maintain high standards of professional conduct.
- Engage in an ongoing process of self-reflection, realizing that personal characteristics, biases, and beliefs have an impact on children and families.
- Be open to new ideas and be willing to learn from the suggestions of others.
- Continue to learn, grow, and contribute as a professional.
- Honor the ideals and principles of the NAEYC Code of Ethical Conduct.

_____

[4]This Statement of Commitment is not part of the Code but is a personal acknowledgment of the individual's willingess to embrace the distinctive values and moral obligations of the field of early childhood care and education. It is recognition of the moral obligations that lead to an individual becoming part of the profession.

NAEYC CODE OF ETHICAL CONDUCT SUPPLEMENT FOR EARLY CHILDHOOD PROGRAM ADMINISTRATORS

Administrators of programs for young children are responsible for overseeing all program operations, serving as leaders in their programs, and representing the field to the community. Early childhood program administrators are called upon to sustain relationships with a wide variety of clients. They interact with and have responsibilities to children, families, program personnel, governing boards and sponsoring agencies, funders, regulatory agencies, their community, and the profession.

Program administrators deal with unique responsibilities and ethical challenges in the course of managing and guiding their programs and assume leadership roles within and beyond their programs. As managers and leaders, they are called upon to share their professional knowledge and expertise with families, personnel, governing boards, and others; demonstrate empathy for the families and children they serve; and communicate respect for the skills, knowledge, and expertise of teaching staff and other personnel. Administrators accept primary responsibility for executing the program's mission as well as developing and carrying out program policies and procedures that support that mission. They also make a commitment to continue their own professional development and the continuing education of the personnel in the program they lead. Administrators also may be advocates for all children

being able to gain access to quality programming. Some of the challenges faced by administrators involve balancing their obligations to support and nurture children with their responsibility to address the needs and safeguard the rights of families and personnel and respond to the requirements of their boards and sponsoring agencies.

PURPOSE OF THE SUPPLEMENT

Like those in the field who work directly with young children, program administrators are regularly called upon to make decisions of a moral and ethical nature. The NAEYC Code of Ethical Conduct (revised 2005) is a foundational document that maps the ethical dimensions of early childhood educators' work in early care and education programs. Program administrators share the ethical obligations assumed by all early childhood educators—obligations that are reflected in the core values, ideals, and principles set forth in the Code. Administrators embrace the central commitment of the early care and education field—and the Code—to ensure the well-being and support the healthy development of young children. Given the nature of their responsibilities, however, administrators face some additional ethical challenges. Conflicts often surface in the areas of enrollment policies; dealings with personnel; and relationships with families, licensors, governing boards, sponsoring agencies, and others in the community. The existing Code is a valuable resource that addresses many of the ethical issues encountered by administrators. However, it does not provide all of the guidance that they need to address the unique ethical issues that arise in their work. This Supplement offers additional core values, ideals, and principles related to the frequently recurring ethical issues encountered by administrators.

Source: National Association for the Education of Young Children. 2006. *Position Statement Supplement. Code of Ethical Conduct. Supplement for Early Childhood Program Administrators.* Washington, DC: Author. Online: http://www.naeyc.org/about/positions/pdf/PSETH05_supp.pdf. Reprinted with permission from the National Association for the Education of Young Children.
Adopted by the National Association for Family Child Care

CORE VALUES

In addition to the core values spelled out in the NAEYC Code of Ethical Conduct, early childhood program administrators commit themselves to the following additional core values.

We make a commitment to

- Recognize that we have many responsibilities—to children, families, personnel, governing boards, sponsoring agencies, funders, regulatory agencies, the community, and the profession—and that the well-being of the children in our care is our primary responsibility, above our obligations to other constituencies.
- Recognize the importance of and maintain a humane and fulfilling work environment for personnel and volunteers.
- Be committed to the professional development of staff.

CONCEPTUAL FRAMEWORK

This document sets forth a conception of early childhood program administrators' professional responsibilities in five areas, some of which differ from those identified in the NAEYC Code. Each section addresses an area of professional relationships: (1) with children, (2) with families, (3) with personnel, (4) with sponsoring agencies and governing boards, and (5) with the community and society. The items in each section address the unique ethical responsibilities of administrators in early care and education settings.

IDEALS AND PRINCIPLES

This Supplement identifies additional **ideals** that reflect exemplary practice (our aspirations) and **principles** describing practices that are required, prohibited, or permitted. The principles guide conduct and assist practitioners in resolving ethical dilemmas. Together, the ideals and principles are intended to direct practitioners to questions that, when responsibly answered, provide the basis for conscientious decision making. While the Code and this Supplement provide specific direction for addressing some ethical dilemmas, many others will require early childhood program administrators to combine the guidance of the Code and/or this Supplement with their best professional judgment.

The ideals and principles in the Code and this Supplement present a shared framework of professional responsibility that affirms our commitment to the core values of our field. The Code and the Supplement publicly acknowledge the responsibilities that early childhood professionals assume and, in so doing, support ethical behavior in our work. Practitioners who face situations with ethical dimensions are urged to seek guidance in the applicable parts of the Code/Supplement and in the spirit that informs the whole.

The ideals and principles in this Supplement are based on early childhood program administrators' descriptions of ethical dilemmas they have encountered in their work. They are designed to inspire and guide administrators toward actions that reflect the field's current understanding of ethical responsibility.

The Supplement also includes items from the NAEYC Code that directly relate to the work of administrators—some are duplicates of Code ideals or principles, and some are adaptations. Items from the Code that are repeated or adapted for this Supplement are cross-referenced with their corresponding ideals and principles, with the Code references indicated in parentheses. Other items that expand and extend the NAEYC Code were written specifically for this Supplement.

(Note: There is not necessarily a corresponding principle for each ideal.)

DEFINITIONS

The following definitions are used in this Supplement:

Administrator

The individual responsible for planning, implementing, and evaluating a child care, preschool, kindergarten, or primary grade program. The administrator's title may vary, depending on the program type or sponsorship of the program. Common titles include director, site manager, administrator, program manager, early childhood coordinator, and principal. (*Note:* The definition of *administrator* and other relevant text in this Supplement are consistent with the Leadership and Management standard of the NAEYC Early Childhood Program Standards and Accreditation Criteria.)

Personnel

Staff members employed, directed, or supervised by an administrator. Here, unless otherwise noted, *personnel* includes all program staff and volunteers providing services to children and/or families. (*Note:* Because program administrators may be supervisors and not employers, we have adopted the terms *personnel* and *staff* in lieu of *employees* for this Supplement to the Code.)

1. Ethical Responsibilities to Children   The early childhood program administrator's paramount responsibility is to ensure that programs for children provide settings that are safe, healthy, nurturing, and responsive for each child. Administrators are committed to establishing and maintaining programs that support children's development and learning; promote respect for individual differences; and help children learn to live, play, and work cooperatively. Administrators are also committed to ensuring that the program promotes children's self-awareness, competence, self-worth, resiliency, and physical well-being.

Ideals

I-1.1—To ensure that children's needs are the first priority in administrative decisionmaking, recognizing that a child's well-being cannot be separated from that of his/her family.

I-1.2—To provide a high-quality program based on current knowledge of child development and best practices in early care and education.

Principles

P-1.1—We shall place the welfare and safety of children above other obligations (for example, to families, program personnel, employing agency, community). *This item takes precedence over all others in this Supplement.*

P-1.2—We shall ensure that the programs we administer are safe and developmentally appropriate in accordance with standards of the field, including those developed and endorsed by NAEYC and other professional associations.

P-1.3—We shall have clearly stated policies for the respectful treatment of children and adults in all contacts made by staff, parents, volunteers, student teachers, and other adults. We shall appropriately address incidents that are not consistent with our policies.

P-1.4—We shall support children's well-being by encouraging the development of strong bonds between children and their families and between children and their teachers.

P-1.5—We shall support children's well-being by promoting connections with their culture and communities.

P-1.6—We shall make every effort to provide the necessary resources (staff, consultation, equipment, and so on) to ensure that all children, including those with special needs, can benefit from the program.

P-1.7—We shall ensure that there is a plan for appropriate transitions for children when they enter our program, move from one classroom to another within our program, and when they leave.

P-1.8—We shall apply all policies regarding our obligations to children consistently and fairly.

P-1.9—We shall review all program policies set forth by sponsoring agencies and governing bodies to ensure that they are in the best interest of the children.

P-1.10—We shall express our professional concerns about directives from the sponsoring agency or governing body when we believe that a mandated practice is not in the best interest of children.

P-1.11—If we determine that a policy does not benefit children, we shall work to change it. If we determine that a program policy is harmful to children, we shall suspend its implementation while working to honor the intent of the policy in ways that are not harmful to children.

2. Ethical Responsibilities to Families   The administrator sets the tone for the program in establishing and supporting an understanding of the family's role in their children's development. Administrators strive to promote communication, cooperation, and collaboration between the home and the program in ways that enhance each child's development. Because administrators provide the link between the family and direct services for children, they often encounter ethical issues in this area of responsibility.

Ideals

I-2.1—To design programs and policies responsive to diverse families.

I-2.2—To serve as a resource for families by providing information and referrals to services in the larger community.

I-2.3—To advocate for the needs and rights of families in the program and the larger community.

I-2.4—To support families in their role as advocate for their children and themselves.

I-2.5—To create and maintain a climate of trust and candor that enables parents/guardians to speak and act in the best interest of their children.

Principles

P-2.1—We shall work to create a respectful environment for and a working relationship with all families, regardless of family members' sex, race, national origin, religious belief or affiliation, age, marital status/family structure, disability, or sexual orientation.

P-2.2—We shall provide families with complete and honest information concerning program philosophy, educational practices, and the services provided.

P-2.3—We shall make every attempt to communicate information in ways that are accessible by every family served.

P-2.4—We shall establish clear operating policies and make them available to families in advance of their child entering the program.

P-2.5—We shall develop enrollment policies that clearly describe admission policies and priorities.

P-2.6—We shall develop policies that clearly state the circumstances under which a child or family may be asked to leave the program. We shall refuse to provide services for children only if the program will not benefit them or if their presence jeopardizes the ability of other children to benefit from the program or prevents personnel from doing their jobs.

P-2.7—We shall assist families in finding appropriate alternatives when we believe their children cannot benefit from the program or when their presence jeopardizes the ability of other children to benefit from the program or prevents personnel from doing their jobs.

P-2.8—We shall apply all policies regarding obligations to families consistently and fairly.

P-2.9—In decisions concerning children and programs, we shall draw upon our relationships with families as well as each family's knowledge of their child. (See also P-3.7 in this Supplement.)

P-2.10—We shall respond to families' requests to the extent that the requests are congruent with program philosophy, standards of good practice, and the resources of the program. We shall not honor any request that puts a child in a situation that would create physical or emotional harm.

P-2.11—We shall work to achieve shared understanding between families and staff members. In disagreements, we shall help all parties express their particular needs and perspectives. (Note: This is repeated in Section 3 [P-3.16] to emphasize the responsibility to both staff and family members.)

3. Ethical Responsibilities to Personnel Early childhood program administrators are managers with the responsibility for providing oversight for all program operations, as well as serving as leaders in early care and education programs. They are responsible for creating and maintaining a caring, cooperative workplace that respects human dignity, promotes professional satisfaction, and models positive relationships. Administrators must exemplify the highest possible standards of professional practice both within and beyond the program. Ethical responsibilities to personnel include those that are related to working with staff they supervise and/or employ as well as the unions or groups that represent these staff.

The ethical dimensions of the administrator's personnel responsibilities begin with and are built specifically on Section III, Part C, of NAEYC's Code of Ethical Conduct, *Responsibilities to Employees.*

Ideals

I-3.1—To create and promote policies and working conditions that are physically and emotionally safe and foster mutual respect, cooperation, collaboration, competence, well-being, confidentiality, and self-esteem. (I-3C.1)

I-3.2—To create and maintain a climate of trust and candor that enables staff to speak and act in the best interest of children, families, and the field of early care and education. (I-3C.2)

I-3.3—To coach and mentor staff, helping them realize their potential within the field of early care and education.

I-3.4—To strive to secure adequate and equitable compensation (salary and benefits) for those who work with or on behalf of young children. (I-3C.3)

I-3.5—To encourage and support continual development of staff in becoming more skilled and knowledgeable practitioners. (I-3C.4)

Principles

P-3.1—We shall provide staff members with safe and supportive working conditions that respect human dignity, honor confidences, and permit them to carry out their responsibilities through performance evaluation, written grievance procedures, constructive feedback, and opportunities for continuing professional development and advancement. (P-3C.2)

P-3.2—We shall develop and maintain comprehensive written personnel policies that define program standards. These policies shall be given to new staff members and shall be easily accessible and available for review by all staff members. (P-3C.3)

P-3.3—We shall apply all policies regarding our work with personnel consistently and fairly.

P-3.4—We shall be familiar with and abide by the rules and regulations developed by unions or other groups representing the interests or rights of personnel in our programs.

P-3.5—We shall support and encourage personnel in their efforts to implement programming that enhances the development and learning of the children served.

P-3.6—We shall act immediately to prevent staff from implementing activities or practices that put any child in a situation that creates physical or emotional harm.

P-3.7—In decisions concerning children and programs, we shall draw upon the education, training, experience, and expertise of staff members. (P-3C.1) (See also P-2.9 in this Supplement.)

P-3.8—We shall work to ensure that ongoing training is available and accessible, represents current understandings of best practice, and is relevant to staff members' responsibilities.

P-3.9—We shall inform staff whose performance does not meet program expectations of areas of concern and, when possible, assist in improving their performance. (P-3C.4)

P-3.10—We shall provide guidance, additional professional development, and coaching for staff whose practices are not appropriate. In instances in which a staff member cannot satisfy reasonable expectations for practice, we shall counsel the staff member to pursue a more appropriate position.

P-3.11—We shall conduct personnel dismissals, when necessary, in accordance with all applicable laws and regulations. We shall inform staff who are dismissed of the reasons for termination. When a dismissal is for cause, justification must be based on evidence of inadequate or inappropriate behavior that is accurately documented, current, and available for the staff member to review. (P-3C.5)

P-3.12—In making personnel evaluations and recommendations, we shall make judgments based on fact and relevant to the interests of children and programs. (P-3C.6)

P-3.13—We shall make hiring, retention, termination, and promotion decisions based solely on a person's competence, record of accomplishment, ability to carry out the responsibilities of the position, and professional preparation specific to the developmental levels of children in his/her care. (P-3C.7)

P-3.14—We shall not make hiring, retention, termination, and promotion decisions based on an individual's sex, race, national origin, religious beliefs or other affiliations, age, marital status/family structure, disability, or sexual orientation. We shall be familiar with and observe laws and regulations that pertain to employment discrimination. (Aspects of this principle do not apply to programs that have a lawful mandate to determine eligibility based on one or more of the criteria identified above.) (P-3C.8)

P-3.15—We shall maintain confidentiality in dealing with issues related to an employee's job performance and shall respect an employee's right to privacy regarding personal issues. (P-3C.9)

P-3.16—We shall work to achieve shared understandings between families and staff members. In disagreements, we shall help all parties express their particular needs and perspectives. (*Note:* This is repeated from Section 2 [P-2.11] to emphasize the responsibility to both staff and family members.)

4. Ethical Responsibilities to Sponsoring Agencies and Governing Bodies   Programs providing early care and education operate under a variety of public and private auspices with diverse governing structures and missions. All early childhood program administrators are responsible to their governing and funding bodies. Administrators ensure the program's stability and reputation by recruiting, selecting, orienting, and supervising personnel; following sound fiscal practices; and securing and maintaining licensure and accreditation. Administrators are also responsible for overseeing day-to-day program operations and fostering positive relationships among children, families, staff, and the community.

Administrators' responsibilities to sponsoring agencies and governing bodies are optimally met in a collaborative manner. Administrators establish and maintain partnerships with sponsoring agency representatives, board members, and other stakeholders to design and improve services for children and their families.

Ideals

I-4.1—To ensure to the best of our ability that the program pursues its stated mission.

I-4.2—To provide program leadership that reflects best practices in early care and education and program administration.

I-4.3—To plan and institute ongoing program improvements.

I-4.4—To be ambassadors within the community, creating goodwill for program sponsors as well as for the program itself.

I-4.5—To advocate on behalf of children and families in interactions with sponsoring agency staff and governing body members for high-quality early care and education programs and services for children.

Principles

P-4.1—We shall ensure compliance with all relevant regulations and standards.

P-4.2—We shall do our jobs conscientiously, attending to all areas that fall within the scope of our responsibility.

P-4.3—We shall manage resources responsibly and accurately account for their use.

P-4.4—To ensure that the program's sponsoring agency and governing body are prepared to make wise decisions, we shall thoroughly and honestly communicate necessary information.

P-4.5—We shall evaluate our programs using agreed-upon standards and report our findings to the appropriate authority.

P-4.6—In presenting information to governing bodies we shall make every effort to preserve confidentiality regarding children, families, and staff unless there is a compelling reason for divulging the information.

1. Ethical Responsibilities to Community, Society, and the Field of Early Childhood Education   Like those of all early childhood educators, administrators' responsibilities to the community include cooperating with agencies and professionals that share the responsibility for children, supporting families in gaining access to services provided by those agencies and professionals, and assisting in the development of community programs and services.

Early childhood program administrators often have the knowledge, expertise, and education to assume leadership roles. For this reason, they are responsible to the community, society, and the field of early childhood education for promoting the education and well-being of young children and their families.

Ideals

1-5.1—To provide the community with high-quality early care and education programs and services. (I-4.1)

I-5.2—To serve as a community resource, spokesperson, and advocate for quality programming for young children.

I-5.3—To uphold the spirit as well as the specific provisions of applicable regulations and standards.

I-5.4—To increase the awareness of the public and policy makers about the importance of the early years and the positive impact of high-quality early care and education programs on society.

I-5.5—To advocate on behalf of children and families for high-quality programs and services for children and for professional development for the early childhood workforce.

I-5.6—To join with other early childhood educators in speaking with a clear and unified voice for the values of our profession on behalf of children, families, and early childhood educators.

I-5.7—To be an involved and supportive member of the early childhood profession.

I-5.8—To further the professional development of the field of early childhood education and to strengthen its commitment to realizing its core values as reflected in NAEYC's Code of Ethical Conduct and this Supplement. (I-4.8).

I-5.9—To ensure that adequate resources are provided so that all provisions of the Code of Ethical Conduct and this Supplement can be implemented.

Principles

P-5.1—We shall communicate openly and truthfully about the nature and extent of services that we provide. (P-4.1)

P-5.2—We shall apply for, accept, and work in positions for which we are personally well-suited and professionally qualified. We shall not offer services that we do not have the competence, qualifications, or resources to provide. (P-4.2)

P-5.3—We shall carefully check references and not hire or recommend for employment any person whose competence, qualifications, or character makes him or her unsuited for the position. (P-4.3)

P-5.4—When we make a personnel recommendation or serve as a reference, we shall be accurate and truthful.

P-5.5—We shall be objective and accurate in reporting the knowledge upon which we base our program practices. (P-4.4)

P-5.6—We shall be knowledgeable about the appropriate use of assessment strategies and instruments and interpret results accurately to families. (P-4.5)

P-5.7—We shall be familiar with laws and regulations that serve to protect the children in our programs and be vigilant in ensuring that these laws and regulations are followed. (P-4.6)

P-5.8—We shall hold program staff accountable for knowing and following all relevant standards and regulations.

P-5.9—When we become aware of a practice or situation that endangers the health, safety, or well-being of children, we have an ethical responsibility to protect children or inform parents and/or others who can. (P-4.7)

P-5.10—We shall not participate in practices in violation of laws and regulations that protect the children in our programs. (P-4.8)

P-5.11—When we have evidence that an early childhood program is violating laws or regulations protecting children, we shall report the violation to appropriate authorities who can be expected to remedy the situation. (P-4.9)

P-5.12—We shall be honest and forthright in communications with the public and with agencies responsible for regulation and accreditation.

P-5.13—When a program violates or requires its employees to violate NAEYC's Code of Ethical Conduct, it is permissible, after fair assessment of the evidence, to disclose the identity of that program (P-4.10)

P-5.14—When asked to provide an informed opinion on issues, practices, products, or programs, we shall base our opinions on relevant experience, knowledge of child development, and standards of best practice.

The core NAEYC Code of Ethical Conduct is online at www.naeyc.org/about/positions/PSETH05.asp

RECOMMENDED FURNITURE, FURNISHINGS, AND MATERIALS

PART 1: FURNITURE AND FURNISHINGS

- Chairs (8", 10", 12", and 14" heights) as appropriate for the children served. At least one chair is needed for each child to sit comfortably at meals, snacks, and for other table activities.
- Tables (16", 18", 20", and 22" heights) as appropriate for the children served. There needs to be a place for all children to sit at the tables comfortably at meals, snacks, and other table activities.
- Cribs and cots.
- Changing table (with stairs for toddlers and 2's) and hands-free trash can.
- A loft.
- Movable risers.
- Children's rocking chairs, easy chairs, stools, and/or benches.
- Low open shelves for blocks, puzzles, manipulatives, writing materials, etc. Consider ones that close and lock if your facility is shared by another program.
- Book storage. Consider book pockets, bins, or other units that display the front of children's books.
- Closed storage for books, puzzles, manipulatives, art supplies, and other instructional materials not currently in use.
- Cubbies for children's coats, book bags, and other belongings. Storage for school agers needs to be larger.
- Storage for adult's coats and personal possessions.
- Adult-sized chairs including gliders or rocking chairs, hammocks, sofas, and easy chairs, particularly in infant and toddler rooms.
- Bulletin boards, dividers (bulletin boards, flannel boards, screens).

PART 2: CLASSROOM MATERIALS

MATERIALS FOR INFANTS AND TODDLERS

Materials for Young Infants (birth–about 8 months)

Young infants explore with their senses. These kinds of toys are appropriate:

- Balls (clutch, nipple, and texture)
- Banners and streamers (especially outside)
- Bells (to firmly attach to wrist or shoes)
- Soft-bodied dolls, puppets, and stuffed toys. Take care that eyes are well attached and that nothing on them or their clothes could come off and be a choking hazard
- Plastic keys on a ring
- Unbreakable mirrors mounted on or close to the floor
- Mobiles—be sure they are interesting to look at from the baby's perspective
- Photographs of them, their families, and other interesting images such as flowers, animals, and the like
- Rattles, squeak and squeeze toys, and others designed for mouthing and teething. They need to be easy to wash and sanitize
- Recordings of the kind of instumental and vocal music they hear at home including popular music, classical music, and lullabies
- Wind chimes

Materials for Mobile Infants (about 8–18 months)

These older infants are becoming mobile. They are now crawling, cruising, and walking on their own. They are learning about their bodies and what they can do. They enjoy a wide variety of materials that they can act upon. They are learning about their own abilities, about cause and effect, and about the world around them.

Toys for Active Play

- Balls (large rubber, soft beach, dimpled balls and others designed for infants and toddlers)
- Blocks (large lightweight)
- Boxes to carry, crawl into and out of, to fill and to dump
- Bubbles (for the teacher to blow)
- Climbing structures designed for crawlers and early walkers with ramps, slides, and stairs
- Exercise mats for tumbling and jumping
- Pounding bench
- Push/pull toys
- Sand and sand toys (cups, buckets, spoons, funnels), especially for outside
- Steering wheels (two or more) attached side-by-side to structures for pretend play
- Tricycles to scoot (that don't steer)
- Tunnels
- Wagons

Materials to Manipulate

- Blocks (large vinyl or other lightweight blocks)
- Cars/trucks/trains/planes. Be careful all wheels are securely fastened and will not come off.
- Containers such as pails, buckets, pots and pans, muffin tins, to fill and sort (take care nothing can become a choking hazard)
- Latch-and-lock boards
- Peg boards with large pegs
- Pop-up toys and jack-in-the boxes
- Push/pull toys
- Puzzles with knobs
- Shape sorters
- Stacking and nesting toys

Materials to Support Creative Expression

- Crayons (large washable and nontoxic)
- Glue
- Markers (washable and nontoxic)—be very careful with lids, they are choking hazards
- Paintbrushes (short handled)
- Paints (washable finger paints, washable tempera)
- Paper (construction, manila and white drawing paper, newsprint, and finger paint)
- Recordings of the kinds of instrumental and vocal music they hear at home including popular music, classical music, and lullabies.
- Rhythm and percussion instruments such as drums, bells, tambourines, wooden blocks, sticks, and xylophones. Be certain all are well made and that nothing can fall out of the shakers.
- Scarves for dancing
- Sponges for painting

Toys to Support Make-Believe

- Cars/trucks/trains/planes. Be carefull all wheels are securely fastened and will not come off.
- Dolls (washable), blankets, bottles
- Dress-up clothes for girls and boys including scarves and pieces of fabric that can be used creatively
- Figures to be used with blocks such as animals, people, and vehicles
- Furniture for playing house including refrigerator, sink, stove, table and chairs, doll bed with blankets
- Plastic keys on a ring
- Purses and briefcases
- Toy telephones

Materials That Support Language and Literacy Development

- A wide selection of board books: storybooks with and without words, concept books, books with drawings, and others with photographs. Some with things to feel, flaps to open, and so on.
- Books on CD
- Puppets

Materials for Toddlers (18–36 months)

These children enjoy active play indoors and out! They are becoming more social, are busily mastering language, and are beginning to enjoy make-believe. They enjoy many of the materials listed for younger children, but it is now appropriate to offer additional play opportunities so they can master their growing skills and competencies.

Toys for Active Play

- Balls of various sizes for throwing and kicking
- Beanbags and target
- Blocks (large vinyl or other lightweight blocks)
- Boxes, cardboard (to carry and crawl in)
- Bubbles (for the teacher to hold)
- Buckets, pails, pots and pans and things to put in them (to support filling and dumping)
- Climbing equipment—both indoors and out
- Exercise mats for tumbling, somersaults, and so on
- Push/pull toys
- Rocking toys (rocking boat and rocking horse)
- Steerable tricycles, with and without pedals
- Tunnels
- Wagons, wheelbarrows, boxes to push and pull

Materials to Manipulate

- Play dough
- Large Legos and other simple building materials
- Tray puzzles with a limited number of pieces (some with knobs)
- Sewing and lacing cards with yarn and laces
- Peg boards with large pegs
- Sand and sand toys (pails, sieves and sifters, measuring cups and spoons, funnels, sand wheels)
- Shape sorters
- Stacking and nesting toys
- Water table and water play toys (for pouring, straining, and floating)

Materials to Support Creative Expression

- Crayons (washable and nontoxic)
- Easel
- Glue
- Magazines (for cutting)
- Markers (washable and nontoxic)
- Paintbrushes (long and short handled)
- Paints (watercolors, washable finger paints, washable tempera)
- Paper (construction, manila and white drawing paper, newsprint, and finger paint)
- Recordings of the kinds of instrumental and vocal music they hear at home including popular music, classical music, and lullabies.
- Rhythm and percussion instruments such as drums, bells, tambourines, wooden blocks, sticks,

and xylophones. Be certain all are well made and that nothing can fall out of the shakers.
- Scarves for dancing to music
- Scissors (blunt-ended and soft-handled)
- Sponges (for painting)
- Stamp pad (with washable ink) and stamps

Toys to Support Make-Believe

- Cars/trucks/trains/planes. Be carefull all wheels are securely fastened and will not come off.
- Cash register and shopping cart
- Washable dolls with easy-on, easy-off clothes
- Dollhouse, farm, airport, and other sets to support pretend play
- Dress up clothes for girls and boys including scarves and pieces of fabric that can be used creatively
- Furniture for playing house including refrigerator, sink, stove, table and chairs, doll bed with blankets, high chair, stroller, play food, empty and clean food containers, pots and pans, plastic dishes, housecleaning tools such as mop and broom
- Plastic keys on a ring
- Purses and briefcases
- Toy telephones

Materials That Support Language and Literacy Development

- A wide selection of board books: storybooks with and without words, concept books, books with drawings, and others with photographs. Some with things to feel, flaps to open, and so on.
- Books on CD at a listening station
- Puppets
- A wide selection of paper—lined and unlined writing paper, note cards, calendars, shopping lists, and so on
- A selection of pencils, washable markers, washable pens, and so on.

MATERIALS FOR PRESCHOOLERS

The Block Center

The main materials for indoor block areas are unit blocks, so named because each block is the unit size ($1^3/_8$" $\times$ $2^3/_4$" $\times$ $5^1/_2$" for standard-size unit blocks) or a multiple or fraction of one of the dimensions of that unit. Hollow blocks are the main materials for outdoor block areas. Factory-made accessories designed specifically as accessories for block play are better than those not so designed because they are in correct proportion to the blocks. Figures of people and other accessories, if appropriate, should be multicultural. Children can also make their own accessories. Materials to include in the block center/areas are as follows:

Accessories
- art materials for making accessories or for decorating structures
- cars, trucks, busses, and/or trains
- farm products
- figures of people or animals
- furniture
- traffic signs
- transportation items
- miscellaneous materials—colored cubes, empty wooden thread spools, small sticks, pretty stones and shells; samples of carpet and tile squares

Block shelves (for indoors) and bins or carts (for outdoors)

Props for dramatic play including blueprints or house plans and hard hats

Children's books related to buildings

Adult picture books (i.e. coffee table books) related to buildings

Pictures of buildings in the neighborhood, buildings visited on field trips, other buildings of interest

Pencils, paper, Post-it® notes, for drawing or writing about building

Outdoor hollow blocks or corrugated cardboard blocks

Steering wheel (attached to a stable structure for pretend play)

The Dramatic Play Center

Besides requiring adequate floor space, all dramatic play centers need adequate storage for equipment and materials. Carpet, although not essential, helps control noise and provides warmth and softness.

Preschool children prefer realistic props that can support many themes for dramatic play. Dolls, puppets, books, and pictures should meet multicultural and antibias criteria. Categories of equipment and materials to consider include the following.

Digital and toy cameras

Dress-up clothes and tools of the trade community workers (e.g., doctor's bag and stethoscope) and costumes for reenacting stories

Doll items (table and two to four chairs; doll furniture—high chair, bed or cradle, carriage, chest of drawers)

Housekeeping equipment and supplies such as

- refrigerator
- stove
- sink
- cabinet for dishes
- washer/dryer
- closet for doll clothes
- cooking supplies
  - pots, pans, and mixing bowls including cupcake and cake pans
  - unbreakable plates, bowls, coffee cups, and serving dishes
  - mixing spoons, funnels, and flatware
  - play food including dishes familiar to your children
  - food containers like yogurt cups, milk and juice cartons, spice bottles provided by children's families (and familiar to them because they come from home)
- housecleaning tools
  - broom
  - dust mop
  - dustpan, clothesline and clothespins; pictures and other home-decorating items
  - empty soap dispensers
- vase with flowers
- tablecloth
- Baby dolls and dolls that are "kids"
- Dress-up clothes for boys and girls
  - skirts and blouses
  - party dresses
  - men's shirts and suit coats
  - shoes and boots including workshoes and athletic shoes
  - small suitcase
  - neckties, scarves and ribbons
  - jewelry, purses
- Fabric (several strips 2 or 3 yd in length that can be used imaginatively)
- Accessories
  - rubber hose
  - steering wheels
  - PVC pipe
  - old faucets

- door locks
- springs
- keys
- pulleys
- bells
- scales
- alarm clock
- cash register and play money
- paintbrushes
- paper bags
- light switches
- paper punch for tickets

Dollhouse, community, farm, service station, and similiar play sets

Mirrors (full-length and handheld)

Pictures of community workers

Puppets and puppet theater

Reading/writing materials (appropriate for theme)

Rocking chair

Stuffed animals

Telephone, cell phone, adding machine, remote control

Computer keyboard and monitor (inoperable)

The Art Center

Aprons with snaps or Velcro

Chalk in various colors and diameters

Chalkboards and erasers

Cookie cutters and molds

Crayons

Design block sets

Display boards and tables

Drying rack

Easels (two or three working sides with a tray for holding paint containers on each side)

Food coloring

Found materials for collage work (beads, buttons, cellophane, cloth, flat corks, sewing trims, wallpaper scraps, wrapping paper scraps, yarn)

Hole punch

Magazines for collages

Markers (washable felt-tip, various colors)

Paint (fluorescent paint, finger paint, powdered or premixed tempera paint, watercolor sets)

Paintbrushes (1/2 in. and 1 in. thick with short and long handles)

Nonspill paint jars

Many kinds of paper including 18" × 24" construction paper; corrugated paper; crepe paper; 18" × 24" white and manila drawing paper; finger paint paper or glazed shelf paper; 18" × 24" newsprint; poster board; tissue paper

Paper bags

Paste and glue

Paste brushes and sticks

Colored pencils

Pictures of children engaging in art activities, reproductions of famous paintings, and pictures of sculpture and architecture

Pipecleaners

Plastic squeeze bottles

Play-Doh® (store bought or home made)

Printing blocks or stamps

Recipes for finger paints, modeling materials, and so on

Rolling pins

Rulers

Scissors (adult shears and right- and left-handed scissors for children)

Scissors rack

Sponges

Stickers in assorted shapes for making designs and pictures

Stories and poems with themes of color, shape, size, beauty of nature, and so on

Teacher supplies (art gum erasers; glue; masking and transparent tape; paper cutter; pins for bulletin boards; rubber cement; shears; stapler)

Templates

Textured materials (for tactile experiences)

Weaving materials

White board, washable dry-erase markers, and erasers

Yarn (various colors) and yarn needles

The Music Center

Equipment and materials for music may include the following:

Autoharp

Books—picture books about music, dancing and marching, and environmental sounds, and illustrated song books (for children), music song books and music appreciation books (for teacher use)

Capes, full skirts, scarves, band uniforms for marching and dancing

Listening stations with CD players and headsets

Melodic instruments (chromatic bells, electronic keyboard, xylophones)

Music cart

Piano and piano bench

Pictures of musicians, musical instruments, dancers, bands, orchestras

Racks or other containers for CDs

Rhythm instruments (drums, claves, triangles, tambourines, cymbals, tom-toms, hand bells, jingle sticks, wrist bells, ankle bells, shakers, maracas, rhythm sticks, tone blocks, castanets, sand blocks, sounder, finger cymbals, gong bell)

The Sand and Water Table

Aprons and plastic smocks

Dishwashing detergent

Food coloring

Mops, brooms, sponges (for cleanup)

Sand (white and brown)

Sand/water table

Sand toys

- cartons
- cookie cutters
- cups
- dishes, plastic
- funnels
- ladles
- marbles
- measuring cups, plastic
- pans, pitchers
- plastic animals and people
- plastic flowers
- rocks
- salt or spice shakers, plastic
- sand combs
- sand dolls
- sand molds
- sand pails
- sand wheels
- screens, plastic
- shells
- shovels
- sieves

- sifters
- spoons
- strainers
- tubes, cardboard, plastic, PVC
- vehicles—cars, trucks, bulldozers, tractors
- watering cans

Water play table

Water play toys

- aquarium nets
- balls—Ping-Pong, plastic, and rubber
- bath toys
- bowls, plastic
- bulb baster
- cooking whisk
- corks
- detergent squeeze bottles
- dolls, washable
- fishing bobbers
- funnels
- hose
- marbles
- measuring cups, plastic
- medicine droppers
- pitchers, small plastic
- rocks
- shaving brushes
- shells
- sponges
- strainers
- Styrofoam trays
- watering cans
- water wheels

Water pump for indoor water play table

MATERIALS FOR PRESCHOOLERS AND PRIMARY-AGE CHILDREN

Carpentry or Woodworking Center

Bar clamps

C-clamps (variety of)

Cloth, leather, Styrofoam®, cardboard, cork, bottle caps, and other scraps to nail on wood

Claw hammers of differing weights and sizes

Hand drill and assorted drill bits

Hard hats

Magnet (tied to a string for picking up dropped nails)

Nails (thin nails with good-sized heads because thick nails tend to split wood)

Paints (water based)

Pencils (heavy, soft leaded)

Pliers

Ruler and yardstick used as a straightedge more than for measuring

Safety goggles

Sandpaper of various grades (some can be wrapped around and tacked to blocks)

Saws (crosscut and coping)

Soap bar (rubbed across the sides of a saw to make it slide more easily)

Tacks

Tri-square

Vises (attached to workbench)

Wire (hand pliable)

Wood (scraps of soft wood, such as white pine, poplar, fir, and basswood with no knots), doweling, wood slats, wooden spools, and cross sections of tree stumps

Wood glue

Workbench or worktable (drawers for sandpaper and nails are desirable)

Young children cannot handle and should not use a rasp, screwdriver and screws, a plane, a brace and bits, a file, an ax or hatchet, metal sheets, tin snips, or power tools

The Science/Mathematics Center

Animal cages (for animals such as small mammals, insects, amphibians)

Animals (e.g., small mammals, insects, fish)

Aquarium (equipped with air pump and hose, filter, gravel, light, thermometer; fish net; aquarium guide)

Beads (for pattern work and for developing an understanding of geometric concepts)

Binoculars

Bird feeder for outside

Books and pictures (bird identification books and other books with science and mathematics themes)

Bubble-making materials and recipes

Calculators suitable for young children

Chick incubator

Collecting nets

Collections (e.g., rocks, bird nests, insects, seashells)

Counting discs

Counting frame

Cuisenaire rods

Cylinders graduated in diameter, height, and both diameter and height (i.e., Montessori)

Design cubes and cards

Digital camera

Directional compass

Dominoes (number)

Dowel rods in graduated lengths

Fabric, wallpaper, and cabinet- and floor-covering samples (patterns)

Flannel board figures illustrating science and mathematics concepts (like fractions, life cycles of the butterfly, etc.)

Flashlights

Gardening tools (child sized)

Geoboards

Geometric shape puzzles

Kaleidoscope

Magnets (bar, horseshoe)

Magnifying lenses (handheld and tripod)

Measuring equipment (*linear measuring*—rulers, yardsticks, tapes; measuring cups and spoons; *scales*—balance, bathroom, postal or food; *time instruments*—sundial, egg timer, clocks; weather *gauges*—rain gauge, thermometer)

Mirrors (unbreakable)

Miscellaneous materials (string, tape, plastic containers of assorted sizes, boxes, buckets, sponges, straws, dippers, bags, and hardware gadgets)

Models (e.g., animals, space equipment, simple machines)

Numerals (e.g., cards, insets, kinesthetic, puzzles, numerals to step on)

Objects to count

Parquetry blocks and cards (also called attribute blocks)

Pegboards and pegs (for developing number and geometric concepts)

Pictures with science themes

Plants, seeds, and bulbs with planting pots, soil, fertilizer, and watering cans

Playing cards

Prisms

Puzzles with science and mathematics themes

Seed box (a transparent container for viewing root growth)

Simple machines

Sorting box

Sound-producing objects

Stacking and nesting materials (for size concepts)

Terrariums (woodland and desert)

Tubing (plastic or PVC)

Vases

Weather vane

Writing materials

The Cooking Center

Aluminum foil

Aprons

Baking pans (various sizes including muffin pans)

Blender

Can opener

Centerpieces for special occasions

Cookie sheets

Cooling racks

Cutters (biscuit and cookie)

Cutting boards

Dishcloths, towels, and sponges

Dish drainer

Dishpan

Dishwashing detergent

Egg separator

Electric griddle

Electric mixer

Electric skillet

Flatware (forks, spoons)

Garbage bags

Gelatin molds

Grater

Ice cream maker

Kitchen scissors

Knives

Measuring cups (liquid and dry)

Microwave oven

Mixing bowls (metal and plastic)

Mixing spoons

Napkins

Nutrition charts

Pantry items (staples such as cooking oil, flour, salt, and sugar)

Paper dishes (plates, bowls, cups)

Paper towels

Vegetable peelers

Pictures of foods, kitchens, and people eating in different settings

Pitchers

Place mats, tablecloths, table runners

Plastic bags (resealable)

Popcorn popper

Popsicle sticks

Pot holders

Pot scrubbers

Recipe books for children

Recipe cards (individual cards for each step; poster with entire recipe)

Refrigerator with freezer

Rolling pin

Rotary eggbeater

Rubber scraper or spatula

Sauce pans (various sizes)

Serving trays

Sifter

Skillet

Storage containers (canisters, microwave dishes, refrigerator dishes)

Stove (hot plate or toaster oven may substitute)

Strainer

Straws

Thermometer

Timer

Toothpicks

Wax paper

Wet wipes

Whisk

Manipulatives and Small Contruction Toys

Accessories for small construction toys (e.g., Lego® vehicles)

Banks ("piggy" or boxes with small slots or holes for dropping small disks or marbles)

Beads for stringing

Bolt and nut boards

Construction toys (interlocking blocks, snap blocks, Junior Erector set, miniature hollow blocks, miniature unit blocks, Tinkertoys®)

Cylinder boards (Montessori)

Design materials (design cubes and cards, parquetry blocks and cards, plastic mosaics)

Dressing materials (e.g., dolls, frames, shoes with laces)

Insets (also called shape boards)

Lacing cards

Latch frames or lock boxes

Paper punch

Pegs and pegboards

Puzzles with storage racks

Sectioned boxes

Sewing cards or plastic canvas, yarn and needles

The Language, Literacy, and Writing Center

Alphabet letters (e.g., alphabet insets, kinesthetic letters, magnetic letters, letters to step on)

Books and recordings of stories

Computers and word processing software

Flannel and magnetic boards

Games and materials for developing letter and sound awareness

Globes and maps

Lotto (covering many subjects)

Numerals (e.g., numeral insets, kinesthetic numerals, magnetic numerals, numerals to step on)

Perceptual and conceptual development games and materials (absurdities, missing parts, sequencing, opposites, classification)

Paper of many kinds and sizes including recipe cards, envelopes, shopping lists, note cards, and so on

Picture dominoes

Pictures and flannel or magnetic representations of finger plays, poems, and stories

Puppets and a puppet theater

Puzzles for developing literacy knowledge (e.g., having story themes; rhyming words, sequencing)

Signs and labels

Writing materials (e.g., paper, chalkboards, porcelain boards, markers, crayons), many kinds of pencils and washable pens

MATERIALS FOR SCHOOL-AGE CHILD CARE

Furniture

Storage for coats and school backpacks

Parent communication center

Quiet Area

Books (reference books or materials on CD for doing homework and a selection of trade books for leisure reading)

Listening station with CD player and headphones

Mazes

Newspapers and children's magazines

Recordings (music and stories)

Word puzzles (e.g., crossword puzzles)

Games and Manipulatives

Board games (e.g., Monopoly®, Scrabble®, chess, checkers, Chinese checkers, Life®, Clue®, bingo, and tic-tac-toe)

Electronic games. Take care to select nonviolent and developmentally appropriate titles.

Card games (e.g., Fish)

Interlocking blocks (e.g., Legos®)

Jacks

Magnetic building sets

Parquetry blocks, design blocks, and design cards

Puzzles (jigsaw with 100 to 500 pieces)

Woodworking

See the recommendations for preschoolers and primary-age children.

Arts and Crafts

See the recommendations for preschoolers and primary-age children.

Materials for Hobbies

Items needed would depend on specific hobbies.

Writing Supplies

Chalk

Chalkboards or white boards

Computer and printer

Dry erase markers for white board (be sure they are non-toxic)

Paper (various types)

Pencils with pencil sharpeners

Computers and Technology

Calculators

Computers with Internet access (with appropriate parental controls) and selected software

CDs, DVDs, and VCRs

Television with DVD and VCR players

Outside

Ball game equipment (e.g., basketball, softball, dodgeball, kick ball, volleyball, soccer)

Marbles

Riding equipment (e.g., bicycles, skates, skateboards)

Sand/water/mud: See the recommendations for preschool and primary-age children.

POISONOUS PLANTS

This is a list of common plants that might be in your environment that have been involved in plant poisonings. It is not exhaustive but identifies some of the most commonly occurring plants that can be dangerous to children.

COMMON PLANTS THAT CAN CAUSE SKIN IRRITATION OR DERMATITIS

Do not let children touch these plants.

> Bull nettle (*Cnidoscolus stimulosus*)
> Spotted spurge (*Euphorbia maculata*)
> Trumpet creeper (*Campsis radicans*)
> Poison oak (*Toxicodendron pubescens*)
> Poison ivy (*Toxicodendron radicans*)
> Wood nettle (*Laportea canadensis*)

COMMON PLANTS THAT CAN BE POISONOUS IF EATEN

Indoor Plants

Aroids (*Dieffenbachia, Monstera, Philodendron, Spathiphyllum*)	Leaves
Mistletoe (*Phoradendron serotinum*)	Berries
Poinsettia (*Euphorbia pulcherrima*)	Milky sap

Adapted from *Poisonous Plant Resource Sheet for Child Care Providers* (n.d.). Alexander Krings, Herbarium, Department of Botany, NC State University, Raleigh, NC 27695-7612. Used with permission. Available on-line at www.cals.ncsu.edu/plantbiology/ncsc/Poisonplants/resourcesheet.pdf

Outdoor Plants

Trees

Black cherry (*Prunus serotina*)	All parts, except ripe fruit flesh
Black locust (*Robinia pseudoacacia*)	Inner bark, twigs, young leaves, seeds
Mulberry (*Morus* spp.)	Unripe fruits and milky sap

Shrubs and bedding plants

Azalea (*Rhododendron* spp.)	All parts
Boxwood (*Buxus* spp.)	Leaves
Caladium (*Caladium* spp.)	All parts
Cardinal flower (*Lobelia cardinalis*)	All parts
Castor-bean (*Ricinus communis*)	Seeds
Heavenly-bamboo (*Nandina domestica*)	Berries (potentially)
Hollies (*Ilex* spp.)	Berries, when eaten in quantity
Hydrangea (*Hydrangea* spp.)	Bark, leaves, flower buds
Jimsonweed (*Datura stramonium*)	All parts
Lantana (*Lantana camara*)	Unripe fruits
Lobelia (*Lobelia* spp.)	All parts
Madagascar periwinkle (*Catharanthus roseus*)	All parts
Mountain-laurel (*Kalmia latifolia*)	All parts
Oleander (*Nerium oleander*)	All parts
Pokeweed (*Phytolacca americana*)	All mature parts
Rhododendron (*Rhododendron* spp.)	All parts

Sheep-laurel, Lamb-kill (*Kalmia* spp.)	All parts
Tomato (*Lycopersicon esculentum*)	Stems and leaves

Vines

English ivy (*Hedera helix*)	All parts
Hyacinth bean (*Dolichos lablab*)	Pods and seeds
Peppervine (*Ampelopsis arborea*)	Unknown, caution with berries
Porcelain berry (*Ampelopsis brevipedunculata*)	Unknown, caution with berries
Sweet Pea (*Lathyrus* spp.)	Seeds
Vetchling (*Lathyrus* spp.)	Seeds
Virginia creeper (*Parthenocissus quinquefolia*)	Berries
Yellow Allamanda (*Allamanda cathartica*)	All parts
Yellow kessamine (*Gelsemium sempervirens*)	All parts
Wisteria (*Wisteria* spp.)	Seeds

How To Avoid Plant Poisoning

These steps will help you keep the children in your care safe.

1. Learn to recognize and name the dangerous plants around your facility.
2. Keep plants and plant parts away from infants and young children.
3. Teach children to keep unknown plants and plant parts out of their mouths.
4. Teach children to recognize poison ivy and other dermatitis-causing plants.
5. Do not allow children to make "tea" from leaves or suck nectar from flowers.
6. Do not rely on pets, birds, squirrels, or other animals to indicate nonpoisonous plants.
7. Label garden seeds and bulbs and store out of reach of children
8. Be proactive. If unsure of whether or not a plant around your facility is poisonous, ask an expert.

In Case of Emergencies

Call a physician or your local Poison Control Center immediately! Be prepared to provide the following information:

1. Name of the plant, if known
2. What parts and how much were eaten
3. How long ago was it eaten
4. Age of individual
5. Symptoms observed
6. A good description of the plant. Save the specimen for identification by an expert.

GOVERNING BOARD PROFILE WORKSHEETS

Governing Board Profile Worksheet—Sample 1

Current Board Directors	Term ending 2009			Term ending 2010			Term ending 2011		
	Alex T.	Jane R.	Tom F.	Lisa S.	Tina C.	Art P.	Stan B.	Maria S.	Albert B.
GENDER:									
• Female		X		X	X			X	
• Male	X		X			X	X		X
AGE:									
• 20–35		X				X			X
• 36–55	X			X			X	X	
• 56+			X		X				
RACE/ETHNICITY:									
• African American	X			X	X				X
• Caucasian		X	X			X			
• Native American								X	
• Hispanic							X		
• Asian-American									
• Other:									
RESIDES IN THE:									
• City		X		X		X		X	
• Suburbs	X		X				X		X
• Rural Areas					X				
CONSTITUENCY:									
• Parent	X			X			X		
• Civic/Business			X			X			X
• Educator		X						X	
• Community					X				X
• Other:									
SKILLS:									
• Fund-raising			X	X	X				X
• Public Relations		X						X	
• Strategic Planning	X						X		X
• Financial	X		X						
• Personnel						X			
• Laws/ Regulations/ Accreditation	X			X		X	X	X **Certified Teacher**	
• Education Expertise									
OTHER:									

Governing Board Profile Worksheet—Sample 2

Categories to Consider	Mike M.	Leo J.	Jane G.	Allen S.	Doris G.
Area of expertise/professional skills:					
• Organizational and financial management				X	X
• Community development		X	X	X	X
• Administration				X	X
• Academic/education					
• Business/corporate					
• Accounting/ Banking/Investments					
• Fund-raising (both experienced fund-raisers and those with leverage in getting funds)					
• Laws/regulations		X	X		
• Accreditation					
• Governmental agency representative		X	X		
• Marketing		X	X		
• Personnel					
• Physical plant (architecture, engineer)					
• Strategic or long-range planning					
• Public relations					
• Real-estate	X		X	X	
• Community resident		X	X	X	X
• Parent of child in school		X		X	
• Business owner					
Demographics:					
• Under 35	X				
• From 35 to 50		X	X	X	X
• From 51 to 65					
• Over 65					
• Female			X		X
• Male	X	X		X	
• Physical disability					
• Race/ethnic background					
• Asian		X			
• African American				X	X
• Hispanic					
• Native American					
• Caucasian	X		X		
• Geographic location					
• City dweller	X		X	X	X
• Suburbanite		X			

Categories to Consider	Mike M.	Leo J.	Jane G.	Allen S.	Doris G.
• Financial position					
• Salaried	X		X		
• Hourly employee					
• Enrolled in college					
• Philanthropic reputation		X			
• Eligible for free/reduced lunch	X			X	X

From *Creating an Effective Charter School Governing Board Guidebook,* by F. Martinelli, 2000, St. Paul, MN: Charter Friends National Network. Used with permission. Available on-line at http://www.uscharterschools.org/governance/

GOVERNING BOARD
JOB DESCRIPTION AND AGREEMENT

SAMPLE BOARD DIRECTOR POSITION DESCRIPTION AND STATEMENT OF COMMITMENT

1. Attend regular meetings of the board, which are scheduled to last two hours. The board meets at least six (6) times per year. Be accessible for personal contact in between board meetings.
2. Provide leadership to board committees. Each board member is expected to serve as an active member of at least one committee. Committee work may require additional meetings and the completion of assigned tasks. At present the board's committees are: program handbooks and policies, resource development/fundraising, strategic planning, board development, personnel, finance, and executive.
3. Commit to supporting fundraising and resource development activities.
4. Responsibly review and act upon committee recommendations brought to the board for action.
5. Prepare in advance for board meetings; take responsibility for becoming informed about upcoming issues.
6. Tap into personal and professional skills, relationships, and knowledge for the advancement of the program.

I am aware that this board position description is an expression of good faith and provides a common ground from which board members can operate. Additional information describing the program's mission, program of early care and education, and board responsibilities is contained in the board orientation materials and bylaws which I have read.

_____   _____
Board Member's Signature   Date

Adapted from Martinelli, F. (2000) *Creating an Effective Charter School Governing Board Guidebook*. St. Paul, MN: Charter Friends National Network. Used with permission. Available on-line at http://www.uscharterschools.org/governance/

PROFESSIONAL ORGANIZATIONS OF INTEREST TO EARLY CHILDHOOD EDUCATORS

Alliance for Early Childhood Finance
www.earlychildhoodfinance.org

American Academy of Pediatrics
www.aap.org

American Montessori Society
www.amshq.org

Association Montessori International/USA
www.montessori-ami.org

Campaign for Commercial Free Childhood
www.commercialfreechildhood.org

The Center for the Child Care Workforce
www.ccw.org

The Center for Early Childhood Leadership
www.nl.edu/cecl

Child Care Action Campaign
www.childcareaction.org

Child Care Law Center
www.childcarelaw.org

Child Welfare League of America
www.cwla.org

Children's Defense Fund
www.childrensdefense.org

Council of Chief State School Officers
www.ccsso.org

Council for Exceptional Children
www.cec.sped.org

Council for Professional Recognition
www.cdacouncil.org

Division for Early Childhood of the Council
for Exceptional Children
www.dec-sped.org

Early Head Start National Resource Center
www.ehsnrc.org/

Families and Work Institute
www.familiesandwork.org

Food and Nutrition Information Center
www.nal.usda.gov/fnic

Foundation for Child Development
www.fcd-us.org/

High/Scope Educational Research
Foundation
www.highscope.org

International Reading Association
www.ira.org

National Association for Bilingual Education
www.nabe.org

National Association for Child Care
Resource and Referral Agencies
www.naccrra.org

National Association of Early Childhood
Specialists in State Departments of
Education (NAECS/SDE)
naecs.crc.uiuc.edu

National Association of Early Childhood
Teacher Educators
www.naecte.org

National Association for the Education of
Young Children
www.naeyc.org

National Association for Family Child Care
www.nafcc.org

National Association for Sick Child Daycare
www.nascd.com

National Association of State Boards of Education
www.nasbe.org

National Association of State Directors of Special Education
www.nasdse.org

National Black Child Development Institute
www.nbcdi.org

National Center for Children in Poverty
www.nccp.org/

National Child Care Information Center
www.nccic.org

National Coalition for Campus Children's Centers
www.campuschildren.org

National Head Start Association
www.nhsa.org

The National Institute for Early Education Research
nieer.org

National Latino Children's Institute
www.nlci.org

National PTA
www.pta.org

National After School Association
www.naaweb.org

National Women's Law Center
www.nwlc.org/

Society for Research in Child Development
www.srcd.org

Southern Early Childhood Association
southernearlychildhood.org/

Special Education Resources for General Educators
serge.ccsso.org

The Urban Institute
www.urban.org

Zero to Three: National Center for Infants, Toddlers, and Families
www.zerotothree.org

Chapter 1

ACF (Administration for Children and Families). (2007). Head Start Act. Retrieved May 24, 2008, from http://eclkc.ohs.acf.hhs.gov/hslc/Program%20Design%20and%20Management/Head%20Start%20Requirements/Head%20Start%20Act/headstartact.html

American Automobile Association. (n.d.). AAA Newsroom: Diamond rating system. Retrieved May 24, 2008, from www.aaanewsroom.net/Main/Default.asp?CategoryID=9&SubCategoryID=22&ContentID=86.

Annie E. Casey Foundation. (2006). *2006 Kids Count Data Book*. Baltimore, MD: Author. Retrieved May 24, 2008, from http://www.aecf.org/upload/publicationfiles/da36221056.pdf

Annie E. Casey Foundation. (2007). *2007 Kids Count Data Book*. Baltimore, MD: Author. Retrieved May 24, 2008, from http://www.aecf.org/upload/publicationfiles/da36221056.pdf

Barnett, W. S. (1995). Long-term effects of early childhood programs on cognitive and school outcomes. *Future of Children, 5*(3), 25–50.

Barnett, W. S., Hustedt, J. T., Hawkinson, L. E., & Robin, K. B. (2006). *The state of preschool 2006*. New Brunswick, NJ: The National Institute for Early Education Research.

Beierlein, J. G., & Van Horn, J. E. (n.d.). Providing child care for mildly ill children. Madison, WI: Wisconsin Child Care Improvement Project. Retrieved May 24, 2008, from www.wccip.org/tips/mildly_ill/mildly_ill.html

Brown-Lyons, M., Robertson, A., & Layzer, J. (2001). Kith and kin—Informal child care: Highlights from recent research. New York: National Center for Children in Poverty. Retrieved May 24, 2008, from www.nccp.org/publications/pdf/text_377.pdf

Burchinal, M. R., Roberts, J. E., Nabors, L. A., & Bryant, D. M. (1996). Quality of center child care and infant cognitive and language development. *Child Development, 67*, 606–620.

California Department of Education. (2006). *The infant/toddler learning and development program guidelines*. Sacramento, CA: Author. Retrieved May 24, 2008, from www.cde.ca.gov/re/pn/fd/documents/itguidelines.pdf

Carnegie Corporation of New York. (1994). Starting points: Executive summary of the report of the Carnegie Corporation of New York Task Force on Meeting the Needs of Young Children. *Young Children, 49*(5), 58–61.

Center for Law and Social Policy & Children's Defense Fund. (2006). Child welfare in the United States. Retrieved May 24, 2008, from www.childrensdefense.org/site/DocServer/Child_Welfare_In_the_United_States06.pdf?docID=3512

Center on the Developing Child at Harvard University. (2007). *A science-based framework for early childhood policy: Using evidence to improve outcomes in learning, behavior, and health for vulnerable children. Retrieved May 24, 2008, from* www.developingchild.harvard.edu

Children's Defense Fund. (2006). *Improving children's health: Understanding children's health disparities and promising approaches to address them*. Washington, DC: Author. Retrieved May 24, 2008, from www.childrensdefense.org/site/DocServer/CDF_Improving_Children_s_Health_FINAL.pdf?docID=1781

Committee for Economic Development, Research, and Policy. (1987). *Children in need: Investment strategies for the educationally disadvantaged, Executive summary*. New York: Author.

Committee for Economic Development, Research, and Policy. (1991). *The unfinished agenda: A new vision for child development and education*. New York: Author.

Committee for Economic Development, Research, and Policy. (1993). *Why child care matters: Preparing young children for a more productive America*. New York: Author.

Cost, Quality, and Child Outcomes Study Team. (1995). *Cost, quality, and child outcomes in child care centers, public report* (2nd ed.). Denver: Economics Department, University of Colorado/Denver.

Cranley Gallagher, K. (2005). Brain research and early childhood development—A primer for developmentally appropriate practice. *Young Children, 60*(4), 12–20.

Dulewicz, V., & Higgs, M. (2005). Assessing leadership styles and organizational context. *Journal of Managerial Psychology, 20*(2), 105–123.

Garbarino, J., & Ganzel, B. (2000). The human ecology of early risk. In J. P. Shonkoff & S. J. Meisels (Eds.), *Handbook of early childhood intervention* (2nd ed., pp. 76–93). New York: Cambridge University Press.

Helburn, S. W., & Culkin, M. L. (1995a). *Cost, quality, and child outcomes in child care centers: Executive summary*. Denver: University of Colorado at Denver.

Helburn, S. W., & Culkin, M. L. (1995b). Costs, quality, and child outcomes in child care centers: Key findings and recommendations. *Young Children, 50*(4), 40–44.

Lerman, R. I., & Schmidt, S. R. (1999). *An overview of economic, social, and demographic trends affecting the U.S. Labor Market*. Washington, DC: The Urban Institute. Retrieved February 14, 2008, from www.urban.org/url.cfm?ID=409203

Meisels, S. J., & Shonkoff, J. P. (2000). Early childhood intervention. In J. P. Shonkoff & S. J. Meisels (Eds.), *Handbook of early childhood intervention* (2nd ed., pp. 3–34). New York: Cambridge University Press.

National Association for Regulatory Administration (NARA) & Technical Assistance Center (NCCIC). (2006). *The 2005 child care licensing study.* Conyers, GA: Author. Retrieved May 24, 2008, from http://nara.affiniscape.com/associations/4734/files/2005%20Licensing%20Study%20Final%20Report_Web.pdf

National Association for the Education of Young Children Academy for Early Childhood Program Accreditation (2005). NAEYC Early Childhood Program Standards. Washington, DC: Author. Retrieved May 24, 2008, from http://www.naeyc.org/academy/standards/

National Association for the Education of Young Children. (1991). *Early childhood teacher education guidelines.* Washington, DC: Author.

National Center for Educational Statistics. (2006). Initial results from the 2005 NHES early childhood program participation survey: Table 5: Mean number of hours per week of care for children from birth through age 5 and not yet in kindergarten, by arrangement and family characteristics: 2005. Retrieved May 24, 2008, from nces.ed.gov/pubs2006/earlychild/tables/table_5.asp?referrer=report

NICHD Early Child Care Research Network. (1998). Early child care and self-control, compliance, and problem behavior at twenty-four and thirty-six months. *Child Development, 69,* 1145–1170.

Olson, L. (2002). Starting early. Quality counts 2002: Building blocks for success. *Education Week, 21*(17), 10–12, 14, 16, 18–22.

Paulsell, D., Mekos, D., Del Grosso, P., Rowand, C., & Banghart, P. (2006). *Strategies for supporting quality in kith and kin child care: Findings from the Early Head Start enhanced home visiting pilot evaluation.* Princeton, NJ: Mathematica Policy Research, Inc. Retrieved May 24, 2008, from www.mathematica-mpr.com/publications/PDFs/kithkinquality.pdf

Ramey, C. T., & Ramey, S. L. (1998). Early intervention and early experience. *American Psychologist, 58,* 109–120.

Rolnick, A., & Grunewald, R. (2003). Early childhood development: Economic development with a high public return. *Fedgazette,* Federal Reserve Bank of Minneapolis, March. Retrieved May 24, 2008, from http://minneapolisfed.org/pubs/fedgaz/03-03/earlychild.cfm

Sameroff, A. J., & Fiese, B. H. (2000). Transactional regulation: The development ecology of early intervention. In J. P. Shonkoff & S. J. Meisels (Eds.), *Handbook of early childhood intervention* (2nd ed., pp. 135–159). New York: Cambridge University Press.

Schumacher, R., Hamm, K., Goldstein. A. & Lombardi, J. (2006). *Starting off right: Promoting child development from birth in state early care and education initiatives.* Washington, DC: Center for Law and Social Policy. Retrieved May 24, 2008, from www.clasp.org/ChildCareAndEarly Education/StartingOffRight/5008_Clasp.pdf

Schweinhart, L. J., Montie, J., Xiang, Z., Barnett, W. S., Belfield, C. R., & Nores, M. (2005). *Lifetime effects: The High/Scope Perry Preschool study through age 40* (Monographs of the High/Scope Educational Research Foundation, 14). Ypsilanti, MI: High/Scope Press.

Shonkoff, J. P., & Phillips, D. A. (Eds.). (2000). *From neurons to neighborhoods: The science of early childhood development.* Washington, DC: National Academy Press.

U.S. Census Bureau. (2006). American Community Survey. Retrieved May 24, 2008, from factfinder.census.gov/servlet/STTable?_bm=y&-geo_id=01000US&-qr_name=ACS_2006_EST_G00_S2301&-ds_name=ACS_2006_EST_G00_

U.S. Department of Education, Office of Special Education and Rehabilitative Services, Office of Special Education Programs. (2007). *27th Annual (2005) Report to Congress on the Implementation of the Individuals with Disabilities Education Act,* Vol. 1. Washington, DC: Author.

U.S. Department of Health and Human Services (2006). *Promoting quality in afterschool programs through state child care regulations.* Washington, DC: Author. Retrieved May 24, 2008, from www.nccic.org/afterschool/childcareregs.pdf

Urban Institute. (2004). *Primary child care arrangements for children under age 5 with employed mothers.* Washington, DC: Author. Retrieved May 24, 2008, from www.urban.org/publications/900706.html.

Zero to Three. (2007). *The infant-toddler set-aside of the child care and development block grant: Improving quality child care for infants and toddlers.* Washington, DC: Author. Retrieved May 24, 2008, from www.zerotothree.org/site/DocServer/Jan_07_Child_Care_Fact_Sheet.pdf?docID=2621

Zinzeleta, E., & Little, N. K. (1997). How do parents really choose early childhood programs? *Young Children, 52*(7), 8–11.

Chapter 2

Barnett, W. S. (1986). Methodological issues in economic evaluation of early intervention programs. *Early Childhood Research Quarterly, 1,* 249–268.

Barnett, W. S., Frede, E. C., Mobasher, H., & Mohr, P. (1987). The efficacy of public preschool programs and the relationship of program quality to program efficacy. *Educational Evaluation and Policy Analysis, 10*(1), 37–39.

Bowman, B. T. (1986). Birthday thoughts. *Young Children, 41*(2), 3–8.

Bredekamp, S. (Ed.). (1987). *Developmentally appropriate practice in early childhood programs serving children from birth through age 8* (Exp. ed.). Washington, DC: National Association for the Education of Young Children.

Bronfenbrenner, U. (1979). *The ecology of human development: Experiments by nature and design.* Cambridge, MA: Harvard University Press.

Bronfenbrenner, U. (1986). Ecology of the family as a context for human development: Research perspectives. *Developmental Psychology, 22,* 723–742.

Bronfenbrenner, U. (1989). Ecological systems theory. In R. Vasta (Ed.), *Six theories of child development: Revised formulations and current issues. Annals of child development: A research annual* (Vol. 6, pp. 187– 249). Greenwich, CT: JAI.

Buysse, V., & Wesley, P. W. (2006). *Evidence-Based Practice in the Early Childhood Field.* Washington, DC: Zero to Three Press.

Bryant, D. M., Clifford, R. M., & Peisner, E. S. (1991). Best practices for beginners: Developmental appropriateness in kindergarten. *American Educational Research Journal, 28,* 783–803.

Charlesworth, R., Hart, C. H., Burts, D. C., Thomasson, R. H., Mosley, J., & Fleege, P. O. (1993). Measuring the developmental appropriateness of kindergarten teachers' beliefs and practices. *Early Childhood Research Quarterly, 8,* 255–276.

Clark, C. M., & Peterson, P. L. (1986). Teachers' thought processes. In M. C. Wittrock (Ed.), *Handbook of research on teaching* (3rd ed., pp. 255–296). New York: Macmillan.

Cole, M. (1998). *Cultural psychology: A once and future discipline.* Cambridge, MA: Belknap Press.

Dewey, J. (1897). My pedagogic creed. *School Journal, 54,* 77–80.

Egan, K. (1983). *Education and psychology: Plato, Piaget, and scientific psychology.* New York: Teachers College Press.

Erikson, E. H. (1950). *Childhood and society.* New York: Norton.

Frost, J. L. (1992a). *Play and playscapes.* Albany, NY: Delmar.

Gardner, H. (1983). *Frames of mind: Theory of multiple intelligences.* New York: Basic Books.

Gardner, H. (1999). *The disciplined mind: What all students should understand.* New York: Simon & Schuster.

Gesell, A. (1931). Maturation and patterning of behavior. In C. Murchinson (Ed.), *A handbook of child psychology* (pp. 209–235). Worchester, MA: Clark University Press.

Goncu, A. (Ed.). (1999). *Children's engagement in the world: Sociocultural perspectives.* London: Cambridge University Press.

Guralnick, M. J. (1988). Efficacy research in early childhood intervention programs. In S. L. Odom & M. B. Karnes (Eds.), *Early intervention for infants and children with handicaps: An empirical base* (pp. 75–88). Baltimore: Brookes.

Harms, T. O., Cryer, D., & Clifford, R. M. (2003). *Infant/Toddler Environment Rating Scale—Revised.* New York: Teachers College Press.

Harms, T. O., & Clifford, R. M., & Cryer, D. (1998). *Early Childhood Environment Rating Scale—Revised.* New York: Teachers College Press.

Harms, T. O., Jacobs, E. V., & White, D. R. (1995). *School-Age Care Environment Rating Scale.* New York: Teachers College Press.

Harms, T. O., & Clifford, R. M. (1989). *The Family Day Care Rating Scale.* New York: Teachers College Press.

Haskins, R. (1989). Beyond metaphors: The efficacy of early childhood education. *American Psychologist, 44,* 247–282.

Hauser-Cram, P. (1990). Designing meaningful evaluations of early childhood services. In S. Meisels & J. Shonkoff (Eds.), *Handbook of early childhood intervention* (pp. 583–602). New York: Cambridge University Press.

Hemmeter, M. L., Maxwell, K. L., Ault, M. J., & Schuster, J. W. (2001). *Assessment of practices in early elementary classrooms.* New York: Teachers College Press.

Hitz, M. C., & Wright, D. (1988). Kindergarten issues: A practitioners' survey. *Principal, 67*(5), 28–30.

Horowitz, F. D., & O'Brien, M. (1989). In the interest of the nation: A reflective essay on the state of our knowledge and the challenges before us. *American Psychologist, 44,* 441–445.

Hunt, J. M. (1961). *Intelligence and experience.* New York: Ronald.

Jacobs, F. (1988). The five-tiered approach to evaluation: Context and implementation. In H. B. Weiss & F. H. Jacobs (Eds.), *Evaluating family programs* (pp. 37–68). New York: Aldine DeGruyter.

Jersild, A. T. (1946). *Child development and the curriculum.* New York: Teachers College Press.

Jorde-Bloom, P. (1988). Assess the climate of your center: Use the early childhood work environment survey. *Early Childhood Education Journal.* 15(4), 9–11.

Kagan, S. L. (1991a). Excellence in early childhood education: Defining characteristics and next decade strategies. In S. L. Kagan (Ed.), *The care and education of America's young children: Obstacles and opportunities* (pp. 237–258). Chicago: University of Chicago Press.

Katz, L. G. (1984b). The professional preschool teacher. In L. G. Katz (Ed.), *More talks with teachers* (pp. 27–42). Urbana, IL: ERIC Clearinghouse on Elementary and Early Childhood Education.

Katz, L. G. (1991a). Pedagogical issues in early childhood education. In S. L. Kagan (Ed.), *The care and education of America's young children: Obstacles and opportunities* (pp. 50–68). Chicago: University of Chicago Press.

Katz, L. G. (1999). *Multiple perspectives on the quality of programs for young children.* Hong Kong: Keynote address at the International Conference of the World Organization for Early Childhood Education, March 20–21, 1999. (ERIC Document Reproduction Service No. ED428868)

Kohlberg, L., & Mayer, R. (1972). Development as the aim of education. *Harvard Educational Review, 42,* 449–496.

Kostelnik, M. J. (1992). Myths associated with developmentally appropriate programs. *Young Children, 47*(4), 17–23.

McNamara, C. (1997–2006). Strategic planning (in nonprofit or for-profit organizations). Retrieved March 21, 2008, at www.managementhelp.org/plan_dec/str_plan/str_plan.htm

Meisels, S. J. (1985). The efficacy of early intervention: Why are we still asking these questions? *Topics in Early Childhood Special Education, 5,* 1–12.

Meshanko, R. (1996). What should our mission statement say? Idealist.org. Retrieved March 21, 2008, at www.idealist.org/en/faq/66-22/5-5

Miller, L. B., Bugbee, M. R., & Hyberton, D. W. (1985). Dimensions of preschool: The effects of individual experience. In I. E. Sigel (Ed.), *Advances in applied developmental psychology* (Vol. 1, pp. 25–90). Norwood, NJ: Ablex.

National Association for the Education of Young Children & the National Association of Early Childhood Specialists in State Departments of Education. (1991). Guidelines for appropriate curriculum content and assessment in programs serving children ages 3 through 8: A position statement. *Young Children, 46*(3), 21–38.

National Association for the Education of Young Children. (1997). NAEYC position statement. Developmentally appropriate practice in early childhood programs serving children from birth through age 8. In S. Bredekamp & C. Copple (Eds.), *Developmentally appropriate practice in early childhood programs* (Rev. ed., pp. 3–30). Washington, DC: Author.

Nilsen, B. A. (2000). *Week by week: Plans for observing and recording young children.* Albany, NY: Delmar.

Oakes, P. D., & Caruso, D. A. (1990). Kindergarten teachers' use of developmentally appropriate practices and attitudes about authority. *Early Education and Development, 1,* 445–457.

Plomin, R. (1997). *Behavioral genetics.* New York: Freeman.

Pogrow, S. (1996, September 25). On scripting the classroom. *Education Week,* pp. 20, 52.

Powell, D. R. (1987a). Comparing preschool curricula and practices: The state of research. In S. L. Kagan & E. F. Zigler (Eds.), *Early schooling: The national debate* (pp. 190–211). New Haven, CT: Yale University Press.

Powell, D. R. (1987c). Methodological and conceptual issues in research. In S. L. Kagan, D. R. Powell, B. Weissbourd, & E. F. Zigler (Eds.), *America's family support system* pp. 311–328). New Haven, CT: Yale University Press

Rogoff, B., & Chavajay, P. (1995). What's become of research on the cutural basis of cognitive development? *American Psychologist, 50,* 859–877.

Rusher, A. S., McGrevin, C. Z., & Lambiotte, J. G. (1992). Belief systems of early childhood teachers and their principals regarding early childhood education. *Early Childhood Research Quarterly, 7,* 277–296.

Sigel, I. E. (1990). Psychoeducational intervention: Future directions. *Merrill-Palmer Quarterly, 36,* 159–172.

Skinner, B. F. (1938). *The behavior of organisms: An experimental analysis.* Upper Saddle River, NJ: Prentice Hall.

Smith, B. S. (1997). Communication as a curriculum guide: Moving beyond ideology to democracy in education. *Childhood Education, 73,* 232–233.

Sommerville, C. J. (1982). *The rise and fall of childhood.* Beverly Hills, CA: Sage.

Spodek, B. (1987). Thought processes underlying preschool teachers' classroom decisions. *Early Child Care and Development, 28,* 197–208.

Spodek, B. (1991). Early childhood curriculum and cultural definitions of knowledge. In B. Spodek & O. N. Saracho (Eds.), *Yearbook in early childhood education: Vol. 2. Issues in early education* (pp. 1–20). New York: Teachers College Press.

Stott, E., & Bowman, B. (1996). Child development knowledge: A slippery base for practice. *Early Childhood Research Quarterly, 11,* 169–183.

Swadener, B. B., & Kessler, S. (Eds.). (1991). Reconceptualizing early childhood education [Special issue]. *Early Education and Development, 2*(2).

Vygotsky, L. S. (1978). *Mind in society* (M. Cole, S. Schribner, V. John-Steiner, & E. Souberman, Trans.). Cambridge, MA: Harvard University Press.

Weikart, D. P. (1981). Effects of different curricula in early childhood intervention. *Educational Evaluation and Policy Analysis, 3,* 25–35.

Weikart, D. P. (1983). A longitudinal view of preschool research effort. In M. Perlmutter (Ed.), *Development and policy concerning children with special needs. The Minnesota Symposia on Child Psychology* (Vol. 16, pp. 175–196). Hillsdale, NJ: Erlbaum.

Wood, D. J., Bruner, J., & Ross, G. (1976). The role of tutoring in problem solving. *Journal of Child Psychology and Psychiatry, 17,* 89–100.

Wolery, R. A., & Odom, S. L. (2000). An administrator's guide to preschool inclusion. Chapel Hill: University of North Carolina, FPG Child Development Center, Early Childhood Research Institute on Inclusion.

Chapter 3

ACF (Administration for Children and Families). (2007). Head Start Act as amended. Retrieved May 23, 2008, from eclkc.ohs.acf.hhs.gov/hslc/Program%20Design%20and%20Management/Head%20Start%20Requirements/Head%20Start%20Act/

American Academy of Pediatrics, American Public Health Association, and National Resource Center for Health and Safety in Child Care. (2002a). *Caring for our children: National health and safety performance standards: Guidelines for out-of-home child care programs* (2nd ed.). Elk Grove Village, IL: American Academy of Pediatrics and Washington, DC: American Public Health Association. Retrieved May 23, 2008, from nrc.uchsc.edu/CFOC/index.html

American Academy of Pediatrics, American Public Health Association, and National Resource Center for Health and Safety in Child Care. (2002b). *Stepping stones to using caring for our children* (2nd Ed.). Elk Grove Village, IL: American Academy of Pediatrics and Washington, DC: American Public Health Association. Retrieved May 23, 2008, from nrc.uchsc.edu/STEPPING/index.htm

Bloom, P. J. (1989). *The Illinois directors' study: A report to the Illinois Department of Children and Family Services.* Evanston, IL: National College of Education, Early Childhood Professional Development Project.

Bloom, P. J. (1996). The quality of work life in early childhood programs: Does accreditation make a difference? In S. Bredekamp & B. A. Willer (Eds.), *NAEYC accreditation: A decade of learning and the years ahead.* Washington, DC: National Association for the Education of Young Children.

Bredekamp, S., & Copple, C. (Eds.). (1997). *Developmentally appropriate practice in early childhood programs: Revised.* Washington, DC: National Association for the Education of Young Children.

Caruso, J. J. (1991). Supervisors in early childhood programs: An emerging profile. *Young Children, 46*(6), 20–26.

Charlesworth, R., Hart, C. H., Burts, D. C., & DeWolf, M. (1993). The LSU studies: Building a research base for developmentally appropriate practice. In S. Reifel (Ed.), *Advances in early education and day care: Perspectives in developmentally appropriate practice* (Vol. 5, pp. 3–28). Greenwich, CT: JAI.

The Children's Foundation. (2001). *2001 family child care licensing study*. Washington, DC: Author.

The Children's Foundation. (2002). *2002 child care center licensing study*. Washington, DC: Author

Class, N. E. (1968). *Licensing of child care facilities by state welfare departments*. Washington, DC: U.S. Department of Health, Education & Welfare, Children's Bureau.

Cost, Quality, and Child Outcomes Study Team (1995). *Cost, quality, and child outcomes in child care centers, Public report*. Denver: Economics Department, University of Colorado-Denver.

Council of Chief State School Officers. (2006). The words we use: A glossary of terms for early childhood education standards and assessment. Retrieved May 23, 2008, from www.ccsso.org/projects/scass/projects/early_childhood_education_assessment_consortium/publications_and_products/2840.cfm

Darling-Hammond, L. (1998). Teachers and teaching: Testing policy hypotheses from a National Commission report. *Educational Researcher, 27*(1), 5–16.

Darling-Hammond, L., Wise, A. E., & Klein, S. P. (1999). *A license to teach: Raising standards for teaching*. San Francisco: Jossey-Bass.

Early, D. M.; Bryant, D. M.; Pianta, R. C.; Clifford, R. M.; Burchinal, M. R.; Ritchie, S.; Howes, C.; Barbarin, O. (2006). Are teachers' education, major, and credentials related to classroom quality and children's academic gains in pre-kindergarten? *Early Childhood Research Quarterly (21)*2, 174–195.

Education Commission of the States. (2002). State-funded pre-kindergarten programs: Curriculum, accreditation, and parental involvement standards. Retrieved May 23, 2008, from www.ecs.org/dbsearches/Search_Info/EarlyLearning Reports.asp?tbl=table8

Epstein, A. S. (1999). Pathways to quality in Head Start, public school, and private nonprofit early childhood programs. *Journal of Research in Childhood Education, 13*(2), 101–119.

Fields, M., & Mitchell, A. (2007, June). ECE/Elementary Licensure Survey. Paper presented at the midyear conference of the National Association for Early Childhood Teacher Educators, Pittsburgh, PA.

Fischer, J. L., & Eheart, B. K. (1991). Family day care: A theoretical basis for improving quality. *Early Childhood Research Quarterly, 6,* 549–563.

Freeman, N. K., & Feeney, S. (2006). The new face of early care and education: Who are we? Where are we going? *Young Children, 61*(5), 10–16.

Goldstein, L. S. (1997). Between a rock and a hard place in the primary grades: The challenge of providing developmentally appropriate early childhood education in an Elementary School Setting. *Early Childhood Research Quarterly, 12,* 3–27.

Gormley, W. T., Jr. (1997). Regulatory enforcement: Accommodations and conflict in four states. *Public Administration Review, 57,* 285–293.

Harms, T., Clifford, R., & Cryer, D. (2005). *Early childhood environment rating scale* (Rev.). New York: Teachers College Press.

Herr, J., Johnson, R. D., & Zimmerman, K. (1993). Benefits of accreditation: A study of directors' perceptions. *Young Children, 48*(4), 32–35.

Howes, C. (1997). Children's experiences in center-based child care as a function of teacher background and adult-child ratio. *Merrill-Palmer Quarterly, 43,* 404–425.

Kontos, S., & File, N. (1992). Conditions of employment, job satisfaction, and job commitment among early intervention personnel. *Journal of Early Intervention, 16,* 155–165.

Kontos, S., Howes, C., & Galinsky, E. (1997). Does training make a difference to quality in family child care? *Early Childhood Research Quarterly, 12,* 351–372.

Mancke, J. B. (1972). Liability of school districts for the negligent acts of their employees. *Journal of Law and Education, 1,* 109–127.

Mitchell, A. (1988). *The Public School Early Childhood Study: The district survey*. New York: Bank Street College Press.

Mitchell, A. (2000). The case for credentialing directors now and considerations for the future. In M. L. Culkin (Ed.), *Managing quality in young children's programs: The leader's role* (pp. 152–169). New York: Teachers College Press.

Mitchell, A. W. (2005). *Stair steps to quality: A guide for states and communities developing quality rating systems for early care and education*. Alexandria, VA: United Way Success by 6™.

Morgan, G. G. (1986). Gaps and excesses in the regulation of child care: Report of a panel. *Review of Infectious Diseases, 8,* 634–643.

Morgan, G. G. (1996). Licensing and accreditation: How much quality is "quality"? In S. Bredekamp & B. A. Wilier (Eds.), *NAEYC accreditation: A decade of learning and the years ahead* (pp. 129–138). Washington, DC: National Association for the Education of Young Children.

Morgan, G. G. (1997). *Taking the lead: Director credentialing information packet*. Boston: Wheelock College, Center for Career Development in Early Care and Education.

Morgan, G. G. (2000a). The director as a key to quality. In M. L. Culkin (Ed.), *Managing quality in young children's programs: The leader's role* (pp. 40–58). New York: Teachers College Press.

Morgan, G. G. (2000b). A profession for the 21st century. In M. L. Culkin (Ed.), *Managing quality in young children's programs: The leader's role* (pp. 133–151). New York: Teachers College Press.

National Association for the Education of Young Children. (1983, 1992, 1997). *Position statement: Licensing and public regulation of early childhood programs*. Washington, DC: Author. Retrieved May 23, 2008, from www.naeyc.org/about/positions/pdf/PSLIC98.PDF

National Association for the Education of Young Children. (1998a). *Accreditation criteria and procedures of the National Association for the Education of Young Children*. Washington, DC: Author.

National Association for the Education of Young Children. (1998b). NAEYC position statement on licensing and public regulation of early childhood programs. *Young Children, 53*(1), 43–50.

National Association for the Education of Young Children Academy for Early Childhood Program Accreditation. (2005). NAEYC Early Childhood Program Standards. Washington, DC: Author. Retrieved May 23, 2008, from www.naeyc.org/academy/standards/

National Association of Child Care Resource and Referral Agencies. (2007). We can do better: NACCRRA's Ranking of State Child Care Center Standards and Oversight. Retrieved May 23, 2008, from www.naccrra.org/policy/scorecard.php

National Association for Regulatory Administration & Technical Assistance Center. (2006). *The 2005 child care licensing study.* Conyers, GA: Author. Retrieved May 23, 2008, from http://nara.affiniscape.com/associations/4734/files/2005%20Licensing%20Study%20Final%20Report_Web.pdf

National Child Care Information Center. (2006). Quality rating systems: Definition and statewide systems. Retrieved May 23, 2008, from www.nccic.org/pubs/qrs-defsystems.html

National Child Care Information Center. (2007). Quick Facts: Quality rating systems. Distributed at the 2007 annual meeting of the Southern Early Childhood Association (SECA), Jacksonville, FL.

National Resource Center for Health and Safety in Child Care. (2002). Stepping stones to using *Caring for Our Children, 2nd Ed.* Compliance/Comparison Checklist. Retrieved May 23, 2008, from nrc.uchsc.edu

Scott, L. C. (1983). Injury in the classroom: Are teachers liable? *Young Children, 38*(6), 10–18.

Snider, M. H., & Fu, V. R. (1990). The effects of specialized education and job experience on early childhood teachers' knowledge of developmentally appropriate practice. *Early Childhood Research Quarterly, 5,* 68–78.

Snow, C. W., Teleki, J. K., & Reguero-de-Atiles, J. T. (1996). Child care center licensing standards in the United States: 1981 to 1995. *Young Children, 51*(6), 36–41.

Stipek, D. J., & Byler, S. (1997). Early childhood education teachers: Do they practice what they preach? *Early Childhood Research Quarterly, 12,* 305–325.

Surr, J. (1992). Early childhood programs and the Americans with Disabilities Act (ADA). *Young Children, 47*(2), 18–21.

Talley, K. (1997). National accreditation: Why do some programs stall in self-study? *Young Children, 52*(3), 31–37.

U. S. Department of Health and Human Services. (2006). *Promoting quality in afterschool programs through state child care regulations.* Accessed May 23, 2008 from www.nccic.acf.hhs.gov/afterschool/childcareregs.pdf

U.S. General Accounting Office. (2000). *Child care state efforts to enforce safety and health requirements* (GAO/HEHS-OO-28). Washington, DC: Author.

West, L. S. (April, 2001). *The influence of principals on the institutionalization of developmentally appropriate practices: A multiple case study.* (ERIC Document Reproduction Service No. ED456543). Paper presented at the annual meeting of the American Educational Research Association, Seattle, WA.

Chapter 4

Aronson, S. S. (Ed.). (2002). *Healthy young children: A manual for programs.* Washington, DC: National Association for the Education of Young Children.

Child Care Partnership Project: T.E.A.C.H. Early Childhood© Project. (n.d.). Retrieved May 23, 2008, from www.childcareservices.org/ps/teach.html

National Association for Regulatory Administration & Technical Assistance Center. (2006). *The 2005 child care licensing study.* Conyers, GA: Author. Retrieved May 23, 2008, from http://nara.affiniscape.com/displaycommon.cfm?an=1&subarticlenbr=104

National Association for the Education of Young Children. (n.d.). Position Statements on Ethical Conduct. Retrieved May 23, 2008, from www.naeyc.org/about/positions/ethical_conduct.asp

U.S. Department of Agriculture. (2000). *Food Guide Pyramid for Young Children—A daily guide for 2- to 6-year-olds.* Washington, DC: U.S. Department of Agriculture Center for Nutrition Policy & Promotion. Retrieved May 23, 2008, from http://www.cnpp.usda.gov/Publications/MyPyramid/OriginalFoodGuidePyramids/FGP4Kids/FGP4KidsTipsBook.pdf

U.S. Department of Education. (n.d.). Family Educational Rights and Privacy Act (FERPA). Retrieved May 23, 2008, from www.ed.gov/policy/gen/guid/fpco/ferpa/index.html

U.S. Department of Justice. (n.d.). Americans with Disabilities Act ADA Home Page. Retrieved May 23, 2008, from www.usdoj.gov/crt/ada/adahom1.htm

U.S. Department of Justice. (n.d.). Commonly asked questions about child care centers and the Americans with Disabilities Act. Retrieved May 23, 2008, from www.ada.gov/childq&a.htm

U.S. Department of Labor. (n.d.). Compliance Assistance—Family and Medical Leave Act (FMLA). Retrieved May 23, 2008, from http://www.dol.gov/esa/whd/fmla/

U.S. Equal Employment Opportunity Commission. (n.d.). Retrieved May 23, 2008, from www.eeoc.gov/

Chapter 5

Abbott-Shim, M. S. (1990). In-service training: A means to quality care. *Young Children, 45*(2), 14–18.

Anthony, M. A. (1998). Stages of director development. *Child Care Information Exchange, 123,* 81–83.

Ashton-Warner, S. (1963). *Teacher.* New York: Simon & Schuster.

Balaban, N. (1992). The role of the child care professional in caring for infants, toddlers, and their families. *Young Children, 47*(5), 66–71.

Bandura, A. (1982). Self-efficacy mechanisms in human agency. *American Psychologists, 37,* 122–147.

Barker, L., Wahlers, K., Watson, K., & Kibler, R. (1987). *Groups in process*. Upper Saddle River, NJ: Prentice Hall.

Barnett, W. S. (2003). Low wages-low quality: Solving the real preschool teacher crisis. Retrieved November 30, 2004, from nieer.org/resources/policybriefs/3.pdf

Bellm, D., Whitebook, M., & Hnatiuk, P. (1997). *The early childhood mentoring curriculum: A handbook for mentors*. Washington, DC: Center for the Child Care Workforce.

Bloom, P. J. (1995). Shared decision making: The centerpiece of participatory management. *Young Children, 50*(4), 55–60.

Bloom, P. J. (1997a). *A great place to work: Improving conditions for staff in young children's programs* (Rev. ed.). Washington, DC: National Association for the Education of Young Children.

Bloom, P. J. (1997b). Navigating the rapids: Directors reflect on their careers and professional development. *Young Children, 52*(7), 32–38.

Bloom, P. J. (2000a). *Circle of influence: Implementing shared decision making and participative management*. Lake Forest, IL: New Horizons.

Bloom, P. J. (2000b). Images from the field: How directors view their organizations, their roles, and their jobs. In M. L. Culkin (Ed.), *Managing quality in young children's programs: The leader's role* (pp. 59–77). New York: Teachers College Press.

Bloom, P. J. (2000c). *Workshop essentials: Planning and presenting dynamic workshops*. Lake Forest, IL: New Horizons.

Bloom, P. J., Sheerer, M., & Britz, J. (1991). *Blueprint for action: Achieving center-based change through staff development*. Mt. Rainer, MD: Gryphon.

Bredekamp, S. (1990). *Regulating child care quality: Evidence from NAEYC's accreditation system*. Washington, DC: National Association for the Education of Young Children.

Brown, N. H., & Manning, J. P. (2000). Core knowledge for directors. In M. L. Culkin (Ed.), *Managing quality in young children's programs: The leader's role* (pp. 78–96). New York: Teachers College Press.

Carnegie Corporation of New York. (1994). Starting points: Executive summary of the report of the Carnegie Corporation of New York Task Force on Meeting the Needs of Young Children. *Young Children, 49*(5), 58–61.

Carter, M. (1992). Honoring diversity: Problems and possibilities for staff and organization. In B. Neugebauer (Ed.), *Alike and different: Exploring our humanity with children* (Rev. ed., pp. 70–81). Washington, DC: National Association for the Education of Young Children.

Carter, M. (1993). Developing a cultural disposition in teachers. *Child Care Information Exchange, 90,* 52–55.

Carter, M., & Curtis, D. (1998). *The visionary director: A handbook for dreaming, organizing, and improvising in your center*. St. Paul, MN: Redleaf.

Caruso, J. J., & Fawcett, M. T. (1999). *Supervision in early childhood education: A developmental perspective* (2nd ed.). New York: Teachers College Press.

Center for Career Development in Early Care and Education at Wheelock College. (2000). *The power of mentoring*. Boston: Wheelock College, Institute for Leadership and Career Initiatives.

Center for Child Care Workforce (2004). Current data on the salaries and benefits of the U.S. early childhood education workforce. Washington, D.C.: Center for the Child Care Workforce.

Cinnamond, J., & Zimpher, N. (1990). Reflectivity as a function of community. In R. Clift, W. Houston, & M. Pugach (Eds.), *Encouraging reflective practice in education* (pp. 57–72). New York: Teachers College Press.

Clarke-Stewart, A., & Gruber, C. (1984). Day care forms and features. In R. C. Ainslie (Ed.), *Quality variations in day care* (pp. 35–62). New York: Praeger.

Clyde, M., & Rodd, J. (1989). Professional ethics: There's more to it than meets the eye. *Early Child Development and Care, 53,* 1–12.

Collins, J. E., & Porras, J. I. (1994). *Built to last: Successful habits of visionary companies*. New York: Harper Business.

Cost, Quality, and Child Outcomes Study Team. (1995). *cost, quality, and child outcomes in child care centers, Public report* (2nd ed.). Denver: Economics Department, University of Colorado-Denver, .

Council for Early Childhood Professional Recognition. (1996). *The Child Development Associate system and competency standards: Pre-school caregivers in center-based programs*. Washington, DC: Author.

Cuffaro, H. (1995). *Experimenting with the world: John Dewey and the early childhood classroom*. New York: Teachers College Press.

Curbow, B., Spratt, K., Ungaretti, A., McDonnell, K., & Breckler, S. (2001). Development of the child care worker job stress inventory. *Early Childhood Research Quarterly, 15*(4), 515–535.

Deery-Schmitt, D. M., & Todd, C. M. (1995). A conceptual model for studying turnover among family child care providers. *Early Childhood Research Quarterly, 10,* 121–143

Drucker, P. (1990). *Managing the nonprofit organization: Principles and practices*. New York: HarperCollins.

Duff, R. E., Brown, M. H., & Van Scoy, I. J. (1995). Reflection and self-evaluation: Keys to professional development. *Young Children, 50*(4), 81–88.

Early, D. M., Maxwell K. L., Burchinal, M., Alva, S., Bender, R. H., Bryant, D., Cai, K., Clifford, R. M., Ebanks, C., Griffin, J. A., Henry, G. T., Howes, C., Iriondo-Perez, J., Jeon, Hyun-Joo, Mashburn, A. J., Peisner-Feinberg, E., Pianta, R. C., Vandergrift, N., Zill, N. (2007). Teachers' education, classroom quality, and young children's academic skills: Results from seven studies of preschool programs. *Child Development, 78*(2), 558–580.

Elicker, J., & Fortner-Wood, C. (1995). Adult-child relationships in early childhood programs. *Young Children, 51*(1), 69–78.

Feeney, S., & Christensen, D. (1979). *Who am I in the lives of children?* New York: Merrill/Macmillan.

Freeman, N. K., & Brown, M. H. (2000). Evaluating the child care director: The collaborative professional assessment process. *Young Children, 55*(5), 20–28.

Galinsky, E., Howes, C., Kontos, S., & Shinn, M. (1994). The study of children in family child care and relative care: Key findings and policy recommendations. *Young Children, 50*(1), 58–61.

Griffin, G. A. (Ed.). (1999). *The education of teachers: Ninety-eighth yearbook of the National Society for the Study of Education*. Chicago: University of Chicago Press.

Hale, C.M., Knopf, H., Kemple, K.M. (2006). Tackling teacher turnover in childcare: Understanding causes and consequences, identifying solutions. *Childhood Education, 82,* 219–226.

Hayden, J. (1996). *Management of early childhood services: An Australian perspective*. Wadsworth Falls, NSW: Social Science Press.

Hebbeler, K. (1995). *Shortages in professions working with young children with disabilities and their families*. Chapel Hill, NC: National Early Childhood Technical Assistance System.

Hennig, M., & Jardin, A. (1976). *The managerial woman*. New York: Pocket Books.

Hewes, D. W. (2000). Looking back: How the role of the director has been understood, studied, and utilized in ECE programs, policy, and practice. In M. L. Culkin (Ed.), *Managing quality in young children's programs: The leader's role* (pp. 23–39). New York: Teachers College Press.

Honig, A. S. (1993). Mental health for babies: What do theory and research teach us? *Young Children, 48*(3), 69–76.

Howes, C., & Hamilton, C. E. (1992). Children's relationships with caregivers: Mothers and child care teachers. *Child Development, 63,* 867–878.

Hoy, W., & Miskel, C. (1987). *Educational administration*. New York: Random House.

Hurst, B., Wilson, C., & Cramer, G. (1998). Professional teaching portfolios: Tools for reflection, growth, and advancement. *Phi Delta Kappan, 79,* 578–582.

Isenberg, J. P. (1999). *The state of the art in early childhood professional preparation*. Washington, DC: National Institute on Early Childhood Development and Education.

Jones, E. (1986). *Teaching adults: An active learning approach*. Washington, DC: National Association for the Education of Young Children.

Jones, E., & Nimmo, J. (1994). *Emergent curriculum*. Washington, DC: National Association for the Education of Young Children.

Jorde-Bloom, P. (1995). Shared decision making: The centerpiece of participatory management. *Young Children, 50*(4), 55–60.

Jorde-Bloom, P. (1997). Leadership: Defining the elusive. *Leadership Quest, 1*(1), 12–15.

Kagan, S. L. (1994). Leadership: Rethinking it—Making it happen. *Young Children, 49*(5), 50–54.

Kagan, S. L., & Bowman, B. T. (1997). Leadership in early care and education: Issues and challenges. In S. L. Kagan & B. T. Bowman (Eds.), *Leadership in early care and education* (pp. 3–8). Washington, DC: National Association for the Education of Young Children.

Kagan, S. L., Rivera, A. M., Brigham, N., & Rosenblum, S. (1992). *Collaboration: Cornerstones of an early childhood system*. New Haven, CT: Yale University, Bush Center in Child Development and Social Policy.

Katz, L. G., (1995). *Talks with teachers of young children: A collection*. Norwood, NJ: Ablex.

Kelley, R. (1991). *The power of followership: How to create leaders who people want to follow and followers who lead themselves*, New York: Doubleday.

Kisker, E. E., Hofferth, S. L., Phillips, D. A., & Farquhar, E. (1991). *A profile of child care settings: Early education and child care in 1990*. Washington, DC: U.S. Department of Education.

Kremer-Hazon, L., & Ben-Peretz, M. (1996). Becoming a teacher: The transition from teacher's college to classroom life. *International Review of Education, 32*(4), 413–422.

Latimer, D. J. (1994). Involving grandparents and other older adults in the preschool classroom. *Dimensions of Early Childhood, 22*(2), 26–30.

Lawler, E. E., Mohrman, S. A., & Ledford, G. E., Jr. (1992). *Employee involvement and total quality management*. San Francisco: Jossey-Bass.

Likert, R. (1967). *The human organization*. New York: McGraw-Hill.

Manlove, E. E. (1993). Multiple correlates of burnout in child care workers. *Early Childhood Research Quarterly, 8,* 499–518.

Manlove, E. E. (1994). Conflict and ambiguity over work roles: The impact on child care worker burnout. *Early Education and Development, 5,* 41–55.

Marshall, N., Creps, C, Burstein, N. Glantz, E, Roberson, W. W., & Barnett, S. (2001). *The cost and quality of full day, year-round early care and education in Massachusetts: Preschool classrooms*. (ERIC Document Reproduction Service No. ED475638)

McClelland, J. (1986). Job satisfaction of child care workers: A review. *Child Care Quarterly, 15,* 82–89.

Morgan, G. G. (1999). *The bottom line for children's programs: What you need to know to manage the money*. Watertown, MA: Steam Press.

Morgan, G. G. (2000). The director as a key to quality. In M. L. Culkin (Ed.), *Managing quality in young children's programs: The leader's role* (pp. 40–58). New York: Teachers College Press.

Morrison, A. M. (1992). *The new leaders: Guidelines on leadership diversity in America*. San Francisco: Jossey-Bass.

National Association for the Education of Young Children. (1988). Early childhood teacher education. Traditions and trends: An executive summary of colloquium proceedings. *Young Children, 44*(1), 53–57.

National Association for the Education of Young Children Academy for Early Childhood Program Accreditation. (2005). NAEYC Early Childhood Program Standards. Washington, DC: Author. Retrieved February 18, 2008, from http://www.naeyc.org/academy/standards/

Neugebauer, R. (2000). What is management ability? In M. L. Culkin (Ed.), *Managing quality in young children's programs: The leader's role* (pp. 97–111). New York: Teachers College Press.

Newman, M., Rutter, R. A., & Smith, M. S. (1989). Organizational factors that affect school sense of efficacy, community, and expectations. *Sociology of Education, 62,* 221–238.

Newman, S. B., Vander Ven, K., & Ward, C. R. (1992). *Guidelines for the productive employment of older adults in child care.* Pittsburgh, PA: Generations Together.

Olson, L. (2002). Starting early. Quality counts 2002: Building blocks for success. *Education Week, 21*(17), 10–12, 14, 16, 18–22.

Phillips, D., Mekos, D., Scarr, S., McCartney, K., & Abbott-Shim, M. (2000). Within and beyond the classroom door: Assessing quality in child care centers. *Early Childhood Research Quarterly, 15*(4), 475–496.

Piscitelli, B. (2000). Practicing what we preach: Active learning in the development of early childhood professionals. In N. J. Yelland (Ed.), *Promoting meaningful learning: Innovations in educating early childhood professionals* (pp. 37–46). Washington, DC: National Association for the Education of Young Children.

Pratt, C. (1948). *I learn from children.* New York: Simon & Schuster.

Quality, compensation, and affordability. The updated staffing study: A valuable resource for advocates. (1998). *Young Children, 53*(5), 42–43.

Rand, M. K. (2000). *Giving it some thought: Cases for early childhood practice.* Washington, DC: National Association for the Education of Young Children.

Rodd, J. (1998). *Leadership in early childhood: The pathway to professionalism* (2nd ed.). New York: Teachers College Press.

Rosenholtz, S. J., Bassler, D., & Hoover-Dempsey, K. (1986). Organizational conditions of teacher learning. *Teaching and Teacher Education, 2*(2), 91–104.

Schiller, P., & Dyke, P. C. (2001). *The pratical guide to quality child care.* Beltsville, MD: Gryphon.

Schneider, A. M. (1991, November). *Mentoring women and minorities into positions of educational leadership: Gender differences and implications for mentoring.* Houston, TX: Paper presented at the Annual Conference of the National Council of States on Inservice Education. (ERIC Document Reproduction Service No. ED344843).

Sciarra, D. J., & Dorsey, A. G. (1998). *Developing and administering child care centers* (4th ed.). Albany, NY: Delmar.

Shoemaker, C. J. (2000). *Leadership and management of programs for young children* (2nd ed.). Upper Saddle River, NJ: Merrill/Prentice Hall.

Smylie, M. (1992). Teacher participation in school decision making: Assessing willingness to participate. *Educational Evaluation and Policy Analysis, 14*(1), 53–67.

Snow, C. W., Teleki, J. K., & Reguero-de-Atiles, J. T. (1996). Child care center licensing standards in the United States: 1981 to 1995. *Young Children, 51*(6), 36–41.

Spodek, B. (1996). The professional development of early childhood teachers. *Early Child Development and Care, 115,* 115–124.

Stonehouse, A., & Woodrow, C. (1992). Professional issues: A perspective on their place in pre-service education for early childhood. *Early Child Development and Care, 78,* 207–223.

Stott, E., & Bowman, B. (1996). Child development knowledge: A slippery base for practice. *Early Childhood Research Quarterly, 11,* 169–183.

Taking the Lead Initiative. (1999). *The many faces of leadership.* Boston: Wheelock College, Center for Career Development in Early Care and Education, Taking the Lead Initiative.

Taking the Lead Initiative. (2000). *The power of mentoring.* Boston: Wheelock College, Center for Career Development in Early Care and Education, Taking the Lead Initiative.

Tertell, E. A., Klein, S. M., & Jewett, J. L. (Eds.). (1998). *When teachers reflect: Journeys toward effective, inclusive practice.* Washington, DC: National Association for the Education of Young Children.

Trawick-Smith, J., & Lambert, L. (1995). The unique challenges of the family child care provider: Implications for professional development. *Young Children, 50*(3), 25–32.

Vander Ven, K. (1988). Pathways to professional effectiveness for early childhood educators. In B. Spodek, O. N. Saracho, & D. L. Peters (Eds.), *Professionalism and the early childhood practitioner* (pp. 137–160). New York: Teachers College Press.

Wesley, P. W. (2002). Early intervention consultants in the classroom: Simple steps for building strong collaboration. *Young Children, 57*(4), 30–35.

Whitebook, M. (2001). Working for worthy wages: The child care movement, 1970–2001. Retrieved March 16, 2004, from www.ccw.org/about_wage.html

Whitebook, M., & Sakai, L. (2003). Turnover begets turnover: An examination of job and occupational instability among child care center staff. *Early Childhood Research Quarterly, 18,* 273–293.

Whitebook, M., Hnatiuk, P., & Bellm, D. (1994). *Mentoring in early care and education: Refining an emerging career path.* Washington, DC: Center for the Child Care Workforce.

Whitebook, M., Howes, C., & Phillips, D. A. (1990). *Who cares? Child care teachers and the quality of care in America* (Final Report of the National Child Care Staffing Study). Oakland, CA: Child Care Employee Project.

Whitebook, M., Howes, C., Phillips, D. A., & Pemberton, C. (1991). Who cares? Child care teachers and the quality of child care in America. In K. M. Paciorek & J. H. Munro (Eds.), *Annual editions, Early childhood education 91/92* (pp. 20–24). Guilford, CT: Dushkin/McGraw-Hill.

Whitebook, M., Sakai, L., Gerber, E., & Howes, C. (2001). Then & now: Changes in child care staffing, 1994–2000 (Technical Report). Washington DC: Center for the Child Care Workforce.

Willer, B. (Ed.). (1994). A conceptual framework for early childhood professional development: NAEYC position statement, adopted November 1993. In J. Johnson & J. B. McCracken (Eds.), *The early childhood career lattice: Perspectives on professional development* (pp. 4–21). Washington, DC: National Association for the Education of Young Children.

Chapter 6

Adams, P. K., & Taylor, M. K. (1985). *A learning center approach to infant education* (ERIC Document Reproduction Service No. ED253315). Columbus, GA: Columbus College, School of Education.

Americans with Disabilities Act. Retrieved May 23, 2008, from www.usdoj.gov/crt/ada/adahom1.htm. Information for child care centers is available from www.ada.gov/childq&a.htm

Baker, K. R. (1968). Extending the indoors outside. In S. Sunderlin & N. Gray (Eds.), *Housing for early childhood education* (pp. 59–70). Olney, MD: Association for Childhood Education International.

Beaty, J. J. (1996). *Preschool appropriate practices* (2nd ed.). Orlando, FL: Harcourt, Brace.

Bergen, D., Reid, R., & Torelli, L. (2001). *Educating and caring for very young children. The infant/toddler curriculum.* New York: Teachers College Press.

Berry, P. (1993). Young children's use of fixed playground equipment. *International Play Journal, 1,* 115–131.

Bodrova, E., & Leong, D. J. (2003). Do play and foundational skills need to compete for the teacher's attention in an early childhood classroom? *Young Children, 58*(3), 10–17.

Boutte, G., Van Scoy, I., & Hendley, S. G. (1996). Multicultural and nonsexist prop boxes. *Young Children, 52*(1), 34–39.

Bredekamp, S., & Copple, C. (Eds.). (1997). *Developmentally appropriate practice in early childhood programs: Revised.* Washington, DC: National Association for the Education of Young Children.

Caples, S. E. (1996). Some guidelines for preschool design. *Young Children, 51*(4), 14–21.

Cataldo, C. Z. (1982). Very early childhood education for infants and toddlers. *Childhood Education, 58,* 149–154.

Cavallaro, C. C., Haney, M., & Cabello, B. (1993). Developmentally appropriate strategies for promoting full participation in early childhood settings. *Topics in Early Childhood Special Education, 13,* 293–307.

Clarke-Stewart, A., & Gruber, C. (1984). Day care forms and features. In R. C. Ainslie (Ed.), *Quality variations in day care* (pp. 35–62). New York: Praeger.

Cost, Quality, and Child Outcomes Study Team. (1995). *Cost, quality, and child outcomes in child care centers, Public report* (2nd ed.). Denver: Economics Department, University of Colorado-Denver.

Cryer, D., Harms, T., & Riley, C. (2003). *All about the ECERS-R: A detailed guide in words and pictures to be used with the ECERS-R.* Lewisville, NC: Pact House Publishing.

Curtis, D., & Carter, M. (2003). Designs for living and learning: Transforming early childhood environments. St. Paul, MN: Redleaf Press.

DeBord, K., Hestenes, L. L., Moore, R. C., Cosco, N., & McGinnis, J. R. (2002). Paying attention to the outdoor environment is as important as preparing the indoor environment. *Young Children, 57*(3), 32–35.

Edwards, L., & Torcellini, P. (2002). *A literature review of the effects of natural light on building occupants.* Golden, CO: National Renewable Energy Laboratory. Retrieved May 23, 2008, from http://www.nrel.gov/docs/fy02osti/30769.pdf

Forman, G., & Fyfe, B. (1998). Negotiated learning through design, documentation, and discourse. In C. Edwards, L. Gandini, & G. Forman (Eds.) *The hundred languages of children: The Reggio Emilia approach— advanced reflections* (2nd ed., pp. 239–260). Greenwich, CT: Ablex.

Frost, J. L. (1992). *Play and playscapes.* Albany, NY: Delmar.

Frost, J. L., Wortham, S. C., & Reifel, S. (2001). *Play and child development.* Upper Saddle River, NJ: Merrill/Prentice Hall.

Frost, J., Wortham, S., & Reifel, S. (2007). *Play and child development* (3rd ed.). Upper Saddle River, NJ: Merrill/Prentice Hall.

Gonzalez-Mena, J. & Eyer, D. W. (2007). *Infants, toddlers, and caregivers* (7th ed.). Boston: McGraw Hill.

Greenman, J. T. (1988). *Caring spaces, learning places: Children's environments that work.* Redmond, WA: Exchange Press.

Greenman, J. T., & Stonehouse, A. (1996). *Prime times: A handbook for excellence in infant and toddler programs.* St. Paul, MN: Redleaf.

Guddemi, M., & Eriksen, H. (1992). Designing outdoor learning environments for and with children. *Dimensions of Early Childhood, 20*(4), 15–24, 40.

Harms, T., Clifford, R., & Cryer, D., (2005). *The Early Childhood Environment Rating Scale* (Rev.). New York: Teachers College Press.

Harms, T., Cryer, D., & Clifford, R. M. (2003). *The Infant/Toddler Environment Rating Scale* (Rev. ed.). New York: Teachers College Press.

Harms, T., Jacobs, E. V., & White, D. R. M. (1996). *The School-Age Care Environment Rating Scale—Revised.* New York: Teachers College Press.

Henniger, M. L. (1993). Enriching the outdoor play experience. *Childhood Education, 70,* 87–90.

Henniger, M. L. (1994). Planning for outdoor play. *Young Children, 49*(4), 10–15.

Hohmann, C., & Buchleitner, W. (1992). *Learning environment.* Ypsilanti, MI: High/Scope Press.

Howes, C. (1983). Caregiver behavior in center and family day care. *Journal of Applied Developmental Psychology, 4,* 99–107.

Hyson, M. C. (1994). *The emotional development of young children: Building an emotion-centered curriculum.* New York: Teachers College Press.

Isbell, R., & Exelby, B. (2001). *Early learning environments that work.* Beltsville, MD: Gryphon.

Jensen, B. J., & Bullard, J. A. (2002). The mud center: Recapturing childhood. *Young Children, 57*(3), 16–19.

Johnson, J. E., Christie, J. F., & Yawkey, T. D. (1987). *Play and early childhood development.* Glenview, IL: Scott, Foresman.

Johnson, L. C. (1987). The developmental implications of home environments. In C. S. Weinstein & T. G. David (Eds.), *Spaces for children: The built environment and child development* (pp. 139–173). New York: Plenum.

Katz, L. G., & Chard, S. C. (2000). *Engaging children's minds The project approach* (2nd ed.). Norwood, NJ: Ablex.

Kennedy, D. (1991). The young child's experience of space and child care center design: A practical meditation. *Children's Environments Quarterly, 8*(1), 37–48.

Klein, T. P., Wirth, D., & Linas, K. (2003). Play: Children's context for development. *Young Children, 58*(3), 38–45.

Koralek, D. (2002). Let's go outside! Outdoor settings for play and learning. *Young Children, 57*(3), 8–9.

Kostelnik, M. J., Soderman, A. K., & Whiren, A. P. (2007). *Developmentally appropriate curriculum: Best practices in early childhood education* (4th ed.). Upper Saddle River, NJ: Merrill/Prentice Hall.

Lally, J. R., Griffin, A., Fenichel, E., Segal, M. M., Szanton, E. S., & Weissbourd, B. (1995). *Caring for infants and toddlers in groups: Developmentally appropriate practice*. Arlington, VA: Zero to Three.

Lally, J. R., Provence, S., Szanton, E., & Weissbourd, B. (1986). Developmentally appropriate care for children from birth to age 3. In S. Bredekamp (Ed.), *Developmentally appropriate practice in early childhood programs serving children from birth through age 8* (Exp. ed., pp. 17–33). Washington, DC: National Association for the Education of Young Children.

Lally, J. R. & Stewart, J. (1990). *Infant/toddler caregiving: A guide to setting up environments*. Sacramento, CA: Far West Laboratory for Educational Development and California Department of Education Press.

Laufer, R. S., & Wolfe, M. (1977). Privacy as a concept and a social issue: A multidimensional developmental theory. *Journal of Social Issues, 33*(3), 22–42.

Lowman, L. H., & Ruhmann, L. H. (1998). Simply sensational spaces: A multi-"s" approach to toddler environments. *Young Children, 53*(3), 11–17.

Meltz, B. F. (1990, December 4). A little privacy: Children need a space to call their own. *Tallahassee Democrat,* p. D1.

Myhre, S. M. (1993). Enhancing your dramatic-play area through the use of prop boxes. *Young Children, 48*(5), 6–11.

National Association for the Education of Young Children. (1998). *Accreditation criteria and procedures of the National Association for the Education of Young Children.* Washington, DC: Author.

National Association for the Education of Young Children Academy for Early Childhood Program Accreditation. (2005). *NAEYC Early Childhood Program Standards.* Washington, DC: Author. Retrieved May 23, 2008, from http://www.naeyc.org/academy/standards/

Neill, S. R. St. J., & Denham, E. J. M. (1982). The effects of preschool building design. *Educational Research, 24*(2), 107–111.

Olds, A. R. (2001). *Child care design guide*. New York: McGraw-Hill.

Osmon, F. (1971). *Patterns for designing children's centers.* New York: Educational Facilities Laboratories.

Perry, J. P. (2003). Making sense of outdoor pretend play. *Young Children, 58*(3), 26–30.

Poest, C. A., Williams, J. R., Witt, D. D., & Atwood, M. E. (1990). Challenge me to move: Large muscle development in young children. *Young Children, 45*(5), 4–10.

Prescott, E. (1984). The physical setting of day-care. In J. T. Greenman & R. W. Fuqua (Eds.), *Making day care better* (pp. 44–65). New York: Teachers College Press.

Prescott, E. (1987). The environment as organizer of intent in child-care. In C. S. Weinstein & T. G. David (Eds.), *Spaces for children: The built environment and child development* (pp. 73–86). New York: Plenum.

Read, M. A. (2007). Sense of place in early childhood environments. *Early Childhood Education Journal, 34*(6), 387–392.

Rivkin, M. S. (1995). *The great outdoors: Restoring children's right to play outside*. Washington, DC: National Association for the Education of Young Children.

Runyan, C., Gray, D., Kotch, J., & Kreuter, M. (1991). Analysis of U.S. child care safety regulations. *American Journal of Public Health, 81,* 981–985.

Sallis, J., McKenzie, T., Kolody, B., Lewis, M., Marshall, S., & Rosengard, P. (1999). Effects of health-related physical education on academic achievement: Project Spark. *Research Quarterly in Exercise and Sport, 70*(2), 127–134.

Sandall, S. R. (2003) Play modifications for children with disabilities. *Young Children, 58*(3), 54–55.

Schreiber, M. E. (1996). Lighting alternatives: Considerations for child care centers. *Young Children, 51*(4), 11–13.

Shade, D. D. (1996). Software evaluation. *Young Children, 51*(6), 17–21.

Sosna, D. (2000). More about woodworking with young children. *Young Children, 55*(2), 38–39.

Stewart, I. S. (1982). The real world of teaching two-year-old children. *Young Children, 37*(5), 3–13.

Sussman, C. (1998). Out of the basement: Discovering the value of child care facilities. *Young Children, 53*(1), 10–17.

Talbot, J., & Frost, J. L. (1989). Magical playscapes. *Childhood Education, 66,* 11–19.

Tarr, P. (2004). Consider the walls. *Young Children 59*(3), 88–92.

Thompson, D., & Hudson, S. (2003). The inside information about safety surfacing. *Young Children, 58*(2), 108–111.

Tilbury, D. (1994). The critical learning years for environmental education. In R. A. Wilson (Ed.), *Environmental education at the early childhood level* (pp. 11–13). Washington, DC: North American Association for Environmental Education.

Tinsworth, D., & McDonald, J. (2001). *Special study: Injuries and deaths associated with children's playground equipment.* Washington, DC: U.S. Consumer Product Safety Commission.

Trawick-Smith, J. (1992). How the classroom environment affects play and development: Review of the research. *Dimensions of Early Childhood, 20*(2), 27–30.

U.S. Consumer Project Safety Commission. (2008). *Public playground safety handbook*. Retrieved May 22, 2008, from www.cpsc.gov/CPSCPUB/PUBS/325.pdf

Wallach, F., & Afthinos, I. D. (1990). *An analysis of the state codes for licensed day care centers focused on playgrounds and supervision*. New York: Total Recreation Management Services.

Wallach, F., & Edelstein, S. (1991). *Analysis of state regulations for elementary schools focused on playgrounds and supervision*. New York: Total Recreation Management Services.

West, S., & Cox, A. (2001). *Sand and water play: Simple, creative activities for young children*. Beltsville, MD: Gryphon.

Wilson, R. A., Kilmer, S. J., & Knauerhase, V. (1996). Developing an environmental outdoor play space. *Young Children, 51*(6), 56–61.

Winter, S. M., Bell, M. J., & Dempsey, J. D. (1994). Creating play environments for children with special needs. *Childhood Education, 71,* 28–32.

Chapter 7

Adams, G., & Poersch, N. O. (1997). Who cares? State commitment to child care and early education. *Young Children, 52*(4), 66–69.

Adams, G., Schulman, K., & Ebb, N. (1998). *Locked doors: States struggling to meet the needs of low-income working families*. Washington, DC: Children's Defense Fund.

Barbett, S., & Korb, R. A. (1999). *Current funds, revenues, and expenditures of degree-granting institutions: Fiscal Year 1996*. Washington, DC: U.S. Department of Education, Office of Educational Research and Improvement.

Barnett, S. W., Hustedt, J. T., Friedman, A. H., Boyd, J. S., & Ainsworth, P. (2007). *The state of preschool 2007*. New Brunswick, NJ: National Institute for Early Education Research.

Barnett, W. S., Hustedt, J. T., Hawkinson, L.E., & Robin, K. B. (2006). *The state of preschool 2006*. New Brunswick, NJ: The National Institute for Early Education Research.

Bellm, D., Breuning, G. S., Lombardi, J., & Whitebook, M. (1992). On the horizon: New policy initiatives to enhance child care staff compensation. *Young Children, 47*(5), 39–42.

Blau, D. M., & Hagy, A. P. (1998). The demand for quality in child care. *Journal of Political Economy, 106,* 104–146.

Brandon, R. N., Kagan, S. L., & Joesch, J. M. (2000). *Design choices: Universal financing for early care and education*. Seattle: University of Washington.

Carnegie Corporation of New York. (1996). *Years of promise: A comprehensive learning strategy for America's children*. New York: Author.

Casper, L. M. (1995). *What does it cost to mind our preschoolers?* Current Population Reports (U.S. Bureau of the Census publications No. 70–52). Washington, DC: U.S. Government Printing Office.

Center for the Child Care Workforce. (2000). *Current data on child care salaries and benefits in the United States*. Washington, DC: Author.

Cost, Quality, and Child Outcomes Study Team. (1995). *Cost, quality, and child outcomes in child care centers, Public report* (2nd ed.). Denver: Economics Department, University of Colorado-Denver, .

Education Week. (2000, January). *Special report: Quality counts 2000: Who should teach?* Washington, DC: Editorial Projects in Education, Inc.

Einbinder, S. D., & Bond, J. T. (1992). *Five million children: 1992 update*. New York: National Center for Children in Poverty.

Greenman, J. T., & Johnson, N. (1993). *Child care center management*. Minneapolis: Greater Minneapolis Day Care Association.

Hayes, C. D., Palmer, J. L., & Zaslow, M. (1990). *Who cares for America's children: Child care policy for the 1990s*. Washington, DC: National Academy Press.

Helburn, S. W. (Ed.). (1995). *Cost, quality, and child outcomes in child care centers*. Technical report. Denver: University of Colorado at Denver, Department of Economics, Center for Research in Economics and Social Policy.

Hill-Scott, K. (2000). Leadership in child development programs: Prospects for the future. In M. L. Culkin (Ed.), *Managing quality in young children's programs* (pp. 203–220). New York: Teachers College Press.

Howes, C., Smith, E., & Galinsky, E. (1998). *The Florida child care quality improvement study: 1996 report*. New York: Families and Work Institute.

Kagan, S. L. (2000). Financing the field: From mistakes to high stakes. *Young Children, 55*(3), 4–5.

Mitchell, A., & Morgan, G. G. (2001). *New perspectives on compensation strategies*. Boston: Wheelock College, Institute for Leadership and Career Initiatives.

Mitchell, A., Stoney, L., & Dichter, H. (1997). *Financing child care in the United States: An illustrative catalog of current strategies*. Philadelphia: Ewing Marion Kauffman Foundation and the Pew Charitable Trusts.

Morgan, G. G. (1999). *The bottom line for children's programs: What you need to know to manage the money*. Watertown, MA: Steam Press.

National Association for the Education of Young Children Policy Brief. (2001). Financing the early childhood education system. *Young Children, 56*(4), 54–57.

National Center for Education Statistics. (1997). *The condition of education 1997*. Washington, DC: U.S. Department of Education.

National Research Council. (2001). *Eager to Learn: Educating Our Preschoolers*. B T. Bowman, S. Donovan, and M. S Burns (Eds.). Washington, DC: National Academy Press.

Neugebauer, R. (1993a). Employer interest in child care growing and diversifying. *Child Care Information Exchange, 94,* 66–72.

Neugebauer, R. (1993b). State-of-the-art thinking on parent fee policies. *Child Care Information Exchange, 94,* 4–12.

Odom, S. L., Wolery, R. A., Lieber, J., & Horn, E. (2002). In S. L. Odom (Ed.), *Widening the circle: Including children with disabilities in preschool programs* (pp. 120–136). New York: Teachers College Press.

Olenick, M. (1986). *The relationship between day-care quality and selected social policy variables.* Unpublished doctoral dissertation, University of California, Los Angeles.

Olson, L. (2002). Starting early. Quality counts 2002: Building blocks for success. *Education Week, 21*(17), 10–12, 14, 16, 18–22.

Powell, I., Eisenberg, D. R., Moy, L., & Vogel, J. (1994). Costs and characteristics of high-quality early childhood education programs. *Child and Youth Care Forum, 23,* 103–118.

Queralt, M., & Witte, A. D. (1998). Influences on neighborhood supply of child care in Massachusetts. *Social Service Review, 17,* 17–47.

Rohacek, M. H., & Russell, S. D. (1998). Public policy report. Child care subsidy yields returns. *Young Children, 53*(2), 68–71.

Sandham, J. L. (2002). Adequate financing. Quality counts 2002: Building blocks for success. *Education Week, 21*(17), 43–46.

Schulman, K., & Adams, G. (1998). *The high cost of child care puts quality care out of reach for many families.* Washington, DC: Children's Defense Fund.

Schulman, K., & Blank, H. (2002). State child care assistance policies. *Young Children, 57*(1), 66–69.

Schulman, K., Blank, H., & Ewen, D. (2001). *A fragile foundation: State child care assistance policies.* Washington, DC: Children's Defense Fund.

Sosinsky, L. S., Lord, H., Zigler, E. (2007). For-profit/nonprofit differences in center-based child care quality: Results from the National Institute of Child Health and Human Development Study of Early Care and Youth Development. *Journal of Applied Developmental Psychology, 28* (5–6), 390–410.

Stephens, K. (1991). *Confronting your bottom line: Financial guide for child care centers.* Redmond, WA: Exchange Press.

Stoney, L. (1999). Looking into new mirrors: Lessons for early childhood finance and system building. *Young Children, 54*(3), 54–57.

Stoney, L., & Greenberg, M. (1996). The financing of child care: Current and emerging trends. Special issue on financing child care. *Future of Children, 6*(2), 83–102.

U.S. Bureau of Labor Statistics. (1996). *Occupational employment statistics* (OES) *program survey.* Washington, DC: U.S. Department of Labor.

U.S. Bureau of the Census. (1997). *Who's minding our preschoolers?* Washington, DC: U.S. Department of Commerce.

U.S. Department of Health and Human Services. (1999). *Access to child care for low-income working families.* Washington, DC: Author.

Vandell, D. L., & Wolfe, B. (2000). *Child care quality: Does it matter and does it need to be improved?* Washington, DC: Department of Health and Human Services.

Verstegen, D. A. (1994). The new wave of school finance litigation. *Phi Delta Kappan, 76,* 243–250.

Washington Update. (2001). A balancing act—surpluses, tax cuts, and investments: Can we have all three? *Young Children, 56*(2), 75.

Whitebook, M., & Eichberg, A. (2002). Finding a better way: Defining policies to improve child care workforce compensation. *Young Children, 57*(3), 66–72.

Whitebook, M. (2002). *Working for worthy wages. The child care compensation movement, 1970–2001.* New York: Foundation for Child Development.

Willer, B. (1990). Estimating the full cost of quality. In B. Willer (Ed.), *Reaching the full cost of quality in early childhood programs* (pp. 1–8). Washington, DC: National Association for the Education of Young Children.

Willer, B. (1992). An overview of the demand and supply of child care in 1990. *Young Children, 47*(2), 19–22.

Chapter 8

American Marketing Association. (2007). *Marketing Definitions.* Retrieved December 20, 2007, from http://www.marketingpower.com/content4620.php

Godin, S. (2002). *Purple Cow.* New York: Portfolio.

Hiam, A. (2004). *Marketing for Dummies* (2nd ed.). Indianapolis, IN: Wiley Publishing.

Lamb, C. W., Hair, J. F., McDaniel, C. (2006). *Essentials of Marketing* (6th Ed.). Winfield, KS: Southwestern College Press.

McNamara, C. (2007). *All About Marketing.* Retrieved December 20, 2007, from http://www.managementhelp.org/mrktng/mrktng.htm

Wisconsin Child Care Improvement Network, Inc. (2007), *Marketing your child care program.* Retrieved December 20, 2007, from www.wccip.org/tips/business/marketing.html

Chapter 9

Bailey, D. B., Jr., Burchinal, M., & McWilliam, R. A. (1993). Age of peers and early childhood development. *Child Development, 64,* 848–862.

Behrmann, M. M., & Lahm, E. A. (1994). Computer applications in early childhood special education. In J. L. Wright & D. D. Shade (Eds.), *Young children: Active learners in a technological age* (pp. 105–120). Washington, DC: National Association for the Education of Young Children.

Bergen, D. (1994). Teaching strategies: Developing the art and science of team teaching. *Childhood Education, 70,* 300–301.

401

Bergen, D., & Coscia, J. (2001). *Brain research and childhood education: Implications for educators.* Olney, MD: Association for Childhood Education International.

Betz, C. (1994). Beyond time-out: Tips from a teacher. *Young Children, 49*(3), 10–14.

Bingham, A. A. (1995). *Exploring the multi-age classroom.* York, ME: Stenhouse.

Bontá P., & Silverman, B. (1993). Making learning entertaining. In N. Estes & M. Thomas (Eds.), *Rethinking the roles of technology in education* (pp. 1150–1152). Cambridge: Massachusetts Institute of Technology.

Bove, C. (1999). *L'inserimento del banbino al nido.* (Welcome the child into infant care): Perspectives from Italy. *Young Children, 54*(2), 32–34.

Bredekamp, S., & Copple, C. (Eds.). (1997). *Developmentally appropriate practice in early childhood programs: Revised.* Washington, DC: National Association for the Education of Young Children.

Bredekamp, S., & Rosegrant, T. (1995). Reaching potentials through national standards: Panacea or pipe dream? In S. Bredekamp & T. Rosegrant (Eds.), *Reaching potentials: Transforming early childhood curriculum and assessment* (Vol. 2, pp. 5–14). Washington, DC: National Association for the Education of Young Children.

Bromer, J. (1999). Cultural variations in child care: Values and actions. *Young Children, 54*(6), 72–78.

Burchinal, M. R., Roberts, J. E., Nabors, L. A., & Bryant, D. M. (1996). Quality of center child care and infant cognitive and language development. *Child Development, 67,* 606–620.

Caldwell, B. M. (1991). Continuity in the early years: Transitions between grades and systems. In S. L. Kagan (Ed.), *The care and education of America's young children: Obstacles and opportunities* (pp. 69–90). Chicago: University of Chicago Press.

Cardelle-Elawar, M., & Wetzel, K. (1995). Students and computers as partners in developing students' problem-solving skills. *Journal of Research on Computing in Education, 27,* 378–401.

Carlisle, A. (2001). Using multiple intelligences theory to assess early childhood curricula. *Young Children, 56*(6), 77–83.

Chaille, C., & Britain, L. (1997). *The young child as scientist: A constructivist approach to early childhood science education.* New York: Longman.

Chipman, M. (1997). Valuing cultural diversity in the early years: Social imperatives and pedagogical insights. In J. P. Isenberg & M. R. Jalongo (Eds.), *Major trends and issues in early childhood education* (pp. 43–55). New York: Teachers College Press.

Clements, D. H. (1994). The uniqueness of the computer as a learning tool: Insights from research and practice. In J. L. Wright & D. D. Shade (Eds.), *Young children: Active learners in a technological age* (pp. 31–50). Washington, DC: National Association for the Education of Young Children.

Clements, D. H., & Nastasi, B. K. (1992). Computers and early childhood education. In M. Gettinger, S. N. Elliott, & T. R.

Kratochwill (Eds.), *Preschool and early childhood treatment directions* (pp. 187–246). Hillsdale, NJ: Erlbaum.

Clements, D. H., & Nastasi, B. K. (1993). Electronic media and early childhood education. In B. Spodek (Ed.), *Handbook of research on the education of young children* (pp. 251–275). New York: Macmillan.

Clements, D. H., Sarama, J., & DiBiase, A.-M. (Eds.). (2003). *Engaging young children in mathematics: Findings of the 2000 National Conference on Standards for Preschool and Kindergarten Mathematics Education.* Mahwah, NJ: Erlbaum.

Clewett, A. S. (1988). Guidance and discipline: Teaching young children appropriate behavior. *Young Children, 43*(4), 25–36.

DeBord, K., & Regueros-de-Atiles, J. (1991). *Teacher perceptions of mixed-age groupings of children.* Research report. (ERIC Document Reproduction Service No. ED360047)

Denning, R., & Smith, P. (1997). Cooperative learning and technology. *Journal of Computers in Mathematics and Science Teaching, 16,* 177–200.

Derman-Sparks, L. (1992). Reaching potentials through antibias, multicultural curriculum. In S. Bredekamp & T. Rosegrant (Eds.), *Reaching potentials: Appropriate curriculum and assessment for young children* (Vol. 1, pp. 114–127). Washington, DC: National Association for the Education of Young Children.

Derman-Sparks, L., & A.B.C. Task Force. (1989). *Anti-bias curriculum: Tools for empowering young children.* Washington, DC: National Association for the Education of Young Children.

DeVries, R., Reese-Learned, H., & Morgan, P. (1991). Sociomoral development in direct-instruction, eclectic, and constructivist kindergartens: A study of children's enacted interpersonal understanding. *Early Childhood Research Quarterly, 6,* 473–517.

Dewey, J. (1916). *Democracy and education: An introduction to the philosophy of education.* New York: Macmillan.

Dodge, D. T., Jablon, J., & Bickart, T. S. (1994). *Constructing curriculum for the primary grades.* Washington, DC: Teaching Strategies.

Edmiaston, R., Dolezal, V., Doolittle, S., Erickson, C., & Merritt, S. (2000). Developing individualized education programs for children in inclusive settings: A developmentally appropriate framework. *Young Children, 55*(4), 36–41.

Elicker, J., & Mathur, S. (1997). What do they do all day? Comprehensive evaluation of a full-day kindergarten. *Early Childhood Research Quarterly, 12,* 459–480.

Elkind, D. (1998). Computers for infants and young children. *Child Care Information Exchange, 123,* 44–46.

Essa, E. L., Favre, K., Thweatt, G., & Waugh, S. (1999). Continuity of care for infants and toddlers. *Early Child Development and Care, 148,* 11–19.

Fedor v. Mauwehu Council of Boy Scouts, 143 A.2d 466 (Conn. 1958).

Ferguson, D. L. (1995). The real challenge of inclusion: Confessions of a "rabid inclusionist." *Phi Delta Kappan, 77,* 281–287.

Friedman, S. L., & Haywood, H. C. (Eds.). (1994). *Developmental follow-up: Concepts, domains, and methods.* San Diego: Academic Press.

Fromberg, D. P. (2002). *Play and meaning in early childhood education.* Boston: Allyn & Bacon.

Frost, J. L., Wortham, S. C., & Reifel, S. (2001). *Play and child development.* Upper Saddle River, NJ: Merrill/Prentice Hall.

Fuchs, D., & Fuchs, L. S. (1998). Inclusion versus full inclusion. *Childhood Education, 74,* 309–316.

Galley, M. (2002). State policies on kindergarten are all over the map. Quality counts 2002: Building blocks for success. *Education Week, 21*(17), 45.

Gardner, H. (1993). *Multiple intelligences: The theory in practice.* New York: Basic/HarperCollins.

Gartrell, D. J. (1995). Misbehavior or mistaken behavior? *Young Children, 50*(5), 27–34.

Gartrell, D. J. (1998). *A guidance approach for the encouraging classroom.* Albany, NY: Delmar.

Gartrell, D. J. (2000). *What the kids said today.* St. Paul, MN: Redleaf.

Gormley, W. T., Jr. (1995). *Everybody's children: Child care as a public problem.* Washington, DC: The Brookings Institution.

Greenman, J. T. (2001). *What happened to the world? Helping children cope in turbulent times.* South Watertown, MA: Bright Horizons Family Solutions.

Hale, J. E. (1994). *Unbank the fire: Vision for the education of African American children.* Baltimore: Johns Hopkins University Press.

Hart, C. H., & Burts, D. C., & Charlesworth, R. (Eds.). (1997). *Integrated curriculum and developmentally appropriate practice—Birth to age eight.* Albany: State University of New York Press.

Hatch, J. A. (2002). Accountability shovedown: Resisting the standards movement in early education. *Phi Delta Kappan, 83,* 457–462.

Hatch, J. A., & Freeman, E. B. (1988). Who's pushing whom? Stress and kindergarten. *Phi Delta Kappan, 70,* 145–147.

Haugland, S. W. (1992). Effects of computer software on preschool children's developmental gains. *Journal of Computing in Childhood Education, 3*(1), 15–30.

Haugland, S. W. (1999). What role should technology play in young children's learning? *Young Children, 54*(6), 26–31.

Haugland, S. W., & Wright, J. L. (1997). *Young children and technology: A world of discovery.* Boston: Allyn & Bacon.

Head Start Bureau. (2001). Head Start child outcomes framework. *Head Start Bulletin,* no. 70. Washington, DC: U.S. Department of Health and Human Services, Administrator for Children and Families. Available online at www .headstartinfo.org/pdf/im00_18a.pdf

Healy, J. M. (1998). *Failure to connect: How computers affect our child's minds—For better and worse.* New York: Simon & Schuster.

Helburn, S. W. (Ed.). (1995). *Cost, quality, and child outcomes in child care centers.* Technical report. Denver: University of Colorado at Denver, Department of Economics, Center for Research in Economics and Social Policy.

Helm, J. H., & Katz, L. G. (2001). *Young investigators: The project approach in the early years.* New York: Teachers College Press.

Helping young children in frightening times. (2001). *Young Children, 56*(6), 6–7.

Hemmeter, M. L., & Grisham-Brown, J. (1997). Developing children's language skills in inclusive early childhood classrooms. *Dimensions of Early Childhood, 25*(3), 6–13.

Henry, G. T., Rickman, D. K. (2007). Effects of peers on early education outcomes. *Economics of Education Review, 26,* 100–112.

Hess, R., & McGarvey, L. (1987). School-relevant effects of educational uses of microcomputers in kindergarten classrooms and homes. *Journal of Educational Computing Research, 3,* 269–287.

Hitz, R., & Driscoll, A. (1988). Praise or encouragement? *Young Children, 43*(5), 6–13.

Hohmann, M., & Weikart, D. P. (1995). *Educating young children: Active learning practices for preschool and child care programs.* Ypsilanti, MI: High/Scope Press.

Honig, A. S. (1995). Singing with infants and toddlers. *Young Children, 50*(5), 72–78.

Honig, A. S. (2002). *Secure relationships: Nurturing infant/ toddler attachment in early care settings.* Washington, DC: National Association for the Education of Young Children.

Howes, C. (1997). Children's experiences in center-based child care as a function of teacher background and adult-child ratio. *Merrill-Palmer Quarterly, 43,* 404–425.

Howes, C., & Norris, D. (1997). Adding two school age children: Does it change quality in family child care? *Early Childhood Research Quarterly, 12,* 327–342.

Howes, C., Phillips, D., & Whitebook, M. (1992). Thresholds of quality: Implications for the social development of children in center–based child care. *Child Development, 63,* 449–460.

Hunt, P., & Goetz, L. (1997). Research on inclusive educational programs, practices, and outcomes for students with severe disabilities. *Journal of Special Education, 31,* 3–29.

Hyman, I. (1997). *The case against spanking.* San Francisco: Jossey-Bass.

International Reading Association & National Association for the Education of Young Children. (2000). Joint position statement. In S. B. Neuman, C. Copple, & S. Bredekamp, *Learning to read and write* (pp. 1–26). Washington, DC: National Association for the Education of Young Children. Available online at www.naeyc.org/resources/position_statements/psreadO .htm

Isenberg, J. P., & Jalongo, M. R. (2000). *Creative expression and play in early childhood* (3rd ed.). Upper Saddle River, NJ: Merrill/Prentice Hall.

Isenberg, J. P., & Quisenberry, N. (2002). A position paper of the Association for Childhood Education International. Play: Essential for all children. *Childhood Education, 79,* 33–39.

Jacobson, L. (2002). Defining quality. Quality counts 2002: Building blocks for success. *Education Week, 21*(17), 24–28, 30–31.

Jones, B., Valdez, G., Norakowski, J., & Rasmussen, C. (1994). *Designing learning and technology for educational reform.* Oakbrook, IL: North Central Regional Educational Laboratory.

Jones, E., & Nimmo, J. (1994). *Emergent curriculum.* Washington, DC: National Association for the Education of Young Children.

Kagan, S. L., & Neuman, M. J. (1997). Highlights of the Quality 2000 initiative: Not by chance. *Young Children, 52*(6), 54–62.

Katz, L. G. (1991). *Readiness: Children and schools.* Urbana, IL: ERIC Clearinghouse on Elementary and Early Childhood Education. (ERIC Document Reproduction Service No. ED330495)

Katz, L. G. (1995a). A developmental approach to the education of young children: Basic principles. *International School Journal, 14*(2), 49–60.

Katz, L. G., (1995b). *Talks with teachers of young children: A collection.* Norwood, NJ: Ablex.

Katz, L. G., & Chard, S. C. (2000). *Engaging children's minds: The project approach* (2nd ed.). Norwood, NJ: Ablex.

Katz, L. G., Evangelou, D., & Hartman, J. A. (1990). *The case for mixed-age grouping in early education.* Washington, DC: National Association for the Education of Young Children.

Katz, L. G., & McClellan, D. E. (1997). *Fostering children's social competence: The teacher's role.* Washington, DC: National Association for the Education of Young Children.

Kilpatrick, W. H. (1918). The project method. *Teachers College Record, 19,* 319–335.

King, E. W., Chipman, M., & Cruz-Jansen, M. (1994). *Educating young children in a diverse society.* Boston: Allyn & Bacon.

Knapp, M. S. (Ed.). (1995). *Teaching for meaning in high-poverty classrooms.* New York: Teachers College Press.

Kohn, A. (2001). Five reasons to stop saying "Good Job!" *Young Children, 56*(5), 24–28.

Kontos, S., Howes, C., & Galinsky, E. (1997). Does training make a difference to quality in family child care? *Early Childhood Research Quarterly, 12,* 351–372.

Kontos, S., Howes, C., Shinn, M., & Galinsky, E. (1995). *Quality in family child care and relative care.* New York: Teachers College Press.

Kromhout, O. M., & Butzin, S. M. (1993). Integrating computers into the elementary school curriculum: An evaluation of nine Project CHILD model schools. *Journal of Research on Computing in Education, 26*(1), 55–69.

Krueger, A. (1999). Experimental estimates of education production functions. *Quarterly Journal of Economics, 114,* 497–532.

Lally, J. R. (1995). The impact of child care policies and practices on infant/toddler identity formation. *Young Children, 51*(1), 58–67.

Lamb, M. E. (1998). Non-parental child care: Context, quality, correlates. In W. Damon, I. E. Sigel, & K. A. Renninger (Eds.), *Handbook of child psychology: Vol. 4. Child psychology in practice* (5th ed., pp. 73–134). New York: Wiley.

Lemerise, T. (1993). Piaget, Vygotsky, and Logo. *Computing Teacher, 20*(4), 24–28.

Lynch, E. W., & Hanson, M. J. (Eds.). (1998). *Developing cross-cultural competence: A guide for working with children and their families* (2nd ed.). Baltimore: Brookes.

Mallory, B. L. (1998). Educating young children with developmental differences: Principles of inclusive practices. In C. Seefeldt & A. Galper (Eds.), *Continuing issues in early childhood education* (2nd ed., pp. 213–237). Upper Saddle River, NJ: Merrill/Prentice Hall.

Mallory, B. L., & New, R. S. (1994). *Diversity and developmentally appropriate practice.* New York: Teachers College Press.

Marcon, R. A. (1992). Differential effects of three preschool models on inner-city 4-year-olds. *Early Childhood Research Quarterly, 7,* 517–530.

Marion, M. (1999). *Guidance of young children.* Upper Saddle River, NJ: Merrill/Prentice Hall.

Marshall, H. H. (1995). Beyond "I like the way . . ." *Young Children, 50*(2), 26–28.

McCormick, L., & Feeney, S. (1995). Modifying and expanding activities for children with disabilities. *Young Children, 50*(4), 10–17.

Miller, L. G., & Albrecht, K. M. (2000). *Innovations: The comprehensive infant curriculum.* Beltsville, MD: Gryphon.

Mitchell, A., & David, J. (Eds.). (1992). *Explorations with young children: A curriculum guide for the Bank Street College of Education.* Mt. Rainer, MD: Gryphon.

Modigliani, K. (1990). *Assessing the quality of family child care: A comparison of five instruments.* Boston: Wheelock College, Family Child Care Project.

Moore, L., & Brown, D. L. (1996). The mixed-age approach: A public school perspective. *Dimensions of Early Childhood, 24*(2), 4–10.

Morrow, L. M., Strickland, D. S., & Woo, D. G. (1998). *Literacy instruction in half- and whole-day kindergarten.* Newark, DE: International Reading Association.

Mosteller, F. (1995). The Tennessee study of class size in the early school grades. *Future of Children, 5,* 113–127.

Nastasi, B. K., & Clements, D. H. (1994). Effectance motivation, perceived scholastic competence, and higher-order thinking in two cooperative computer environments. *Journal of Educational Computing Research, 10,* 241–267.

National Association for the Education of Young Children. (1995). *National Association for the Education of Young Children position statement: Responding to linguistic and cultural diversity: Recommendations for effective early childhood education.* Washington, DC: Author.

National Association for the Education of Young Children. (1996a). *Guidelines for preparation of early childhood professionals.* Washington, DC: Author.

National Association for the Education of Young Children. (1996b). *What are the benefits of high-quality early childhood programs?* (Brochure). Washington, DC: Author.

National Association for the Education of Young Children. (2005). *Accreditation criteria and procedures of the National Academy of Early Childhood programs.* Washington, DC: Author.

National Association for the Education of Young Children & the National Association of Early Childhood Specialists in State Departments of Education. (1991). Guidelines for appropriate curriculum content and assessment in programs serving children ages 3 through 8: A position statement. *Young Children, 46*(3), 21–38.

National Association for the Education of Young Children & the National Association of Early Childhood Specialists in State Departments of Education. (2002). *A joint position statement. Early learning standards: Creating the conditions for success.* Washington, DC & Alexandria, VA: Authors. Available online at www.naeyc.org/resources/position_statements/creating/conditions.asp

National Center for Education Statistics. (2000). *America's kindergartners: Findings from the Early Childhood Longitudinal Study, Kindergarten Class of 1998–99, Fall 1998.* Washington, DC: U.S. Department of Education. Available online at http://nces.ed.gov/pubs2001/2001023.pdf

National Council of Teachers of Mathematics. (2000). *Principles and standards for school mathematics.* Reston, VA: Author. Available online at standards.nctm.org/document/index.htm

National Council of Teachers of Mathematics & National Association for the Education of Young Children. (2002). *Early childhood mathematics: Promoting good beginnings.* Washington, DC: National Association for the Education of Young Children. Available online at www.naeyc.org/resources/position_statements/psmath.htm

National Research Council. (2001). *Eager to Learn: Educating Our Preschoolers.* B T. Bowman, S. Donovan, and M. S. Burns (Eds.). Washington, DC: National Academy Press.

National Research Council. (1999). *How people learn: Brain, mind, experience, and school.* Washington, DC: National Academy Press.

Neuman, S. B., Copple, C., & Bredekamp, S. (2000). *Learning to read and write: Developmentally appropriate practices for young children.* Washington, DC: National Association for the Education of Young Children.

NICHD Early Child Care Research Network. (1996). Characteristics of infant care: Factors contributing to positive caregiving. *Early Childhood Research Quarterly, 11,* 269–306.

NICHD Early Child Care Research Network. (1998). Early child care and self-control, compliance, and problem behavior at twenty-four and thirty-six months. *Child Development, 69,* 1145–1170.

NICHD Early Child Care Research Network. (2000). The relation of child care to cognitive and language development. *Child Development, 71,* 958–978.

Novick, R. (1998). The comfort corner: Fostering resiliency and emotional intelligence. *Childhood Education, 74,* 200–204.

Papert, S. (1993). *The children's machine: Rethinking school in the age of the computer.* New York: Basic Books.

Peth-Pierce, R. (2001). *A good beginning: Sending America's children to school with the social and emotional competence they need to succeed.* Monograph based on two papers commissioned by the Child Mental Health Foundations and Agencies Network (FAN). Chapel Hill: University of North Carolina.

Phillips, C. B. (1994a). The challenge of training and credentialing early childhood educators. *Phi Delta Kappan, 76,* 214–217.

Phillips, C. B. (1994b). The movement of African-American children through sociocultural contexts: A case of conflict resolution. In B. L. Mallory & R. S. New (Eds.), *Diversity and developmentally appropriate practices: Challenges for early childhood education* (pp. 137–154). New York: Teachers College Press.

Phillips, D. A., & Crowell, N. A. (Eds.). (1994). *Cultural diversity in early education: Results of a workshop.* Washington, DC: National Academy Press.

Piaget, J. (1959). *Language and thought of the child* (3rd ed.). London: Routledge & Kegan Paul.

Raikes, H. (1996). A secure base for babies: Applying attachment concepts to the infant care setting. *Young Children, 51*(5), 59–67.

Raver, C. (2002). Emotions matter: Making the case for the role of young children's emotional development for early school readiness. *SRCD Social Policy Report, 16*(3). Ann Arbor, MI: Society for Research in Child Development.

Rofrano, F. (2002). "I care for you": A reflection on caring as infant curriculum. *Young Children, 57*(1), 49–51.

Rosegrant, T., & Bredekamp, S. (1992). Planning and implementing transformational curriculum. In S. Bredekamp & T. Rosegrant (Eds.), *Reaching potentials: Appropriate curriculum and assessment for young children* (Vol. 1, pp. 66–73). Washington, DC: National Association for the Education of Young Children.

Rushton, S., & Larkin, L. (2001). Shaping the learning environment: Connecting brain research to developmentally appropriate practices. *Early Childhood Education Journal, 29*(1), 25–33.

Russell-Fox, J. (1997). Together is better: Specific tips on how to include children with various types of disabilities. *Young Children, 52*(4) 81–83.

Salovey, P., & Sluyter, D. (Eds.). (1997). *Emotional development and emotional intelligence: Educational implications.* New York: Basic.

Santrock, J. (2003). *Children* (7th ed.). Boston: McGraw-Hill.

Shepard, L. A., Kagan, S. L., & Wurtz, E. (1998). Goal One Early Childhood Assessments Resource Group recommendations. *Young Children, 53*(3), 52–54.

Shonkoff, J. P., & Phillips, D. A. (Eds.). (2000). *From neurons to neighborhoods: The science of early childhood development.* Washington, DC: National Academy Press.

Small, M. (1998). *Our babies, ourselves: How biology and culture shape the way we parent.* New York: Anchor Books.

Smith, T. E. C., & Dowdy, C. A. (1998). Educating young children with disabilities using responsible inclusion. *Childhood Education, 74,* 317–320.

Stipek, D., & Byler, P. (1997). Early childhood education teachers: Do they practice what they preach? *Early Childhood Research Quarterly, 12,* 305–325.

Sullivan, A. K., & Strang, H. R. (2002/03). Bibliotherapy in the classrooms: Using literature to promote the development of emotional intelligence. *Childhood Education, 79,* 74–80.

Swick, K., Van Scoy, I., & Boutte, G. (1994). Multicultural learning through family involvement. *Dimensions of Early Childhood, 22*(4), 17–21.

Taylor, B. J. (1999). *A child goes forth: A curriculum guide for preschool children.* Upper Saddle River: Merrill/Prentice Hall.

Theilheimer, R. (1993). Something for everyone: Benefits of mixed-age grouping for children, parents, and teachers. *Young Children, 48*(5), 82–87.

Thoman, E. (1987). *Born dancing: How intuitive parents understand their baby's unspoken language.* New York: Harper & Row.

Thompson, P. W. (1992). Notations, conventions, and constraints: Contributions to effective use of concrete materials in elementary mathematics. *Journal of Research in Mathematics Education, 23,* 123–147.

Thompson, R. A. (1997). Early sociopersonality development. In W. Damon (Series Ed.) & N. Eisenberg (Vol. Ed.), *Handbook of child psychology: Vol. 3. Social, emotional, and personality development* (5th ed., pp. 25–104). New York: Wiley.

Vance, E., & Weaver, P. J. (2002). *Class meetings: Young children solving problems together.* Washington, DC: National Association for the Education of Young Children.

Veenman, S. (1995). Cognitive and non-cognitive effects of multigrade and multi-age classes: A best-evidence synthesis. *Review of Educational Research, 65,* 319–381.

Vygotsky, L. S. (1978). *Mind in society* (M. Cole, S. Schribner, V. John-Steiner, & E. Souberman, Trans.). Cambridge, MA: Harvard University Press.

Wagenblast v. Odessa School Dist., 758 P. 2d 968 (Wash. 1988).

Wardle, F. (1999). In praise of developmentally appropriate practice. *Young Children, 54*(6), 4–12.

Wien, C. A. (1996). Time, work, and developmentally appropriate practice. *Early Childhood Research Quarterly, 11,* 377–403.

Wien, C. A., & Kirby-Smith, S. (1998). Untiming the curriculum: A case study of removing clocks from the program. *Young Children, 53*(5), 8–13.

Williams, K. C. (1997). "What do you wonder?" Involving children in curriculum planning. *Young Children, 52*(6), 78–81.

Wolery, M., Strain, P. S., & Bailey, D. B., Jr. (1992). Reaching potentials of children with special needs. In S. Bredekamp & T. Rosegrant (Eds.), *Reaching potentials: Appropriate curriculum and assessment for young children* (Vol. 1, pp. 92–111). Washington, DC: National Association for the Education of Young Children.

Wolfe, J., & Brandt, R. (1998). What we know from brain research. *Educational Leadership, 56*(3), 8–14.

Yell, M., & Shriner, J. (1997). The IDEA amendments of 1997: Implications for special and general education teachers, administrators, and teacher trainers. *Focus on Exceptional Children, 30*(1), 2–19.

Chapter 10

American Academy of Family Physicians, American Academy of Pediatrics, American College of Physicians, and American Osteopathic Association. (2007). Consensus Statement: *Joint Principles of the Patient-Centered Medical Home.* Retrieved May 23, 2008, from www.medicalhomeinfo.org/Joint%20Statement.pdf

American Academy of Pediatrics, American Public Health Association, and National Resource Center for Health and Safety in Child Care. (2002). *Caring for our children: National health and safety performance standards: Guidelines for out-of-home child care programs* (2nd ed.). Elk Grove Village, IL: American Academy of Pediatrics and Washington, DC: American Public Health Association. Retrieved May 24, 2008, from nrc.uchsc.edu/CFOC/index.html

Anderson, P. M., & Butcher, K. F. (2006). Childhood obesity: Trends and potential causes. In C. Paxson, E. Donahue, C. T. Orleans, & J. A. Grisso (Eds.), *Childhood obesity. The future of children, 16*(1), 19–45. Princeton, NJ: The Woodrow Wilson School of Public and International Affairs and the Bookings Institution. Retrieved January 12, 2008, from www.futureofchildren.org/information2826/information_show.htm?doc_id=351457

Austin, J. S. (2000). When a child discloses sexual abuse: Immediate and appropriate teacher responses. *Childhood Education, 77,* 2–5.

Bar-Or, O. (2000). Juvenile obesity, physical activity, and lifestyle changes. *The Physician and Sports Medicine, 28*(11), 51–58.

Berk, L. (2008). *Infants and children: Prenatal through middle childhood (6th ed.).* Boston, MA: Pearson/Allyn & Bacon.

Bhattacharya, J., & Currie, J. (2001). Youths and nutrition risk: Malnourished or misnourished? In J. Gruber (Ed.), *Risky behavior among youths: An economic analysis* (pp. 483–521). Chicago: University of Chicago Press.

Birch, L. L., Johnson, S. L., & Fisher, J. A. (1995). Children's eating: The development of food acceptance patterns. *Young Children, 50*(2), 71–78.

Brennan, P., Mednick, S., & Kandal, E. (1991). Congenital determinants of violence and property offending. In D. J. Pepler & K. H. Rubin (Eds.), *The development and treatment of childhood aggression* (pp. 87–90). Hillsdale, NJ: Erlbaum.

Child Welfare League of America. (1945). *Day-care: A partnership of three professions.* Washington, DC: Author.

Cosgrove, M. S. (1991). Cooking in the classroom: The doorway to nutrition. *Young Children, 46*(3), 43–46.

Cost, Quality, and Child Outcomes Study Team. (1995). *Cost, quality, and child outcomes in child care centers, Public report* (2nd ed.). Denver: Economics Department, University of Colorado-Denver.

Cryer, D., Harms, T., & Riley, C. (2003). *All about the ECERS-R: A detailed guide in words and pictures to be used with the ECERS-R.* Lewisville, NC: Pact House Publishing.

Dahl, K. (1998). Why cooking in the classroom? *Young Children, 53*(1), 81–83.

Dehghan, M., Akhtar-Danesh, N., & Merchant, A. T. (2005). Childhood obesity, prevalence and prevention. *Nutrition Journal 4*(24). Retrieved May 24, 2008, from www.nutritionj.com/content/4/1/24/

Division of Early Childhood of the Council for Exceptional Children. (2006). Position Statement: Identification of and Intervention with Challenging Behavior. Missoula, MT: Author. Retrieved May 24, 2008, from www.dec-sped.org/pdf/positionpapers/PositionStatement_ChallBeh.pdf

Dooling, M. V., & Ulione, M. S. (2000). Health consultation in child care: A partnership that works. *Young Children, 55*(2), 23–26.

Drake, M. M. (1992). Menu evaluation, nutrient intake of young children, and nutrition knowledge of menu planners in child care centers in Missouri. *Journal of Nutrition Education, 24,* 145–148.

Federal Interagency Forum on Child and Family Statistics. (2002). *America's children: Key national indicators of well-being 2002.* Washington, DC: U.S. Government Printing Office.

Gabbard, C. (2000). Physical education. Should it be part of the core curriculum? *Principal, 79*(3), 29–31.

Goals 2000: Educate America Act. (1994). Washington, DC: One Hundred Third Congress. Retrieved May 23, 2008, from www.ed.gov/legislation/GOALS2000/TheAct/index.html

Harms, T. O. (1992). Designing settings to support high-quality care. In B. Spodek & O. N. Saracho (Eds.), *Yearbook in early childhood education: Vol. 3. Issues in child care* (pp. 169–186). New York: Teachers College Press.

Himle, M. B., Miltenberger, R G., Gatheridge, B. J., & Flessner, C. A. (2004). An evaluation of two procedures for training skills to prevent gun play in children. *Pediatrics 113*(1), 70–77. Retrieved May 24, 2008, from pediatrics.aappublications.org/cgi/reprint/113/1/70

Holland, M. (2004). "That food makes me SICK": Managing food allergies and intolerances in early childhood settings. *Young Children 59*(2), 42–46.

Honig, A. S. (1993). Mental health for babies: What do theory and research teach us? *Young Children, 48*(3), 69–76.

Howell, N. M. (1999). Cooking up a learning community with corn, beans, and rice. *Young Children, 54*(5), 36–38.

Huettig, C. I., Sanborn, C. F., MiMarco, N., Popejoy, A., & Rich, S. (2004). The O generation: Our youngest children are at risk for obesity. *Young Children, 59*(2), 50–55.

Javernick, E. (1988). Johnny's not jumping: Can we help obese children? *Young Children, 43*(2), 18–23.

Kaplan, P. (1998). *The human odyssey.* Pacific Grove, CA: Brooks & Cole.

Karp, R., Martin, R., Sewell, T., Manni, J., & Heller, A. (1992). Growth and academic achievement in inner-city kindergarten children. *Clinical Pediatrics, 31,* 336–340.

Klefstad, J. (1995). Cooking in the kindergarten. *Young Children, 50*(6), 32–33.

Lanphear, B. (2001). Blood lead levels below "acceptable" value linked with IQ deficits, according to new study. *LEAD Action News, 8*(3). Retrieved May 24, 2008, from www.lead.org.au/lanv8n3/lanv8n3-3.html

Levin, D. E. (2003). *Teaching young children in violent times: Building a peaceable classroom.* Cambridge, MA: Educators for Social Responsibility and National Association for the Education of Young Children.

Linn, S.(2004). *Consuming kids: The hostile takeover of childhood.* New York: The New Press.

Loewy, M. (1998). Suggestions for working with fat children in schools. *Professional School Counseling, 1*(4), 18–23.

Lozoff, B., Jimenez, E., Hagen, J., Mollen, E., & Wolf, A. W. (2000). Poorer behavior and developmental outcome more than 10 years after treatment for iron deficiency in infancy. *Pediatrics, 105*(4), E51.

Lozoff, B., Klein, N. K., Nelson, E. C., McClish, D. K., Manuel, M., & Chacon, M. E. (1998). Behavior of infants with iron-deficiency anemia. *Child Development, 69*(1), 24–36.

Mayo Clinic Staff (2007). Hand washing: An easy way to prevent infection. Retrieved May 24, 2008, from www.mayoclinic.com/health/hand-washing/HQ00407

McBride, N. (n.d.) Child safety is more than a slogan: "Stranger Danger" warnings not effective at keeping children safe. National Center for Missing and Exploited Children. Retrieved May 24, 2008, from www.missingkids.com/missingkids/servlet/NewsEventServlet?LanguageCountry=en_US&PageId=2034

Mikkelsen, E. J. (1997). Responding to allegations of sexual abuse in child care and early childhood education programs. *Young Children, 52*(3), 47–51.

Morgan, B., & Gibson, R. K. (1991). Nutritional and environmental interactions in brain development. In R. K. Gibson & A. C. Petersen (Eds.), *Brain maturation and cognitive development: Comparative cross-cultural perspectives* (pp. 91–106). New York: Aldine De Gruyter.

Murray, C. G. (2000). Learning about children's social and emotional needs at snack time—Nourishing the body, mind, and spirit of each child. *Young Children, 55*(2), 43–52.

National Association for the Education of Young Children. (1997). NAEYC position statement on the prevention of child abuse in early childhood programs and the responsibilities of early childhood professionals to prevent child abuse. *Young Children, 52*(3), 42–46.

National Association for the Education of Young Children Academy for Early Childhood Program Accreditation. (2005). NAEYC Early Childhood Program Standards. Washington, DC: Author. Retrieved May 25, 2008, from http://www.naeyc.org/academy/standards/

National Association for Regulatory Administration (NARA) & Technical Assistance Center (NCCIC). (2006). *The 2005 child care licensing study.* Conyers, GA: Author. Retrieved May 23, 2008, from http://nara.affiniscape.com/associations/4734/files/2005%20Licensing%20Study%20Final%20Report_Web.pdf

National Education Goals Panel. (1997). *Getting a Good Start in School.* Washington DC: U.S. Government Printing Office. Retrieved May 24, 2008, from www.ncrel.org/sdrs/areas/issues/envrnmnt/go/go4negp.htm

Nahikian-Nelms, M. L., Syler, G., & Mogharrehan, C. N. (1994). Pilot assessment of nutrition practices in a university child care program. *Journal of Nutrition Education, 26*(5), 238–240.

Nokes, C., van den Bosch, C., & Bundy, D. (1998). *The effects of iron deficiency and anemia on mental health and motor performance, educational achievement, and behavior in children.* Washington, DC: International Nutritional Anemia Consulting Group.

Nord, M., Andrews, M., & Carlson, S. (2007). *Household food security in the United States, 2006.* Washington, DC. United States Department of Agriculture. Retrieved May 23, 2008, from www.ers.usda.gov/publications/err49/

Perry, P. (2001). Sick kids. *American Way, 4,* 64–65.

Pond-Smith, D., Richarz, S. H., & Gonzalez, N. (1992). A survey of food service operations in child care centers in Washington State. *Journal of the American Dietetic Association, 92,* 483–484.

Powell, L. M., Szczypka, G., Chaloupka, & Braunschweig, F. J. (2007). Nutritional Content of TV Food Advertisements Seen by Children and Adolescents in the US. *Pediatrics,* 120(3), 576–83.

Rideout, V., & Hamel, E. (2006). *The media family: Electronic media in the lives of infants, toddlers, preschoolers and their parents.* Menlo Park, CA: Henry J. Kaiser Family Foundation

Shore, R. (1997). *Rethinking the brain: New insights into early development.* New York: Families and Work Institute.

Simmons, B. J., Stalsworth, K., & Wentzel, H. (1999). Television violence and its effects on young children. *Early Childhood Education Journal, 26*(3), 149–153.

Slaby, R. G., Roedell, W. C., Arezzo, D., & Hendrix, K. (1995). *Early violence prevention: Tools for teachers of young children.* Washington, DC: National Association for the Education of Young Children.

Stanford, B. H., & Yamamoto, K. (Eds.). (2001). *Children and stress: Understanding and helping.* Olney, MD: Association for Childhood Education International.

Stoneham, L. (2001). Diabetes on a rampage. *Texas Medicine, 97*(11), 42–48.

Strupp, B. J., & Levitsky, D. A. (1995). Enduring cognitive effects of early maturation: A theoretical reappraisal. *Journal of Nutrition, 125,* 2221S–2232S.

Swadener, S. (1995). Nutrition education for preschool children. *Journal of Nutrition Education, 27,* 291–297.

U. S. Department of Agriculture. (2005). *Dietary Guidelines for Americans.* Washington, DC: Author Retrieved May 23, 2008, from www.health.gov/dietaryguidelines/dga2005/document/default.htm

U.S. Department of Education. (2001). *Twenty-third annual report to Congress on the implementation of the Individuals with Disabilities Education Act.* Washington, DC: Author.

United States Breastfeeding Committee. (2002). Breastfeeding and child care (issue paper). Raleigh, NC: United States Breastfeeding Committee. Retrieved May 24, 2008, from www.usbreastfeeding.org/Issue-Papers/Childcare.pdf

Vermeer, H. J., & van IJzendoorn, M. H. (2006). Children's elevated cortisol levels at daycare: A review and meta-analysis. *Early Childhood Research Quarterly, 21*(3), 390–401.

Wardle, F. (1990). Bunny ears and cupcakes for all: Are parties developmentally appropriate? *Child Care Information Exchange, 74,* 39–42.

Whitebook, M., Howes, C., & Phillips, D. A. (1998). *Who cares? Child care teachers and the quality of child care in America* (Final report, National Child Care Staffing Study). Washington, DC: Center for the Child Care Workforce.

Chapter 11

American Educational Research Association, American Psychological Association, & National Council on Measurement in Education. (1999). *Standards for educational and psychological testing.* Washington, DC: American Educational Research Association.

American Educational Research Association. (2000). *Position statement on high stakes testing.* Washington, DC: Author.

Association of Childhood Education International. (1991). On standardized testing. *Childhood Education, 67,* 132–142.

Beaty, J. J. (2002). *Observing development of the young child* (5th ed.). Upper Saddle River, NJ: Merrill/Prentice Hall.

Bentzen, W. (2000). *Seeing young children: A guide to observing and recording behaviors.* Albany, NY: Delmar.

Bergen, D. (1993/94). Authentic performance assessments. *Childhood Education, 70,* 99, 102.

Bowman, B. T. (1990). Child care: Challenges for the 90's. *Dimensions, 18*(4), 27, 29–31.

Bredekamp, S., & Copple, C. (Eds.). (1997). *Developmentally appropriate practice in early childhood programs: Revised.* Washington, DC: National Association for the Education of Young Children.

Bricker, D., Pretti-Frontczak, K., Johnson, J., Straka, E., Capt, B., Slentz, K., & Waddell, M. (2002). Administration Guide. *Assessment, Evaluation, and Programming System for Infants and Children.* Baltimore, MD: Brookes Publishing.

Burnette, J. (1998). *Reducing the disproportionate representation of minority students in special education* (ERIC/OSEP Digest #E566). Reston, VA: ERIC Clearinghouse on Disabilities and Gifted Education. (ERIC Document Reproduction Service No. ED417501)

Charlesworth, R., Hart, C. H., Burts, D. C., & DeWolf, M. (1993). The LSU studies: Building a research base for developmentally appropriate practice. In S. Reifel (Ed.), *Advances in early education and day care: Perspectives in developmentally appropriate practice* (Vol. 5, pp. 3–28). Greenwich, CT: JAI.

Cohen, D. H., Stern, V., & Balaban, N. (1997). *Observing and recording the behavior of young children* (4th ed.). New York: Teachers College Press.

Coleman, M. R., Buysse, V., & Neitzel, J. (2006). *Recognition and response: An early intervening system for young children at risk for learning disabilities. Full Report.* Chapel Hill: The University of North Carolina at Chapel Hill, FPG Child Development Institute.

Council of Chief State School Officers. (1995). *Moving toward accountability for results: A look at ten states' efforts*. Washington, DC: Author.

Dahlberg, G., & Asen, G. (1994). Evaluation and regulation: A question of empowerment. In P. Moss & A. Pence (Eds.), *Valuing quality in early childhood services* (pp. 157–171). New York: Teachers College Press.

Danielson, C., & Abrutyn, L. (1997). *An introduction to using portfolios in the classroom*. Alexandria, VA: Association for Supervision and Curriculum Development.

Darling-Hammond, L., & Falk, B. (1997). Using standards and assessments to support student learning. *Phi Delta Kappan, 79,* 190–199.

Greenspan, S. I., & Weider, S. (1998). *The child with special needs: Encouraging intellectual and emotional growth*. Reading, MA: Perseus Books.

Grisham-Brown, J. L., Hallam, R. & Brookshire, R. (2006). Using authentic assessment to evidence children's progress towards early learning standards. *Early Childhood Education Journal, 34*(1), 47–53.

Grisham-Brown, J. L., Hemmeter, M. L., & Pretti-Frontczak, K. L. (2005*). Blended Practices for Teaching Young Children in Inclusive Settings*. B. Himme, MD: Paul Brookes Publishing Company.

Gronlund, G. (1998). Portfolios as an assessment tool: Is collection of work enough? *Young Children, 53*(3), 4–10.

Helm, J. H., Beneke, S., & Steinheimer, K. (1998). *Windows on learning: Documenting young children's work*. New York: Teachers College Press.

High/Scope Educational Research Foundation (2001). *Preschool Child Observation Record*. Ypsilanti, MI: High/Scope Press.

High/Scope Educational Research Foundation (2002). *The Child Observation Record for Infants and Toddlers*. Ypsilanti, MI: High/Scope Press.

Irwin, D. M., & Bushnell, M. M. (1980). *Observational strategies for child study*. New York: Holt, Rinehart, and Winston.

Kagan, S. L. (2000). Making assessment count . . . What matters? *Young Children, 55*(2), 4.

Kagan, S. L., Rosenkoetter, S., & Cohen, N. E. (Eds.). (1997). *Considering child-based outcomes for young children: Definitions, desirability, feasibility, and next steps*. New Haven, CT: Yale University, Bush Center in Child Development and Social Policy.

Kohn, A. (2000). *The case against standardized testing: Raising the scores, running the schools*. Portsmouth, NH: Heinemann.

Kohn, A. (2001). Fighting the tests: Turning frustration into action. *Young Children, 56*(2), 19–24.

Lambert, R. G. (2003). Considering purpose and intended use when making evaluations of assessments: A response to Dickinson, *Educational Researcher, 32*, pp. 23–26.

Langhorst, B. H. (1989). *Assessment in early childhood: A consumer's guide*. Portland, OR: Northwest Regional Educational Laboratory.

Martin, S. (1998). *Take a look: Observation and portfolio assessment in early childhood*. Reading, MA: Addison-Wesley.

Meisels, S. J., & Atkins-Burnett, S. (1994). *Developmental Screening in Early Childhood: A Guide* (4th ed.). Washington, DC: National Association for the Education of Young Children.

Meisels, S. J., & Atkins-Burnett, S. (2000). The elements of early childhood assessment. In J. P. Shonkoff & S. J. Meisels (Eds.), *Handbook of early childhood intervention* (2nd ed., pp. 231–257). New York: Cambridge University Press.

Meisels, S. J., Dorfman, A., & Steele, D. (1995). Equity and excellence in group-administered and performance-based assessments. In M. T. Nettles & A. L. Nettles (Eds.), *Equity in educational assessment and testing* (pp. 196–211). Boston: Kluwer Academic Publishers.

Meisels, S. J., Jablon, J. R., Marsden, D. B., Dichtelmiller, M. L., Dorfman, A. B., & Steele, D. M. (1994). *An overview: The Work Sampling System*. Ann Arbor, MI: Rebus.

Meisels, S., Dichtelmiller, M., Jablon, J., Dorfman, A., & Marsden, D. (1997). *Work sampling in the classroom: A teacher's manual. The Work Sampling System*. Ann Arbor, MI: Rebus.

National Association for the Education of Young Children & the National Association of Early Childhood Specialists in State Departments of Education. (2003). *Position Statement: Early childhood curriculum, assessment, and program evaluation: Building an effective, accountable system in programs for children birth through age 8*. Washington DC: National Association for the Education of Young Children.

National Association for the Education of Young Children & the National Association of Early Childhood Specialists in State Departments of Education. (2007). Joint Position Statement. *Early Childhood Curriculum, Assessment, and Program Evaluation: Building and effective, accountable system in programs for children birth through age 8*. Retrieved November 9, 2007, from http://www.naeyc.org/about/positions/pdf/pscape.pdf

National Association for the Education of Young Children Academy for Early Childhood Program Accreditation. (2005). NAEYC Early Childhood Program Standards. Washington, DC: Author. Retrieved February 18, 2008, from http://www.naeyc.org/academy/standards/

National Association of Early Childhood Specialists in State Departments of Education. (2001). *Still unacceptable trends in kindergarten entry and placement*. Denver, CO: Author.

National Association of School Psychologists. (1999). *Position statement on early childhood assessment*. Bethesda, MD: Author.

National Research Council. (1997). *Educating one and all: Students with disabilities and standards-based reform*. Washington, DC: National Academy Press.

National Research Council. (1999). *High stakes testing for tracking, promotion, and graduation*. Washington, DC: National Academy Press.

Nicholson, S., & Shipstead, S. G. (2002). *Through the looking glass: Observations in the early childhood classroom* (3rd ed.). Upper Saddle River, NJ: Merrill/Prentice Hall.

Nilsen, B. A. (2000). *Week by week: Plans for observing and recording young children*. Albany, NY: Delmar.

Nilsen, B. A. (2008). *Week by week: Plans for observing and recording young children* (4th ed). Albany, NY: Delmar.

Nuttall, E. V., Romero, I., & Kalesnik, J. (Eds.). (1999). *Assessing and screening preschoolers: Psychological and educational dimensions* (2nd ed.). Boston: Allyn & Bacon.

Peel, J., & McCary, C. E. (1997). Visioning the "little red schoolhouse" for the 21st century. *Phi Delta Kappan, 78,* 698–705.

Piaget, J. (1952). *The origins of intelligence in children.* New York: Norton.

Rhodes, L., & Nathenson Mejia, S. (1992). Anecdotal records: A powerful tool for organizing literacy assessment. *Reading Teacher, 45,* 502–509.

Roskos, K. A., & Neuman, S. B. (1994). Of scribbles, schemas, and storybooks: Using literacy albums to document young children's literacy growth. *Young Children, 49*(2), 78–85.

Schorr, L. B. (1994). The case for shifting to results-based accountability. In N. Young, S. Gardner, L. Coley, L. Schorr, & C. Bruner (Eds.), *Making a difference: Moving to outcome-based accountability for comprehensive service reforms* (pp. 13–28). Falls Church, VA: National Center for Service Integration.

Shepard, L. A. (1994). The challenges of assessing young children appropriately. *Phi Delta Kappan, 76,* 206–212.

Shepard, L. A., Kagan, S. L., & Wurtz, E. (1998a). Goal One Early Childhood Assessments Resource Group recommendations. *Young Children, 53*(3), 52–54.

Shepard, L. A., Kagan, S. L., & Wurtz, E. (Eds.). (1998b). *Principles and recommendations for early childhood assessments.* Washington, D.C: National Education Goals Panel.

Southern Early Childhood Association. (1990/1996/2000). *Assessing Development and Learning in Young Children.* Retrieved August 31, 2003, from http://www.seca50.org/position_assessment.html.

Stiggins, R. (1991). *Facing the challenge of the new era of assessment.* Portland, OR: Northwest Evaluation Association.

Trister-Dodge, D., Colker, L. J., & Heroman, C. (2003) *Creative Curriculum Developmental Continuum Assessment Toolkit for Ages 3–5.* Washington DC: Teaching Strategies Inc.

Chapter 12

ACF (Administration for Children and Families). (2007). Head Start Act. Retrieved May 24, 2008, from http://eclkc.ohs.acf.hhs.gov/hslc/Program%20Design%20and%20Management/Head%20Start%20Requirements/Head%20Start%20Act/headstartact.html

Alexander, K. L., & Entwisle, D. R. (1988). Achievement in the first two years of school: Pattern and processes. *Monographs for the Society of Research in Child Development, 53*(2). (Serial No. 218)

Allan, L. L. (1997). Do you resent and stonewall parents— Matthew's line. *Young Children, 52*(4), 72–74.

Allen, M., Brown, P., & Finlay, B. (1992). *Helping children by strengthening families.* Washington, DC: Children's Defense Fund.

Bermudez, A., & Marquez, J. (1996). An examination of a four-way collaborative to increase parental involvement in the schools. *The Journal of Educational Issues of Language Minority Students, 16,* 1–16.

Birckmayer, J., Cohen, J., Jensen, I. J., & Variano, D. A. (2005). Kyle lives with his Granny—Where are his Mommy and Daddy? *Young Children 60*(3), 100–104.

Boutte, G. S., Keepler, D. L., Tyler, V. S., & Terry, B. Z. (1992). Effective techniques for involving "difficult" parents. *Young Children, 47*(3), 19–22.

Bredekamp, S., & Copple, C. (Eds.). (1997). *Developmentally appropriate practice in early childhood programs: Revised.* Washington, DC: National Association for the Education of Young Children.

Bronfenbrenner, U. (1979). *The ecology of human development: Experiments by nature and design.* Cambridge, MA: Harvard University Press.

Bronfenbrenner, U. (1986). Ecology of the family as a context for human development: Research perspectives. *Developmental Psychology, 22,* 723–742.

Bronfenbrenner, U., & Morris, P. A. (1998). The ecology of developmental process. In W. Damon (Series Ed.) & R. M. Lerner (Vol. Ed.), *Handbook of child psychology: Vol. 1. Theoretical models of human development* (pp. 993–1028). New York: Wiley.

Caldwell, B. M. (1985). What is quality child care? In B. M. Caldwell & A. Hillard (Eds.), *What is quality child care?* (pp. 1–16). Washington, DC: National Association for the Education of Young Children.

Cherlin, A. (1999). Going to extremes: Family structure, children's well-being, and social science. *Demography, 36,* 421–428.

Christian, L. G. (2007). Understanding families: Applying family systems theory to early childhood practice. In *Spotlight on Young Children and Families* (pp. 4–11). Washington, DC: National Association for the Education of Young Children.

Clay, J. W. (2004). Creating safe, just places to learn for children of lesbian and gay parents: The NAEYC Code of Ethics in action. *Young Children, 59*(6), 34–38.

Coleman, M. (1997). Families and schools: In search of common ground. *Young Children, 52*(5), 14–21.

Coleman, M., & Wallinga, C. (2000). Connecting families and classrooms using family involvement webs. *Childhood Education, 76,* 209–214.

Coleman, M., & Wallinga, C. (2000). Teacher training in family involvement: An interpersonal approach. *Childhood Education, 76,* 76–81.

Comer, J. P., & Haynes, N. M. (1991). Parent involvement in schools: An ecological approach. *The Elementary School Journal, 91,* 271–278.

Cunningham, B. (1994). Portraying fathers and other men in the curriculum. *Young Children, 49*(6), 4–13.

Daniel, J. (1996). Family-centered work and child care. *Young Children, 51*(6), 2.

Davies, D. (1991). Schools reaching out: Family, school, and community partnerships for student success. *Phi Delta Kappan, 72,* 376–382.

Diffily, D., & Morrison, K. (Eds.). (1997). *Family-friendly communication for early childhood programs*. Washington, DC: National Association for the Education of Young Children.

Division for Early Childhood Task Force on Recommended Practices. (1993). *DEC recommended practices: Indicators of quality in programs for infants and young children with special needs and their families*. Reston, VA: Council for Exceptional Children.

Dodd, E. L., & Brock, D. R. (1994). Building partnerships with families through home-learning activities. *Dimensions of Early Childhood, 22*(2), 37–39, 46.

Edkin, K., & Lein, L. (1997). *Making ends meet: How single mothers survive welfare and low wage work*. New York: Sage.

Epstein, J. L. (1991). Paths to partnerships: What we can learn from federal, state, district, and school initiatives. *Phi Delta Kappan, 72,* 344–349.

Epstein, J. L. (1995). School/family/community partnerships. *Phi Delta Kappan, 76,* 701–712.

Epstein, J. L. (2001). *School, family, and community partnerships: Preparing educators and improving schools*. Boulder, CO: Westview.

Epstein, J. L., & Sanders, M. (1998). What we learn from international studies of school-family-community partnerships. *Childhood Education, 74,* 392–394.

Epstein, J. L., Sanders, M. G., Simon, B. S., Salinas, K. C., Jansorn, N. R., & Van Voorhis, F. L. (2002). *School, family, and community partnerships: Your handbook for action* (2nd ed.). Thousand Oaks, CA: Corwin.

Fagan, J. (1994). Mother and father involvement in day care centers serving infants and young toddlers. *Early Child Development and Care, 103,* 95–101.

Fagan, J. (1996). Principles for developing male involvement programs in early childhood settings: A personal experience. *Young Children, 51*(4), 64–71.

Feeney, S., & Sysko, L. (1986). Professional ethics in early childhood education: Survey results. *Young Children, 42*(1), 15–20.

Fox-Barnett, M., & Meyer, T. (1992). The teacher's playing at my house this week. *Young Children, 47*(2), 45–50.

Freeman, N. K. (1998). Look to the east to gain a new perspective, understand cultural differences, and appreciate cultural diversity. *Early Childhood Education Journal, 26*(2), 79–82. Also available online at www.pbs.org/kcts/preciouschildren/earlyed/read_east.html

Freeman, N. K., & Knopf, H. T. (2007). Learning to speak with a professional voice: Initiating preservice teachers into being a resource for parents. *Journal of Early Childhood Teacher Education, 28(2),* 141–152.

Galinsky, E. (1987). *The six stages of parenthood*. Reading, MA: Addison-Wesley.

Galinsky, E. (1988). Parents and teacher-caregivers: Sources of tension, sources of support. *Young Children, 43*(3), 4–12.

Garbarino, J., & Abramowitz, R. H. (1992). *Children and families in the social environment* (2nd ed.). New York: Aldine.

García Coll, C., & Magnuson, K. (2000). Cultural differences as sources of developmental vulnerabilities and resources.

In J. P. Shonkoff & S. J. Meisels (Eds.), *Handbook of early childhood intervention* (2nd ed., pp. 94–114). New York: Cambridge University Press.

Gibbs, N. (2005, February 21). Parents behaving badly: Inside the new classroom power struggle: What teachers say about pushy moms and dads who drive them crazy. *Time,* 40–48.

Gonzalez-Mena, J. (2002). *The child in the family and community* (3rd ed.). Upper Saddle River, NJ: Merrill/Prentice Hall.

Gonzalez-Mena, J. (2007). *50 early childhood strategies for working and communicating with diverse families*. Upper Saddle River, NJ: Merrill/Prentice Hall.

Gonzalez-Mena, J. (2008). Diversity in early care and education: Honoring differences (5th ed.). New York: McGraw-Hill.

Gottlieb, H. (2005). Board diversity: A bigger issue than you think. Help 4 NonProfits: Community Driven Institute. Retrieved February 20, 2008, from www.help4nonprofits.com/NP_Bd_Diversity_Art.htm

Greenberg, P. (1989). Parents as partners in young children's development and education: A new American fad? Why does it matter? *Young Children, 44*(4), 61–75.

Hall, E. T. (1977). *Beyond culture*. Garden City, NY: Anchor Press/Doubleday.

Hanhan, S. F. (2003). Parent-teacher communication: Who's talking? In G. Olsen & M. L. Fuller (Eds.), *Home-school relations: Working successfully with parents and families* (2nd ed., pp. 111–133). Boston: Allyn & Bacon.

Harms, T. O., Cryer, D., & Clifford, R. M. (2003). *Infant/Toddler Environment Rating Scale—Revised*. New York: Teachers College Press.

Harms, T., Clifford, R., & Cryer, D., (2005). *The Early Childhood Environment Rating Scale* (Rev.) New York: Teachers College Press.

Harms, T., Jacobs, E. V., & White, D. R. (1996). *The School-Age Care Environment Rating Scale* (Rev. ed.). New York: Teachers College Press.

Heckman, J. J. (1999). *Policies to foster human capital*. Aaron Wildavsky Forum, Richard and Rhoda Goldman School of Public Policy: University of California at Berkeley. Retrieved on February 20, 2008, from www.ounceofprevention.org/includes/tiny_mce/plugins/filemanager/files/Fostering%20Human%20Capital.pdf

Henrich, C. C., & Blackman-Jones, R. (2006). Parent involvement in preschool. In E. Zigler, W. S. Gilliam, & S. M. Jones (Eds.), *A vision for universal preschool education* (pp. 149–168). New York: Cambridge University Press.

High/Scope Educational Research Foundation. (1992). *High/Scope Child Observation Record*. Ypsilanti, MI: High/Scope Press.

Hohmann, M., & Weikart, D. P. (1995). *Educating young children: Active learning practices for preschool and child care programs*. Ypsilanti, MI: High/Scope Press.

Hoover-Dempsey, K. V., & Sandler, H. M. (1997). Why do parents become involved in their children's education? *Review of Educational Research, 67,* 3–42.

Johnston, L., & Mermin, J. (1994). Easing children's entry to school: Home visits help. *Young Children, 49*(5), 62–68.

Keyser, J. (2006). *From parents to partners: Building a family-centered early childhood program.* St. Paul, MN: Redleaf Press.

Kirmani, M. H. (2007). Empowering culturally and linguistically diverse children and families. *Young Children, 62*(6), 94–98.

Kontos, S., & Dunn, L. (1989). Attitudes of caregivers, maternal experiences with day care, and children's development. *Journal of Applied Developmental Psychology, 10,* 37–51.

Kontos, S., & Wells, W. (1986). Attitudes of caregivers and the day care experiences of families. *Early Childhood Research Quarterly, 1,* 47–67.

Kostelnik, M. J., Soderman, A. K., & Whiren, A. P. (2007). *Developmentally appropriate curriculum: Best practices in early childhood education.* Upper Saddle River, NJ: Merrill/Prentice Hall.

Kraft, S., & Snell, M. (1980). Parent-teacher conflict: Coping with parental stress. *Pointer, 24,* 29–37.

Larner, M. (1996). Parents' perspectives on quality in early care and education. In S. Kagan & N. Cohen (Eds.), *Reinventing early care and education: A vision for quality systems* (pp. 21–42). San Francisco: Jossey-Bass.

Lawrence-Lightfoot, S. (2003). *The essential conversation: What parents and teachers can learn from each other.* New York: Ballentine Books.

Leavitt, R. L. (1987). *Invisible boundaries: An interpretive study of parent-provider relationship.* Chicago: Spencer Foundation. (ERIC Document Reproduction Service No. ED299035)

Lee, V. E., & Burkam, D. T. (2002). *Inequality at the starting gate: Social background differences in achievement as children begin school.* Washington, DC: Economic Policy Institute.

Levine-Coley, R. (1998). Children's socialization experiences and functioning in single-mother households: The importance of fathers and other men. *Child Development, 69,* 219–230.

Marcon, R. A. (1994a). Doing the right thing for children: Linking research and policy reform in the District of Columbia Public Schools. *Young Children, 50*(1), 8–11.

Marcon, R. A. (1994b). *Early learning and early identification follow-up study: Transition from the early to the later childhood grades. 1990–93.* Washington, DC: District of Columbia Public Schools, Center for Systemic Change.

Meisels, S. J., Jablon, J. R., Marsden, D. B., Dichtelmiller, M. L., Dorfman, A. B., & Steele, D. M. (1994). *An overview: The Work Sampling System.* Ann Arbor, MI: Rebus.

Meisels, S. J., Marsden, D. B, & Stetson, C. (2000). *Winning ways to learn, Ages 3, 4 & 5: 600 great ideas for children.* New York: Goddard Press.

Murphy, D. M. (1997). Parent and teacher plan for the child. *Young Children, 52*(4), 32–36.

National Association for the Education of Young Children Academy for Early Childhood Program Accreditation. (2005). NAEYC Early Childhood Program Standards. Washington, DC: Author. Retrieved February 18, 2008, from http://www.naeyc.org/academy/standards/

National Association for the Education of Young Children. (1993). Washington update. The United Nations Convention on the Rights of the Young Child. *Young Children, 48*(6), 65.

National Association for the Education of Young Children. (1994). *Principles to link by: Integrated service systems that are community-based and school-linked.* Washington, DC: Author

National Association for the Education of Young Children. (1995). *National Association for the Education of Young Children position statement: Responding to linguistic and cultural diversity. Recommendations for effective early childhood education.* Washington, DC: Author.

National Association for the Education of Young Children. (2001). *NAEYC guidelines revision. NAEYC standards for early childhood professional preparation.* Washington, DC: Author.

National Association for the Education of Young Children. (2003). *NAEYC Standards for Early Childhood Professional Preparation: Associate Degree Programs.* Washington, DC: National Association for the Education of Young Children. Retrieved February 20, 2008, from naeyc.org/faculty/pdf/2003.pdf

National Association for the Education of Young Children. (2006). *Code of Ethical Conduct: Supplement for Early Childhood Program Administrators.* Washington, DC: Author. Retrieved February 20, 2008, from www.naeyc.org/about/positions/PSETH05_supp.asp

National PTA. (2000). *Building successful partnerships: A guide for developing parent and family involvement programs.* Indianapolis, IN: National Educational Service.

National Research Council. (2001). *Eager to learn: Educating our preschoolers.* B. Bowman, M. S. Donovan, & M. S. Burns (Eds.), Washington, DC: National Academy Press.

Neilsen, L. E., & Finkelstein, J. M. (1993). A new approach to parent conferences. *Teaching K–8, 24*(1), 90–92.

Neuman, S. B., Hagedorn, T., Celano, D., & Daly, P. (1995). Toward a collaborative approach to parent involvement in early education: A study of teenage mothers in an African-American community. *American Educational Research Journal, 32,* 801–824.

NICHD Early Child Care Research Network. (1997). Child care in the first year of life. *Merrill-Palmer Quarterly, 43,* 340–360.

Pena, D. (2000). Parent involvement: Influencing factors and implications. *Journal of Educational Research, 94,* 42–54.

Pogoloff, S. M. (2004). Facilitate positive relationships between parents and professionals. *Intervention in School & Clinic, 40*(2), 116–120.

Powell, D. R. (1987). Day care as a family support system. In S. L. Kagan, D. R. Powell, B. Weissbourd, & E. F. Zigler (Eds.). *America's family support programs: Perspectives and prospects* (pp. 115–132). New Haven, CT: Yale University Press.

Powell, D. R. (1989). *Families and early childhood programs.* Washington, DC: National Association for the Education of Young Children.

Powell, D. R. (1991). How schools support families: Critical policy tensions. *Elementary School Journal, 91,* 307–319.

Powell, D. R., & Gerde, H. K. (2006). Considering kindergarten families. In D. F. Gullo(Ed.), *K today: Teaching and learning in the kindergarten year* (pp. 26–34). Washington, DC: National Association for the Education of Young Children.

Raab, M., & Dunst, D. J. (1997). Early childhood program assessment scales and family support practices. In S. Reifel (Series Ed.) & C. J. Dunst & M. Wolery (Vol. Eds.), *Advances in early education and day care: Vol 8. Family policy and practice in early education and child care programs* (pp. 105–131). Greenwich, CT: JAI.

Rolnick, A., & Grunewald, R. (2003). Early childhood development: Economic development with a high public return. *Fedgazette,* Federal Reserve Bank of Minneapolis, March. Retrieved February 20, 2008, from http://minneapolisfed.org/pubs/fedgaz/03-03/earlychild.cfm

Sciarra, D. J., & Dorsey, A. G. (1998). *Developing and administering child care centers* (4th ed.). Albany, NY: Delmar.

Seplocha, H. (2004). Partnerships for learning: Conferencing with families. *Young Children, 59*(5), 96–98.

Shores, E. F., & Grace, C. (1998). *The portfolio book: A step-by-step guide for teachers.* Beltsville, MD: Gryphon.

Smith, J. R., Brooks-Gunn, J., & Klebanov, P. K. (1997). Consequences of living in poverty for young children's cognitive and verbal ability and early school achievement. In G. J. Duncan & J. Brooks-Gunn (Eds.), *Consequences of growing up poor* (pp. 132–189). New York: Sage.

Stamp, L. N., & Groves, M. M. (1994). Strengthening the ethic of care: Planning and supporting family involvement. *Dimensions of Early Childhood, 22*(2), 5–9.

Stevenson, D. L., & Baker, D. P. (1987). The family-school relation and the child's school performance. *Child Development, 58,* 1348–1357.

Stevenson, H. W., Chen, C., & Uttal, D. H. (1990). Beliefs and achievement: A study of Black, White, and Hispanic children. *Child Development, 61,* 508–523.

Stewart, I. S. (1982). The real world of teaching two-year-old children. *Young Children, 37*(5), 3–13.

Stipek, D., Milburn, S., Clements, D., & Daniels, D. H. (1992). Parents' beliefs about appropriate education for young children. *Journal of Applied Developmental Psychology, 13,* 293–310.

Swick, K. J., & Williams, R. D. (2006). An analysis of Bronfenbrenner's bio-ecological perspective for early childhood educators: Implications for working with families experiencing stress. *Early Childhood Education Journal, 33*(5), 371–378.

Taylor, B. J. (1999). *A child goes forth: A curriculum guide for preschool children.* Upper Saddle River: Merrill/Prentice Hall.

Vander Ven, K. (1988). Pathways to professional effectiveness for early childhood educators. In B. Spodek, O. N. Saracho, & D. L. Peters (Eds.), *Professionalism and the early childhood practitioner* (pp. 137–160). New York: Teachers College Press.

Vygotsky, L. S. (1978). *Mind in society* (M. Cole, S. Schribner, V. John-Steiner, & E. Souberman, Trans.). Cambridge, MA: Harvard University Press.

White, B. (1988). *Educating infants and toddlers.* Lexington, MA: Lexington Books.

Workman, S. H., & Gage, J. A. (1997). Family-school partnerships: A family strengths approach. *Young Children, 52*(4), 10–14.

Zigler, E. F. (1989). Addressing the nation's child care crisis: The school of the twenty-first century. *American Journal of Orthopsychiatry, 59,* 484–491.

Chapter 13

ACF (Administration for Children and Families). (2007). Head Start Act. Retrieved May 24, 2008, from http://eclkc.ohs.acf.hhs.gov/hslc/Program%20Design%20and%20Management/Head%20Start%20Requirements/Head%20Start%20Act/headstartact.html

Barnett, W. S., Hustedt, J. T., Hawkinson, L. E. & Robin, K. B. (2007). *The state of preschool in 2006.* New Brunswick, NJ: National Institute for Early Education Research.

Blank, H. K. (1997). Advocacy leadership. In S. L. Kagan & B. T. Bowman (Eds.), *Leadership in early care and education* (pp. 39–45). Washington, DC: National Association for the Education of Young Children.

Bowman, B. T. (1995). The professional development challenge: Supporting young children and families. *Young Children, 51*(1), 30–34.

Charlesworth, R., & DeBoer, B. B. (2000). An early childhood teacher moves from DIP to DAP: Self-study as a useful research method for teacher researcher and university professor collaboration. *Journal of Early Childhood Teacher Education, 21*(2), 149–154.

Clifford, R. M. (1997). Partnerships with other professionals. *Young Children, 52*(5), 2–3.

Cochran-Smith, M., & Lytle, S. L. (1999). The teacher research movement: A decade later. *Educational Researcher, 28*(7), 15–25.

Cooney, M. H., Buchanan, M., & Parkinson, D. (2001). Teachers as researchers: Classroom inquiry initiatives at undergraduate and graduate levels in early childhood education. *Journal of Early Childhood Teacher Education, 22*(3), 151–159.

Ellison, C., & Barbour, N. (1992). Changing child care systems through collaborative efforts: Challenges for the 1990s. *Child and Youth Care Forum, 21,* 299–316.

Feeney, S. (1995). Professionalism in early childhood teacher education: Focus on ethics. *Journal of Early Childhood Teacher Education, 16*(3), 13–15.

Feeney, S., & Freeman, N. K. (1999/2005). *Ethics and the early childhood educator: Using the NAEYC Code.* Washington, DC: National Association for the Education of Young Children.

Feeney, S., Freeman, N. K., & Moravick, E. (2000). *Teaching the NAEYC Code of Ethical Conduct: Activity sourcebook.* Washington, DC: National Association for the Education of Young Children.

Feeney, S., & Kipnis, K. (1989). *Code of Ethical Conduct and Statement of Commitment.* Washington, DC: National Association for the Education of Young Children.

Hankins, K. H. (1998). Cacophony to symphony: Memoirs in teacher research. *Harvard Educational Review, 68,* 80–95.

Jacobson, L., & A. Simpson (2007). Communicating about early childhood education: Lessons from working with the news media. *Young Children, 62*(3), 89–93.

Kagan, S. L., & Cohen, N. E. (1997). *Not by chance: Creating an early care and education system for America's children. Full report, the Quality 2000 Initiative.* New Haven, CT: Bush Center in Child Development and Social Policy.

Kagan, S. L., & Neuman, M. J. (1997). Conceptual leadership. In S. L. Kagan & B. T. Bowman (Eds.), *Leadership in early care and education* (pp. 59–64). Washington, DC: National Association for the Education of Young Children.

Katz, L. (1995). The nature of professions: Where is early childhood education? In L. Katz. *Talks with teachers of young children: A collection* (pp. 219–235). Norwood, NJ: Ablex.

Levine, M. (1992). Observations on the early childhood profession. *Young Children, 47*(2), 50–51.

Moran, M. J. (2007). Collaborative action research and project work: Promising practices for developing collaborative inquiry among early childhood preservice teachers. *Teaching and Teacher Education, 23*(4), 418–431.

Muenchow, S. (1997). Commentary. In S. L. Kagan & B. T. Bowman (Eds.), *Leadership in early care and education* (pp. 46–47). Washington, DC: National Association for the Education of Young Children.

Nanus, B. (1992). *Visionary leadership.* San Francisco: Jossey-Bass.

National Association for the Education of Young Children. (2004). *Code of Ethical Conduct and Statement of Commitment: Supplement for Early Childhood Adult Educators.* Washington, DC: Author. Retrieved May 24, 2008, from www.naeyc.org/about/positions/ethics04.asp

National Association for the Education of Young Children. (2005b). *Code of Ethical Conduct and Statement of Commitment.* Washington, DC: Author. Retrieved May 24, 2008, from naeyc.org/about/positions/PSETH05.asp

National Association for the Education of Young Children. (2006). *Code of Ethical Conduct and Statement of Commitment: Supplement for Early Childhood Program Administrators.* Washington, DC: Author. Retrieved May 24, 2008, from www.naeyc.org/about/positions/PSETH05_supp.asp

National Association for the Education of Young Children Academy for Early Childhood Program Accreditation. (2005a). NAEYC Early Childhood Program Standards. Washington, DC: Author. Retrieved May 24, 2008, from http://www.naeyc.org/academy/standards/

National Association for the Education of Young Children and the National Council of Teachers of Mathematics. (n.d.). *Early childhood mathematics: Promoting good beginnings.* Retrieved May 24, 2008, from www.naeyc.org/about/positions/psmath.asp

National Association for Regulatory Administration & Technical Assistance Center. (2006). *The 2005 child care licensing study.* Conyers, GA: Author. Retrieved May 24, 2008, from http://nara.affiniscape.com/associations/4734/files/2005%20Licensing%20Study%20Final%20Report_Web.pdf

Paley, V. G. (1981). *Wally's stories.* Cambridge, MA: Harvard University Press.

Perreault, J. (1991). Society as extended family: Giving a childhood to every child. *Dimensions, 19*(4), 3–8, 31.

Robinson, A., & Stark, D. R. (2002). *Advocates in action: Making a difference for young children.* Washington, DC: National Association for the Education of Young Children.

Stonehouse, A. (1994). *Not just nice ladies.* Castle Hill, New South Wales, Australia: Pademelon Press.

Stremmel, A. J., & Hill, L. T. (1999). Towards multicultural understanding: A reflective journey. In V. R. Fu & A. J. Stremmel (Eds.), *Affirming diversity through democratic conversations* (pp. 141–155). Upper Saddle River, NJ: Merrill/Prentice Hall.

AUTHOR INDEX

A

Abbott-Shim, M. S., 87, 106, 110
Abramowitz, R. H., 317
Abrutyn, L., 298, 299
Adams, G., 176, 177, 180
Adams, P. K., 138
Afthinos, I. D., 163
Ainsworth, P., 175
Akhtar-Danesh, N., 247
Albrecht, K. M., 229
Alexander, K. L., 316
Allan, L. L., 338
Allen, M., 334
Anderson, P. M., 247
Andrews, M., 246
Anthony, M. A., 91
Arezzo, D., 268
Aronson, S. S., 70
Asen, G., 291
Ashton-Warner, S., 110
Atkins-Burnett, S., 280, 289, 290
Atwood, M. E., 155
Ault, M. J., 33
Austin, J. S., 268

B

Bailey, D. B., Jr., 213, 236
Baker, D. P., 312, 313, 316
Baker, K. R., 157
Balaban, N., 93, 298
Bandura, A., 104
Banghart, P., 6
Barbett, S., 192
Barbour, N., 345
Barker, L., 101
Barnett, W. S., 3, 20, 21, 86, 175,
    180, 341
Bar-Or, O., 247
Bassler, D., 109
Beaty, J. J., 141, 285, 295
Behrmann, M. M., 227
Beierlein, J. G., 8
Bell, M. J., 132
Bellm, D., 109, 176
Bender, R. H., 87
Beneke, S., 297

Ben-Peretz, M., 109
Bentzen, W., 285
Bergen, D., 131, 216, 242, 281
Berk, L., 246
Bermudez, A., 310
Berry, P., 161
Betz, C., 233
Bhattacharya, J., 247
Bickart, T. S., 219
Bingham, A. A., 236
Birch, L. L., 248
Birckmayer, J., 313, 332
Blackman-Jones, R., 310, 317
Blank, H. K., 193, 346
Blau, D. M., 177
Bloom, P. J., 45, 48, 88, 90, 91, 99, 101,
    102, 103, 104, 110
Bodrova, E., 155
Bond, J. T., 181
Bontá, P., 228
Boutte, G. S., 141, 214, 318
Bove, C., 229
Bowman, B. T., 20, 30, 100, 101, 291,
    351
Boyd, J. S., 175
Brandon, R. N., 178
Brandt, R., 222, 233
Braunschweig, F. J., 247
Breckler, S., 86
Bredekamp, S., 19, 45, 108, 168, 212,
    214, 215, 221, 238, 241, 281, 308
Brennan, P., 267
Breuning, G. S., 176
Bricker, D., 289
Brigham, N., 101
Britain, L., 221
Britz, J., 99, 108
Brock, D. R., 329
Bromer, J., 214
Bronfenbrenner, U., 17, 20, 308, 309,
    310
Brooks-Gunn, J., 313
Brookshire, R., 281
Brown, D. L., 237
Brown-Lyons, M., 6
Brown, M. H., 90, 113

Brown, N. H., 90, 100
Brown, P., 334
Bruner, J., 18
Bryant, D. M., 3, 33, 87, 235
Buchanan, M., 349
Buchleitner, W., 131
Bugbee, M. R., 21
Bullard, J. A., 160
Bundy, D., 247
Burchinal, M. R., 3, 87, 235, 236
Burkam, D. T., 310, 313
Burnette, J., 289
Burts, D. C., 45, 219, 291
Bushnell, M. M., 285
Butcher, K. F., 247
Butzin, S. M., 228
Buysse, V., 16
Byler, P., 241, 242

C

Cabello, B., 132
Caldwell, B. M., 241, 310
Caples, S. E., 127
Cardelle-Elawar, M., 227
Carlisle, A., 222
Carlson, S., 246
Carter, M., 88, 90, 101, 110, 125,
    130, 133
Caruso, D. A., 33
Caruso, J. J., 45, 88, 90, 91, 113, 115
Casper, L. M., 174, 176
Cataldo, C. Z., 138
Cavallaro, C. C., 132
Celano, D., 317
Chaille, C., 221
Chaloupka, F. J., 247
Chard, S. C., 130, 222, 223, 243
Charlesworth, R., 33, 45, 219, 291, 349
Chavajay, P., 20
Chen, C., 316
Cherlin, A., 313
Chipman, M., 213, 214
Christensen, D., 93
Christian, L. G., 313, 315, 316, 325
Christie, J. F., 160
Cinnamond, J., 110

Clark, C. M., 31
Clarke-Stewart, A., 87
Class, N. E., 39
Clay, J. W., 313
Clements, D. H., 219, 227, 228, 317
Clewett, A. S., 232
Clifford, R. M., 32, 33, 50, 131, 309, 350
Clyde, M., 104
Cochran-Smith, M., 349
Cohen, D. H., 298
Cohen, J., 313
Cohen, N. E., 290
Cole, M., 18
Coleman, M. R., 305, 313
Colker, L. J., 288, 299
Collins, J. E., 102
Comer, J. P., 317
Cooney, M. H., 349
Copple, C., 45, 168, 212, 214, 221, 241, 281, 308
Coscia, J., 216
Cosco, N., 157
Cosgrove, M. S., 258
Cox, A., 143
Cramer, G., 99
Cranley Gallagher, K., 4
Crowell, N. A., 214
Cruz-Jansen, M., 213
Cryer, D., 32, 33, 50, 131, 132, 264, 309
Cuffaro, H., 108
Culkin, M. L., 9
Cunningham, B., 332
Curbow, B., 86
Currie, J., 247
Curtis, D., 88, 90, 101, 125, 133

D

Dahlberg, G., 291
Dahl, K., 258
Daly, P., 317
Daniel, J., 317
Daniels, D. H., 317
Danielson, C., 298, 299
Darling-Hammond, L., 46, 291
David, J., 219
Davies, D., 316
DeBoer, B. B., 349
DeBord, K., 157, 236
Deery-Schmitt, D. M., 86
Dehghan, M., 247
Del Grosso, P., 6
Dempsey, J. D., 132
Denham, E. J. M., 132
Denning, R., 227
Derman-Sparks, L., 213, 214
DeVries, R., 221

Dewey, J., 16, 18, 222
DeWolf, M., 45, 291
DiBiase, A.-M., 219
Dichtelmiller, M. L., 299
Dichter, H., 174
Diffily, D., 330
Dodd, E. L., 329
Dodge, D. T., 219
Dolezal, V., 213
Dooling, M. V., 262
Doolittle, S., 213
Dorfman, A. B., 281, 299
Dorsey, A. G., 90, 317, 332
Dowdy, C. A., 212
Drake, M. M., 251
Driscoll, A., 233
Drucker, P., 101
Duff, R. E., 113
Dulewicz, V., 11
Dunn, L., 318
Dunst, D. J., 308
Dyke, P. C., 90

E

Early, D. M., 46, 87
Ebb, N., 177
Edelstein, S., 163
Edkin, K., 313
Edmiaston, R., 213
Edwards, L., 127
Egan, K., 18
Eheart, B. K., 46
Eichberg, A., 193
Einbinder, S. D., 181
Eisenberg, D. R.
Elicker, J., 93, 242
Elkind, D., 227
Ellison, C., 345
Entwisle, D. R., 316
Epstein, A. S., 46
Epstein, J. L., 310, 311, 312, 316, 317, 318, 333
Erickson, C., 213
Eriksen, H., 160
Erikson, E. H., 18
Essa, E. L., 231
Evangelou, D., 236
Ewen, D., 193
Exelby, B., 130, 146
Eyer, D. W., 128, 137, 152, 153, 158

F

Fagan, J., 332
Falk, B., 291
Farquhar, E., 110
Favre, K., 231

Fawcett, M. T., 88, 90, 91, 113, 115
Feeney, S., 47, 93, 234, 238, 316, 340, 342
Ferguson, D. L., 212
Fields, M., 46
Fiese, B. H., 5
File, N., 46
Finkelstein, J. M., 324
Finlay, B., 334
Fischer, J. L., 46
Fisher, J. A., 248
Flessner, C. A., 274
Fortner-Wood, C., 93
Fox-Barnett, M., 329
Frede, E. C., 21
Freeman, E. B., 241
Freeman, N. K., 47, 90, 314, 316, 340, 342
Friedman, A. H., 175
Friedman, S. L., 240
Fromberg, D. P., 222
Frost, J. L., 33, 155, 156, 157, 158, 160, 226
Fuchs, D., 212
Fuchs, L. S., 212
Fu, V. R., 56

G

Gabbard, C., 247
Gage, J. A., 316
Galinsky, E., 46, 112, 193, 234, 240, 315, 316
Galley, M., 242
Ganzel, B., 5
Garbarino, J., 5, 317
García Coll, C., 314
Gardner, H., 17, 20, 222
Gartrell, D. J., 232, 233
Gatheridge, B. J., 274
Gerber, E., 86
Gerde, H. K., 310, 313
Gesell, A., 16
Gibbs, N., 309
Gibson, R. K., 246
Godin, S., 208
Goetz, L., 212
Goldstein, L. S., 45
Goncu, A., 20
Gonzalez-Mena, J., 128, 137, 152, 153, 158, 311, 312, 313, 314, 315, 316, 317, 318, 325, 332, 335
Gonzalez, N., 251
Gormley, W. T., Jr., 43, 235
Gottlieb, H., 335, 336
Grace, C., 336
Gray, D., 163

Greenberg, M., 176
Greenberg, P., 314, 315, 332
Greenman, J. T., 126, 132, 138, 174, 234
Greenspan, S. I., 289, 291
Griffin, G. A., 93
Grisham-Brown, J. L., 213, 281
Gronlund, G., 300
Groves, M. M., 331
Gruber, C., 87
Grunewald, R., 2, 335
Guddemi, M., 160
Guralnick, M. J., 21

H

Hagedorn, T., 317
Hagen, J., 247
Hagy, A. P., 177
Hair, J. F., 203
Hale, J. E., 241
Hale-Jinks, C.M., 85, 86
Hallam, R., 281
Hall, E. T., 314
Hamel, E., 247
Hamilton, C. E., 87
Haney, M., 132
Hanhan, S. F., 321
Hankins, K. H., 349
Hanson, M. J., 212
Harms, T. O., 32, 33, 50, 131, 132, 153, 263, 264, 309
Hart, C. H., 45, 219, 291
Hartman, J. A., 236
Haskins, R., 20
Hatch, J. A., 241
Haugland, S. W., 227, 228
Hauser-Cram, P., 21
Hawkinson, L. E., 3, 180, 341
Hayden, J., 88
Hayes, C. D., 189
Haynes, N. M., 317
Haywood, H. C., 240
Healy, J. M., 226
Hebbeler, K., 85
Heckman, J. J., 335
Helburn, S. W., 9, 240
Heller, A., 247
Helm, J. H., 223, 297
Hemmeter, M. L., 33, 213, 281
Hendley, S.G., 141
Hendrix, K., 268
Henniger, M. L., 155, 160
Hennig, M., 100
Henrich, C. C., 310, 317
Henry, G. T., 236
Heroman, C., 288, 299
Herr, J., 48
Hess, R., 227

Hestenes, L. L., 157
Hewes, D. W., 90
Hiam, A., 205
Higgs, M., 11
Hill, L. T., 349
Hill-Scott, K., 174
Himle, M. B., 274
Hitz, M. C., 33
Hitz, R., 233
Hnatiuk, P., 109
Hofferth, S. L., 110
Hohmann, C., 131
Hohmann, M., 219, 226, 316
Holland, M., 248
Honig, A. S., 93, 231, 268
Hoover-Dempsey, K. V., 109, 318
Horn, E., 175
Horowitz, F. D., 21
Howell, N. M., 258
Howes, C., 46, 86, 87, 112, 131, 193, 234, 235, 240, 271
Hoy, W., 101
Hudson, S., 131
Huettig, C. I., 247
Hunt, J. M., 18
Hunt, P., 212
Hurst, B., 99
Hustedt, J. T., 3, 175, 180, 341
Hyberton, D. W., 21
Hyman, I., 232
Hyson, M. C., 132

I

Irwin, D. M., 285
Isbell, R., 130, 146
Isenberg, J. P., 93, 221, 222

J

Jablon, J. R., 219, 299
Jacobs, E. V., 21, 33, 131, 309
Jacobs, F., 21, 33
Jacobson, L., 217, 345, 346, 348
Jalongo, M. R., 222
Jardin, A., 100
Javernick, E., 247
Jensen, B. J., 160
Jensen, I. J., 313
Jersild, A. T., 17
Jewett, J. L., 108
Jimenez, E., 247
Joesch, J. M., 178
Johnson, J. E., 160
Johnson, L. C., 132
Johnson, N., 174
Johnson, R. D., 48
Johnson, S. L., 248
Johnston, L., 329

Jones, B., 221
Jones, E., 95, 105, 108, 215, 222, 223, 238
Jorde-Bloom, P., 90, 101, 108

K

Kagan, S. L., 20, 100, 101, 178, 194, 214, 241, 280, 290, 304, 350
Kalesnik, J., 289
Kandal, E., 267
Kaplan, P., 268
Karp, R., 247
Katz, L. G., 19, 31, 34, 90, 106, 108, 130, 212, 217, 222, 223, 232, 236, 237, 340
Keepler, D. L., 318
Kelley, R., 101
Kemple, K. M., 85
Kennedy, D., 132
Kessler, S., 19
Keyser, J., 311, 314, 318, 329
Kibler, R., 101
Kilmer, S. J., 155
Kilpatrick, W. H., 22
King, E. W., 213
Kipnis, K., 342
Kirby-Smith, S., 238
Kirmani, M. H., 314
Kisker, E. E., 110
Klebanov, P. K., 313
Klefstad, J., 258
Klein, S. M., 108
Klein, S. P., 46
Klein, T. P., 155
Knapp, M. S., 222
Knauerhase, V., 155
Knopf, H. T., 85, 316
Kohlberg, L., 18
Kohn, A., 232, 291, 292
Kontos, S., 46, 112, 234, 240, 315, 318
Koralek, D., 155
Korb, R. A., 192
Kostelnik, M. J., 19, 135, 315
Kotch, J., 163
Kraft, S., 315
Kremer-Hazon, L., 109
Kreuter, M., 163
Kromhout, O. M., 228
Krueger, A., 235

L

Lahm, E. A., 227
Lally, J. R., 126, 131, 137, 152, 158, 231
Lamb, C. W., 203
Lambert, L., 105, 111
Lambert, R. G., 288
Lambiotte, J. G., 35

Lamb, M. E., 231
Langhorst, B. H., 291
Lanphear, B., 272
Larkin, L., 222, 233
Larner, M., 308
Latimer, D. J., 110
Laufer, R. S., 132
Lawler, E. E., 100
Lawrence-Lightfoot, S., 326
Layzer, J., 6
Leavitt, R. L., 315
Ledford, G. E., Jr., 100
Lee, V. E., 313
Lein, L., 313
Lemerise, T., 228
Leong, D. J., 155
Lerman, R. I., 2
Levin, D. E., 268
Levine-Coley, R., 313
Levine, M., 345
Levitsky, D. A., 246
Lieber, J., 175
Likert, R., 102
Linas, K., 155
Linn, S., 247
Little, N. K., 9
Loewy, M., 247
Lombardi, J., 176
Lord, H., 176
Lowman, L. H., 138
Lozoff, B., 247
Lynch, E. W., 212
Lytle, S. L., 349

M

Magnuson, K., 314
Mallory, B. L., 213
Mancke, J. B., 58
Manlove, E. E., 86
Manni, J., 247
Manning, J. P., 90, 100
Marcon, R. A., 221, 222, 310
Marion, M., 232, 233
Marquez, J., 310
Marsden, D. B., 299, 330
Marshall, H. H., 233
Marshall, N., 87
Martin, R., 247
Martin, S., 294, 295
Mathur, S., 242
Maxwell, K. L., 33, 87
Mayer, R., 18
McBride, N., 274
McCartney, K., 87
McCary, C. E., 291
McClellan, D. E., 222, 232
McClelland, J., 86

McCormick, L, 234, 238
McDaniel, C., 203
McDonald, J., 164
McDonnell, K., 86
McGarvey, L., 227
McGinnis, J. R., 157
McGrevin, C. Z., 35
McNamara, C., 203
McWilliam, R. A., 236
Mednick, S., 267
Meisels, S. J., 5, 21, 280, 281, 288, 289, 290, 291, 290, 299, 326, 330
Mekos, D., 6, 87
Meltz, B. F., 132
Merchant, A. T., 247
Mermin, J., 329
Merritt, S., 213
Meshanko, R., 29
Meyer, T., 329
Mikkelsen, E. J., 268
Milburn, S., 317
Miller, L. B., 21
Miller, L. G., 229
Miltenberger, R G., 274
Miskel, C., 101
Mitchell, A., 45, 46, 49, 50, 174, 192, 219
Mobasher, H., 21
Modigliani, K., 214
Mogharrehan, C. N., 258
Mohrman, S. A., 100
Mohr, P., 21
Mollen, E., 247
Moore, L., 237
Moore, R. C., 157
Moran, M. J., 349
Moravick, E., 342
Morgan, B., 246
Morgan, G. G., 39, 42, 44, 45, 88, 90, 186, 187, 188, 189, 192
Morgan, P., 221
Morrison, A. M., 100
Morrison, K., 330
Morris, P. A., 310
Morrow, L. M., 242
Mosteller, F., 235
Moy, L., 175
Muenchow, S., 346
Murphy, D. M., 317
Murray, C. G., 248
Myhre, S. M., 141

N

Nabors, L. A., 3, 235
Nahikian-Nelms, M. L., 258
Nanus, B., 350
Nastasi, B. K., 227, 228

Nathenson-Mejia, S., 282
Neill, S. R., 132
Neilsen, L. E., 324
Neitzel, J., 305
Neugebauer, R., 90, 175, 177
Neuman, M. J., 214, 350
Neuman, S. B., 241, 298, 317
Newman, M., 109
Newman, S. B., 99
New, R. S., 213
Nilsen, B. A., 33, 285, 295, 297
Nimmo, J., 105, 215, 222, 223, 238
Nokes, C., 247
Norakowski, J., 221
Nord, M., 246
Norris, D., 235
Novick, R., 232
Nuttall, E. V., 289

O

Oakes, P. B., 33
O'Brien, M., 21
Odom, S. L., 16, 175
Olds, A. R., 124, 126, 127, 128, 129, 130, 131, 132, 135, 154, 155, 156, 163
Olenick, M., 176
Olson, L., 2, 108, 174, 181
Osmon, F., 161

P

Paley, V. G., 349
Palmer, J. L., 189
Papert, S., 227
Parkinson, D., 349
Paulsell, D., 6
Peel, J., 291
Peisner, E. S., 33
Pemberton, C., 86
Pena, D., 310
Perreault, J., 350
Perry, J. P., 155, 160
Perry, P., 247
Peterson, P. L., 31
Peth-Pierce, R., 231, 241
Phillips, C. B., 214
Phillips, D. A., 2, 4, 86, 87, 110, 214, 235, 240, 242, 271
Piaget, J., 236, 284
Piscitelli, B., 108
Plomin, R., 16
Poersch, N. O., 180
Poest, C. A., 155
Pogoloff, S. M., 318
Pond-Smith, D., 251
Popejoy, A., 247
Porras, J. I., 102

Powell, D. R., 21, 310, 311, 313, 316, 317
Powell, I., 175, 176, 189
Powell, L. M., 247
Pratt, C., 110
Prescott, E., 129, 146
Pretti-Frontczak, K. L., 281
Provence, S., 131

Q

Queralt, M., 177
Quisenberry, N., 221

R

Raab, M., 308
Raikes, H., 231
Ramey, C. T., 3
Ramey, S. L., 3
Rand, M. K., 108
Rasmussen, C., 221
Raver, C., 241
Read, M. A., 125
Reese-Learned, H., 221
Reguero-de-Atiles, J. T., 43, 85, 236
Reid, R., 131
Reifel, S., 155, 157, 226
Rhodes, L., 282
Richarz, S. H., 251
Rich, S., 247
Rickman, D. K., 236
Rideout, V., 247
Riley, C., 132, 264
Rivera, A. M., 101
Rivkin, M. S., 155
Roberts, J. E., 3, 235
Robertson, A., 6
Robin, K. B., 3, 180, 341
Robinson, A., 344, 345, 346, 348
Rodd, J., 100, 102, 103, 104
Roedell, W. C., 268
Rofrano, F., 231
Rogoff, B., 20
Rohacek, M. H., 177
Rolnick, A., 2, 335
Romero, I., 289
Rosegrant, T., 215, 238
Rosenblum, S., 101
Rosenholtz, S. J., 109
Rosenkoetter, S., 290
Roskos, K. A., 298
Ross, G., 18
Rowand, C., 6
Ruhmann, L. H., 138
Runyan, C., 163
Rusher, A. S., 35
Rushton, S., 222, 233

Russell-Fox, J., 213
Russell, S. D., 177
Rutter, R. A., 109

S

Sakai, L., 86, 87
Sallis, J., 155
Salovey, P., 231
Sameroff, A. J., 5
Sanborn, C. F., 247
Sandall, S. R., 166
Sanders, M. G., 318
Sandham, J. L., 179, 180
Sandler, H. M., 318
Santrock, J., 222
Sarama, J., 219
Scarr, S., 87
Schiller, P., 90
Schmidt, S. R., 2
Schneider, A. M., 109
Schorr, L. B., 290
Schreiber, M. E., 127
Schulman, K., 176, 177, 193
Schuster, J. W., 33
Schweinhart, L. J., 2
Sciarra, D. J., 90, 317, 332
Scott, L. C., 58
Seplocha, H., 318, 327
Sewell, T., 247
Shade, D. D., 157, 170, 219
Sheerer, M., 99, 108
Shepard, L. A., 241, 280, 281, 292, 304
Shinn, M., 112, 240
Shoemaker, C. J., 104
Shonkoff, J. P., 2, 4, 5, 240, 242
Shore, R., 267
Shores, E. F., 327
Shriner, J., 213
Sigel, I. E., 21
Silverman, B., 228
Simmons, B. J., 268
Simpson, A., 345, 346, 348
Skinner, B. F., 17
Slaby, R. G., 268
Sluyter, D., 231
Small, M., 231
Smith, B. S., 18
Smith, E., 193
Smith, J. R., 313
Smith, M. S., 109
Smith, P., 227
Smith, T. E. C., 212
Snell, M., 315
Snider, M. H., 46
Snow, C. W., 43, 85

Soderman, A. K., 135, 315
Sommerville, C. J., 18
Sosinsky, L. S., 176
Sosna, D., 144
Spodek, B., 19, 31, 93
Spratt, K., 86
Stalsworth, K., 268
Stamp, L. N., 331
Stanford, B. H., 268
Stark, D. R., 344, 345, 346, 348
Steele, D. M., 281
Steinheimer, K., 297
Stephens, K., 189
Stern, V., 298
Stetson, C., 330
Stevenson, D. L., 312, 313, 316
Stevenson, H. W., 316
Stewart, J., 126, 137, 152, 158
Stiggins, R., 291
Stipek, D., 241, 242, 317
Stoneham, L., 247
Stonehouse, A., 90, 138, 340
Stoney, L., 174, 176, 191, 192
Stott, E., 20, 101
Strain, P. S., 213
Strang, H. R., 232
Stremmel, A. J., 349
Strickland, D. S., 242
Strupp, B. J., 246
Sullivan, A. K., 232
Surr, J., 56
Sussman, C., 126
Swadener, B. B., 19
Swadener, S., 258
Swick, K. J., 214, 312, 315
Syler, G., 258
Sysko, L., 316
Szanton, E. S., 131
Szczypka, G., 247

T

Talbot, J., 155
Talley, K., 49
Tarr, P., 126
Taylor, B. J., 228, 327
Taylor, M. K., 138
Teleki, J. K., 43, 85
Terry, B. Z., 318
Tertell, E. A., 108
Theilheimer, R., 236
Thoman, E., 231
Thompson, D., 131
Thompson, P. W., 227
Thompson, R. A., 231
Thweatt, G., 231

Tilbury, D., 155
Tinsworth, D., 164
Todd, C. M., 86
Torcellini, P., 127
Torelli, L., 131, 137, 139, 140, 149, 150, 151
Trawick-Smith, J., 105, 111, 131, 132
Trister-Dodge, D., 288
Tyler, V. S., 318

U
Ulione, M. S., 262
Ungaretti, A., 86
Uttal, D. H., 316

V
Valdez, G., 221
Vance, E., 233
Vandell, D. L., 192
van den Bosch, C., 247
Vander Ven, K., 90, 315
Van Horn, J. E., 8
van IJzendoorn, M. H., 268
Van Scoy, I. J., 113, 141, 214
Variano, D. A., 313
Veenman, S., 236
Vermeer, H. J., 268
Verstegen, D. A., 180
Vogel, J., 175
Vygotsky, L. S., 17, 18, 20, 214, 226, 236, 308

W
Wahlers, K., 101
Wallach, F., 163
Wallinga, C., 318
Wardle, F., 214, 254
Watson, K., 101
Waugh, S., 231
Weaver, P. J., 233
Weider, S., 289, 291
Weikart, D. P., 21, 219, 226, 316
Weissbourd, B., 131
Wells, W., 315
Wentzel, H., 268
Wesley, P. W., 16, 93
West, L. S., 45
West, S., 143
Wetzel, K., 227
Whiren, A. P., 135
White, B., 311
Whitebook, M., 86, 87, 109, 112, 176, 193, 235, 271
White, D. R., 33, 131, 309
Wien, C. A., 238
Willer, B., 113, 175, 176
Williams, J. R., 155
Williams, K. C., 222, 236
Williams, R. D., 312, 315
Wilson, C., 99
Wilson, R. A., 155
Winter, S. M., 132

Wirth, D., 155
Wise, A. E., 46
Witt, D. D., 155
Witte, A. D., 177
Wolery, M., 213
Wolery, R. A., 16, 175
Wolf, A. W., 247
Wolfe, B., 193
Wolfe, J., 222, 233
Wolfe, M., 132
Wood, D. J., 18
Woo, D. G., 242
Woodrow, C., 90
Workman, S. H., 316
Wortham, S. C., 155, 157, 226
Wright, D., 33
Wright, J. L., 227
Wurtz, E., 241, 280, 304

Y
Yamamoto, K., 268
Yawkey, T. D., 160
Yell, M., 213

Z
Zaslow, M., 189
Zigler, E. F., 176, 317
Zimmerman, K., 48
Zimpher, N., 110
Zinzeleta, E., 9

A

Ability grouping, 236
Academy for Early Childhood Program Accreditation, 48
Accident reports, 319, 322
Accreditation
    accrediting associations, 49
    advocacy and, 46
    collaboration, community-school-family and, 45
    defined, 47
    vs. licensing, 48
    NAEYC steps in, 48–49
    program evaluation and, 47–49
        self-study in, 111, 112
    of public schools, 49
    staff development and, 111, 112
Action alerts, 348
Action research, 349
Active learning, 108
Acts of omission/commission, 274
Administrative manual
    described, 62
    information included in, 81–82
Administrative mechanisms, 178
Administrators. *See* Directors
Adult–child ratio, 235
Adult lounge/rest area, 154
Advisory committees, 335–337
Advocacy
    accreditation and, 46
    action alerts, 348
    briefing papers, 346
    collective, 345
    concrete examples, 348
    defined, 343
    effective, 345–346
    individual/personal, 344–345
    key facts handouts, 347
    in licensing laws and procedures, 44
    NAEYC *Statement of Commitment,* 343–344
    position statements, 346
    private-sector, 345
    public policy, 345
    talking points, 346
Affirmative action, 94–95
American Academy of Pediatrics (AAP), 38, 43

American Automobile Association (AAA), 9–10
American Educational Research Association, 279
American Marketing Association, 198
American Montessori Society (AMS), 47
American Psychological Association, 279
American Public Health Association (APHA), 38
American Red Cross, 262
Americans with Disabilities Act (ADA), 7, 56, 69, 94, 166
Anecdotal records, 282–283, 284
    entries, 294, 295
Anticipatory concept web, 223–225
Archival portfolio, 299
Art center, 142, 143, 374–375
Articles of incorporation, 54
Assessment. *See also* Observations; Record keeping; Reporting
    Assessment, Evaluation, and Programming System for Infants and Children (2nd Edition), 289
    authentic, 281–282, 304
        tools for structuring, 288–289
    Creative Curriculum, 288
    defined, 279
    developmental screening, 280–281
    diagnostic, 289
    documentation methods and, 281–282, 283
    vs. evaluation, 279
    formative, 280
    health, 260–262
    interview method of, 114, 286–287
    job performance (*See* Job performance assessments)
    needs assessment surveys, 106
    professional associations' call for, 279
    program evaluation measures, 106
    purposes for, 304, 305
    Recognition and Response, 305
    reliability of, 281
    responsible, characteristics of, 279–280
    risk, 274
    samples of children's work, 287
    summative, 289–290 (*See also* Assessment tests, standardized)

    validity of, 281
    Work Sampling System, 288
Assessment, Evaluation, and Programming System for Infants and Children (2nd Edition), 289
Assessment of Practices in Early Elementary Classrooms (APEEC), 33
Assessment tests, standardized
    concerns about, 290–291
    criterion-referenced measure, 290
    description of, 290
    matrix sampling, 292
    norm-referenced measure, 290
    position statements on, 292
Assets, 182
Assistant teachers, 92. *See also* Primary program personnel
Association of Childhood Education International, 279
Association of Christian Schools International (ACSI), 49
Atelier/atelieristas, 142
Authentic assessment, 281–282, 304
    tools for structuring, 288–289

B

Background information records, 293–294
Behavioral-environmental view, 17
Block center, 138–141, 373
Block grant, 179
Board of directors, 335–337
Bona fide occupational qualifications (BFOQ), 56
Break-even analysis, 186
Bricks and Mortar Act, 182
Briefing paper, 346
Budgeting
    budget comparison report, 190
    budget projection, 187
    definition of budget, 187
    formats, 188, 191–192
    operating budget, 188
    regulations, 187
    reporting, 190
    start-up budget, 188
    statement of financial position, 190
    types of budgets, 187–188
    writing, 189–190

Building codes, 38
Bureau of Citizenship and Immigration
    Services, 98
Bureau of Labor Statistics, 183
Bylaws, 54

C

Cameras, 169–170
*Campaign for Commercial Free Child-
    hood,* 344–355
Capacity, 6, 154
Capital support, 182
*Caring for Our Children: National
    Health and Safety Performance
    Standards: Guidelines for Out-of-
    Home Child Care,* 38
Carnegie Institute, 190
Carpentry or woodworking center, 144,
    376
Case managers, 93
Catalog of Federal Domestic Assistance,
    182
Categorical grant, 179
Ceilings, 129
Center for Child Care Workforce, 86
Certificate of incorporation, 54
Certificate of Occupancy, 37–38
Chains, 55
Checklist for Rating Developmentally
    Appropriate Practice in Kinder-
    garten Classrooms, 33
Checklists, 114, 294–295, 296
Child and Adult Care Food Program
    (CACFP), 193, 248, 250, 252–253.
    See also U.S. Department of Agri-
    culture (USDA)
Child care
    family, 5–6
    fees, subsidized, 177, 180, 181
    group homes, 6
    for infants (*See* Infant care)
    large family homes, 5–6
    school-age child care (*See* School-age
        child care [SACC])
    special needs (*See* Special needs
        child care)
    special services in, 7–8
    for toddlers (*See* Toddler care)
    types of, most common, 5
Child Care and Development Block
    Grant (CCDBG), 181, 193
Child Care and Development Fund
    (CCDF), 7, 177, 180
Child care center, defined, 5, 39.
    See also Learning/activity centers
Child Care Improvement Grants (Family
    Support Act), 193
Child Care Resource and Referral
    Agencies (CCR&Rs), 9

Child Care Tax Credits Outreach Cam-
    paign, 177
Child Development Associate (CDA),
    41, 45, 47, 113, 341, 342
Childhood Education International
    (ACEI), 346
Child outcomes, 217–218
Children's books
    purchasing, 168–169
    suppliers of, 353
Children's Day Care Health and
    Improvement Act, 181
Child Tax Credit, 177
Civil Rights Acts of 1964, 56, 58, 99
Class celebrations, 230
Classroom displays, 320
Cleaning and sanitation, 264, 265
Cleanup/fix-up workdays, 329
Coach, rolls of, 10–11. *See also* Directors
Code of ethics, defined, 361
Collaboration, community-school-family
    accreditation and, 45
    advisory committees and governing
        boards, 335–337
    ill-prepared communities, 337
    school's role in linking families with
        communities, 334–335
Collaboration, director-staff
    communication skills, 104–105
    conflicts, 104–105
    decision making, 102–103
    efforts, motivating, 103–104
    leadership roles in, 103
    responsibilities, delegating, 105
    steps in, 103
Collaboration, family-school. *See also*
        Communication, family-staff
    barriers to, 312–314
        cultural diversity, 313–314
        family structure, 313
        linguistic diversity, 314
        socioeconomic backgrounds, 313
    benefits of, 310–312
    challenges of, 316–318
    classroom visits, 329
    concepts, skills, and attitudes of
        teachers and, 316, 317
    guidelines for creating partnerships,
        308–309
    home visits, 328–329
    ill-prepared teachers and, 316
    models, family-centered, 337
    newsletters, 329–330
    notes, informal, 331
    parent education and family resource
        support programs, 333–334
    parent involvement in, 309–310
    social events, 331
    telephone conversations, 330

tension/conflict and, 314–315
    videos, program, 331
    volunteers, family, 331–333
    Web site, program, 331
    workshops or workdays, 329–330
Collective advocacy, 345
Colors, 126–127
Committee on Early Childhood Peda-
    gogy, 193, 216
Communication, family-staff. *See also*
        Conferences, family-staff
    accident reports, 319, 322
    classroom displays, 320
    effective communication, suggestions
        for, 318–319
    family area and, 319–321
    initial family visit, 321
    logs, 319, 320
    open house or curriculum night,
        322–324
    regulations, 42
    special topics meetings, 324
    spring or autumn orientation, 321–322
Community
    ethical responsibilities to, 360–361
    staff and, influence on, 99–100
    values in program planning, 15–16
Computers
    DAP use of, 226–227
    general benefits of, 227
    program implementation and,
        226–228
    purchasing, 169–170
Concrete examples, 348
Conferences, family-staff
    effective, guidelines for, 325–327
    reporting, individual, 303–304
    scheduled individual, 324–325, 327
    specially called individual, 325, 328
Constructivist view, 17
Contracts
    employment, 116–117
    financial, 181
    fiscal regulations, 55
Cooking center, 144–145, 377–378
Corporations, 53–55
Cost, Quality, and Child Outcomes
    Study Team, 7, 107–108, 175
Costs of early childhood programs, 174.
    See also Financing early childhood
        programs
    capital *vs.* operating, 178
    to family, 176–178
    fixed and variable, 178
    foregone income, 178
    government contributions, 175–176
    hidden, 178
    joint, 178
    for labor, 176

Costs of early childhood programs (*continued*)
  local program, 178
  marginal, 178
  multi-child discounts, 177
  policies and procedures, 70
  quality and, 175, 176
  start-up, 178
  tax credits and deductions, 175, 176
  varied costs of different programs, 175
  volunteers and donations, 176
Council on Accreditation (COA), 49
Creative Curriculum, 288
Credentialing, 44
  administrator qualifications, 44–46
  education subject areas required to receive, 47–49
  NAEYC's core competencies, 45–46
Crime coverage, 119
Criminal history records checks, 98
Criterion-referenced measure, 290
Cubbies, 150–151
Cultural diversity, 313–314
Culturally competent or sensitive, 31
Cumulative records, 298
Curriculum, 20, 211
  emergent, 215
  implementing (*See* Program implementation)
  integrated curriculum approach, 219, 220–222
  models, 21
  nutrition, 258
  organizing, 218–222
  themes *vs.* projects, 222–224
  theory as program informant, 20–21

D
Database management system, 170
Decision making
Declining grant, 182
Dependent Care Assistance Program (DCAP), 177, 185
Dependent Care Tax Credit, 177
Deregulation, 179
Developmentally Appropriate Practices (DAP), 212
  empirical studies of, 33
  environment of local programs, 213–215
  implementing, lack of, 241–242
  interests and needs of children, 212–213
  knowledge of children, 212
  NAEYC position statements on, 19, 212, 221–222
  standards, 215–217
  teaching strategies, 241–242
Developmental screening, 280–281, 289, 305

Diagnostic assessment, 289
Diapering areas, 152
Directors. *See also* Collaboration, director-staff
  administrator qualifications, 44–46
  board of, 335–337
  definition and job description of, 88
  development of, stages of, 91–92
  educational coordinator, 88
  executive, 88
  head teacher, 88
  leadership and management components, 88
  leadership styles, 11–12
  NAEYC's core competencies, 45–46
  personal qualifications of, 90, 92
  professional qualifications of, 90
  program, 88
  qualifications of, 44–46
  roles and responsibilities of, 10–11, 88–90
  supervisor, 88
Direct revenue sources, 179
Disabilities, caring for children with. *See* Illnesses and disabilities, caring for children with
Discipline, 42
Display areas, 130
Display portfolio, 298
Division for Early Childhood (DEC), 309
Documentation methods of assessment, 281–282, 283
Dramatic play center, 141–142, 373–374
Drill-and-practice software, 227

E
Eager to Learn: Educating Our Preschoolers, 240, 308
Early care and education programs, 4–5. *See also* Learning/activity centers
  influences of, 3–4
  types of, 4–5
Early Childhood Environment Rating Scale: Revised Edition (ECERS), 32–33
Early Childhood Mathematics: Promoting Good Beginnings, 346
Early Childhood Professional Preparation Accreditation Criteria, 309
Early Childhood Program Standards and Accreditation Criteria, revised, 48
Early Head Start, 181, 337
Early intervention specialists, 93
Early learning guidelines (ELGs), 215–216
Early Learning Opportunities Act, 181
Early learning standards, 215–216
Earned Income Tax Credit, 177
Economic Employment Opportunity Commission (EEOC), 95, 117
Eddie Eagle educational program, 274

Effective motivation, 228
Elementary and Secondary Education Act (ESEA), 180
Emergencies, preparing for, 273–274
Emotional illiteracy, 231–232
Employer identification number, 55
Employment and Training Administration, 183
Endowment, 182, 186
Entry/exit areas, 125–126
Environment
  of facility, 155
  of local programs, 213–215
Environment Rating Scales, 309
Epistemological beliefs, 16
Equipment and materials, 166–167
  children's books, 168–169
  computers, cameras, and related hardware/software, 169–170
  furniture and furnishings, suggested, 370
  for infants and toddlers, 371–373
  instructional materials, 168
  inventory of, 167–168
  kits and sets, 168
  for preschoolers, 373–376
    and primary-age children, 376–379
  purchasing guidelines, 167–168
  regulations, 41
  for school-age child care, 379
  suppliers of, 352–353
  for zones, playground, 161–162
Ethics. *See also* NAEYC Code of Ethical Conduct
  defined, 362
  ethical dilemma, 362
  ethics, 362
  professional, 362
Ethics and the Early Childhood Educator, 342
Evaluation, program
  accreditation, 47–49
  vs. assessment, 279
  formal, 32–33
  goal development and, 30–31
  internally stimulated *vs.* external mandates, 33–34
  intuitive, 31–32
  negative effects of, overcoming, 34
Even Start, 337
Event sampling, 285
Executive director, 88

F
Facility checklist, 22, 23–26
Facility design, indoor space. *See also* Learning/activity centers; Playgrounds and outdoor space
  adult lounge/rest area, 154
  capacity, deterring anticipated, 154

ceilings, 129
children's cubbies, 150–151
colors, 126–127
diapering areas, 152
display, 130
entry/exit areas, 125–126
environmental control, 155
equipment and materials, caring for,
    170 (*See also* Equipment and
    materials)
family reception area, 154
floor plans, recommended steps in
    creating, 153
floors, 128
food preparation, feeding and dining
    areas, 152–153
furniture and other essentials,
    132–135
insurance, 171
isolation areas, 153–154
issues to consider, 123–124
lease arrangements, 125
lighting, 127
napping areas, 153
office, 154
planning committee, 124
professional library, 154
progress of, steps in, 124–125
rooms
    arrangement of, 131–132
    shape of, 131
    size of, 130–131
sharing space, 125
sound, 127–128
special needs, accommodating, 166
staff workroom, 154
storage, 129–130
toileting areas, 152
walls, 129
Faculty. *See* Staff
Fair Labor Standards Act of 1938, 57
Families, collaborating with. *See* Collab-
    oration, community-school-family;
    Collaboration, family-school
Family and Medical Leave Act (FMLA), 57
Family area, 319–321
Family child care, defined, 5–6
Family Day Care Rating Scale (FDCRS),
    33
Family discussion groups, 333–334
Family Educational Rights and Privacy
    Act (FERPA), 70, 75, 300
Family grouping, 236
Family handbook
    administration, 77
    business and financial issues, 80
    described, 62
    developing or revising, 66–68
    families, 80–81
    health and safety, 78–80

program overview, 77
program services, 77
public relations and marketing, 81
records, 80
services to children, 77–78
Family reception area, 154
Family resource and support programs,
    334
Federal financing, 180, 181–182
    contracts and grants, 181, 182–183
    obtaining, 182
    programs, 181–182
    securing, 182–183
    vouchers, 181
Federal Insurance Contributions Act
    (FICA), 117
FICA tax, 119, 185
Field trips, 229–230
Financial management, 26–27
Financial report, 182
Financing early childhood programs.
    See also Federal financing
    administrative mechanisms, 178
    categorical grant, 179
    coherence in, lack of, 193–194
    direct revenue sources, 179
    employer assistance, 185
    fees, tuition, and miscellaneous
        sources, 185–187
    financing mechanisms, 178
    foundation support, 184
    general revenue sharing, 179
    government and foundation, 178–179
    indirect revenue sources, 179
    local support, 179
    NAEYC system for, 193
    proposal planning, 183–184
    public school, of kindergarten and
        primary programs, 179–180
    state support, 179–180
        for prekindergarten programs,
        180–181
    subsidies, 177, 191–193
    workforce compensation, 193
Financing mechanisms, 178
Fire safety, 38
First aid
    kit, contents of, 273
    staff training, 269
First days, 229
Fiscal regulations
    contracts, 55
    IRS regulations, 55–56
Fixed schedules, 237–238
Flexible schedules, 238
Floor plans, 149–150, 153
Floors, 128
Food preparation. *See also* Nutrition
    feeding and dining areas, 152–153
    meal planning, 170

Food service regulations, 42
Forced-choice rating scale, 295, 296
Formal evaluation, 32–33
Formative assessment, 280
Formative evaluation, 32
Franchises, 55
Free play, 171
*From Neurons to Neighborhoods: The
    Science of Early Childhood
    Development,* 240
Full inclusion, 242
Functional literacy, 216
Funding
    Head Start, 180, 181, 215
    reporting requirements, 301, 302
Furniture and other essentials, 132–135

G
Gardens, 161
General Educational Development
    (GED), 41
General partnership, 52
General-purpose grant, 182
General revenue sharing, 179
Goal 1 Early Childhood Assessments
    Resource Group, 304
Goals
    of child outcomes, 217–218
    of program development, 30–31
Goal statement, 217
Golden Rule, 18
Good Start Grow Smart, 2
Governing boards
    collaboration between communities,
        schools, and families, 335–337
    job description and agreement, 385
    profile worksheets, 382–384
Graded system of grouping, 236
Grants, 181, 182–183
Grassroots fund-raising, 183
Group child care homes, 6
Grouping decisions, 234–237
    ability grouping, 236
    adult–child ratio, 235
    family grouping, 236
    graded system, 236
    mixed-age grouping, 236, 237
    multi-age grouping, 236
    NAEYC definition of group, 234
    nongraded approach, 236
    patterns, 236–237
    size of group, 234–235

H
*Handbook for Public Playground
    Safety,* 163, 164
Hand washing, 263–264
Head Start
    Child Outcomes Framework, 218
    Civil Rights Act and, 47

Head Start (*continued*)
 creating partnerships with families, 308
 family-centered collaboration, principles and components of, 337
 family participation in programs, 331
 funding, 180, 181, 215
 Improving Head Start Act of 2007, 341
 insurance needs, 171
 length of sessions and, 237
 Management Fellows program, 45
 organizational structure and authority, 66
 Performance Standards, 308, 312
 Privacy Act of 1974 and, 120
 purpose of, 2, 5
 record collections, 120, 298
 staff credentials, 45
 stakeholders' participation in governing bodies, guidelines for, 335
 teacher qualifications in, 45, 47
Head teacher, 88
Health. *See also* Illnesses and disabilities, caring for children with; Safety
 assessment of, 260–262
 blood-borne pathogens, 264
 care, providing, 266
 cleaning and sanitation, 264, 265
 communicating with families, 264, 266
 defined, 259
 family handbook policies and procedures, 78–80
 hand washing, 263–264
 infections, preventing, 262
 paid sick leave for staff, 271
 policies and procedures, 70
 recommended practices, 263–264
 regulations, 41–42
 services, securing, 262
 staff illnesses and injuries, protecting against, 271
 staff manual policies and procedures, 74–75
 vulnerability of children, 262–263
Health insurance and hospital-medical insurance, 119
Healthy Young Children, 70
Heating, cooling, and ventilating, 155
High/Scope Child Observation Record (COR), 288, 304
High/Scope Foundation, 47
High/Scope Program Quality Assessment (PQA), 32
Home visits, 328–329, 333
Human resources, 45

I
Illnesses and disabilities, caring for children with
 exposure notice, sample of, 266
 first aid training for staff, 269
 issues to consider, 267
 medications, administering, 267
 mental health, promoting, 267–268, 269
 mildly ill, 7–8
 neglect and abuse, 269–271
Improving Head Start Act of 2007, 341
Inclusion, 7, 242–243
Indirect revenue sources, 179
Individual Education Plan (IEP), 212, 267
Individual Family Services Plan (IFSP), 212–213, 267
Individual/personal advocacy, 344–345
Individuals with Disabilities Education Act (IDEA), 19, 181, 212, 213, 267
Infant care, 7
 active play, toys for, 371
 creative expression, materials to support, 371–372
 language and literacy development, materials to support, 372
 learning/activity centers, 136–138
 make-believe, toys to support, 372
 manipulation, materials to support, 371
 nutrition, 249–250, 251
 outdoor areas for, 158–159
Infant Toddler Child Observation Record, 288
Infant/Toddler Environment Rating Scale: Revised Edition (ITERS), 33
Infections, preventing, 262
Informal care, defined, 6
Injury report form, 275–276
In-kind contribution, 183, 186
Inserimento, 229
Insurance, 117
 crime coverage, 119
 health insurance and hospital-medical insurance, 119
 liability insurance, 119
 purchasing, 171
 records, 120
 state unemployment insurance, 119
 workers' compensation insurance, 118–119
Integrated curriculum approach, 219, 220–222
Integrated learning systems (ILSs), 227
Internal Revenue Code, 185
Internal Revenue Service. *See* IRS regulations

International Reading Association (IRA), 216
Interviews
 assessment, 114, 286–287
 recruits, 95, 98–99
Intuitive evaluation, 31–32
IRS regulations
 employer identification number, 55–56
 tax returns, 56
 Withholding Exemption Certificates and IRS Form 1099, 56
Isolation areas, 153–154

J
Job performance assessments
 concerns, 115–116
 criteria for, 113
 formative, 113
 frequency of, 115
 observing and recording methods, 113–114
 purposes of, 113
 rating scales, 114–115
 records, 120
 steps in, 115–116
 summative, 113
Job Training Partnership Act, 193

K
Key facts handouts, 347
Kindergarten and primary programs. *See also* Preschool learning/activity centers
 computer use, 227
 financing for, 179–180
 prekindergarten programs, financing for, 180–181
"Kith-and-kin" providers, 6

L
Lag costs, 188
Language, literacy, writing and book center, 145, 147, 378–379
Large family child care homes, defined, 5–6
Laws. *See also* Licensing laws and procedures
 Americans with Disabilities Act (ADA), 7, 56, 69, 94
 Civil Rights Acts of 1964, 56, 58, 99
 Fair Labor Standards Act of 1938, 57
 Family and Medical Leave Act (FMLA), 57
 that protect children in addition to licensing, 57–58
 that protect staff and program, 56–57
 vulnerabilities to legal action, 57–58
Leader, rolls of, 10. *See also* Directors

Learning/activity centers. *See also* Facility design, indoor space; Preschool learning/activity centers
 general criteria for, 135–136
 for infants and toddlers, 136–140
 for primary-level children, 146–147, 376–379
 scheduling, 238, 239
 for school-age children, 147–148, 151, 379
Lease arrangements, 125
Least restrictive environment (LRE), 242
Liability insurance, 119
Library, facility, 154
Licensed Capacity Reports, 6
Licensing laws and procedures
 advocacy and, 44
 for child care centers, laws and procedures, 40
 codes, 43
 defined, 39
 features of, 39
 introduction to, 40
 minimal quality regulations, 39
 organization and administration, 40–41
 overview of, 41
 and program accreditation, comparison of, 48
 requirements, 63
 staff training in, 43
 vs. accreditation, 48
Life Safety Code Handbook of the National Fire Protection Association (NFPA), 38
Lighting, 126, 127
Limited liability company (LLC), 53
Limited partnership, 52–53
Linguistic diversity, 314
Literacy and mathematics standards, 216–217
Log entries, 294, 295, 319, 320

M
Management Fellows program (Head Start), 45
Manager, rolls of, 10. *See also* Directors
Mandated reporters, 57
Manipulatives and small construction toy center, 145, 146, 378
Marketing
 defined, 198
 facility design, 200–201
 importance of, 197–198
 initial point of contact, strategies for, 207–208
 market research, 203
 market segmentation strategy, 198

perception of services and interactions, 198–199
 plan, 197, 203–204
 policies and procedures, 71
 print media, guidelines for, 206–207
 Purple Cow products and services, 208–209
 service delivery, 201–203
 strategies, internal and external, 205–206
 web site design, 207
Matching grant, 183
Materials workshops, 329
Matrix sampling, 292
Maturational view, 16–17
Medications, administering, 267
Meetings, special topics, 324
Mental health
 poverty and, 267
 promoting, 267–268, 269
Mentoring
 defined, 108
 effective, requirements for, 109–110
 models and processes, 109
 performance supervision and, 109
 professional development, 108–109
 professionalism, 348
 quality circles, 109
 values of, 109
Mind in society theory, Vygotsky's, 18
Mission statement, developing, 28–29, 212
Mixed-age grouping, 236, 237
Morality, defined, 362
Multi-age grouping, 236
Music center, 142–143, 375
MyPyramid.gov, 249–251

N
NAEYC Code of Ethical Conduct
 children, ethical responsibilities to, 356–357
 colleagues, ethical responsibilities to, 358
  co-workers, 359
  employees, 359–360
  employers, 359
 community and society, ethical responsibilities to, 360–361
 conceptual framework, 356
 core values, 355
 Ethics and the Early Childhood Educator, 342
 families, ethical responsibilities to, 357–358
 policies and procedures, 61–63
 preamble, 355
 professionalism, 341–343

research with young children, 349
 Statement of Commitment, 342, 343–344, 355
 Supplement for Program Administrators, 342, 363
  conceptual framework, 364
  core values, 364
  definitions, 364–369
  ideals and principles, 364
  purpose of, 363
 Teaching the NAEYC Code of Ethical Conduct, 342
Napping areas, 153
Narratives, 113–114
 report letters, 302–303
National Accreditation Commission for Early Care and Education Programs (NAC), 49
National After School Association (NAA), 49
National Association for Family Child Care (NAFCC), 49
National Association for Regulatory Administration (NARA), 6
National Association for the Education of Young Children (NAEYC). *See also NAEYC Code of Ethical Conduct*
 accreditation criteria
  Academy for Early Childhood Program Accreditation, 48
  Early Childhood Professional Preparation Accreditation Criteria, 309
  Early Childhood Program Standards and Accreditation Criteria, revised, 48
  for health services, 262
  for outdoor activity areas, 156
  Program Accreditation Standards, 3, 37, 45, 48–49, 64, 156, 246, 248, 341, 342
  steps in, 48–49
  teachers' preparation, knowledge, and skills, 64
 antidiscriminatory policy, 95
 director competencies, 90
 early childhood defined by, 5
 financing, system for, 193
 Governing Board, 48
 group defined by, 92, 234
 Healthy Young Children, 70
 partnerships with families, creating, 308
 position statements, 346
  on assessment tests, standardized, 292
  DAP, 19, 212, 221–222, 308

National Association for the Education of Young Children (*continued*)
DEC, 309
on early learning standards, 241
on ethical assessment, 280
on goals, 217
on literacy development, 216
on mathematics, 217
on technology and young children, 227
primary program personnel, definitions, 92
responsible assessment, 279
staff assessment criteria, 113
standards
for early childhood professional preparation, 93
Early Childhood Program Standards, 308
Statement of Commitment, 343–344
Teaching Young Children, 330
National Association of Child Care Resource and Referral Agencies (NACCRA), 39–40
National Association of Early Childhood Specialists in State Departments of Education (NAECS/SDE), 18, 44, 217, 241, 279, 280, 292
National Association of School Psychologists, 279
National Board of Professional Teaching Standards (NBPTS), 46–47
National Center for Education Statistics, 179
National Child Care Information Center (NCCIC), 6, 215
National Council of Teachers of Mathematics (NCTM), 217, 346
National Council on Measurement in Education, 279
National Early Childhood Program Accreditation (NECPA), 49
National Education Goals Panel, 304
National Institute for Early Education Research, 180
National Lutheran School Accreditation (NLSA), 49
National Research Council (NRC), 216
National Resource Center for Health and Safety in Child Care and Early Education (NRCHSCCEE), 38, 40, 42
National Sanitation Foundation (NSF), 256
National School Lunch Program, 248
National Women's Law Center, 177
Naturalistic observations, 282–284
Neglect and abuse
risk factors for, 269
signs of, 270–271

Newsletters, 329–330
No Child Left Behind (NCLB), 2, 46, 180, 181–182, 193, 215
Nongraded approach to grouping, 236
Norm-referenced measure, 290
Notes, informal, 331
Not-for-profit corporations, 54–55
Notification contract, 116
Numerical rating scale, 295, 297
Nutrition, 246–247
children with special needs, 255
education, 257–259
facilities and equipment, 256
food service options, 256
hunger statistics, 246
infants, 250, 251
meals and snacks, 248, 251, 254–255
MyPyramid.gov, 249–251
purchasing food, 256–257
regulations, 42
sanitation requirements, 257
staff requirements, 256
young children, 251, 252–254

O
Objectives-based evaluation, 32
Observations. *See also* Observing and recording methods
advantages/disadvantages of, 282
anecdotal record, 282–283, 284
event sampling, 285
High/Scope Child Observation Record (COR), 288
Infant Toddler Child Observation Record, 288
naturalistic, 282–284
Revised Preschool Child Observation Record, 288
running record, 284
structured, 285–286
time sampling, 285, 286
Observing and recording methods, 113–114
checklists, 114
interview procedures, 114, 286–287
narratives, 113–114
portfolios, 114
rating scales, 114–115
Occupational Safety & Health Administration (OSHA), 264, 269
Office of facility, 154
Open area, playground, 161
Open-ended software, 228
Open house or curriculum night, 322–324
Operating-support grant, 183
Operations management, 22
Orientation programs, 333
spring or autumn, 321–322

P
Parent education and family resource programs, 333–334
Partial inclusion, 242
Pedagogical beliefs, 16, 45
Performance records, 294–297
Performance supervision, 109
Permission Marketing, 208
Personal Responsibility and Work Opportunity Act of 1996, 180
Personnel. *See* Primary program personnel; Staff
Personnel services
contract and terms of employment, 116–117
essential functions, 117
insurance and retirement plans, 117–119
job description, 117, 118
Planning committee, facility design, 124
Plants, poisonous, 380–381
Playgrounds and outdoor space. *See also* Equipment and materials
equipment hazards, 164–165
fencing, 156
gardens, 161
infant and toddler areas, 158–159
location, 155–156
for older children, 159
open area, 161
plan for, 161
play structures, 162
road for wheeled toys, 161
safety regulations, 163–166
sandpit or sandbox, 161
separating play areas, 164
shade and shelter, 157
size, 156
special needs, accommodating, 166
storage, 157
supervision, 163–164
surface, 157
surface materials, 165–166
terrain, 156–157
water areas, 161
zones, 160–162
Poisonous plants, 380–381
Policies and procedures. *See also* NAEYC *Code of Ethical Conduct;* Policy and procedure categories
administrative manual, 62, 81–82
antidiscriminatory, 95
below standards licensing codes, 43, 44
developing, responsible parties for, 65–66
established, using, 68
family handbook (*See* Family handbook)

importance of, 65
licensing requirements, 63
program exemptions, 43, 44
public agency regulations, 44
staff credentials, 44–46
staff manual (*See* Staff manual)
staff qualifications, 43, 44
viable, characteristics of, 68–69
of voluntary standards, 64
Policy and procedure categories
administration, 69
business and financial issues, 70
families, 70–71
health and safety, 70
personnel policies, 69
program overview, 69
program services, 69
public relations and marketing, 71
record keeping, 70
services to children, 69–70
Portfolios
archival, 299
display, 298
job performance assessments, 114
process, 299
in record keeping, 298–300
showcase, 298
working, 299
Position statements, 346
Poverty
cycle of, breaking, 27
hunger statistics, 246
during infancy and early childhood,
effects of, 4
mental health and, 267
minorities and, 4
subsidized child care fees, 177, 180,
181
telephone communications and, 330
Pregnancy Discrimination Act of 1978,
69
Preschool learning/activity centers
art center, 142, 143, 374–375
block center, 138–141, 373
carpentry or woodworking center,
144, 376
cooking center, 144–145, 377–378
dramatic play center, 141–142,
373–374
floor plan, 149–150
language, literacy, writing and book
center, 145, 147, 378–379
manipulatives and small construction
toy center, 145, 146, 378
music center, 142–143, 375
outdoor areas for, 158–159
private spaces, 146
science and mathematics center, 144,
376–377

special interest areas, 146
water and sand center, 143–144,
375–376
Primary program personnel. *See also*
Professional development; Staff
case manager, 93
directors (*See* Directors)
early intervention specialists, 93
NAEYC definitions for teaching staff,
92
primary program, 92–94
qualifications of, 93
records, 119–120
role of, 92–93
services (*See* Personnel services)
substitute teachers, 94
support program, 93–94
Privacy Act of 1974, 120
Private ownership, 50
chains, 55
comparisons between, 51
corporations, 53–55
franchises, 55
general partnership, 52
limited liability company (LLC), 53
limited partnership, 52–53
proprietorship/sole proprietorship, 52
Private-sector advocacy, 345
Private spaces, 146
Process portfolio, 299
Process quality, 9
Professional development. *See also* Job
performance assessments
accreditation and program evaluation, self-study in, 111, 112
discussions, 110, 111
formal education, encouraging, 108
group activities, providing, 110
mentoring (*See* Mentoring)
needs assessment, 105–106, 107
professional affiliations, urging, 112
resources/tools for, suppliers of,
353
staff development activities, 106,
107–108
workshops and consultations,
110–111
Professionalism. *See also* Advocacy
commitments, moving from short- to
long-term, 350
continuum for, 340–341
mentoring, 348
moving from "programs" to "systems," 349
NAEYC Code of Ethical Conduct,
reliance on, 341–343
preparation for, 341
programs to systems, moving from,
349

promoting, 340
research involvement, 349
vision, moving from particularistic to
universal, 350
Program directors. *See* Directors
Program implementation, 19, 224–225
classroom transitions, effective, 228
computers and other technologies,
using, 226–228
other aspects of, 234
physical care routines, providing, 228
special times, planning for, 228–230
supportive relationships, developing,
231–234
teaching strategies, 225
Program planning, 19. *See also* Costs of
early childhood programs; Developmentally Appropriate Practices
(DAP); Standards
community values, considering, 15–16
curriculum (*See* Curriculum)
evaluation of, 30–34
financial management, 26–27
goals, 217–218
grouping decisions, 234–237
mission statement, developing,
28–29, 212
operations management, 22
philosophy of program, developing,
16
scheduling decisions, 237–238,
239–240
services offered, 21–22
staff responsibilities, determining,
238, 240
standards (*See* Standards)
theory and philosophy of early childhood, reviewing, 16–19
vision, developing, 27–28, 212
Proposal planning, 183
writing, 183–184
Proprietorship/sole proprietorship, 52
Psychosocial theory, Erikson's, 18
Public agency regulations, 44
Public policy advocacy, 345
Public relations, policies and procedures, 71, 76, 81
Purple Cow, 208

Q
Quality
characteristics of, 9
collaboration and, 308–309
concerns over, 8
parent choice and, 9–10
process, 9
quality rating system (QRS), 9–10
structural, 9
Quality circles, 109

Quality rating systems (QRS), 9–10, 49–50
  elements of, 50
  fiscal regulations, 55–56
  laws that protect children in addition to licensing, 57–58
  laws that protect staff and program, 56–57
  legal requirements, 50
  private programs, legal existence of, 50–55

R

Rating scales
  assessment, 114–115, 295–297
  Environment Rating Scales, 309
  forced-choice, 295, 296
  numerical, 295, 297
  semantic differential, 295, 296
Recognition and Response, 305
Record keeping
  advantages of, 292–293
  anecdotal entries, 294, 295
  background information records, 293–294
  checklists, 294–295, 296
  cumulative records, 298
  disadvantages of, 293
  family handbook policy and procedures, 80
  FERPA and, 300
  Head Start, 120, 298
  log entries, 294, 295
  not-for-profit corporations, 55
  performance records, 294–297
  personnel records, 119–120
  policies and procedures, 70
  portfolios, 298–300
  Privacy Act of 1974, 120
  rating scales, 295–297
  referral records, 297–298
  staff manual policy and procedures, 75
  summary records, 298
Recruiting staff members
  advertising, 95
  affirmative action, 94–95
  antidiscriminatory policy, 95
  application, sample, 96–97
  criminal history records checks, 98
  documentations and credentials, obtaining, 95, 98–99
  employment eligibility verification, 98
  hiring, 99
  interviewing, steps in, 95, 98–99
  introductory letter and reference form, sample, 98

materials for recruitment, gathering, 95
  negligent hire, 98
  references, obtaining, 95, 97–98
Referral records, 297–298
Reflective practice, 108
Reggio Emilia schools, 142
Regulations. *See also* Licensing laws and procedures; Policies and procedures
  activities and equipment, 42
  building codes, fire safety, and sanitation, 38
  child care centers, 39–42, 163
  defined, 37
  discipline, 42
  facilities, supplies, equipment, and transportation, 41
  family child care regulations, 42–43
  licensing, 39, 48, 63
  nutrition and food services, 42
  opening process, overview of, 41
  organization and licensing procedures, 40–41
  parent involvement and communication, 42
  public agency, 44
  registration, 43
  specialized teacher qualifications, 47–49
  staff, 41
  teacher qualifications/certifications, 46–47
  types of, 37–38
  zoning, 38
Reporting
  assessment data, facilitating through, 301–302, 305
  individual conferences, 303–304
  methods of, selecting, 302–304
  narrative report letters, 302–303
  practices, developing, 301, 304
  purposes of, determining, 301
The Republic, 18
Research
  action, 349
  market, 203
Resource centers, 334
Retirement plans, 117, 119
  Federal Insurance Contributions Act (FICA), 117
  Social Security coverage, 118
Revised Preschool Child Observation Record, 288
Risk assessment, 274
Road for wheeled toys, playground, 161
Rooms in facility
  arrangement of, 131–132

shape of, 131
  size of, 130–131
Running record, 284

S

Safety
  acts of omission/commission, 274
  emergencies, preparing for, 273–274
  family handbook policies and procedures, 78–80
  fire, 38
  first aid kit, contents of, 273
  injury report form, 275–276
  limits for children, setting, 271–272
  playgrounds and outdoor space, 163–166
  policies and procedures, 70, 272–273
  regulations, 41–42, 163
  risk assessment, 274
  staff manual policies and procedures, 74–75
  teaching children to be safe, 274
Sandpit or sandbox, playground, 161
Sanitation, 38
Scaffolding, 18, 226
Scheduling, 237–238, 239–240
  child care center schedules, 238
  defined, 237
  fixed schedules, 237–238
  flexible schedules, 238
  length of session, 237
  school-age child care program schedules, 238
  staff responsibilities, 238–240
  time and arranging activities, 237–238
  toddler schedules, 238
School-Age Care Environment Rating Scale (SACERS), 33
School-age child care (SACC)
  cost of programs, 175
  defined, 7
  equipment and materials for, 379
  learning/activity centers for, 147–148, 151, 379
  scheduling, 238, 240
Science and mathematics center, 144, 376–377
Screening, developmental, 280–281, 289, 305
Seed grant or seed money, 183
Self-contained special education, 242
Self-improvement programs, 334
Self-study, 48
Semantic differential rating scale, 295, 296
Service delivery planning sheet, 22
Sharing space, 125

Showcase portfolio, 298
Social competence
  defined, 232
  external controls, reducing, 232–233
  sense of community, building, 233
Social constructivism, 17
Social Security coverage, 118, 185
Socioeconomic backgrounds, 313. *See also* Poverty
Software
  benefits of, 227–228
  for business management, suppliers of, 354
  for computers/cameras, purchasing, 169–170
  suppliers of, 353
  drill-and-practice, 227
  integrated learning systems (ILSs), 227
  open-ended, 228
Sound, 127–128
Southern Association of Colleges and Schools, 49
Southern Early Childhood Association (SECA), 279, 346
Special interest areas, 146
Special needs child care. *See also* Illnesses and disabilities, caring for children with
  facility accommodations, 166
  inclusion, 7, 242–243
  nutrition, 255
  services in, 7–8
  special interest areas, 146
Special times, planning for, 228–230
  class celebrations, 230
  field trips, 229–230
  first days, 229
Special topics meetings, 324
Spring or autumn orientation, 321–322
Staff. *See also* Collaboration, director-staff; Primary program personnel
  community foundation and, influence on, 99–100
  compensation, 86
  credentials, 44–46
  culturally relevant vision, creating and communicating, 101–102
  for food service, 256
  illnesses and injuries, protecting against, 271
  for licensing, 43
  needs assessment, 94
  paid sick leave, 271
  paid sick leave for, 271
  policies, 69
  recruiting (*See* Recruiting staff members)

regulations, 41
responsibilities, determining, 238, 240
shortages, 85–87
stress, 86
training (*See* Staff training)
trends, 85
turnover rate, 86
work climate, 100–101
workroom, 154
Staff manual
  administration, 72
  business and financial issues, 75
  described, 62
  developing or revising, 66–68
  families, 75–76
  health and safety, 74–75
  personnel policies, 72–73
  program overview, 71
  program services, 71–72
  public relations and marketing, 76
  records, 75
  services to children, 73–74
Staff training. *See also* Job performance assessments
  first aid, 269
  formal education, encouraging, 108
  inadequate, 86–87
  individualized, 106
  mentoring (*See* Mentoring)
  needs assessment survey, 107
  performance supervision, 109
  professional affiliations, urging, 112
  professional development resources, use of, 112
  quality circles, 109
  self-study in accreditation and program evaluation, 111, 112
  workshops and consultation, 110–111, 112
Stakeholders
  collaborating with, 45, 103
  on governing boards, 335
  mission statement and, 29
  ownership, 11
  values and, 15
  vision and, 27, 28
Standards
  benefits of, 240–241
  defined, 37, 215
  early learning standards, 215–216
  inclusion, considering, 242–243
  literacy and mathematics standards, 216–217
  recommendations for, 241
  teaching strategies and DAP, 241–242
  voluntary, requirements addressed by, 64
Standards-based evaluation, 32

Statement of financial position, 190
State unemployment insurance, 119
Storage areas
  indoors, 129–130
  outdoors, 157
Strangulation, 164
Stressful events, children who experience, 233–234
Structural quality, 9
Structured observations, 285–286
Subsidies, 177, 191–193
Sudden infant death syndrome (SIDS), 153
Summary records, 298
Summative assessment, 113, 289–290. *See also* Assessment tests, standardized
Summative evaluation, 32
Supervisors, 88. *See also* Directors
Supportive relationships, developing, 231
  caring as infant/toddler curriculum, 231
  children who experience stressful events, supporting, 233–234
  emotional literacy, nurturing, 231–232
  social competence, encouraging, 232–233
Support programs
  family discussion groups, 333–334
  family resource and support programs, 334
  home-visiting programs, 333
  orientation programs, 333
  personnel, 93–94
  resource centers, 334
  self-improvement programs, 334
Surface materials, playground, 165
  inorganic loose material, 165–166
  organic loose material, 165
  unitary material, 166
System, defined, 6

T
Talking points, 346
Taxes. *See also* IRS regulations
  credits and deductions, 175, 176, 185
  rate of taxation, 179–180
T.E.A.C.H.© Early Childhood© Project, 73, 343
Teacher aides, 92
Teachers. *See also* Primary program personnel
  assistant, defined, 92
  child-initiated activities and scaffolding, 226
  concepts, skills, and attitudes of, 316, 317

Teachers (*continued*)
  defined, 92
  head, 88
  Head Start qualifications, 45, 47
  ill-prepared, 316
  NAEYC accreditation criteria, 64
  qualifications/certifications, 46–47
  specialized, 47–49
  substitute, 94
  teacher-directed activities, 225–226
  teaching strategies, 225–226
Teachers Belief Statements, the Instructional Activities Scale, 33
Teaching the NAEYC Code of Ethical Conduct, 342
Teaching Young Children, 330
Telephone conversations, 330
Temporary Assistance to Needy Families (TANF), 177, 181
Tenure contract, 116
Theory and philosophy of early childhood
  behavioral-environmental view, 17
  constructivist view, 17
  ecological perspectives, 17–18
  maturational view, 16–17
  philosophical positions, 18
  psychological theories, 16–17
  vs. scientific evidence, 16
  social constructivism, 17
  synthesis of theories and philosophies, 19
  theory as program informant, 20–21
Time sampling, 285, 286
Toddler care, 7, 372
  active play, toys for, 372
  computers and, 226–227
  creative expression, materials to support, 372–373
  language and literacy development, materials to support, 373
  learning/activity centers, 136–138
  make-believe, toys to support, 373
  manipulation, materials to support, 372
  nutrition (*See* Nutrition)
  outdoor areas for, 158–159
  scheduling, 238, 239
Toileting areas, 152

U
U.S. Bureau of the Census, 183
U.S. Consumer Product Safety Commission (CPSC), 163, 164, 272
U.S. Department of Agriculture (USDA)
  CACFP, 193, 248, 250, 252–253
  food service equipment standards, 256
  hunger statistics, 246
  Infant Meal Pattern, 249–250
  Meal Pattern for Young Children, 251
  MyPyramid.gov, 249–251
  National School Lunch Program, 248
U.S. Department of Commerce, 183
U.S. Department of Defense (DOD), 40
U.S. Department of Education, 7
U.S. Department of Health and Human Services, 183
U.S. Department of Justice, 69, 98
U.S. Department of Labor, 183
U.S. Equal Employment Opportunity Commission, 69
United Way, 186, 262
Use zones, 164. *See also* Zones, playground
Utilization rate, 186

V
Values
  core, 362
  defined, 361
Videos
  for children, suppliers of, 353
  program, 331
Vision
  crisis change or transformational change, 101–102
  culturally relevant, creating and communicating, 101–102
  developing, 27–28, 212
  moving from particularistic to universal, 350
  stakeholders and, 27, 28
Volunteers, family, 331–332
  appropriate roles for, 332–333
  occasional, 333
Vouchers, 181

W
Walls, 129
Water and sand center, 143–144, 375–376
Water areas, playground, 161
Web concept, 223
  anticipatory, 223–225
Wisconsin Child Care Improvement Project (WCCIP)
  1998, 206
  2007, 205
Withholding Exemption Certificates and IRS Form 1099, 56
Workers' compensation insurance, 118–119
Working portfolio, 299
Work Sampling System, 288, 304
Workshops or workdays, 329–330
Worthy Wage Campaign, 86

Z
Zero to Three, 321
Zone of proximal development (ZPD), 18, 226
Zones, playground, 160
  arranging, criteria for, 160
  equipment for, 161–162
Zoning regulations, 38